*Movie Song Catalog*

# Movie Song Catalog

*Performers and Supporting Crew
for the Songs Sung in 1460
Musical and Nonmusical Films,
1928–1988*

*by*

RUTH BENJAMIN
ARTHUR ROSENBLATT

McFarland & Company, Inc., Publishers
*Jefferson, North Carolina, and London*

**British Library Cataloguing-in-Publication data are available**

**Library of Congress Cataloguing-in-Publication Data**

Benjamin, Ruth, 1934–
    Movie song catalog : the songs, performers and songwriters film
-by-film, 1928–1988 / by Ruth Benjamin and Arthur Rosenblatt.
        p.    cm.
    Includes indexes.
    ISBN 0-89950-764-6 (lib. bdg. : 50# alk. paper) ∞
    1. Motion picture music—United States—Bibliography.   2. Motion
picture music—Great Britain—Bibliography.   3. Popular music—
Bibliography.   I. Rosenblatt, Arthur.   II. Title.
ML128.M7B46   1993
016.78242'1542—dc20                                                    92-56630
                                                                              CIP
                                                                              MN

Manufactured in the United States of America

McFarland & Company, Inc., Publishers
    Box 611, Jefferson, North Carolina 28640

*For Judy,*
*Petra and Paul*

# Contents

# Foreword

My husband, Arthur Rosenblatt, is an architect. I am a novelist and former editor. What, you may be asking yourself, made two such people decide to put together a book about popular songs in the movies? The answer boils down to a single word: love.

In 1939, when Arthur was eight years old, living with his parents and older brother in Brooklyn, he made a startling discovery: at the Museum of Modern Art in Manhattan was a basement theater that showed silent movies. From that time on, he spent several days a week after school riding the subway to Manhattan (a nickel in those days), returning home only to stay up most of the night doing homework. (Years later the delightful man named Arthur Kleiner who had played piano accompaniment to those films at the museum was a neighbor of ours.)

My husband was hooked, and this passion continues to grow. Our library shelves are stuffed with biographies of movie moguls and songwriters; one special cupboard contains a burgeoning collection of cassette tapes—Noël Coward, Kurt Weill, George Gershwin, Cole Porter. Life without the movies and music would, to him, be quite colorless.

His tastes and mine are somewhat different, though they often coincide. While he was watching Louise Brooks in the basement of the Museum of Modern Art, or lunching out of a paper bag on Saturdays in his seat at the Navarre Theater (also known as the Itch) on Coney Island Avenue in Brooklyn, my best girlfriend and I were a couple of boroughs away, in Jackson Heights, Queens, at our local moviehouse on Northern Boulevard. When I was 10 years old, my dearest wish was to actually live 24 hours a day at the movies. What bliss! Put a musical in front of me and I was dazzled, enthralled. I not only came out humming the songs, but I spent a good portion of my 30 cents a week allowance on song sheets so that I could memorize the words to the current popular tunes; I still remember hundreds of them. The rest of my allowance had to be stretched to cover Bing Crosby records, Rita Hayworth and Deanna Durbin coloring books, and the splendid movie magazines which I devoured from cover to cover, believing every word, then cut up to paste the photos of my favorite stars meticulously and alphabetically into several fat scrapbooks. (I wish I had them now.)

Since then, of course, movies have changed dramatically (pun intended) and so has popular music. In the fifties, we danced to early rock and roll; in the sixties and seventies we listened—not always enthusiastically, I admit—to the music our kids adored, blaring out from the increasingly sophisticated sound systems in their bedrooms. But some of that music was awfully good, and I'll never forget the day in 1968 when the four of us went to see a group called the Beatles in *The Yellow Submarine*.

The idea for this book was born one Sunday afternoon as my husband and I were strolling along Fifth Avenue, having just attended a rarely shown English musical, vintage 1937, in the basement theater of the Museum of Modern Art. The film was called *Head Over Heels*, and it starred one of his all-time favorite actresses, Jessie Matthews. We began reminiscing, as we often do, about movies in general and about the songs that were in those movies. And who sang them.

The subject remained in the back of our minds, to surface again on another more recent Sunday after a trip to London where we'd visited the exciting new Museum of the Moving Image. "I wonder if there's a book that lists movie songs," I said. We happened to be passing a bookshop, so we went in and looked. There were books about movies, and books about songs. But we couldn't find anything in that shop or in any other that was exactly like the one we had in mind, the one we wanted to read ourselves.

So gradually this book came into being, compiled by an architect and a novelist with love and affection.

*Ruth Benjamin*

# Introduction

In the past few years, the videocassette has become to the motion picture what the paperback has long been to the book. The oldest and newest of films are now accessible to wide audiences via the VCR. And people still catch movies on television or visit local theaters and revival houses. For the casual viewer, for the serious buff, for the pop music lover, this book is intended to help the viewer identify the songs, the songwriters and the singers in movies he or she has seen, plans to see or simply wants to know about.

Credits roll past too quickly or, especially on the small screen, are virtually unintelligible to the eye. Here, listed alphabetically by film and indexed by song, can be found thousands of the tunes, together with their composers and lyricists, that have been sung (and dubbed) on screen or soundtrack by the famous and the forgotten in American and British films, musical and non-musical, from the earliest talkies of 1928 to the latest rock 'n' roll of 1988. Which adds up to 60 years of movie songs.

From the major studios, we have included movies that have, with varying degrees of success, been adapted from Broadway musicals, sometimes using a different combination of songs; movies that contain songs written by prominent lyricists and composers, or that are introduced by well-known singing stars, or that have won awards and become best-selling records and then standards; movies that may not be artistic triumphs but whose songs strongly reflect their times, be those times the Roaring '20s, the Depression of the 1930s, the wartime patriotism of the '40s, the so-called silent era of Joe McCarthy's '50s, the swinging '60s and '70s or the selfish '80s; and movies that for one reason or another we have found appealing and interesting, or even unappealing and interesting, including some that are rarely seen but feature gems of songs by well known composers. For example, in the very appealing class, from the British musical *Evergreen* (1934) comes "Dancing on the Ceiling" written by Rodgers and Hart and performed by Jessie Matthews.

Within these categories are Westerns and comedies, from Roy Rogers to Woody Allen, as well as dramas, biopics, rock musicals and concert films. We include theme music and title songs, if they are sung. We omit short subjects, operas, serials, animated films and television movies.

In selecting the 1,460 films listed here, we have consulted and been guided by the work of authorities in the fields of pop music and film, such as Nat Shapiro, Bruce Pollock, David Ewen, Leslie Halliwell, Leonard Maltin, Stanley Green, Roy Hemming and many others. Research material has come from a number of sources, British and American: reference volumes; libraries and study centers such as those at the Museum of Modern Art, the New York Public Library and the British Film Institute; record archives at ASCAP and BMI and the ARChive of Contemporary Music; and soundtrack albums and the films themselves. And special thanks to those kind and helpful souls who assisted us in our search for just the right detail to fill in another piece of the huge jigsaw puzzle that has turned out to be this book. We hope it will be informative to use and as much fun to read as it was to compile, that it will whet curiosity as well as aid reminiscence and win a few bets along the way. We look forward to hearing from readers with comments, corrections and additions.

# How to Use This Book

The reader will find an alphabetical listing of 1,460 films made in the years 1928 through 1988. Each numbered entry is made up of the film's vital statistics followed by its songs, its singers and its songwriters. Entries are sometimes preceded by pertinent or intriguing sidelights about the film's history, performers or music. They are sometimes followed by samplings of what reviewers at *Variety* or *The New York Times* said about the movie when it opened.

The vital statistics of each film (and their abbreviations) include:

1) Entry number. Used to identify the film in the indexes.

2) Title. The name under which the movie was released.

3) Country of origin. United States (US) or Great Britain (GB).

4) Year of release. Here we have followed Leonard Maltin's *TV Movies and Video Guide*, which uses as its criterion the year a film was first shown in theaters.

5) Whether the film was made in black and white (BW) or color (C). We've pretended colorization doesn't exist.

6) Running time in minutes. This varies from source to source. Films have been cut mercilessly to fit program space; we have tried to use release times.

7) The director (D).

8) The music director (MD).

9) The music score (MS).

10) The name of the company or studio that produced, released or distributed the film (P), followed by the names of its producers in parenthesis.

11) The orchestras or bands featured in the film (Orch).

12) Music Backup (MB). Usually vocal groups of various sizes that sang behind solo performers in some or all of their songs.

13) Vocals. The dubber who sang on the soundtrack for the on-screen performer.

14) Performer. When all or most of the songs were sung by the same person or group we have listed the name only once to avoid repetition. If others performed as well, their names appear in parentheses following the song title.

15) Alternate or television titles. Sometimes titles of movies were changed for distribution in another country, or for television or other purposes. We have listed as many of these as possible, though there are undoubtedly some we have missed.

As far as the body of an entry is concerned, each song title is followed by the name(s) of its performer(s) in parentheses, then by its lyricist and composer (WM), and sometimes by its arranger (Arr.).

For purposes of avoiding needless repetition, whenever more than one song was written by the same composers, it is separated from the next song by a semicolon.

A slash separates songs written by different writers.

When all the words and or all the music are by the same hand, the name appears only once at the very end of the entry.

It was not uncommon for a songwriter to use a pseudonym. Occasionally a performer used an alternate name. In these entries, the most well-known name is given. The birth name will appear in brackets.

At the back of the book are three alphabetical indexes, listing by entry number the performers, the songwriters and the songs.

# The Films

**1 Aaron Slick from Punkin Crick.** US, 1952, C, 95 m. D: Claude Binyon, MD: Robert Emmett Dolan, P: Paramount (William Perlberg, George Seaton). GB Title: Marshmallow Moon.

*I'd Like to Baby You* (Chorus); *Life Is a Beautiful Thing* (Dinah Shore, Minerva Urecal); *Marshmallow Moon* (Dinah Shore, Alan Young, Male Quartet); *My Beloved* (Robert Merrill, Dinah Shore); *Purt' Nigh But Not Plumb* (Dinah Shore, Alan Young); *Saturday Night in Punkin Crick* (Dinah Shore, Alan Young, Chorus); *Soda Shop* (Dinah Shore, Alan Young, Chorus); *Step Right Up* (Chick Chandler, Veda Ann Borg, Robert Merrill, Martha Stewart); *Still Water* (Robert Merrill, Dinah Shore, Chorus); *Why Should I Believe in Love?* (Dinah Shore) WM: Jay Livingston and Ray Evans.

"Undisturbed by anything more sophisticated than Technicolor and ... routine songs." —Bosley Crowther, *The New York Times.*

**2 Abbott and Costello Meet the Mummy.** US, 1955, BW, 79 m. D: Charles Lamont, MS: Joseph Gershenson, P: Universal (Howard Christie).

*You Came a Long Way from St. Louis* (Peggy King) W: Bob Russell— M: John Benson Brooks.

**3 About Last Night.** US, 1986, C, 113 m. D: Edward Zwick, MS: Miles Goodman, P: Tri-Star (Jason Brett, Stuart Oken).

*If Anybody Had a Heart* (John Waite) WM: John David Souther and Danny Kortchmar / *If We Can Get Through the Night* (Paul Davis) WM: Brock Walsh / *Living Inside My Heart* (Bob Seger) WM: Bob Seger / *Natural Love* (Sheena Easton) WM: Tom Snow and Cynthia Weil / *Shape of Things to Come* (Hall and Oates) WM: John Oates / *So Far So Good* (Sheena Easton) WM: Tom Snow and Cynthia Weil / *Step by Step* (J.D. Souther) WM: John David Souther and Karla Bonoff / *'Til You Love Somebody* (Michael Henderson) WM: Bob Marlette and Sue Shifrin / *Trials of the Heart* (Nancy Shanks) WM: Thom Bishop, Michael Day and Rocky Maffit / *True Love* (The Del Lords) WM: Scott Kempner / *Words Into Action* (Jermaine Jackson) WM: Mike Lesson and Peter Vale.

**4 About Mrs. Leslie.** US, 1954, BW, 104 m. D: Daniel Mann, MS: Victor Young, P: Paramount (Hal B. Wallis). Performer: Shirley Booth.

*I'm in the Mood for Love* W: Dorothy Fields—M: Jimmy McHugh / *Kiss the Boys Goodbye* W: Frank Loesser—M: Victor Schertzinger.

"The strains of soap opera are unmistakably clear." —A.H. Weiler, *The New York Times.*

**5 Above Suspicion.** US, 1943, BW, 90 m. D: Richard Thorpe, MS: Bronislau Kaper, P: MGM (Victor Saville).

*A Bird in a Gilded Cage* (Joan Crawford, Fred MacMurray) W: Arthur J. Lamb—M: Harry von Tilzer.

**6 Absolute Beginners.** GB, 1986, C, 107 m. D: Julien Temple, P: Virgin (Stephen Woolley, Chris Brown).

*Absolute Beginners* (David Bowie)

1

WM: David Bowie / *Have You Ever Had It Blue?* (Style Council) WM: Paul Weller / *Having It All (Eighth Wonder)* WM: Patsy Kensit, Godson and Beauchamp / *Killer Blow* (Sade) WM: Sade Adu, Booth and Stabbins / *Quiet Life* (Ray Davies) WM: Ray Davies / *Riot City* (Jerry Dammers) WM: Jerry Dammers / *Rodrigo Bay* (Working Week) WM: Booth, Stabbins and Roberts / *Selling Out* (Slim Gaillard) WM: Tot Taylor, Julien Temple and Slim Gaillard / *That's Motivation* (David Bowie) WM: David Bowie / *Va Va Voom* (Gil Evans) WM: Gil Evans.

"Daring attempt to portray the birth of teenagedom in London, 1958, almost exclusively through song." — *Variety.*

"A movie about style — the 50's roots of 80's clothes and music echoed through 40's musicals." — Caryn James, *The New York Times.*

**7  Across 110th Street.** US, 1972, C, 102 m. D: Barry Shear, MS: J.J. Johnson, P: UA (Fouad Said, Ralph Serpe). Performers: Bobby Womack and Peace.

*Across 110th Street; Do It Right; Hang On In There; If You Don't Want My Love; Quicksand* WM: Bobby Womack and J.J. Johnson.

**8  Adam's Rib.** US, 1949, BW, 100 m. D: George Cukor, MS: Miklos Rozsa, P: MGM (Lawrence Weingarten).

*Farewell, Amanda* (David Wayne) WM: Cole Porter.

**9  The Adventures of Hajji Baba.** US, 1954, C, 94 m. D: Don Weis, MS: Dimitri Tiomkin, P: AA (Walter Wanger).

*Hajji Baba* (Nat King Cole) W: Ned Washington — M: Dimitri Tiomkin.

**10  The Adventures of Sherlock Holmes.** US, 1939, BW, 85 m. D: Alfred L. Werker, MS: Cyril Mockridge, P: TCF (Gene Markey). GB Title: Sherlock Holmes.

*I Do Like to Be Beside the Seaside* (Basil Rathbone) WM: John A. Glover-Kind.

**11  Affair in Trinidad.** US, 1952, BW, 98 m. D: Vincent Sherman, MS: Morris Stoloff and George Duning, P: Columbia (Vincent Sherman). Vocals: Jo Ann Greer for Rita Hayworth. Performer: Rita Hayworth.

*I've Been Kissed Before; Trinidad Lady* W: Bob Russell — M: Lester Lee.

**12  An Affair to Remember.** US, 1957, C, 115 m. D: Leo McCarey, MD: Lionel Newman, MS: Hugo Friedhofer, P: TCF (Jerry Wald). Vocals: Marni Nixon for Deborah Kerr.

The title song was sung over the titles by Vic Damone, then within the film by Marni Nixon who had also dubbed Deborah Kerr's voice the previous year in the film version of Rodgers and Hammerstein's "The King and I."

*An Affair to Remember* (Vic Damone, Deborah Kerr); *The Tiny Scout* (Deborah Kerr, Chorus); *Tomorrow Land* (Deborah Kerr, Chorus); *You Make It Easy to Be True* (Cary Grant, Deborah Kerr, Male Quartet) W: Harold Adamson and Leo McCarey — M: Harry Warren.

**13  The Affairs of Susan.** US, 1945, BW, 110 m. D: William A. Seiter, MS: Frederick Hollander, P: Paramount (Hal B. Wallis).

*If You Knew Susie* (George Brent, Dennis O'Keefe, Don DeFore, Rita Johnson, Walter Abel) WM: B.G. De Sylva and Joseph Meyer.

**14  After the Fox.** GB-US-Italy, 1966, C, 103 m. D: Vittorio De Sica, P: UA (John Bryan).

*After the Fox* (Peter Sellers, The Hollies) W: Hal David — M: Burt Bacharach.

**15  After the Thin Man.** US, 1936, BW, 113 m. D: W.S. Van Dyke II, MS: Herbert Stothart and Edward Ward, P: MGM (Hunt Stromberg). Performer: Dorothy McNulty.

Mariana Dorothy McNulty went

on to become Penny Singleton, best known as Dagwood's wife, Blondie, in the popular movie series.

*Blow That Horn* W: Robert Wright and George "Chet" Forrest—M: Walter Donaldson / *Smoke Dreams* W: Arthur Freed—M: Nacio Herb Brown.

**16 Agatha.** GB, 1979, C, 98 m. D: Michael Apted, MS: Johnny Mandel, P: Warner (Jarvis Astaire, Gavrik Losey).

*Close Enough for Love* (Pattie Brooks) W: Paul Williams—M: Johnny Mandel / *They Didn't Believe Me* (Vanessa Redgrave) W: Herbert Reynolds [Michael E. Rourke]—M: Jerome Kern.

**17 Alexander's Ragtime Band.** US, 1938, BW, 105 m. D: Henry King, MD: Alfred Newman, P: TCF (Harry Joe Brown).

A flock of stars and Irving Berlin songs added up to one of the most popular musical movies of the 1930s. For the first time a songwriter's name appeared above the title of a film and ahead of any of the actors in the credits.

*Alexander's Ragtime Band* (Alice Faye, Tyrone Power, Don Ameche, Jack Haley); *All Alone* (Alice Faye); *Blue Skies* (Alice Faye, Ethel Merman); *Easter Parade* (Don Ameche); *Everybody's Doin' It* (Alice Faye, Wally Vernon, Dixie Dunbar); *Everybody Step* (Ethel Merman); *For Your Country and My Country* (Douglas Fowley); *Heat Wave* (Ethel Merman, Chorus); *I Can Always Find a Little Sunshine at the YMCA* (The King's Men); *Marie* (Chorus); *My Walking Stick* (Ethel Merman); *Now It Can Be Told* (Alice Faye, Don Ameche); *Oh, How I Hate to Get Up in the Morning* (Jack Haley, Chorus); *Pack Up Your Sins and Go to the Devil* (Ethel Merman); *A Pretty Girl Is Like a Melody* (Ethel Merman); *Ragtime Violin* (Jane Jones, Mel Kalish, Otto Fries); *Remember* (Alice Faye); *Say It with Music* (Ethel Merman); *That International Rag* (Alice Faye, Wally Vernon, Chick Chandler); *This Is the Life* (Wally Vernon); *We're on Our Way to France* (Chorus); *What'll I Do?* (Chorus); *When the Midnight Choo-Choo Leaves for Alabam'* (Alice Faye, Tyrone Power, Don Ameche) WM: Irving Berlin.

"A grand filmusical which stirs and thrills." — *Variety.*

**18 Alfie.** GB, 1966, C, 114 m. D: Lewis Gilbert, MS: Sonny Rollins, P: Paramount (Lewis Gilbert).

Sonny Rollins, the tenor-sax musician, wrote the original score used in this film. No songs appeared in it. Only later did Hal David and Burt Bacharach compose *Alfie,* which was recorded first by British performer Cilla Black, and then, for American audiences, by Cher. Her version, added to the soundtrack of the film shown in the US, was thus qualified to be nominated as Best Song at the Academy Awards in 1966.

*Alfie* (Cher) W: Hal David—M: Burt Bacharach.

**19 Alice Doesn't Live Here Anymore.** US, 1975, C, 113 m. D: Martin Scorsese, MS: Richard LaSalle, P: Warner (David Susskind, Audrey Maas).

*All the Way from Memphis* (Mott the Hoople) WM: Ian Hunter / *Cuddle Up a Little Closer* (Betty Grable) W: Otto Harbach—M: Karl Hoschna / *Daniel* (Elton John) WM: Elton John and Bernie Taupin / *I've Got a Crush on You* (Ellen Burstyn) W: Ira Gershwin —M: George Gershwin / *Jeepster* (T-Rex) WM: Marc Bolan / *You'll Never Know* (Alice Faye) W: Mack Gordon —M: Harry Warren.

**20 Alice's Adventures in Wonderland.** GB, 1972, C, 96 m. D: William Sterling, P: TCF (Derek Horne).

*Curioser and Curioser* (Fiona Fullerton); *Dum and Dee Dance* (Fiona Fullerton); *I've Never Been This Far Before* (Fiona Fullerton); *The Last Word is Mine* (Fiona Fullerton, Michael Crawford); *The Me I Never Knew* (Fiona

Fullerton); *The Moral Song* (Peter Bull); *Off with Their Heads* (Flora Robson); *The Pun Song* (Robert Helpman, Peter Sellers, Dudley Moore) W: Don Black—M: John Barry / *They Told Me* (Michael Crawford); *Will You Walk a Little Faster?* (Michael Hordern, Spike Milligan) W: Lewis Carroll—M: John Barry / *You've Gotta Know When to Stop* (Davy Kaye) W: Don Black—M: John Barry.

**21 Alice's Restaurant.** US, 1969, C, 111 m. D: Arthur Penn, MD: Fred Hellerman, P: UA (Joe Manduke, Hillard Elkins).

*Alice's Restaurant Massacree* (Arlo Guthrie) WM: Arlo Guthrie / *Amazing Grace* (Lee Hays, Chorus) WM: John Newton—Arr: Arlo Guthrie and Garry Sherman / *Car Song* (Arlo Guthrie, Pete Seeger) WM: Woody Guthrie / *Chilling of the Evening* (Arlo Guthrie); *Highway in the Wind* (Arlo Guthrie); *I'm Going Home* (Arlo Guthrie); *Motorcycle Song* (Arlo Guthrie); *Now and Then* (Arlo Guthrie) WM: Arlo Guthrie / *Pastures of Plenty* (Pete Seeger) WM: Woody Guthrie / *Songs to Aging Children* (Joni Mitchell) WM: Joni Mitchell.

**22 All Hands on Deck.** US, 1961, C, 98 m. D: Norman Taurog, MD: Lionel Newman, MS: Cyril Mockridge, P: TCF (Oscar Brodney). Performer: Pat Boone.

*All Hands on Deck; I've Got It Made; Somewhere There's Home; There's No One Like You* WM: Jay Livingston and Ray Evans.

**23 All That Jazz.** US, 1979, C, 123 m. D: Bob Fosse, MS: Ralph Burns, P: Columbia/TCF (Robert Alan Aurthur, Daniel Melnick).

*After You've Gone* (Leland Palmer) W: Henry Creamer—M: Turner Layton / *Bye Bye Love* (Ben Vereen, Roy Scheider) WM: Felice Bryant and Boudleaux Bryant / *Everything Old Is New Again* (Peter Allen) WM: Peter Allen and Carole Bayer Sager / *On Broadway* (George Benson) WM: Barry Mann, Cynthia Weil, Jerry Leiber and Mike Stoller / *A Perfect Day* (Harry Nilsson) / *Some of These Days* (Erzsebet Foldi) WM: Shelton Brooks / *Take Off with Us* (Sandahl Bergman, Chorus) WM: Stan Lebowsky and Fred Tobias / *There'll Be Some Changes Made* (Ann Reinking) W: Billy Higgins—M: W. Benton Overstreet / *There's No Business Like Show Business* (Ethel Merman) WM: Irving Berlin / *Who's Sorry Now* (Chorus) WM: Bert Kalmar, Harry Ruby and Ted Snyder.

**24 All This and World War II.** US, 1976, BW/C, 88 m. D: Susan Winslow, MD: Lou Reizner, P: TCF (Sanford Lieberson, Martin J. Machat).

*Because* (Lynsey De Paul); *Carry That Weight* (The Bee Gees); *Come Together* (Tina Turner); *A Day in the Life* (Frankie Valli); *The Fool on the Hill* (Helen Reddy); *Get Back* (Rod Stewart); *Getting Better* (Status Quo); *Golden Slumbers* (The Bee Gees); *Help!* (Henry Gross); *Hey Jude* (The Brothers Johnson); *I Am the Walrus* (Leo Sayer); *Let It Be* (Leo Sayer); *The Long and Winding Road* (Leo Sayer); *Lovely Rita* (Roy Wood); *Lucy in the Sky with Diamonds* (Elton John); *Magical Mystery Tour* (Ambrosia); *Nowhere Man* (Jeff Lynne); *Polythene Pam* (Roy Wood); *She Came In Through the Bathroom Window* (The Bee Gees); *She's Leaving Home* (Bryan Ferry); *Strawberry Fields Forever* (Peter Gabriel); *Sun King* (The Bee Gees); *We Can Work It Out* (The Four Seasons); *When I'm Sixty-Four* (Keith Moon); *With a Little Help from My Friends* (Jeff Lynne); *Yesterday* (David Essex) WM: John Lennon and Paul McCartney.

"Neither the war nor the songs emerge victorious or especially memorable ... an unresolved tussle between realism, seemingly weak satire and the tunes so dear to the Woodstock generation." —A.H. Weiler, *The New York Times*.

**25 All Through the Night.** US, 1942, BW, 107 m. D: Vincent Sherman,

MS: Adolph Deutsch, P: Warner (Hal B. Wallis, Jerry Wald). Performer: Kaaren Verne.

*All Through the Night* W: Johnny Mercer—M: Arthur Schwartz / *Cherie, I Love You So* WM: Lillian Goodman.

**26 An Alligator Named Daisy.** GB, 1957, C, 88 m. D: J. Lee-Thompson, MS: Stanley Black, P: Rank (Raymond Stross).

*In Love for the Very First Time* (Diana Dors) WM: Jack Woodman and Paddy Roberts.

**27 Almost Summer.** US, 1978, C, 88 m. D: Martin Davidson, MS: Charles Lloyd and Ron Altbach, P: Universal (Rob Cohen). Performers: Mike Love and Celebration.

*Almost Summer* WM: Brian Wilson, Alan Jardine and Mike Love / *Cruisin'* WM: Mike Love / *It's O.K.* WM: Brian Wilson and Mike Love / *Sad Sad Summer* WM: Mike Love / *She Was a Lady* (Fresh) WM: Bill Pratt / *Summer in the City* WM: John B. Sebastian, Steve Boone and Mark Sebastian / *We Are the Future* (High Inergy) WM: Mel Bolton, James Holiday, Troy Laws and Friendly Womack.

**28 Always in My Heart.** US, 1942, BW, 92 m. D: Jo Graham, MS: Heinz Roemheld, P: Warner (Walter McEwen, William Jacobs).

*Always in My Heart* (Gloria Warren) W: Kim Gannon—M: Ernesto Lecuona.

**29 American Graffiti.** US, 1973, C, 110 m. D: George Lucas, P: Universal (Francis Ford Coppola, Gary Kurtz).

*Ain't That a Shame* (Fats Domino) WM: Antoine "Fats" Domino and Dave Bartholomew / *All Summer Long* (The Beach Boys) WM: Brian Wilson / *Almost Grown* (Chuck Berry) WM: Chuck Berry / *At the Hop* (Flash Cadillac and The Continental Kids) WM: John Madara, Arthur Singer and Dave White / *Barbara Ann* (The Regents) WM: Fred Fassert / *Book of Love* (The Monotones) WM: Warren Davis, George Malone and Charles Patrick / *Chantilly Lace* (The Big Bopper) WM: J.P. Richardson / *Come Go with Me* (The Del Vikings) WM: Clarence E. Quick / *Crying in the Chapel* (Sonny Till and The Orioles) WM: Artie Glenn / *Do You Wanna Dance?* (Bobby Freeman) WM: Bobby Freeman / *Fannie Mae* (Buster Brown) WM: Clarence L. Lewis, Morris Levy and Waymon Glasco / *Gee!* (The Crows) WM: Viola Watkins, Daniel Norton and William Davis / *Get a Job* (The Silhouettes) WM. Earl T. Beal, Raymond W. Edwards, William F. Horton and Richard A. Lewis / *Goodnight, Well It's Time to Go* (The Spaniels) WM: Calvin Carter and James Hudson / *The Great Pretender* (The Platters) WM: Buck Ram / *Heart and Soul* (The Cleftones) W: Frank Loesser—M: Hoagy Carmichael / *I Only Have Eyes for You* (The Flamingos) W: Al Dubin—M: Harry Warren / *Johnny B. Goode* (Chuck Berry) WM: Chuck Berry / *Little Darlin'* (The Diamonds) WM: Maurice Williams / *Love Potion Number Nine* (The Clovers) WM: Jerry Leiber and Mike Stoller / *Maybe Baby* (Buddy Holly) WM: Buddy Holly and Norman Petty / *Only You* (The Platters) WM: Buck Ram and Ande Ram / *Party Doll* (Buddy Knox) WM: Jimmy Bowen and Buddy Knox / *The Peppermint Twist* (Joey Dee and The Starliters) WM: Joey Dee and Henry Glover / *Rock Around the Clock* (Bill Haley and His Comets) WM: Max C. Freedman and Jimmy De Knight / *Runaway* (Del Shannon) WM: Del Shannon [Charles Westover] and Max Crook / *See You in September* (The Tempos) W: Sid Wayne—M: Sherman Edwards / *She's So Fine* (Flash Cadillac and The Continental Kids) WM: K. Moe and L. Phillips / *Since I Don't Have You* (The Skyliners) W: James Beaumont, Janet Vogel, Joseph Verscharen, Walter Lester and John Taylor—M: Joseph Rock and Lennie Martin / *Sixteen*

*Candles* (The Crests) WM: Luther Dixon and Allyson R. Khent / *Smoke Gets in Your Eyes* (The Platters) W: Otto Harbach—M: Jerome Kern / *Stay* (Maurice Williams) WM: Maurice Williams / *The Stroll* (The Diamonds) WM: Clyde Otis and Nancy Lee / *Surfin' Safari* (The Beach Boys) WM: Brian Wilson and Mike Love / *Teen Angel* (Mark Dinning) WM: Jean Surrey and Red Surrey / *That'll Be the Day* (Buddy Holly) WM: Jerry Allison, Buddy Holly and Norman Petty / *A Thousand Miles Away* (The Heartbeats) WM: James Sheppard and William Miller / *To the Aisle* (The Five Satins) WM: Stuart Wiener and Billy Dawn Smith / *Why Do Fools Fall in Love?* (Frankie Lymon and The Teenagers) WM: Morris Levy and Frankie Lymon / *Ya Ya* (Lee Dorsey) WM: Lee Dorsey, Clarence Lewis and Morgan Robinson / *You're Sixteen* (Johnny Burnette) WM: Richard M. Sherman and Robert B. Sherman.

"Walter Murch's outstanding sound collage—an unending stream of early rock platter hits—complements in the aural department." —*Variety*.

**30 American Hot Wax.** US, 1978, C, 91 m. D: Floyd Mutrux, MD: Kenny Vance, P: Paramount (Art Linson).

*Bye Bye Love* (The Everly Brothers) WM: Felice Bryant and Boudleaux Bryant / *Charlie Brown* (The Coasters) WM: Jerry Leiber and Mike Stoller / *Do You Wanna Dance?* (Bobby Freeman) WM: Bobby Freeman / *Goodnight, Well It's Time to Go* (The Spaniels) WM: Calvin Carter and James Hudson / *Great Balls of Fire* (Jerry Lee Lewis) WM: Jack Hammer and Otis Blackwell / *Hey, Little Girl* (Clark Otis) WM: Bobby Stevenson and Otis Blackwell / *Hushabye* (The Mystics) WM: Doc Pomus and Mort Shuman / *I Put a Spell on You* (Screamin' Jay Hawkins) WM: Jay Hawkins / *La Bamba* (Ritchie Valens) WM: William Clauson / *Little Darlin'* (The

Diamonds) WM: Maurice Williams / *Little Star* (The Elegants) WM: Vito Picone and Arthur Venosa / *Maybe* (The Delights) WM: George Goldner / *Mr. Lee* (The Delights) WM: Heather Dixon, Helen Gathers, Emma Ruth Pought, Laura Webb and Jannie Pought / *Oh Boy* (Buddy Holly) WM: Sonny West, Bill Tilghman and Norman Petty / *Reelin' and Rockin'* (Chuck Berry) WM: Chuck Berry / *Rock and Roll Is Here to Stay* (The Planotones) WM: Dave White / *Roll Over Beethoven* (Chuck Berry) WM: Chuck Berry / *Sea Cruise* (Frankie Ford) WM: Huey P. Smith / *Since I Don't Have You* (The Chesterfields) W: James Beaumont, Janet Vogel, Joseph Verscharen, Walter Lester and John Taylor—M: Joseph Rock and Lennie Martin / *Sincerely* (The Moonglows) WM: Harvey Fuqua and Alan Freed / *Sixty Minute Man* (The Dominoes) WM: William Ward and Rose Marks / *Splish Splash* (Bobby Darin) WM: Bobby Darin and Jean Murray / *Stay* (Maurice Williams and The Zodiacs) WM: Maurice Williams / *Summertime Blues* (Eddie Cochran) WM: Eddie Cochran and Jerry Capehart / *Sweet Little Sixteen* (Chuck Berry) WM: Chuck Berry / *That Is Rock and Roll* (The Chesterfields) WM: Jerry Leiber and Mike Stoller / *That's Why* (Jackie Wilson) WM: Berry Gordy, Jr., Gwen Gordy and Tyran Carlo [Billy Davis, Sr.] / *There Goes My Baby* (The Drifters) WM: Benjamin Nelson, Lover Patterson and George Treadwell / *A Thousand Miles Away* (The Heartbeats) WM: James Sheppard and William Miller / *Tutti Frutti* (Little Richard) WM: Richard Penniman, Dorothy La Bostrie and Joe Lubin / *When You Dance* (The Turbans) WM: Andrew Jones and Leroy Kirkland / *Whispering Bells* (The Del Vikings) WM: Clarence E. Quick and F. Lowry / *Whole Lotta Shakin' Goin' On* (Jerry Lee Lewis) WM: Dave Williams and Sunny David / *Why Do Fools Fall in Love?* (Frankie Lymon and The Teenagers) WM: Morris Levy and Frankie Lymon / *Willie and the Hand Jive* (Johnny Otis) WM: Johnny Otis / *Zoom* (The Cadillacs) WM: Esther Navarro.

**31 An American in Paris.** US, 1951, C, 113 m. D: Vincente Minnelli, MD: Johnny Green, P: MGM (Arthur Freed).

*By Strauss* (Gene Kelly, Oscar Levant, Georges Guetary); *Embraceable You* (Gene Kelly); *I Got Rhythm* (Gene Kelly, Lucien Planzoles, Christian Pasques, Anthony Mazola) W: Ira Gershwin—M: George Gershwin / *I'll Build a Stairway to Paradise* (Georges Guetary) W: B.G. De Sylva and Arthur Francis [Ira Gershwin]—M: George Gershwin / *Nice Work If You Can Get It* (Georges Guetary); *Our Love Is Here to Stay* (Gene Kelly); *S'Wonderful* (Georges Guetary, Gene Kelly); *Tra La La* (Gene Kelly, Oscar Levant) W: Ira Gershwin—M: George Gershwin.

"One of the most imaginative musical confections turned out by Hollywood. . . . Gershwin's music gets boffo treatment throughout." —*Variety*.

"Spangled with pleasant little patches of amusement and George Gershwin tunes." —Bosley Crowther, *The New York Times*.

**32 An American Werewolf in London.** US, 1981, C, 97 m. D: John Landis, MS: Elmer Bernstein, P: Universal (George Folsey, Jr.).

*Bad Moon Rising* (Credence Clearwater) WM: John C. Fogerty / *Blue Moon* (The Marcels, Sam Cooke, Bobby Vinton) W: Lorenz Hart—M: Richard Rodgers.

**33 Americathon.** US, 1979, C, 86 m. D: Neil Israel, MS: Tom Scott, P: UA (Joe Roth).

*Chelsea* (Elvis Costello); *Crawlin' to the U.S.A.* (Elvis Costello) WM: Elvis Costello / *Don't You Ever Say No* (Zane Buzby) WM: David Pomeranz and L. Catherine Cohen / *Get a Move On* (Eddie Money) WM: Eddie Money and Phil Collins / *Gold* (Harvey Kor-

man) WM: David Pomeranz / *It's a Beautiful Day* (The Beach Boys) WM: Mike Love and Alan Jardine / *Open Up Your Heart* (Eddie Money) WM: Eddie Money / *Without Love* (Nick Lowe) WM: Nick Lowe.

**34 Anastasia.** US, 1956, C, 105 m. D: Anatole Litvak, MS: Alfred Newman, P: TCF (Buddy Adler).

*Anastasia* (Pat Boone) W: Paul Francis Webster—M: Alfred Newman.

"The musical score is very good. Put this one in a class with 'Mayerling'." —Bosley Crowther, *The New York Times*.

**35 Anchors Aweigh.** US, 1945, C, 140 m. D: George Sidney, MS: George Stoll, P: MGM (Joe Pasternak).

*Anchors Aweigh* (Chorus) W: Alfred Hart Miles and Royal Lovell — M: Charles A. Zimmerman / *The Charm of You* (Frank Sinatra); *I Begged Her* (Frank Sinatra, Gene Kelly); *I Fall in Love Too Easily* (Frank Sinatra) W: Sammy Cahn—M: Jule Styne / *If You Knew Susie* (Frank Sinatra, Gene Kelly) WM: B.G. De Sylva and Joseph Meyer—Add. W: Sammy Cahn / *Jealousy* (Kathryn Grayson) W: Vera Bloom—M: Jacob Gade / *Lullaby* (Frank Sinatra) W: Mrs. Natalia MacFarren—M: Johannes Brahms / *My Heart Sings* (Kathryn Grayson) W: Harold Rome—M: "Jamblan" Henri Herpin / *Waltz Serenade* (Kathryn Grayson) W: Earl K. Brent—M: Peter Ilyich Tchaikovsky / *We Hate to Leave* (Frank Sinatra, Gene Kelly, Chorus); *What Makes the Sunset?* (Frank Sinatra) W: Sammy Cahn—M: Jule Styne / *The Worry Song* (Gene Kelly) W: Ralph Freed—M: Sammy Fain.

"Solid musical fare. ...the songs are extremely listenable." —*Variety*.

**36 And the Angels Sing.** US, 1944, BW, 96 m. D: George Marshall, MS: Victor Young, P: Paramount (E.D. Leshin). Vocals: Julie Gibson for Diana Lynn.

*Bluebirds in My Belfry* (Betty Hutton); *For the First Hundred Years* (Betty Hutton, Dorothy Lamour, Diana Lynn, Mimi Chandler); *His Rocking Horse Ran Away* (Betty Hutton); *It Could Happen to You* (Dorothy Lamour, Fred MacMurray); *Knockin' on Your Own Front Door* (Betty Hutton, Dorothy Lamour, Diana Lynn, Mimi Chandler) W: Johnny Burke—M: James Van Heusen.

**37  Andy Hardy Meets Debutante.** US, 1940, BW, 86 m. D: George B. Seitz, P: MGM. Performer: Judy Garland.

*Alone* W: Arthur Freed—M: Nacio Herb Brown / *I'm Nobody's Baby* WM: Benny Davis, Milton Ager and Lester Santly.

**38  Andy Hardy's Private Secretary.** US, 1941, BW, 101 m. D: George B. Seitz, P: MGM.

*I've Got My Eyes on You* (Kathryn Grayson) WM: Cole Porter.

**39  Animal Crackers.** US, 1930, BW, 98 m. D: Victor Heerman, P: Paramount.

*Hooray for Captain Spaulding* (Groucho Marx, Zeppo Marx, Robert Greig, Margaret Dumont, Chorus) WM: Bert Kalmar and Harry Ruby / *My Old Kentucky Home* (Groucho Marx, Zeppo Marx, Chico Marx) WM: Stephen Collins Foster / *Some of These Days* (Lillian Roth) WM: Shelton Brooks / *Why Am I So Romantic?* (Lillian Roth, Hal Thompson) WM: Bert Kalmar and Harry Ruby.

**40  Annie.** US, 1982, C, 128 m. D: John Huston, MD: Ralph Burns, P: Columbia (Ray Stark).

*Dumb Dog* (Aileen Quinn); *Easy Street* (Carol Burnett, Bernadette Peters, Tim Curry); *I Don't Need Anything But You* (Aileen Quinn, Albert Finney); *I Think I'm Gonna Like It Here* (Aileen Quinn, Ann Reinking, Chorus); *It's the Hard-Knock Life* (Aileen Quinn, Toni Ann Gisondi, Chorus); *Let's Go to the Movies* (Aileen Quinn, Ann Reinking, Albert Finney, Chorus); *Little Girls* (Carol Burnett); *Maybe* (Aileen Quinn, Albert Finney, Chorus); *Sandy* (Aileen Quinn, Chorus); *Sign* (Carol Burnett, Albert Finney); *Tomorrow* (Aileen Quinn, Albert Finney, Edward Herrmann, Lois DeBanzie, Chorus); *We Got Annie* (Ann Reinking, Lu Leonard, Geoffrey Holder, Roger Minami, Chorus); *You're Never Fully Dressed Without a Smile* (Peter Marshall, Nancy Sinclair, Loni Ackerman, Murphy Cross) W: Martin Charnin—M: Charles Strouse.

"Aside from the memorable *Tomorrow* the show's songs weren't that much in the first place and four new tunes penned for the $35 million film aren't any better." —*Variety.*

**41  Annie Get Your Gun.** US, 1950, C, 107 m. D: George Sidney, MD: Adolph Deutsch, P: MGM (Arthur Freed).

Ethel Merman was Annie Oakley in the stage production.

*Anything You Can Do* (Betty Hutton, Howard Keel); *Colonel Buffalo Bill* (Keenan Wynn, Benay Venuta, Howard Keel); *Doin' What Comes Natur'lly* (Betty Hutton, Children); *The Girl That I Marry* (Howard Keel); *I Got the Sun in the Morning* (Betty Hutton); *I'm an Indian Too* (Betty Hutton); *My Defenses Are Down* (Howard Keel); *There's No Business Like Show Business* (Betty Hutton, Howard Keel, Keenan Wynn, Louis Calhern); *They Say It's Wonderful* (Betty Hutton, Howard Keel); *You Can't Get a Man with a Gun* (Betty Hutton) WM: Irving Berlin.

"Socko musical entertainment on film, just as it was on the Broadway stage [in 1946]." —*Variety.*

"A whale of a musical picture." —Bosley Crowther, *The New York Times.*

**42  Annie Hall.** US, 1977, C, 94 m. D: Woody Allen, P: UA (Fred T. Gallo). Performer: Diane Keaton.

*It Had to Be You* W: Gus Kahn—M: Isham Jones / *Seems Like Old Times* WM: Carmen Lombardo and John Jacob Loeb.

43 **Any Which Way You Can.**
US, 1980, C, 116 m. D: Buddy Van
Horn, P: Warner (Fritz Manes).

*Acapulco* (Johnny Duncan) WM:
Larry Collins and Mary Leath / *Any
Way You Want Me* (Gene Watson)
WM: L. Ofman / *Any Which Way You
Can* (Glen Campbell) WM: Milton
Brown, Steve Dorff and Snuff Garrett
/ *Beers to You* (Ray Charles, Clint East-
wood) WM: Steve Dorff, Snuff Gar-
rett, Sandy Pinkard and John Durrill /
*Cotton-Eyed Clint* (The Texas Opera
Company) WM: Steve Dorff and Snuff
Garrett / *Cow Patti* (Jim Stafford) WM:
Jim Stafford / *The Good Guys and the
Bad Guys* (John Durrill) WM: John
Durrill and Snuff Garrett / *One Too
Many Women in Your Life* (Sondra
Locke) WM: John Durrill and Phil
Everly / *Orangutan Hall of Fame* (Cliff
Crofford) WM: Cliff Crofford and
Snuff Garrett / *Too Loose* (Sondra
Locke) WM: Milton Brown, Steve
Dorff and Snuff Garrett / *Whiskey
Heaven* (Fats Domino) WM: Cliff
Crofford, John Durrill and Snuff Gar-
rett / *You're the Reason God Made Okla-
homa* (David Frizzell, Shelly West)
WM: Larry Collins and Sandy Pinkard.

44 **Anything Goes.** US, 1936,
BW, 92 m. D: Lewis Milestone, MD:
Victor Young, P: Paramount (Benja-
min Glazer). TV Title: Tops Is the
Limit.

*Anything Goes* (Ethel Merman); *I
Get a Kick Out of You* (Ethel Merman)
WM: Cole Porter / *Moonburn* (Bing
Crosby) W: Edward Heyman—M:
Hoagy Carmichael / *My Heart and I*
(Bing Crosby) W: Leo Robin—M:
Frederick Hollander / *Sailor Beware*
(Bing Crosby, Chorus) W: Leo
Robin—M: Richard A. Whiting /
*Shanghai-Di-Ho* (Ethel Merman, Bing
Crosby) W: Leo Robin—M: Frederick
Hollander / *There'll Always Be a Lady
Fair* (Bing Crosby, Chill Wills and The
Avalon Boys, Chorus); *You're the Top*
(Ethel Merman, Bing Crosby) WM:
Cole Porter.

"Ethel Merman has been brought
over from the original cast to sing *I Get
a Kick Out of You* just as Mr. Porter
meant her to, and Bing Crosby is an acceptable substitute for the show's
William Gaxton in almost every sub-
division except that in which he joins
Miss Merman in *You're the Top*. It
doesn't seem possible, but Mr. Crosby
croons it." —Frank S. Nugent, *The
New York Times.*

45 **Anything Goes.** US, 1956,
C, 106 m. D: Robert Lewis, MD:
Joseph J. Lilley, P: Paramount (Robert
Emmett Dolan).

*All Through the Night* (Bing
Crosby); *Anything Goes* (Mitzi Gay-
nor); *Blow, Gabriel, Blow* (Mitzi Gay-
nor, Bing Crosby, Donald O'Connor,
Zizi Jeanmaire, Chorus); *I Get a Kick
Out of You* (Mitzi Gaynor, Bing
Crosby, Zizi Jeanmaire); *It's De-Lovely*
(Mitzi Gaynor, Donald O'Connor)
WM: Cole Porter / *A Second-Hand
Turban and a Crystal Ball* (Bing
Crosby, Donald O'Connor); *Ya Gotta
Give the People Hoke* (Bing Crosby,
Donald O'Connor); *You Can Bounce
Right Back* (Donald O'Connor) W:
Sammy Cahn—M: James Van Heusen
/ *You're the Top* (Mitzi Gaynor, Bing
Crosby, Donald O'Connor, Zizi Jean-
maire) WM: Cole Porter.

"Standard musical comedy. Mr.
Porter's noted ditties have not suffered.
They are as bubbly and memorable as
ever." —A.H. Weiler, *The New York
Times.*

46 **Apache Country.** US, 1952,
62 m. D: George Archainbaud, MD:
Paul Mertz, P: Columbia (Armand
Schaefer).

*Cold Cold Heart* (Gene Autry)
WM: Hank Williams.

47 **April Love.** US, 1957, C, 97
m. D: Henry Levin, MD: Lionel Newman, P: TCF (David Weisbart). MB:
Chorus. Performers: Pat Boone and
Shirley Jones.

*April Love; The Bentonville Fair;
Clover in the Meadow* (Pat Boone); *Do*

*It Yourself; Give Me a Gentle Girl* W: Paul Francis Webster—M: Sammy Fain.

"The tunes are sweet, lilting and practically sketch the plot." —Howard Thompson, *The New York Times.*

**48  Arise My Love.** US, 1940, BW, 113 m. D: Mitchell Leisen, MS: Victor Young, P: Paramount (Arthur Hornblow, Jr.).

*Dream Lover* (Claudette Colbert) W: Clifford Grey—M: Victor Schertzinger.

**49  Arthur.** US, 1981, C, 97 m. D: Steve Gordon, MS: Burt Bacharach, P: Warner/Orion (Robert Greenhut). Performer: Dudley Moore.

*Arthur's Theme* (Christopher Cross) WM: Carole Bayer Sager, Christopher Cross, Peter Allen and Burt Bacharach / *Blue Moon* W: Lorenz Hart—M: Richard Rodgers / *If You Knew Susie* WM: B.G. De Sylva and Joseph Meyer / *Santa Claus Is Coming to Town* WM: Haven Gillespie and J. Fred Coots.

**50  Artists and Models.** US, 1955, C, 109 m. D: Frank Tashlin, MS: Walter Scharf, P: Paramount (Hal B. Wallis).

*Artists and Models* (Chorus); *Innamorata* (Dean Martin, Shirley MacLaine); *The Lucky Song* (Dean Martin); *When You Pretend* (Dean Martin, Jerry Lewis); *You Look So Familiar* (Dean Martin) W: Jack Brooks—M: Harry Warren.

**51  As Long As They're Happy.** GB, 1957, C, 76 m. D: J. Lee Thompson, MS: Stanley Black, P: Rank (Raymond Stross).

*Be My Guest* (Jerry Wayne); *Crazy Little Mixed-Up Heart* (Jean Carson); *Cry* (Jack Buchanan); *Hokey-Pokey Polka* (Diana Dors, Jack Buchanan); *I Don't Know Whether to Laugh or to Cry Over You* (Jerry Wayne, Jack Buchanan); *Liza's Eyes* (Jerry Wayne); *Quiet Little Rendezvous* (Jean Carson); *You Started Something* (Jerry Wayne) WM: Sam Coslow.

**52  As Young As You Feel.** US, 1951, BW, 77 m. D: Harmon Jones, MS: Cyril Mockridge, P: TCF (Lamar Trotti).

*You Make Me Feel So Young* (Chorus) W: Mack Gordon—M: Josef Myrow.

**53  Ask Any Girl.** US, 1959, C, 101 m. D: Charles Walters, MS: Jeff Alexander, P: MGM (Joe Pasternak).

*I'm in the Mood for Love* (Chorus) W: Dorothy Fields—M: Jimmy McHugh.

**54  At Long Last Love.** US, 1975, C, 118 m. D: Peter Bogdanovich, MD: Lionel Newman, MS: Artie Butler, P: TCF (Peter Bogdanovich).

*At Long Last Love* (Duilio Del Prete, Madeline Kahn, Burt Reynolds, Cybill Shepherd); *But in the Morning, No!* (Eileen Brennan, John Hillerman, Burt Reynolds, Cybill Shepherd); *Find Me a Primitive Man* (Madeline Kahn); *Friendship* (Duilio Del Prete, Madeline Kahn, Burt Reynolds, Cybill Shepherd); *From Alpha to Omega* (Duilio Del Prete, Madeline Kahn); *I Get a Kick Out of You* (Cybill Shepherd); *I Loved Him* (Madeline Kahn, Cybill Shepherd); *It's De-Lovely* (Burt Reynolds, Cybill Shepherd); *Just One of Those Things* (Duilio Del Prete, Burt Reynolds, Cybill Shepherd); *Let's Misbehave* (Burt Reynolds, Cybill Shepherd); *Most Gentlemen Don't Like Love* (Eileen Brennan, Madeline Kahn, Cybill Shepherd); *A Picture of Me Without You* (Duilio Del Prete, Madeline Kahn, Burt Reynolds, Cybill Shepherd); *Poor Young Millionaire* (Burt Reynolds, John Hillerman); *Well, Did You Evah?* (Duilio Del Prete, Madeline Kahn, Burt Reynolds, Cybill Shepherd, Mildred Natwick, Chorus); *Which* (Eileen Brennan, Cybill Shepherd); *You're the Top* (Duilio Del Prete, Madeline Kahn, Burt Reynolds, Cybill Shepherd) WM: Cole Porter.

"Peter Bogdanovich's experiment with a mostly-singing 1930's upper-class romance, is a disappointing and embarrassing waste of talent.... The principals sang their numbers while being filmed, with orchestrations dubbed in later, in an attempt to eliminate the lifelessness of post-sync when it is done poorly. On the basis of this experiment, pre-recording can rest its case." — *Variety.*

**55  At the Circus.** US, 1939, BW, 87 m. D: Edward Buzzell, MD: Franz Waxman, P: MGM (Mervyn LeRoy).

*Lydia, the Tattooed Lady* (Groucho Marx); *Step Up and Take a Bow* (Kenny Baker); *Two Blind Loves* (Kenny Baker, Florence Rice) W: E.Y. Harburg—M: Harold Arlen.

**56  Athena.** US, 1954, C, 96 m. D: Richard Thorpe, MD: George Stoll, P: MGM (Joe Pasternak).

*Athena* (Chorus) WM: Bert Pollack, Hugh Martin and Ralph Blane / *The Girl Next Door* (Vic Damone); *Harmonize* (Jane Powell, Louis Calhern, Vic Damone, Debbie Reynolds); *Imagine* (Debbie Reynolds, Vic Damone); *I Never Felt Better* (Debbie Reynolds, Jane Powell, Chorus); *Love Can Change the Stars* (Debbie Reynolds, Jane Powell, Vic Damone, Chorus); *Venezia* (Vic Damone); *Vocalize* (Jane Powell) WM: Hugh Martin and Ralph Blane.

**57  Atlantic City.** US, 1944, BW, 87 m. D: Ray McCarey, P: Republic (Albert J. Cohen). Orch: Paul Whiteman; Louis Armstrong.

*After You've Gone* (Constance Moore) W: Henry Creamer—M: Turner Layton / *Ain't Misbehavin'* (Louis Armstrong) W: Andy Razaf—M: Thomas "Fats" Waller and Harry Brooks / *By the Beautiful Sea* (Constance Moore) W: Harold Atteridge—M: Harry Carroll / *Mister Gallagher and Mister Shean* (Jack Benny, Al Shean) WM: Ed Gallagher and Al Shean / *Nobody's Sweetheart Now* (Belle Baker) WM: Gus Kahn, Ernie Erdman, Billy Meyers and Elmer Schoebel / *On a Sunday Afternoon* (Constance Moore)

W: Andrew B. Sterling—M: Harry von Tilzer.

**58  Atlantic City.** Canada-France-US, 1980, C, 104 m. D: Louis Malle, MS: Michel Legrand, P: Cine-Neighbour/Selta Films (Denis Heroux). Alt. Title: Atlantic City, U.S.A.

*Atlantic City, My Old Friend* (Ann Burns, Marie Burns, Jean Burns) WM: Paul Anka.

**59  Autumn Leaves.** US, 1956, BW, 108 m. D: Robert Aldrich, MS: Hans Salter, P: Columbia (William Goetz).

*Autumn Leaves* (Nat King Cole) Eng. W: Johnny Mercer—Fr. W: Jacques Prevert—M: Joseph Kosma.

"At the beginning and at the end, the singer Nat King Cole gives a soggy sound-track rendering of the ballad *Autumn Leaves.*" —Bosley Crowther, *The New York Times.*

**60  The Awakening.** US, 1928, BW, 105 m. D: Victor Fleming, P: UA.

Only one song appeared in this early talkie, and was hardly noticed at the time. In 1937, however, with a faster pace and a vocal by Jack Leonard, Tommy Dorsey and His Orchestra turned the same song into a standard.

*Marie* (Unbilled Female Singer) WM: Irving Berlin.

"The first showing of this picture was under the auspices of the Boys' Club of New York. The orchestra of the Boys' Club gave nice renditions of Elgar's *Pomp and Circumstance*, Grieg's *Ingrid's Lament*, and *Marie*, a theme song, specially composed by Irving Berlin to accompany the picture." — Mordaunt Hall, *The New York Times.*

**61  The Awful Truth.** US, 1937, BW, 92 m. D: Leo McCarey, MD: Morris Stoloff, P: Columbia (Leo McCarey).

*Home on the Range* (Irene Dunne, Ralph Bellamy) WM: Unknown / *I Don't Like Music* (Irene Dunne); *My Dreams Have Gone with the Wind* (Irene Dunne, Joyce Compton) W: Milton Drake—M: Ben Oakland.

**62  Babes in Arms.** US, 1939, BW, 96 m. D: Busby Berkeley, MD: George Stoll, P: MGM (Arthur Freed).

*Babes in Arms* (Judy Garland, Mickey Rooney, Betty Jaynes, Douglas McPhail, Chorus) W: Lorenz Hart—M: Richard Rodgers / *Broadway Rhythm* (Judy Garland, Betty Jaynes) W: Arthur Freed—M: Nacio Herb Brown / *Daddy Was a Minstrel Man* (Judy Garland) WM: Roger Edens / *The Darktown Strutters' Ball* (Chorus) WM: Shelton Brooks / *De Camptown Races* (Chorus) WM: Stephen Collins Foster / *Figaro* (Judy Garland) WM: Roger Edens / *God's Country* (Judy Garland, Mickey Rooney, Betty Jaynes, Douglas McPhail, Chorus) W: E.Y. Harburg—M: Harold Arlen / *Good Morning* (Judy Garland, Mickey Rooney) W: Arthur Freed—M: Nacio Herb Brown / *I Cried for You* (Judy Garland) WM: Arthur Freed, Gus Arnheim and Abe Lyman / *Ida, Sweet As Apple Cider* (Mickey Rooney) W: Eddie Leonard—M: Eddie Munson / *I'm Just Wild About Harry* (Judy Garland, Mickey Rooney, Chorus) WM: Noble Sissle and Eubie Blake / *Moonlight Bay* (Chorus) W: Edward Madden—M: Percy Wenrich / *Mr. Bones* (Judy Garland, Mickey Rooney, Douglas McPhail, Chorus) / *Oh, Susanna* (Judy Garland, Mickey Rooney, Chorus) WM: Stephen Collins Foster / *Where or When* (Judy Garland, Betty Jaynes, Douglas McPhail) W: Lorenz Hart—M: Richard Rodgers / *You Are My Lucky Star* (Betty Jaynes) W: Arthur Freed—M: Nacio Herb Brown.

"Film version of the Rodgers and Hart [1937] musical has been considerably embellished in its transfer to the screen. . . . It's a greatly enhanced piece of entertainment." —*Variety.*

**63  Babes in Toyland.** US, 1961, C, 105 m. D: Jack Donohue, MD: George Bruns, P: Buena Vista (Walt Disney).

Victor Herbert's first musical

opened on Broadway in October 1903, with lyrics and book by Glen Mac-Donough. A 1934 MGM film version starred Laurel and Hardy.

*A Castle in Spain* (Ray Bolger); *Floretta* (Tommy Sands, Chorus); *The Forest of No Return* (Chorus); *Go to Sleep, Slumber Deep* (Tommy Sands, Annette Funicello); *I Can't Do This Sum* (Annette Funicello); *Just a Toy* (Tommy Sands, Annette Funicello); *Just a Whisper Away* (Tommy Sands, Annette Funicello); *Lemonade* (Chorus); *Never Mind, Bo Peep* (Ann Jillian, Annette Funicello, Mary McCarty, Chorus); *Slowly He Sank to the Bottom of the Sea* (Henry Calvin); *Toyland* (Chorus); *We Won't Be Happy Till We Get It* (Ray Bolger, Henry Calvin); *The Workshop Song* (Ed Wynn, Chorus) W: Glen MacDonough and Mel Leven—M: Victor Herbert—Arr: George Bruns.

**64  Babes on Broadway.** US, 1941, BW, 118 m. D: Busby Berkeley, MD: George Stoll, P: MGM (Arthur Freed).

*Anything Can Happen in New York* (Mickey Rooney, Ray McDonald, Richard Quine) W: E.Y. Harburg—M: Burton Lane / *Babes on Broadway* (Judy Garland, Mickey Rooney, Virginia Weidler, Ray McDonald, Richard Quine, Annie Rooney, Chorus) W: Ralph Freed—M: Burton Lane / *Blackout Over Broadway* (Judy Garland, Mickey Rooney, Chorus); *Bombshell from Brazil* (Judy Garland, Mickey Rooney, Chorus) WM: Roger Edens / *By the Light of the Silvery Moon* (Chorus) W: Edward Madden—M: Gus Edwards / *Chin Up! Cheerio! Carry On!* (Judy Garland, Chorus) W: E.Y. Harburg—M: Burton Lane / *Franklin D. Roosevelt Jones* (Judy Garland, Chorus) WM: Harold Rome / *Hoedown* (Judy Garland, Mickey Rooney, Chorus) W: Ralph Freed—M: Roger Edens / *How About You?* (Judy Garland, Mickey Rooney) W: Ralph Freed—M: Burton Lane / *I've Got Rings on My Fingers* (Judy Garland) W: R.P. Weston and F.J. Barnes—M: Maurice Scott / *Mama Yo Quiero* (Mickey Rooney) Eng. W: Al Stillman—Span. WM: Jararaca Paiva and Vincente Paiva / *Mary's a Grand Old Name* (Judy Garland, Chorus) WM: George M. Cohan / *She Is Ma Daisy* (Mickey Rooney) WM: Harry Lauder and J.D. Harper / *Waiting for the Robert E. Lee* (Judy Garland, Chorus) W: L. Wolfe Gilbert—M: Lewis F. Muir / *The Yankee Doodle Boy* (Judy Garland, Mickey Rooney) WM: George M. Cohan.

**65 Baby, Take a Bow.** US, 1934, BW, 76 m. D: Harry Lachman, MD: Samuel Kaylin, P: Fox (Winfield Sheehan).

*On Accounta I Love You* (Shirley Temple) W: Bud Green—M: Sam H. Stept.

**66 Baby, the Rain Must Fall.** US, 1965, BW, 100 m. D: Robert Mulligan, MS: Elmer Bernstein, P: Columbia (Alan J. Pakula).

*Baby, the Rain Must Fall* (The We Three); *Shine for Me* (The We Three); *Treat Me Right* (Jim and Johnny) W: Ernie Sheldon—M: Elmer Bernstein.

**67 Back to the Beach.** US, 1987, C, 92 m. D: Lyndall Hobbs, P: Paramount (Frank Mancuso, Jr.).

*Absolute Perfection* (Private Domain, Pato Banton) WM: Jack Butler and Paul Shaffer / *California Sun* (Frankie Avalon) WM: Morris Levy and Henry Glover / *Catch a Ride* (Eddie Money) WM: David Kahne / *Jamaica Ska* (Annette Funicello, Fishbone) WM: Byron Lee / *Papa-Oom-Mow-Mow* (Pee-wee Herman) WM: Al Frazier, Carl White, John Earl Harris and Turner Wilson, Jr. / *Sign of Love* (Almee Mann) WM: Mark Goldenberg and J. Condos / *Sun, Sun, Sun, Sun, Sun* (Marti Jones) WM: David Kahne / *Surfin' Bird* (Pee-wee Herman) WM: Al Frazier, Carl White, John Earl Harris and Turner Wilson, Jr. / *Wooly Bully* (Dave Edmunds, Chorus) WM: Domingo Samudio.

**68 Back to the Future.** US, 1985, C, 116 m. D: Robert Zemeckis, MS: Alan Silvestri, P: Universal (Bob Gale, Neil Canton).

*The Power of Love* (Huey Lewis) WM: Chris Hayes, Huey Lewis and Johnny Colla.

**69 Ball of Fire.** US, 1941, BW, 111 m. D: Howard Hawks, MS: Alfred Newman, P: RKO (Samuel Goldwyn). Orch: Gene Krupa.

*Drumboogie* (Barbara Stanwyck) WM: Gene Krupa and Roy Eldridge.

**70 The Band Wagon.** US, 1953, C, 112 m. D: Vincente Minnelli, MS: Adolph Deutsch, P: MGM (Arthur Freed). Vocals: India Adams for Cyd Charisse.

Originally a Broadway revue, the 1931 cast included Fred Astaire and his sister Adele, Frank Morgan and Helen Broderick.

*By Myself* (Fred Astaire); *High and Low* (Chorus); *I Guess I'll Have to Change My Plan* (Fred Astaire, Jack Buchanan); *I Love Louisa* (Fred Astaire, Nanette Fabray, Chorus); *Louisiana Hayride* (Nanette Fabray, Chorus); *New Sun in the Sky* (Cyd Charisse); *A Shine on Your Shoes* (Fred Astaire); *Something to Remember You By* (Chorus); *That's Entertainment* (Fred Astaire, Nanette Fabray, Cyd Charisse, Jack Buchanan, Oscar Levant); *Triplets* (Fred Astaire, Nanette Fabray, Jack Buchanan); *You and the Night and the Music* (Chorus) W: Howard Dietz—M: Arthur Schwartz.

"Bids for recognition as one of the best musical films ever made." —Bosley Crowther, *The New York Times.*

**71 Bang the Drum Slowly.** US, 1973, C, 97 m. D: John Hancock, MS: Stephen Lawrence, P: Paramount (Maurice Rosenfield, Lois Rosenfield).

*Bang the Drum Slowly* (Bobby Gosh) W: Bruce Hart—M: Stephen Lawrence.

**72 Banjo on My Knee.** US, 1936, BW, 96 m. D: John Cromwell,

MD: Arthur Lange, P: TCF (Nunnally Johnson). MB: The Hall Johnson Choir.

*St. Louis Blues* (The Hall Johnson Choir) WM: W.C. Handy / *There's Something in the Air* (Tony Martin); *Where the Lazy River Goes By* (Barbara Stanwyck, Tony Martin); *With a Banjo on My Knee* (Buddy Ebsen, Walter Brennan) W: Harold Adamson—M: Jimmy McHugh.

**73    The Barkleys of Broadway.** US, 1949, C, 109 m. D: Charles Walters, MD: Lennie Hayton, P: MGM (Arthur Freed).

*Manhattan Downbeat* (Fred Astaire, Chorus); *My One and Only Highland Fling* (Ginger Rogers, Fred Astaire); *Shoes with Wings On* (Fred Astaire); *They Can't Take That Away from Me* (Fred Astaire); *A Weekend in the Country* (Ginger Rogers, Fred Astaire, Oscar Levant); *You'd Be Hard to Replace* (Fred Astaire) W: Ira Gershwin—M: Harry Warren.

"The songs are ordinary." — *Variety.*

"They make old-time magic with *You'd Be Hard to Replace* and they drift into realms of rapture with *They Can't Take That Away from Me.*" —Bosley Crowther, *The New York Times.*

**74    Bathing Beauty.** US, 1944, C, 101 m. D: George Sidney, MS: Johnny Green, P: MGM (Jack Cummings). Orch: Xavier Cugat; Harry James.

*Bim Bam Boom* (Lina Romay) WM: John A. Camacho, Noro Morales and Harold Adamson / *I Cried for You* (Helen Forrest) WM: Arthur Freed, Gus Arnheim and Abe Lyman / *I'll Take the High Note* (Red Skelton, Helen Forrest, Jean Porter, Janis Paige, Carlos Ramirez, Buddy Moreno) WM: Harold Adamson and Johnny Green / *Loch Lomond* (Chorus) WM: Unknown / *Magic Is the Moonlight* (Carlos Ramirez) Eng. W: Charles Pasquale—Span. WM: Maria Grever.

**75    Beach Blanket Bingo.** US, 1965, C, 98 m. D: William Asher, P: AIP (James H. Nicholson, Samuel Z. Arkoff).

*Beach Blanket Bingo* (Annette Funicello, Frankie Avalon) WM: Jerry Styner and Guy Hemrick / *The Cycle Set* (The Hondells) WM: Gary Usher and Roger Christian / *Fly Boy* (Linda Evans); *The Good Times* (Frankie Avalon); *I Am My Ideal* (Harvey Lembeck); *I Think You Think* (The Hondells); *It Only Hurts When I Cry* (Donna Loren); *New Love* (Linda Evans); *You'll Never Change Him* (Annette Funicello) WM: Jerry Styner and Guy Hemrick.

**76    Beach Party.** US, 1963, C, 101 m. D: William Asher, MS: Les Baxter, P: AIP (James H. Nicholson, Samuel Z. Arkoff).

*Beach Party* (Annette Funicello, Frankie Avalon) WM: Gary Usher and Roger Christian / *Don't Stop Now* (Annette Funicello, Frankie Avalon) WM: Robert Marcucci and Russell Faith / *Promise Me Anything* (Annette Funicello, Chorus) WM: Jerry Styner and Guy Hemrick / *Secret Surfin' Spot* (Dick Dale and The Deltones); *Surfin' and A-Swingin'* (Dick Dale and The Deltones) WM: Gary Usher and Roger Christian / *Treat Him Nicely* (Annette Funicello) WM: Jerry Styner and Guy Hemrick.

**77    Beat Street.** US, 1984, C, 106 m. D: Stan Lathan, MS: Harry Belafonte, P: Orion (David V. Picker, Harry Belafonte).

*Baptize the Beat* (System) WM: Michael Murphy and David Frank / *Beat Street Breakdown* (Grand Master Melle Mel and The Furious Five) WM: Melvin Glover and Reggie Griffin / *Beat Street Strut* (Juicy) WM: Eumir Deodato, Alan Palanker, Milton G. Barnes and Katreese Barnes / *Breakers Revenge* (Arthur Baker) WM: Arthur Baker / *Strangers in a Strange World* (Jenny Burton, Patrick Jude) WM: Jack Holmes / *This Could Be the Night* (Cindy Mizelle) WM: Arthur

Baker, Tina B. Evan, Carl Sturken and Chris Lord-Alge / *Us Girls* (Sharon Green, Lisa Counts, Debbie D.) WM: Ross Levinson and Debora Hooper.

**78 Beau James.** US, 1957, C, 105 m. D: Melville Shavelson, MS: Joseph J. Lilley, P: Paramount (Jack Rose). Vocals: Imogene Lynn for Vera Miles.

*His Honor, the Mayor of New York* (Jimmy Durante) W: Sammy Cahn— M: Joseph J. Lilley / *Manhattan* (Vera Miles, Bob Hope) W: Lorenz Hart— M: Richard Rodgers / *The Sidewalks of New York* (Bob Hope, Jimmy Durante, Chorus) W: James W. Blake—M: Charles B. Lawlor / *Someone to Watch Over Me* (Vera Miles) W: Ira Gershwin—M: George Gershwin / *When We're Alone* (Bob Hope, Vera Miles, Chorus) WM: Will Jason and Val Burton / *Will You Love Me in December?* (Bob Hope) W: James J. Walker—M: Ernest R. Ball.

**79 The Beautiful Blonde from Bashful Bend.** US, 1949, C, 77 m. D: Preston Sturges, MS: Cyril Mockridge, P: TCF (Preston Sturges).

*The Beautiful Blonde from Bashful Bend* (Male Singers) WM: Don George and Lionel Newman / *Every Time I Meet You* (Male Singers) WM: Mack Gordon and Josef Myrow / *In the Gloaming* (Betty Grable, Rudy Vallee) WM: Annie Fortesque Harrison and Meta Orred.

**80 Because They're Young.** US, 1960, BW, 102 m. D: Paul Wendkos, MS: Johnny Williams, P: Columbia (Jerry Bresler).

*Because They're Young* (James Darren) W: Aaron Schroeder and Wally Gold—M: Don Costa / *Swingin' School* (Bobby Rydell) WM: Kal Mann, Bernie Lowe and Dave Appell.

**81 Because You're Mine.** US, 1952, C, 103 m. D: Alexander Hall, MD: Johnny Green, P: MGM (Joe Pasternak).

*All the Things You Are* (Mario Lanza) W: Oscar Hammerstein II—M: Jerome Kern / *Because You're Mine* (Mario Lanza, Doretta Morrow); *Be My Love* (Doretta Morrow) W: Sammy Cahn—M: Nicholas Brodszky / *Granada* (Mario Lanza) Eng. W: Dorothy Dodd—Span. WM: Augustin Lara / *Lee-Ah-Loo* (Mario Lanza) W: John Lehman—M: Ray Sinatra / *The Lord's Prayer* (Mario Lanza) W: From the Bible—M: Albert Hay Malotte / *The Song Angels Sing* (Mario Lanza) W: Paul Francis Webster—M: Irving Aaronson / *You Do Something to Me* (Mario Lanza, Doretta Morrow) WM: Cole Porter.

**82 Bedknobs and Broomsticks.** US, 1971, C, 117 m. D: Robert Stevenson, MD: Irwin Kostel, P: Walt Disney (Bill Walsh).

*Age of Not Believing* (Angela Lansbury); *The Beautiful Briny* (Angela Lansbury, David Tomlinson, Chorus); *Don't Let Me Down* (Angela Lansbury); *Eglantine* (Angela Lansbury, David Tomlinson); *The Old Home Guard* (Chorus); *Portobello Road* (David Tomlinson, Chorus); *Portobello Street Dance* (David Tomlinson); *A Step in the Right Direction* (Angela Lansbury); *Substitutiary* (Angela Lansbury, David Tomlinson, Chorus); *With a Flair* (David Tomlinson) WM: Robert B. Sherman and Richard M. Sherman.

**83 The Beggar's Opera.** GB, 1953, C, 94 m. D: Peter Brook, MD: Muir Mathieson, P: British Lion (Herbert Wilcox, Laurence Olivier). Vocals: Adele Leigh for Dorothy Tutin; John Cameron for George Devine; Jennifer Vyvyan for Daphne Anderson; Joan Cross for Margot Grahame; Edith Coates for Mary Clare and Athene Seyler.

*And the Beef We Have Roasted and Ate* (George Devine, Stanley Holloway); *And We Shall See Spinning Together* (Laurence Olivier); *At the Gallows I'll Serve Her with Pleasure* (Laurence Olivier); *Can Love Be Controlled by Advice?* (Dorothy Tutin); *Come, Sweet Lass* (Laurence Olivier,

Daphne Anderson); *Feed the Dear Heart* (Dorothy Tutin, Daphne Anderson); *Fill Every Glass* (Chorus); *How Happy Would I Be with Either* (Laurence Olivier); *How Shall I Change a Dull Day?* (Dorothy Tutin); *If the Heart of a Man* (Laurence Olivier); *I'm Like a Skiff on the Ocean Toss'd* (Daphne Anderson); *In the Days of My Youth* (Athene Seyler, Stanley Holloway, Daphne Anderson); *Man May Escape from Rope and Gun* (Laurence Olivier); *My Heart Was So Free* (Laurence Olivier); *No Power on Earth* (Dorothy Tutin); *O Cruel Cruel Cruel Case* (Laurence Olivier); *O Lucy, What Made You Sink So Low?* (Stanley Holloway, George Devine, Athene Seyler); *O Ponder Well* (Dorothy Tutin); *O What Pain It Is to Part* (Dorothy Tutin, Laurence Olivier); *Paddington Green* (Stanley Holloway); *Pretty Polly Say* (Laurence Olivier); *Reprieve* (Chorus); *Rest You, Sleep You* (Dorothy Tutin); *Since Laws Were Made for Ev'ry Degree* (Laurence Olivier); *To Arms* (Chorus); *Were I Laid on When I Was Down Greenland Coast* (Dorothy Tutin, Laurence Olivier); *What Now, Madam Flirt?* (Daphne Anderson, Dorothy Tutin); *Would I Might Be Hang'd* (Daphne Anderson, Dorothy Tutin); *Youth's the Season Made for Joy* (Laurence Olivier) W: John Gay and Christopher Fry—M: Sir Arthur Bliss.

"An example of the uneasy partnership between screen and opera. . . . At constant intervals events are brought to a standstill by the John Gay lyrics and attractive though they are in their own right, they do not merge too happily in the film." — *Variety.*

**84   The Belle of New York.** US, 1952, C, 82 m. D: Charles Walters, MD: Adolph Deutsch, P: MGM (Arthur Freed). Vocals: Anita Ellis for Vera-Ellen.

*Baby Doll* (Fred Astaire); *Bachelor Dinner Song* (Fred Astaire, Chorus); *A Bride's Wedding Day Song* (Vera-Ellen); *I Wanna Be a Dancin' Man* (Fred Astaire) W: Johnny Mercer—M: Harry Warren / *Let a Little Love Come In* (Alice Pearce, Vera-Ellen, Fred Astaire, Chorus) WM: Roger Edens / *Naughty But Nice* (Vera-Ellen, Alice Pearce); *Oops* (Fred Astaire); *Seeing's Believing* (Fred Astaire); *When I'm Out with the Belle of New York* (Chorus) W: Johnny Mercer—M: Harry Warren.

"A couple of bright production numbers . . . a couple of Johnny Mercer lyrics, attached to some Harry Warren tunes, and that is about the total—outside of Vera-Ellen and Mr. A." —Bosley Crowther, *The New York Times.*

**85   Belle of the Nineties.** US, 1934, BW, 73 m. D: Leo McCarey, P: Paramount (William LeBaron). Orch: Duke Ellington. Performer: Mae West.

*American Beauty* W: Sam Coslow—M: Arthur Johnston / *The Memphis Blues* W: George A. Norton—M: W.C. Handy / *My Old Flame; Troubled Waters; When a St. Louis Woman Comes Down to New Orleans* W: Sam Coslow—M: Arthur Johnston.

**86   Bells Are Ringing.** US, 1960, C, 127 m. D: Vincente Minnelli, MD: Andre Previn, P: MGM (Arthur Freed).

Judy Holliday and Sydney Chaplin led the cast in the 1956 Broadway musical presentation by The Theatre Guild.

*Bells Are Ringing* (Chorus); *Better Than a Dream* (Judy Holliday, Dean Martin); *Do It Yourself* (Dean Martin); *Drop That Name* (Judy Holliday, Chorus); *Hello, Hello There* (Judy Holliday); *I Met a Girl* (Dean Martin); *I'm Going Back* (Judy Holliday); *It's a Perfect Relationship* (Judy Holliday); *It's a Simple Little System* (Eddie Foy, Jr.); *Just in Time* (Judy Holliday, Dean Martin); *The Midas Touch* (Hal Linden); *Mu-Cha-Cha* (Judy Holliday, Doria Avila); *The Party's Over* (Judy Holliday) W: Betty Comden and Adolph Green—M: Jule Styne.

"Jule Styne's bright score has been

vibrantly adapted and conducted by Andre Previn." — *Variety*.

"Jule Styne's songs . . . sound as if they might have been done by that song-writing dentist." — Bosley Crowther, *The New York Times*.

**87 The Bells of St. Mary's.** US, 1945, BW, 126 m. D: Leo McCarey, MS: Robert Emmett Dolan, P: RKO (Leo McCarey). Performer: Bing Crosby.

*Adeste Fidelis* Eng. W: Frederick Oakeley — Latin WM: John Francis Wade / *Aren't You Glad You're You?* W: Johnny Burke — M: James Van Heusen / *The Bells of St. Mary's* W: Douglas Furber — M: Emmett Adams / *In the Land of Beginning Again* W: Grant Clarke — M: George W. Meyer.

**88 Ben.** US, 1972, C, 95 m. D: Phil Karlson, MS: Walter Scharf, P: Cinerama (Mort Briskin). Performer: Michael Jackson.

*Ben* W: Don Black — M: Walter Scharf / *Everybody's Somebody's Fool* WM: G. Hampton, R. Adams and A. Adams / *Greatest Show on Earth* WM: Jerry Marcellino and Mel Larson / *In Our Small Way* WM: B. Verdi and Christine Yarian / *My Girl* WM: William "Smokey" Robinson and Ronald White / *People Make the World Go Round* WM: Thom Bell and Linda Creed / *Shoo Be Doo Be Doo Da Day* WM: Henry Cosby, Sylvia Moy and Stevie Wonder / *We've Got a Good Thing Going* WM: The Corporation / *What Goes Around Comes Around* WM: A. Strokes, D.L. Meyers, F. Witherspoon and L. Allen / *You Can Cry on My Shoulder* WM: Berry Gordy.

**89 Benji.** US, 1974, C, 86 m. D: Joe Camp, MS: Euel Box, P: Mulberry Square (Joe Camp).

*I Feel Love* (Charlie Rich) W: Betty Box — M: Euel Box.

**90 Bernardine.** US, 1957, C, 95 m. D: Henry Levin, MS: Lionel Newman, P: TCF (Samuel G. Engel). Performer: Pat Boone.

*Bernardine* WM: Johnny Mercer /

*Love Letters in the Sand* W: Nick Kenny and Charles Kenny — M: J. Fred Coots / *Technique* WM: Johnny Mercer.

**91 Best Foot Forward.** US, 1943, C, 95 m. D: Edward Buzzell, MD: Lennie Hayton, P: MGM (Arthur Freed). Orch: Harry James. Vocals: Gloria Grafton for Lucille Ball.

*Alive and Kicking* (Nancy Walker); *Buckle Down, Winsocki* (Tommy Dix, Chorus); *Ev'ry Time* (Virginia Weidler); *My First Promise* (Beverly Tyler); *The Three B's* (June Allyson, Nancy Walker, Gloria De Haven); *Three Men on a Date* (Tommy Dix, Kenny Bowers, Jack Jordan); *Wish I May, Wish I Might* (June Allyson, Gloria De Haven, Kenny Bowers, Jack Jordan, Sara Haden, Donald MacBride, Chorus); *You're Lucky* (Lucille Ball) WM: Ralph Blane and Hugh Martin.

**92 Best Friends.** US, 1982, C, 116 m. D: Norman Jewison, MS: Michel Legrand, P: Warner (Norman Jewison).

*How Do You Keep the Music Playing* (Patti Austin, James Ingram) W: Marilyn Bergman and Alan Bergman — M: Michel Legrand.

**93 The Best Little Whorehouse in Texas.** US, 1982, C, 114 m. D: Colin Higgins, MS: Patrick Williams, P: Universal/RKO (Thomas L. Miller, Edward K. Milkis, Robert L. Boyett).

*The Aggie Song* (Chorus); *Hard Candy Christmas* (Dolly Parton) WM: Carol Hall / *I Will Always Love You* (Dolly Parton) WM: Dolly Parton / *A Lil' Ole Bitty Pissant Country Place* (Dolly Parton, Theresa Merritt, Chorus); *The Sidestep* WM: Carol Hall / *Sneakin' Around* (Dolly Parton, Burt Reynolds) WM: Dolly Parton / *Texas Has a Whorehouse in It* (Dom DeLuise, Chorus); *20 Fans* (Jim Nabors, Chorus); *Watchdog Report* (Chorus) WM: Carol Hall.

**94 The Best Things in Life Are Free.** US, 1956, C, 104 m. D: Michael Curtiz, MS: Lionel Newman,

P: TCF (Henry Ephron). Vocals: Eileen Wilson for Sheree North.

Saga of the illustrious songwriting team of Buddy De Sylva, Lew Brown and Ray Henderson. Their song, *Lucky Day*, was used to advertise Lucky Strike cigarettes on the popular radio program "Your Hit Parade."

*The Best Things in Life Are Free* (Gordon MacRae, Ernest Borgnine, Sheree North, Dan Dailey); *The Birth of the Blues* (Gordon MacRae); *Black Bottom* (Sheree North, Chorus); *Button Up Your Overcoat!* (Gordon MacRae, Ernest Borgnine, Sheree North, Dan Dailey); *Don't Hold Everything* (Gordon MacRae, Ernest Borgnine, Dan Dailey); *Good News* (Gordon MacRae, Ernest Borgnine, Dan Dailey); *Here Am I—Broken Hearted* (Gordon MacRae, Ernest Borgnine, Dan Dailey); *If I Had a Talking Picture of You* (Byron Palmer); *It All Depends on You* (Gordon MacRae, Sheree North); *Just a Memory* (Sheree North, Chorus); *Lucky Day* (Dan Dailey); *Lucky in Love* (Gordon MacRae, Ernest Borgnine, Dan Dailey) W: B.G. De Sylva and Lew Brown / *Sonny Boy* (Norman Brooks) W: Al Jolson, B.G. De Sylva and Lew Brown / *Sunny Side Up* (Sheree North) W: B.G. De Sylva and Lew Brown / *This Is the Missus* (Sheree North) W: Lew Brown / *Together* (Dan Dailey, Phyllis Avery); *Without Love* (Sheree North); *You Try Somebody Else* (Sheree North, Roxanne Arlen) W: B.G. De Sylva and Lew Brown. M: Ray Henderson.

"It's a sparkling string of hits that's presented with all the nostalgic attention they deserve." — *Variety.*

"The best thing in life yesterday, apart from some good, thumping tunes, was Miss North." — Howard Thompson, *The New York Times.*

**95   The Best Years of Our Lives.** US, 1946, BW, 172 m. D: William Wyler, MS: Hugo Friedhofer, P: RKO (Samuel Goldwyn). Performer: Hoagy Carmichael.

*Among My Souvenirs* W: Edgar Leslie—M: Horatio Nicholls [Lawrence Wright] / *Lazy River* WM: Hoagy Carmichael and Sidney Arodin.

**96   Better Off Dead.** US, 1985, C, 98 m. D: Savage Steve Holland, MS: Rupert Hine, P: Warner (Michael Jaffe).

*Arrested By You* (Rupert Hine) WM: Torrence Merdur and Rupert Hine / *Come to Your Rescue* (Thinkman, with Matthew Harte) WM: Jeannette Therese Obstoj and Rupert Hine / *Dancing in Isolation* (Teri Nunn, Rupert Hine) WM: Torrence Merdur and Rupert Hine / *A Little Luck* (E.G. Daily) WM: Angela Rubin / *One Way Love* (E.G. Daily) WM: Steve Goldstein, Duane Hitchings, Craig Krampf and Eric Nelson / *Shine* (Martin Ansell) WM: Martin Ansell / *With One Look* (Rupert Hine, Cy Curnin) WM: Torrence Merdur and Rupert Hine.

**97   Between Two Women.** US, 1944, BW, 83 m. D: Willis Goldbeck, P: MGM (Willis Goldbeck).

*I'm in the Mood for Love* (Gloria De Haven) W: Dorothy Fields—M: Jimmy McHugh.

**98   Beyond the Valley of the Dolls.** US, 1970, C, 109 m. D: Russ Meyer, P: TCF (Russ Meyer).

*Beyond the Valley of the Dolls* (The Sandpipers); *Come with the Gentle People* (Carrie Nations) WM: Stu Phillips and Bob Stone / *Find It* (Carrie Nations) WM: Lynn Carey and Stu Phillips / *Girl from the City* (The Strawberry Alarm Clock); *I'm Comin' Home* (The Strawberry Alarm Clock) WM: Paul Marshall / *In the Long Run* (Carrie Nations); *Look On Up at the Bottom* (Carrie Nations) WM: Stu Phillips and Bob Stone / *Once I Had Love* (Carrie Nations) WM: Stu Phillips and Lynn Carey / *Sweet Talkin' Candy Man* (Carrie Nations) WM: Stu Phillips and Bob Stone.

**99   The Big Beat.** US, 1958, C, 82 m. D: Will Cowan, MD: Henry Mancini, MS: Joseph Gershenson, P:

Universal (Will Cowan). Orch: Harry James; Russ Morgan.

*As I Love You* (Alan Copeland) WM: Jay Livingston and Ray Evans / *The Big Beat* (Fats Domino) WM: Antoine "Fats" Domino and Dave Bartholomew / *Call Me* (Gogi Grant) W: Bernard Gasso—M: Irving Fields / *Can't Wait* (The Del Vikings) WM: Grace Saxon and Barry Mirkin / *Come Go with Me* (The Del Vikings) WM: Clarence E. Quick / *I'm Walkin'* (Fats Domino) WM: Antoine "Fats" Domino and Dave Bartholomew / *It's Great When You're Doing a Show* (Rose Marie, The Lancers, The Paulette Sisters) / *I Waited So Long* (Jeri Southern, Cal Tjader Quintet) WM: Jay Livingston and Ray Evans / *Lazy Love* (Gogi Grant) W: Bernard Gasso—M: Irving Fields / *Little Darlin'* (The Diamonds) WM: Maurice Williams / *Take My Heart* (The Four Aces) WM: Al Alberts and Dave Mahoney / *Where Mary Go* (The Diamonds) WM: Diane Lampert and John Gluck, Jr. / *You're Being Followed* (The Mills Brothers) W: Charles Tobias—M: Arthur Altman / *You've Never Been in Love* (Gogi Grant) WM: Alan Copeland and Jack Lloyd.

**100   Big Boy.** US, 1930, BW, 68 m. D: Alan Crosland, P: Warner. MB: The Monroe Jubilee Singers. Performer: Al Jolson.

*Go Down Moses* WM: Unknown / *Hooray for Baby and Me* W: Sidney D. Mitchell and Archie Gottler—M: George W. Meyer / *I Got Shoes* WM: Unknown / *Little Sunshine* W: Sidney D. Mitchell and Archie Gottler—M: George W. Meyer / *Liza Lee; Tomorrow Is Another Day* WM: Bud Green and Sam H. Stept.

**101   The Big Broadcast.** US, 1932, BW, 78 m. D: Frank Tuttle, P: Paramount. Orch: Cab Calloway; Vincent Lopez.

*Crazy People* (The Boswell Sisters) WM: Edgar Leslie and James V. Monaco / *Dinah* (Bing Crosby) W: Sam M.

Lewis and Joe Young—M: Harry Akst / *Goodbye Blues* (The Mills Brothers) W: Dorothy Fields and Arnold Johnson—M: Jimmy McHugh / *Here Lies Love* (Bing Crosby, Arthur Tracy) W: Leo Robin—M: Ralph Rainger / *It Was So Beautiful* (Kate Smith) W: Arthur Freed—M: Harry Barris / *Kickin' the Gong Around* (Cab Calloway) W: Ted Koehler—M: Harold Arlen / *Minnie the Moocher* (Cab Calloway, Chorus) WM: Cab Calloway, Irving Mills and Clarence Gaskill / *Please* (Bing Crosby, Stuart Erwin) W: Leo Robin—M: Ralph Rainger / *Tiger Rag* (The Mills Brothers) W: Harry DeCosta—M: The Original Dixieland Jazz Band / *Trees* (Donald Novis) W: Joyce Kilmer—M: Oscar Rasbach / *When the Moon Comes Over the Mountain* (Kate Smith) W: Howard Johnson—M: Harry M. Woods / *Where the Blue of the Night* (Bing Crosby) WM: Roy Turk, Bing Crosby and Fred E. Ahlert.

**102   The Big Broadcast of 1936.** US, 1935, BW, 97 m. D: Norman Taurog, P: Paramount (Benjamin Glazer). Orch: Ray Noble; Ina Ray Hutton. Vocals: Kenny Baker for Henry Wadsworth.

*Double Trouble* (Lyda Roberti, Jack Oakie, Henry Wadsworth, Chorus) W: Leo Robin—M: Ralph Rainger and Richard A. Whiting / *It's the Animal in Me* (Ethel Merman) W: Mack Gordon—M: Harry Revel / *I Wished on the Moon* (Bing Crosby) W: Dorothy Parker—M: Ralph Rainger / *Miss Brown to You* (The Nicholas Brothers, Chorus); *Why Dream?* (Henry Wadsworth, Harold Nicholas) W: Leo Robin—M: Ralph Rainger and Richard A. Whiting.

**103   The Big Broadcast of 1938.** US, 1938, BW, 90 m. D: Mitchell Leisen, MS: Boris Morros, P: Paramount (Harlan Thompson). Orch: Shep Fields and His Rippling Rhythm.

*Don't Tell a Secret to a Rose* (Tito Guizar); *Mama, That Moon Is Here Again* (Martha Raye); *Thanks for the*

*Memory* (Bob Hope, Shirley Ross) W: Leo Robin—M: Ralph Rainger / *Truckin'* (Martha Raye) W: Ted Koehler—M: Rube Bloom / *The Waltz Lives On* (Bob Hope, Shirley Ross, Chorus); *You Took the Words Right Out of My Heart* (Dorothy Lamour, Leif Erickson) W: Leo Robin—M: Ralph Rainger / *Zuni Zuni* (Tito Guizar) WM: Tito Guizar.

"The smash production number is *The Waltz Lives On*, which is a fanciful bit of terp and song that carries the waltz strain through the past 100 years." — *Variety*.

**104 The Big Chill.** US, 1983, C, 103 m. D: Lawrence Kasdan, MS: John Williams, P: Columbia (Michael Shamberg).

*Ain't Too Proud to Beg* (The Temptations) WM: Eddie Holland and Norman Whitfield / *Good Lovin'* (The Young Rascals) WM: Rudy Clark and Arthur Resnick / *I Heard It Through the Grapevine* (Marvin Gaye) WM: Norman Whitfield and Barrett Strong / *I Second That Emotion* (Smokey Robinson and The Miracles) WM: William "Smokey" Robinson and Alfred Cleveland / *Joy to the World* (Three Dog Night) WM: Hoyt Axton / *My Girl* (The Temptations) WM: William "Smokey" Robinson and Ronald White / *Tell Him* (The Exciters) WM: Bert Russell / *The Tracks of My Tears* (Smokey Robinson and The Miracles) WM: Warren Moore, William "Smokey" Robinson and Marvin Tarpin / *A Whiter Shade of Pale* (Procul Harum) WM: Gary Brooker and Keith Reid / *You Make Me Feel Like a Natural Woman* (Aretha Franklin) WM: Carole King, Jerry Wexler and Gerry Goffin.

**105 The Big City.** US, 1948, BW, 103 m. D: Norman Taurog, MS: George Stoll, P: MGM (Joe Pasternak). Vocals: Marni Nixon for Margaret O'Brien.

*Don't Blame Me* (Betty Garrett) W: Dorothy Fields—M: Jimmy McHugh / *God Bless America* (Lotte Lehmann, Margaret O'Brien, Chorus) WM: Irving Berlin / *I'm Gonna See a Lot of You* (Betty Garrett) W: Janice Torre—M: Fred Spielman / *The Kerry Dance* (Lotte Lehmann, Margaret O'Brien) W: James Lyman Molloy—M: Unknown / *Lullaby* (Lotte Lehmann, Margaret O'Brien) W: Mrs. Natalia MacFarren—M: Johannes Brahms / *Ok'l Baby Dok'l* (Betty Garrett) W: Inez James—M: Sidney Miller / *Shoo Shoo, Baby* (The Page Cavanaugh Trio) WM: Phil Moore / *What'll I Do* (Danny Thomas) WM: Irving Berlin.

**106 The Big Store.** US, 1941, BW, 80 m. D: Charles F. Riesner, MS: George Stoll, P: MGM (Louis K. Sidney).

*If It's You* (Tony Martin) WM: Ben Oakland, Artie Shaw and Milton Drake / *Rock-a-Bye Baby* (Virginia O'Brien) WM: Effie I. Crockett / *Sing While You Sell* (Groucho Marx, Chorus); *Tenement Symphony* (Tony Martin) W: Sid Kuller and Ray Golden—M: Hal Borne.

**107 The Big Street.** US, 1942, BW, 88 m. D: Irving Reis, MS: Roy Webb, P: RKO (Damon Runyon). Vocal: Martha Mears for Lucille Ball. Orch: Ozzie Nelson.

*Who Knows* (Lucille Ball) W: Mort Greene—M: Harry Revel.

**108 The Big TNT Show.** US, 1966, BW, 93 m. D: Larry Peerce, MD: Phil Spector, P: AIP (Phil Spector).

*Bells of Rhymney* (The Byrds) W: Idris Davies—M: Pete Seeger / *Be My Baby* (The Ronettes) WM: Jeff Barry, Ellie Greenwich and Phil Spector / *Bo Diddley* (Bo Diddley) WM: Ellas McDaniel / *The Break* (Bo Diddley) / *Dang Me* (Roger Miller) WM: Roger Miller / *Downtown* (Petula Clark) WM: Tony Hatch / *Do You Believe in Magic?* (The Lovin' Spoonful) WM: John B. Sebastian / *Engine, Engine Number Nine* (Roger Miller); *England Swings* (Roger Miller) WM: Roger Miller / *Five*

*Hundred Miles* (Joan Baez) WM: Bobby Bare, Hedy West and Charlie Williams / *Georgia on My Mind* (Ray Charles) W: Stuart Gorrell—M: Hoagy Carmichael / *It's Gonna Work Out Fine* (Ike and Tina Turner) WM: Rose Marie McCoy and Sylvia McKinney / *King of the Road* (Roger Miller) WM: Roger Miller / *Let the Good Times Roll* (Ray Charles) WM: Leonard Lee / *Mr. Tambourine Man* (The Byrds) WM: Bob Dylan / *My Sweet Joy* (Donovan) / *Road Runner* (Bo Diddley) WM: Ellas McDaniel / *Summer Day Reflection* (Donovan) / *Turn! Turn! Turn!* (The Byrds) WM: Pete Seeger / *The Universal Soldier* (Donovan) WM: Buffy Sainte-Marie / *What'd I Say?* (Ray Charles) WM: Ray Charles / *You Didn't Have to Be So Nice* (The Lovin' Spoonful) WM: John B. Sebastian and Steve Boone / *You've Lost That Lovin' Feelin'* (Joan Baez) WM: Phil Spector, Barry Mann and Cynthia Weil.

**109  The Big Town.** US, 1987, C, 109 m. D: Ben Bolt, MS: Michael Melvoin, P: Columbia (Martin Ransohoff, Don Carmody).

*Big Town* (Ronnie Self) / *Drown in My Own Tears* (Ray Charles) WM: Henry Glover / *Fever* (Little Willie John) WM: John Davenport, Otis Blackwell and Eddie Cooley / *Goodnight My Love* (Jesse Belvin) WM: George Motola and John Marascalco / *Home of the Blues* (Johnny Cash) WM: Johnny Cash, Glenn Douglas and Vic McAlpin / *Jim Dandy* (LaVerne Baker) WM: Lincoln Chase / *Mack the Knife* (Bobby Darin) Eng. W: Marc Blitzstein—M: Kurt Weill / *Ruby Baby* (The Drifters) WM: Jerry Leiber and Mike Stoller / *Shake, Rattle and Roll* (Big Joe Turner) WM: Charles Calhoun [Jesse Stone] / *Since I Met You Baby* (Ivory Joe Hunter) WM: Ivory Joe Hunter.

"Like the actors, the music and other 1950's trappings resemble tacky artificial decorations hung on the story." —Caryn James, *The New York Times*.

**110  Big Wednesday.** US, 1978, C, 119 m. D: John Milius, MS: Basil Poledouris, P: Warner (Buzz Feitshans). TV Title: Summer of Innocence.

*Do You Wanna Dance?* (Bobby Freeman) WM: Bobby Freeman / *He's a Rebel* (The Crystals) WM: Gene Pitney / *La Bamba* (Trini Lopez) WM: William Clauson / *The Loco-Motion* (Little Eva) WM: Gerry Goffin and Carole King / *Money* (Barrett Strong) WM: Janie Bradford and Berry Gordy, Jr. / *Sherry* (The Four Seasons) WM: Bob Gaudio / *The Twist* (Chubby Checker) WM: Hank Ballard / *Will You Love Me Tomorrow* (Carole King) WM: Gerry Goffin and Carole King.

**111  The Bigamist.** US, 1953, BW, 80 m. D: Ida Lupino, MS: Leith Stevens, P: Filmmakers (Collier Young).

*It Wasn't the Stars That Thrilled Me* (Matt Dennis) W: David Gilliam—M: Matt Dennis.

**112  Billy Jack.** US, 1971, C, 114 m. D: T.C. Frank [Tom Laughlin], MS: Mundell Lowe, P: Warner (Mary Rose Solti).

*One Tin Soldier* (Coven) WM: Dennis Lambert and Brian Potter / *The Ring Song* (Katy Moffatt) WM: Katy Moffatt.

**113  Billy Rose's Jumbo.** US, 1962, C, 123 m. D: Charles Walters, MD: George Stoll, P: MGM (Joe Pasternak, Martin Melcher). Vocals: James Joyce for Stephen Boyd. Alt. Title: Jumbo.

*The Circus Is on Parade* (Doris Day, Martha Raye, Jimmy Durante, Chorus); *Little Girl Blue* (Doris Day); *The Most Beautiful Girl in the World* (Stephen Boyd, Jimmy Durante); *My Romance* (Doris Day); *Over and Over Again* (Doris Day, Chorus) W: Lorenz Hart—M: Richard Rodgers / *Sawdust, Spangles and Dreams* (Doris Day, Martha Raye, Jimmy Durante, Stephen Boyd) WM: Roger Edens / *This Can't Be Love* (Doris Day, Jimmy Durante,

Stephen Boyd); *Why Can't I?* (Doris Day, Martha Raye) W: Lorenz Hart— M: Richard Rodgers.

"One of the final productions ever seen in the old N.Y. Hippodrome, 'Jumbo' was a dull book musical of the 1935 season. The showmanship of Metro has turned the combo musical and circus into a great film entertainment." — *Variety.*

**114  The Birds and the Bees.** US, 1956, C, 94 m. D: Norman Taurog, MS: Walter Scharf, P: Paramount (Paul Jones).

*The Birds and the Bees* (Mitzi Gaynor, George Gobel); *La Parisienne* (Mitzi Gaynor) W: Mack David— M: Harry Warren.

**115  The Birth of the Blues.** US, 1941, BW, 85 m. D: Victor Schertzinger, MD: Robert Emmett Dolan, P: Paramount (B.G. De Sylva, Monta Bell). Orch: Jack Teagarden.

*The Birth of the Blues* (Bing Crosby) W: B.G. De Sylva and Lew Brown— M: Ray Henderson / *By the Light of the Silvery Moon* (Bing Crosby) W: Edward Madden— M: Gus Edwards / *Cuddle Up a Little Closer* (Mary Martin) W: Otto Harbach— M: Karl Hoschna / *The Memphis Blues* (Bing Crosby) W: George A. Norton— M: W.C. Handy / *My Melancholy Baby* (Bing Crosby) W: George A. Norton— M: Ernie Burnett / *Saint James Infirmary* (Jack Teagarden) WM: Joe Primrose / *S-h-i-n-e* (Bing Crosby) W: Cecil Mack and Lew Brown— M: Ford Dabney / *St. Louis Blues* (Ruby Elzy) WM: W.C. Handy / *Tiger Rag* (Bing Crosby) W: Harry DeCosta— M: The Original Dixieland Jazz Band / *The Waiter and the Porter and the Upstairs Maid* (Mary Martin, Bing Crosby, Jack Teagarden) WM: Johnny Mercer / *Waiting at the Church* (Mary Martin) W: Fred W. Leigh— M: Henry E. Pether / *Wait 'Til the Sun Shines, Nellie* (Mary Martin, Bing Crosby) W: Andrew B. Sterling— M: Harry von Tilzer.

**116  Bitter Sweet.** GB, 1933, BW, 93 m. D: Herbert Wilcox, P: British and Dominion/UA (Herbert Wilcox).

The melody for the song *I'll See You Again* came to Noel Coward as he sat waiting in traffic in a New York City taxi. The rest of the score, which had been eluding him, then followed smoothly and without difficulty. The operetta opened in both London and New York in 1929 and was an enormous success.

*Dear Little Cafe* (Anna Neagle, Fernand Gravet); *If You Could Only Come with Me* (Fernand Gravet); *I'll See You Again* (Anna Neagle, Fernand Gravet); *Tell Me, What Is Love?* (Anna Neagle, Chorus); *Zigeuner* (Anna Neagle) WM: Noel Coward.

"Continuity takes many liberties with the operetta script, usually without improving it. ... Coward's score, hailed at the time of the stage presentation as brilliant, is a part of the picture and helps its class tone." — *Variety.*

**117  Bitter Sweet.** US, 1940, C, 92 m. D: W.S. Van Dyke II, P: MGM (Victor Saville).

*Dear Little Cafe* (Jeanette MacDonald, Nelson Eddy); *If You Could Only Come with Me* (Nelson Eddy); *I'll See You Again* (Jeanette MacDonald, Nelson Eddy); *Ladies of the Town* (Jeanette MacDonald, Muriel Goodspeed, Pamela Randall) WM: Noel Coward / *Love in Any Language Means Oui Oui* (Jeanette MacDonald, Nelson Eddy) W: Gus Kahn— M: Noel Coward / *Tell Me, What Is Love?* (Jeanette MacDonald, Nelson Eddy); *Tokay* (Nelson Eddy); *Zigeuner* (Jeanette MacDonald) WM: Noel Coward.

**118  The Blackboard Jungle.** US, 1955, BW, 101 m. D: Richard Brooks, MS: Charles Wolcott, P: MGM (Pandro S. Berman).

The first use of a rock song in a movie soundtrack.

*Rock Around the Clock* (Bill Haley and His Comets) WM: Max C. Freedman and Jimmy De Knight.

**119 Blazing Saddles.** US, 1974, C, 93 m. D: Mel Brooks, MS: John Morris, P: Warner (Michael Herzberg).

*Blazing Saddles* (Frankie Laine, Chorus) W: Mel Brooks—M: John Morris / *The French Mistake* (Men); *I'm Tired* (Madeline Kahn, Men) WM: Mel Brooks.

**120 Blessed Event.** US, 1932, BW, 83 m. D: Roy Del Ruth, P: Warner (Ray Griffith).

*I'm Making Hay in the Moonlight* (Dick Powell) W: Tot Seymour—M: Jesse Greer.

**121 Blind Date.** US, 1987, C, 93 m. D: Blake Edwards, MS: Henry Mancini, P: Tri-Star (Tony Adams).

*Anybody Seen Her?* (Billy Vera and The Beaters) WM: Billy Vera / *Crash, Bang Boom* (Hubert Tubbs) WM: Peter Bunetta and Joe Erickson / *Let You Get Away* (Billy Vera and The Beaters); *Oh, What a Nite* (Billy Vera and The Beaters) WM: Billy Vera / *Simply Meant to Be* (Gary Morris, Jennifer Warnes) WM: Shannon Rubicam, George Merrill and Henry Mancini / *Talked About Lover* (Keith L'Niere) WM: Keith L'Niere and Larry Brown / *Treasures* (Stanley Jordan) WM: Stanley Jordan.

**122 The Blob.** US, 1958, C, 86 m. D: Irvin S. Yeaworth, Jr., MS: Jean Yeaworth, P: Paramount (Jack H. Harris). GB Title: Son of Blob.

*The Blob* (The Five Blobs) W: Mack David—M: Burt Bacharach.

"Intriguing is the title number. ... It's sung offscreen by a harmony group as the credits unreel." —*Variety.*

**123 Blonde Venus.** US, 1932, BW, 97 m. D: Josef von Sternberg, MS: Oscar Poteker, P: Paramount. Performer: Marlene Dietrich.

*Hot Voodoo* W: Sam Coslow—M: Ralph Rainger / *I Couldn't Be More Annoyed* W: Leo Robin—M: Richard A. Whiting / *You Little So-and-So* W: Sam Coslow—M: Ralph Rainger.

**124 Blowing Wild.** US, 1953, BW, 90 m. D: Hugo Fregonese, P: Warner (Milton Sperling).

*Blowing Wild* (Frankie Laine) W: Paul Francis Webster—M: Dimitri Tiomkin.

**125 The Blue Angel.** Germany, 1930, BW, 103 m. D: Josef von Sternberg, P: UFA (Erich Pommer). Performer: Marlene Dietrich.

*Blonde Woman; Falling in Love Again; They Call Me Wicked Lola; This Evening, Children* Eng. W: Sammy Lerner—M: Frederick Hollander.

"Dietrich's final rendition of the main song astride a chair, as she tosses it with almost a sneer on her face at the low-brow mob in the sailors' dive, is something of a classic." —*Variety.*

**126 The Blue Angel.** US, 1959, C, 107 m. D: Edward Dmytryk, MS: Hugo Friedhofer, P: TCF (Jack Cummings). Performer: May Britt.

*Falling in Love Again* Eng. W: Sammy Lerner—M: Frederick Hollander / *Lola-Lola* WM: Jay Livingston and Ray Evans.

**127 Blue Collar.** US, 1978, C, 114 m. D: Paul Schrader, MS: Jack Nitzsche, P: Universal (Don Guest).

*Goodbye, So Long* (Ike and Tina Turner) WM: Ike Turner / *Hard Workin' Man* (Captain Beefheart) WM: Ry Cooder, Paul Schrader and Jack Nitzsche / *Saturday Night Special* (Lynyrd Skynyrd) WM: Edward King and Ronnie Van Zant / *Wang Dang Doodle* (Howlin' Wolf) WM: Willie Dixon.

**128 The Blue Gardenia.** US, 1953, BW, 90 m. D: Fritz Lang, MD: Raoul Kraushaar, P: Warner (Alex Gottlieb).

*Blue Gardenia* (Nat King Cole) WM: Bob Russell and Lester Lee.

**129 Blue Hawaii.** US, 1961, C, 101 m. D: Norman Taurog, MS: Joseph J. Lilley, P: Paramount (Hal B. Wallis). MB: The Jordanaires. Performer: Elvis Presley.

*Almost Always True* WM: Fred Wise and Ben Weisman / *Aloha Oe* WM: Queen Liliuokalani / *Beach Boy*

*Blues* WM: Sid Tepper and Roy C. Bennett / *Blue Hawaii* W: Leo Robin—M: Ralph Rainger / *Can't Help Falling in Love* WM: Hugo Peretti, Luigi Creatore and George Weiss / *Hawaiian Sunset* WM: Sid Tepper and Roy C. Bennett / *The Hawaiian Wedding Song* W: Al Hoffman and Dick Manning—M: Charles E. King / *Island of Love*; *Ito Eats* WM: Sid Tepper and Roy C. Bennett / *K-u-u-i-po* WM: Hugo Peretti, Luigi Creatore and George Weiss / *Moonlight Swim* WM: Sylvia Dee and Ben Weisman / *No More* WM: Don Robertson and Hal Blair / *Rock-a-Hula Baby* WM: Fred Wise, Dolores Fuller and Ben Weisman / *Slicin' Sand* WM: Sid Tepper and Roy C. Bennett.

**130  Blue Skies.** US, 1946, C, 104 m. D: Stuart Heisler, MD: Robert Emmett Dolan, P: Paramount (Sol C. Siegel).

*All by Myself* (Bing Crosby, Joan Caulfield); *Always* (Chorus); *Any Bonds Today?* (Bing Crosby); *Blue Skies* (Bing Crosby); *A Couple of Song and Dance Men* (Fred Astaire, Bing Crosby); *Everybody Step* (Bing Crosby); *Getting Nowhere* (Bing Crosby); *Heat Wave* (Olga San Juan, Chorus); *How Deep Is the Ocean?* (Bing Crosby, Chorus); *I'll See You in C-U-B-A* (Olga San Juan, Bing Crosby); *I've Got My Captain Working for Me Now* (Billy De Wolfe, Bing Crosby); *The Little Things in Life* (Bing Crosby); *Not for All the Rice in China* (Bing Crosby); *A Pretty Girl Is Like a Melody* (Chorus); *Puttin' on the Ritz* (Fred Astaire); *Russian Lullaby* (Bing Crosby, Male Quartet); *Serenade to an Old Fashioned Girl* (Joan Caulfield, Chorus); *This Is the Army, Mr. Jones* (Bing Crosby); *White Christmas* (Bing Crosby); *You'd Be Surprised* (Olga San Juan); *You Keep Coming Back Like a Song* (Bing Crosby) WM: Irving Berlin.

"Fred Astaire's *Puttin' on the Ritz* (originally written for Harry Richman) is the musical standout." —*Variety*.

**131  The Blue Veil.** US, 1951, BW, 113 m. D: Curtis Bernhardt, MS: Franz Waxman, P: RKO (Raymond Hakim). Performer: Joan Blondell.

*Daddy* WM: Bobby Troup / *I Couldn't Sleep a Wink Last Night* W: Harold Adamson—M: Jimmy McHugh / *There'll Be Some Changes Made* W: Billy Higgins—M: W. Benton Overstreet.

**132  Blue Velvet.** US, 1986, C, 120 m. D: David Lynch, MS: Angelo Badalamenti, P: De Laurentiis (Fred Caruso).

Singer Ketty Lester left nurses' training to study music. She made her singing debut at the Purple Onion in San Francisco. *Love Letters* was her first million-selling record in 1962.

*Blue Velvet* (Bobby Vinton) WM: Bernie Wayne and Lee Morris / *In Dreams* (Roy Orbison) WM: Roy Orbison / *Love Letters* (Ketty Lester) W: Edward Heyman—Victor Young.

**133  The Blues Brothers.** US, 1980, C, 130 m. D: John Landis, MD: Ira Newborn, P: Universal (Robert K. Weiss).

*Everybody Needs Somebody to Love* (Dan Aykroyd, John Belushi) WM: Jerry Wexler, Bert Berns and Solomon Burke / *Gimme Some Lovin'* (Dan Aykroyd, John Belushi) WM: Steve Winwood, Muff Winwood and Spencer Davis / *I'm Walkin'* (Fats Domino) WM: Antoine "Fats" Domino and Dave Bartholomew / *Jailhouse Rock* (Dan Aykroyd, John Belushi) WM: Jerry Leiber and Mike Stoller / *Minnie the Moocher* (Cab Calloway) WM: Cab Calloway, Irving Mills and Clarence Gaskill / *The Old Landmark* (James Brown) WM: A.M. Brunner / *Shake a Tail Feather* (Ray Charles) W: Verlie Rice—M: Andre Williams and Otha Hayes / *She Caught the Katy* (Dan Aykroyd, John Belushi) WM: Taj Mahal and Yank Rachel / *Sweet Home Chicago* (Dan Aykroyd, John Belushi) WM: Woody Payne / *Theme from Rawhide* (Dan Aykroyd, John Belushi)

W: Ned Washington—M: Dimitri Tiomkin / *Think* (Aretha Franklin) WM: Aretha Franklin and Ted White.

"Film's greatest pleasure comes from watching the likes of James Brown, Cab Calloway, Ray Charles and especially Aretha Franklin do their musical things." —*Variety.*

**134 Blues for Lovers.** GB, 1966, BW, 89 m. D: Paul Henried, MS: Ray Charles and Stanley Black, P: TCF (Herman Blaser) GB Title: Ballad in Blue. MB: The Raelettes. Performer: Ray Charles.

*Cry,* which became singer Johnnie Ray's first big hit, was written by a night watchman at a dry cleaning company in Pittsburgh who entered it in an amateur competition in 1951.

*Careless Love* WM: W.C. Handy and Spencer Williams / *Cry* WM: Churchill Kohlman / *Hallelujah, I Love Her So* WM: Ray Charles / *I Got a Woman* WM: Ray Charles and Renald J. Richard / *Let the Good Times Roll* WM: Leonard Lee / *Light Out of Darkness* WM: Stanley Black / *Talkin' About You* / *That Lucky Old Sun* W: Haven Gillespie—M: Beasley Smith / *Unchain My Heart* WM: Freddy James and Agnes Jones / *What'd I Say?* WM: Ray Charles.

**135 Bob and Carol and Ted and Alice.** US, 1969, C, 104 m. D: Paul Mazursky, MS: Quincy Jones, P: Columbia (Larry Tucker).

*What the World Needs Now Is Love* (Jackie De Shannon) W: Hal David—M: Burt Bacharach.

**136 Body Slam.** US, 1987, C, 89 m. D: Hal Needham, P: Hemdale (Shel Lytton, Mike Curb).

*American Way* (Kick) WM: David Hallowren / *Bad News Travels Fast* (Bachman Turner Overdrive) WM: Randy Bachman / *Body Slam* (Debbie Lytton) WM: Michael Lloyd / *Book of Love* (Frankie Valli and The Four Seasons) WM: Warren Davis, George Malone and Charles Patrick / *My Body Keeps Changin' My Mind* (Moses

Tyson, Jr.) WM: Leslie Pearl and Darryl Tyson, Jr. / *Push* (Kick) WM: David Hallowren / *Rock 'n' Roll Heart* (Kick) WM: Jack D'Amore and Peter Beckett / *Takin' Care of Business* (Bachman Turner Overdrive) WM: Randy Bachman / *The Time Is Right* (Jimmy Scarlett and The Dimensions) WM: Michael Lloyd.

**137 Born Free.** GB, 1966, C, 96 m. D: James Hill, MS: John Barry, P: Columbia/Open Road (Carl Foreman)/High Road (Sam Jaffe, Paul Radin).

*Born Free* (Matt Monro) W: Don Black—M: John Barry.

**138 Born to Dance.** US, 1936, BW, 105 m. D: Roy Del Ruth, MD: Alfred Newman, P: MGM (Jack Cummings).

Cole Porter's first film score.

*Easy to Love* (James Stewart, Frances Langford); *Entrance of Lucy James* (Chorus); *Hey, Babe, Hey!* (Eleanor Powell, James Stewart, Frances Langford, Una Merkel, Buddy Ebsen, Sid Silvers); *I've Got You Under My Skin* (Virginia Bruce); *Love Me, Love My Pekingese* (Virginia Bruce, Raymond Walburn, Chorus); *Rap Tap on Wood* (Eleanor Powell, The Foursome); *Rolling Home* (James Stewart, Buddy Ebsen, Sid Silvers, The Foursome, Chorus); *Swingin' the Jinx Away* (Frances Langford, Buddy Ebsen, The Foursome, Chorus) WM: Cole Porter.

"Comedy breaks into song and song gives place to dancing with the swift and effortless ease of the changing of partners at the six-day bicycle races. ... No fewer than seven Cole Porter compositions, most of them destined to a good measure of the ephemeral fame of modern song hits, punctuate the proceedings." —John T. McManus, *The New York Times.*

**139 The Boy Friend.** GB, 1971, C, 135 m. D: Ken Russell, MD: Ian Whittaker, Peter Greenwell and Peter Maxwell Davies, P: MGM (Ken Russell).

*All I Do Is Dream of You* (Twiggy) W: Arthur Freed—M: Nacio Herb Brown / *The Boy Friend* (Twiggy, Chorus); *Fancy Forgetting* (Bryan Pringle, Moyra Fraser); *I Could Be Happy with You* (Twiggy, Christopher Gable); *It's Never Too Late to Fall in Love* (Max Adrian, Georgina Hale); *It's Nicer in Nice* (Barbara Windsor, Chorus); *Perfect Young Ladies* (Barbara Windsor, Antonia Ellis, Georgina Hale, Sally Bryant, Caryl Little); *Poor Little Pierette* (Twiggy, Moyra Fraser, Chorus); *The Riviera* (Chorus); *A Room in Bloomsbury* (Twiggy, Christopher Gable); *Safety in Numbers* (Antonia Ellis, Tommy Tune, Brian Murphy, Graham Armitage, Murray Melvin, Christopher Gable); *Sur La Plage* (Barbara Windsor, Chorus); *Won't You Charleston with Me?* (Antonia Ellis, Tommy Tune) WM: Sandy Wilson / *You Are My Lucky Star* (Twiggy) W: Arthur Freed—M: Nacio Herb Brown / *The You-Don't-Want-to-Play-with-Me Blues* (Moyra Fraser, Bryan Pringle, Chorus) WM: Sandy Wilson.

"Ken Russell's ... version of Sandy Wilson's 1950's musical about the 1920's ... is not so much an adaptation as almost total transformation—honorable transformation, for the most part." —Roger Greenspun, *The New York Times.*

**140  Boy on a Dolphin.** US, 1957, C, 111 m. D: Jean Negulesco, MS: Hugo Friedhofer, P: TCF (Samuel G. Engel).

*Boy on a Dolphin* (Julie London) Eng. W: Paul Francis Webster—Greek W: J. Fermanoglou—M: Takis Morakis.

**141  The Boys from Syracuse.** US, 1940, BW, 73 m. D: A. Edward Sutherland, MS: Frank Skinner, P: Universal (Jules Levey).

Eddie Albert and Burl Ives were in the original 1938 stage production of this adaptation of Shakespeare's 'Comedy of Errors.'

*Falling in Love with Love* (Allan Jones, Rosemary Lane); *The Greeks Have No Word for It* (Martha Raye); *He and She* (Martha Raye, Joe Penner); *Sing for Your Supper* (Martha Raye); *Who Are You?* (Allan Jones) W: Lorenz Hart—M: Richard Rodgers.

"Raye, provided with the swell Rodgers and Hart tunes, gets good opportunity to use her pipes. ... Allan Jones capably acts and warbles his way through the top characterization." —*Variety.*

**142  Boys' Town.** US, 1938, BW, 96 m. D: Norman Taurog, MS: Edward Ward, P: MGM (John W. Considine, Jr.).

*Drink to Me Only with Thine Eyes* (Chorus) W: Ben Jonson—M: Unknown, possibly Colonel R. Mellish / *Silent Night* (Chorus) W: Joseph Mohr—M: Franz Gruber.

**143  Breakfast at Tiffany's.** US, 1961, C, 115 m. D: Blake Edwards, MS: Henry Mancini, P: Paramount (Martin Jurow, Richard Shepherd).

*Moon River* (Audrey Hepburn) W: Johnny Mercer— M: Henry Mancini.

**144  Breaking Glass.** GB, 1980, C, 104 m. D: Brian Gibson, MD: Tony Visconti, P: Paramount (Davina Belling, Clive Parsons). Performer: Hazel O'Connor.

*Big Brother; Black Man; Calls the Tune; Come Into the Air; Eighth Day; Give Me an Inch; If Only; Monsters in Disguise; One More Time* (Victy Silva); *Top of the Wheel; Who Needs It?; Will You?; Writing on the Wall* WM: Hazel O'Connor.

**145  The Breaking Point.** US, 1950, BW, 97 m. D: Michael Curtiz, MD: Ray Heindorf, P: Warner (Jerry Wald).

*Please Don't Talk About Me When I'm Gone* (Patricia Neal) W: Sidney Clare—M: Sam H. Stept.

**146  Brigadoon.** US, 1954, C, 108 m. D: Vincente Minnelli, MD: Johnny Green, P: MGM (Arthur Freed). Vocals: John Gustafson for

Jimmy Thompson; Carole Richards for Cyd Charisse.

*Almost Like Being in Love* (Gene Kelly); *Brigadoon* (Chorus); *Down on MacConnachy Square* (Chorus); *The Heather on the Hill* (Gene Kelly); *I'll Go Home with Bonnie Jean* (Jimmy Thompson, Van Johnson, Gene Kelly, Chorus); *Once in the Highlands* (Chorus); *Waitin' for My Dearie* (Cyd Charisse, Chorus) W: Alan Jay Lerner—M: Frederick Loewe.

"In transferring 'Brigadoon,' a click as a [1947] Broadway musical play, to the screen, Metro has medium success. It's a fairly entertaining tune-film of mixed appeal." — *Variety.*

**147  Bright Eyes.** US, 1934, BW, 83 m. D: David Butler, MS: Samuel Kaylin, M: Fox (Sol M. Wurtzel). MB: St. Luke's Chorister.

*On the Good Ship Lollipop* (Shirley Temple) W: Sidney Clare—M: Richard A. Whiting.

**148  Bright Lights, Big City.** US, 1988, C, 110 m. D: James Bridges, MS: Donald Fagen, P: UA (Mark Rosenberg, Sydney Pollack).

*Bright Lights, Big City* (Donald Fagen) WM: Jimmy Reed / *Century's End* (Donald Fagen) WM: Donald Fagen and T. Meher / *Divine Emotions* (Narada) WM: N.M. Walden and J. Cohen / *Good Love* (Prince) WM: Prince / *Ice Cream Days* (Jennifer Hall) WM: Jennifer Hall and A. Tarney / *Kiss and Tell* (Bryan Ferry) WM: Bryan Ferry / *Love Attack* (Konk) WM: S. Dawson and G. "Love" Jay / *Obsessed* (The Noise Club) WM: O. Lieber / *Pleasure, Little Treasure* (Depeche Mode) WM: Martin L. Gore / *Pump Up the Volume* (M/A/R/R/S) WM: Martyn Young and Steve Young / *True Faith* (New Order) WM: New Order and Stephan Hague.

**149  Bright Road.** US, 1953, BW, 69 m. D: Gerald Mayer, P: MGM (Sol Baer Fielding).

*Suzanne* (Harry Belafonte) WM: Harry Belafonte and Millard Thomas.

**150  Bringing Up Baby.** US, 1938, BW, 102 m. D: Howard Hawks, MS: Roy Webb, P: RKO (Howard Hawks).

*I Can't Give You Anything But Love, Baby* (Katharine Hepburn, Cary Grant) W: Dorothy Fields—M: Jimmy McHugh.

**151  The Broadway Melody.** US, 1929, BW/C, 104 m. D: Harry Beaumont, P: MGM (Irving Thalberg).

Hollywood's first musical film and first score written specifically for the screen. Its stars and chorus were imported from Broadway and vaudeville; it premiered in Hollywood at Grauman's Chinese Theater on February 1, 1929, and opened in New York at the Astor Theater on February 8. The prodigiously talented songwriter Arthur Freed later became the prodigiously talented producer of musicals for MGM.

*The Boy Friend* (Anita Page, Bessie Love); *The Broadway Melody* (Charles King, Anita Page, Bessie Love); *Harmony Babies* (Bessie Love, Anita Page); *The Love Boat* (James Burrows) W: Arthur Freed—M: Nacio Herb Brown / *Truthful Parson Brown* (Biltmore Trio) WM: Willard Robinson / *The Wedding of the Painted Doll* (James Burrows); *You Were Meant for Me* (Charles King) W: Arthur Freed—M: Nacio Herb Brown.

"This alternately lachrymose, laughable and bellicose feature is called 'The Broadway Melody,' a title that refers to a song composed and rendered by the leading male character." —Mordaunt Hall, *The New York Times.*

**152  Broadway Melody of 1936.** US, 1935, BW, 103 m. D: Roy Del Ruth, MD: Alfred Newman, P: MGM (John W. Considine, Jr.). Vocals: Marjorie Lane for Eleanor Powell.

*All I Do Is Dream of You* (Unidentified Singer); *The Broadway Melody* (Harry Stockwell); *Broadway Rhythm* (Frances Langford); *I've Got a Feelin'*

*You're Foolin'* (Robert Taylor, June Knight, Frances Langford); *On a Sunday Afternoon* (Vilma Ebsen, Buddy Ebsen, Chorus); *Sing Before Breakfast* (Vilma Ebsen, Buddy Ebsen, Eleanor Powell); *You Are My Lucky Star* (Eleanor Powell, Frances Langford) W: Arthur Freed—M: Nacio Herb Brown.

"Songs are all good. *Broadway Rhythm* ... is a corking creation." — *Variety.*

**153 Broadway Melody of 1938.** US, 1937, BW, 110 m. D: Roy Del Ruth, MD: George Stoll, P: MGM (Jack Cummings). MB: The Robert Mitchell Boychoir.

*The Broadway Melody* (Chorus); *Everybody Sing* (Judy Garland, Sophie Tucker, Barnett Parker, Chorus); *Follow in My Footsteps* (Eleanor Powell, George Murphy, Buddy Ebsen); *I'm Feelin' Like a Million* (Eleanor Powell, George Murphy) W: Arthur Freed—M: Nacio Herb Brown / *Some of These Days* (Sophie Tucker) WM: Shelton Brooks / *You Made Me Love You* (Judy Garland) W: Joseph McCarthy—M: James V. Monaco—Arr: Roger Edens / *Your Broadway and My Broadway* (Sophie Tucker, Charles Igor Gorin, Chorus); *Yours and Mine* (Judy Garland, Eleanor Powell) W: Arthur Freed—M: Nacio Herb Brown.

"Judy sings a plaint to Clark Gable's photograph which is close to great screen acting. Then, to top it off, Soph does *Your Broadway and My Broadway*, with lyrics which bring in the great names of the past generation." — *Variety.*

**154 Broadway Melody of 1940.** US, 1940, BW, 102 m. D: Norman Taurog, MD: Alfred Newman, P: MGM (Jack Cummings).

*Begin the Beguine* (Lois Hodnett, The Music Maids); *Between You and Me* (George Murphy) WM: Cole Porter / *I Am the Captain* (Eleanor Powell, Chorus) WM: Roger Edens / *I Concentrate on You* (Douglas McPhail); *I've Got My Eyes on You* (Fred Astaire);

*Please Don't Monkey with Broadway* (Fred Astaire, George Murphy) WM: Cole Porter.

**155 Broadway Rhythm.** US, 1944, C, 114 m. D: Roy Del Ruth, MD: Johnny Green, P: MGM (Jack Cummings). Orch: Tommy Dorsey.

*All in Fun* (George Murphy); *All the Things You Are* (Ginny Simms) W: Oscar Hammerstein II—M: Jerome Kern / *Amor* (Ginny Simms) Eng. W: Sunny Skylar—Span. W: Ricardo Mendez—M: Gabriel Ruiz / *Brazilian Boogie* (Lena Horne) WM: Hugh Martin and Ralph Blane / *Ida, Sweet as Apple Cider* (Kenny Bowers) W: Eddie Leonard—M: Eddie Munson / *I Love Corny Music* (Charles Winninger) W: Don Raye—M: Gene de Paul / *In Other Words* (George Murphy) W: Oscar Hammerstein II—M: Jerome Kern / *Irresistible You* (Ginny Simms, George Murphy); *Milkman, Keep Those Bottles Quiet* (Nancy Walker, Ben Blue) W: Don Raye—M: Gene de Paul / *Oh You Beautiful Doll* (Charles Winninger) W: A. Seymour Brown—M: Nat D. Ayer / *Pretty Baby* (Gloria De Haven, Charles Winninger, Kenny Bowers) W: Gus Kahn—M: Tony Jackson and Egbert Van Alstyne / *Seventeen* (George Murphy) W: Oscar Hammerstein II—M: Jerome Kern / *Somebody Loves Me* (Lena Horne) W: B.G. De Sylva and Ballard MacDonald—M: George Gershwin / *That Lucky Fellow* (George Murphy) W: Oscar Hammerstein II—M: Jerome Kern / *What Do You Think I Am* (Gloria De Haven, Kenny Bowers) WM: Hugh Martin and Ralph Blane.

"A typical backstage filmusical wheeled out in the usual Metro elaborate and colorful style. ... Lena Horne socks over two songs ... and both are smartly presented for maximum effect." — *Variety.*

**156 Broadway Thru a Keyhole.** US, 1933, BW, 90 m. D: Lowell Sherman, MD: Alfred Newman, P: UA (William Goetz, Raymond Griffith).

*Doin' the Uptown Lowdown* (Frances Williams); *I Love You Pizzicato* (Russ Columbo, Constance Cummings); *When You Were a Girl on a Scooter and I Was a Boy on a Bike* (Constance Cummings, Eddie Foy, Jr., Chorus); *You're My Past, Present and Future* (Russ Columbo) W: Mack Gordon—M: Harry Revel.

**157 Bronco Billy.** US, 1980, C, 119 m. D: Clint Eastwood, MD: Snuff Garrett and Steve Dorff, P: Warner (Neal Dubrovsky, Dennis Hackin).

*Bar Room Buddies* (Clint Eastwood, Merle Haggard) WM: Cliff Crofford, Snuff Garrett, Steve Dorff and Milton Brown / *Bayou Lullaby* (Penny De Haven) WM: Cliff Crofford and Snuff Garrett / *Bronco Billy* (Ronnie Milsap) WM: Snuff Garrett, Steve Dorff and Milton Brown / *Cowboys and Clowns* (Ronnie Milsap) WM: Snuff Garrett, Steve Dorff, Gary Harju and Larry Herbstritt / *Misery and Gin* (Merle Haggard) WM: John Durrill and Snuff Garrett / *Stardust Cowboy* (The Reinsmen) WM: Cliff Crofford and Snuff Garrett.

**158 Buck Benny Rides Again.** US, 1940, BW, 82 m. D: Mark Sandrich, P: Paramount (Mark Sandrich).

*Drums in the Night* (Lillian Cornell); *My Kind of Country* (Lillian Cornell); *My! My!* (Eddie "Rochester" Anderson); *Say It* (Ellen Drew, Virginia Dale, Lillian Cornell) W: Frank Loesser—M: Jimmy McHugh.

**159 Buck Privates.** US, 1941, BW, 84 m. D: Arthur Lubin, MD: Charles Previn, P: Universal (Alex Gottlieb). Performers: The Andrews Sisters. GB Title: Rookies.

*Boogie Woogie Bugle Boy; Bounce Me Brother with a Solid Four* WM: Don Raye and Hughie Prince / *I'll Be with You in Apple Blossom Time* W: Neville Fleeson—M: Albert von Tilzer / *You're a Lucky Fellow, Mr. Smith* WM: J. Francis "Sonny" Burke, Don Raye and Hughie Prince.

**160 Buddy Buddy.** US, 1981, C, 96 m. D: Billy Wilder, MS: Lalo Schifrin, P: MGM (Jay Weston).

*Cecilia* (Michael Dees) W: Herman Ruby—M: Dave Dreyer.

**161 The Buddy Holly Story.** US, 1978, C, 113 m. D: Steve Rash, MD: Joe Renzetti, P: Columbia (Fred Bauer). Performer: Gary Busey.

Buddy Holly, born Charles Hardin Holly in Lubbock, Texas, on September 7, 1936, used the name Charles Hardin as a pseudonym for some of the songs he wrote. In 1956 he met Norman Petty, who for a while was his co-writer and manager of his group, The Crickets.

*Chantilly Lace* (Gailard Sartain) WM: J.P. Richardson / *Everyday* WM: Buddy Holly and Norman Petty / *I'm Gonna Love You Too* WM: Joe B. Mauldin, Norman Petty and Niki Sullivan / *It's So Easy; Listen to Me; Maybe Baby; Not Fade Away* WM: Buddy Holly and Norman Petty / *Oh Boy* WM: Sonny West, Bill Tilghman and Norman Petty / *Peggy Sue* WM: Buddy Holly, Norman Petty and Jerry Allison / *Rave On* WM: Sonny West, Bill Tilghman and Norman Petty / *Rock Around with Ollie Vee* WM: Sonny Curtis / *That'll Be the Day* WM: Buddy Holly, Norman Petty and Jerry Allison / *True Love Ways* WM: Buddy Holly and Norman Petty / *Well All Right* WM: Joe B. Mauldin, Buddy Holly, Norman Petty and Jerry Allison / *Whole Lotta Shakin' Goin' On* (Jerry Zaremba) WM: Dave Williams and Sunny David / *Words of Love* WM: Buddy Holly.

"Smacks of realism in almost every respect. ... The musical numbers ... were recorded live, using 24 tracks, and there was no studio rerecording." — *Variety*.

**162 Bull Durham.** US, 1988, C, 108 m. D: Ron Shelton, MS: Michael Convertino, P: Orion (Thom Mount, Mark Burg).

*All Night Dance* (Bennie Wallace and Dr. John, with Stevie Ray Vaughan)

WM: Bennie Wallace / *Born to Be Bad* (George Thorogood and The Destroyers) WM: George Thorogood / *Can't Tear It Up Enuff* (The Fabulous Thunderbirds) WM: Kim Wilson / *Centerfield* (John Fogerty) WM: John C. Fogerty / *I Got Loaded* (Los Lobos) WM: Camille Bob / *Love Ain't No Triple Play* (Bennie Wallace and Dr. John, with Bonnie Raitt) WM: Bennie Wallace and Mac "Dr. John" Rebennack / *Middle of Nowhere* (House of Schock) WM: G. Schlock and V. DeGeneras / *So Long Baby, Goodbye* (The Blasters) WM: David Alvin / *Try a Little Tenderness* (Bennie Wallace and Dr. John) WM: Harry M. Woods, Jimmy Campbell and Reg Connelly / *A Woman Loves a Man* (Joe Cocker) WM: Dan Hartman and Charlie Midnight / *You Done Me Wrong* (Pat McLaughlin) WM: Pat McLaughlin.

**163  Bundle of Joy.** US, 1956, C, 98 m. D: Norman Taurog, MS: Josef Myrow, P: RKO (Edmund Grainger).

*All About Love* (Eddie Fisher, Chorus); *Bundle of Joy* (Eddie Fisher); *I Never Felt This Way Before* (Debbie Reynolds, Eddie Fisher); *Lullaby in Blue* (Debbie Reynolds, Eddie Fisher); *Some Day Soon* (Eddie Fisher); *What's So Good About Good Morning* (Debbie Reynolds, Nita Talbot); *Worry About Tomorrow Tomorrow* (Debbie Reynolds, Eddie Fisher, Nita Talbot) W: Mack Gordon—M: Josef Myrow.

"Its music and so-called dances are depressingly lacking in class." —Bosley Crowther, *The New York Times.*

**164  Bus Stop.** US, 1956, C, 96 m. D: Joshua Logan, MS: Alfred Newman and Cyril Mockridge, P: TCF (Buddy Adler).

*The Bus Stop Song* (The Four Lads) WM: Ken Darby / *That Old Black Magic* (Marilyn Monroe) W: Johnny Mercer—M: Harold Arlen.

**165  Buster.** GB, 1988, C, 102 m. D: David Green, MS: Anne Dudley, P:

Hemdale (Norma Heyman).

*Big Noise* (Phil Collins) WM: Lamont Dozier and Phil Collins / *A Groovy Kind of Love* (Phil Collins) WM: Toni Wine and Carole Bayer Sager / *How Do You Do It* (Gerry and The Pacemakers) WM: Mitch Murray / *I Got You Babe* (Sonny and Cher) WM: Sonny Bono / *I Just Don't Know What to Do with Myself* (Dusty Springfield) W: Hal David—M: Burt Bacharach / *Just One Look* (The Hollies) WM: Gregory Carroll and Doris Payne / *Loco in Acapulco* (The Four Tops) WM: Lamont Dozier and Phil Collins / *Robbery* (Anne Dudley) / *Sweets for My Sweet* (The Searchers) WM: Doc Pomus and Mort Shuman / *Two Hearts* (Phil Collins) WM: Lamont Dozier and Phil Collins / *Will You Still Be Waiting?* (Anne Dudley).

"A little extra dividend is the Four Tops song heard on the soundtrack as the Edwardses supposedly live it up in Acapulco." —Janet Maslin, *The New York Times.*

**166  Butch Cassidy and the Sundance Kid.** US, 1969, C, 112 m. D: George Roy Hill, MS: Burt Bacharach, P: TCF (John Foreman). Performer: B.J. Thomas.

*On a Bicycle Built for Joy; Raindrops Keep Fallin' on My Head* W: Hal David—M: Burt Bacharach.

**167  By the Light of the Silvery Moon.** US, 1953, C, 102 m. D: David Butler, MD: Ray Heindorf, MS: Max Steiner, P: Warner (William Jacobs).

*Ain't We Got Fun?* (Doris Day, Gordon MacRae, Russell Arms) W: Gus Kahn and Raymond B. Egan—M: Richard A. Whiting / *Be My Little Baby Bumble Bee* (Gordon MacRae) W: Stanley Murphy—M: Henry I. Marshall / *By the Light of the Silvery Moon* (Doris Day, Gordon MacRae) W: Edward Madden—M: Gus Edwards / *If You Were the Only Girl in the World* (Doris Day, Gordon MacRae) W: Clifford Grey—M: Nat D. Ayer / *I'll Forget You* (Doris Day) W: Annelu Burns—

M: Ernest R. Ball / *Just One Girl* (Gordon MacRae) W: Karl Kennett—M: Lyn Udall / *King Chanticleer* (Doris Day) W: A.S. Brown—M: Nat D. Ayer / *Meet Me in St. Louis, Louis* (Leon Ames) W: Andrew B. Sterling—M: Kerry Mills / *Your Eyes Have Told Me So* (Doris Day, Gordon MacRae) W: Gus Kahn and Egbert Van Alstyne—M: Walter Blaufuss.

**168  Bye Bye Birdie.** US, 1963, C, 112 m. D: George Sidney, MD: Johnny Green, P: Columbia (Fred Kohlmar, George Sidney).

Before it was a movie it was the first Broadway hit musical about rock and roll, opening on April 14, 1960, with Dick Van Dyke and Chita Rivera as its leads.

*Bye Bye Birdie* (Ann-Margret, Paul Lynde, Mary LaRoche, Bryan Russell); *Honestly Sincere* (Jesse Pearson); *How Lovely to Be a Woman* (Ann-Margret); *Hymn for a Sunday Evening* (Ann-Margret, Paul Lynde, Mary LaRoche, Bryan Russell); *Kids* (Dick Van Dyke, Paul Lynde, Maureen Stapleton, Bryan Russell); *A Lot of Livin' to Do* (Ann-Margret, Jesse Pearson, Bobby Rydell); *One Boy* (Ann-Margret, Janet Leigh, Bobby Rydell); *One Last Kiss* (Ann-Margret, Jesse Pearson, Bobby Rydell); *Put On a Happy Face* (Dick Van Dyke, Janet Leigh); *Rosie* (Ann-Margret, Dick Van Dyke, Janet Leigh, Bobby Rydell); *The Telephone Hour* (Bobby Rydell, The Sweet Apple Teenagers); *We Love You, Conrad* (Ann-Margret, Chorus) W: Lee Adams—M: Charles Strouse.

"The songs fit in nicely ... Rydell gets the right kind of chance to warble. Ann-Margret ... is a wow." —*Variety*.

**169  Cabaret.** US, 1972, C, 128 m. D: Bob Fosse, MD: Ralph Burns, P: AA (Cy Feuer). Vocals: Mark Lambert for Oliver Collignon.

*Cabaret* (Liza Minnelli); *Heiraten* (Greta Keller); *If You Could See Her* (Joel Grey); *Maybe This Time* (Liza Minnelli); *Mein Herr* (Liza Minnelli); *Money* (Liza Minnelli, Joel Grey); *Tomorrow Belongs to Me* (Oliver Collignon); *Two Ladies* (Joel Grey, Angelika Koch, Louise Quick); *Willkommen* (Joel Grey, Chorus) W: Fred Ebb—M: John Kander.

"Not so much a movie musical as it is a movie with a lot of music in it. Several numbers from the Broadway show [1966] have been dropped, and some new, and better ones added." —Roger Greenspun, *The New York Times*.

**170  Cabin in the Sky.** US, 1943, BW, 100 m. D: Vincente Minnelli, MD: George Stoll, P: MGM (Arthur Freed). Orch: Duke Ellington. MB: The Hall Johnson Choir.

*Cabin in the Sky* (Ethel Waters, Eddie "Rochester" Anderson) W: John Latouche—M: Vernon Duke / *Happiness Is a Thing Called Joe* (Ethel Waters) W: E.Y. Harburg—M: Harold Arlen / *Honey in the Honeycomb* (Lena Horne, Ethel Waters) W: John Latouche—M: Vernon Duke / *Life's Full of Consequence* (Lena Horne, Eddie "Rochester" Anderson); *Li'l Black Sheep* (Ethel Waters) E.Y. Harburg—M: Harold Arlen / *Old Ship of Zion* (Kenneth Spencer) WM: Unknown / *S-h-i-n-e* (John W. Bubbles) W: Cecil Mack and Lew Brown—M: Ford Dabney / *Taking a Chance on Love* (Ethel Waters) W: John Latouche and Ted Fetter—M: Vernon Duke.

"Every inch as sparkling and satisfying as was the original stage production back in 1940. ... The main thing is that Miss Waters is on hand, for there are songs to be sung ... and in that respect she is incomparable." —Thomas M. Pryor, *The New York Times*.

**171  The Caddy.** US, 1953, BW, 95 m. D: Norman Taurog, MS: Joseph J. Lilley, P: Paramount (Paul Jones).

*The Gay Continental* (Jerry Lewis); *It's a Whistlin' Kinda Mornin'* (Dean Martin); *One Big Love* (Dean Martin); *That's Amore* (Dean Martin, Jerry Lewis, Barbara Bates, Argentina Bru-

netti); *What Would You Do Without
Me?* (Dean Martin, Jerry Lewis);
*You're the Right One* (Dean Martin) W:
Jack Brooks—M: Harry Warren.
**172  Caddyshack.** US, 1980, C,
99 m. D: Harold Ramis, MS: Johnny
Mandel, P: Orion (Douglas Kenney).
*I'm Alright* (Kenny Loggins) WM:
Kenny Loggins.
**173  The Caine Mutiny.** US,
1954, C, 125 m. D: Edward Dmytryk,
MS: Max Steiner, P: Columbia (Stan-
ley Kramer).
*I Can't Believe That You're in Love
with Me* (May Wynn) W: Clarence Gas-
kill—M: Jimmy McHugh.
**174  Cairo.** US, 1942, BW, 101
m. D: W.S. Van Dyke II, MD: Herbert
Stothart, P: MGM (Joseph L. Man-
kiewicz).
*Avalon* (Jeanette MacDonald,
Robert Young) WM: Al Jolson, B.G.
De Sylva and Vincent Rose / *Beautiful
Ohio* (Jeanette MacDonald, Chorus)
W: Ballard MacDonald—M: Mary
Earl [Robert A. King] / *Buds Won't Bud*
(Ethel Waters) W: E.Y. Harburg—M:
Harold Arlen / *Cairo* (Jeanette Mac-
Donald, Chorus) W: E.Y. Harburg—
M: Arthur Schwartz / *From the Land of
the Sky Blue Water* (Jeanette Mac-
Donald, Chorus) W: Nelle Richmond
Eberhart—M: Charles Wakefield Cad-
man / *Home Sweet Home* (Jeanette
MacDonald, Chorus) W: John Howard
Payne—M: Sir Henry Bishop / *Keep the
Light Burning Bright in the Harbor*
(Jeanette MacDonald) W: E.Y. Har-
burg—M: Arthur Schwartz / *Waiting
for the Robert E. Lee* (Ethel Waters) W:
L. Wolfe Gilbert—M: Lewis F. Muir.
**175  Calamity Jane.** US, 1953,
C, 101 m. D: David Butler, MD: Ray
Heindorf, P: Warner (William Jacobs).
*Secret Love*, introduced here by
Doris Day, received an Academy
Award for Best Film Song of 1953.
*The Black Hills of Dakota* (Doris
Day, Quartet); *The Deadwood Stage*
(Doris Day); *Higher Than a Hawk*
(Howard Keel); *I Can Do Without You*

(Doris Day, Howard Keel); *Just Blew
In from the Windy City* (Doris Day);
*Secret Love* (Doris Day); *'Tis Harry I'm
Plannin' to Marry* (Doris Day, Quar-
tet); *A Woman's Touch* (Doris Day) W:
Paul Francis Webster—M: Sammy
Fain.
"A number of the ... songs sug-
gest other scores of other years." —
*Variety.*
**176  California.** US, 1946, C, 97
m. D: John Farrow, MS: Victor Young,
P: Paramount (Seton I. Miller).
*California* (Chorus); *Said I to My
Heart, Said I* (Barbara Stanwyck) W:
E.Y. Harburg—M: Earl Robinson.
**177  California Dreaming.** US,
1979, C, 92 m. D: John Hancock, MS:
Fred Karlin, P: AIP (Christian Whit-
taker).
*Among the Yesterdays* (Burton
Cummings) W: Robb Royer—M: Fred
Karlin / *California Dreaming* (America)
WM: John E.A. Phillips and Michelle
G. Phillips / *Come On and Get Ready*
(Henry Small) WM: Vincent Albano /
*Everybody's Dancin'* (Henry Small);
*Forever* (Michelle Phillips); *I'm in Love
Again* (Pat Upton) WM: Fred Karlin /
*Keep It in the Family* (Burton Cum-
mings) WM: Burton Cummings / *Pass
You By* (Flo and Eddie) W: Robb
Royer—M: Fred Karlin / *See It My
Way* (FDR) WM: Fred Karlin.
**178  Call Me Madam.** US,
1953, C, 117 m. D: Walter Lang, MD:
Alfred Newman, P: TCF (Sol C.
Siegel). Vocals: Carole Richards for
Vera-Ellen.
Ethel Merman led the cast in the
1950 Broadway production.
*The Best Thing for You* (Ethel Mer-
man, George Sanders); *Can You Use
Any Money Today?* (Ethel Merman);
*The Hostess with the Mostes' on the Ball*
(Ethel Merman); *It's a Lovely Day To-
day* (Vera-Ellen, Donald O'Connor);
*Marrying for Love* (George Sanders);
*The Ocarina* (Vera-Ellen); *Something to
Dance About* (Vera-Ellen, Donald
O'Connor); *That International Rag*

(Ethel Merman); *What Chance Have I with Love?* (Donald O'Connor); *You're Just in Love* (Ethel Merman, Donald O'Connor) WM: Irving Berlin.

"With all the melodious wit and gusto in its passel of Irving Berlin songs, it is obvious that the one and only 'Madame' and Ambassadress to Lichtenburg—the indispensable, indestructible Miss Merman—is the reason for the buoyance in this show." —Bosley Crowther, *The New York Times.*

**179   Camelot.** US, 1967, C, 178 m. D: Joshua Logan, MD: Ken Darby and Alfred Newman, P: Warner (Jack L. Warner). Vocals: Gene Merlino for Franco Nero.

The 1960 Broadway cast included Julie Andrews, Richard Burton, Robert Goulet and Roddy McDowall.

*Camelot* (Richard Harris, Chorus); *C'est Moi* (Franco Nero); *Follow Me* (Chorus); *Guenevere* (Chorus); *How to Handle a Woman* (Richard Harris); *If Ever I Would Leave You* (Franco Nero); *I Loved You Once in Silence* (Vanessa Redgrave, Franco Nero); *I Wonder What the King Is Doing Tonight?* (Richard Harris); *The Lusty Month of May* (Vanessa Redgrave, Chorus); *The Simple Joys of Maidenhood* (Vanessa Redgrave); *Then You May Take Me to the Fair* (Vanessa Redgrave, Peter Bromilow, Gary Marshall, Anthony Rogers); *What Do the Simple Folk Do?* (Vanessa Redgrave, Richard Harris) W: Alan Jay Lerner—M: Frederick Loewe.

"The music is played and sung with great charm, but the settings are vastly overdone." —Bosley Crowther, *The New York Times.*

**180   Cameo Kirby.** US, 1930, BW, 55 m. D: Irving Cummings, P: Fox. Performers: J. Harold Murray and Norma Terris.

*After a Million Dreams* W: Edgar Leslie—M: Walter Donaldson / *I'm a Peaceful Man* (Charles Morton, Stepin Fetchit) WM: Fred Strauss and Ed Brady / *Romance; Tankard and Bowl* W:

Edgar Leslie—M: Walter Donaldson.

**181   Can-Can.** US, 1960, C, 131 m. D: Walter Lang, MD: Nelson Riddle, P: TCF (Jack Cummings).

*C'est Magnifique* (Frank Sinatra, Shirley MacLaine); *Come Along with Me* (Shirley MacLaine); *I Love Paris* (Chorus); *It's All Right with Me* (Frank Sinatra, Louis Jourdan); *Just One of Those Things* (Maurice Chevalier); *Let's Do It* (Frank Sinatra, Shirley MacLaine); *Live and Let Live* (Louis Jourdan, Maurice Chevalier); *Maidens Typical of France* (Juliet Prowse, Chorus); *Montmart'* (Frank Sinatra, Maurice Chevalier, Chorus); *You Do Something to Me* (Louis Jourdan) WM: Cole Porter.

"The musical score has been enhanced with three Cole Porter songs that were not in the original Broadway musical [1953]—*Let's Do It, Just One of Those Things* and *You Do Something to Me.*" —*Variety.*

"The music has been reduced to snatches." —Bosley Crowther, *The New York Times.*

**182   Can't Help Singing.** US, 1944, C, 89 m. D: Frank Ryan, MD: Jerome Kern and Hans Salter, P: Universal (Frank Ross).

*Any Moment Now* (Deanna Durbin); *Californ-i-ay* (Deanna Durbin, Robert Paige, Chorus); *Can't Help Singing* (Deanna Durbin, Robert Paige, Chorus); *Elbow Room* (Robert Paige, Chorus); *More and More* (Deanna Durbin); *Swing Your Sweetheart* (Chorus) W: E.Y. Harburg—M: Jerome Kern.

**183   Can't Stop the Music.** US, 1980, C, 118 m. D: Nancy Walker, MD: Horace Ott, P: EMI (Allan Carr).

*Can't Stop the Music* (The Village People) WM: Jacques Morali, Henri Belolo, Phil Hurtt and Beauris Whitehead / *Gimme a Break* (The Ritchie Family) WM: Jacques Morali, Henri Belolo, The Ritchie Family / *I Love You to Death* (The Village People); *Liberation* (The Village People) WM: Jacques

Morali, Henri Belolo, Phil Hurtt and Beauris Whitehead / *Magic Night* (The Village People); *Milkshake* (The Village People) WM: Jacques Morali, Henri Belolo and Victor Willis / *Samantha* (David London); *Sophistication* (The Ritchie Family); *Sound of the City* (David London) WM: Jacques Morali, Henri Belolo and Phil Hurtt / *Y.M.C.A.* (The Village People) WM: Jacques Morali, Henri Belolo and Victor Willis.

**184  Captain January.** US, 1936, BW, 75 m. D: David Butler, MS: Louis Silvers, P: TCF (Darryl F. Zanuck).

*At the Codfish Ball* (Shirley Temple, Buddy Ebsen, Guy Kibbee); *Early Bird* (Shirley Temple) W: Sidney D. Mitchell—M: Lew Pollack / *The Right Somebody to Love* (Shirley Temple, Chorus) W: Jack Yellen—M: Lew Pollack.

**185  Captains Courageous.** US, 1937, BW, 116 m. D: Victor Fleming, MS: Franz Waxman, P: MGM (Louis D. Lighton).

*Don't Cry Little Fish* (Spencer Tracy) W: Gus Kahn—M: Franz Waxman.

**186  Carefree.** US, 1938, BW, 80 m. D: Mark Sandrich, MD: Victor Baravelle, P: RKO (Pandro S. Berman). MB: Robert B. Mitchell and His St. Brendan's Boys.

*Change Partners* (Fred Astaire); *I Used to Be Color Blind* (Fred Astaire); *The Yam* (Ginger Rogers, Fred Astaire) WM: Irving Berlin.

**187  Carmen Jones.** US, 1954, C, 105 m. D: Otto Preminger, MD: Herschel Burke Gilbert, P: TCF (Otto Preminger). Vocals: Marilyn Horne for Dorothy Dandridge; Le Vern Hutcherson for Harry Belafonte; Bernice Peterson for Diahann Carroll; Marvin Hayes for Joe Adams; Brock Peters for Roy Glenn; Joe Crawford for Nick Stewart.

Hammerstein's updated version of Bizet's opera 'Carmen' opened on Broadway in December 1943 and ran for 502 performances.

*Beat Out Dat Rhythm on a Drum* (Pearl Bailey); *Card Song* (Dorothy Dandridge, Pearl Bailey, Chorus); *Dat's Love* (Dorothy Dandridge); *Dere's a Cafe on de Corner* (Dorothy Dandridge); *Dis Flower* (Harry Belafonte); *Duet* (Dorothy Dandridge, Harry Belafonte, Chorus); *Lift 'Em Up and Put 'Em Down* (Chorus); *My Joe* (Olga James); *Send Them Along* (Chorus); *Stan' Up an' Fight* (Joe Adams); *Whizzin' Away Along de Track* (Dorothy Dandridge, Nick Stewart, Diahann Carroll, Roy Glenn, Pearl Bailey); *You Talk Jus' Like My Maw* (Harry Belafonte, Olga James) W: Oscar Hammerstein II—M: Georges Bizet.

"There is nothing wrong with the music  except that it does not fit the people or the words." —Bosley Crowther, *The New York Times.*

**188  Carnegie Hall.** US, 1947, BW, 134 m. D: Edgar G. Ulmer, P: UA (Boris Morros, William LeBaron). Orch: Harry James; Vaughn Monroe.

*Beware My Heart* (Vaughn Monroe) WM: Sam Coslow.

**189  Carousel.** US, 1956, C, 128 m. D: Henry King, MD: Alfred Newman, P: TCF (Henry Ephron).

The second collaboration of Rodgers and Hammerstein opened on Broadway in 1945 and in London in 1950.

*Blow High, Blow Low* (Cameron Mitchell, Chorus); *If I Loved You* (Gordon MacRae, Shirley Jones); *June Is Bustin' Out All Over* (Claramae Turner, Barbara Ruick, Chorus); *Mister Snow* (Barbara Ruick); *A Real Nice Clambake* (Claramae Turner, Barbara Ruick, Robert Rounseville, Cameron Mitchell, Chorus); *Soliloquy* (Gordon MacRae); *Stonecutters Cut It on Stone* (Cameron Mitchell, Chorus); *There's Nothin' So Bad for a Woman* (Cameron Mitchell); *What's the Use of Wond'rin?* (Shirley Jones, Chorus); *When the Children Are Asleep* (Barbara Ruick, Robert

Rounseville); *You'll Never Walk Alone* (Claramae Turner, Shirley Jones, Chorus); *You're a Queer One, Julie Jordan* (Shirley Jones, Barbara Ruick) W: Oscar Hammerstein II—M: Richard Rodgers.

"Musical numbers are all in extremely good taste. ... The stars of 'Carousel' remain Rodgers and Hammerstein." —*Variety.*

**190 Casablanca.** US, 1942, BW, 102 m. D: Michael Curtiz, MD: Leo F. Forbstein, MS: Max Steiner, P: Warner (Hal B. Wallis). Performer: Dooley Wilson.

*As Time Goes By* WM: Herman Hupfeld / *It Had to Be You* W: Gus Kahn—M: Isham Jones / *Knock on Wood* W: Jack Scholl—M: M.K. Jerome.

**191 Casbah.** US, 1948, BW, 94 m. D: John Berry, P: Universal (Erik Charell).

*For Every Man There's a Woman* (Yvonne de Carlo, Tony Martin); *Hooray for Love* (Yvonne de Carlo, Tony Martin); *It Was Written in the Stars* (Tony Martin); *What's Good About Goodbye?* (Tony Martin) W: Leo Robin—M: Harold Arlen.

**192 Casey's Shadow.** US, 1978, C, 116 m. D: Martin Ritt, MS: Patrick Williams, P: Columbia (Ray Stark).

*Let Me Go Till I'm Gone* (Dobie Gray) W: Will Jennings—M: Patrick Williams.

**193 Casino Royale.** GB, 1967, C, 130 m. D: John Huston, Ken Hughes, Robert Parrish, Joe McGrath and Val Guest, P: Columbia (Charles K. Feldman, Jerry Bresler).

*The Look of Love* (Dusty Springfield) W: Hal David—M: Burt Bacharach.

**194 The Cat and the Fiddle.** US, 1934, BW/C, 90 m. D: William K. Howard, P: MGM (Bernard Hyman).

Jeanette MacDonald's first MGM musical after her move from Paramount was based on the 1931 operetta which ran on Broadway for 395 performances.

*Don't Ask Me Not to Sing* (Chorus); *Ha! Cha Cha* (Vivienne Segal); *I Watch the Love Parade* (Jeanette MacDonald, Ramon Novarro); *A New Love Is Old* (Jeanette MacDonald, Vivienne Segal, Ramon Novarro); *The Night Was Made for Love* (Jeanette MacDonald, Ramon Novarro); *One Moment Alone* (Jeanette MacDonald, Vivienne Segal, Ramon Novarro); *Poor Pierrot* (Jeanette MacDonald, Ramon Novarro, Chorus); *She Didn't Say Yes* (Jeanette MacDonald); *Try to Forget* (Jeanette MacDonald, Ramon Novarro) W: Otto Harbach—M: Jerome Kern.

"The only thing remaining of merit is the music." —*Variety.*

**195 Cat Ballou.** US, 1965, C, 96 m. D: Elliot Silverstein, MS: Frank DeVol, P: Columbia (Harold Hecht).

*The Ballad of Cat Ballou* (Nat King Cole, Stubby Kaye) W: Mack David—M: Jerry Livingston.

**196 Cat People.** US, 1982, C, 118 m. D: Paul Schrader, MS: Giorgio Moroder, P: RKO/Universal (Charles Fries).

*Cat People* (David Bowie) WM: David Bowie and Giorgio Moroder.

**197 Catch My Soul.** US, 1974, C, 95 m. D: Patrick McGoohan, MS: Tony Joe White, P: TCF (Richard Rosenbloom, Jack Good). Alt. Titles: To Catch a Spy; Santa Fe Satan.

*Backwoods Preacher* (Tony Joe White) WM: Tony Joe White / *Book of Prophecy* (Richie Havens); *Catch My Soul* (Lance Le Gault, Chorus) WM: Tony Joe White and Jack Good / *Chug a Lug* (Bonnie Bramlett) WM: Delaney Bramlett / *Eat the Bread, Drink the Wine* (Lance Le Gault, Chorus) WM: Tony Joe White and Jack Good / *I Found Jesus* (Delaney Bramlett, Chorus) WM: Delaney Bramlett / *Looking Back* (Tony Joe White, Chorus) WM: Tony Joe White and Delaney Bramlett / *Lust of the Blood* (Lance Le Gault) WM: Ray Pohlman and Jack Good / *Open Our Eyes* (Richie Havens)

WM: Leon Lumkins / *Othello* (Tony Joe White, Chorus) WM: Tony Joe White / *Put Out the Light* (Richie Havens) WM: Ray Pohlman and Jack Good / *Run, Shaker, Run* (Richie Havens, Chorus) WM: Unknown / *That's What God Said* (Delaney Bramlett) WM: Delaney Bramlett / *Tickle His Fancy* (Susan Tyrrell) WM: Emile Dean Zoghby and Jack Good / *Wash Us Clean* (Tony Joe White, Chorus) WM: Tony Joe White and Jack Good / *Working on a Building* (Richie Havens) WM: Tony Joe White.

**198   Centennial Summer.** US, 1946, C, 102 m. D: Otto Preminger, MD: Alfred Newman, P: TCF (Otto Preminger). Vocals: Louanne Hogan for Jeanne Crain.

Jerome Kern's last score; he died several months before the opening of this film on July 10, 1946, at the Roxy Theater in New York.

*All Through the Day* (Jeanne Crain, Larry Stevens, Cornel Wilde, Linda Darnell, William Eythe) W: Oscar Hammerstein II / *Centennial* (Chorus) W: Leo Robin / *Cinderella Sue* (Avon Long, Chorus) W: E.Y. Harburg / *In Love in Vain* (Jeanne Crain, William Eythe); *Railroad Song* (Walter Brennan, Jeanne Crain, Eddie Dunn, Harry Strang, Dorothy Gish, Napoleon Whiting, Buddy Swan, Lois Austin, Frances Morris); *The Right Romance* (Jeanne Crain); *Up with the Lark* (Jeanne Crain, Dorothy Gish, Constance Bennett, Linda Darnell, Walter Brennan, Buddy Swan, Kathleen Howard, Cornel Wilde, Napoleon Whiting, Chorus) W: Leo Robin. M: Jerome Kern.

"The Jerome Kern score, while sometimes pleasant, is very poorly used, since the show is neither blessed with voices nor sparked with fresh musical routines." —Bosley Crowther, *The New York Times*.

**199   A Certain Smile.** US, 1958, C, 106 m. D: Jean Negulesco, MS: Alfred Newman, P: TCF (Henry Ephron).

*A Certain Smile* (Johnny Mathis) W: Paul Francis Webster—M: Sammy Fain.

**200   Change of Habit.** US, 1969, C, 93 m. D: William Graham, MS: William Goldenberg, P: Universal (Joe Connelly). Performer: Elvis Presley.

*Change of Habit* WM: Ben Weisman and Buddy Kaye / *Have a Happy* WM: Ben Weisman, Buddy Kaye and Dolores Fuller / *Let Us Pray* WM: Ben Weisman and Buddy Kaye / *Rubberneckin'* W: Dory Jones—M: Bunny Warren.

**201   Change of Heart.** US, 1934, BW, 74 m. D: John G. Blystone, MD: Louis de Francesco, P: Fox.

The first of many roles for Dick Foran. In 1936 he became a singing cowboy in Warner Bros. Westerns; in other films he played the nice guy who didn't get the girl.

*So What?* (Dick Foran) WM: Harry Akst.

**202   Charade.** US, 1963, C, 114 m. D: Stanley Donen, MS: Henry Mancini, P: Universal (Stanley Donen).

*Charade* (Chorus) W: Johnny Mercer—M: Henry Mancini.

**203   Charro.** US, 1969, C, 98 m. D: Charles Marquis Warren, MS: Hugo Montenegro, P: National General (Charles Marquis Warren).

*Charro* (Elvis Presley) WM: Billy Strange and Mac Davis.

**204   Chastity.** US, 1969, C, 98 m. D: Alessio de Paola, MS: Sonny Bono, P: AIP (Sonny Bono).

*Chastity's Song* (Cher) WM: Elyse Weinberg.

**205   The Chicken Chronicles.** US, 1977, C, 95 m. D: Francis Simon, MD: Ken Lauber, P: Avco Embassy (Walter Shenson).

*Buy for Me the Rain* (The Nitty Gritty Dirt Band) W: Greg Copeland—M: Steve Noonan / *Everyday with You Girl* (Classics IV) WM: Buddy Buie and James B. Cobb / *On the Road Again* (Canned Heat) WM: Allen Wilson and

Floyd Jones / *Put a Little Love in Your Heart* (Jackie DeShannon) WM: Jimmy Holiday, Randy Myers and Jackie DeShannon / *Sea's Getting Rough* (Boffalong) / *Spooky* (Classics IV) WM: Harry Middlebrooks and Mike Shapiro / *Stormy* (Classics IV) WM: Buddy Buie and James B. Cobb.

**206  A Child Is Waiting.** US, 1963, BW, 102 m. D: John Cassavetes, MS: Ernest Gold, P: UA (Stanley Kramer).

*Snowflakes* (Judy Garland) WM: Marjorie Kurtz.

**207  China Gate.** US, 1957, BW, 97 m. D: Samuel Fuller, MS: Victor Young and Max Steiner, P: TCF (Samuel Fuller).

*China Gate* (Nat King Cole) W: Harold Adamson—M: Victor Young.

**208  Chisum.** US, 1970, C, 111 m. D: Andrew V. McLaglen, MS: Dominic Frontiere, P: Warner (Michael Wayne, Andrew J. Fenady).

*Turn Me Around* (Merle Haggard) W: Norman Gimbel—M: Dominic Frontiere.

**209  Chitty Chitty Bang Bang.** GB, 1968, C, 142 m. D: Ken Hughes, MS: Irwin Kostal, P: UA (Albert R. Broccoli).

*Chitty Chitty Bang Bang* (Dick Van Dyke, Sally Ann Howes, Adrian Hill, Heather Ripley, Chorus); *Chu-Chi Face* (Gert Frobe, Anna Quayle); *Doll on a Music Box* (Sally Ann Howes); *Hushabye Mountain* (Dick Van Dyke, Sally Ann Howes); *Lovely Lonely Man* (Sally Ann Howes); *Me Ol' Bam-Boo* (Dick Van Dyke, Chorus); *Posh!* (Lionel Jeffries); *The Roses of Success* (Lionel Jeffries, Men); *Toot Sweets* (Dick Van Dyke, Sally Ann Howes, Adrian Hill, Heather Ripley); *Truly Scrumptious* (Dick Van Dyke, Sally Ann Howes, Adrian Hill, Heather Ripley); *You Two* (Dick Van Dyke, Adrian Hill, Heather Ripley) WM: Richard M. Sherman and Robert B. Sherman.

**210  The Chocolate Soldier.** US, 1941, BW, 102 m. D: Roy Del Ruth, MS: Herbert Stothart and Bronislau Kaper, P: MGM (Victor Saville).

*My Hero* (Rise Stevens, Nelson Eddy); *Sympathy* (Rise Stevens, Nelson Eddy); *Ti-ra-la-la* (Rise Stevens, Chorus) W: Stanislaus Stange—M: Oscar Straus / *While My Lady Sleeps* (Nelson Eddy, Chorus) W: Gus Kahn—M: Bronislau Kaper.

**211  A Chorus Line.** US, 1985, C, 113 m. D: Richard Attenborough, P: Embassy/Polygram (Cy Feuer, Ernest Martin).

The original musical was produced by Joseph Papp and presented by the New York Shakespeare Festival Public Theatre, where it opened on May 21, 1975.

*At the Ballet* (Vicki Frederick, Michelle Johnston, Pam Klinger); *Dance 10 Looks 3* (Audrey Landers); *I Can Do That* (Charles McGowan); *I Hope I Get It* (Chorus); *Let Me Dance for You* (Alyson Reed); *Nothing* (Yamil Borges); *One* (Chorus); *Surprise Surprise* (Gregg Burge); *What I Did for Love* (Alyson Reed) W: Edward Kleban—M: Marvin Hamlisch.

**212  Christine.** US, 1983, C, 111 m. D: John Carpenter, MS: John Carpenter, P: Columbia (Richard Kobritz).

*Bad to the Bone* (George Thorogood and The Destroyers) / *Bony Moronie* (Larry Williams) WM: Larry Williams / *I Wonder Why* (Dion and The Belmonts) W: Ricardo Weeks—M: Melvin Anderson / *Keep A-Knockin'* (Little Richard) WM: Richard Penniman, Bert Mays and J. Mayo Williams / *Little Bitty Pretty One* (Thurston Harris and The Sharps) WM: Robert Byrd / *Not Fade Away* (Buddy Holly and The Crickets) WM: Buddy Holly and Norman Petty / *Pledging My Love* (Johnny Ace) WM: Ferdinand Washington and Don Robey / *Rock and Roll Is Here to Stay* (Danny and The Juniors) WM: Dave White.

**213  Christmas Holiday.** US, 1944, BW, 93 m. D: Robert Siodmak, MS: Hans J. Salter, P: Universal (Felix

Jackson). Performer: Deanna Durbin.
*Always* WM: Irving Berlin / *Spring Will Be a Little Late This Year* WM: Frank Loesser.

**214  Chuck Berry Hail! Hail! Rock 'n' Roll.** US, 1987, C, 120 m. D: Taylor Hackford, P: Universal (Stephanie Bennett, Chuck Berry). Performer: Chuck Berry.

*Almost Grown; Around and Around; Back in the U.S.A.* (Chuck Berry, Linda Ronstadt); *Brown Eyed Handsome Man* (Chuck Berry, Robert Cray); *Carol* (Chuck Berry, Keith Richard) WM: Chuck Berry / *A Cottage for Sale* W: Larry Conley—M: Willard Robison / *I'm Thru with Love* W: Gus Kahn—M: Matt Malneck and Fud Livingston / *Johnny B. Goode* (Chuck Berry, Julian Lennon); *Little Queenie; Maybellene; Memphis, Tennessee; Nadine; No Particular Place to Go; Rock and Roll Music* (Chuck Berry, Etta James); *Roll Over Beethoven; Sweet Little Sixteen; Too Much Monkey Business; Wee Wee Hours* (Chuck Berry, Eric Clapton) WM: Chuck Berry.

"A joyous docu that effortlessly weaves luminary rock interviews with performance footage mostly shot at Berry's 60th birthday bash concert at the Fox Theatre St. Louis." — *Variety.*

**215  The Cincinnati Kid.** US, 1965, C, 113 m. D: Norman Jewison, MS: Lalo Schifrin, P: MGM (Martin Ransohoff, John Calley).

*The Cincinnati Kid* (Ray Charles) W: Dorcas Cochran—M: Lalo Schifrin.

**216  Cinderella Liberty.** US, 1973, C, 117 m. D: Mark Rydell, MS: John Williams, P: TCF (Mark Rydell).

*Nice to Be Around* (Paul Williams) W: Paul Williams—M: John Williams.

**217  Circus of Horrors.** GB, 1960, C, 89 m. D: Sidney Hayers, P: Anglo Amalgamated (Norman Priggen).

*Look for a Star* (Garry Miles) WM: Tony Hatch [Mark Anthony].

**218  Clambake.** US, 1967, C, 98

m. D: Arthur Nadel, MS: Jeff Alexander, P: UA (Arnold Laven, Arthur Gardner, Jules Levy). Vocals: Ray Walker for Will Hutchins. Performer: Elvis Presley.

*Clambake* WM: Sid Wayne and Ben Weisman / *Confidence* WM: Sid Tepper and Roy C. Bennett / *The Girl I Never Loved* WM: Randy Starr / *Hey, Hey, Hey* WM: Joy Byers / *A House That Has Everything* WM: Sid Tepper and Roy C. Bennett / *Who Needs Money?* (Elvis Presley, Will Hutchins) WM: Randy Starr / *You Don't Know Me* WM: Cindy Walker and Eddy Arnold.

**219  Clash by Night.** US, 1952, BW, 105 m. D: Fritz Lang, MS: Roy Webb, P: RKO (Harriet Parsons).

*I Hear a Rhapsody* (Tony Martin) WM: George Fragos, Jack Baker and Dick Gasparre.

**220  Claudine.** US, 1974, C, 92 m. D: John Berry, P: TCF (Hannah Weinstein). Performers: Gladys Knight and The Pips.

*Hold On; Make Yours a Happy Home; The Makings of You; Mr. Welfare Man; On and On; To Be Invisible* WM: Curtis Mayfield.

**221  Cleopatra Jones.** US, 1973, C, 89 m. D: Jack Starrett, P: Warner (William Tennant, Max Julien).

*It Hurts So Good* (Millie Jackson) WM: Phillip Mitchell / *Love Doctor* (Millie Jackson) WM: Jackie Avery / *Theme from Cleopatra Jones* (Joe Simon) WM: Joe Simon.

**222  The Clock.** US, 1945, BW, 90 m. D: Vincente Minnelli, MS: George Bassman, P: MGM (Arthur Freed). GB Title: Under the Clock.

*That's How I Need You* (James Gleason) W: Joseph McCarthy and Joe Goodwin—M: Al Piantadosi / *Whispering* (Chorus) WM: John Schonberger, Richard Coburn and Vincent Rose.

**223  A Clockwork Orange.** GB, 1971, C, 137 m. D: Stanley Kubrick, MS: Walter Carlos, P: Warner (Bernard Williams).

*Cockles and Mussels, Alive, Alive,
O!* (Paul Farrell) WM: Unknown / *I
Want to Marry a Lighthouse Keeper*
(Erika Eigen) WM: Erika Eigen /
*Singin' in the Rain* (Malcolm Mc-
Dowell, Gene Kelly) W: Arthur
Freed — M: Nacio Herb Brown.

**224   C'mon Let's Live a Little.**
US, 1967, C, 85 m. D: David Butler,
MD: Don Ralke, P: Paramount (June
Starr, John Hertelandy).

*Back Talk* (Jackie DeShannon,
Bobby Vee); *Baker Man* (Jackie De-
Shannon); *C'mon Let's Live a Little*
(Suzie Kaye); *For Granted* (Jackie
DeShannon); *Instant Girl* (Bobby
Vee); *Let's Go-Go* (Eddie Hodges);
*Over and Over* (Jackie DeShannon,
Bobby Vee); *Tonight's the Night* (The
Pair Extraordinaire); *Way Back Home*
(Ethel Smith, Don Crawford); *What
Fool This Mortal Be* (Bobby Vee) WM:
Don Crawford.

**225   Coal Miner's Daughter.**
US, 1980, C, 125 m. D: Michael
Apted, MD: Owen Bradley, P: Univer-
sal (Bob Larsen).

*Amazing Grace* (Chorus) WM:
John Newton / *Back in Baby's Arms*
(Sissy Spacek, Beverly D'Angelo) WM:
Bob Montgomery / *Blue Moon of Ken-
tucky* (Levon Helm) WM: Bill Monroe
/ *Coal Miner's Daughter* (Sissy Spacek)
WM: Loretta Lynn / *Crazy* (Beverly
D'Angelo) WM: Willie Nelson / *The
Great Titanic* (Sissy Spacek) WM: Un-
known / *Honky-Tonk Girl* (Sissy
Spacek) WM: Loretta Lynn / *I Fall to
Pieces* (Sissy Spacek) W: Hank Coch-
ran — M: Harlan Howard / *One's on the
Way* (Sissy Spacek) WM: Shel Silver-
stein / *Sweet Dreams* (Beverly D'An-
gelo) WM: Don Gibson / *There He Goes*
(Sissy Spacek) WM: Eddie Miller,
Durwood Haddock and W.S. Steven-
son / *Walkin' After Midnight* (Beverly
D'Angelo) W: Don Hecht — M: Alan
Block / *You Ain't Woman Enough to
Take My Man* (Sissy Spacek); *You're
Lookin' at Country* (Sissy Spacek) WM:
Loretta Lynn.

"Both Spacek and D'Angelo deserve a special nod for doing all their
own singing with style and accuracy."
— *Variety.*

**226   Cocktail.** US, 1988, C, 100
m. D: Roger Donaldson, MS: J. Peter
Robinson, P: Touchstone (Ted Field,
Robert W. Cort).

*All Shook Up* (Ry Cooder) WM:
Elvis Presley and Otis Blackwell / *Don't
Worry, Be Happy* (Bobby McFerrin)
WM: Bobby McFerrin / *Hippy Hippy
Shake* (The Georgia Satellites) WM:
Charles Romero / *Kokomo* (The Beach
Boys) WM: Mike Love, Terry Melcher,
John Phillips and Scott MacKenzie /
*Oh, I Love You So* (Preston Smith)
WM: Preston Smith / *Powerful Stuff*
(The Fabulous Thunderbirds) WM:
Wally Wilson, Michael Henderson and
Robert S. Field / *Rave On* (John
Cougar Mellencamp) WM: Sonny
West, Norman Petty and Bill Tilghman
/ *Since When* (Robbie Nevil) WM:
Robbie Nevil and Brock Walsh / *Tutti
Frutti* (Little Richard) WM: Richard
Penniman, Dorothy La Bostrie and Joe
Lubin / *Wild Again* (Starship) WM:
John Bettis and Michael Clark.

**227   The Cocoanuts.** US, 1929,
BW, 96 m. D: Joseph Santley and Robert Florey, MD: Frank Tours, P: Paramount (Walter Wanger, Monta Bell).

The first Marx Brothers movie,
and the first Irving Berlin movie score.
*Tale of the Shirt* was set to the *Toreador
Song* from Bizet's 'Carmen.'

*Florida by the Sea* (Chorus); *The
Monkey Doodle-Doo* (Mary Eaton);
*Tale of the Shirt* (Basil Ruysdael,
Chorus); *When My Dreams Come True*
(Oscar Shaw, Mary Eaton) WM: Ir-
ving Berlin.

"Here is a musical talker, with the
musical background, music, songs and
girls, taken from the [1925] Broadway
stage success with the Marxes. . . . Only
Irving Berlin song of merit is the theme
number, *When Our Dreams Come True*,
good enough musically, but as trite in
idea as the title suggests." — *Variety.*

"Fun puts melody in the shade."
—Mordaunt Hall, *The New York Times.*

**228   Cold Turkey.** US, 1971, C, 99 m. D: Norman Lear, MS: Randy Newman, P: UA (Norman Lear, Bud Yorkin).

*He Gives Us All His Love* (Randy Newman) WM: Randy Newman.

**229   Colleen.** US, 1936, BW, 89 m. D: Alfred E. Green, P: Warner (Robert Lord).

*A Boulevardier from the Bronx* (Jack Oakie); *An Evening with You* (Dick Powell); *I Don't Have to Dream Again* (Dick Powell); *You Gotta Know How to Dance* (Ruby Keeler) W: Al Dubin—M: Harry Warren.

**230   College Swing.** US, 1938, BW, 86 m. D: Raoul Walsh, P: Paramount (Lewis Gensler). GB Title: Swing, Teacher, Swing.

*College Swing* (Betty Grable, Martha Raye, Skinnay Ennis) M: Hoagy Carmichael / *Howdja Like to Love Me?* (Bob Hope, Martha Raye) M: Burton Lane / *I Fall in Love with You Every Day* (John Payne, Florence George) M: Manning Sherwin / *Moments Like This* (Florence George) M: Burton Lane / *You're a Natural* (Gracie Allen) M: Manning Sherwin. W: Frank Loesser.

"A medley of vaude specialties, bits and numbers strung together in not too happy a manner." —*Variety.*

**231   Colors.** US, 1988, C, 120 m. D: Dennis Hopper, MS: Herbie Hancock, P: Orion (Robert H. Solo).

*Butcher Shop* (Kool G. Rap) WM: N.T. Wilson and M. Williams / *Colors* (Ice-T) WM: Ice-T and Afrika Islam / *Everywhere I Go* (Rick James) WM: Rick James / *Go On Girl* (Roxanne Shante) WM: A. Hardy and M. Williams / *Let the Rhythm Run* (Salt-N-Pepa) WM: Fingerprints / *Mad Mad World* (7A3) WM: E. Bouldin, S. Bouldin and J. Rivers / *A Mind Is a Terrible Thing to Waste* (M.C. Shan) WM: S. Moltke and M. Williams / *Paid in Full* (Eric B. and Rakim) WM: E. Barrier and W. Griffin / *Raw* (Big Daddy Kane) WM: A. Hardy and M. Williams / *Six Gun* (Decadent Dub Team) WM: D. Williams and J. Liles.

**232   Come and Get It.** US, 1936, BW, 99 m. D: Howard Hawks and William Wyler, MS: Alfred Newman, P: Samuel Goldwyn (Merritt Hulburd). Alt. Title: Roaring Timber.

*Aura Lee* (Frances Farmer) W: W.W. Fosdick—M: George R. Poulton.

**233   Come Back Charleston Blue.** US, 1972, C, 100 m. D: Mark Warren, MS: Donny Hathaway, P: Warner (Samuel Goldwyn, Jr.).

*Come Back Charleston Blue* (Donny Hathaway, Valerie Simpson) W: Al Cleveland and Quincy Jones—M: Donny Hathaway.

**234   Come Blow Your Horn.** US, 1963, C, 112 m. D: Bud Yorkin, MS: Nelson Riddle, P: Paramount (Norman Lear, Bud Yorkin).

*Come Blow Your Horn* (Frank Sinatra) W: Sammy Cahn—M: James Van Heusen.

**235   Come Fly with Me.** US, 1963, C, 109 m. D: Henry Levin, MS: Lyn Murray, P: MGM (Anatole De Grunwald).

*Come Fly with Me* (Frankie Avalon) W: Sammy Cahn—M: James Van Heusen.

**236   Come Next Spring.** US, 1956, C, 92 m. D: R.G. Springsteen, MS: Max Steiner, P: Republic (Herbert J. Yates).

*Come Next Spring* (Tony Bennett) W: Lenny Adelson—M: Max Steiner.

**237   Come September.** US, 1961, C, 112 m. D: Robert Mulligan, MS: Hans J. Salter, P: Universal (Robert Arthur).

*Multiplication* (Bobby Darin) WM: Bobby Darin.

**238   Come to the Stable.** US, 1949, BW, 94 m. D: Henry Koster, MD: Lionel Newman, MS: Cyril Mockridge, P: TCF (Samuel G. Engel).

*Through a Long and Sleepless Night* (Hugh Marlowe, Dorothy Patrick,

Louis Jean Heydt) W: Mack Gordon—M: Alfred Newman.

**239 Coming Home.** US, 1978, C, 128 m. D: Hal Ashby, P: UA (Bruce Gilbert, Jerome Hellman).

*Bookends* (Simon and Garfunkel) WM: Paul Simon / *Born to Be Wild* (Steppenwolf) WM: Mars Bonfire [Dennis Edmonton] / *Call on Me* (Big Brother and The Holding Company, with Janis Joplin) WM: Deadric Malone / *Follow* (Richie Havens) / *For What It's Worth* (Buffalo Springfield) WM: Stephen Stills / *Hey Jude* (The Beatles) WM: John Lennon and Paul McCartney / *Jumpin' Jack Flash* (The Rolling Stones) WM: Mick Jagger and Keith Richard / *Just Like a Woman* (Bob Dylan) WM: Bob Dylan / *Manic Depression* (Jimi Hendrix) / *My Girl* (The Rolling Stones) WM: William "Smokey" Robinson and Ronald White / *No Expectations* (The Rolling Stones) WM: Mick Jagger and Keith Richard / *Once I Was* (Tim Buckley) / *Out of Time* (The Rolling Stones); *Ruby Tuesday* (The Rolling Stones) WM: Mick Jagger and Keith Richard / *Save Me* (Aretha Franklin) / *Strawberry Fields Forever* (The Beatles) WM: John Lennon and Paul McCartney / *Sympathy for the Devil* (The Rolling Stones) WM: Mick Jagger and Keith Richard / *Time Has Come Today* (The Chambers Brothers) W: Joseph Chambers—M: Willie Chambers / *White Rabbit* (Jefferson Airplane) WM: Grace Slick.

"Mr. Ashby has poured music over the movie like a child with a fondness for maple syrup on his pancakes." —Vincent Canby, *The New York Times.*

**240 The Competition.** US, 1980, C, 129 m. D: Joel Oliansky, MS: Lalo Schifrin, P: Columbia (William Sackheim).

*People Alone* (Randy Crawford) W: Will Jennings—M: Lalo Schifrin.

**241 Coney Island.** US, 1943, C, 96 m. D: Walter Lang, MS: Alfred Newman, P: TCF (William Perlberg). MB: Chorus. Performer: Betty Grable.

Composer Ralph Rainger died in October 1942 when the plane taking him from Hollywood to New York collided in midair with a second aircraft. He was 41 years old and had composed nearly 200 songs, mainly with lyricist Leo Robin.

*Cuddle Up a Little Closer* W: Otto Harbach—M: Karl Hoschna / *Lulu from Louisville* W: Leo Robin—M: Ralph Rainger / *Pretty Baby* W: Gus Kahn—M: Tony Jackson and Egbert Van Alstyne / *Put Your Arms Around Me, Honey* W: Junie McCree—M: Albert von Tilzer / *Take It from There; There's Danger in a Dance* W: Leo Robin—M: Ralph Rainger / *When Irish Eyes Are Smiling* W: Chauncey Olcott and George Graff, Jr.—M: Ernest R. Ball / *Who Threw the Overalls in Mrs. Murphy's Chowder?* (Charles Winninger, Chorus) WM: George L. Giefer.

**242 A Connecticut Yankee in King Arthur's Court.** US, 1949, C, 107 m. D: Tay Garnett, MD: Victor Young, P: Paramount (Robert Fellows). GB Title: A Yankee in King Arthur's Court.

*Busy Doing Nothing* (Bing Crosby, William Bendix, Cedric Hardwicke); *If You Stub Your Toe on the Moon* (Bing Crosby); *Once and for Always* (Bing Crosby, Rhonda Fleming); *When Is Sometime?* (Bing Crosby) W: Johnny Burke—M: James Van Heusen.

**243 Convoy.** US, 1978, C, 110 m. D: Sam Peckinpah, MS: Chip Davis, P: UA (Robert M. Sherman).

*Blanket on the Ground* (Billie Jo Spears) WM: Roger Bowling / *Convoy* (C.W. McCall) W: C.W. McCall [William D. Fries]—M: Louis "Chip" Davis / *Cowboys Don't Get Lucky All the Time* (Gene Watson) / *Don't It Make My Brown Eyes Blue?* (Crystal Gayle) WM: Richard Leigh / *I Cheated on a Good Woman's Love* (Billy Crash Craddock) / *Keep on the Sunny Side* (Doc Watson) / *Lucille* (Kenny Rogers) WM: Hal Bynum and Roger Bowling / *Okie from Muskogee* (Merle Haggard) WM:

Merle Haggard and Roy Burris / *Southern Nights* (Glen Campbell) WM: Allen Toussaint / *Walk Right Back* (Anne Murray) WM: Sonny Curtis.

**244   Cooley High.** US, 1975, C, 107 m. D: Michael Schultz, MS: Freddie Perren, P: AIP (Steve Krantz).

*Baby Love* (The Supremes) WM: Eddie Holland, Lamont Dozier and Brian Holland / *Beechwood 4-5789* (The Marvellettes) WM: William Stevenson, George Gordy and Marvin Gaye / *Dancing in the Street* (Martha and The Vandellas) WM: William Stevenson and Marvin Gaye / *Fingertips* (Little Stevie Wonder) WM: Henry Crosby and Clarence Paul / *I Can't Help Myself* (The Four Tops) WM: Eddie Holland, Lamont Dozier and Brian Holland / *Luther's Blues* (Luther Allison) / *Mickey's Monkey* (Smokey Robinson and The Miracles) WM: Eddie Holland, Lamont Dozier and Brian Holland / *Money* (Barrett Strong) WM: Janie Bradford and Berry Gordy, Jr. / *My Girl* (The Temptations) WM: William "Smokey" Robinson and Ronald White / *Ooh Baby Baby* (Smokey Robinson and The Miracles) WM: William "Smokey" Robinson and Warren Moore / *Reach Out, I'll Be There* (The Four Tops); *Road Runner* (Junior Walker and The All Stars) WM: Eddie Holland, Lamont Dozier and Brian Holland / *So Hard to Say Goodbye to Yesterday* (G.C. Cameron) / *Stop! in the Name of Love* (The Supremes) WM: Eddie Holland, Lamont Dozier and Brian Holland.

**245   Copacabana.** US, 1947, BW, 92 m. D: Alfred E. Green, MS: Edward Ward, P: UA (Sam Coslow).

*Fifi* (Carmen Miranda) WM: Sam Coslow / *Go West, Young Man* (Groucho Marx, The Famous Copa Girls) W: Bert Kalmar—M: Harry Ruby / *He Hasn't Got a Thing to Sell* (Carmen Miranda, Andy Russell); *Je Vous Aime* (Carmen Miranda, Andy Russell); *Let's Do the Copacabana* (Carmen Miranda, Groucho Marx,

The Famous Copa Girls); *My Heart Was Doing a Bolero* (Andy Russell); *Stranger Things Have Happened* (Andy Russell, Gloria Jean) WM: Sam Coslow / *Tico Tico* (Carmen Miranda) Eng. W: Ervin Drake—Portuguese W: Aloysio Oliveira—M: Zequinha Abreu / *We Come to the Copa* (The Famous Copa Girls) WM: Sam Coslow.

"Furnished with all the usual fixtures of a Hollywood night-club film—meaning chorus girls, musical numbers, cardboard characters and an idiotic plot." —Bosley Crowther, *The New York Times*.

**246   The Cotton Club.** US, 1984, C, 127 m. D: Francis Coppola, MS: John Barry, P: Zoetrope/Orion (Robert Evans).

*Am I Blue?* (Ethel Waters) WM: Grant Clarke and Harry Akst / *Between the Devil and the Deep Blue Sea* (Louis Armstrong) W: Ted Koehler—M: Harold Arlen / *The Blues I Love to Sing* (Adelaide Hall) / *Copper Colored Gal* (Gregory Hines) W: Benny Davis—M: J. Fred Coots / *Creole Love Call* (Patricia Baskerville) WM: Duke Ellington / *I Can't Give You Anything But Love, Baby* (Ethel Waters) W: Dorothy Fields—M: Jimmy McHugh / *Ill Wind* (Lonette McKee) W: Ted Koehler—M: Harold Arlen / *I Must Have That Man* (Adelaide Hall) W: Dorothy Fields—M: Jimmy McHugh / *Just a Crazy Song* (Bill "Bojangles" Robinson) / *Lazybones* (Midge Williams) WM: Johnny Mercer and Hoagy Carmichael / *Minnie the Moocher* (Larry Marshall) WM: Cab Calloway, Irving Mills and Clarence Gaskill / *Serenade to a Wealthy Widow* (Reginald Foresythe) WM: Dorothy Fields, Jimmy McHugh and Reginald Foresythe / *When You're Smiling* (Louis Armstrong) WM: Mark Fisher, Joe Goodwin and Larry Shay.

"The best things in the film are its musical numbers, but though 'The Cotton Club' is loaded with period music, it becomes overwhelmed by the general sloppiness of everything that's going on." —Vincent Canby, *The New York Times.*

**247  The Countess of Monte Cristo.** US, 1948, BW, 77 m. D: Frederick de Cordova, P: Universal (John Beck). Performer: Olga San Juan.

The last of Sonja Henie's ice-skating films was a remake of a 1933 Universal musical with Fay Wray and Paul Lucas.

*Count Your Blessings; Friendly Polka; Who Believes in Santa Claus?* WM: Jack Brooks and Saul Chaplin.

**248  The Country Girl.** US, 1954, BW, 104 m. D: George Seaton, MD: Joseph J. Lilley, MS: Victor Young, P: Paramount (William Perlberg).

*Dissertation on the State of Bliss* (Bing Crosby, Jacqueline Fontaine); *It's Mine, It's Yours* (Bing Crosby); *The Land Around Us* (Bing Crosby, Chorus); *The Search Is Through* (Bing Crosby) W: Ira Gershwin—M: Harold Arlen.

**249  The Court Jester.** US, 1956, C, 101 m. D: Norman Panama and Melvin Frank, P: Paramount (Norman Panama, Melvin Frank). Performer: Danny Kaye.

*I'll Take You Dreaming; Life Could Not Better Be* WM: Sylvia Fine and Sammy Cahn / *The Maladjusted Jester* WM: Sylvia Fine / *My Heart Knows a Lovely Song; Outfox the Fox* WM: Sylvia Fine and Sammy Cahn.

"A major assist comes from the ... songs of which there are five all tuned to the Kaye talent." —*Variety.*

**250  Cover Girl.** US, 1944, C, 107 m. D: Charles Vidor, MD: Morris Stoloff, P: Columbia (Arthur Schwartz). Vocals: Martha Mears for Rita Hayworth.

*Cover Girl* (Chorus); *Long Ago and Far Away* (Gene Kelly, Rita Hayworth) W: Ira Gershwin—M: Jerome Kern / *Make Way for Tomorrow* (Gene Kelly, Rita Hayworth, Phil Silvers) W: Ira Gershwin and E.Y. Harburg—M: Jerome Kern / *Poor John* (Rita Hayworth)

WM: Fred W. Leigh and Harry E. Pether / *Put Me to the Test* (Gene Kelly, Phil Silvers, Chorus); *The Show Must Go On* (Rita Hayworth, Leslie Brooks, Chorus); *Sure Thing* (Rita Hayworth, Chorus); *Who's Complaining?* (Rita Hayworth, Phil Silvers, Leslie Brooks, Chorus) W: Ira Gershwin—M: Jerome Kern.

"Score ... is of high caliber." —*Variety.*

**251  The Cowboy and the Lady.** US, 1938, BW, 91 m. D: H.C. Potter, MS: Alfred Newman, P: UA (Samuel Goldwyn).

*The Cowboy and the Lady* (Harry Davenport) WM: Arthur Quenzer, L. Wolfe Gilbert and Lionel Newman.

**252  Cowboy from Brooklyn.** US, 1938, BW, 80 m. D: Lloyd Bacon, P: Warner (Louis F. Edelman). Performer: Dick Powell.

While at work on this film, Richard Whiting had a heart attack and died at age 46. The music was completed by Harry Warren.

*Cowboy from Brooklyn* W: Johnny Mercer—M: Harry Warren / *I'll Dream Tonight* (Dick Powell, Priscilla Lane); *I've Got a Heart Full of Music; Ride, Tenderfoot, Ride* W: Johnny Mercer—M: Richard A. Whiting.

**253  Cowboy Serenade.** US, 1942, BW, 66 m. D: William Morgan, MD: Raoul Kraushaar, P: Republic (Harry Grey). Performer: Gene Autry.

*The Cowboy Serenade* WM: Rich Hall / *Sweethearts or Strangers* WM: Jimmie Davis, Lou Wayne and Don Marcotte / *Tahiti Honey* WM: Jule Styne, George H. Brown and Sol Meyer.

**254  Criminal Court.** US, 1946, BW, 63 m. D: Robert Wise, P: RKO. Performer: Martha O'Driscoll.

*I Couldn't Sleep a Wink Last Night; A Lovely Way to Spend an Evening* W: Harold Adamson—M: Jimmy McHugh.

**255  Cross My Heart.** US, 1946, BW, 83 m. D: John Berry, MS: Robert

Emmett Dolan, P: Paramount (Harry Tugend). Performer: Betty Hutton.

*Cross My Heart* WM: Robert Emmett Dolan and Larry Neill / *Does Baby Feel All Right?; How Do You Do It?; It Hasn't Been Chilly in Chile; Love Is the Darndest Thing; That Little Dream Got Nowhere* W: Johnny Burke—M: James Van Heusen.

**256  Crossroads.** US, 1986, C, 96 m. D: Walter Hill, P: Columbia (Mark Carliner). Performer: Ry Cooder.

*Cotton Needs Pickin'* WM: Frank Frost, Richard Holmes, Otis Taylor and John Price / *Crossroads* WM: Robert Johnson / *Down in Mississippi* WM: J.B. Lenoir / *Feelin' Bad Blues* WM: Ry Cooder / *He Made a Woman Out of Me; Nitty Gritty Mississippi* WM: Fred Burch and Donald Hill / *See You in Hell, Blind Boy* WM: Ry Cooder / *Somebody's Callin' My Name* WM: Unknown—Arr: Ry Cooder / *Viola Lee Blues* WM: Noah Lewis / *Walkin' Away Blues* WM: Sonny Terry and Ry Cooder / *Willy Brown Blues* WM: Joe Seneca and Ry Cooder.

**257  Cruisin' down the River.** US, 1953, C, 79 m. D: Jack Corrick, P: Columbia (Jonie Taps).

The title song won the 1945 'Write a Song Contest' in England.

*Come Home, Father* (Chorus) WM: Henry Clay Work / *Cruising down the River* (Dick Haymes, Chorus) W: Eily Beadel—M: Nell Tollerton / *Pennies from Heaven* (Dick Haymes) W: Johnny Burke—M: Arthur Johnston / *She Is More to Be Pitied Than Censured* (Chorus) WM: William B. Gray / *Sing, You Sinners* (Billy Daniels) WM: Sam Coslow and W. Franke Harling / *There Goes That Song Again* (Dick Haymes) W: Sammy Cahn—M: Jule Styne.

**258  Curly Top.** US, 1935, BW, 75 m. D: Irving Cummings, MD: Oscar Bradley, P: Fox (Winfield Sheehan).

*Animal Crackers in My Soup* (Shirley Temple) W: Ted Koehler and Irving Caesar / *Curly Top* (John Boles) W: Ted Koehler / *It's All So New to Me* (John Boles) W: Ted Koehler and Irving Caesar / *The Simple Things in Life* (Rochelle Hudson) W: Ted Koehler / *When I Grow Up* (Shirley Temple, Billy Gilbert, Arthur Treacher) W: Edward Heyman—M: Ray Henderson.

"When Shirley is singing her *Animal Crackers* song or . . . breaking into an *Off to Buffalo* routine, 'Curly Top' is completely bearable." —Andre Sennwald, *The New York Times*.

**259  Daddy Long Legs.** US, 1955, C, 130 m. D: Jean Negulesco, MS: Alfred Newman, P: TCF (Samuel G. Engel). Orch: Ray Anthony.

One of the earlier film versions of this Jean Webster story was 'Curly Top,' made in 1935 with Shirley Temple.

*C-A-T Spells Cat* (Leslie Caron, Chorus); *Daddy Long Legs* (Chorus); *Dream* (Fred Astaire, Chorus); *How I Made the Team* (Fred Astaire); *Sluefoot* (Fred Astaire, Chorus); *Something's Gotta Give* (Fred Astaire, Leslie Caron); *Texas Romp and Square Dance* (Fred Astaire, Chorus); *Welcome Egghead* (Chorus) WM: Johnny Mercer.

**260  Daddy's Gone A-Hunting.** US, 1969, C, 108 m. D: Mark Robson, MS: John Williams, P: Warner (Mark Robson).

*Daddy's Gone A-Hunting* (Lyn Roman) W: Dory Previn—M: John Williams.

**261  Dames.** US, 1934, BW, 90 m. D: Ray Enright and Busby Berkeley, MD: Leo F. Forbstein, P: Warner (Robert Lord).

*Dames* (Dick Powell, Chorus); *The Girl at the Ironing Board* (Joan Blondell, Chorus); *I Only Have Eyes for You* (Dick Powell, Ruby Keeler, Chorus) W: Al Dubin—M: Harry Warren / *Try to See It My Way* (Dick Powell, Joan Blondell, Chorus) W: Mort Dixon—M: Allie Wrubel / *When You Were a Smile on Your Mother's Lips* (Dick Powell) W: Irving Kahal—M: Sammy Fain.

"Three sets of songwriters fashioned a corking score." —*Variety*.

**262　Damn Yankees.** US, 1958, C, 110 m. D: George Abbott and Stanley Donen, MD: Ray Heindorf, P: Warner (George Abbott, Stanley Donen). GB Title: What Lola Wants.

Gwen Verdon originated the role of Lola in the hit Broadway show of 1955, and thereby became a star.

*Goodbye, Old Girl* (Robert Shafer, Tab Hunter); *Heart* (Russ Brown, James Komack, Albert Linville, Nathaniel Frey, Jean Stapleton); *A Little Brains, a Little Talent* (Gwen Verdon); *Shoeless Joe from Hannibal Mo.* (Rae Allen, Chorus); *Six Months Out of Every Year* (Shannon Bolin, Robert Shafer, Chorus); *There's Something About an Empty Chair* (Shannon Bolin, Robert Shafer); *Those Were the Good Old Days* (Ray Walston); *Two Lost Souls* (Tab Hunter, Gwen Verdon); *Whatever Lola Wants* (Gwen Verdon); *Who's Got the Pain?* (Gwen Verdon, Bob Fosse) WM: Richard Adler and Jerry Ross.

"Still held in prominence is the . . . musical score—a tuneful, storytelling assortment of gag songs and ballads. . . . To add to the original score is one new tune, *The Empty Chair*, a sorrowful creation that makes little impression." —*Variety.*

**263　A Damsel in Distress.** US, 1937, BW, 101 m. D: George Stevens, MD: Victor Baravalle, P: RKO (Pandro S. Berman).

*A Foggy Day* (Fred Astaire); *I Can't Be Bothered Now* (Fred Astaire); *The Jolly Tar and the Milkmaid* (Fred Astaire, Jan Duggen, Mary Dean, Pearl Amatore, Betty Rome, Chorus); *Nice Work If You Can Get It* (Fred Astaire, Jan Duggen, Mary Dean, Pearl Amatore); *Sing of Spring* (Chorus); *Stiff Upper Lip* (Gracie Allen); *Things Are Looking Up* (Fred Astaire) W: Ira Gershwin—M: George Gershwin.

**264　Dance, Girl, Dance.** US, 1940, BW, 90 m. D: Dorothy Arzner, MS: Edward Ward, P: RKO (Erich Pommer). Performer: Lucille Ball.

*The Beer Barrel Polka* WM: Lew Brown, Taromir Vejvoda and Wladimir A. Timm / *Jitterbug Bite* WM: Robert Wright, George "Chet" Forrest and Ed Ward / *Morning Star* (Male Singer); *Mother, What Do I Do Now?* WM: Robert Wright and George "Chet" Forrest.

**265　Dancing in the Dark.** US, 1949, C, 92 m. D: Irving Reis, MS: Alfred Newman, P: TCF (George Jessel). Performer: Betsy Drake.

*Dancing in the Dark; I Love Louisa; New Sun in the Sky; Something to Remember You By* W: Howard Dietz—M: Arthur Schwartz.

"A very fine score is pretty much thrown away." —Bosley Crowther, *The New York Times.*

**266　Dancing Lady.** US, 1933, BW, 94 m. D: Robert Z. Leonard, MD: Louis Silvers, P: MGM (David O. Selznick).

*Everything I Have Is Yours* (Joan Crawford, Art Jarrett); *Heigh-Ho, the Gang's All Here* (Fred Astaire, Joan Crawford) W: Harold Adamson—M: Burton Lane / *Hey, Young Fella, Close Your Old Umbrella* (Chorus) W: Dorothy Fields—M: Jimmy McHugh / *Hold Your Man* (Winnie Lightner) W: Arthur Freed—M: Nacio Herb Brown / *Let's Go Bavarian* (Fred Astaire, Joan Crawford) W: Harold Adamson—M: Burton Lane / *My Dancing Lady* (Art Jarrett) W: Dorothy Fields—M: Jimmy McHugh / *That's the Rhythm of the Day* (Nelson Eddy) W: Lorenz Hart—M: Richard Rodgers.

"The dancing of Fred Astaire and Miss Crawford is most graceful and charming. . . . There are several tuneful songs." —Mordaunt Hall, *The New York Times.*

**267　The Dancing Pirate.** US, 1936, C, 83 m. D: Lloyd Corrigan, MD: Alfred Newman, P: RKO/Pioneer (John Speaks).

The Royal Cansinos, Rita Hayworth's dancing family, appeared in this film.

*Are You My Love?* (Steffi Duna);

*When You're Dancing the Waltz* (Steffi Duna, Charles Collins) W: Lorenz Hart—M: Richard Rodgers.

"A light and amusing trifle in song, dance and comedy." —B.R. Crisler, *The New York Times.*

**268  Danger—Love at Work.** US, 1937, BW, 81 m. D: Otto Preminger, MD: David Buttolph, P: TCF (Harold Wilson).

*Danger—Love at Work* (Jack Haley, Ann Sothern) WM: Mack Gordon and Harry Revel.

**269  Dangerous Nan McGrew.** US, 1930, BW, 71 m. D: Malcolm St. Clair, P: Paramount. Performer: Helen Kane.

*Aw! C'mon, Whatta Ya Got to Lose?* W: Leo Robin—M: Richard A. Whiting / *Dangerous Nan McGrew; I Owe You* WM: Al Goodhart and Don Hartman / *Once a Gypsy Told Me* WM: Irving Kahal, Sammy Fain and Pierre Norman.

**270  Dangerous When Wet.** US, 1953, C, 95 m. D: Charles Walters, MD: George Stoll, P: MGM (George Wells).

*Ain't Nature Grand* (Esther Williams, Fernando Lamas, Denise Darcel, Jack Carson, Charlotte Greenwood, William Demarest); *I Got Out of Bed on the Right Side* (Esther Williams, Fernando Lamas, Charlotte Greenwood, William Demarest, Barbara Whiting, Donna Corcoran); *I Like Men* (Barbara Whiting); *In My Wildest Dreams* (Fernando Lamas) W: Johnny Mercer—M: Arthur Schwartz.

**271  Dark City.** US, 1950, BW, 88 m. D: William Dieterle, MS: Franz Waxman, P: Paramount (Hal B. Wallis). Performer: Lizabeth Scott.

*I Don't Want to Walk Without You, Baby* W: Frank Loesser—M: Jule Styne / *I'm in the Mood for Love* W: Dorothy Fields—M: Jimmy McHugh / *That Old Black Magic* W: Johnny Mercer—M: Harold Arlen.

**272  Dark Victory.** US, 1939, BW, 106 m. D: Edmund Goulding, MS: Max Steiner, P: Warner (David Lewis).

*Oh, Give Me Time for Tenderness* (Bette Davis, Vera Van) W: Elsie Janis—M: Edmund Goulding.

**273  Darling Lili.** US, 1970, C, 136 m. D: Blake Edwards, MS: Henry Mancini, P: Paramount (Blake Edwards, Owen Crump). Performer: Julie Andrews.

*Darling Lili* (Chorus); *The Girl in No Man's Land; I'll Give You Three Guesses* W: Johnny Mercer—M: Henry Mancini / *It's a Long Way to Tipperary* (Chorus) WM: Jack Judge and Harry Williams / *Keep the Home Fires Burning* WM: Ivor Novello and Lena Guilbert-Ford / *The Little Birds* (Chorus) W: Johnny Mercer—M: Henry Mancini / *Pack Up Your Troubles in Your Old Kit Bag* W: George Asaf—M: Felix Powell / *Skol* (Chorus); *Smile Away Each Rainy Day; Whistling Away the Dark; Your Goodwill Ambassador* (Gloria Paul) W: Johnny Mercer—M: Henry Mancini.

"Andrews' best moments are her singing sequences." —*Variety.*

**274  A Date with Judy.** US, 1948, C, 113 m. D: Richard Thorpe, MD: George Stoll, P: MGM (Joe Pasternak). Orch: Xavier Cugat.

*Cuanto Le Gusta* (Carmen Miranda) W: Ray Gilbert—M: Gabriel Ruiz / *Home Sweet Home* (Jane Powell, Selena Royle, Jerry Hunter) W: John Howard Payne—M: Sir Henry Bishop / *I'm Cookin' with Gas* (Carmen Miranda) / *I'm Strictly on the Corny Side* (Jane Powell, Scotty Beckett) W: Stella Unger—M: Alec Templeton / *It's a Most Unusual Day* (Jane Powell, Elizabeth Taylor) W: Harold Adamson—M: Jimmy McHugh / *Judaline* (Jane Powell, Scotty Beckett, Male Quartet) WM: Don Raye and Gene de Paul / *Love Is Where You Find It* (Jane Powell) W: Earl K. Brent—M: Nacio Herb Brown / *Through the Years* (Jane Powell, George Cleveland) W: Edward Heyman—M: Vincent Youmans.

**275 Davy Crockett, King of the Wild Frontier.** US, 1955, C, 93 m. D: Norman Foster, MS: George Bruns, P: Walt Disney (Bill Walsh).

*The Ballad of Davy Crockett* (Fess Parker) W: Tom Blackburn—M: George Bruns.

**276 A Day at the Races.** US, 1937, BW, 111 m. D: Sam Wood, MS: Franz Waxman, P: MGM (Irving Thalberg, Max Siegel, Lawrence Weingarten). Orch: Duke Ellington. Performer: Allan Jones.

*All God's Chillun Got Rhythm* (Ivie Anderson, Crinoline Choir); *Blue Venetian Waters; A Message from the Man in the Moon; Tomorrow Is Another Day* W: Gus Kahn—M: Walter Jurmann and Bronislau Kaper.

**277 The Day of the Locust.** US, 1975, C, 144 m. D: John Schlesinger, MS: John Barry, P: Paramount (Jerome Hellman, Sheldon Shrager).

*Hot Voodoo* (Paul Jabara) W: Sam Coslow—M: Ralph Rainger / *Isn't It Romantic?* (Michael Dees) W: Lorenz Hart—M: Richard Rodgers / *I Wished on the Moon* (Nick Lucas) W: Dorothy Parker—M: Ralph Rainger / *Jeepers Creepers* (Louis Armstrong) W: Johnny Mercer—M: Harry Warren / *Sing, You Sinners* (Pamela Myers) WM: Sam Coslow and W. Franke Harling.

**278 Days of Wine and Roses.** US, 1962, BW, 117 m. D: Blake Edwards, MS: Henry Mancini, P: Warner (Martin Manulis).

*Days of Wine and Roses* (Andy Williams, Chorus) W: Johnny Mercer—M: Henry Mancini.

**279 Dead Reckoning.** US, 1947, BW, 100 m. D: John Cromwell, MD: Morris Stoloff, MS: Marlin Skiles, P: Columbia (Sidney Biddell).

*Either It's Love or It Isn't* (Lizabeth Scott) WM: Allan Roberts and Doris Fisher.

**280 The Decline of Western Civilization.** US, 1981, C, 105 m. D: Penelope Spheeris, P: Spheeris Films (Gordon Brown, Jeff Prettyman).

*Back Against the Wall* (Circle Jerks) WM: Morris / *Beverly Hills* (Circle Jerks) WM: Circle Jerks / *Beyond and Back* (X) WM: John Doe and Exene / *Depression* (Black Flag) WM: Greg Ginn / *Fear Anthem* (Fear) / *Gluttony* (Alice Bag Band) WM: Craig Lee / *I Don't Care About You* (Fear) WM: Lee Ving / *I Just Want Some Skank* (Circle Jerks) WM: Circle Jerks / *I Love Livin' in the City* (Fear) WM: Lee Ving / *Johny Hit and Run Pauline* (X) WM: John Doe and Exene / *Manimal* (Germs) WM: Darby Crash / *Red Tape* (Circle Jerks) WM: Morris and Hetson / *Revenge* (Black Flag) WM: Greg Ginn / *Underground Babylon* (Catholic Discipline) WM: Bessy and Meade / *We're Desperate* (X) WM: John Doe and Exene / *White Minority* (Black Flag) WM: Greg Ginn.

**281 Decline of Western Civilization Part II: The Metal Years.** US, 1988, C, 90 m. D: Penelope Spheeris, P: New Line Cinema (Jonathan Dayton, Valerie Faris).

*The Bathroom Wall* (Faster Pussycat) WM: Taime Down / *Born to Be Wild* (Lizzy Borden) WM: Mars Bonfire [Dennis Edmonton] / *The Brave* (Metal Church) WM: K. Vanderhoff and C. Wells / *Colleen* (Seduce) WM: Andrews, Black and Burns / *Cradle to the Grave* (Motorhead) WM: Ian Kilmister, Burston, Phil Campbell and Phil Taylor / *Foaming at the Mouth* (Rigor Mortis) WM: Harrison, Orr, Scaccia and Corbitt / *In My Darkest Hour* (Megadeath) WM: Dave Mustaine and Dave Ellefson / *The Prophecy* (Queensryche) WM: DeGarmo; *Under My Wheels* (Alice Cooper, with Axl Rose, Slash and Izzy of Guns 'n' Roses) WM: Michael Bruce, Dennis Dunaway and Bob Erzin / *You Can Run But You Can't Hide* (Armored Saint) WM: Armored Saint.

**282 The Deep.** US, 1977, C, 123 m. D: Peter Yates, MS: John Barry, P: Columbia (Peter Guber).

*Disco Calypso* (Beckett) / *Theme*

*from The Deep* (Donna Summer) WM: John Barry and Donna Summer.

**283  Deep in My Heart.** US, 1954, C, 132 m. D: Stanley Donen, P: MGM (Roger Edens).

*Auf Wiedersehn* (Helen Traubel) W: Herbert Reynolds / *Deep in My Heart, Dear* (Chorus) W: Dorothy Donnelly / *Goodbye, Girls* (Jose Ferrer) / *I Love to Go Swimmin' with Wimmen* (Gene Kelly, Fred Kelly) W: Ballard MacDonald / *It* (Ann Miller, Chorus) W: Otto Harbach and Oscar Hammerstein II / *The Jazzadoo* (Jose Ferrer) / *Leg of Mutton* (Helen Traubel, Jose Ferrer) W: Roger Edens / *Lover, Come Back to Me* (Tony Martin, Joan Weldon) W: Oscar Hammerstein II / *Mr. and Mrs.* (Rosemary Clooney, Jose Ferrer) W: Cyrus Wood / *My Fat Fatima* (Jose Ferrer) / *One Alone* (Cyd Charisse) W: Otto Harbach and Oscar Hammerstein II / *The Road to Paradise* (Vic Damone) W: Rida Johnson Young / *Serenade* (William Olvis) W: Dorothy Donnelly / *Softly, As in a Morning Sunrise* (Helen Traubel, Tamara Toumanova, Chorus); *Stouthearted Men* (Helen Traubel); *When I Grow Too Old to Dream* (Jose Ferrer, Chorus) W: Oscar Hammerstein II / *Will You Remember?* (Jane Powell, Vic Damone) W: Rida Johnson Young / *Your Land and My Land* (Howard Keel) W: Dorothy Donnelly / *You Will Remember Vienna* (Helen Traubel) W: Oscar Hammerstein II—M: Sigmund Romberg.

"This medley of melodies, which is designed to pretend to tell a story of Mr. Romberg's successful career, runs more to showy presentation of the more familiar of the composer's tunes." —Bosley Crowther, *The New York Times*.

**284  The Delicate Delinquent.** US, 1957, BW, 100 m. D: Don McGuire, MS: Buddy Bregman, P: Paramount (Jerry Lewis).

*By Myself* (Jerry Lewis) W: Howard Dietz—M: Arthur Schwartz.

**285  Delicious.** US, 1931, BW, 106 m. D: David Butler, P: Fox (Winfield Sheehan).

Ira and George Gershwin went to Hollywood in 1930 to write the songs for this Janet Gaynor–Charles Farrell picture, then left again, not to return for five years.

*Blah-Blah-Blah* (El Brendel, Manya Roberti, Chorus); *Delishious* (Raul Roulien); *Katinkitschke* (Janet Gaynor, El Brendel, Chorus); *Somebody from Somewhere* (Janet Gaynor); *Welcome to the Melting Pot* (Janet Gaynor) W: Ira Gershwin—M: George Gershwin.

**286  The Desert Song.** US, 1929, BW/C, 106 m. D: Roy Del Ruth, MS: Sigmund Romberg, P: Warner.

*The Desert Song* (John Boles, Carlotta King); *French Military Marching Song* (Carlotta King); *My Little Castagnette* (Marie Wells); *One Alone* (John Boles); *One Flower* (Robert E. Guzman, Jack Pratt); *The Riff Song* (John Boles); *Romance* (Carlotta King); *Sabre Song* (John Boles, Carlotta King); *Song of the Brass Key* (Marie Wells, Jack Pratt); *Then You Will Know* (John Boles, Carlotta King) W: Otto Harbach and Oscar Hammerstein II—M: Sigmund Romberg.

"The first audible film operetta came to the screen of Warners Theatre last night. . . . The singing . . . is good, and it would be a great deal better if the theatre reproducing device was tuned down a little. . . . John Boles . . . has a voice that is quite pleasing. Carlotta King . . . is rather overwhelming." —Mordaunt Hall, *The New York Times*.

**287  The Desert Song.** US, 1943, C, 96 m. D: Robert Florey, MS: Heinz Roemheld, P: Warner (Robert Florey).

*The Desert Song* (Dennis Morgan); *Fifi's Song* (George Dobbs); *French Military Marching Song* (Irene Manning); *One Alone* (Dennis Morgan, Irene Manning); *One Flower* (Dennis Morgan, Chorus); *The Riff Song* (Dennis Morgan, Chorus); *Romance* (Irene Manning) W: Otto Harbach and Oscar

Hammerstein II—M: Sigmund Romberg.

"Despite modernization . . . basic entertainment qualities . . . are retained." —*Variety.*

**288 The Desert Song.** US, 1953, C, 110 m. D: H. Bruce Humberstone, MD: Max Steiner, P: Warner (Rudi Fehr).

*The Desert Song* (Kathryn Grayson, Gordon MacRae) W: Otto Harbach and Oscar Hammerstein II—M: Sigmund Romberg / *Gay Parisienne* (Kathryn Grayson, Gordon MacRae) W: Jack Scholl—M: Serge Walter / *Long Live the Night* (Kathryn Grayson, Gordon MacRae) W: Mario Sylva—M: Sigmund Romberg / *One Alone* (Gordon MacRae, Kathryn Grayson); *One Flower* (Kathryn Grayson, Chorus); *The Riff Song* (Gordon MacRae, Chorus); *Romance* (Kathryn Grayson) W: Otto Harbach and Oscar Hammerstein II—M: Sigmund Romberg.

"Both story and the songs are well-worn. Latter wear their age with charm and are nicely delivered." —*Variety.*

**289 Designing Woman.** US, 1957, C, 118 m. D: Vincente Minnelli, MS: Andre Previn, P: MGM (Dore Schary). Performer: Dolores Gray.

*Music Is Better Than Words* W: Roger Edens—M: Andre Previn / *There'll Be Some Changes Made* W: Billy Higgins—M: W. Benton Overstreet.

**290 Desire.** US, 1936, BW, 96 m. D: Frank Borzage, MS: Frederick Hollander, P: Paramount (Ernst Lubitsch).

*Awake in a Dream* (Marlene Dietrich) W: Leo Robin—M: Frederick Hollander.

**291 The Desk Set.** US, 1957, C, 103 m. D: Walter Lang, MS: Cyril Mockridge, P: TCF (Henry Ephron). GB Title: His Other Woman.

*Night and Day* (Katharine Hepburn) WM: Cole Porter.

**292 Destry Rides Again.** US, 1939, BW, 94 m. D: George Marshall, MD: Charles Previn, MS: Frank Skinner, P: Universal (Joe Pasternak). Performer: Marlene Dietrich.

*Li'l Joe the Wrangler* (Marlene Dietrich, Charles Winninger, Chorus); *See What the Boys in the Back Room Will Have; You've Got That Look* W: Frank Loesser—M: Frederick Hollander.

**293 Detour.** US, 1945, BW, 69 m. D: Edgar G. Ulmer, MS: Leo Erdody, P: PRC (Leon Fromkess).

*I Can't Believe That You're in Love with Me* (Claudia Drake) W: Clarence Gaskill—M: Jimmy McHugh.

**294 Diamond Horseshoe.** US, 1945, C, 107 m. D: George Seaton, P: TCF (William Perlberg). Orch: Carmen Cavallaro. Orig. Title: Billy Rose's Diamond Horseshoe.

*The Aba Daba Honeymoon* (Willie Solar) W: Arthur Fields—M: Walter Donovan / *Carrie Marry Harry* (Beatrice Kay, William Gaxton) W: Junie McCree—M: Albert von Tilzer / *I'd Climb the Highest Mountain* (Dick Haymes) WM: Lew Brown and Sidney Clare / *In Acapulco* (Betty Grable); *I Wish I Knew* (Dick Haymes, Betty Grable) W: Mack Gordon—M: Harry Warren / *Let Me Call You Sweetheart* (Beatrice Kay) WM: Beth Slater Whitson and Leo Friedman / *The More I See You* (Dick Haymes, Betty Grable) W: Mack Gordon—M: Harry Warren / *My Melancholy Baby* (Dick Haymes) W: George A. Norton—M: Ernie Burnett / *A Nickel's Worth of Jive* (Betty Grable); *Play Me an Old Fashioned Melody* (Betty Grable, William Gaxton, Beatrice Kay) W: Mack Gordon—M: Harry Warren / *Shoo Shoo, Baby* (Betty Grable) WM: Phil Moore / *You'll Never Know* (Betty Grable) W: Mack Gordon—M: Harry Warren.

**295 Diamonds Are Forever.** GB, 1971, C, 119 m. D: Guy Hamilton, MS: John Barry, P: UA (Harry Saltzman, Albert R. Broccoli).

*Diamonds Are Forever* (Shirley Bassey) W: Don Black—M: John Barry.

**296 Dimples.** US, 1936, BW, 78 m. D: William A. Seiter, MD: Louis Silvers, P: TCF (Darryl F. Zanuck, Nunnally Johnson). MB: The Hall Johnson Choir. Performer: Shirley Temple.

*Dixie-Anna* W: Ted Koehler—M: Jimmy McHugh / *Get on Board* WM: Unknown / *He Was a Dandy; Hey, What Did the Bluejay Say?; Picture Me Without You* W: Ted Koehler—M: Jimmy McHugh / *Swing Low, Sweet Chariot* (The Hall Johnson Choir) WM: Unknown.

"Her Little Eva performance is shameless bathos, and so is the love song she sings with her arms twined around the suffering neck of Mr. Morgan." —Frank S. Nugent, *The New York Times.*

**297 Diner.** US, 1982, C, 110 m. D: Barry Levinson, MS: Bruce Brody and Ivan Kral, P: MGM (Jerry Weintraub).

*Ain't Got No Home* (Clarence Henry) WM: Clarence Henry / *Beyond the Sea* (Bobby Darin) W: Jack Lawrence—M: Charles Trenet / *Come Go with Me* (The Del Vikings) WM: Clarence E. Quick / *Don't Be Cruel* (Elvis Presley) WM: Otis Blackwell and Elvis Presley / *Dream Lover* (Bobby Darin) WM: Bobby Darin / *Fascination* (Jane Morgan) W: Dick Manning—M: F.D. Marchetti / *Goodbye Baby* (Jack Scott) WM: Jack Scott / *Honey Don't* (Carl Perkins) / *It's All in the Game* (Tommy Edwards) W: Carl Sigman—M: Charles Gates Dawes / *I Wonder Why* (Dion and The Belmonts) W: Ricardo Weeks—M: Melvin Anderson / *Mr. Blue* (The Fleetwoods) WM: Dewayne Blackwell / *Reconsider Baby* (Lowell Fulson) WM: Lowell Fulson / *Somethin' Else* (Eddie Cochran) WM: Bob Cochran and Sharon Sheeley / *Take Out Some Insurance* (Jimmy Reed) / *A Teenager in Love* (Dion and The Belmonts) WM: Doc Pomus and Mort Shuman / *A Thousand Miles Away* (The Heartbeats) WM: James Shep-

pard and William Miller / *Where or When* (Dick Haymes) W: Lorenz Hart—M: Richard Rodgers / *Whole Lotta Loving* (Fats Domino) WM: Antoine "Fats" Domino and Dave Bartholomew / *Whole Lotta Shakin' Goin' On* (Jerry Lee Lewis) WM: Dave Williams and Sunny David.

**298 Dirty Dancing.** US, 1987, C, 97 m. D: Emile Ardolino, MD: John Morris, P: Vestron (Linda Gottlieb).

*Be My Baby* (The Ronettes) WM: Phil Spector, Ellie Greenwich and Jeff Barry / *Big Girls Don't Cry* (The Four Seasons) WM: Bob Crewe and Bob Gaudio / *Cry to Me* (Solomon Burke) WM: Bert Russell [Bert Berns] / *Do You Love Me?* (The Contours) WM: Berry Gordy, Jr. / *Hey Baby* (Bruce Channel, Margaret Cobb) WM: Bruce Channel and Margaret Cobb / *Hungry Eyes* (Eric Carmen) WM: Frankie Previte and John DeNicola / *In the Still of the Nite* (The Five Satins) WM: Fred Parris / *Love Is Strange* (Mickey and Sylvia) WM: Ethel Smith, Mickey Baker and Sylvia Robinson / *Love Man* (Otis Redding) WM: Otis Redding / *Overload* (Zappacosta) WM: A. Zappacosta and M. Luciani / *She's Like the Wind* (Patrick Swayze, Wendy Fraser) WM: Patrick Swayze and Stacey Widelitz / *Some Kind-a Wonderful* (The Drifters) WM: Gerry Goffin and Carole King / *Stay* (Maurice Williams and The Zodiacs) WM: Maurice Williams / *These Arms of Mine* (Otis Redding) WM: Otis Redding / *The Time of My Life* (Bill Medley, Jennifer Warnes) WM: Frankie Previte, John DeNicola and Donald Markowitz / *Where Are You Tonight?* (Tom Johnston) WM: Mark Scola / *Will You Love Me Tomorrow* (The Shirelles) WM: Gerry Goffin and Carole King / *Wipe Out* (The Surfaris) WM: Ron Wilson, James Fuller, Robert Berryhill and Patrick Connolly / *Yes* (Merry Clayton) WM: T. Fryer, N. Cavanaugh and T. Graf / *You Don't Own Me* (Blow Monkeys) WM: John Madara and Dave White.

"The movie makes a lot of good use of period music, to which some not very evocative new songs have been added." —Vincent Canby, *The New York Times.*

**299 The Disorderly Orderly.** US, 1964, C, 90 m. D: Frank Tashlin, MS: Joseph J. Lilley, P: Paramount (Paul Jones).

*The Disorderly Orderly* (Sammy Davis, Jr.) W: Earl Shuman—M: Leon Carr.

**300 Divine Madness.** US, 1980, C, 94 m. D: Michael Ritchie, P: Warner (Michael Ritchie). MB: The Harlettes [Jocelyn Brown, Ula Hedwig, Diva Gray]. Performer: Bette Midler.

*Big Noise from Winnetka* W: Gil Rodin and Bob Crosby—M: Bob Haggart and Ray Bauduc / *The Boogie Woogie Bugle Boy* WM: Don Raye and Hughie Prince / *Chapel of Love* WM: Phil Spector, Ellie Greenwich and Jeff Barry / *Do You Wanna Dance?* WM: Bobby Freeman / *E Street Shuffle* / *Fire Down Below* WM: Bob Seger / *I Shall Be Released* WM: Bob Dylan / *Leader of the Pack* WM: George Morton, Ellie Greenwich and Jeff Barry / *My Way* WM: Paul Anka / *The Rose* WM: Amanda McBroom / *Shiver Me Timbers* WM: Tom Waites / *Stay with Me* WM: Jerry Ragovoy and George Weiss / *Summer* WM: Bobby Goldsboro / *You Can't Always Get What You Want* WM: Mick Jagger and Keith Richard.

"After years of honing her act in gay baths and on concert stages, Bette Midler in 1980 committed it to film in four days at the Pasadena Calif. Civic Auditorium. 'Because this is the time capsule version of my show,' she tells the aud, 'I might as well do everything I know.' Well, she doesn't quite do everything but she does not stint on energy and showmanship." —*Variety.*

**301 Dixie.** US, 1943, C, 89 m. D: A. Edward Sutherland, MS: Robert Emmett Dolan, P: Paramount (Paul Jones). Performer: Bing Crosby.

*Dixie* WM: Daniel Decatur Emmett / *A Horse That Knows His Way Back Home; If You Please; Kinda Peculiar Brown; Miss Jemima Walks Home; She's from Missouri; Sunday, Monday or Always* W: Johnny Burke—M: James Van Heusen.

**302 Do You Love Me?** US, 1946, C, 91 m. D: Gregory Ratoff, P: TCF (George Jessel). Orch: Harry James. Performer: Dick Haymes.

*As If I Didn't Have Enough on My Mind* W: Charles Henderson—M: Lionel Newman and Harry James / *Do You Love Me?* WM: Harry Ruby / *I Didn't Mean a Word I Said* W: Harold Adamson—M: Jimmy McHugh / *Moonlight Propaganda* WM: Herb Magidson and Matt Malneck.

**303 Doctor Dolittle.** US, 1967, C, 152 m. D: Richard Fleischer, MD: Lionel Newman and Alex Courage, P: TCF (Arthur P. Jacobs).

*After Today* (Anthony Newley); *At the Crossroads* (Samantha Eggar); *Beautiful Things* (Anthony Newley, Samantha Eggar); *Doctor Dolittle* (Anthony Newley, William Dix, Children); *Fabulous Places* (Anthony Newley, Samantha Eggar, Rex Harrison); *I Think I Like You* (Samantha Eggar, Rex Harrison); *I've Never Seen Anything Like It* (Richard Attenborough); *Like Animals* (Rex Harrison); *My Friend the Doctor* (Anthony Newley, Chorus); *Something in Your Smile* (Rex Harrison); *Talk to the Animals* (Rex Harrison); *The Vegetarian* (Rex Harrison); *When I Look in Your Eyes* (Rex Harrison); *Where Are the Words?* (Anthony Newley) WM: Leslie Bricusse.

"Music and lyrics, while containing no smash hits, are admirably suited to the scenario." —*Variety.*

**304 Dr. Strangelove: or How I Learned to Stop Worrying and Love the Bomb.** GB, 1964, BW, 93 m. D: Stanley Kubrick, MS: Laurie Johnson, P: Columbia (Victor Lyndon).

*We'll Meet Again* (Vera Lynn) WM: Ross Parker and Hugh Charles.

**305  Dodge City.** US, 1939, C, 105 m. D: Michael Curtiz, MS: Max Steiner, P: Warner (Robert Lord). MB: Chorus. Performer: Ann Sheridan.

*Ise Gwine Back to Dixie* WM: C.A. White / *Little Brown Jug* WM: Joseph E. Winner.

**306  $ (Dollars).** US, 1972, C, 119 m. D: Richard Brooks, MS: Quincy Jones, P: Columbia (M.J. Frankovich). GB Title: The Heist.

*Do It to It* (Little Richard); *Money Is* (Little Richard) WM: Quincy Jones / *When You're Smiling* (Roberta Flack) WM: Mark Fisher, Joe Goodwin and Larry Shay.

**307  The Dolly Sisters.** US, 1945, C, 114 m. D: Irving Cummings, MD: Alfred Newman, P: TCF (George Jessel).

*Arrah Go On, I'm Gonna Go Back to Oregon* (John Payne, Chorus) W: Sam M. Lewis and Joe Young—M: Bert Grant / *Carolina in the Morning* (Betty Grable, June Haver) W: Gus Kahn—M: Walter Donaldson / *The Darktown Strutters' Ball* (Betty Grable, June Haver) WM: Shelton Brooks / *Don't Be Too Old-Fashioned* (Betty Grable, June Haver, Chorus) W: Mack Gordon—M: James V. Monaco / *Give Me the Moonlight* (Betty Grable, John Payne, Chorus) W: Lew Brown—M: Albert von Tilzer / *I Can't Begin to Tell You* (Betty Grable, John Payne, June Haver) W: Mack Gordon—M: James V. Monaco / *I'm Always Chasing Rainbows* (Betty Grable, John Payne) W: Joseph McCarthy—M: Harry Carroll / *Oh, Frenchy!* (Chorus) W: Sam Ehrlich—M: Con Conrad / *On the Mississippi* (Male Quartet) W: Ballard MacDonald—M: Harry Carroll and Arthur Fields / *Powder, Lipstick and Rouge* (Betty Grable, June Haver, Chorus) W: Mack Gordon—M: Harry Revel / *The Sidewalks of New York* (Betty Grable, June Haver) WM: James W. Blake and Charles B. Lawlor /

*Smiles* (Chorus) W: J. Will Callahan—M: Lee G. Roberts / *The Vamp* (Betty Grable, June Haver) WM: Byron Gay / *We've Been Around* (Betty Grable, June Haver) W: Mack Gordon—M: Charles Henderson.

**308  Dondi.** US, 1961, BW, 100 m. D: Albert Zugsmith, P: AA (Albert Zugsmith, Gus Edson). Performer: Patti Page.

*Dondi* W: Earl Shuman—M: Mort Garson / *Jingle Bells* WM: J.S. Pierpont / *Meadow in the Sky* W: Earl Shuman—M: Mort Garson.

**309  Donovan's Reef.** US, 1963, C, 109 m. D: John Ford, MS: Cyril Mockridge, P: Paramount (John Ford).

*Silent Night* (Dorothy Lamour) W: Joseph Mohr—M: Franz Gruber.

**310  Don't Fence Me In.** US, 1945, BW, 71 m. D: John English, MD: Morton Scott and Dale Butts, P: Republic. MB: Bob Nolan and The Sons of the Pioneers. Performer: Roy Rogers.

*Along the Navajo Trail* WM: Larry Markes, Dick Charles and Eddie De Lange / *Don't Fence Me In* WM: Cole Porter / *The Last Round-Up* WM: Billy Hill / *My Little Buckaroo* W: Jack Scholl—M: M.K. Jerome / *Tumbling Tumbleweeds* WM: Bob Nolan.

**311  Don't Knock the Rock.** US, 1956, BW, 84 m. D: Fred F. Sears, MD: Fred Karger, P: Columbia (Sam Katzman). MB: Dave Appell and His Applejacks.

*Calling All Comets* (Bill Haley and His Comets) WM: Bill Haley, Milt Gabler and Rudy Pompilli / *Don't Knock the Rock* (Bill Haley and His Comets, Alan Dale) WM: Fred Karger and Robert E. Kent / *Gonna Run* (Alan Dale) WM: D'Attili and De Jesus / *Goofin' Around* (Bill Haley and His Comets) WM: Francis Beecher and John Grande / *Hook, Line and Sinker* (Bill Haley and His Comets) WM: Bill Haley, George Khoury and Ed Bonner / *Hot Dog, Buddy, Buddy* (Bill Haley and His Comets) WM: Bill Haley / *I*

*Cry More* (Alan Dale) W: Hal David— M: Burt Bacharach / *Long Tall Sally* (Little Richard) WM: Enotris Johnson, Robert Blackwell and Richard Penniman / *Rip It Up* (Little Richard) WM: Robert Blackwell and John Marascalco / *Rockin' on Sunday Night* (The Treniers) WM: Holtzman and Ellis / *Tutti-Frutti* (Little Richard) WM: Richard Penniman, Dorothy La Bostrie and Joe Lubin / *You're So Right* (Alan Dale) WM: D'Attili and De Jesus.

"What is rock 'n' roll? Well, to one comparatively middle-aged man who made the awful mistake of grabbing a seat down front, it goes thump, *thump*, thump, *thump*. The audience roared it right back, number for number." —Howard Thompson, *The New York Times*.

**312 Don't Knock the Twist.** US, 1962, BW, 86 m. D: Oscar Rudolph, P: Columbia (Sam Katzman).

*Bo Diddley* (The Carroll Brothers) WM: Ellas McDaniel / *The Bristol Stomp* (The Dovells); *Don't Knock the Twist* (Chubby Checker); *Do the New Continental* (The Dovells) WM: Kal Mann and Dave Appell / *The Duke of Earl* (Gene Chandler) WM: Earl Edwards, Bernie Williams and Eugene Dixon / *The Fly* (Chubby Checker) WM: John Madara and Dave White / *I Love to Twist* (Chubby Checker) WM: Kal Mann and Bernie Lowe / *La Paloma Twist* (Chubby Checker) WM: Kal Mann / *Little Altar Boy* (Vic Dana) WM: Howlett Smith / *Mashed Potato Time* (Dee Dee Sharp) WM: Jon Sheldon and Harry Land / *Slow Twistin'* (Chubby Checker, Dee Dee Sharp) WM: Jon Sheldon / *Yesiree* (Linda Scott) WM: Linda Scott.

**313 Double Dynamite.** US, 1951, BW, 80 m. D: Irving Cummings, Jr., MS: Leigh Harline, P: RKO (Irving Cummings, Jr.). Alt. Title: It's Only Money.

*It's Only Money* (Frank Sinatra, Groucho Marx, Jane Russell); *Kisses and Tears* (Frank Sinatra, Jane Russell) W: Sammy Cahn—M: Jule Styne.

**314 Double or Nothing.** US, 1937, BW, 95 m. D: Theodore Reed, P: Paramount (Benjamin Glazer).

*After You* (Bing Crosby, Frances Faye, Martha Raye) WM: Sam Coslow and Al Siegel / *All You Want to Do Is Dance* (Bing Crosby) W: Johnny Burke—M: Arthur Johnston / *It's On, It's Off* (Martha Raye) WM: Sam Coslow and Al Siegel / *It's the Natural Thing to Do* (Bing Crosby) W: Johnny Burke—M: Arthur Johnston / *Listen My Children and You Shall Hear* (Martha Raye) W: Ralph Freed—M: Burton Lane / *The Moon Got in My Eyes* (Bing Crosby) W: Johnny Burke—M: Arthur Johnston / *Smarty* (Bing Crosby) W: Ralph Freed—M: Burton Lane.

**315 Double Trouble.** US, 1967, C, 90 m. D: Norman Taurog, MS: Jeff Alexander, P: MGM (Judd Bernard, Irwin Winkler). Performer: Elvis Presley.

*Baby, If You'll Give Me All of Your Love* WM: Joy Byers / *City by Night* WM: Bill Giant, Bernie Baum and Florence Kaye / *Could I Fall in Love* WM: Randy Starr / *Double Trouble* WM: Doc Pomus and Mort Shuman / *I Love Only One Girl* WM: Sid Tepper and Roy C. Bennett / *Long Legged Girl* WM: J. Leslie McFarland and Winfield Scott / *Old MacDonald Had a Farm* WM: Unknown—Arr: Randy Starr / *There Is So Much World to See* WM: Sid Tepper and Ben Weisman.

**316 Down Among the Sheltering Palms.** US, 1953, C, 87 m. D: Edmund Goulding, MS: Leigh Harline, P: TCF (Fred Kohlmar).

*All of Me* (Gloria De Haven) WM: Seymour Simons and Gerald Marks / *I'm the Ruler of a South Sea Island* (William Lundigan, David Wayne); *What Make de Difference?* (Mitzi Gaynor); *Who Will It Be When the Time Comes?* (Jane Greer) W: Ralph Blane—M: Harold Arlen.

**317 Down Argentine Way.** US, 1940, C, 94 m. D: Irving Cummings,

P: TCF (Harry Joe Brown). Orch: Bando da Lua. MB: Six Hits and A Miss. Vocals: Carlos Albert (in Spanish) for Don Ameche.

*Down Argentina Way* (Carmen Miranda, Betty Grable, Don Ameche, Henry Stephenson, J. Carrol Naish, Chris Pin Martin, Leonid Kinskey, Charlotte Greenwood, The Nicholas Brothers, Chorus) W: Mack Gordon— M: Harry Warren / *Mama Yo Quiero* (Carmen Miranda) Eng. W: Al Stillman—Span. WM: Jararaca Paiva and Vincente Paiva / *Nenita* (Leonid Kinskey, Trio); *Sing to Your Senorita* (Charlotte Greenwood, Leonid Kinskey) W: Mack Gordon—M: Harry Warren / *South American Way* (Carmen Miranda) W: Al Dubin—M: Jimmy McHugh / *Two Dreams Met* (Betty Grable, Don Ameche, Pepe Guizar, Chorus) W: Mack Gordon—M: Harry Warren.

**318  Dreamboat.** US, 1952, BW, 83 m. D: Claude Binyon, MS: Cyril Mockridge, P: TCF (Sol C. Siegel). Performer: Ginger Rogers.

*I Can't Begin to Tell You* W: Mack Gordon—M: James V. Monaco / *You'll Never Know* W: Mack Gordon—M: Harry Warren.

**319  Du Barry Was a Lady.** US, 1943, C, 101 m. D: Roy Del Ruth, MD: George Stoll, P: MGM (Arthur Freed). Orch: Tommy Dorsey. MB: The Pied Pipers, with Dick Haymes and Jo Stafford. Vocals: Martha Mears for Lucille Ball.

The original 1939 Broadway hit musical included Bert Lahr, Ethel Merman and Betty Grable.

*Do I Love You?* (Gene Kelly) WM: Cole Porter / *Du Barry Was a Lady* (Lucille Ball, Chorus) W: Ralph Freed—M: Burton Lane / *Friendship* (Red Skelton, Lucille Ball, Gene Kelly, Virginia O'Brien, Rags Ragland, Zero Mostel) WM: Cole Porter / *I Love an Esquire Girl* (Red Skelton) WM: Ralph Freed, Roger Edens and Lew Brown / *Katie Went to Haiti* (Jo Stafford, Dick Haymes, The Pied Pipers) WM: Cole Porter / *Madam, I Love Your Crepe Suzettes* (Red Skelton) WM: Ralph Freed, Burton Lane and Lew Brown / *Salome* (Virginia O'Brien) WM: Roger Edens.

"Gene Kelly, whose forte is terping, suffers from the histrionic and singing demands of his role and lack of opportunity to make with the feet. O'Brien is disappointing, too, except for the one tune she's given ... in which she literally sparkles." — *Variety*.

**320  The Duchess of Idaho.** US, 1950, C, 98 m. D: Robert Z. Leonard, MD: George Stoll, P: MGM (Joe Pasternak).

*Baby, Come Out of the Clouds* (Lena Horne) WM: Lee Pearl and Henry Nemo / *Choo Choo Choo to Idaho* (Van Johnson, Chorus); *Of All Things* (Connie Haines and The Jubalaires); *You Can't Do Wrong Doing Right* (Van Johnson) WM: Al Rinker and Floyd Huddleston.

**321  Duck Soup.** US, 1933, BW, 70 m. D: Leo McCarey, P: Paramount.

*The Country's Going to War* (The Marx Brothers, Chorus); *Hail, Hail Freedonia* (Chorus); *The Laws of My Administration* (Groucho Marx, Margaret Dumont, Chorus); *When the Clock on the Wall Strikes Ten* (Zeppo Marx, Margaret Dumont, Chorus) WM: Bert Kalmar and Harry Ruby.

"Music and lyrics through which much of the action is in rhyme and song, serve to carry the story along rather than to stand out on pop song merit on their own." — *Variety*.

**322  Duel in the Sun.** US, 1946, C, 130 m. D: King Vidor, MS: Dimitri Tiomkin, P: Selznick (David O. Selznick). Performer: Gregory Peck.

*Gotta Get Me Somebody to Love* WM: Allie Wrubel / *I've Been Workin' on the Railroad* WM: Unknown.

**323  Duffy's Tavern.** US, 1945, BW, 97 m. D: Hal Walker, MS: Robert Emmett Dolan, P: Paramount (Joseph Sistrom, Danny Dare).

*The Hard Way* (Betty Hutton);

*Swinging on a Star* (Dorothy Lamour, Betty Hutton, Bing Crosby, Sonny Tufts, Diana Lynn, Arturo De Cordova) W: Johnny Burke—M: James Van Heusen / *You Can't Blame a Gal for Trying* (Cass Daley) WM: Ben Raleigh and Bernie Wayne.

**324 The Duke Wore Jeans.** GB, 1958, BW, 89 m. D: Gerald Thomas, MD: Roland Shaw, P: Anglo Amalgamated (Peter Rogers). Performer: Tommy Steele.

*Family Tree; Hair-Down Hoe-Down; Happy Guitar; It's All Happening; Photograph* (Tommy Steele, June Laverick); *Princess; Thanks a Lot; What Do You Do* WM: Jimmy Bennett [Tommy Steele], Michael Pratt and Lionel Bart.

**325 East Side of Heaven.** US, 1939, BW, 90 m. D: David Butler, P: Universal (Herbert Polesie). Performer: Bing Crosby.

*East Side of Heaven; Hang Your Heart on a Hickory Limb* (Bing Crosby, Jane Jones, The Music Maids); *Sing a Song of Sunbeams; That Sly Old Gentleman* W: Johnny Burke—M: James V. Monaco.

**326 Easter Parade.** US, 1948, C, 103 m. D: Charles Walters, MD: Johnny Green, P: MGM (Arthur Freed).

*Better Luck Next Time* (Judy Garland); *A Couple of Swells* (Judy Garland, Fred Astaire); *Drum Crazy* (Fred Astaire); *Easter Parade* (Judy Garland, Fred Astaire, Chorus); *Everybody's Doin' It* (Chorus); *A Fella with an Umbrella* (Judy Garland, Peter Lawford); *The Girl on the Magazine Cover* (Richard Beavers, Chorus); *Happy Easter* (Fred Astaire, Chorus); *I Love a Piano* (Judy Garland); *It Only Happens When I Dance with You* (Judy Garland, Fred Astaire); *I Want to Go Back to Michigan* (Judy Garland); *Ragtime Violin* (Fred Astaire); *Shaking the Blues Away* (Ann Miller); *Snooky Ookums* (Judy Garland, Fred Astaire); *Steppin' Out with My Baby* (Fred Astaire); *When the Midnight*

*Choo Choo Leaves for Alabam'* (Judy Garland, Fred Astaire) WM: Irving Berlin.

"Technicolor and Irving Berlin's score, including seven new songs, serve as sturdy props." —Thomas M. Pryor, *The New York Times.*

"Highpoint of comedy is reached when Astaire and Garland team for vocals and footwork on *A Couple of Swells.*" —*Variety.*

**327 Easy Come, Easy Go.** US, 1967, C, 95 m. D: John Rich, MS: Joseph J. Lilley, P: Paramount (Hal B. Wallis). MB: The Jordanaires. Performer: Elvis Presley.

*Easy Come, Easy Go* WM: Sid Wayne and Ben Weisman / *I'll Take Love* WM: Dolores Fuller and Mark Barkan / *The Love Machine* WM: Gerald Nelson, Fred Burch and Chuck Taylor / *Sing, You Children; Yoga Is as Yoga Does* (Elvis Presley, Elsa Lanchester) WM: Gerald Nelson and Fred Burch / *You Gotta Stop* WM: Bill Giant, Bernie Baum and Florence Kaye.

**328 Easy Rider.** US, 1969, C, 95 m. D: Dennis Hopper, P: Columbia (Peter Fonda).

*Ballad of Easy Rider* (Roger McGuinn) WM: Roger McGuinn / *Born to Be Wild* (Steppenwolf) WM: Mars Bonfire [Dennis Edmonton] / *Don't Bogart Me* (Fraternity of Men) WM: Elliot Ingber and Larry Warner / *If Six Was Nine* (The Jimi Hendrix Experience) WM: Jimi Hendrix / *If You Want to Be a Bird* (The Holy Modal Rounders) WM: Antonia Duren / *It's Alright, Ma* (Roger McGuinn) WM: Bob Dylan / *I Wasn't Born to Follow* (The Byrds) WM: Gerry Goffin and Carole King / *Kyrie Eleison* (The Electric Prunes) WM: David Axelrod / *Let's Turkey Trot* (Little Eva) WM: Gerry Goffin and Jack Keller / *The Pusher* (Steppenwolf) WM: Hoyt Axton / *The Weight* (The Band) WM: Jaime Robbie Robertson.

**329 Easy to Love.** US, 1953, C,

96 m. D: Charles Walters, MD: Lennie Hayton and George Stoll, P: MGM (Joe Pasternak). Performer: Tony Martin.

*Coquette* W: Gus Kahn—M: Johnny Green and Carmen Lombardo / *Didja Ever?* W: Mann Curtis—M: Vic Mizzy / *Easy to Love* WM: Cole Porter / *That's What a Rainy Day Is For* W: Mann Curtis—M: Vic Mizzy.

**330   The Eddie Cantor Story.** US, 1953, C, 116 m. D: Alfred E. Green, MD: Ray Heindorf, P: Warner (Sidney Skolsky). Vocals: Eddie Cantor for Keefe Brasselle. Performer: Keefe Brasselle.

*Be My Little Baby Bumblebee* W: Stanley Murphy—M: Henry I. Marshall / *Bye, Bye, Blackbird* W: Mort Dixon—M: Ray Henderson / *How Ya Gonna Keep 'Em Down on the Farm?* W: Sam M. Lewis and Joe Young—M: Walter Donaldson / *Ida, Sweet as Apple Cider* W: Eddie Munson—M: Eddie Leonard / *If I Was a Millionaire* W: Will D. Cobb—M: Gus Edwards / *If You Knew Susie* WM: B.G. De Sylva and Joseph Meyer / *Ma, He's Making Eyes at Me* W: Sidney Clare—M: Con Conrad / *Makin' Whoopee* W: Gus Kahn—M: Walter Donaldson / *Margie* W: Benny Davis—M: Con Conrad and J. Russel Robinson / *Now's the Time to Fall in Love* WM: Al Sherman and Al Lewis / *Oh, You Beautiful Doll* W: A. Seymour Brown—M: Nat D. Ayer / *One Hour with You* W: Leo Robin—M: Richard A. Whiting / *Pretty Baby* W: Gus Kahn—M: Tony Jackson and Egbert Van Alstyne / *Row, Row, Row* W: William Jerome—M: James V. Monaco / *Will You Love Me in December* W: James J. Walker—M: Ernest R. Ball / *Yes Sir, That's My Baby* W: Gus Kahn—M: Walter Donaldson / *Yes! We Have No Bananas* WM: Frank Silver and Irving Cohn / *You Must Have Been a Beautiful Baby* W: Johnny Mercer—M: Harry Warren.

"Although it . . . is weighted with the songs and shows he helped make famous, 'The Eddie Cantor Story' is slightly less than a colorful illustration of the reasons for its hero's greatness." —A.H. Weiler, *The New York Times*.

**331   Electra Glide in Blue.** US, 1973, C, 113 m. D: James William Guercio, MS: James William Guercio, P: UA (James William Guercio, Rupert Hitzig).

*Free from the Devil* (Madura) WM: Alan De Carlo / *Meadow Mountain Top* (Mark Spoelstra) WM: Mark Spoelstra / *Most of All* (The Marcels) WM: Alan Freed and Harvey Fuqua / *Song of Sad Bottles* (Mark Spoelstra) WM: Mark Spoelstra / *Tell Me* (Terry Kath) WM: James William Guercio.

"Guercio at one time played with the rock group of Frank Zappa and brings that balladlike, terse feel of rock to this extremely well-played and mounted pic." —*Variety*.

**332   The Electric Horseman.** US, 1979, C, 120 m. D: Sydney Pollack, MS: Dave Grusin, P: Columbia/Universal (Ray Stark). Performer: Willie Nelson.

*Hands on the Wheel* / *Mammas, Don't Let Your Babies Grow Up to Be Cowboys* WM: Ed Bruce and Patsy Bruce / *Midnight Rider* WM: Greg Allman and Kim Payne / *My Heroes Have Always Been Cowboys* WM: Sharon Vaughan.

**333   Elvis on Tour.** US, 1972, C, 93 m. D: Pierre Adidge and Robert Abel, P: MGM (Pierre Adidge, Robert Abel). MB: Kathy Westmorland; The Sweet Inspirations; J.D. Sumner and The Stamps Quartet. Performer: Elvis Presley.

*All My Trials* WM: Unknown / *Amen* WM: Unknown / *Battle Hymn of the Republic* W: Julia Ward Howe—M: William Steffe / *A Big Hunk O' Love* WM: Aaron Schroeder and Sid Wyche / *Bosom of Abraham* WM: William Johnson, George McFadden and Ted Brooks / *Bridge Over Troubled Water* WM: Paul Simon / *Burning Love* WM: Dennis Linde / *Can't Help Falling in*

*Love* WM: Hugo Peretti, Luigi Creatore and George Weiss / *Dixie* WM: Daniel Decatur Emmett / *Don't Be Cruel* WM: Otis Blackwell and Elvis Presley / *For the Good Times* WM: Kris Kristofferson / *Funny How Time Slips Away* WM: Willie Nelson / *I Got a Woman* WM: Ray Charles / *I, John* WM: William Johnson, George McFadden and Ted Brooks / *Johnny B. Goode* WM: Chuck Berry / *Lawdy Miss Clawdy* WM: Lloyd Price / *Lead Me, Guide Me* WM: Doris Akers / *Lighthouse* (The Stamps) / *Love Me Tender* W: Vera Matson and Elvis Presley—M: George R. Poulton / *Memories* WM: Billy Strange and Mac Davis / *Mystery Train* WM: Herman Parker and Sam Phillips / *Never Been to Spain* WM: Hoyt Axton / *Polk Salad Annie* WM: Tony Joe White / *Proud Mary* WM: John C. Fogerty / *Ready Teddy* WM: John Marascalco and Robert Blackwell / *Separate Ways* WM: Bobby "Red" West and Richard Mainegra / *See See Rider* WM: Ma Rainey / *Suspicious Minds* WM: Mark James / *Sweet Sweet Spirit* (The Stamps) / *That's All Right* WM: Arthur Crudup / *Until It's Time for You to Go* WM: Buffy Sainte Marie / *You Gave Me a Mountain* WM: Marty Robbins.

**334  Elvis—That's the Way It Is.** US, 1970, C, 97 m. D: Denis Sanders, P: MGM (Herbert F. Soklow). MB: Millie Kirkham; The Sweet Inspirations; The Imperials. Performer: Elvis Presley.

*All Shook Up* WM: Otis Blackwell and Elvis Presley / *Blue Suede Shoes* WM: Carl Lee Perkins / *Bridge Over Troubled Water* WM: Paul Simon / *Can't Help Falling in Love* WM: Hugo Peretti, Luigi Creatore and George Weiss / *Crying Time* WM: Buck Owens / *Heartbreak Hotel* WM: Mae Boren Axton and Tommy Durden / *How the Web Was Woven* WM: Clive Westlake and David Most / *I Just Can't Help Believin'* WM: Barry Mann and Cynthia Weil / *I've Lost You* WM: Kenneth Howard and Alan Blaikley / *Little Sister* WM: Doc Pomus and Mort Shuman / *Love Me Tender* WM: Vera Matson and Elvis Presley—M: George R. Poulton / *Mary in the Morning* WM: Johnny Cymbal and Michael Rashkow / *Mystery Train* WM: Herman Parker and Sam Phillips / *The Next Step Is Love* WM: Paul Evans and Paul Parnes / *One Night* WM: Dave Bartholomew and Pearl King / *Patch It Up* WM: Eddie Rabbitt and Rory Bourke / *Polk Salad Annie* WM: Tony Joe White / *Stranger in the Crowd* WM: Winfield Scott / *Suspicious Minds* WM: Mark James / *Sweet Caroline* WM: Neil Diamond / *That's All Right* WM: Arthur Crudup / *Tiger Man* WM: Joe Hill Louis and Sam Burns / *What'd I Say* WM: Ray Charles / *Words* WM: Barry Gibb, Robin Gibb and Maurice Gibb / *You Don't Have to Say You Love Me* W: Vicki Wickham and Simon Napier-Bell—M: P. Donaggio / *You've Lost That Lovin' Feelin'* WM: Phil Spector, Barry Mann and Cynthia Weil.

**335  The Emperor Jones.** US, 1933, BW, 72 m. D: Dudley Murphy, MD: Frank Tours, MS: J. Rosamund Johnson, P: UA (John Krimsky). MB: The Hall Johnson Choir. Performer: Paul Robeson.

*I'm Travelin'; John Henry; Now Let Me Fly* WM: Unknown / *Water Boy* WM: Avery Robinson.

"Mr. Robeson adds to the interest of one or two opening scenes by his singing." —Mordaunt Hall, *The New York Times.*

**336  Emperor of the North.** US, 1973, C, 118 m. D: Robert Aldrich, MS: Frank DeVol, P: TCF (Stan Hough). Orig. Title: Emperor of the North Pole.

*A Man and a Train* (Marty Robbins) W: Hal David—M: Frank DeVol.

**337  The Emperor Waltz.** US, 1948, C, 106 m. D: Billy Wilder, MS: Victor Young, P: Paramount (Charles Brackett). Performer: Bing Crosby.

*The Emperor Waltz* W: Johnny Burke—M: Johann Strauss / *Friendly Mountains* WM: Unknown—Arr: Johnny Burke / *I Kiss Your Hand, Madame* German W: Fritz Rotter—Eng. W: Sam M. Lewis and Joe Young—M: Ralph Erwin / *The Kiss in Your Eyes* W: Johnny Burke—M: Richard Heuberger.

**338   Endless Love.** US, 1981, C, 115 m. D: Franco Zeffirelli, MS: Jonathan Tunick, P: Universal (Dyson Lovell).

*Dreamin'* (Cliff Richard) WM: Alan Tarney and Leo Sayer / *Dreaming of You* (Diana Ross, Lionel Richie); *Endless Love* (Diana Ross, Lionel Richie) WM: Lionel Richie, Jr. / *I Was Made for Lovin' You* (Kiss) WM: Paul Stanley, Vini Poncia and Desmond Child.

**339   Evergreen.** GB, 1934, BW, 90 m. D: Victor Saville, MD: Louis Levy, P: Gaumont-British (Michael Balcon).

Jessie Matthews and Sonnie Hale brought an earlier version of this Rodgers and Hart musical to the London stage in 1930.

*Daddy Wouldn't Buy Me a Bow-Wow* (Jessie Matthews) WM: Joseph Tabrar / *Dancing on the Ceiling* (Jessie Matthews); *Dear Dear* (Jessie Matthews, Barry Mackay); *If I Give In to You* (Jessie Matthews) W: Richard Rodgers—M: Lorenz Hart / *I Wouldn't Leave My Little Wooden Hut for You* (Jessie Matthews, Betty Balfour) WM: Charles Collins and Tom Mellor / *Over My Shoulder* (Jessie Matthews); *Tinkle Tinkle Tinkle* (Sonnie Hale); *When You've Got a Little Springtime in Your Heart* (Jessie Matthews) WM: Harry M. Woods.

"The most pleasurable musical comedy yet offered us by the ambitious British screen industry . . . most likable when Miss Matthews is adjusting her nimble and lyric style to the music of Richard Rodgers, Lorenz Hart and Harry M. Woods." —Andre Sennwald, *The New York Times*.

**340   Every Night at Eight.** US, 1935, BW, 81 m. D: Raoul Walsh, P: Paramount (Walter Wanger).

*Every Night at Eight* (Frances Langford, Patsy Kelly) W: Dorothy Fields—M: Jimmy McHugh / *I Feel a Song Coming On* (Frances Langford, Alice Faye, Harry Barris, Patsy Kelly) W: Dorothy Fields and George Oppenheimer—M: Jimmy McHugh / *I'm in the Mood for Love* (Frances Langford); *Speaking Confidentially* (Frances Langford, Alice Faye, Patsy Kelly); *Take It Easy* (Frances Langford, Alice Faye, Patsy Kelly) W: Dorothy Fields—M: Jimmy McHugh / *Then You've Never Been Blue* (Frances Langford) W: Sam M. Lewis and Joe Young—M: Ted Fiorito.

**341   Every Which Way But Loose.** US, 1978, C, 114 m. D: James Fargo, MD: Steve Dorff, P: Warner (Robert Daley).

*Behind Closed Doors* (Charlie Rich) WM: Kenny O'Dell / *Coca Cola Cowboy* (Mel Tillis) WM: Irving Dain, Steve Dorff, James S. Pinkard, Jr., and Sam Atchley / *Don't Say You Don't Love Me No More* (Sondra Locke, Phil Everly) WM: Phil Everly and J. Paige / *Every Which Way But Loose* (Eddie Rabbitt) WM: Milton Brown, Steve Dorff and Snuff Garrett / *I Can't Say No to a Truck Drivin' Man* (Carol Chase) WM: Cliff Crofford / *I'll Wake You When I Get Home* (Charlie Rich) WM: Steve Dorff and Milton Brown / *I Seek the Night* (Sondra Locke) WM: Neil Diamond / *Monkey See, Monkey Do* (Cliff Crofford) WM: Cliff Crofford and Snuff Garrett / *Red Eye Special* (Larry Collins) WM: Larry Collins, Steven Pinkard and Snuff Garrett / *Send Me Down to Tucson* (Mel Tillis) WM: Cliff Crofford and Snuff Garrett / *A Six Pack to Go* (Hank Thompson) WM: Hank Thompson, J. Lowe and D. Hart.

**342   Everybody Sing.** US, 1938, 80 m. D: Edwin L. Marin, MS: William Axt, P: MGM (Harry Rapf).

*Cosi Cosa* (Allan Jones) W: Ned Washington—M: Bronislau Kaper and Walter Jurmann / *Down on Melody Farm* (Judy Garland); *The One I Love* (Allan Jones); *Rigoletto* (Allan Jones, Judy Garland, Reginald Gardiner, Lynne Carver) W: Gus Kahn—M: Bronislau Kaper and Walter Jurmann / *Swing Low, Sweet Chariot* (Judy Garland) WM: Unknown—Arr: Roger Edens / *Swing Mr. Mendelssohn* (Judy Garland, Chorus) W: Gus Kahn—M: Bronislau Kaper and Walter Jurmann.

"Excellent film musical with fresh ideas and a corking cast for the top spots." — *Variety.*

**343  Everything I Have Is Yours.** US, 1952, C, 92 m. D: Robert Z. Leonard, MD: David Rose, P: MGM (George Wells).

*Derry Down Dilly* (Marge Champion) W: Johnny Mercer—M: Johnny Green / *Everything I Have Is Yours* (Monica Lewis) W: Harold Adamson—M: Burton Lane / *Like Monday Follows Sunday* (Marge Champion, Gower Champion) WM: Clifford Grey, Rex Newman, Douglas Furber and Johnny Green / *17,000 Telephone Poles* (Monica Lewis, Chorus) WM: Saul Chaplin.

**344  Everything Is Rhythm.** GB, 1936, BW, 73 m. D: Alfred Goulding, P: Associated British (Joe Rock).

London-born singer, band leader and clarinet player Harry Roy was known as the "King of Hotcha." His marriage in 1935 to Elizabeth Brooke, the beautiful daughter of Sir Charles Vyner Brooke, White Rajah of Sarawak, caused a sensation. For a short while she sang with Roy's band, under the name "Princess Pearl," but their marriage did not last.

*Black Minnie's Got the Blues* (Harry Roy, Mabel Mercer, Chorus) W: Jack Meskill—M: Cyril Ray / *Cheerful Blues* (Harry Roy) WM: Harry Roy / *The Internationale* (Harry Roy) W: Jack Meskill—M: Cyril Ray / *Life Is Empty Without Love* (Princess Pearl, Harry Roy) WM: Harry Roy / *Make Some Music* (Harry Roy, Chorus) W: Jack Meskill—M: Cyril Ray / *No Words No Anything* (Harry Roy, Ivor Moreton, Bill Curie) WM: Harry Roy / *Sky High Honeymoon* (Princess Pearl, Harry Roy, Chorus); *You're the Last Word in Love* (Harry Roy, Phyllis Thackeray, Ivor Moreton) W: Jack Meskill—M: Cyril Ray.

**345  Evil Under the Sun.** GB, 1982, C, 102 m. D: Guy Hamilton, MS: Cole Porter, P: EMI (John Brabourne, Richard Goodwin).

*You're the Top* (Diana Rigg) WM: Cole Porter.

"Diana Rigg as the stage star makes it believable in one short song-and-dance scene that she really is such a star." — *Variety.*

**346  Expresso Bongo.** GB, 1960, BW, 108 m. D: Val Guest, MD: Robert Farnon, P: British Lion/Britannia (Val Guest). Performers: Cliff Richard and The Shadows.

*Bongo Blues / Love / The Shrine on the Second Floor* WM: Julian More, David Heneker and Monty Norman / *A Voice in the Wilderness* WM: Norrie Paramor and Bunny Lewis.

"The songs are intended to spoof the whole business of pop crooning but they come over, in Richard's larynx, as completely feasible entries into the pop market." — *Variety.*

**347  Eyes of Laura Mars.** US, 1978, C, 103 m. D: Irvin Kershner, MS: Artie Kane, P: Columbia (Jon Peters).

*Burn* (Michalski and Oosterveen) WM: George Michalski and Niki Oosterveen / *Let's All Chant* (The Michael Zager Band) WM: Alvin Fields and Michael Zager / *Love Theme from Eyes of Laura Mars* (Barbra Streisand) W: John Desautels—M: Karen Lawrence / *Native New Yorker* (Odyssey) WM: Sandy Linzer and Denny Randell / *Shake Your Booty* (K.C. and The Sunshine Band) WM: Harry Wayne Casey and Richard Finch.

**348  The Fabulous Dorseys.**
US, 1947, BW, 88 m. D: Alfred E.
Green, MS: Leo Shuken, P: UA
(Charles R. Rogers). Orch: Tommy
Dorsey; Jimmy Dorsey; Paul White-
man.

*Green Eyes* (Helen O'Connell,
Bob Eberly) Spanish W: Adolfo
Utrera—Eng. W: L. Wolfe Gilbert—
M: Nilo Menendez / *Marie* (Janet
Blair, Stuart Foster, Chorus) WM: Ir-
ving Berlin / *The Object of My Affection*
(Janet Blair) WM: Pinky Tomlin, Coy
Poe and Jimmie Grier / *To Me* (Janet
Blair, William Lundigan) W: Don
George—M: Allie Wrubel.

**349  A Face in the Crowd.** US,
1957, BW, 125 m. D: Elia Kazan, MS:
Tom Glazer, P: Warner (Elia Kazan).
Performer: Andy Griffith.

*A Face in the Crowd; Free Man in
the Morning* W: Budd Schulberg—M:
Tom Glazer / *Just a Closer Walk with
Thee* WM: Red Foley / *Just Plain Folks*
(Male Group); *Mama Guitar*; *Old
Fashioned Marriage* (Female Trio);
*Vitajex Jingle* (Female Trio) W: Budd
Schulberg—M: Tom Glazer.

**350  The Facts of Life.** US,
1960, BW, 103 m. D: Melvin Frank,
MS: Leigh Harline, P: UA (Norman
Panama).

*The Facts of Life* (Steve Lawrence,
Eydie Gorme) WM: Johnny Mercer.

**351  Fallen Angel.** US, 1945,
BW, 97 m. D: Otto Preminger, MS:
David Raksin, P: TCF (Otto Premin-
ger).

*The Cubanola Glide* (Alice Faye)
W: Vincent P. Bryan—M: Harry von
Tilzer / *Slowly* (Dick Haymes) W: Ker-
mit Goell—M: David Raksin.

**352  Fame.** US, 1980, C, 133 m.
D: Alan Parker, P: MGM (David De
Silva, Alan Marshall).

*Dogs in the Yard* (Paul McCrane)
WM: Dominic Bugatti and Frank
Musker / *Fame* (Irene Cara, Chorus)
W: Dean Pitchford—M: Michael Gore
/ *Hot Lunch Jam* (Irene Cara, Chorus)
W: Lesley Gore and Robert F. Coles-

berry—M: Michael Gore / *I Sing the
Body Electric* (Chorus) W: Dean Pitch-
ford—M: Michael Gore / *Is It Okay If
I Call You Mine?* (Paul McCrane)
WM: Paul McCrane / *Out Here on My
Own* (Irene Cara) W: Lesley Gore—M:
Michael Gore / *Red Light* (Linda Clif-
ford, Chorus) W: Dean Pitchford—M:
Michael Gore.

"Frequently breaks into song, into
big, noisy, raucous musical interludes
to which Mr. Parker brings his utmost
flair. Those numbers don't always fit
the film, but no one seems to care." —
Janet Maslin, *The New York Times.*

**353  The Family Jewels.** US,
1965, C, 100 m. D: Jerry Lewis, MS:
Pete King, P: Paramount (Jerry Lewis).

*This Diamond Ring* (Gary Lewis
and The Playboys) WM: Al Kooper,
Irwin Levine and Bob Brass.

**354  The Family Way.** GB,
1966, C, 114 m. D: Roy Boulting, MS:
Paul McCartney, P: Warner (John
Boulting, Roy Boulting).

*Love in the Open Air* (Paul Mc-
Cartney) WM: Paul McCartney.

**355  Fancy Pants.** US, 1950, C,
92 m. D: George Marshall, MS: Van
Cleave, P: Paramount (Robert Welch).

*Home Cookin'* (Bob Hope, Lucille
Ball) WM: Jay Livingston and Ray
Evans.

**356  Farewell, My Lovely.** US,
1975, C, 97 m. D: Dick Richards, MS:
David Shire, P: Avco Embassy (George
Pappas, Jerry Bruckheimer).

*I've Heard That Song Before* (Edra
Gale) W: Sammy Cahn—M: Jule
Styne.

**357  The Farmer Takes a Wife.**
US, 1953, C, 81 m. D: Henry Levin,
MD: Lionel Newman, MS: Cyril
Mockridge, P: TCF (Frank P. Rosen-
berg).

*Can You Spell Schenectady?* (Eddie
Foy, Jr.); *On the Erie Canal* (Betty
Grable, Dale Robertson); *Somethin'
Real Special* (Betty Grable, Dale Rob-
ertson); *Today, I Love Ev'rybody* (Betty
Grable, Chorus); *We're Doin' It for the*

*Natives in Jamaica* (Thelma Ritter, John Carroll, Chorus); *We're in Business* (Betty Grable, Dale Robertson, Gwen Verdon, Chorus); *With the Sun Warm Upon Me* (Dale Robertson) W: Dorothy Fields—M: Harold Arlen.

"The tuning is unimpressive and the terp numbers are lacking in bounce." — *Variety*.

**358  Fast Break.** US, 1979, C, 107 m. D: Jack Smight, P: Columbia (Stephen Friedman).

*Go for It* (Billy Preston and Syreeta) W: Carol Connors—M: David Shire / *He Didn't Stay* (Syreeta) WM: Carol Connors and James Di Pasquale / *More Than Just a Friend* (Billy Preston); *With You I'm Born Again* (Billy Preston and Syreeta) W: Carol Connors—M: David Shire.

**359  Fast Forward.** US, 1985, C, 110 m. D: Sidney Poitier, MS: Tom Scott and Jack Hayes, P: Columbia (John Patrick Veitch).

*Breakin' Out* (John Scott Clough) / *Curves* (Deco) WM: Preston Glass and Michael Warden / *Do You Want It Right Now* (Siedah Garrett) WM: China Burton and Nick Straker / *Fast Forward* (John Scott Clough, Kip Lennon) WM: Brock Walsh, Tom Bahler, John Van Tongeren and Bunny Hull / *How Do You Do* (John Scott Clough, Kip Lennon) WM: Brock Walsh and Mark Vieha / *Showdown* (John Scott Clough, Kip Lennon) WM: Jellybean, Toni C. and Stephen Bray / *Survive* (John Scott Clough) / *Taste* (Deco) WM: Siedah Garrett and Swanson / *That's Just the Way It Is* (Narada Michael Williams).

**360  The Fastest Guitar Alive.** US, 1968, C, 87 m. D: Michael Moore, P: MGM (Sam Katzman). Performer: Roy Orbison.

*The Fastest Guitar Alive; Good Time Party; Medicine Man; Pistolero; River; Rollin' On* WM: Bill Dees and Roy Orbison / *Snuggle Huggle* WM: Robert E. Kent and Fred Karger / *Whirlwind* WM: Bill Dees and Roy Orbison.

**361  Fate Is the Hunter.** US, 1964, BW, 106 m. D: Ralph Nelson, MS: Jerry Goldsmith, P: TCF (Aaron Rosenberg).

*No Love, No Nothin'* (Jane Russell) W: Leo Robin—M: Harry Warren.

**362  Father Goose.** US, 1964, C, 115 m. D: Ralph Nelson, MS: Cy Coleman, P: Universal (Robert Arthur).

*Pass Me By* (Digby Wolfe) W: Carolyn Leigh—M: Cy Coleman.

**363  Father Is a Bachelor.** US, 1950, BW, 84 m. D: Norman Foster and Abby Berlin, MS: Arthur Morton, P: Columbia (S. Sylvan Simon).

*Big Rock Candy Mountain* (William Holden, Chorus) WM: Unknown.

**364  Ferry 'Cross the Mersey.** GB, 1965, BW, 88 m. D: Jeremy Summers, MD: George Martin, P: UA (Michael Holden). Performers: Gerry and The Pacemakers.

*Baby You're So Good to Me; Fall in Love; Ferry 'Cross the Mersey* WM: Gerry Marsden / *I Got a Woman* (The Black Knights) WM: Griffiths / *I'll Be There; I'll Wait for You* WM: Gerry Marsden / *I Love You Too* (The Fourmost) / *Is It Love?* (Cilla Black) / *It's Gonna Be All Right* WM: Gerry Marsden / *Shake a Tail Feather* (Earl Royce and The Olympics) W: Verlie Rice—M: Andre Williams and Otha Hayes / *She's the Only Girl for Me; Think About Love; This Thing Called Love* WM: Gerry Marsden / *Why Don't You Love Me?* (The Blackwells) WM: McDermott, Trimnell, Little and Gormall / *Why Oh Why* WM: Gerry Marsden.

"The British pop rock group known as Gerry and the Pacemakers have made an unabashed imitation of the Beatles. They could have done a lot worse." —Eugene Archer, *The New York Times*.

**365  Fiddler on the Roof.** US, 1971, C, 181 m. D: Norman Jewison, MD: John Williams, P: UA (Norman Jewison).

The show opened at the Imperial Theatre on Broadway on September 22, 1964, and ran for 3,242 performances.

*Anatevka* (Topol, Norma Crane, Paul Mann, Molly Picon, Chorus); *Chavelah* (Topol); *Do You Love Me?* (Topol, Norma Crane); *Far from the Home I Love* (Michele Marsh); *If I Were a Rich Man* (Topol); *Matchmaker, Matchmaker* (Rosalind Harris, Michele Marsh, Neva Small); *Miracle of Miracles* (Leonard Frey); *Sabbath Prayer* (Topol, Norma Crane, Chorus); *Sunrise, Sunset* (Topol, Norma Crane, Michael Glazer, Michele Marsh, Chorus); *Tevye's Dream* (Topol, Norma Crane, Patience Collier, Ruth Madoc, Chorus); *To Life* (Topol, Paul Mann, Chorus); *Tradition* (Topol, Chorus); *Wedding Celebration* (Chorus) W: Sheldon Harnick—M: Jerry Bock.

"Not quite all the life is gone. The . . . score is practically all there, and it's one mixed marriage—between Tin Pan Alley and Jewish folk music—that really works." —Vincent Canby, *The New York Times*.

**366   The Fiendish Plot of Dr. Fu Manchu.** GB, 1980, C, 108 m. D: Piers Haggard, MS: Marc Wilkinson, P: Orion (Zev Braun, Lelan Nolan).

*On the Good Ship Lollipop* (Helen Mirren) W: Sidney Clare—M: Richard A. Whiting / *Rock Fu* (Peter Sellers).

**367   55 Days at Peking.** US-Spain, 1963, C, 150 m. D: Nicholas Ray, MS: Dimitri Tiomkin, P: AA (Samuel Bronston).

*So Little Time* (Andy Williams) W: Paul Francis Webster—M: Dimitri Tiomkin.

**368   Fight for Your Lady.** US, 1937, BW, 67 m. D: Ben Stoloff, P: RKO (Albert Lewis).

*Blame It on the Danube* (Ida Lupino, John Boles) WM: Harry Akst and Frank Loesser.

**369   Fighting Coast Guard.** US, 1951, BW, 86 m. D: Joseph Kane, MS: David Buttolph, P: Republic (Joseph Kane).

*Home on the Range* (The Sons of the Pioneers) WM: Unknown.

**370   A Fine Mess.** US, 1986, C, 88 m. D: Blake Edwards, MS: Henry Mancini, P: Columbia (Tony Adams).

*Can't Help Falling in Love* (Christine McVie) WM: Hugo Peretti, Luigi Creatore and George Weiss / *Easier Said Than Done* (Chico De Barge) WM: William Linton and Larry Huff / *A Fine Mess* (The Temptations) W: Dennis Lambert—M: Henry Mancini / *I'm Gonna Be a Wheel Someday* (Los Lobos) WM: Dave Bartholomew and Antoine "Fats" Domino / *Love's Closing In* (Nick Jameson) / *Moving So Close* (Second Generation) / *Slow Down* (Billy Vera and The Beaters) WM: Lawrence E. Williams / *Walk Like a Man* (The Mary Jane Girls) WM: Bob Crewe and Bob Gaudio / *Wishful Thinking* (Smokey Robinson).

**371   Fingers.** US, 1978, C, 91 m. D: James Toback, P: Brut (George Barrie).

*Angel of the Morning* (Merrilee Rush) WM: Chip Taylor / *Baby Talk* (Jan and Dean) WM: Melvin H. Schwartz / *Summertime, Summertime* (The Jamies) WM: Tom Jameson and Sherm Feller.

**372   Finian's Rainbow.** US, 1968, C, 145 m. D: Francis Ford Coppola, MD: Ray Heindorf, P: Warner (Joseph Landon).

The Broadway musical opened on January 10, 1947.

*The Begat* (Keenan Wynn, Avon Long, Jester Hairston, Roy Glenn); *How Are Things in Glocca Morra?* (Petula Clark, Fred Astaire, Don Francks, Tommy Steele, Barbara Hancock, Chorus); *If This Isn't Love* (Petula Clark, Fred Astaire, Don Francks, Chorus); *Look to the Rainbow* (Petula Clark, Fred Astaire, Don Francks, Chorus); *Old Devil Moon* (Petula Clark, Don Francks); *Something Sort of Grandish* (Petula Clark, Tommy Steele); *That Great Come-and-Get-It Day* (Petula Clark, Don

Francks, Chorus); *When I'm Not Near the Girl I Love* (Tommy Steele); *When the Idle Poor Become the Idle Rich* (Petula Clark, Fred Astaire, Chorus) W: E.Y. Harburg—M: Burton Lane.

"It is not just that the musical is dated. ... It is that it has been done listlessly and even tastelessly." — Renata Adler, *The New York Times*.

**373 Fire Down Below.** GB, 1957, C, 116 m. D: Robert Parrish, MS: Arthur Benjamin, P: Columbia (Irving Allen, Albert R. Broccoli).

*Fire Down Below* (Jeri Southern) W: Ned Washington—M: Lester Lee.

**374 First Love.** US, 1939, BW, 84 m. D: Henry Koster, MD: Charles Previn, MS: Frank Skinner, P: Universal (Joe Pasternak). Performer: Deanna Durbin.

*Amapola* W: Albert Gamse—M: Joseph M. Lacalle / *Home Sweet Home* W: John Howard Payne—M: Sir Henry Bishop / *Spring in My Heart* W: Ralph Freed—M: Johann Strauss—Adapted by: Hans Salter.

**375 The Five Pennies.** US, 1959, C, 117 m. D: Melville Shavelson, MD: Leith Stevens, P: Paramount (Jack Rose, Sylvia Fine). Vocals: Eileen Wilson for Barbara Bel Geddes.

*Battle Hymn of the Republic* (Danny Kaye, Louis Armstrong) W: Julia Ward Howe—M: William Steffe / *Bill Bailey, Won't You Please Come Home* (Danny Kaye, Louis Armstrong) WM: Hugh Cannon / *The Five Pennies* (Danny Kaye, Louis Armstrong, Susan Gordon); *Good Night, Sleep Tight* (Danny Kaye, Louis Armstrong, Barbara Bel Geddes) WM: Sylvia Fine / *Indiana* (Danny Kaye) W: Ballard MacDonald—M: James F. Hanley / *Jingle Bells* (Danny Kaye) WM: J.S. Pierpont / *Lullaby in Ragtime* (Danny Kaye, Barbara Bel Geddes) WM: Sylvia Fine / *The Music Goes 'Round and 'Round* (Danny Kaye, Susan Gordon) W: Red Hodgson—M: Edward Farley and Michael Riley / *My Blue Heaven* (Bob

Crosby) W: George Whiting—M: Walter Donaldson / *Paradise* (Bob Crosby) W: Gordon Clifford—M: Nacio Herb Brown / *When the Saints Go Marching In* (Danny Kaye, Louis Armstrong) W: Katherine E. Purvis—M: James M. Black—Arr: Sylvia Fine.

"The tune-filled story . . . is highly palatable schmaltz served up with a Dixieland beat." —A.H. Weiler, *The New York Times*.

**376 The Flame.** US, 1947, BW, 97 m. D: John H. Auer, MD: Cy Feuer, MS: Heinz Roemheld, P: Republic (Herbert J. Yates, John H. Auer).

*Love Me or Leave Me* (Constance Dowling) W: Gus Kahn—M: Walter Donaldson.

**377 The Flame and the Flesh.** US, 1954, C, 104 m. D: Richard Brooks, MD: George Stoll, P: MGM (Joe Pasternak). Performer: Carlos Thompson.

*By Candlelight; Languida; No One But You; Peddler Man* W: Jack Lawrence—M: Nicholas Brodszky.

**378 Flaming Star.** US, 1960, C, 101 m. D: Don Siegel, MD: Lionel Newman, MS: Cyril Mockridge, P: TCF (David Weisbart). MB: The Jordanaires. Performer: Elvis Presley.

*Cane and a High Starched Collar* WM: Sid Tepper and Roy C. Bennett / *Flaming Star* WM: Sid Wayne and Sherman Edwards.

**379 Flamingo Road.** US, 1949, BW, 94 m. D: Michael Curtiz, MS: Max Steiner, P: Warner (Jerry Wald).

*If I Could Be with You One Hour Tonight* (Joan Crawford) WM: Henry Creamer and James P. Johnson.

**380 Flap.** US, 1970, C, 106 m. D: Carol Reed, MS: Marvin Hamlisch, P: Warner (Jerry Adler). GB Title: The Last Warrior.

*If Nobody Loves* (Kenny Rogers and The First Edition) WM: Estelle Levitt and Marvin Hamlisch.

**381 Flashdance.** US, 1983, C,

96 m. D: Adrian Lyne, MS: Giorgio Moroder, P: Paramount (Don Simpson, Jerry Bruckheimer).

*Flashdance Love Theme* (Helen St. John) / *Flashdance... What a Feeling* (Irene Cara) W: Keith Forsey and Irene Cara—M: Giorgio Moroder / *Gloria* (Laura Branigan) Eng. W: Trevor Veitch—Ital. WM: Giancarlo Bigazzi and Umberto Tozzi / *He's a Dream* (Shandi) WM: Shandi Sinnamon and Ronald Magness / *I'll Be Here Where the Heart Is* (Kim Carnes) WM: Kim Carnes and Duane Hitchings / *Imagination* (Laura Branigan) WM: Michael Boddicker, Jerry Hey, Phil Ramone and Michael Sembello / *Lady, Lady, Lady* (Joe Esposito) W: Keith Forsey—M: Giorgio Moroder / *Manhunt* (Karen Kamon) WM: Richard Gilbert and Doug Cotler / *Maniac* (Michael Sembello) WM: Michael Sembello and Dennis Matkosky / *Romeo* (Donna Summer) WM: Pete Bellotte and Sylvester Levay / *Seduce Me Tonight* (Cycle V) W: Keith Forsey—M: Giorgio Moroder.

"Pretty much like looking at MTV for 96 minutes." — *Variety.*

**382   The Fleet's In.** US, 1942, BW, 93 m. D: Victor Schertzinger, P: Paramount (Paul Jones). Orch: Jimmy Dorsey.

*Arthur Murray Taught Me Dancing in a Hurry* (Betty Hutton, Eddie Bracken); *The Fleet's In* (Betty Jane Rhodes, Chorus); *If You Build a Better Mousetrap* (Betty Hutton, Helen O'Connell, Bob Eberly); *I Remember You* (Dorothy Lamour, Helen O'Connell, Bob Eberly, Chorus); *Not Mine* (Dorothy Lamour, Betty Hutton, Eddie Bracken); *Tangerine* (Helen O'Connell, Bob Eberly); *Tomorrow You Belong to Uncle Sam* (Cass Daley); *When You Hear the Time Signal* (Dorothy Lamour) W: Johnny Mercer—M: Victor Schertzinger.

"There are no production numbers but an overdose of vocalists, backed by the Dorsey band." — *Variety.*

**383   Fletch.** US, 1985, C, 96 m. D: Michael Ritchie, MS: Harold Faltermeyer, P: Universal (Alan Greisman, Peter Douglas).

*Bit by Bit* (Stephanie Mills) W: Franne Golde—M: Harold Faltermeyer / *Name of the Game* (Dan Hartman) WM: Dan Hartman and Charlie Midnight.

**384   Flower Drum Song.** US, 1961, C, 133 m. D: Henry Koster, MD: Alfred Newman and Ken Darby, P: Universal (Ross Hunter). Vocals: B.J. Baker for Nancy Kwan; Marilyn Horne for Reiko Sato; John Dodson for Kam Tong.

*Chop Suey* (Juanita Hall, James Shigeta, Patrick Adiarte, Jack Soo); *Don't Marry Me* (Miyoshi Umeki, Jack Soo); *Fan Tan Fannie* (Nancy Kwan); *Gliding Through My Memoree* (Victor Sen Yung); *Grant Avenue* (Nancy Kwan); *A Hundred Million Miracles* (Miyoshi Umeki, Kam Tong, Chorus); *I Am Going to Like It Here* (Miyoshi Umeki); *I Enjoy Being a Girl* (Nancy Kwan); *Love, Look Away* (Reiko Sato); *The Other Generation* (Benson Fong, Juanita Hall, Patrick Adiarte); *Sunday* (Miyoshi Umeki, Jack Soo); *You Are Beautiful* (James Shigeta) W: Oscar Hammerstein II—M: Richard Rodgers.

"As in most R & H enterprises, the meat is in the musical numbers. There are some bright spots in this area but ... the effect isn't overpowering." — *Variety.*

**385   Flying Down to Rio.** US, 1933, BW, 89 m. D: Thornton Freeland, MD: Max Steiner, P: RKO (Merian C. Cooper, Louis Brock).

The first Fred and Ginger pairing, and the last score Vincent Youmans wrote for films or the theater. Ill with tuberculosis for many years, he died in 1946 at the age of 48.

*The Carioca* (Etta Moten); *Flying Down to Rio* (Fred Astaire, Chorus); *Music Makes Me* (Ginger Rogers); *Orchids in the Moonlight* (Raul Roulien)

W: Gus Kahn and Edward Eliscu — M: Vincent Youmans.

"The main point . . . is the screen promise of Fred Astaire. The mike is kind to his voice and as a dancer he remains in a class by himself." — *Variety*.

**386 FM.** US, 1978, C, 105 m. D: John A. Alonzo, P: Universal (Rand Holston). Alt. Title: Citizens' Band.

*American Girl* (Tom Petty and The Heartbreakers) / *Baby Come Back* (Player) WM: Peter Beckett and John Crowley / *Bad Man* (Randy Meisner) WM: John David Souther and Glenn Frey / *Breakdown* (Tom Petty and The Heartbreakers) WM: Tom Petty / *Cold as Ice* (Foreigner) WM: Mick Jones and Lou Gramm / *Do It Again* (Steely Dan) WM: Walter Becker and Donald Fagen / *Don't Stop* (Fleetwood Mac) WM: Christine McVie / *Feels Like the First Time* (Foreigner) WM: Mick Jones / *Fly Like an Eagle* (Steve Miller) WM: Steve Miller / *FM* (Steely Dan) WM: Walter Becker and Donald Fagen / *Green Grass and High Times* (The Outlaws) WM: Hugh Thomasson / *Hollywood* (Boz Scaggs) WM: William Scaggs and Michael Omartian / *It Keeps You Runnin'* (The Doobie Bros.) WM: Michael McDonald / *Just the Way You Are* (Billy Joel) WM: Billy Joel / *The Key to My Kingdom* (B.B. King) WM: Maxwell Davis, Claude Baum and Joe Josea / *Lido Shuffle* (Boz Scaggs) WM: David Paich and William Scaggs / *Life in the Fast Lane* (The Eagles) WM: Glenn Frey, Don Henley and Joe Walsh / *Life's Been Good* (Joe Walsh) WM: Joe Walsh / *Livingston Saturday Night* (Jimmy Buffett) WM: Jimmy Buffett / *Love Me Tender* (Linda Ronstadt) W: Elvis Presley and Vera Matson — M: George R. Poulton / *More Than a Feeling* (Boston) WM: Tom Scholz / *Night Moves* (Bob Seger) WM: Bob Seger / *Poor Poor Pitiful Me* (Linda Ronstadt) WM: Warren Zevon / *Ridin' the Storm Out* (REO Speedwagon) / *Sentimental Lady* (Bob Welch) WM: Bob Welch / *Slow Ride* (Foghat) WM:

Dave Peverett / *There's a Place in the World for a Gambler* (Dan Fogelburg) WM: Dan Fogelburg / *Tumbling Dice* (Linda Ronstadt) WM: Mick Jagger and Keith Richard / *We Will Rock You* (Queen) WM: Brian May and Freddy Mercury / *Your Smiling Face* (James Taylor) WM: James Taylor.

**387 Folies Bergere.** US, 1935, BW, 84 m. D: Roy Del Ruth, MD: Alfred Newman, P: TCF (Darryl F. Zanuck, William Goetz, Raymond Griffith). GB Title: The Man from the Folies Bergere.

*Ghost of a Chance* (Maurice Chevalier) W: Ned Washington and Bing Crosby — M: Victor Young / *I Was Lucky* (Maurice Chevalier, Ann Sothern) French W: Andre Hornez — Eng. W: Jack Meskill — M: Jack Stern / *Rhythm of the Rain* (Maurice Chevalier, Ann Sothern, Chorus); *Singing a Happy Song* (Maurice Chevalier, Ann Sothern, Chorus) W: Jack Meskill — M: Jack Stern / *Valentine* (Maurice Chevalier) Eng. W: Herbert Reynolds [Michael E. Rourke] — French W: Albert Willemetz — M: Henri Christine / *You Took the Words Right Out of My Mouth* (Maurice Chevalier) W: Harold Adamson — M: Burton Lane.

"Ann Sothern . . . sings and dances with Chevalier and makes a definite sock impression." — *Variety*.

**388 Follow a Star.** GB, 1960, BW, 104 m. D: Robert Asher, MS: Philip Green, P: Rank (Hugh Stewart). MB: Chorus. Performer: Norman Wisdom.

*The Bath Song; Follow a Star* WM: Norman Wisdom / *Give Me a Night in June* WM: Philip Green and Miller / *I Love You* WM: Norman Wisdom.

**389 Follow That Dream.** US, 1962, C, 110 m. D: Gordon Douglas, MS: Hans J. Salter, P: UA (David Weisbart). Performer: Elvis Presley.

*Angel* WM: Sid Tepper and Roy C. Bennett / *Follow That Dream* WM: Fred Wise and Ben Weisman / *Home Is Where the Heart Is* WM: Sherman

Edwards and Hal David / *I'm Not the Marrying Kind* WM: Mack David and Sherman Edwards / *On Top of Old Smokey* WM: Pete Seeger / *Sound Advice* (Arthur O'Connell) WM: Bill Giant, Bernie Baum and Florence Kaye / *What a Wonderful Life* WM: Sid Wayne and Jay Livingston.

**390 Follow the Band.** US, 1943, BW, 60 m. D: Jean Yarbrough, P: Universal (Paul Malvern). Orch: Skinnay Ennis.

*Ain't Misbehavin'* (Mary Beth Hughes) W: Andy Razaf—M: Thomas "Fats" Waller and Harry Brooks / *The Army Air Corps Song* (The Bombardiers) WM: Robert Crawford / *Don't Tread on the Tail of Me Coat* (The King's Men) WM: Unknown / *Hilo Hattie* (Hilo Hattie) WM: Harold Adamson and Johnny Noble / *My Devotion* (The King Sisters, Alvino Rey) WM: Roc Hillman and Johnny Napton / *My Melancholy Baby* (Frances Langford) W: George A. Norton—M: Ernie Burnett / *Rosie the Riveter* (The King Sisters, Alvino Rey) WM: Redd Evans and John Jacob Loeb / *Spellbound* (Ray Eberle); *Swingin' the Blues* (Mary Beth Hughes) WM: Everett Carter and Milton Rosen.

**391 Follow the Boys.** US, 1944, BW, 122 m. D: A. Edward Sutherland, P: Universal (Charles K. Feldman). Orch: Ted Lewis; Freddie Slack; Charlie Spivak; Louis Jordan.

*The Beer Barrel Polka* (The Andrews Sisters) WM: Lew Brown, Jaromir Vejvoda and Wladimir A. Timm / *Bei Mir Bist Du Schoen* (The Andrews Sisters) WM: Sammy Cahn, Jacob Jacobs, Saul Chaplin and Sholom Secunda / *A Better Day Is Coming* (Chorus) W: Sammy Cahn—M: Jule Styne / *Beyond the Blue Horizon* (Jeanette MacDonald) W: Leo Robin —M: Richard A. Whiting and W. Franke Harling / *The Bigger the Army and the Navy* (Sophie Tucker) WM: Jack Yellen / *The House I Live In* (The Delta Rhythm Boys) W: Lewis Allan—M:

Earl Robinson / *I'll Be with You in Apple Blossom Time* (The Andrews Sisters) W: Neville Fleeson—M: Albert von Tilzer / *I'll Get By* (Dinah Shore) W: Roy Turk—M: Fred E. Ahlert / *I'll See You in My Dreams* (Jeanette MacDonald) W: Gus Kahn—M: Isham Jones / *I'll Walk Alone* (Dinah Shore) W: Sammy Cahn—M: Jule Styne / *Is You Is, Or Is You Ain't, Ma Baby?* (Louis Jordan) WM: Billy Austin and Louis Jordan / *Kittens with Their Mittens Laced* (Donald O'Connor, Peggy Ryan) WM: Inez James, Sidney Miller and Buddy Pepper / *Pennsylvania Polka* (The Andrews Sisters) WM: Lester Lee and Zeke Manners / *Shoo Shoo Baby* (The Andrews Sisters) WM: Phil Moore / *Some of These Days* (Sophie Tucker) WM: Shelton Brooks / *Tonight* (Chorus) W: Kermit Goell—M: Walter Donaldson / *Vict'ry Polka* (The Andrews Sisters) W: Sammy Cahn—M: Jule Styne.

**392 Follow the Fleet.** US, 1936, BW, 110 m. D: Mark Sandrich, MD: Max Steiner, P: RKO (Pandro S. Berman).

*But Where Are You?* (Harriet Hilliard); *Get Thee Behind Me Satan* (Harriet Hilliard); *I'd Rather Lead a Band* (Fred Astaire); *I'm Putting All My Eggs in One Basket* (Ginger Rogers, Fred Astaire); *Let's Face the Music and Dance* (Fred Astaire); *Let Yourself Go* (Ginger Rogers, Betty Grable, Jennie Gray, Joy Hodges); *We Saw the Sea* (Fred Astaire, Chorus) WM: Irving Berlin.

"There are seven songs which is a bit too much. ... The score on the whole is pleasant but save for *Face the Music* ... not particularly distinguished." *—Variety.*

"Even though it is not the best of their series it still is good enough to take the head of this year's class in song and dance entertainment. ... Mr. Berlin ... was not at his best when he composed the battery of tunes." — Frank S. Nugent, *The New York Times.*

**393 Follow Thru.** US, 1930, C, 93 m. D: Laurence Schwab and Lloyd Corrigan, P: Paramount (Laurence Schwab, Frank Mandel). Orch: George Olsen.

The movie was a version of the 1929 Broadway show that provided Jack Haley with his first important comic role.

*Button Up Your Overcoat!* (Zelma O'Neal, Jack Haley) W: B.G. De Sylva and Lew Brown—M: Ray Henderson / *It Must Be You* (Nancy Carroll, Charles "Buddy" Rogers, Zelma O'Neal, Jack Haley) WM: Edward Eliscu and Manning Sherwin / *I Want to Be Bad* (Nancy Carroll, Zelma O'Neal); *Then I'll Have Time for You* (Margaret Lee, Don Tomkins) W: B.G. De Sylva and Lew Brown—M: Ray Henderson / *We'd Make a Peach of a Pair* (Nancy Carroll, Charles "Buddy" Rogers) W: George Marion, Jr.—M: Richard A. Whiting.

**394 Follow Your Heart.** US, 1936, BW, 82 m. D: Aubrey Scotto, MD: Hugo Riesenfeld, P: Republic (Nat Levene).

*Follow Your Heart* (Marion Talley, Michael Bartlett) W: Sidney D. Mitchell / *Magnolias in the Moonlight* (Michael Bartlett); *Who Minds About Me?* (Clarence Muse, The Hall Johnson Choir) W: Walter Bullock—M: Victor Schertzinger.

**395 Footlight Parade.** US, 1933, BW, 104 m. D: Lloyd Bacon and Busby Berkeley, MD: Leo F. Forbstein, P: Warner (Hal B. Wallis).

*Ah, the Moon Is Here* (Dick Powell, Frank McHugh); *By a Waterfall* (Dick Powell, Ruby Keeler, Chorus) W: Irving Kahal—M: Sammy Fain / *Honeymoon Hotel* (Dick Powell, Ruby Keeler, Chorus); *Shanghai Lil* (James Cagney, Ruby Keeler, Chorus) W: Al Dubin—M: Harry Warren / *Sittin' on a Backyard Fence* (Ruby Keeler, Billy Taft, Chorus) W: Irving Kahal—M: Sammy Fain.

"Not as good as '42nd Street' and 'Gold Diggers' but ... the hokum *Honeymoon Hotel* and *Shanghai Lil* are punchy and undeniable." —*Variety*.

**396 Footlight Serenade.** US, 1942, BW, 80 m. D: Gregory Ratoff, MD: Charles Henderson, P: TCF (William LeBaron).

*Are You Kidding?* (Betty Grable); *I Heard the Birdies Sing* (Betty Grable, Chorus); *I'll Be Marching to a Love Song* (Betty Grable, Victor Mature, John Payne); *I'm Still Crazy for You* (Betty Grable, John Payne) W: Leo Robin—M: Ralph Rainger.

**397 Footloose.** US, 1984, C, 107 m D: Herbert Ross, MS: Miles Goodman and Becky Shargo, P: Paramount (Lewis J. Rachmil, Craig Zadan).

*Almost Paradise* (Mike Reno, Ann Wilson) M: Eric Carmen / *Dancing in the Sheets* (Shalamar) M: Bill Wolfer / *Footloose* (Kenny Loggins) M: Kenny Loggins / *The Girl Gets Around* (Sammy Hagar) M: Sammy Hagar / *Holding Out for a Hero* (Bonnie Tyler) M: Jim Steinman / *I'm Free* (Kenny Loggins) M: Kenny Loggins / *Let's Hear It for the Boy* (Deniece Williams) M: Tom Snow / *Never* (Moving Pictures) M: Michael Gore / *Somebody's Eyes* (Karla Bonoff) M: Tom Snow. W: Dean Pitchford.

"Mainly a youth-oriented rock picture, complete with big-screen reminders of what's hot today in music video." —*Variety*.

**398 For Love of Ivy.** US, 1968, C, 102 m. D: Daniel Mann, MS: Quincy Jones, P: Cinerama (Edgar J. Scherick, Jay Weston).

*For Love of Ivy* (Shirley Horn) W: Bob Russell—M: Quincy Jones / *My Side of the Sky* (Terry Cashman, Gene Pistilli, Tommy West) WM: Terry Cashman, Gene Pistilli, Tommy West and Quincy Jones / *You Put It on Me* (B.B. King) W: Maya Angelou—M: Quincy Jones.

**399 For Me and My Gal.** US, 1942, BW, 104 m. D: Busby Berkeley, MD: George Stoll and Roger Edens, P: MGM (Arthur Freed).

*After You've Gone* (Judy Garland) W: Henry Creamer—M: Turner Layton / *Ballin' the Jack* (Judy Garland, Gene Kelly) W: Jim Burris—M: Chris Smith / *By the Beautiful Sea* (Judy Garland, George Murphy, Ben Blue, Chorus) W: Harold Atteridge—M: Harry Carroll / *Do I Love You?* (Marta Eggerth) W: E. Ray Goetz—M: Henri Christine / *For Me and My Gal* (Judy Garland, Gene Kelly, Chorus) W: Edgar Leslie and E. Ray Goetz—M: George W. Meyer / *Goodbye Broadway, Hello France* (Judy Garland, Gene Kelly, Ben Blue, Chorus) W: C. Francis Reisner and Benny Davis—M: Billy Baskette / *How Ya Gonna Keep 'Em Down on the Farm?* (Judy Garland, Chorus) W: Sam M. Lewis and Joe Young—M: Walter Donaldson / *It's a Long Way to Tipperary* (Judy Garland) WM: Jack Judge and Harry Williams / *Oh! Frenchy* (Gene Kelly, Ben Blue) W: Sam Ehrlich—M: Con Conrad / *Oh, You Beautiful Doll* (George Murphy, Lucille Norman) W: A. Seymour Brown—M: Nat D. Ayer / *Pack Up Your Troubles* (Judy Garland) W: George Asaf—M: Felix Powell / *Smiles* (Judy Garland) W: J. Will Callahan—M: Lee Roberts / *Strike Up the Band* (Judy Garland) W: Ira Gershwin—M: George Gershwin / *Tell Me* (Lucille Norman) W: J. Will Callahan—M: Max Kortlander / *There's a Long Long Trail* (Chorus) W: Stoddard King—M: Zo Elliott / *Till We Meet Again* (Lucille Norman, Judy Garland, Chorus) W: Raymond B. Egan—M: Richard A. Whiting / *What Are You Going to Do to Help the Boys?* (Ben Blue, Chorus) W: Gus Kahn—M: Egbert Van Alstyne / *When Johnny Comes Marching Home* (Judy Garland) WM: Patrick S. Gilmore [Louis Lambert]—Arr: Roger Edens / *When You Wore a Tulip* (Judy Garland, Gene Kelly) W: Jack Mahoney—M: Percy Wenrich / *Where Do We Go from Here?* (Judy Garland, Chorus) W: Howard Johnson—M: Percy Wenrich.

"Great chunks of dripping nostalgia and gobs of wistfulness are being tossed from the screen by this one in a cascade of memorable song." —Bosley Crowther, *The New York Times*.

**400   For the Love of Benji.** US, 1977, C, 84 m. D: Joe Camp, P: Mulberry Square (Ben Vaughn).

*Sunshine Smiles* (Charlie Rich) W: Betty Box and Joe Camp—M: Euel Box.

**401   For the Love of Mary.** US, 1948, BW, 90 m. D: Frederick de Cordova, MS: Frank Skinner, P: Universal (Robert Arthur). Performer: Deanna Durbin.

*I'll Take You Home Again, Kathleen* WM: Thomas Westendorf / *Moonlight Bay* W: Edward Madden—M: Percy Wenrich.

**402   For Your Eyes Only.** GB, 1981, C, 127 m. D: John Glen, MS: Bill Conti, P: UA (Albert R. Broccoli).

*For Your Eyes Only* (Sheena Easton) W: Michael Leeson—M: Bill Conti.

**403   A Foreign Affair.** US, 1948, BW, 116 m. D: Billy Wilder, MS: Frederick Hollander, P: Paramount (Charles Brackett). Performer: Marlene Dietrich.

*Black Market; Illusions* WM: Frederick Hollander / *Iowa Corn Song* (Jean Arthur) WM: E. Riley, G. Botsford, R. Lockard and G. Hamilton / *Ruins of Berlin* WM: Frederick Hollander.

"She gives the Dietrich s.a. treatment to three Frederick Hollander tunes, lyrics of which completely express the cynical undertones of the film." —*Variety*.

**404   Forever Darling.** US, 1956, C, 96 m. D: Alexander Hall, MS: Bronislau Kaper, P: MGM (Desi Arnaz).

*Forever Darling* (Desi Arnaz, The Ames Brothers) W: Sammy Cahn—M: Bronislau Kaper.

**405   Forty Little Mothers.** US, 1940, BW, 90 m. D: Busby Berkeley, P: MGM (Harry Rapf).

*Little Curly Hair in a High Chair* (Eddie Cantor) W: Charles Tobias—M: Nat Simon / *You Were Meant for Me* (Chorus) W: Arthur Freed—M: Nacio Herb Brown.

**406 Forty-Second Street.** US, 1933, BW, 89 m. D: Lloyd Bacon and Busby Berkeley, MD: Leo F. Forbstein, P: Warner (Darryl F. Zanuck).

*Forty-Second Street* (Ruby Keeler, Dick Powell); *It Must Be June* (Bebe Daniels, Dick Powell, Chorus); *Shuffle Off to Buffalo* (Ruby Keeler, Clarence Nordstrom, Ginger Rogers, Una Merkel, Chorus); *Young and Healthy* (Dick Powell, Toby Wing, Chorus); *You're Getting to Be a Habit with Me* (Bebe Daniels) W: Al Dubin—M: Harry Warren.

"The liveliest and one of the most tuneful screen musical comedies that has come out of Hollywood." —Mordaunt Hall, *The New York Times.*

**407 Foul Play.** US, 1978, C, 116 m. D: Colin Higgins, MS: Charles Fox, P: Paramount (Thomas L. Miller, Edward K. Milkis).

*Ready to Take a Chance Again* (Barry Manilow) W: Norman Gimbel—M: Charles Fox / *Stayin' Alive* (The Bee Gees) WM: Barry Gibb, Maurice Gibb and Robin Gibb.

**408 Four Jills in a Jeep.** US, 1944, BW, 89 m. D: William A. Seiter, P: TCF (Irving Starr). Orch: Jimmy Dorsey.

*The Caissons Go Rolling Along* (Chorus) WM: Edmund L. Gruber / *Crazy Me* (Carole Landis) W: Harold Adamson—M: Jimmy McHugh / *Cuddle Up a Little Closer* (Betty Grable) W: Otto Harbach—M: Karl Hoschna / *How Blue the Night* (Dick Haymes); *How Many Times Do I Have to Tell You?* (Dick Haymes) W: Harold Adamson—M: Jimmy McHugh / *I Yi Yi Yi Yi* (Carmen Miranda) W: Mack Gordon—M: Harry Warren / *No Love, No Nothin'* (Phil Silvers) W: Leo Robin—M: Harry Warren / *You'll Have to Swing It* (Martha Raye, Chorus) WM:

Sam Coslow / *You'll Never Know* (Alice Faye) W: Mack Gordon—M: Harry Warren / *You Send Me* (Dick Haymes, Chorus) W: Harold Adamson—M: Jimmy McHugh.

**409 Fox Movietone Follies of 1929.** US, 1929, BW/C, 82 m. D: David Butler, MD: Arthur Kay, P: William Fox. Orig. Title: William Fox Movietone Follies of 1929. GB Title: Movietone Follies of 1929.

*Big City Blues* (Lola Lane); *The Breakaway* (Sue Carol, Jeanette Dancey, Chorus); *That's You, Baby* (David Percy, Sharon Lynn, Sue Carol, David Rollins, Jackie Cooper, Dixie Lee, Frank Richardson, Bobby Burns, Chorus); *Walking with Susie* (Frank Richardson, Chorus); *Why Can't I Be Like You?* (Dixie Lee) W: Sidney D. Mitchell and Archie Gottler—M: Con Conrad.

**410 Frankie and Johnny.** US, 1966, C, 87 m. D: Frederick de Cordova, MD: Fred Karger, P: UA (Edward Small). MB: The Jordanaires. Vocals: Eileen Wilson for Donna Douglas. Performer: Elvis Presley.

*Beginner's Luck* WM: Sid Tepper and Roy C. Bennett / *Chesay* (Elvis Presley, Harry Morgan, Chorus) WM: Fred Karger, Sid Wayne and Ben Weisman / *Come Along* WM: David Hess / *Down by the Riverside* WM: Unknown / *Everybody Come Aboard* WM: Bill Giant, Bernie Baum and Florence Kaye / *Frankie and Johnny* (Elvis Presley, Harry Morgan, Donna Douglas, Sue Ane Langdon, Chorus) WM: Unknown—Arr: Alex Gottlieb, Fred Karger and Ben Weisman / *Hard Luck* WM: Sid Wayne and Ben Weisman / *Look Out, Broadway* (Elvis Presley, Harry Morgan, Donna Douglas, Audrey Christie) WM: Fred Wise and Randy Starr / *Petunia, the Gardener's Daughter* (Elvis Presley, Donna Douglas) WM: Sid Tepper and Roy C. Bennett / *Please Don't Stop Loving Me* WM: Joy Byers / *Shout It Out* WM: Bill Giant, Bernie Baum and Florence Kaye

/ *What Every Woman Lives For* WM: Doc Pomus and Mort Shuman / *When the Saints Go Marching In* W: Katherine E. Purvis—M: James M. Black.

**411  The French Line.** US, 1954, C, 102 m. D: Lloyd Bacon, MD: Lionel Newman, P: RKO (Edmund Grainger).

*Any Gal from Texas* (Jane Russell, Mary McCarty); *Comment Allez-Vous?* (Gilbert Roland); *The French Line* (Chorus); *Lookin' for Trouble* (Jane Russell); *Wait Till You See Paris* (Gilbert Roland); *Well, I'll Be Switched* (Jane Russell); *What Is This That I Feel?* (Jane Russell); *With a Kiss* (Gilbert Roland) W: Ralph Blane and Robert Wells—M: Josef Myrow.

**412  Friendly Persuasion.** US, 1956, C, 140 m. D: William Wyler, MS: Dimitri Tiomkin, P: AA (William Wyler). Performer: Pat Boone.

The original title of the theme song, *Thee I Love*, was also to have been the name of the movie. Pat Boone was then an unknown performer whom Tiomkin had heard on Arthur Godfrey's TV show.

*Coax Me a Little; Friendly Persuasion; Indiana Holiday; Marry Me, Marry Me; The Mocking Bird in the Willow Tree* W: Paul Francis Webster—M: Dimitri Tiomkin.

**413  Friends.** GB, 1971, C, 102 m. D: Lewis Gilbert, P: Paramount (Lewis Gilbert). Performer: Elton John.

*Can I Put You On; A Day in the Country; Four Moods; Friends; Honey Roll; I Meant to Do My Work Today; Michelle's Song; Seasons Reprise* WM: Elton John and Bernie Taupin.

**414  Fright Night.** US, 1985, C, 105 m. D: Tom Holland, MS: Brad Fiedel, P: Columbia (Herb Jaffe).

*Armies of the Night* (Sparks) WM: Ron Mael and Russell Mael / *Boppin' Tonight* (Fabulous Fontaines) WM: Gary Goetzman and Mike Piccirillo / *Come to Me* (Brad Feidel) WM: Brad Feidel / *Fright Night* (J. Geils Band) WM: J. Lamont / *Give It Up* (Evelyn "Champagne" King) WM: D. Matkosky and B. Caldwell / *Good Man in a Bad Time* (Ian Hunter) WM: M. Tanner and J. Reede / *Let's Talk* (Devo) WM: Mark Mothersbaugh / *Rock Myself to Sleep* (April Wine) WM: Kimberley Rew and V. De la Cruz / *Save Me Tonight* (White Sister) WM: M. Leib and G. Brandon / *You Can't Hide from the Beast Inside* (Autograph) WM: S. Plunkett.

**415  From Russia with Love.** GB, 1963, C, 118 m. D: Terence Young, MS: John Barry, P: UA (Harry Saltzman, Albert R. Broccoli).

*From Russia with Love* (Matt Munroe) WM: Lionel Bart.

**416  The Front.** US, 1976, C, 94 m. D: Martin Ritt, MS: Dave Grusin, P: Columbia (Martin Ritt, Charles H. Joffe).

*Young at Heart* (Frank Sinatra) W: Carolyn Leigh—M: Johnny Richards.

**417  The Fugitive Kind.** US, 1959, BW, 135 m. D: Sidney Lumet, MS: Kenyon Hopkins, P: UA (Martin Jurow, Richard A. Shepherd, Pennebaker).

*Not a Soul* (Marlon Brando) W: Tennessee Williams—M: Kenyon Hopkins.

**418  Fun in Acapulco.** US, 1963, C, 97 m. D: Richard Thorpe, MS: Joseph J. Lilley, P: Paramount (Hal B. Wallis). MB: The Jordanaires; The Four Amigos. Performer: Elvis Presley.

*Bossa Nova Baby* WM: Jerry Leiber and Mike Stoller / *The Bullfighter Was a Lady* WM: Sid Tepper and Roy C. Bennett / *El Toro* WM: Bill Giant, Bernie Baum and Florence Kaye / *Fun in Acapulco* WM: Sid Wayne and Ben Weisman / *Guadalajara* WM: Pepe Guizar / *I Think I'm Gonna Like It Here* WM: Don Robertson and Hal Blair / *Marguerita* WM: Don Robertson / *Mexico* (Elvis Presley, Larry Domasin) WM: Sid Tepper and Roy C. Bennett / *No Room to Rhumba in a Sports Car* WM: Fred Wise and Dick Manning /

*Vino, Dinero Y Amor* WM: Sid Tepper and Roy C. Bennett / *You Can't Say No in Acapulco* WM: Sid Feller, Dorothy Fuller and Lee Morris.

"He sings serviceable songs and wiggles a bit to boot." —*Variety.*

**419 Funny Face.** US, 1957, C, 103 m. D: Stanley Donen, MD: Adolph Deutsch, P: Paramount (Roger Edens).

In 1927, with a different story and only some of the same Gershwin tunes, this was a Broadway and London musical for Fred Astaire and his sister, Adele.

*Bonjour, Paris!* (Fred Astaire, Audrey Hepburn, Kay Thompson) W: Leonard Gershe—M: Roger Edens / *Clap Yo' Hands* (Fred Astaire, Kay Thompson); *Funny Face* (Fred Astaire); *He Loves and She Loves* (Fred Astaire); *How Long Has This Been Going On?* (Audrey Hepburn); *Let's Kiss and Make Up* (Fred Astaire) W: Ira Gershwin—M: George Gershwin / *Marche Funebre* (Unbilled French Singer) WM: Roger Edens / *On How to Be Lovely* (Audrey Hepburn, Kay Thompson) W: Leonard Gershe—M: Roger Edens / *'S Wonderful* (Fred Astaire, Audrey Hepburn) W: Ira Gershwin—M: George Gershwin / *Think Pink!* (Kay Thompson) W: Leonard Gershe—M: Roger Edens.

"A lightly diverting, modish, Parisian-localed tintuner." —*Variety.*

"The songs of George and Ira Gershwin ... have more lilt and frolic in them than if they had been written last year." —Bosley Crowther, *The New York Times.*

**420 Funny Girl.** US, 1968, C, 155 m. D: William Wyler, MD: Walter Scharf, P: Columbia (Ray Stark). Performer: Barbra Streisand.

*Don't Rain on My Parade; Funny Girl; His Love Makes Me Beautiful* W: Bob Merrill—M: Jule Styne / *I'd Rather Be Blue Over You* W: Billy Rose—M: Fred Fisher / *If a Girl Isn't Pretty* (Kay Medford, Mae Questel); *I'm the Great-*

*est Star* W: Bob Merrill—M: Jule Styne / *My Man* Eng. W: Channing Pollock—M: Maurice Yvain / *People; Roller Skate Rag* (Chorus); *Sadie, Sadie* W: Bob Merrill—M: Jule Styne / *Second Hand Rose* W: Grant Clarke—M: James F. Hanley / *The Swan; You Are Woman, I Am Man* (Barbra Streisand, Omar Sharif) W: Bob Merrill—M: Jule Styne.

"The durable songs ... from the [1964] stage score are given fuller enhancement under the flexibility of the cinematic sweep." —*Variety.*

**421 Funny Lady.** US, 1975, C, 137 m. D: Herbert Ross, MD: Peter Matz, P: Columbia (Ray Stark). Performer: Barbra Streisand.

*Am I Blue?* W: Grant Clarke—M: Harry Akst / *Beautiful Face, Have a Heart* (Garrett Lewis) W: Fred Fisher and Billy Rose—M: James V. Monaco / *Blind Date* W: Fred Ebb—M: John Kander / *Clap Hands! Here Comes Charley!* (Ben Vereen, Chorus) W: Billy Rose and Ballard MacDonald—M: Joseph Meyer / *Great Day!* (Barbra Streisand, Chorus) W: Billy Rose and Edward Eliscu—M: Vincent Youmans / *How Lucky Can You Get?* W: Fred Ebb—M: John Kander / *If I Love Again* W: Jack Murray—M: Ben Oakland / *I Found a Million Dollar Baby* W: Billy Rose and Mort Dixon—M: Harry Warren / *If You Want the Rainbow* (Chorus) WM: Billy Rose and Mort Dixon—M: Oscar Levant / *I Got a Code in My Doze* WM: Billy Rose, Fred Hall and Arthur Fields / *I Like Her* (James Caan); *I Like Him; Isn't This Better?* W: Fred Ebb—M: John Kander / *It's Only a Paper Moon* (Barbra Streisand, James Caan, Chorus) W: Billy Rose and E.Y. Harburg—M: Harold Arlen / *Let's Hear It for Me* W: Fred Ebb—M: John Kander / *Me and My Shadow* (James Caan) W: Billy Rose—M: Dave Dreyer and Al Jolson / *More Than You Know* (Barbra Streisand, Shirley Kirkes) W: Billy Rose and Edward Eliscu—M: Vincent Youmans.

**422  A Funny Thing Happened on the Way to the Forum.** US, 1966, C, 99 m. D: Richard Lester, MD: Ken Thorne, P: UA (Melvin Frank).

*Comedy Tonight* (Zero Mostel, Chorus); *The Dirge* (Leon Greene, Chorus); *Everybody Ought to Have a Maid* (Zero Mostel, Phil Silvers, Jack Gilford, Michael Hordern); *Lovely* (Zero Mostel, Jack Gilford, Michael Crawford, Annette Andre); *My Bride* (Leon Greene, Chorus) WM: Stephen Sondheim.

"Mr. Lester seems not to have disturbed the basic structure of the [1962] show, except to remove some of the songs. ... Stephen Sondheim's music and lyrics hold up well, especially *Comedy Tonight* by which Mr. Mostel introduces the characters at the start." —Vincent Canby, *The New York Times*.

**423  G.I. Blues.** US, 1960, C, 104 m. D: Norman Taurog, MS: Joseph J. Lilley, P: Paramount (Hal B. Wallis). MB: The Jordanaires. Performer: Elvis Presley.

*Big Boots* WM: Sid Wayne and Sherman Edwards / *Blue Suede Shoes* WM: Carl Lee Perkins / *Didja Ever* WM: Sid Wayne and Sherman Edwards / *Doin' the Best I Can* WM: Doc Pomus and Mort Shuman / *Frankfort Special* WM: Sid Wayne and Sherman Edwards / *G.I. Blues* WM: Sid Tepper and Roy C. Bennett / *Pocketful of Rainbows* WM: Fred Wise and Ben Weisman / *Shoppin' Around* WM: Sid Tepper, Roy C. Bennett and Aaron Schroeder / *Tonight Is So Right for Love; What's She Really Like?* WM: Sid Wayne and Abner Silver / *Wooden Heart* WM: Fred Wise, Ben Weisman, Kay Twomey and Berthold Kaempfert.

"Elvis Presley warbles 10 wobbly songs." —*Variety*.

**424  "G" Men.** US, 1935, BW, 85 m. D: William Keighley, MD: Leo F. Forbstein, P: Warner (Louis F. Edelman).

*You Bother Me an Awful Lot* (Ann Dvorak) W: Irving Kahal—M: Sammy Fain.

**425  Gaby.** US, 1956, C, 97 m. D: Curtis Bernhardt, MS: Conrad Salinger, P: MGM (Edwin H. Knopf).

*Where or When* (Gloria Wood) W: Lorenz Hart—M: Richard Rodgers.

**426  Gaily, Gaily.** US, 1969, C, 107 m. D: Norman Jewison, MS: Henry Mancini, P: UA/Mirisch. GB Title: Chicago, Chicago.

*Sentimental Dream* (Anita Nye); *There's Enough to Go Around* (Melina Mercouri, Chorus); *Tomorrow Is My Friend* (Jimmie Rodgers, Chorus) W: Alan Bergman and Marilyn Bergman—M: Henry Mancini.

**427  The Gang's All Here.** US, 1943, C, 103 m. D: Busby Berkeley, MD: Alfred Newman, P: TCF (William LeBaron). Orch: Benny Goodman; Bando da Lua. GB Title: The Girls He Left Behind.

Aloysio de Oliveira was a Latin American tenor and leader of Carmen Miranda's band, the Bando da Lua, formed in 1930.

*Brazil* (Aloysio de Oliveira, Carmen Miranda, Chorus) Eng. W: Bob Russell [S.K. Russell]—M: Ary Barroso / *A Journey to a Star* (Alice Faye, Carmen Miranda, Eugene Pallette, Charlotte Greenwood, Edward Everett Horton, Phil Baker, Chorus); *The Lady in the Tutti-Frutti Hat* (Carmen Miranda, Chorus); *Minnie's in the Money* (Benny Goodman); *No Love, No Nothin'* (Alice Faye, Chorus); *Paducah* (Benny Goodman, Carmen Miranda); *The Polka Dot Polka* (Alice Faye); *You Discover You're in New York* (Carmen Miranda, Alice Faye, Phil Baker, Chorus) W: Leo Robin—M: Harry Warren.

"A weak script is somewhat relegated by the flock of tuneful musical numbers that frequently punctuate the picture." —*Variety*.

**428  The Gangster.** US, 1947, BW, 84 m. D: Gordon Wiles, P: Monogram (Maurice King, Frank King).

Belita was Gladys Jepson-Turner, a British ice-skater and dancer who made several movies in Hollywood.

*Paradise* (Belita) WM: Gordon Clifford and Nacio Herb Brown.

**429 Garden of the Moon.** US, 1938, BW, 94 m. D: Busby Berkeley, P: Warner (Louis F. Edelman). Orch: Joe Venuti.

*Confidentially* (John Payne, Mabel Todd); *Garden of the Moon* (Mabel Todd); *The Girl Friend of the Whirling Dervish* (John Payne, Jerry Colonna, Johnny "Scat" Davis, Ray Mayer); *Love Is Where You Find It* (John Payne, Johnny "Scat" Davis) W: Al Dubin and Johnny Mercer—M: Harry Warren.

**430 Gator.** US, 1976, C, 116 m. D: Burt Reynolds, MS: Charles Bernstein, P: UA (Jules Levy, Arthur Gardner).

*Ballad of Gator McClusky* (Jerry Reed) WM: Jerry Reed / *For a Little While* (Bobby Goldsboro) WM: Bobby Goldsboro.

**431 The Gay Desperado.** US, 1936, BW, 85 m. D: Rouben Mamoulian, MS: Alfred Newman, P: UA (Mary Pickford). Performer: Nino Martini.

*Adios Mi Terra* WM: Miguel Sandoval / *Cielito Lindo* WM: Quirino Mendoza y Cortez—Arr: Neil Wilson, Carlo Fernandez and Sebastian Yradier / *Estrelita* WM: Frank La Forge and Manuel Ponce / *Lamento Gitano* WM: Walter Samuels and Leonard Whitcup / *The World Is Mine* WM: Holt Marvell [Eric Maschwitz]—M: George Posford.

**432 The Gay Divorcee.** US, 1934, BW, 107 m. D: Mark Sandrich, MD: Max Steiner, P: RKO (Pandro S. Berman). GB Title: The Gay Divorce.

The movie was based on Cole Porter's 1932 stage musical 'The Gay Divorce,' which starred Fred Astaire and Claire Luce.

*The Continental* (Ginger Rogers, Erik Rhodes, Lillian Miles) W: Herb Magidson—M: Con Conrad / *Don't*

*Let It Bother You* (Unbilled Singer, Chorus); *Let's K-nock K-nees* (Betty Grable, Edward Everett Horton) W: Mack Gordon—M: Harry Revel / *A Needle in a Haystack* (Fred Astaire) W: Herb Magidson—M: Con Conrad / *Night and Day* (Fred Astaire) WM: Cole Porter.

"*The Continental* is the smash song and dance hit. Cole Porter's *Night and Day*, from the original show, is alone retained, and worthily so." —*Variety*.

**433 The Gay Ranchero.** US, 1948, C, 72 m. D: William Witney, MD: Morton Scott, P: Republic (Edward J. White). MB: Bob Nolan and The Sons of the Pioneers.

*A Gay Ranchero* (Roy Rogers, Estelita Rodriguez) Eng. W: Abe Tuvim and Francia Luban—Span. WM: J.J. Espinosa / *Granada* (Tito Guizar) Eng. W: Dorothy Dodd—Span. WM: Augustin Lara / *Wait'll I Get My Sunshine in the Moonlight* (Roy Rogers, Jane Frazee) / *You Belong to My Heart* (Tito Guizar) Eng. W: Ray Gilbert—Span. WM: Augustin Lara.

**434 The Gene Krupa Story.** US, 1959, BW, 101 m. D: Don Weis, MS: Leith Stevens, P: Columbia (Philip A. Waxman). Orch: Gene Krupa. GB Title: Drum Crazy.

*I Love My Baby* (Ruby Lane) W: Bud Green—M: Harry Warren / *Let There Be Love* (James Darren) WM: Ian Grant and Lionel Rand / *Memories of You* (Anita O'Day) W: Andy Razaf—M: Eubie Blake.

**435 Gentlemen Marry Brunettes.** US, 1955, C, 97 m. D: Richard Sale, MS: Robert Farnon, P: UA (Richard Sale, Robert Waterfield). Vocals: Anita Ellis for Jeanne Crain; Paul Carpenter for Scott Brady.

*Ain't Misbehavin'* (Jane Russell, Jeanne Crain, Alan Young) W: Andy Razaf—M: Thomas "Fats" Waller and Harry Brooks / *Daddy* (Jane Russell, Jeanne Crain) WM: Bobby Troup / *Gentlemen Marry Brunettes* (Johnny Desmond) WM: Herbert Spencer and

Earle Hagen / *Have You Met Miss Jones?* (Jane Russell, Jeanne Crain, Rudy Vallee, Alan Young, Scott Brady); *I've Got Five Dollars* (Jane Russell, Scott Brady) W: Lorenz Hart— M: Richard Rodgers / *I Wanna Be Loved by You* (Jane Russell, Jeanne Crain, Rudy Vallee) W: Bert Kalmar— M: Herbert Stothart and Harry Ruby / *My Funny Valentine* (Jeanne Crain, Alan Young, Chorus) W: Lorenz Hart—M: Richard Rodgers / *You're Driving Me Crazy* (Jane Russell, Jeanne Crain) WM: Walter Donaldson.

**436 Gentlemen Prefer Blondes.** US, 1953, C, 91 m. D: Howard Hawks, MD: Lionel Newman, P: TCF (Sol C. Siegel). Performers: Marilyn Monroe and Jane Russell.

*Ain't There Anyone Here for Love?* (Jane Russell) W: Harold Adamson— M: Hoagy Carmichael / *Bye, Bye, Baby*; *Diamonds Are a Girl's Best Friend*; *A Little Girl from Little Rock* W: Leo Robin—M: Jule Styne / *When Love Goes Wrong* W: Harold Adamson—M: Hoagy Carmichael.

"An attractive screen tintuner has been fashioned from the [1949] musical stage hit." —*Variety*.

"Except for one plush production number in which Miss Monroe sings that candid refrain, the theme song of the gold-diggers, *Diamonds Are a Girl's Best Friend*, there is not much class in this picture." —Bosley Crowther, *The New York Times*.

**437 George White's Scandals.** US, 1945, BW, 95 m. D: Felix E. Feist, MS: Leigh Harline, P: RKO (Jack J. Gross, Nat Holt, George White). Orch: Gene Krupa. Performers: Joan Davis and Jack Haley.

*I Wake Up in the Morning* WM: Jack Yellen and Sammy Fain / *Life Is Just a Bowl of Cherries* W: Lew Brown— M: Ray Henderson / *Who Killed Vaudeville?* WM: Jack Yellen and Sammy Fain.

**438 Georgy Girl.** GB, 1966, BW, 100 m. D: Silvio Narizzano, MS: Alexander Faris, P: Columbia (Otto Plaschkes, Robert A. Goldston).

*Georgy Girl* (The Seekers); *I'm Gonna Leave Her* (The Mirage) W: Jim Dale—M: Tom Springfield.

**439 Get Yourself a College Girl.** US, 1964, C, 88 m. D: Sidney Miller, P: MGM (Sam Katzman). GB Title: The Swingin' Set.

*Around and Around* (The Animals) WM: Chuck Berry / *Blue Feeling* (The Animals) WM: Marion Motter / *Bony Moronie* (The Standells) WM: Larry Williams / *Comin' Home Johnny* (The Jimmy Smith Trio) / *Get Yourself a College Girl* (Mary Ann Mobley) WM: Sidney Miller and Fred Karger / *The Sermon* (The Jimmy Smith Trio) / *The Swim* (The Standells) / *The Swingin' Set* (Donnie Brooks) WM: Donnie Brooks, Sidney Miller and Fred Karger / *Talkin' About Love* (Roberta Linn, Freddy Bell and The Bellboys) / *Thinking of You Baby* (The Dave Clark Five); *Whenever You're Around* (The Dave Clark Five) WM: Dave Clark and Mike Smith.

**440 Gidget.** US, 1959, C, 95 m. D: Paul Wendkos, MD: Morris Stoloff, MS: George Duning, P: Columbia (Lewis J. Rachmil). Performers: James Darren and The Four Preps.

*Cinderella; Gidget; The Next Best Thing to Love* W: Patti Washington— M: Fred Karger.

"Three tunes are tossed in at random." —Howard Thompson, *The New York Times*.

**441 Gidget Goes to Rome.** US, 1963, C, 101 m. D: Paul Wendkos, P: Columbia (Jerry Bresler). Performer: James Darren.

*Big Italian Moon; Gegetta* WM: George David Weiss and Al Kasha.

**442 Gigi.** US, 1958, C, 116 m. D: Vincente Minnelli, MD: Andre Previn, P: MGM (Arthur Freed). Vocals: Betty Wand for Leslie Caron.

*Gigi* (Louis Jourdan); *Gossip* (Chorus); *I'm Glad I'm Not Young Anymore* (Maurice Chevalier); *I Remember*

*It Well* (Hermione Gingold, Maurice Chevalier); *It's a Bore* (Maurice Chevalier, Louis Jourdan); *The Night They Invented Champagne* (Leslie Caron, Louis Jourdan, Hermione Gingold); *The Parisiens* (Leslie Caron, Louis Jourdan); *Say a Prayer for Me Tonight* (Leslie Caron); *She Is Not Thinking of Me* (Louis Jourdan); *Thank Heaven for Little Girls* (Maurice Chevalier) W: Alan Jay Lerner—M: Frederick Loewe.

"A musical film that bears such a basic resemblance to 'My Fair Lady' that the authors may want to sue themselves." —Bosley Crowther, *The New York Times*.

"Fritz Loewe's tunes (to Lerner's lyrics) vie with and suggest their memorable 'My Fair Lady' score." — *Variety*.

**443 Gilda.** US, 1946, BW, 110 m. D: Charles Vidor, MD: Morris Stoloff and Marlin Skiles, MS: Hugo Friedhofer, P: Columbia (Virginia Van Upp). Vocals: Anita Ellis for Rita Hayworth. Performer: Rita Hayworth.

*Amado Mio; Put the Blame on Mame* WM: Doris Fisher and Allan Roberts.

**444 Girl Crazy.** US, 1943, BW, 99 m. D: Norman Taurog and Busby Berkeley, MD: George Stoll, P: MGM (Arthur Freed). Orch: Tommy Dorsey. MB: The King's Men. Alt. Title: When the Girls Meet the Boys.

The musical show opened on October 14, 1930. It was Ethel Merman's Broadway debut and the second stage musical for Ginger Rogers. A 1932 film version for RKO starred Bert Wheeler and Robert Woolsey.

*Bidin' My Time* (Judy Garland); *But Not for Me* (Judy Garland, Rags Ragland); *Could You Use Me?* (Judy Garland, Mickey Rooney); *Embraceable You* (Judy Garland, Chorus); *I Got Rhythm* (Judy Garland, Mickey Rooney, Chorus); *Sam and Delilah* (Judy Garland); *Treat Me Rough* (June Allyson, Mickey Rooney, Chorus) W: Ira Gershwin—M: George Gershwin.

**445 Girl Happy.** US, 1965, C, 96 m. D: Boris Sagal, MS: George Stoll, P: MGM (Joe Pasternak). MB: The Jordanaires. Performer: Elvis Presley.

*Cross My Heart and Hope to Die* WM: Sid Wayne and Ben Weisman / *Do Not Disturb* WM: Bill Giant, Bernie Baum and Florence Kaye / *Do the Clam* WM: Sid Wayne, Ben Weisman and Dolores Fuller / *Fort Lauderdale Chamber of Commerce* WM: Sid Tepper and Roy C. Bennett / *Girl Happy* WM: Doc Pomus and Norman Meade / *I've Got to Find My Baby; The Meanest Girl in Town* WM: Joy Byers / *Puppet on a String* WM: Sid Tepper and Roy C. Bennett / *Read All About It* (Nita Talbot, Shelley Fabares) / *Spring Fever* (Elvis Presley, Gary Crosby, Joby Baker, Jimmy Hawkins, Shelley Fabares, Chorus) WM: Bill Giant, Bernie Baum and Florence Kaye / *Startin' Tonight* WM: Lenore Rosenblatt and Victor Millrose / *Wolf Call* WM: Bill Giant, Bernie Baum and Florence Kaye.

**446 The Girl Most Likely.** US, 1957, C, 98 m. D: Mitchell Leisen, MS: Nelson Riddle, P: RKO (Stanley Rubin).

*All the Colors of the Rainbow* (Jane Powell, Keith Andes, Kaye Ballard, Kelly Brown, Chorus); *Crazy Horse* (Jane Powell, Chorus); *The Girl Most Likely* (Chorus); *I Don't Know What I Want* (Jane Powell); *Travelogue* (Jane Powell, Cliff Robertson, Kaye Ballard, Kelly Brown, Chorus); *We Gotta Keep Up with the Joneses* (Jane Powell, Tommy Noonan, Chorus) WM: Hugh Martin and Ralph Blane.

**447 The Girl of the Golden West.** US, 1938, BW, 120 m. D: Robert Z. Leonard, P: MGM (William Anthony McGuire).

*Ave Maria* (Jeanette MacDonald) W: The Bible—M: Charles Gounod, based on Bach / *Liebestraum* (Jeanette MacDonald) W: Gus Kahn—M: Franz Liszt / *Mariache* (Chorus); *Senorita*

(Jeanette MacDonald, Nelson Eddy, Chorus); *Shadows on the Moon* (Jeanne Ellis, Jeanette MacDonald); *Soldiers of Fortune* (Bill Cody, Jr., Nelson Eddy, Chorus); *The West Ain't Wild Anymore* (Buddy Ebsen); *Who Are We to Say* (Nelson Eddy) W: Gus Kahn — M: Sigmund Romberg.

"This musical mustanger finds the stars ... hemmed in by a two-hour melange of the great outdoors, Mexican bandits, early Spanish-Californian atmosphere and musical boredom." — *Variety*.

**448   Girls! Girls! Girls!** US, 1962, C, 106 m. D: Norman Taurog, MS: Joseph J. Lilley, P: Paramount (Hal B. Wallis). MB: The Jordanaires. Performer: Elvis Presley.

*Baby, Baby, Baby* (Stella Stevens) W: Mack David — M: Jerry Livingston / *Because of Love* WM: Ruth Batchelor and Bob Roberts / *A Boy Like Me, a Girl Like You* WM: Sid Tepper and Roy C. Bennett / *Dainty Little Moonbeams* WM: Jerry Leiber and Mike Stoller / *Earth Boy* (Elvis Presley, Ginny Tiu, Elizabeth Tiu) WM: Sid Tepper and Roy C. Bennett / *Girls! Girls! Girls!* WM: Jerry Leiber and Mike Stoller / *I Don't Wanna Be Tied* WM: Bill Giant, Bernie Baum and Florence Kaye / *Mama* (The Four Amigos) WM: Charles O'Curran and Dudley Brooks / *The Nearness of You* (Stella Stevens) W: Ned Washington — M: Hoagy Carmichael / *Never Let Me Go* (Stella Stevens) WM: Jay Livingston and Ray Evans / *Return to Sender* WM: Otis Blackwell and Winfield Scott / *Song of the Shrimp* WM: Sid Tepper and Roy C. Bennett / *Thanks to the Rolling Sea* WM: Ruth Batchelor and Bob Roberts / *The Walls Have Ears* WM: Sid Tepper and Roy C. Bennett / *We'll Be Together* WM: Charles O'Curran and Dudley Brooks / *We're Coming In Loaded* WM: Otis Blackwell and Winfield Scott / *Where Do You Come From?* WM: Ruth Batchelor and Bob Roberts.

**449   Girls Town.** US, 1959, BW, 92 m. D: Charles Haas, MD: Van Alexander, P: MGM (Albert Zugsmith). Alt. Title: The Innocent and the Damned.

*Ave Maria* (Paul Anka) W: Sir Walter Scott — M: Franz Schubert / *Girls Town* (Mamie Van Doren, Paul Anka); *Hey, Mama* (Mamie Van Doren); *I Love You* (Cathy Crosby); *Lonely Boy* (Paul Anka); *A Time to Cry* (Paul Anka) WM: Paul Anka / *Wish It Were Me* (The Platters) WM: Buck Ram.

**450   Glamorous Night.** GB, 1937, BW, 81 m. D: Brian Desmond Hurst, MS: Ivor Novello, P: Associated British (Walter C. Mycroft).

*Fold Your Wings* (Mary Ellis, Trefor Jones); *Glamorous Night* (Mary Ellis); *Shine Through My Dreams* (Trefor Jones); *When the Gypsy Played* (Mary Ellis) W: Christopher Hassall — M: Ivor Novello.

**451   The Glass Bottom Boat.** US, 1966, C, 110 m. D: Frank Tashlin, MS: Frank DeVol, P: MGM (Martin Melcher).

*Que Sera, Sera* (Doris Day) W: Ray Evans — M: Jay Livingston.

**452   The Glass Mountain.** GB, 1950, BW, 94 m. D: Henry Cass, MS: Nino Rota, P: Victoria (John Sutro, Joseph Janni, Fred Zelnik).

*The Song of the Mountains* (Tito Gobbi) WM: Luigi Pigarelli and Toni Ortelli.

**453   The Glass Slipper.** US, 1955, C, 94 m. D: Charles Walters, MS: Bronislau Kaper, P: MGM (Edwin H. Knopf).

*Take My Love* (Michael Wilding) W: Helen Deutsch — M: Bronislau Kaper.

"Makes its best points in the ... score and in the ballets." — *Variety*.

**454   The Glenn Miller Story.** US, 1954, C, 116 m. D: Anthony Mann, MD: Joseph Gershenson and Henry Mancini, P: Universal (Aaron Rosenberg). Orch: The Universal International Studio Orchestra. MB: The Modernaires.

*Basin Street Blues* (Louis Armstrong) WM: Spencer Williams / *Bidin' My Time* (Male Quartet) W: Ira Gershwin—M: George Gershwin / *Chattanooga Choo Choo* (Frances Langford) W: Mack Gordon—M: Harry Warren / *Little Brown Jug* (Chorus) WM: Joseph E. Winner / *Moonlight Serenade* (Ruth Hampton) W: Mitchell Parish—M: Glenn Miller.

**455  Go Into Your Dance.** US, 1935, BW, 89 m. D: Archie L. Mayo, P: Warner (Sam Bischoff). GB Title: Casino De Paree.

*About a Quarter to Nine* (Al Jolson, Chorus); *Casino de Paree* (Al Jolson) W: Al Dubin—M: Harry Warren / *Cielito Lindo* (Al Jolson) WM: Quirino Mendoza y Cortez—Arr: Neil Wilson, Carlo Fernandez and Sebastian Yradier / *Go Into Your Dance* (Al Jolson); *A Good Old-Fashioned Cocktail* (Ruby Keeler); *The Little Things You Used to Do* (Helen Morgan); *Mammy, I'll Sing About You* (Al Jolson); *She's a Latin from Manhattan* (Al Jolson, Sam Hayes) W: Al Dubin—M: Harry Warren.

"Besides everything else, it has Al Jolson in top form, plus a nifty set of songs." —*Variety.*

**456  Go West.** US, 1940, BW, 81 m. D: Edward Buzzell, MD: George Stoll, MS: Bronislau Kaper, P: MGM (Jack Cummings).

*Beautiful Dreamer* (Diana Lewis) WM: Stephen Collins Foster / *Ridin' the Range* (John Carroll, Groucho Marx, Chico Marx) W: Gus Kahn—M: Roger Edens / *You Can't Argue with Love* (Groucho Marx, June McCoy) W: Gus Kahn—M: Bronislau Kaper.

**457  The Godfather.** US, 1972, C, 175 m. D: Francis Ford Coppola, MS: Nino Rota, P: Paramount (Albert S. Ruddy).

*I Have But One Heart* (Al Martino) W: Marty Symes—M: Johnny Farrow.

**458  Godspell.** US, 1973, C, 103 m. D: David Greene, P: Columbia (Edgar Lansbury).

Originally an off–Broadway workshop production presented at La Mama in 1971.

*Alas for You* (Victor Garber); *All for the Best* (Victor Garber, David Haskell, Chorus); *All Good Gifts* (Merrell Jackson, Chorus); *Beautiful City* (Chorus); *Bless the Lord* (Lynn Thigpen, Chorus) WM: Stephen Schwartz / *By My Side* (Katie Hanley, Chorus) W: Jay Hamburger—M: Peggy Gordon / *Day by Day* (Robin Lamont, Chorus); *Light of the World* (Jerry Sroka, Gilmer McCormick, Jeffrey Mylett, Robin Lamont, Chorus); *On the Willows* (Stephen Reinhardt, Richard La Bonte, Victor Garber); *Prepare Ye* (David Haskell, Chorus); *Save the People* (Victor Garber, Chorus); *Turn Back O Man* (Joanne Jonas, Victor Garber, Chorus) WM: Stephen Schwartz.

"A strong Stephen Schwartz score and an infectious joie de vivre conveyed by an energetic, no-name cast." —*Variety.*

"One of the finest production numbers I've seen in years is the exuberant and ironic *All for the Best* which Jesus and John the Baptist sing and dance all over New York." —Vincent Canby, *The New York Times.*

**459  Goin' South.** US, 1978, C, 108 m. D: Jack Nicholson, P: Paramount (Harry Gittes, Harold Schneider).

*Available Space* (Ry Cooder) W: Van Dyke Parks—M: Perry Botkin, Jr.

**460  Goin' to Town.** US, 1935, BW, 74 m. D: Alexander Hall, MD: Andrea Setaro, P: Paramount (William LeBaron). Performer: Mae West.

*He's a Bad, Bad Man; Love Is Love in Any Woman's Heart* WM: Irving Kahal and Sammy Fain / *Now I'm a Lady* WM: Irving Kahal, Sam Coslow and Sammy Fain.

**461  Going Hollywood.** US, 1933, BW, 80 m. D: Raoul Walsh, P: MGM (Walter Wanger).

*After Sundown* (Bing Crosby); *Beautiful Girl* (Bing Crosby); *Cinderella's*

*Fella* (Fifi D'Orsay, Marion Davies); *Going Hollywood* (Bing Crosby) W: Arthur Freed—M: Nacio Herb Brown / *Just an Echo in the Valley* (Bing Crosby) WM: Harry M. Woods, Jimmy Campbell and Reginald Connelly / *Our Big Love Scene* (Bing Crosby); *Temptation* (Bing Crosby); *We'll Make Hay While the Sun Shines* (Bing Crosby, Marion Davies, Chorus) W: Arthur Freed—M: Nacio Herb Brown.

**462  Going My Way.** US, 1944, BW, 126 m. D: Leo McCarey, MS: Robert Emmett Dolan, P: Paramount (Leo McCarey). MB: The Robert Mitchell Boychoir.

*Ave Maria* (Bing Crosby, Rise Stevens) W: Sir Walter Scott—M: Franz Schubert / *The Day After Forever* (Bing Crosby, Jean Heather); *Going My Way* (Bing Crosby, Rise Stevens) W: Johnny Burke—M: James Van Heusen / *Silent Night* (Bing Crosby) W: Joseph Mohr—M: Franz Gruber / *Swinging on a Star* (Bing Crosby) W: Johnny Burke—M: James Van Heusen / *Too-Ra-Loo-Ra-Loo-Ral* (Bing Crosby) WM: James Royce Shannon.

**463  Going Places.** US, 1938, BW, 84 m. D: Ray Enright, P: Warner (Hal B. Wallis). Orch: Louis Armstrong.

*Jeepers, Creepers* (Louis Armstrong, Maxine Sullivan) W: Johnny Mercer—M: Harry Warren / *Mutiny in the Nursery* (Dick Powell, Louis Armstrong, Maxine Sullivan, Anita Louise) WM: Johnny Mercer / *Oh, What a Horse Was Charlie* (Dick Powell, Walter Catlett, Harold Huber, Allen Jenkins) W: Al Dubin and Johnny Mercer—M: Harry Warren / *Say It with a Kiss* (Maxine Sullivan) W: Johnny Mercer—M: Harry Warren.

**464  Gold.** GB, 1974, C, 120 m. D: Peter Hunt, MS: Elmer Bernstein, P: Hemdale (Michael Klinger).

*Wherever Love Takes Me* (Maureen McGovern) W: Don Black—M: Elmer Bernstein.

**465  Gold Diggers of Broad-**

**way.** US, 1929, C, 98 m. D: Roy Del Ruth, P: Warner.

*In a Kitchenette* (Nick Lucas); *Mechanical Man* (Winnie Lightner); *Painting the Clouds with Sunshine* (Nick Lucas); *Song of the Gold Diggers* (Nancy Welford, Chorus); *Tip Toe Through the Tulips with Me* (Nick Lucas) W: Al Dubin—M: Joe Burke.

"Lots of color—Technicolor—lots of comedy, girls, songs, music, dancing, production." —*Variety.*

**466  Gold Diggers of 1933.** US, 1933, BW, 96 m. D: Mervyn LeRoy, MD: Leo F. Forbstein, P: Warner (Hal B. Wallis).

*I've Got to Sing a Torch Song* (Dick Powell); *Pettin' in the Park* (Dick Powell, Ruby Keeler, Aline MacMahon, Billy Barty, Chorus); *Remember My Forgotten Man* (Joan Blondell, Etta Moten, Chorus); *Shadow Waltz* (Dick Powell, Ruby Keeler, Chorus); *We're in the Money* (Ginger Rogers, Chorus) W: Al Dubin—M: Harry Warren.

"Once the numbers get going, nothing else matters." —*Variety.*

**467  Gold Diggers of 1935.** US, 1935, BW, 95 m. D: Busby Berkeley, MD: Leo F. Forbstein, P: Warner (Robert Lord).

*I'm Goin' Shoppin' with You* (Dick Powell, Gloria Stuart); *Lullaby of Broadway* (Dick Powell, Wini Shaw, Chorus); *The Words Are in My Heart* (Dick Powell, Virginia Grey, Chorus) W: Al Dubin—M: Harry Warren.

"Songs this time miss a bit. ... *Lullaby of Broadway* ... runs overboard in footage." —*Variety.*

**468  Gold Diggers of 1937.** US, 1936, BW, 100 m. D: Lloyd Bacon and Busby Berkeley, MD: Leo F. Forbstein, P: Warner (Hal B. Wallis).

*All's Fair in Love and War* (Dick Powell, Joan Blondell, Lee Dixon, Rosalind Marquis, Chorus) W: Al Dubin—M: Harry Warren / *Let's Put Our Heads Together* (Dick Powell, Rosalind Marquis, Glenda Farrell, Victor

Moore, Jack Norton); *Speaking of the Weather* (Dick Powell) W: E.Y. Harburg—M: Harold Arlen / *With Plenty of Money and You* (Dick Powell) W: Al Dubin—M: Harry Warren.

"Dick Powell ... has four outstanding songs, never overdoes them and breaks through with his ballads at the most opportune times." —*Variety*.

**469   Golden Boy.** US, 1939, BW, 99 m. D: Rouben Mamoulian, MD: Morris Stoloff, MS: Victor Young, P: Columbia (William Perlberg).

*Funiculi-Funicula* (William Holden, Lee J. Cobb, Sam Levene, William Strauss) WM: Luigi Denza.

**470   Golden Earrings.** US, 1947, BW, 95 m. D: Mitchell Leisen, MS: Victor Young, P: Paramount (Harry Tugend).

*Golden Earrings* (Murvyn Vye) W: Jay Livingston and Ray Evans—M: Victor Young.

**471   Goldfinger.** GB, 1964, C, 111 m. D: Guy Hamilton, MS: John Barry, P: UA (Harry Saltzman, Albert R. Broccoli).

*Goldfinger* (Shirley Bassey) W: Anthony Newley and Leslie Bricusse—M: John Barry.

**472   The Goldwyn Follies.** US, 1938, C, 120 m. D: George Marshall, MD: Alfred Newman, P: UA (Samuel Goldwyn). Vocals: Virginia Verrill for Andrea Leeds.

At the time of his death on July 11, 1937, George Gershwin was at work on the score for this film. It was completed by Vernon Duke and Oscar Levant.

*Here, Pussy, Pussy* (The Ritz Brothers) WM: Ray Golden and Sid Kuller / *I Love to Rhyme* (Phil Baker, Edgar Bergen and Charlie McCarthy); *I Was Doing All Right* (Ella Logan); *Love Walked In* (Kenny Baker, Helen Jepson, Andrea Leeds); *Our Love Is Here to Stay* (Kenny Baker) W: Ira Gershwin—M: George Gershwin / *Serenade to a Fish* (The Ritz Brothers) / *Spring Again* (Kenny Baker) W: Ira Gershwin—M: Vernon Duke.

**473   The Good Companions.** GB, 1957, C, 104 m. D: J. Lee Thompson, MS: Laurie Johnson, P: Associated British (Hamilton Inglis, J. Lee Thompson).

*The Good Companions* (Janette Scott, John Fraser, Chorus); *If Only* (Janette Scott, Chorus); *Round the World in Eighty Minutes* (Janette Scott, Chorus); *This Kind of Love* (Janette Scott); *Where There's You There's Me* (John Fraser) WM: C.A. Rossi, Paddy Roberts and Geoffrey Parsons.

**474   Good Morning, Vietnam.** US, 1987, C, 120 m. D: Barry Levinson, MS: Alex North, P: Touchstone (Mark Johnson, Larry Brezner).

*Baby, Please Don't Go* (Them) WM: Joe Williams / *California Sun* (The Rivieras) WM: Morris Levy and Henry Glover / *Danger Heartbreak Dead Ahead* (The Marvelettes) WM: Ivy Hunter, Clarence Paul and William Stevenson / *Five O'Clock World* (The Vogues) WM: Allen Reynolds / *The Game of Love* (Wayne Fontana and The Mindbenders) WM: Clint Ballard / *I Get Around* (The Beach Boys) WM: Brian Wilson / *I Got You* (James Brown) WM: James Brown / *Liar, Liar* (The Castaways) WM: James J. Donna / *Nowhere to Run* (Martha Reeves) WM: Eddie Holland, Lamont Dozier and Brian Holland / *Sugar and Spice* (The Searchers) WM: Fred Nightingale / *Warmth of the Sun* (The Beach Boys) / *What a Wonderful World* (Louis Armstrong) WM: George Douglas and George David Weiss.

**475   Good News.** US, 1947, C, 95 m. D: Charles Walters, MD: Lennie Hayton, P: MGM (Arthur Freed). MB: The Williams Brothers.

The movie was based on the 1927 Broadway musical by De Sylva, Brown and Henderson.

An earlier film version was made by MGM in 1930.

*Be a Ladies' Man* (Peter Lawford, Mel Torme, Ray McDonald, Tom Dugan, Lon Tindall); *The Best Things in Life Are Free* (June Allyson, Peter Lawford, Mel Torme) W: B.G. De Sylva and Lew Brown—M: Ray Henderson / *The French Lesson* (June Allyson, Peter Lawford) W: Betty Comden and Adolph Green—M: Roger Edens / *Good News* (Joan McCracken, Chorus); *Just Imagine* (June Allyson); *Lucky in Love* (June Allyson, Peter Lawford, Patricia Marshall, Joan McCracken, Mel Torme) W: B.G. De Sylva and Lew Brown—M: Ray Henderson / *Pass That Peace Pipe* (Joan McCracken, Ray McDonald, Chorus) WM: Ralph Blane, Hugh Martin and Roger Edens / *The Varsity Drag* (June Allyson, Peter Lawford, Chorus) W: B.G. De Sylva and Lew Brown—M: Ray Henderson.

"The old tunes are still full of fragrance." —Bosley Crowther, *The New York Times*.

**476   Good Times.** US, 1967, C, 91 m. D: William Friedkin, P: Columbia (Lindsley Parsons). Performers: Sonny and Cher.

*Don't Talk to Strangers; Good Times; I Got You Babe; I'm Gonna Love You; It's the Little Things; Just a Name; Trust Me* WM: Sonny Bono.

**477   Good to Go.** US, 1986, C, 87 m. D: Blaine Novak, P: Doug Dilge and Sean Ferrer. Video Title: Short Fuse.

*Drop the Bomb* (Trouble Funk) WM: James Avery, Tony Fisher, Robert Reed and T. Reed, Jr. / *E.U. Freeze* (E.U.) WM: G. Elliot / *Good to Go* (Trouble Funk); *I Like It* (Trouble Funk) WM: James Avery, Tony Fisher, Robert Reed and T. Reed, Jr. / *Keys* (Wally Badarou) WM: Wally Badarou / *Make 'Em Move* (Sly Dunbar and Robbie Shakespeare) WM: Robbie Shakespeare, Sly Dunbar, Bernie Worrell, B. Aosim and Bill Laswell / *Meet Me at the Go-Go* (Hot, Cold Sweat) WM: D. Moss / *Movin' and Groovin'* (Redds and The Boys); *Riot Zone* (Ini Kamoze) WM: A. Williams, C. Jones and D. Pearson / *Status Quo* (Donald Banks) WM: W.E. Thompson / *Still Smokin'* (Trouble Funk) WM: James Avery, Tony Fisher, Robert Reed and T. Reed, Jr. / *We Need Money* (Chuck Brown and The Soul Searchers) WM: Chuck Brown, J. Buchanan, D. Tillery, L. Fleming and C. Johnson.

**478   Goodbye, Charlie.** US, 1964, C, 117 m. D: Vincente Minnelli, MS: Andre Previn, P: TCF (David Weisbart).

*Goodbye, Charlie* (Pat Boone); *Seven at Once* (Jerry Wallace) W: Dory Langdon—M: Andre Previn.

**479   The Goodbye Girl.** US, 1977, C, 110 m. D: Herbert Ross, MS: Dave Grusin, P: Warner (Ray Stark).

*Goodbye Girl* (David Gates) WM: David Gates.

**480   Goodbye, Mr. Chips.** GB, 1969, C, 151 m. D: Herbert Ross, MD: John Williams, P: MGM (Arthur P. Jacobs).

*And the Sky Smiled* (Petula Clark); *Apollo* (Petula Clark); *Fill the World with Love* (Peter O'Toole, Chorus); *London Is London* (Petula Clark, Chorus); *Schooldays* (Petula Clark, Chorus); *Walk Through the World* (Petula Clark); *What a Lot of Flowers* (Peter O'Toole); *What Shall I Do with Today?* (Petula Clark); *When I Am Older* (Chorus); *When I Was Younger* (Peter O'Toole); *Where Did My Childhood Go?* (Peter O'Toole); *You and I* (Petula Clark) WM: Leslie Bricusse.

**481   The Graduate.** US, 1967, C, 105 m. D: Mike Nichols, MS: Dave Grusin, P: UA-Embassy (Lawrence Turman). Performers: Simon and Garfunkel.

*April Come She Will; The Big, Bright Green Pleasure Machine; Mrs. Robinson* WM: Paul Simon / *Scarborough Fair-Canticle* WM: Paul Simon and Art Garfunkel / *The Sounds of Silence* WM: Paul Simon.

"A rich, poignant musical score ... has the sound of today's moody youngsters." —Bosley Crowther, *The New York Times*.

**482 The Grapes of Wrath.** US, 1940, BW, 129 m. D: John Ford, MS: Alfred Newman, P: TCF (Darryl F. Zanuck, Nunnally Johnson).

*Red River Valley* (Henry Fonda) WM: Unknown.

**483 The Grass Is Greener.** GB, 1960, C, 105 m. D: Stanley Donen, MD: Muir Mathieson, P: Grandon (Stanley Donen).

*The Stately Homes of England* (Chorus) WM: Noel Coward.

**484 Grease.** US, 1978, C, 110 m. D: Randal Kleiser, MD: Louis St. Louis, P: Paramount (Robert Stigwood, Allan Carr).

*Beauty School Dropout* (Frankie Avalon, Chorus) WM: Warren Casey and Jim Jacobs / *Blue Moon* (Sha Na Na) W: Lorenz Hart—M: Richard Rodgers / *Born to Hand Jive* (Sha Na Na) WM: Warren Casey and Jim Jacobs / *Grease* (Frankie Valli, Chorus) WM: Barry Gibb / *Greased Lightnin'* (John Travolta, Jeff Conaway) WM: Warren Casey and Jim Jacobs / *Hopelessly Devoted to You* (Olivia Newton-John, Chorus) WM: John Farrar / *Hound Dog* (Sha Na Na) WM: Jerry Leiber and Mike Stoller / *Look at Me, I'm Sandra Dee* (Stockard Channing, Olivia Newton-John) WM: Warren Casey and Jim Jacobs / *Love Is a Many-Splendored Thing* (Chorus) W: Paul Francis Webster—M: Sammy Fain / *Rock and Roll Is Here to Stay* (Sha Na Na) WM: Dave White / *Sandy* (John Travolta) W: Scott Simon—M: Louis St. Louis / *Summer Nights* (Olivia Newton-John, John Travolta); *There Are Worse Things I Could Do* (Stockard Channing); *Those Magic Changes* (Sha Na Na); *We Go Together* (Olivia Newton-John, John Travolta, Jeff Conaway, Stockard Channing) WM: Warren Casey and Jim Jacobs / *You're the One That I Want* (Olivia Newton-John, John Travolta) WM: John Farrar.

"The film's score, which is one of the best things about the production, has been liberally supplemented by new material and new-old material." —Vincent Canby, *The New York Times*.

**485 The Great American Broadcast.** US, 1941, BW, 92 m. D: Archie Mayo, MD: Alfred Newman, P: TCF (Kenneth MacGowan).

*Alabamy Bound* (The Ink Spots) W: B.G. De Sylva and Bud Green—M: Ray Henderson / *The Great American Broadcast* (James Newill, Chorus); *I Take to You* (Alice Faye, John Payne, Jack Oakie); *It's All in a Lifetime* (Alice Faye); *Long Ago Last Night* (Alice Faye); *Where You Are* (Alice Faye, John Payne, The Ink Spots) W: Mack Gordon—M: Harry Warren.

**486 The Great Caruso.** US, 1951, C, 109 m. D: Richard Thorpe, MD: Johnny Green and Peter Herman Adler, P: MGM (Joe Pasternak).

*Ave Maria* (Mario Lanza, Chorus) Eng. W: The Bible—French W: Paul Bernard—M: Charles Gounod / *Because* (Mario Lanza) W: Edward Teschemacher—M: Guy d'Hardelot / *The Loveliest Night of the Year* (Ann Blyth) W: Paul Francis Webster—M: Juventino Rosas—Adapted by: Irving Aaronson / *Sweethearts* (Dorothy Kirsten) W: Robert B. Smith—M: Victor Herbert / *'Tis the Last Rose of Summer* (Dorothy Kirsten, Mario Lanza) W: Thomas Moore—M: Richard Alfred Milliken.

**487 The Great Gatsby.** US, 1974, C, 144 m. D: Jack Clayton, MS: Nelson Riddle, P: Paramount (David Merrick). Performer: Nick Lucas.

*Five Foot Two, Eyes of Blue* W: Sam M. Lewis and Joe Young—M: Ray Henderson / *I'm Gonna Charleston Back to Charleston* WM: Roy Turk and Lou Handman / *Tip Toe Through the Tulips with Me* W: Al Dubin—M: Joe Burke / *When You and I Were Seventeen* W: Gus Kahn—M: Charles Rosoff.

**488 The Great Lover.** US, 1949, BW, 80 m. D: Alexander Hall, MS: Joseph J. Lilley, P: Paramount (Edmund Beloin).

*A Thousand Violins* (Rhonda Fleming) WM: Jay Livingston and Ray Evans.

**489   The Great Man.** US, 1956, BW, 92 m. D: Jose Ferrer, MS: Herman Stein, P: Universal (Aaron Rosenberg).

*The Meaning of the Blues* (Julie London) WM: Leah Worth and Bobby Troup.

**490   The Great Race.** US, 1965, C, 150 m. D: Blake Edwards, MS: Henry Mancini, P: Warner (Martin Jurow). Vocals: Jackie Ward for Natalie Wood.

*He Shouldn't-a, Hadn't-a, Oughtn't -a Swang on Me* (Dorothy Provine); *The Sweetheart Tree* (Natalie Wood) W: Johnny Mercer—M: Henry Mancini.

**491   The Great Victor Herbert.** US, 1939, BW, 84 m. D: Andrew L. Stone, MD: Phil Boutelje and Arthur Lange, P: Paramount (Andrew L. Stone).

*Ah, Sweet Mystery of Life* (Allan Jones) W: Rida Johnson Young / *All for You* (Allan Jones, Mary Martin) W: Henry Blossom / *I Love Thee, I Adore Thee* (Allan Jones) W: Harry B. Smith / *I'm Falling in Love with Someone* (Allan Jones, Mary Martin) W: Rida Johnson Young / *I Might Be Your "Once in a While"* (Mary Martin) W: Robert B. Smith / *A Kiss in the Dark* (Mary Martin) W: B.G. De Sylva / *Kiss Me Again* (Susanna Foster); *Neapolitan Love Song* (Allan Jones) W: Henry Blossom / *There Once Was an Owl* (Allan Jones, Mary Martin) W: Harry B. Smith / *Thine Alone* (Allan Jones, Mary Martin) W: Henry Blossom / *To the Land of My Own Romance* (Allan Jones, Susanna Foster) W: Harry B. Smith / *Wonderful Dreams* W: Gus Kahn—M: Victor Herbert.

"A large and splendid and thoroughly light-opera tribute to the Irish genius who introduced poetry into popular music. . . . His music is still inimitably superb." —B.R. Crisler, *The New York Times.*

**492   The Great Waltz.** US, 1938, BW, 102 m. D: Julien Duvivier, MD: Arthur Gutmann, MS: Dimitri Tiomkin, P: MGM (Bernard Hyman).

The only English language film of soprano Miliza Korjus. Born in Poland in 1900, the coloratura enjoyed a European reputation for her operatic and concert work until being tapped by Irving Thalberg to perform in this lush and expensively produced biopic of composer Johann Strauss. Thalberg died before the movie was released.

*Du Und Du* (Miliza Korjus, George Houston, Chorus); *I'm in Love with Vienna* (Curt Bois, Leonid Kinsky, Al Shean, George Houston, Chorus); *One Day When We Were Young* (Miliza Korjus, Fernand Gravet); *Revolutionary March* (Chorus); *Tales from the Vienna Woods* (Miliza Korjus, Fernand Gravet, Christian Rub, Chorus); *There'll Come a Time* (Miliza Korjus); *Voices of Spring* (Miliza Korjus) W: Oscar Hammerstein II—M: Johann Strauss—Adapted and Arr. by: Dimitri Tiomkin.

"Miss Korjus . . . sings her waltzes well enough, yet does not convince us that Strauss has profited noticeably through Oscar Hammerstein's lyrics." —Frank S. Nugent, *The New York Times.*

**493   The Great Waltz.** US, 1972, C, 135 m. D: Andrew L. Stone, P: MGM (Andrew L. Stone). Vocals: Ken Barrie for Horst Bucholz; Joan Baxter for Yvonne Mitchell.

*Crystal and Gold* (Kenneth McKellar); *The Great Waltz in Boston* (Chorus); *Louder and Faster* (Mary Costa, Horst Bucholz); *Love Is Magic* (Mary Costa); *Nightfall* (Kenneth McKellar, Chorus); *Say Yes* (Yvonne Mitchell); *Six Drinks* (Horst Bucholz); *Warm* (Yvonne Mitchell, Horst Bucholz); *Who Are You?* (Mary Costa); *With You Gone* (Kenneth McKellar) W: Robert Wright and George "Chet" Forrest—M: Johann Strauss.

**494   The Great Ziegfeld.** US, 1936, BW, 176 m. D: Robert Z. Leonard, MD: Arthur Lange, P: MGM (Hunt Stromberg). Vocals: Allan Jones for Stanley Morner.

Why Stanley Morner, who later became known as Dennis Morgan, was not allowed to sing for himself is to be wondered at.

*A Circus Must Be Different in a Ziegfeld Show* (Chorus) W: Herb Magidson—M: Con Conrad / *If You Knew Susie* (Buddy Doyle) WM: B.G. De Sylva and Joseph Meyer / *It's Delightful to Be Married* (Luise Rainer, Chorus) W: Anna Held—M: Vincent Scotto / *Look for the Silver Lining* (William Demarest, William Powell) W: B.G. De Sylva—M: Jerome Kern / *My Man* (Fanny Brice) W: Channing Pollock—M: Maurice Yvain / *A Pretty Girl Is Like a Melody* (Stanley Morner, Chorus) WM: Irving Berlin / *Queen of the Jungle* (Fanny Brice, Chorus); *She's a Follies Girl* (Ray Bolger, Chorus) W: Harold Adamson—W: Walter Donaldson / *Shine On, Harvest Moon* (Chorus) WM: Jack Norworth and Nora Bayes / *Won't You Come and Play with Me?* (Luise Rainer) WM: Anna Held / *Yiddle on Your Fiddle* (Fanny Brice) WM: Irving Berlin / *You* (Chorus); *You Gotta Pull Strings* (Chorus); *You Never Looked So Beautiful Before* (Virginia Bruce, Chorus) W: Harold Adamson—M: Walter Donaldson.

"The picture achieves its best moments in the larger sequences devoted to the girls—ballet, chorus and show. At least one of these spectacular numbers, filmed to the music of *A Pretty Girl Is Like a Melody*, with overtones of *Rhapsody in Blue* never has been equaled on the musical comedy stage or screen." —Frank S. Nugent, *The New York Times*.

**495 The Greatest.** US-GB, 1977, C, 101 m. D: Tom Gries, MS: Michael Masser, P: Columbia (John Marshall). Performer: George Benson.

*Greatest Love of All* W: Linda Creed—M: Michael Masser / *I Always Knew I Had It in Me* W: Gerry Goffin—M: Michael Masser.

**496 The Green Pastures.** US, 1936, BW, 90 m. D: William Keighley, MS: Erich Wolfgang Korngold, P: Warner (Henry Blanke). Performers: The Hall Johnson Choir.

*Death's Gwinter Lay His Cold Hands on Me; De Old Ark's A-Moverin'; Go Down, Moses; Joshua Fit de Battle of Jericho; Run, Sinner, Run* WM: Unknown—Arr: Hall Johnson / *When the Saints Go Marching In* W: Katherine E. Purvis—M: James M. Black—Arr: Hall Johnson.

**497 The Grissom Gang.** US, 1971, C, 127 m. D: Robert Aldrich, MS: Gerald Fried, P: ABC (Robert Aldrich).

*I Can't Give You Anything But Love, Baby* (Rudy Vallee) W: Dorothy Fields—M: Jimmy McHugh.

**498 Guess Who's Coming to Dinner.** US, 1967, C, 108 m. D: Stanley Kramer, MD: Frank DeVol, P: Columbia (Stanley Kramer).

*The Glory of Love* (Jacqueline Fontaine, Chorus) WM: Billy Hill.

**499 Gunfight at the O.K. Corral.** US, 1957, C, 122 m. D: John Sturges, MS: Dimitri Tiomkin, P: Paramount (Hal B. Wallis).

*Gunfight at the O.K. Corral* (Frankie Laine) W: Ned Washington—M: Dimitri Tiomkin.

**500 A Guy Named Joe.** US, 1943, BW, 120 m. D: Victor Fleming, MS: Herbert Stothart, P: MGM (Everett Riskin).

*I'll Get By* (Irene Dunne) W: Roy Turk—M: Fred E. Ahlert.

**501 Guys and Dolls.** US, 1955, C, 158 m. D: Joseph L. Mankiewicz, MD: Jay S. Blackton, MS: Cyril Mockridge, P: MGM (Samuel Goldwyn).

The 1950 Broadway musical hit starred Robert Alda and Vivian Blaine as Sky Masterson and Miss Adelaide, with Sam Levene as Nathan Detroit and Stubby Kaye as Nicely-Nicely. Miss Blaine, Mr. Levene and Mr. Kaye repeated their performances in the London production which opened in 1953.

*Adelaide* (Frank Sinatra, Chorus);

*Adelaide's Lament* (Vivian Blaine); *Follow the Fold* (Jean Simmons, Regis Toomey, Chorus); *Fugue for Tinhorns* (Stubby Kaye, Johnny Silver, Danny Dayton); *Guys and Dolls* (Frank Sinatra, Stubby Kaye, Johnny Silver, Chorus); *If I Were a Bell* (Jean Simmons); *I'll Know* (Marlon Brando, Jean Simmons); *Luck Be a Lady* (Marlon Brando, Chorus); *The Oldest Established* (Frank Sinatra, Stubby Kaye, Johnny Silver, George E. Stone, Sheldon Leonard, Chorus); *Pet Me, Poppa* (Vivian Blaine, Chorus); *Sit Down, You're Rockin' the Boat* (Stubby Kaye, Jean Simmons, Kathryn Givney, Alan Hokanson); *Sue Me* (Frank Sinatra, Vivian Blaine); *Take Back Your Mink* (Vivian Blaine, Chorus); *A Woman in Love* (Jean Simmons, Marlon Brando, Renee Renor, Ruben De Fuentes) WM: Frank Loesser.

"This musical comedy classic, based upon a Damon Runyon tale and with wonderful songs by Frank Loesser, gets a great ride all the way." —Bosley Crowther, *The New York Times*.

**502   Gypsy.** US, 1962, C, 149 m. D: Mervyn LeRoy, MD: Frank Perkins, P: Warner (Mervyn LeRoy). Vocals: Marnie Nixon for part of Natalie Wood's singing; Lisa Kirk for part of Rosalind Russell's singing.

The stage musical starring Ethel Merman opened at the Broadway Theatre on May 21, 1959.

*All I Need Is the Girl* (Paul Wallace); *Baby June and Her Newsboys* (Suzanne Cupito, Diane Pace, Boys); *Broadway, Broadway* (Ann Jillian); *Dainty June and Her Farmboys* (Ann Jillian, Boys); *Everything's Coming Up Roses* (Rosalind Russell); *If Mama Was Married* (Natalie Wood, Ann Jillian); *Let Me Entertain You* (Natalie Wood); *Little Lamb* (Natalie Wood); *Mr. Goldstone, I Love You* (Rosalind Russell, Chorus); *Rose's Turn* (Rosalind Russell); *Small World* (Rosalind Russell); *Some People* (Rosalind Russell); *To-gether, Wherever We Go* (Rosalind Russell); *You Gotta Have a Gimmick* (Roxanne Arlen, Faith Dane, Betty Bruce); *You'll Never Get Away from Me* (Rosalind Russell, Karl Malden) W: Stephen Sondheim—M: Jule Styne.

"Rosalind Russell's performance ... deserves commendation." —*Variety*.

"For all Miss Russell's exertions ... she misses the Merman magic." —Bosley Crowther, *The New York Times*.

**503   Hair.** US, 1979, C, 118 m. D: Milos Forman, MS: Galt MacDermot, P: UA (Lester Persky, Michael Butler).

*Abie Boy* (Nell Carter, Charlaine Woodard, Trudy Perkins, Chorus); *Ain't Got No* (Nell Carter, Toney Watkins, Kurt Yaghjian, Chorus); *Air* (Annie Golden, Chorus); *Aquarius* (John Savage, Chorus); *Black Boys/White Boys* (Ellen Foley, Laurie Beechman, Debi Dye, Vincent Carrella, John Maestro, Jim Rosica, Fred Ferrarra); *Donna* (Treat Williams, Chorus); *Easy to Be Hard* (Cheryl Barnes); *Fourscore* (Nell Carter, Charlaine Woodard, Trudy Perkins, Chorus); *Frank Mills* (Suzette Charles); *Good Morning Starshine* (Beverly D'Angelo, Annie Golden, Cheryl Barnes, Don Dacus, Treat Williams, Dorsey Wright); *Hair* (Don Dacus, Treat Williams, Chorus); *Hare Krishna* (Nell Carter, Chorus); *Hashish* (Treat Williams, Chorus); *I Got Life* (Treat Williams, Chorus); *I'm Black* (Dorsey Wright, Don Dacus, Treat Williams, John Savage); *L.B.J.* (Chorus); *Let the Sunshine In* (John D. Robertas, Treat Williams, Chorus); *Manchester* (Treat Williams, John Savage, Chorus); *My Conviction* (Charlotte Rae); *Sodomy* (Don Dacus, Chorus); *3-5-0-0* (Melba Moore, Ron Dyson, Chorus); *What a Piece of Work Is Man* (David Lassley, Alex Paez); *Where Do I Go* (John Savage, Chorus) W: Gerome Ragni and James Rado—M: Galt MacDermot.

"A rollicking musical memoir, as much a recollection of the show as of the period." —Vincent Canby, *The New York Times*.

**504  Hairspray.** US, 1988, C, 96 m. D: John Waters, P: New Line (Rachel Talalay).

*The Bug* (Jerry Dallman and The Knightcaps) WM: Jerry Dallman and Milton Grant / *Foot Stompin'* (The Flares) WM: Aaron Collins / *Hairspray* (Rachel Sweet) WM: Rachel Sweet, Anthony Battaglia and Willa Bassen / *I'm Blue* (The Ikettes) WM: Ike Turner / *I Wish I Were a Princess* (Little Peggy Marsh) WM: George David Weiss, Hugo and Luigi / *The Madison Time* (Eddie Morrison and The Ray Bryant Combo) WM: Eddie Morrison and Ray Bryant / *Mama Didn't Lie* (Jan Bradley) WM: Curtis Mayfield / *Nothing Takes the Place of You* (Toussaint McCall) WM: Toussaint McCall and Patrick Robinson / *Shake a Tail Feather* (The Five Du-Tones) W: Verlie Rice—M: Andre Williams and Otha Hayes / *Town Without Pity* (Gene Pitney) W: Ned Washington—M: Dimitri Tiomkin / *You'll Lose a Good Thing* (Barbara Lynn) WM: Barbara Lynn Ozen.

**505  Half a Sixpence.** GB, 1967, C, 148 m. D: George Sidney, MD: Irwin Kostal, P: Paramount (Charles H. Schneer, George Sidney). Vocals: Marti Webb for Julia Foster.

Tommy Steele played the lead in both the London and Broadway productions in 1963 and 1965; in fact, the musical was written specifically for him.

*All in the Cause of Economy* (Tommy Steele, Chorus); *Flash, Bang, Wallop!* (Tommy Steele, Julia Foster, Chorus); *Half a Sixpence* (Tommy Steele, Julia Foster); *I Don't Believe a Word of It* (Julia Foster); *If the Rain's Got to Fall* (Tommy Steele, Chorus); *I Know What I Am* (Julia Foster); *I'm Not Talking to You* (Tommy Steele, Chorus); *Money to Burn* (Tommy Steele, Chorus); *A Proper Gentleman* (Chorus); *The Race* (Tommy Steele, Chorus); *She's Too Far Above Me* (Tommy Steele) WM: David Heneker.

"The haunting title song and the ebullient *Flash, Bang, Wallop!* remain the showstoppers, and David Heneker's score is a little short of socko tunes elsewhere." — *Variety*.

**506  Hallelujah, I'm a Bum.** US, 1933, BW, 82 m. D: Lewis Milestone, MD: Alfred Newman, P: UA (Joseph M. Schenck). GB Title: Hallelujah, I'm a Tramp. TV Title: Heart of New York.

Because of the offensive connotation of the word "bum" in England, the title for release there was changed, and Jolson filmed two versions of the title song.

*Bumper Found a Grand* (Harry Langdon, Edgar Connor); *Dear June* (Al Jolson); *Hallelujah, I'm a Bum* (Al Jolson); *I'd Do It Again* (Al Jolson); *I Gotta Get Back to New York* (Al Jolson); *Kangaroo Court* (Al Jolson, Harry Langdon, Edgar Connor, Chorus); *Laying the Cornerstone* (Frank Morgan); *My Pal Bumper* (Al Jolson, Harry Langdon, Edgar Connor, Chorus); *What Do You Want with Money?* (Al Jolson); *You Are Too Beautiful* (Al Jolson) W: Lorenz Hart—M: Richard Rodgers.

"The 'rhythmic dialog' and the Lewis Milestonian method of wedding the tempo'd music to the action has its moments ... Jolson's selling of the title song and *You Are Too Beautiful* ... leaves little wanting." — *Variety*.

**507  Halls of Montezuma.** US, 1950, C, 113 m. D: Lewis Milestone, MD: Lionel Newman, MS: Sol Kaplan, P: TCF (Robert Bassler).

*The Marines' Hymn* (Chorus) W: Unknown, poss. Henry C. Davis—M: Jacques Offenbach.

**508  The Hanging Tree.** US, 1959, C, 106 m. D: Delmer Daves, MS: Max Steiner, P: Warner (Martin Jurow, Richard Shepherd).

*The Hanging Tree* (Marty Robbins) W: Mack David—M: Jerry Livingston.

**509  Hannah and Her Sisters.** US, 1986, C, 106 m. D: Woody Allen, P: Orion (Robert Greenhut).

*Bewitched* (Lloyd Nolan, Maureen O'Sullivan) W: Lorenz Hart—M: Richard Rodgers / *I'm in Love Again* (Bobby Short) WM: Cole Porter.

**510  Hans Christian Andersen.** US, 1952, C, 120 m. D: Charles Vidor, MD: Walter Scharf, P: RKO (Samuel Goldwyn). Performer: Danny Kaye.

*Anywhere I Wander; Ice Skating Ballet* (Zizi Jeanmaire, Erik Bruhn); *I'm Hans Christian Andersen; Inch Worm; The King's New Clothes; No Two People* (Danny Kaye, Zizi Jeanmaire); *Thumbelina; The Ugly Duckling; Wonderful Cophenhagen* (Danny Kaye, Joey Walsh) WM: Frank Loesser.

**511  The Happiest Millionaire.** US, 1967, C, 118 m. D: Norman Tokar, MD: Jack Elliott, P: Walt Disney (Bill Anderson).

*Are We Dancing* (John Davidson, Lesley Ann Warren); *Bye Yum Pum Pum* (Joyce Bulifant, Lesley Ann Warren); *Detroit* (John Davidson, Lesley Ann Warren); *Fortuosity* (Tommy Steele); *I Believe in This Country* (Fred MacMurray); *I'll Always Be Irish* (Tommy Steele, Fred MacMurray, Lesley Ann Warren); *Let's Have a Drink on It* (Tommy Steele); *Strengthen the Dwelling* (Fred MacMurray, Chorus); *There Are Those* (Geraldine Page, Gladys Cooper, Tommy Steele); *Valentine Candy* (Lesley Ann Warren); *Watch Your Footwork* (Eddie Hodges, Paul Petersen); *What's Wrong with That* (Fred MacMurray, Lesley Ann Warren); *When a Man Has a Daughter* (Fred MacMurray) WM: Richard M. Sherman and Robert B. Sherman.

**512  Happiness Ahead.** US, 1934, BW, 86 m. D: Mervyn LeRoy, P: First National (Sam Bischoff). Performer: Dick Powell.

*Beauty Must Be Loved* W: Irving Kahal—M: Sammy Fain / *Happiness*

*Ahead; Pop! Goes Your Heart* W: Mort Dixon—M: Allie Wrubel / *The Window Cleaners* (Dick Powell, Frank McHugh) W: Bert Kalmar—M: Harry Ruby.

**513  Happy Anniversary.** US, 1959, BW, 81 m. D: David Miller, MS: Sol Kaplan and Robert Allen, P: UA (Ralph Fields).

*Happy Anniversary* (Mitzi Gaynor) W: Al Stillman—M: Robert Allen.

**514  The Happy Ending.** US, 1969, C, 112 m. D: Richard Brooks, MS: Michel Legrand, P: UA (Richard Brooks).

*What Are You Doing the Rest of Your Life?* (Michael Dees) W: Alan Bergman and Marilyn Bergman—M: Michel Legrand.

**515  Happy Go Lucky.** US, 1943, C, 81 m. D: Curtis Bernhardt, MD: Robert Emmett Dolan, P: Paramount (Harold Wilson).

*The Fuddy Duddy Watchmaker* (Betty Hutton, The Sportsmen); *Happy Go Lucky* (Mary Martin, Dick Powell); *Let's Get Lost* (Mary Martin, Dick Powell); *Murder, He Says* (Betty Hutton); *Sing a Tropical Song* (Dick Powell, Eddie Bracken, Sir Lancelot) W: Frank Loesser—M: Jimmy McHugh / *Ta-Ra-Ra-Boom-De-Ay* (Mary Martin) WM: Henry J. Sayers.

**516  Hard Country.** US, 1981, C, 104 m. D: David Greene, MS: Jimmie Haskell, P: Universal (David Greene, Mack Bing).

*Break My Mind* (Michael Martin Murphy, Chorus) WM: John D. Loudermilk / *Cowboy Cadillac* (Michael Martin Murphy, Chorus) WM: Michael Martin Murphy / *Gonna Love You Anyway* (Tanya Tucker) WM: L. Martine, Jr. / *Hard Country* (Michael Martin Murphy, Kate Moffatt / *I Love You So Much It Hurts* (Jerry Lee Lewis) WM: Floyd Tillman / *Somebody Must Have Loved You Last Night* (Tanya Tucker) WM: K. Bell / *Take It as It Comes* (Michael Martin Murphy, Kate Moffatt) WM: Michael Martin Murphy / *West Texas Waltz* (Joe Ely,

Chorus) WM: B. Hancock / *When I Die Just Let Me Go to Texas* (Tanya Tucker, Chorus) WM: Ed Bruce, Bobby Borchers and Patsy Bruce.

**517 A Hard Day's Night.** GB, 1964, BW, 87 m. D: Richard Lester, MD: George Martin, P: UA (Walter Shenson). Performers: The Beatles.

*All My Loving; And I Love Her; Can't Buy Me Love* WM: John Lennon and Paul McCartney / *Don't Bother Me* WM: George Harrison / *A Hard Day's Night; If I Fell; I'll Cry Instead; I'm Happy Just to Dance with You; I Should Have Known Better; I Want to Be Your Man; She Loves You; Tell Me Why; This Boy* WM: John Lennon and Paul McCartney.

"One musical sequence . . . when the boys tumble wildly out of doors and race eccentrically about a patterned playground to the tune of their song *Can't Buy Me Love* hits a surrealistic tempo that approaches audio-visual poetry." —Bosley Crowther, *The New York Times*.

**518 Hard to Get.** US, 1938, BW, 80 m. D: Ray Enright, P: Warner (Hal B. Wallis). Performer: Dick Powell.

*There's a Sunny Side to Every Situation* W: Al Dubin and Johnny Mercer—M: Harry Warren / *You Must Have Been a Beautiful Baby* W: Johnny Mercer—M: Harry Warren.

**519 Harum Scarum.** US, 1965, C, 86 m. D: Gene Nelson, MD: Fred Karger, P: MGM (Sam Katzman). MB: The Jordanaires. Performer: Elvis Presley. GB Title: Harem Holiday.

*Go East, Young Man; Golden Coins* WM: Bill Giant, Bernie Baum and Florence Kaye / *Harem Holiday* WM: Peter Andredi and Vince Poncia, Jr. / *Hey, Little Girl* WM: Joy Byers / *Kismet* WM: Sid Tepper and Roy C. Bennett / *Mirage* WM: Bill Giant, Bernie Baum and Florence Kaye / *My Desert Serenade* WM: Stan Gelber / *Shake That Tambourine* WM: Bill Giant, Bernie

Baum and Florence Kaye / *So Close, Yet So Far* WM: Joy Byers.

**520 The Harvey Girls.** US, 1946, C, 101 m. D: George Sidney, MD: Lennie Hayton, P: MGM (Arthur Freed). Vocals: Marion Doenges for Cyd Charisse.

*In the Valley* (Judy Garland, Kenny Baker); *It's a Great Big World* (Judy Garland, Cyd Charisse, Virginia O'Brien); *Oh, You Kid* (Angela Lansbury, Chorus); *On the Atchison, Topeka and the Santa Fe* (Judy Garland, Ray Bolger, Margaret O'Brien, Marjorie Main, Ben Carter, Vernon Dent, Jack Clifford, Ray Teal, Chorus); *Swing Your Partner Round and Round* (Judy Garland, Marjorie Main, Chorus); *The Train Must Be Fed* (Selena Royle, Marjorie Main, Chorus); *Wait and See* (Angela Lansbury, Cyd Charisse, Kenny Baker); *The Wild Wild West* (Virginia O'Brien) W: Johnny Mercer— M: Harry Warren.

"Best and most frequently chanted of the . . . tunes is that rattling railroad number that bids fair to live as long as *Casey Jones*." —Bosley Crowther, *The New York Times*.

**521 Hawaii Calls.** US, 1938, BW, 73 m. D: Edward F. Cline, P: RKO (Sol Lesser). Performer: Bobby Breen.

*Aloha Oe* WM: Queen Liliuokalani / *Down Where the Trade Winds Blow; Hawaii Calls* WM: Harry Owens / *Machushla* W: Josephine V. Rowe—M: Dermot MacMurrough.

**522 Head.** US, 1968, C, 86 m. D: Bob Rafelson, MS: Ken Thorne, P: Columbia (Bob Rafelson, Jack Nicholson, Bert Schneider). Performers: The Monkees.

*As We Go Along* WM: Carole King and Toni Stern / *Can You Dig It* WM: Peter Tork / *Circle Sky* WM: Michael Nesmith / *Daddy's Song* WM: Harry Nilsson / *Long Title—Do I Have to Do This All Over Again?* WM: Peter Tork / *Porpoise Song* WM: Gerry Goffin and Carole King.

**523   Head Over Heels in Love.**
GB, 1937, BW, 81 m. D: Sonnie Hale, MD: Louis Levy, P: Gaumont (S.C. Balcon). Performer: Jessie Matthews. GB Title: Head Over Heels.

*Head Over Heels in Love; Looking Around Corners for You; May I Have the Next Romance with You?* (Jessie Matthews, Louis Borrell); *There's That Look in Your Eyes* W: Mack Gordon— M: Harry Revel.

"Miss Matthews has a voice which, in moderation, is reasonably uncloying ... and it was not fair to ask her to carry such dead weights of footage with the unaided larynx. ... The score ... is adequately tuneful." —B.R. Crisler, *The New York Times.*

**524   Heads Up!** US, 1930, BW, 76 m. D: Victor Schertzinger, P: Paramount.

*My Man Is on the Make* (Helen Kane); *A Ship Without a Sail* (Charles "Buddy" Rogers) W: Lorenz Hart— M: Richard Rodgers.

**525   The Heartbreak Kid.** US, 1972, C, 104 m. D: Elaine May, MS: Garry Sherman, P: TCF (Edgar J. Scherick).

*The Heartbreak Kid* (Bill Dean) W: Sheldon Harnick—M: Cy Coleman.

**526   Heidi.** US, 1937, BW, 88 m. D: Allan Dwan, MD: Louis Silvers, P: TCF (Raymond Griffith).

*The First Noel* (Chorus) WM: Unknown / *In My Little Wooden Shoes* (Shirley Temple, Chorus) W: Sidney D. Mitchell—M: Lew Pollack / *Silent Night* (Chorus) W: Joseph Mohr—M: Franz Gruber.

**527   The Helen Morgan Story.** US, 1957, BW, 118 m. D: Michael Curtiz, P: Warner (Martin Rackin). Vocals: Gogi Grant for Ann Blyth. Performer: Ann Blyth. GB Title: Both Ends of the Candle.

*April in Paris* W: E.Y. Harburg— M: Vernon Duke / *Avalon* WM: Al Jolson, B.G. De Sylva and Vincent Rose / *Bill* W: P.G. Wodehouse and Oscar Hammerstein II—M: Jerome Kern /

*Body and Soul* WM: Edward Heyman, Robert Sour, Frank Eyton and Johnny Green / *Breezin' Along with the Breeze* WM: Haven Gillespie, Seymour Simons and Richard A. Whiting / *Can't Help Lovin' Dat Man* W: Oscar Hammerstein II—M: Jerome Kern / *Deep Night* WM: Rudy Vallee and Charlie Henderson / *Do, Do, Do* W: Ira Gershwin—M: George Gershwin / *Do It Again* W: B.G. De Sylva —M: George Gershwin / *Don't Ever Leave Me* W: Oscar Hammerstein II —M: Jerome Kern / *I Can't Give You Anything But Love, Baby* W: Dorothy Fields—M: Jimmy McHugh / *If You Were the Only Girl in the World* W: Clifford Grey—M: Nat D. Ayer / *I'll Get By* W: Roy Turk—M: Fred E. Ahlert / *I've Got a Crush on You* W: Ira Gershwin—M: George Gershwin / *Just a Memory* W: B.G. De Sylva and Lew Brown—M: Ray Henderson / *The Love Nest* W: Otto Harbach—M: Louis A. Hirsch / *The Man I Love* W: Ira Gershwin—M: George Gershwin / *More Than You Know* W: Billy Rose and Edward Eliscu—M: Vincent Youmans / *My Melancholy Baby* W: George A. Norton—M: Ernie Burnett / *My Time Is Your Time* W: Eric Little—M: Leo Dance / *The One I Love Belongs to Somebody Else* W: Gus Kahn—M: Isham Jones / *On the Sunny Side of the Street* W: Dorothy Fields—M: Jimmy McHugh / *Somebody Loves Me* W: B.G. De Sylva and Ballard MacDonald— M: George Gershwin / *Someone to Watch Over Me* W: Ira Gershwin—M: George Gershwin / *Something to Remember You By* W: Howard Dietz— M: Arthur Schwartz / *Speak to Me of Love* Eng. W: Bruce Sievier—French WM: Jean Lenoir / *Sweet Georgia Brown* (Cara Williams) WM: Ben Bernie, Maceo Pinkard and Kenneth Casey / *Why Was I Born?* W: Oscar Hammerstein II—M: Jerome Kern / *You Do Something to Me* WM: Cole Porter.

"The indestructible tunes ...

should generate genuine nostalgia. . . . Gogi Grant lends authenticity to the sound track." —A.H. Weiler, *The New York Times.*

**528  Hello, Dolly!** US, 1969, C, 146 m. D: Gene Kelly, MD: Lennie Hayton, P: TCF (Ernest Lehman).

The musical adaptation of Thornton Wilder's 'The Matchmaker' starring Carol Channing opened at Broadway's St. James Theatre on January 16, 1964, and was still playing when the film opened. Mary Martin headed the cast of the touring company that began a run in London in December 1965.

*Before the Parade Passes By* (Barbra Streisand, Chorus); *Dancing* (Barbra Streisand, Michael Crawford, Danny Lockin, Marianne McAndrew, Chorus); *Elegance* (Michael Crawford, Danny Lockin, Marianne McAndrew); *Hello, Dolly!* (Barbra Streisand, Louis Armstrong, Walter Matthau, Chorus); *It Only Takes a Moment* (Michael Crawford, Marianne McAndrew, Chorus); *It Takes a Woman* (Barbra Streisand, Walter Matthau, Michael Crawford, Danny Lockin, Chorus); *Just Leave Everything to Me* (Barbra Streisand); *Love Is Only Love* (Barbra Streisand); *Put On Your Sunday Clothes* (Barbra Streisand, Tommy Tune, Michael Crawford, Danny Lockin, Joyce Ames, Chorus); *Ribbons Down My Back* (Marianne McAndrew); *So Long, Dearie* (Barbra Streisand) WM: Jerry Herman.

"An expensive, expansive, sometimes exaggerated, sentimental, nostalgic, wholesome, pictorially opulent $20 million filmusical with the charisma of Barbra Streisand in the title role." —*Variety.*

"The Jerry Herman score is generally so routine that it's difficult to distinguish between it and the ones he wrote later for 'Mame' and 'Dear World.'" —Vincent Canby, *The New York Times.*

**529  Hello, Everybody!** US,

1933, BW, 69 m. D: William Seiter, P: Paramount. Performer: Kate Smith.

*Moon Song; Out in the Great Open Spaces; Pickaninnies' Heaven; Queen of Lullaby Land; Twenty Million People* W: Sam Coslow—M: Arthur Johnston.

**530  Hello, Frisco, Hello.** US, 1943, C, 98 m. D: H. Bruce Humberstone, P: TCF (Milton Sperling).

*Bedelia* (Alice Faye, Chorus) W: William Jerome—M: Jean Schwartz / *By the Light of the Silvery Moon* (Alice Faye, Chorus) W: Edward Madden—M: Gus Edwards / *Gee, But It's Great to Meet a Friend from Your Home Town* (June Havoc, Jack Oakie) W: William Tracey—M: James McGavisk / *The Grizzly Bear* (Alice Faye, June Havoc, Jack Oakie, Chorus) WM: Irving Berlin and George Botsford / *Has Anybody Here Seen Kelly?* (Alice Faye, Jack Oakie, Chorus) WM: C.W. Murphy, William Letters, John Charles Moore and William J. McKenna / *Hello, Frisco!* (Alice Faye, June Havoc, John Payne, Jack Oakie) W: Gene Buck—M: Louis A. Hirsch / *It's Tulip Time in Holland* (Kirby Grant, Chorus) W: Dave Radford—M: Richard A. Whiting / *I've Got a Gal in Every Port* (June Havoc, Jack Oakie, Chorus) WM: Unknown / *Ragtime Cowboy Joe* (Alice Faye, June Havoc, Jack Oakie) W: Grant Clarke—M: Maurice Abrahams and Lewis F. Muir / *San Francisco* (Chorus) W: Gus Kahn—M: Bronislau Kaper and Walter Jurmann / *Strike Up the Band, Here Comes a Sailor* (Jack Oakie, Chorus) W: Andrew B. Sterling—M: Charles B. Ward / *Sweet Cider Time* (Alice Faye) W: Joseph McCarthy—M: Percy Wenrich / *They Always Pick on Me* (Alice Faye) W: Stanley Murphy—M: Harry von Tilzer / *You'll Never Know* (Alice Faye) W: Mack Gordon—M: Harry Warren.

**531  Help!** GB, 1965, C, 92 m. D: Richard Lester, MD: George Martin, P: UA (Walter Shenson). Performers: The Beatles.

*Another Girl; Help!* WM: John

Lennon and Paul McCartney / *I Need You* WM: George Harrison / *The Night Before; Ticket to Ride; You're Gonna Lose That Girl; You've Got to Hide Your Love Away* WM: John Lennon and Paul McCartney.

"It is the usual Beatle's music, dished out to an infectious beat." — Bosley Crowther, *The New York Times*.

**532　Her Cardboard Lover.** US, 1942, BW, 93 m. D: George Cukor, MS: Franz Waxman, P: MGM (J. Walter Ruben).

*I Dare You* (Robert Taylor, Frank McHugh) W: Ralph Freed — M: Burton Lane.

**533　Her Lucky Night.** US, 1945, BW, 63 m. D: Edward Lilley, P: Universal (Warren Wilson). Performers: The Andrews Sisters.

*Dance with a Dolly* WM: Terry Shand, Jimmy Eaton and Mickey Leader / *Is You Is, or Is You Ain't, Ma Baby?* WM: Billy Austin and Louis Jordan / *The Polka Polka* WM: Maxine Manners / *Sing a Tropical Song* W: Frank Loesser — M: Jimmy McHugh / *Straighten Up and Fly Right* WM: Irving Mills and Nat King Cole.

**534　Here Come the Waves.** US, 1944, BW, 99 m. D: Mark Sandrich, MD: Robert Emmett Dolan, P: Paramount (Mark Sandrich).

*Ac-cent-tchu-ate the Positive* (Bing Crosby, Sonny Tufts); *I Promise You* (Betty Hutton, Bing Crosby); *Let's Take the Long Way Home* (Betty Hutton, Bing Crosby); *That Old Black Magic* (Bing Crosby); *There's a Fellow Waiting in Poughkeepsie* (Betty Hutton) W: Johnny Mercer — M: Harold Arlen.

**535　Here Comes the Band.** US, 1935, BW, 82 m. D: Paul Sloane, MS: Edward Ward, P: MGM (Lucien Hubbard). Orch: Ted Lewis.

*Headin' Home* (Harry Stockwell) W: Ned Washington — M: Herbert Stothart / *Roll Along, Prairie Moon* (Harry Stockwell) WM: Cecil Mack, Albert von Tilzer and Ted Fiorito / *Tender Is the Night* (Virginia Bruce, Harry Stockwell) W: Harold Adamson — M: Walter Donaldson / *You're My Thrill* (Ted Lewis) W: Ned Washington — M: Burton Lane.

**536　Here Comes the Groom.** US, 1951, BW, 113 m. D: Frank Capra, MD: Joseph J. Lilley, P: Paramount (Frank Capra).

*Bonne Nuit, Good Night* (Bing Crosby) W: Ray Evans — M: Jay Livingston / *In the Cool, Cool, Cool of the Evening* (Bing Crosby, Jane Wyman) W: Johnny Mercer — M: Hoagy Carmichael / *Misto Cristofo Columbo* (Bing Crosby, Dorothy Lamour, Cass Daley, Louis Armstrong, Phil Harris); *Your Own Little House* (Bing Crosby) W: Ray Evans — M: Jay Livingston.

**537　Here We Go Round the Mulberry Bush.** GB, 1968, C, 96 m. D: Clive Donner, P: UA (Clive Donner).

*Am I What I Was or Was I What I Am?* (Traffic) WM: Stevie Winwood, Jim Capaldi and Chris Wood / *Every Little Thing* (The Spencer Davis Group) WM: Spencer Davis and Matthews / *Here We Go Round the Mulberry Bush* (Traffic) WM: Dave Mason, Stevie Winwood, Jim Capaldi and Chris Wood / *It's Been a Long Time* (Andy Ellison) WM: Simon Napier-Bell, Child and Child / *Just Like Me* (The Spencer Davis Group) WM: Spencer Davis / *Looking Back* (The Spencer Davis Group) WM: Spencer Davis and Sawyer / *Picture of Her* (The Spencer Davis Group) WM: Spencer Davis / *Possession* (The Spencer Davis Group) WM: Spencer Davis and Matthews / *Taking Out Time* (The Spencer Davis Group) WM: Spencer Davis and Eddie Hardin / *Utterly Simple* (Traffic) WM: Dave Mason / *Virginal's Dream* (The Spencer Davis Group) WM: Spencer Davis / *Waltz for Caroline* (The Spencer Davis Group) WM: Stevie Winwood.

**538　Hers to Hold.** US, 1943, BW, 94 m. D: Frank Ryan, MD: Charles Previn, MS: Frank Skinner, P:

Universal (Felix Jackson). Performer: Deanna Durbin.

*Begin the Beguine* WM: Cole Porter / *God Bless America* WM: Irving Berlin / *Kashmiri Love Song* WM: Lawrence Hope and Amy Woodeforde-Finden / *Say a Prayer for the Boys Over There* W: Herb Magidson—M: Jimmy McHugh.

**539 Hey Boy! Hey Girl!** US, 1959, BW, 81 m. D: David Lowell Rich, P: Columbia (Harry Romm).

*Autumn Leaves* (Keely Smith, Chorus) Eng. W: Johnny Mercer — French W: Jacques Prevert—M: Joseph Kosma / *A Banana Split for My Baby* (Louis Prima, Chorus) WM: Louis Prima and Stan Irwin / *Fever* (Keely Smith, Louis Prima, Sam Butera and The Witnesses) WM: John Davenport and Eddie Cooley / *Hey Boy! Hey Girl!* (Keely Smith, Louis Prima, Chorus) WM: J. Thomas and Oscar McLollie / *Lazy River* (Keely Smith, Louis Prima, Chorus) WM: Sidney Arodin and Hoagy Carmichael / *Nitey-Nite* (Keely Smith) WM: Louis Prima, Keely Smith and Barbara Belle / *Oh Marie* (Louis Prima, Chorus) WM: Eduardo di Capua / *When the Saints Go Marching In* (Louis Prima, Chorus) W: Katherine E. Purvis—M: James M. Black / *You Are My Love* (Keely Smith) WM: Joe Sauter.

**540 Hey, Let's Twist!** US, 1961, BW, 80 m. D: Greg Garrison, P: Paramount (Harry Romm).

*Hey, Let's Twist!* (Joey Dee and The Starliters) W: Joey Dee and Morris Levy—M: Henry Glover / *It's a Pity to Say Goodnight* (Teddy Randazzo) WM: Billy Reid / *I Wanna Twist* (Kay Armen); *Joey's Blues* (Dave and The Starliters); *Let's Do My Twist* (Jo Ann Campbell) W: Joey Dee and Morris Levy—M: Henry Glover / *Mother Goose Twist* (Teddy Randazzo) WM: Teddy Randazzo, Bobby Weinstein and Billy Barberis / *Peppermint Twist* (Joey Dee and The Starliters) W: Joey Dee—M: Henry Glover / *Roly Poly* (Joey Dee) W: Joey Dee and Morris

Levy—M: Henry Glover / *Shout* (Joey Dee and The Starliters) WM: O'Kelly Isley, Ronald Isley and Rudolph Isley.

**541 High Anxiety.** US, 1977, C, 94 m. D: Mel Brooks, MS: John Morris, P: TCF (Mel Brooks).

*High Anxiety* (Mel Brooks, Chorus); *If You Love Me Baby, Tell Me Loud* (Mel Brooks) WM: Mel Brooks.

**542 High Noon.** US, 1952, BW, 85 m. D: Fred Zinnemann, MS: Dimitri Tiomkin, P: UA (Stanley Kramer).

*High Noon* (Tex Ritter) W: Ned Washington—M: Dimitri Tiomkin.

"Throughout the film is a hauntingly-presented ballad that tells the story of the coming gun duel." — *Variety.*

**543 High School Confidential.** US, 1958, BW, 85 m. D: Jack Arnold, P: MGM (Albert Zugsmith).

*High School Confidential* (Jerry Lee Lewis) WM: Ron Hargrove and Jerry Lee Lewis.

**544 High Society.** US, 1956, C, 107 m. D: Charles Walters, MD: Johnny Green and Saul Chaplin, P: MGM (Sol C. Siegel). Orch: Louis Armstrong.

*High Society Calypso* (Louis Armstrong); *I Love You, Samantha* (Bing Crosby); *Little One* (Bing Crosby, Lydia Reed); *Mind If I Make Love to You?* (Frank Sinatra); *Now You Has Jazz* (Bing Crosby, Louis Armstrong); *True Love* (Bing Crosby, Grace Kelly); *Well, Did You Evah?* (Bing Crosby, Frank Sinatra); *Who Wants to Be a Millionaire?* (Frank Sinatra, Celeste Holm); *You're Sensational* (Frank Sinatra) WM: Cole Porter.

"Porter has whipped up a solid set of songs with which vocal pros like the male stars and Holm do plenty." — *Variety.*

"There are moments of amusement ... when Louis Armstrong and his band are beating out ... tunes ... from old Cole Porter albums or especially written by him for this show." — Bosley Crowther, *The New York Times.*

545 **High, Wide and Handsome.** US, 1937, BW, 112 m. D: Rouben Mamoulian, MD: Boris Morros, P: Paramount (Arthur Hornblow, Jr.). GB Title: Black Gold.

The only musical Hammerstein and Kern ever wrote specifically for the screen.

*Allegheny Al* (Dorothy Lamour, Irene Dunne); *Can I Forget You?* (Irene Dunne); *The Folks Who Live on the Hill* (Irene Dunne); *High, Wide and Handsome* (Irene Dunne); *The Things I Want* (Dorothy Lamour); *Will You Marry Me Tomorrow, Maria?* (William Frawley) W: Oscar Hammerstein II—M: Jerome Kern.

"A spectacular show. ... The songs ... almost seem to have been plucked from the minstrelsy of the pre–Civil War years rather than coined this season. ... Miss Dunne's voice is as delightful as she is." —Frank S. Nugent, *The New York Times*.

546 **Higher and Higher.** US, 1943, BW, 90 m. D: Tim Whelan, MD: Constantin Bakaleinikoff, P: RKO (Tim Whelan).

*Disgustingly Rich* (Chorus) W: Lorenz Hart—M: Richard Rodgers / *I Couldn't Sleep a Wink Last Night* (Frank Sinatra); *I Saw You First* (Frank Sinatra, Marcy McGuire, Barbara Hale); *It's a Most Important Affair* (Chorus); *A Lovely Way to Spend an Evening* (Frank Sinatra); *Minuet in Boogie* (Marcy McGuire, Mel Torme, Chorus); *The Music Stopped* (Frank Sinatra); *Today I'm a Debutante* (Michele Morgan, Jack Haley, Chorus); *You're on Your Own* (Dooley Wilson, Mel Torme, Frank Sinatra, Marcy McGuire, Chorus) W: Harold Adamson—M: Jimmy McHugh.

547 **Hips, Hips, Hooray.** US, 1934, BW, 68 m. D: Mark Sandrich, P: RKO (H.N. Swanson).

*Keep on Doin' What You're Doin'* (Ruth Etting, Bert Wheeler, Robert Woolsey, Dorothy Lee, Thelma Todd); *Keep Romance Alive* (Ruth Etting);

*Tired of It All* (Ruth Etting) W: Bert Kalmar—M: Harry Ruby.

548 **His Butler's Sister.** US, 1943, BW, 94 m. D: Frank Borzage, MS: Hans Salter, P: Universal (Felix Johnson).

*In the Spirit of the Moment* (Deanna Durbin) W: Bernie Grossman —M: Walter Jurmann / *Is It True What They Say About Dixie?* (Iris Adrian, Robin Raymond) WM: Irving Caesar, Sammy Lerner and Gerald Marks / *When You're Away* (Deanna Durbin) W: Henry Blossom—M: Victor Herbert.

549 **Hit the Deck.** US, 1955, C, 112 m. D: Roy Rowland, MD: George Stoll, P: MGM (Joe Pasternak).

A film version of the 1927 Broadway musical was made by RKO in 1930. With a changed story and different songs in 1937 it became "Follow the Fleet" starring Ginger Rogers and Fred Astaire.

*Ciribiribin* (Jane Powell, Tony Martin, Debbie Reynolds, Kay Armen, Vic Damone, Russ Tamblyn) W: Rudolf Thaler—M: Alberto Pestalozza / *Hallelujah* (Jane Powell, Tony Martin, Kay Armen, Vic Damone, Russ Tamblyn, The Jubalaires) W: Leo Robin and Clifford Grey—M: Vincent Youmans / *Happy Birthday to You* (Tony Martin, Vic Damone, Russ Tamblyn, Chorus) WM: Patty Smith Hill and Mildred J. Hill / *I Know That You Know* (Jane Powell, Vic Damone) W: Anne Caldwell—M: Vincent Youmans / *Join the Navy* (Debbie Reynolds, Chorus) W: Leo Robin and Clifford Grey—M: Vincent Youmans / *Keepin' Myself for You* (Ann Miller, Tony Martin) W: Sidney Clare—M: Vincent Youmans / *A Kiss or Two* (Debbie Reynolds, Men); *Lady from the Bayou* (Ann Miller) W: Leo Robin—M: Vincent Youmans / *Lucky Bird* (Jane Powell) W: Leo Robin and Clifford Grey—M: Vincent Youmans / *More Than You Know* (Tony Martin) W: Billy Rose and Edward Eliscu—M: Vincent Youmans / *Sometimes I'm*

*Happy* (Jane Powell, Vic Damone) W: Irving Caesar—M: Vincent Youmans / *Why Oh Why?* (Jane Powell, Tony Martin, Debbie Reynolds, Ann Miller, Vic Damone, Russ Tamblyn) W: Leo Robin and Clifford Grey—M: Vincent Youmans.

"A pretty picture, replete with songs from the old footlight piece, complete with new lyrics and flashy production numbers." — *Variety*.

**550  Hit the Ice.** US, 1943, BW, 82 m. D: Charles Lamont, MD: Charles Previn, P: Universal (Alex Gottlieb). Orch: Johnny Long. Performer: Ginny Simms. Alt. Title: Oh Doctor.

*Happiness Bound; I'd Like to Set You to Music; I'm Like a Fish Out of Water; The Slap Polka* W: Paul Francis Webster—M: Harry Revel.

**551  Hitting a New High.** US, 1937, BW, 85 m. D: Raoul Walsh, P: RKO. Performer: Lily Pons.

*I Hit a New High; Let's Give Love Another Chance; This Never Happened Before; You're Like a Song* W: Harold Adamson—M: Jimmy McHugh.

**552  Hold On!** US, 1966, C, 86 m. D: Arthur Lubin, P: MGM (Sam Katzman). Performers: Herman's Hermits.

*All the Things I Do for You Baby* WM: P.F. Sloan and Steve Barri / *The George and Dragon; Got a Feeling; Gotta Get Away* WM: Sid Wayne, Ben Weisman and Fred Karger / *Hold On!* WM: P.F. Sloan and Steve Barri / *Leaning on the Lamp Post* WM: Noel Gay / *Make Me Happy* WM: Sid Wayne, Ben Weisman and Fred Karger / *A Must to Avoid* WM: P.F. Sloan and Steve Barri / *We Want You Herman* WM: Sid Wayne, Ben Weisman and Fred Karger / *Where Were You When I Needed You* WM: P.F. Sloan and Steve Barri / *Wild Love* WM: Sid Wayne, Ben Weisman and Fred Karger.

**553  Hold That Ghost.** US, 1941, BW, 86 m. D: Arthur Lubin, MS: Hans Salter, P: Universal (Burt

Kelly, Glenn Tryon). Orch: Ted Lewis.

*Aurora* (The Andrews Sisters) WM: Harold Adamson, Mario Lago and Roberto Roberti / *Me and My Shadow* (Ted Lewis) W: Billy Rose—M: Dave Dreyer and Al Jolson / *Sleepy Serenade* (The Andrews Sisters) W: Mort Greene—M: Lou Singer / *When My Baby Smiles at Me* (Ted Lewis) W: Andrew B. Sterling and Ted Lewis—M: Bill Munro.

**554  Hold Your Man.** US, 1933, BW, 86 m. D: Sam Wood, P: MGM (Sam Wood).

*Hold Your Man* (Jean Harlow) W: Arthur Freed—M: Nacio Herb Brown.

**555  A Hole in the Head.** US, 1959, C, 120 m. D: Frank Capra, MS: Nelson Riddle, P: UA (Frank Sinatra).

*All My Tomorrows* (Frank Sinatra); *High Hopes* (Frank Sinatra, Eddie Hodges) W: Sammy Cahn—M: James Van Heusen.

**556  Holiday in Mexico.** US, 1946, C, 127 m. D: George Sidney, P: MGM (Joe Pasternak). Orch: Xavier Cugat. Performer: Jane Powell.

*Ave Maria* W: Sir Walter Scott—M: Franz Schubert / *Italian Street Song* W: Rida Johnson Young—M: Victor Herbert / *I Think of You* WM: Jack Elliott and Don Marcotte.

**557  Holiday Inn.** US, 1942, BW, 101 m. D: Mark Sandrich, MD: Robert Emmett Dolan, P: Paramount (Mark Sandrich). Orch: Bob Crosby's Bobcats. Vocals: Martha Mears for Marjorie Reynolds.

*Abraham* (Bing Crosby, Marjorie Reynolds, Louise Beavers, Chorus); *Be Careful, It's My Heart* (Bing Crosby); *Easter Parade* (Bing Crosby); *Happy Holiday* (Bing Crosby, Marjorie Reynolds, Chorus); *Holiday Inn* (Bing Crosby, Marjorie Reynolds); *I Can't Tell a Lie* (Fred Astaire); *I'll Capture Your Heart Singing* (Bing Crosby, Fred Astaire, Virginia Dale); *Lazy* (Bing Crosby); *Let's Say It with Firecrackers* (Chorus); *Let's Start the New Year Right* (Bing Crosby); *Plenty to Be Thankful For*

(Bing Crosby); *Song of Freedom* (Bing Crosby, Chorus); *White Christmas* (Bing Crosby, Marjorie Reynolds, Chorus); *You're Easy to Dance With* (Fred Astaire, Chorus) WM: Irving Berlin.

"Irving Berlin has fashioned some peach songs to fit the highlight holidays." — *Variety.*

**558  Hollywood Canteen.** US, 1944, BW, 124 m. D: Delmer Daves, MD: Leo F. Forbstein, MS: Ray Heindorf, P: Warner (Alex Gottlieb). Orch: Carmen Cavallaro; Jimmy Dorsey.

In which Roy Rogers introduced the Cole Porter standard *Don't Fence Me In.* The song's idea arose out of a poem written by a mining engineer from Montana named Robert Fletcher, from whom Porter bought the rights for $150 during the 1930s.

*Corns for My Country* (The Andrews Sisters) WM: Leah Worth, Jean Barry and Dick Charles / *Don't Fence Me In* (Roy Rogers and The Sons of the Pioneers, The Andrews Sisters) WM: Cole Porter / *The General Jumped at Dawn* (Golden Gate Quartet) W: Larry Neal — M: Jimmy Mundy / *Hollywood Canteen* (The Andrews Sisters) W: Ted Koehler — M: Ray Heindorf and M.K. Jerome / *Sweet Dreams, Sweetheart* (Joan Leslie, Kitty Carlisle) W: Ted Koehler — M: M.K. Jerome / *Tumbling Tumbleweeds* (The Sons of the Pioneers) WM: Bob Nolan / *We're Having a Baby* (Eddie Cantor, Nora Martin) W: Harold Adamson — M: Vernon Duke / *What Are You Doing the Rest of Your Life* (Jack Carson, Jane Wyman) W: Ted Koehler — M: Burton Lane / *You Can Always Tell a Yank* (Dennis Morgan, Joe E. Brown) W: E.Y. Harburg — M: Burton Lane.

**559  Hollywood Hotel.** US, 1937, BW, 109 m. D: Busby Berkeley, P: Warner (Hal B. Wallis). Orch: Benny Goodman; Raymond Paige.

This movie took its title from Louella Parsons' popular radio variety show. Jerry Cooper was a singer on the show.

*Hooray for Hollywood* (Frances Langford, Johnny "Scat" Davis, Chorus); *I'm Like a Fish Out of Water* (Dick Powell, Rosemary Lane); *I've Hitched My Wagon to a Star* (Dick Powell); *Let That Be a Lesson to You* (Dick Powell, Johnny "Scat" Davis, Rosemary Lane, Mabel Todd, Ted Healy, Chorus); *Silhouetted in the Moonlight* (Dick Powell, Rosemary Lane, Frances Langford, Jerry Cooper); *Sing, You Son of a Gun* (Dick Powell, Chorus) W: Johnny Mercer — M: Richard A. Whiting.

**560  The Hollywood Knights.** US, 1980, C, 95 m. D: Floyd Mutrux, P: Columbia (Richard Lederer).

*Big Girls Don't Cry* (The Four Seasons) WM: Bob Crewe and Bob Gaudio / *Heat Wave* (Martha and The Vandellas) WM: Eddie Holland, Lamont Dozier and Brian Holland / *Hey! Baby* (Bruce Channel) WM: Bruce Channel and Margaret Cobb / *The Midnight Hour* (Wilson Pickett) WM: Wilson Pickett and Steve Cropper / *One Fine Day* (The Chiffons) WM: Gerry Goffin and Carole King / *What'd I Say* (Ray Charles) WM: Ray Charles / *Wipe Out* (The Surfaris) WM: Ron Wilson, James Fuller, Robert Berryhill and Patrick Connolly.

**561  Hollywood or Bust.** US, 1956, C, 95 m. D: Frank Tashlin, MS: Walter Scharf, P: Paramount (Hal B. Wallis). Performer: Dean Martin.

*A Day in the Country; Hollywood or Bust; It Looks Like Love; Let's Be Friendly* W: Paul Francis Webster — M: Sammy Fain.

**562  The Hollywood Revue of 1929.** US, 1929, BW/C, 130 m. D: Charles F. Reisner, P: MGM (Harry Rapf). Vocal: Charles King for Conrad Nagel.

The song *Singin' in the Rain* was introduced here.

*For I'm the Queen* (Marie Dressler) WM: Andy Rice and Martin Broones / *Gotta Feelin' for You* (Joan Crawford, Paul Gibbons, The Biltmore Trio) W:

Jo Trent—M: Louis Alter / *I Never Knew I Could Do a Thing Like That* (Bessie Love, Boys) W: Joe Goodwin—M: Gus Edwards / *Low Down Rhythm* (Jane Purcell) W: Raymond Klages—M: Jesse Greer / *Marie, Polly and Bess* (Marie Dressler, Polly Moran, Bessie Love); *Minstrel Days* (Gus Edwards, Chorus); *Nobody But You* (Cliff Edwards); *Orange Blossom Time* (Charles King) W: Joe Goodwin—M: Gus Edwards / *Singin' in the Rain* (Cliff Edwards, The Rounders, The Brox Sisters); *Tommy Atkins on Parade* (Marion Davies) W: Arthur Freed—M: Nacio Herb Brown / *While Strolling Through the Park One Day* (Cliff Edwards, Gus Edwards, Polly Moran, Marie Dressler, Bessie Love) WM: Ed Haley and Robert A. Keiser / *Your Mother and Mine* (Charles King, Jack Benny, Karl Dane, George K. Arthur) W: Joe Goodwin—M: Gus Edwards / *You Were Meant for Me* (Conrad Nagel) W: Arthur Freed—M: Nacio Herb Brown.

**563 Honeysuckle Rose.** US, 1980, C, 119 m. D: Jerry Schatzberg, P: Warner (Sydney Pollack, Gene Taft). Alt. Title: On the Road Again.

*Angel Eyes* (Willie Nelson, Emmylou Harris) WM: Rodney Crowell / *Angel Flying Too Close to the Ground* (Willie Nelson); *Bloody Mary Morning* (Willie Nelson) WM: Willie Nelson / *Blue Eyes Crying in the Rain* (Willie Nelson) WM: Fred Rose / *Cotton Eyed Joe* (Johnny Gimble); *Fiddlin' Around* (Johnny Gimble) WM: Johnny Gimble / *Heaven or Hell* (Willie Nelson) WM: Willie Nelson / *I Don't Do Windows* (Hank Cochran) WM: Hank Cochran / *If You Could Touch Her at All* (Willie Nelson) WM: L. Clayton / *If You Want Me to Love You* (Amy Irving); *I Guess I've Come to Live Here in Your Eyes* (Willie Nelson); *It's Not Supposed to Be That Way* (Willie Nelson) WM: Willie Nelson / *Jumpin'* (Johnny Gimble, Chorus) WM: Johnny Gimble / *Lovin' Her Was Easier* (Dyan Cannon, Willie Nelson) WM: Kris Kristofferson / *Make the World Go Away* (Hank Cochran, Jeannie Seely) WM: Hank Cochran / *On the Road Again* (Willie Nelson); *Pick Up the Tempo* (Willie Nelson) WM: Willie Nelson / *A Song for You* (Willie Nelson) WM: L. Russell / *So You Think You're a Cowboy* (Emmylou Harris) WM: Hank Cochran and Willie Nelson / *Two Sides to Every Story* (Dyan Cannon, Chorus); *Uncloudy Day* (Willie Nelson, Dyan Cannon, Chorus) WM: Willie Nelson / *Whiskey River* (Willie Nelson) WM: J.B. Shinn III / *Working Man Blues* (Jody Payne) WM: Merle Haggard / *You Show Me Yours* (Willie Nelson, Amy Irving, Chorus) WM: Kris Kristofferson.

"Mr. Nelson's songs become even more of a high point than they should be when everything surrounding the musical numbers feels slack." —Janet Maslin, *The New York Times*.

**564 Honkey Tonk.** US, 1929, BW, 80 m. D: Lloyd Bacon, P: Warner. Performer: Sophie Tucker.

*He's a Good Man to Have Around; I'm Doin' What I'm Doin' for Love; I'm Feathering a Nest; I'm the Last of the Red Hot Mammas* W: Jack Yellen—M: Milton Ager / *Some of These Days* WM: Shelton Brooks.

**565 Honkytonk Man.** US, 1982, C, 122 m. D: Clint Eastwood, MS: Steve Dorff, P: Warner (Clint Eastwood).

*Honkytonk Man* (Marty Robbins, Chorus) WM: DeWayne Blackwell / *In the Jailhouse Now* (Marty Robbins, John Anderson, David Frizzell, Clint Eastwood) WM: Jimmie Rodgers / *No Sweeter Cheater Than You* (Clint Eastwood) WM: Mitchell Torok and Ramona Redd / *One Fiddle, Two Fiddle* (Ray Price, Chorus); *Please Surrender* (David Frizzell, Shelly West, Chorus) WM: John Durrill, Cliff Crofford, Snuff Garrett / *San Antonio Rose* (Ray Price, Chorus) WM: Bob Wills / *These Cotton Patch Blues* (John Anderson) WM: Cliff Crofford / *Turn the Pencil*

*Over* (Porter Wagoner, Chorus); *When I Sing About You* (Clint Eastwood, Chorus) WM: DeWayne Blackwell / *When the Blues Come Around This Evening* (Linda Hopkins) WM: John Durrill and Cliff Crofford.

**566  Horse Feathers.** US, 1932, BW, 68 m. D: Norman Z. McLeod, P: Paramount (Herman J. Mankiewicz).

*Ev'ryone Says "I Love You"* (Groucho Marx, Chico Marx, Zeppo Marx); *Whatever It Is I'm Against It* (Groucho Marx, Zeppo Marx) W: Bert Kalmar — M: Harry Ruby.

"The harp and piano numbers were repeated against the Marxes' personal wishes but by exhibitor demands to the studio. The piano is oke, but the harp reprise of *Everyone Says I Love You* substantiates the boys' opinion that it tends to slow up the comedy."
— *Variety.*

**567  Hotel.** US, 1967, C, 124 m. D: Richard Quine, MS: Johnny Keating, P: Warner (Wendell Mayes).

*This Year* (Carmen McRae) WM: Johnny Keating.

**568  The House Across the Bay.** US, 1940, BW, 86 m. D: Archie Mayo, MS: Werner Janssen, P: UA (Walter Wanger). Performer: Joan Bennett.

*I'll Be a Fool Again* WM: George R. Brown and Irving Actman / *I Still Love to Kiss You Goodnight* W: Walter Bullock — M: Harold Spina / *Walking My Chihuahua* WM: Sidney Clare, Nick Castle and Jule Styne / *You Made Me Fall in Love* WM: Al Siegel.

**569  House Calls.** US, 1978, C, 98 m. D: Howard Zieff, MS: Henry Mancini, P: Universal (Alex Winitsky, Arlene Sellers).

*On the Sunny Side of the Street* (Frankie Laine) W: Dorothy Fields — M: Jimmy McHugh / *Something* (The Beatles) WM: George Harrison.

**570  Houseboat.** US, 1958, C, 110 m. D: Melville Shavelson, MS: George Duning, P: Paramount (Jack Rose).

*Almost in Your Arms* (Sophia Loren); *Bing! Bang! Bong!* (Sophia Loren, Chorus) WM: Jay Livingston and Ray Evans.

**571  How Do I Love Thee?** US, 1970, C, 110 m. D: Michael Gordon, MS: Randy Sparks, P: ABC (Robert Enders, Everett Freeman).

*How Do I Love Thee?* (Randy Sparks) WM: Everett Freeman and Randy Sparks.

**572  How the West Was Won.** US, 1962, C, 155 m. D: Henry Hathaway, John Ford and George Marshall, MS: Alfred Newman, P: MGM (Bernard Smith).

*Battle Hymn of the Republic* (Chorus) W: Julia Ward Howe — M: William Steffe / *He's Linus' Boy* (Chorus) W: Ken Darby — M: Alfred Newman / *Home in the Meadow* (Debbie Reynolds, Chorus) W: Sammy Cahn — M: Unknown — Arr: Robert Emmett Dolan / *How the West Was Won* (Chorus) W: Ken Darby — M: Alfred Newman / *I'm Bound for the Promised Land* (Chorus) WM: Unknown / *On the Banks of the Sacramento* (Chorus) W: Ken Darby — M: Alfred Newman / *Raise a Ruckus Tonight* (Debbie Reynolds, Chorus); *What Was Your Name in the States?* (Debbie Reynolds) WM: Unknown — Arr: Johnny Mercer and Robert Emmett Dolan / *When Johnny Comes Marching Home* (Chorus) WM: Patrick S. Gilmore.

**573  How to Stuff a Wild Bikini.** US, 1965, C, 93 m. D: William Asher, P: AIP (James H. Nicholson, Samuel Z. Arkoff). GB Title: How to Fill a Wild Bikini.

*After the Party* (Chorus); *Better Be Ready* (Annette Funicello); *Follow Your Leader* (Harvey Lembeck, Chorus); *Give Her Lovin'* (The Kingsmen); *How About Us?* (Mickey Rooney, Chorus); *How to Stuff a Wild Bikini* (The Kingsmen); *I'm the Boy Next Door* (Harvey Lembeck); *Madison Avenue* (Mickey Rooney, Brian Donlevy); *The Perfect Boy* (Annette Funicello, Chorus);

*That's What I Call a Healthy Girl* (Chorus); *When Love Comes Swingin' Along* (Annette Funicello) WM: Guy Hemrick and Jerry Styner.

**574 How to Succeed in Business Without Really Trying.** US, 1967, C, 121 m. D: David Swift, MD: Nelson Riddle, P: Mirisch/UA (David Swift).

*Been a Long Day* (Robert Morse, Michele Lee, Rudy Vallee, Kay Reynolds, Anthony Teague, Maureen Arthur, Chorus); *Brotherhood of Man* (Robert Morse, Rudy Vallee, Ruth Kobart, Anthony Teague, Sammy Smith, Chorus); *The Company Way* (Robert Morse, Sammy Smith, Anthony Teague); *Gotta Stop That Man* (Chorus); *Grand Old Ivy* (Robert Morse, Rudy Vallee); *How To* (Robert Morse); *I Believe in You* (Michele Lee, Robert Morse); *Rosemary* (Robert Morse); *A Secretary Is Not a Toy* (John Myhers) WM: Frank Loesser.

"An entertaining, straightforward filming of the [1961] legituner, featuring many thesps in their stage roles. . . . Most of Frank Loesser's literate melodies have been retained." — *Variety*.

"David Swift has done nothing to diminish the wit, the sparkle and the zing of the musical show in transferring it into the movie." — Bosley Crowther, *The New York Times*.

**575 The Hucksters.** US, 1947, BW, 115 m. D: Jack Conway, MS: Lennie Hayton, P: MGM (Arthur Hornblow, Jr.). Vocal: Eileen Wilson for Ava Gardner.

*Don't Tell Me* (Ava Gardner) WM: Buddy Pepper.

**576 Humoresque.** US, 1946, BW, 125 m. D: Jean Negulesco, MD: Franz Waxman, P: Warner (Jerry Wald).

*Embraceable You* (Peg La Centra) W: Ira Gershwin—M: George Gershwin / *What Is This Thing Called Love?* (Peg La Centra); *You Do Something to Me* (Joan Crawford, Peg La Centra) WM: Cole Porter.

"Integration of music and drama ties the two together so tightly there is never a separation. Some 23 classical numbers are included, plus a number of pop pieces used as background for cafe sequences." — *Variety*.

**577 Hush, Hush, Sweet Charlotte.** US, 1965, BW, 133 m. D: Robert Aldrich, MS: Frank DeVol, P: TCF (Robert Aldrich).

*Hush, Hush, Sweet Charlotte* (Al Martino) W: Mack David—M: Frank DeVol.

**578 I Could Go On Singing.** GB, 1963, C, 99 m. D: Ronald Neame, MS: Mort Lindsey, P: UA (Lawrence Turman, Stuart Miller). Performer: Judy Garland.

*By Myself* W: Howard Dietz—M: Arthur Schwartz / *Hello, Bluebird* WM: Cliff Friend / *I Could Go On Singing* W: E.Y. Harburg—M: Harold Arlen / *It Never Was You* W: Maxwell Anderson—M: Kurt Weill.

**579 I Dood It!** US, 1943, BW, 102 m. D: Vincente Minnelli, MD: George Stoll, P: MGM (Jack Cummings). Orch: Jimmy Dorsey. GB Title: By Hook or by Crook.

*Jericho* (Lena Horne) W: Leo Robin—M: Richard Myers / *Star Eyes* (Helen O'Connell, Bob Eberly) WM: Don Raye and Gene de Paul / *Taking a Chance on Love* (Lena Horne) W: John Latouche and Ted Fetter—M: Vernon Duke.

**580 I Dream Too Much.** US, 1935, BW, 95 m. D: John Cromwell, MD: Max Steiner, P: RKO (Pandro S. Berman). Performer: Lily Pons.

*I Dream Too Much; I Got Love; I'm the Echo; The Jockey on the Carousel* W: Dorothy Fields—M: Jerome Kern.

**581 I Love Melvin.** US, 1953, C, 76 m. D: Don Weis, MD: George Stoll, P: MGM (George Wells).

*I Wanna Wander* (Donald O'Connor); *A Lady Loves* (Debbie Reynolds); *Life Has Its Funny Little Ups and Downs* (Noreen Corcoran); *Saturday Afternoon Before the Game* (Chorus); *We Have

*Never Met as Yet* (Debbie Reynolds, Donald O'Connor) W: Mack Gordon—M: Josef Myrow.

**582　I Married an Angel.** US, 1942, BW, 84 m. D: W.S. Van Dyke II, P: MGM (Hunt Stromberg).

*Aloha Oe* (Jeanette MacDonald) WM: Queen Liluokalani / *But What of Truth* (Jeanette MacDonald); *Hey Butcher* (Nelson Eddy) W: Robert Wright and George "Chet" Forrest—M: Herbert Stothart / *I'll Tell the Man in the Street* (Jeanette MacDonald, Nelson Eddy); *I Married an Angel* (Jeanette MacDonald, Nelson Eddy) W: Lorenz Hart—M: Richard Rodgers / *May I Present the Girl?* (Edward Everett Horton); *Now You've Met the Angel* (Nelson Eddy) W: Robert Wright and George "Chet" Forrest—M: Herbert Stothart / *Spring Is Here* (Jeanette MacDonald, Nelson Eddy) W: Lorenz Hart—M: Richard Rodgers / *There Comes a Time* (Edward Everett Horton) W: Robert Wright and George "Chet" Forrest—M: Herbert Stothart / *Tira Lira La* (Chorus) W: Robert Wright and George "Chet" Forrest—M: Richard Rodgers / *To Count Palaffi* (Edward Everett Horton) W: Robert Wright and George "Chet" Forrest—M: Herbert Stothart / *A Twinkle in Your Eye* (Jeanette MacDonald, Binnie Barnes) W: Lorenz Hart, Robert Wright and George "Chet" Forrest—M: Richard Rodgers.

"Mr. Eddy and Miss MacDonald are just not geared to toss a gossamer fable like this one about in the air. Granted they can sing—and they do so, in full voice, loud enough to wake the dead." —Bosley Crowther, *The New York Times.*

**583　I Ought to Be in Pictures.** US, 1982, C, 107 m. D: Herbert Ross, MS: Marvin Hamlisch, P: TCF (Herbert Ross, Neil Simon).

*One Hello* (Dinah Manoff) W: Carole Bayer Sager—M: Marvin Hamlisch.

**584　I Wanna Hold Your Hand.** US, 1978, C, 104 m. D: Robert Zemeckis, MS: Meredith Wilson, P: Universal (Tamara Asseyev, Alex Rose). Performers: The Beatles.

*Boys* WM: Luther Dixon and Wes Farrell / *Do You Want to Know a Secret?; From Me to You; I Saw Her Standing There; I Wanna Be Your Man; I Want to Hold Your Hand; Love Me Do; Misery* WM: John Lennon and Paul McCartney / *Money* WM: Janie Bradford and Berry Gordy, Jr. / *Please Mr. Postman* WM: Brian Holland, Robert Bateman and Freddy C. Gorman / *Please Please Me; P.S. I Love You; She Loves You; Thank You Girl; There's a Place* WM: John Lennon and Paul McCartney / *Till There Was You* WM: Meredith Willson / *Twist and Shout* WM: Bert Russell [Bert Berns] and Phil Medley.

**585　I Was an American Spy.** US, 1951, BW, 85 m. D: Lesley Selander, P: AA (David Diamond).

*Because of You* (Ann Dvorak) W: Arthur Hammerstein—M: Dudley Wilkinson.

**586　Ice Castles.** US, 1979, C, 109 m. D: Donald Wrye, MS: Marvin Hamlisch, P: Columbia (John Kemeny).

*Looking Through the Eyes of Love* (Melissa Manchester) W: Carole Bayer Sager—M: Marvin Hamlisch.

**587　Iceland.** US, 1942, BW, 79 m. D: H. Bruce Humberstone, P: TCF (William LeBaron). Orch: Sammy Kaye. GB Title: Katina.

*I Like a Military Tune* (Sonja Henie); *It's the Lover's Knot* (Jack Oakie, John Payne, Sonja Henie); *Let's Bring New Glory to Old Glory* (Sonja Henie); *There Will Never Be Another You* (Joan Merrill); *You Can't Say No to a Soldier* (Joan Merrill) W: Mack Gordon—M: Harry Warren.

**588　Idiot's Delight.** US, 1939, BW, 105 m. D: Clarence Brown, MS: Herbert Stothart, P: MGM (Hunt Stromberg).

*Abide with Me* (Clark Gable,

Norma Shearer) W: Henry Francis Lyte—M: William Henry Monk / *By the Light of the Silvery Moon* (Clark Gable, Chorus) W: Edward Madden— M: Gus Edwards / *How Strange* (Norma Shearer) W: Gus Kahn—M: Herbert Stothart and Earl K. Brent / *Puttin' on the Ritz* (Clark Gable, Chorus) WM: Irving Berlin.

**589 The Idolmaker.** US, 1980, C, 116 m. D: Taylor Hackford, P: UA (Gene Kirkwood, Howard W. Koch, Jr.). Vocals: Jesse Frederick for Paul Land.

*Baby* (Peter Gallagher); *A Boy and a Girl* (The Sweet Inspirations); *Come and Get It* (Nino Tempo); *Here Is My Love* (Paul Land); *However Dark the Night* (Peter Gallagher); *I Believe It Can Be Done* (Ray Sharkey); *I Can't Tell* (Colleen Fitzpatrick); *I Know Where You're Goin'* (Nino Tempo); *Oo-Wee Baby* (Darlene Love); *Sweet Little Lover* (Paul Land) WM: Jeff Barry.

**590 If a Man Answers.** US, 1962, C, 102 m. D: Henry Levin, MS: Hans Salter, P: Universal (Ross Hunter). Performer: Bobby Darin.

*If a Man Answers; A True, True Love* WM: Bobby Darin.

**591 I'll Cry Tomorrow.** US, 1955, BW, 117 m. D: Daniel Mann, MS: Alex North, P: MGM (Lawrence Weingarten). Performer: Susan Hayward.

*Happiness Is a Thing Called Joe* W: E.Y. Harburg—M: Harold Arlen / *I'm Sitting on Top of the World* W: Sam M. Lewis and Joe Young—M: Ray Henderson / *Sing, You Sinners* W: Sam Coslow—M: W. Franke Harling / *When the Red, Red Robin Comes Bob, Bob, Bobbin' Along* WM: Harry M. Woods.

**592 I'll Get By.** US, 1950, C, 83 m. D: Richard Sale, MD: Lionel Newman, P: TCF (William Perlberg). Orch: Harry James.

*Deep in the Heart of Texas* (Dennis Day) W: June Hershey—Don Swander / *I'll Get By* (Dennis Day, June Haver, Gloria De Haven) W: Roy Turk—M: Fred E. Ahlert / *It's Been a Long, Long Time* (Dan Dailey, June Haver, Gloria De Haven) W: Sammy Cahn—M: Jule Styne / *I've Got the World on a String* (June Haver, Gloria De Haven) W: Ted Koehler—M: Harold Arlen / *Once in a While* (Vocal Quintet) W: Bud Green—M: Michael Edwards / *Taking a Chance on Love* (June Haver, Gloria De Haven) W: John Latouche and Ted Fetter—M: Vernon Duke / *There Will Never Be Another You* (Dennis Day) W: Mack Gordon—M: Harry Warren / *The Yankee Doodle Blues* (June Haver, Gloria De Haven) W: Irving Caesar and B.G. De Sylva—M: George Gershwin / *You Make Me Feel So Young* (Dennis Day) W: Mack Gordon—M: Josef Myrow.

"In this cavalcade of songs, the years from 1939 to 1945 slip by rather gaily. ... [It] adds up to a nice, light entertainment, a sort of disk jockey show with colored pictures." —Thomas M. Pryor, *The New York Times*.

**593 I'll Remember April.** US, 1945, BW, 63 m. D: Harold Young, P: Universal (Gene Lewis).

*Hittin' the Beach Tonite* (Gloria Jean) WM: Marty Roberts and Chic Dornish / *I'll Remember April* (Gloria Jean, Kirby Grant) W: Don Raye and Pat Johnston—M: Gene de Paul.

**594 I'll See You in My Dreams.** US, 1951, BW, 110 m. D: Michael Curtiz, MD: Ray Heindorf, P: Warner (Louis F. Edelman).

*Ain't We Got Fun?* (Doris Day, Danny Thomas, Chorus) W: Gus Kahn and Raymond B. Egan—M: Richard A. Whiting / *Carolina in the Morning* (Patrice Wymore) W: Gus Kahn—M: Walter Donaldson / *I'll See You in My Dreams* (Doris Day, Danny Thomas, Chorus); *It Had to Be You* (Doris Day, Danny Thomas) W: Gus Kahn—M: Isham Jones / *I Wish I Had a Girl* (Doris Day, Chorus) W: Gus Kahn—M: Grace Le Boy Kahn / *Love*

*Me or Leave Me* (Patrice Wymore); *Makin' Whoopee* (Doris Day, Danny Thomas) W: Gus Kahn—M: Walter Donaldson / *Memories* (Danny Thomas) W: Gus Kahn—M: Egbert Van Alstyne / *My Buddy* (Doris Day) W: Gus Kahn—M: Walter Donaldson / *Nobody's Sweetheart* (Doris Day, Danny Thomas) WM: Gus Kahn, Ernie Erdman, Billy Meyers and Elmer Schoebel / *No, No, Nora* (Doris Day) WM: Gus Kahn, Ted Fiorito and Ernie Erdman / *The One I Love Belongs to Somebody Else* (Doris Day, Danny Thomas) W: Gus Kahn—M: Isham Jones / *Pretty Baby* (Doris Day, Danny Thomas) WM: Gus Kahn, Egbert Van Alstyne and Tony Jackson / *Swingin' Down the Lane* (Doris Day, Danny Thomas, Children) W: Gus Kahn—M: Isham Jones / *Toot, Toot, Tootsie!* (Doris Day) WM: Gus Kahn, Ernie Erdman and Dan Russo / *Ukulele Lady* (Chorus) W: Gus Kahn and Raymond B. Egan—M: Richard A. Whiting / *Yes Sir, That's My Baby* (Doris Day, Danny Thomas, Children) W: Gus Kahn—M: Walter Donaldson.

"It's that Danny Thomas ... who lifts and carries off this show. You'll be hearing the singing of his praises as much as the words of Gus Kahn." —Bosley Crowther, *The New York Times.*

**595  I'll Take Romance.** US, 1937, BW, 85 m. D: Edward H. Griffith, MD: M.W. Stoloff and Isaac Van Grove, P: Columbia (Everett Riskin). Performer: Grace Moore.

*A Frangesa* WM: Milton Drake and Marie Costa / *I'll Take Romance* W: Oscar Hammerstein II—M: Ben Oakland.

**596  I'll Take Sweden.** US, 1965, C, 96 m. D: Frederick de Cordova, MS: Jimmie Haskell, P: UA (Edward Small).

*The Bells Keep Ringing* (Frankie Avalon) W: Bobby Beverly—M: By Dunham / *Give It to Me* (Tuesday Weld) W: Jimmie Haskell—M: By Dunham / *I'll Take Sweden* (Frankie Avalon) WM: Diane Lampert and Ken

Lauber / *Nothing Can Compare with You* (Bob Hope) W: Bobby Beverly—M: By Dunham / *Tell Me, Tell Me* (Chorus) W: Jimmie Haskell—M: By Dunham / *There'll Be Rainbows Again* (Frankie Avalon) W: Bobby Beverly—M: By Dunham / *Would Ya Like My Last Name* (Frankie Avalon) WM: Diane Lampert and Ken Lauber.

**597  I'm No Angel.** US, 1933, BW, 87 m. D: Wesley Ruggles, P: Paramount (William LeBaron). Performer: Mae West.

*I'm No Angel; I Want You, I Need You; No One Loves Me Like That Dallas Man of Mine; They Call Me Sister Honky Tonk* WM: Gladys Du Bois, Ben Ellison and Harvey O. Brooks.

"Every now and again West bursts into a song ... but primarily she plays a lion tamer, not a songstress." —*Variety.*

**598  Imagine: John Lennon.** US, 1988, C, 103 m. D: Andrew Solt, P: Warner. Performers: John Lennon; The Beatles.

*The Ballad of John and Yoko* WM: John Lennon and Paul McCartney / *Beautiful Boy* WM: John Lennon / *A Day in the Life; Don't Let Me Down; Help!* WM: John Lennon and Paul McCartney / *Imagine* WM: John Lennon / *In My Life; Julia* WM: John Lennon and Paul McCartney / *Mother* WM: John Lennon / *Revolution* WM: John Lennon and Paul McCartney / *Stand by Me* WM: Ben E. King, Jerry Leiber and Mike Stoller / *Starting Over* WM: John Lennon / *Strawberry Fields Forever* WM: John Lennon and Paul McCartney / *Twist and Shout* WM: Bert Russell and Phil Medley / *Woman* WM: John Lennon.

**599  Imitation of Life.** US, 1959, C, 124 m. D: Douglas Sirk, MS: Frank Skinner, P: Universal (Ross Hunter).

*Imitation of Life* (Nat King Cole) W: Paul Francis Webster—M: Sammy Fain / *Trouble of the World* (Mahalia Jackson) WM: Unknown.

**600 In Gay Madrid.** US, 1930, BW, 78 m. D: Robert Z. Leonard, P: MGM. Performer: Ramon Novarro.

*Dark Night* W: Clifford Grey—M: Herbert Stothart / *Into My Heart* W: Roy Turk—M: Fred E. Ahlert / *Santiago; Smile While We May* W: Roy Turk—M: Clifford Grey.

**601 In Old Chicago.** US, 1938, BW, 95 m. D: Henry King, MD: Louis Silvers, P: TCF (Darryl F. Zanuck, Kenneth MacGowan).

*Carry Me Back to Old Virginny* (Alice Faye, Tyler Brooke, Male Quartet, Chorus) WM: James A. Bland / *I'll Never Let You Cry* (Alice Faye) W: Sidney D. Mitchell—M: Lew Pollack / *In Old Chicago* (Alice Faye, Chorus) W: Mack Gordon—M: Harry Revel / *I've Taken a Fancy to You* (Alice Faye) W: Sidney D. Mitchell—M: Lew Pollack / *Sweet Genevieve* (Alice Brady, Tyrone Power, Don Ameche, Tom Brown, June Storey) WM: George Cooper and Henry Tucker / *Take a Dip in the Sea* (Tyler Brooke, Chorus) W: Sidney D. Mitchell—M: Lew Pollack.

**602 In Person.** US, 1935, BW, 85 m. D: William A. Seiter, MS: Roy Webb, P: RKO (Pandro S. Berman). Performer: Ginger Rogers.

*Don't Mention Love to Me; I Got a New Lease on Life; Out of Sight, Out of Mind* W: Dorothy Fields—M: Oscar Levant.

**603 In the Good Old Summertime.** US, 1949, C, 102 m. D: Robert Z. Leonard, MD: George Stoll, P: MGM (Joe Pasternak).

*I Don't Care* (Judy Garland) W: Jean Lenox—M: Harry O. Sutton / *In the Good Old Summertime* (Spring Byington, Van Johnson, S.Z. Sakall, Chorus) W: Ren Shields—M: George Evans / *Meet Me Tonight in Dreamland* (Judy Garland) W: Beth Slater Whitson—M: Leo Friedman / *Merry Christmas* (Judy Garland) W: Janice Torre— M: Fred Spielman / *Play That Barber Shop Chord* (Judy Garland, Male Quartet) W: William Tracey and Ballard Mac-

Donald—M: Lewis F. Muir / *Put Your Arms Around Me, Honey* (Judy Garland, Van Johnson) W: Junie McCree—M: Albert von Tilzer / *Wait Till the Sun Shines, Nellie* (Male Quartet) W: Andrew B. Sterling—M: Harry von Tilzer.

"Miss Garland is fresh as a daisy. ... her slightly amusing and free-wheeling interpretation of *I Don't Care* brought a burst of applause, which is not a common tribute in a movie house." —Thomas M. Pryor, *The New York Times.*

**604 In the Heat of the Night.** US, 1967, C, 109 m. D: Norman Jewison, MS: Quincy Jones, P: UA (Walter Mirisch).

*In the Heat of the Night* (Ray Charles) W: Marilyn Bergman and Alan Bergman—M: Quincy Jones.

**605 In the Mood.** US, 1987, C, 99 m. D: Phil Alden Robinson, MS: Ralph Burns, P: Kings Road/Lorimar (Gary Adelson, Karen Mack).

*Baby Blues* (Beverly D'Angelo) WM: Ralph Burns / *Dream* (Beverly D'Angelo) WM: Johnny Mercer / *In the Mood* (Jennifer Holliday) WM: Andy Razaf and Joseph Garland.

**606 In the Navy.** US, 1941, BW, 86 m. D: Arthur Lubin, P: Universal (Alex Gottlieb).

*Give Me Some Skin My Friend* (The Andrews Sisters); *Hula Balua* (The Andrews Sisters); *A Sailor's Life* (Lou Costello, Dick Powell, Dick Foran, Chorus); *Starlight, Starbright* (Dick Powell, The Andrews Sisters); *We're in the Navy* (Dick Powell, The Andrews Sisters, Chorus); *You're Off to See the World* (The Andrews Sisters) W: Don Raye—M: Gene de Paul.

**607 Incendiary Blonde.** US, 1945, C, 113 m. D: George Marshall, MS: Robert Emmett Dolan, P: Paramount (Joseph Sistrom).

*The Darktown Strutters' Ball* (Maurice Rocco) WM: Shelton Brooks / *Ida, Sweet as Apple Cider* (Unbilled Singer) W: Eddie Leonard—M: Eddie Munson /*It Had to Be You* (Betty Hutton)

W: Gus Kahn—M: Isham Jones /
*Margie* (Betty Hutton) W: Benny
Davis—M: Con Conrad and J. Russel
Robinson / *Oh by Jingo, Oh by Gee* (Betty Hutton, Chorus) W: Lew Brown—
M: Albert von Tilzer / *Ragtime Cowboy
Joe* (Betty Hutton) W: Grant Clarke—
M: Maurice Abrahams and Lewis F.
Muir / *Row, Row, Row* (Betty Hutton)
W: William Jerome—M: James V.
Monaco / *Sweet Genevieve* (Barry Fitzgerald, Chorus) WM: George Cooper
and Henry Tucker / *What Do You Want
to Make Those Eyes at Me For?* (Betty
Hutton) WM: Joseph McCarthy,
Howard Johnson and James V.
Monaco.

"As tuneful as it is colorful." —
Thomas M. Pryor, *The New York Times*.

**608   Inherit the Wind.** US,
1960, BW, 127 m. D: Stanley Kramer,
MS: Ernest Gold, P: UA (Stanley
Kramer).

*Give Me That Old Time Religion*
(Leslie Uggams) WM: Unknown.

**609   The Inn of the Sixth Happiness.** GB, 1958, C, 158 m. D: Mark
Robson, MS: Malcolm Arnold, P:
TCF (Buddy Adler).

*The Children's Marching Song* (Ingrid Bergman, Chorus) WM: Malcolm
Arnold.

**610   Innocents of Paris.** US,
1929, BW, 69 m. D: Richard Wallace,
P: Paramount (Jesse L. Lasky). Performer: Maurice Chevalier.

*It's a Habit of Mine; Louise; On Top
of the World Alone* W: Leo Robin—M:
Richard A. Whiting / *Valentine* WM:
Herbert Reynolds and Henri Christine
/ *Wait 'Til You See Ma Cherie* W: Leo
Robin—M: Richard A. Whiting.

"Without Chevalier this latest
speciman of audible films would be a
sad affair." —Mordaunt Hall, *The New
York Times*.

**611   Inside Daisy Clover.** US,
1965, C, 128 m. D: Robert Mulligan,
MS: Andre Previn, P: Warner (Alan J.
Pakula). Vocal: Jackie Ward for Natalie
Wood.

*You're Gonna Hear from Me* (Natalie Wood) W: Dory Previn—M: Andre Previn.

**612   The Inspector General.**
US, 1949, C, 102 m. D: Henry Koster,
MD: Johnny Green, P: Warner (Jerry
Wald). Performer: Danny Kaye. Alt.
Title: Happy Times.

*Brodny; Gypsy Drinking Song;
Happy Times; The Inspector General;
Lonely Heart; The Medicine Show;
Onward Onward; Soliloquy for Three
Heads* WM: Sylvia Fine and Johnny
Mercer.

"Especially in his performance of
the several musical turns that are
carefully spotted through the picture
does Mr. Kaye sparkle and shine." —
Bosley Crowther, *The New York Times*.

**613   International House.** US,
1933, BW, 70 m. D: A. Edward Sutherland, P: Paramount. Orch: Cab Calloway.

*My Bluebird's Singing the Blues*
(Baby Rose Marie) W: Leo Robin —M:
Ralph Rainger / *Reefer Man* (Cab Calloway) W: Andy Razaf—M: J. Russel
Robinson / *She Was a China Teacup and
He Was Just a Mug* (Sterling Holloway);
*Thank Heaven for You* (Rudy Vallee) W:
Leo Robin—M: Ralph Rainger.

**614   Interrupted Melody.** US,
1955, C, 106 m. D: Curtis Bernhardt,
MD: Walter Du Cloux, P: MGM
(Jack Cummings). Vocals: Eileen Farrell for Eleanor Parker.

*Over the Rainbow* (Eleanor Parker)
W: E.Y. Harburg—M: Harold Arlen /
*Waltzing Matilda* (Eleanor Parker,
Chorus) W: A.B. Paterson—M: Marie
Cowan.

**615   Irene.** US, 1940, BW/C,
104 m. D: Herbert Wilcox, MD: Anthony Collins, P: RKO (Herbert Wilcox). Orch: Johnny Long.

*Alice Blue Gown* (Anna Neagle,
Martha Tilton, The Dandridge Sisters); *Castle of Dreams* (Chorus); *Irene*
(Chorus); *You've Got Me Out on a Limb*
(Anna Neagle, Stuart Robertson) W:
Joseph McCarthy—M: Harry Tierney.

"Back in 1919-20 a smash musical comedy and then in 1926 a hit First National film starring Colleen Moore, 'Irene' emerges this time as dated celluloidia. . . . *Castle in Your Dreams, Gown* and the title song are still very worthy tunes, from the original score." — *Variety.*

**616   Irish Eyes Are Smiling.** US, 1944, C, 90 m. D: Gregory Ratoff, MD: Alfred Newman and Charles Henderson, P: TCF (Damon Runyon).

*Be My Little Baby Bumble Bee* (June Haver, Chorus) W: Stanley Murphy — M: Henry I. Marshall / *Dear Little Boy of Mine* (Blanche Thebom, Dick Haymes) W: J. Keirn Brennan — M: Ernest R. Ball / *I Don't Need a Million Dollars* (Dick Haymes) W: Mack Gordon — M: James V. Monaco / *I'll Forget You* (Dick Haymes) W: Annelu Burns — M: Ernest R. Ball / *Let the Rest of the World Go By* (Dick Haymes, Male Quartet); *A Little Bit of Heaven* (Leonard Warren) W: J. Keirn Brennan — M: Ernest R. Ball / *Mother Machree* (Blanche Thebom, Chorus) W: Rida Johnson Young — M: Chauncey Olcott and Ernest R. Ball / *Strut Miss Lizzie* (June Haver) WM: Henry Creamer and Turner Layton / *When Irish Eyes Are Smiling* (Dick Haymes) W: Chauncey Olcott and George Graff, Jr. — M: Ernest R. Ball.

"You'd better just count on this one for the songs — and also for little Miss Haver, if you've an eye for a pretty blonde chick." — Bosley Crowther, *The New York Times.*

**617   Istanbul.** US, 1957, C, 84 m. D: Joseph Pevney, MS: Joseph Gershenson, P: Universal (Albert J. Cohen). Performer: Nat King Cole.

*I Was a Little Too Lonely* WM: Jay Livingston and Ray Evans / *When I Fall in Love* W: Edward Heyman — M: Victor Young.

**618   It Happened at the World's Fair.** US, 1963, C, 105 m. D: Norman Taurog, MS: Leith Stevens, P: MGM (Ted Richmond). MB: The

Jordanaires; The Mellow Men. Performer: Elvis Presley.

*Beyond the Bend* WM: Fred Wise, Ben Weisman and Dolores Fuller / *Cotton Candy Land* WM: Ruth Batchelor and Bob Roberts / *Happy Ending* (Elvis Presley, Joan O'Brien) WM: Ben Weisman and Sid Wayne / *How Would You Like to Be* (Elvis Presley, Vicky Tiu) WM: Ben Raleigh and Mark Barkan / *I'm Falling in Love Tonight* WM: Don Robertson / *One Broken Heart for Sale* WM: Otis Blackwell and Winfield Scott / *Relax; Take Me to the Fair* WM: Sid Tepper and Roy C. Bennett / *They Remind Me Too Much of You* WM: Don Robertson / *A World of Our Own* WM: Bill Giant, Bernie Baum and Florence Kaye.

**619   It Happened in Brooklyn.** US, 1947, BW, 105 m. D: Richard Whorf, MS: Johnny Green, P: MGM (Jack Cummings).

Playing the piano offscreen was a 17-year-old newcomer to the music department at MGM named Andre Previn.

*The Brooklyn Bridge* (Frank Sinatra); *I Believe* (Frank Sinatra, Jimmy Durante, Billy Roy); *It's the Same Old Dream* (Frank Sinatra, Chorus); *The Song's Gotta Come from the Heart* (Frank Sinatra, Jimmy Durante); *Time After Time* (Frank Sinatra, Kathryn Grayson); *Whose Baby Are You?* (Frank Sinatra, Peter Lawford) W: Sammy Cahn — M: Jule Styne.

"Interspersed in the story are a group of six new tunes from the able pianos of Sammy Cahn and Jule Styne." — *Variety.*

**620   It Happened One Night.** US, 1934, BW, 105 m. D: Frank Capra, MD: Louis Silvers, P: Columbia (Frank Capra).

*The Man on the Flying Trapeze* (Clark Gable, Chorus) W: George Leybourne — M: Alfred Lee.

**621   It Happened to Jane.** US, 1959, C, 98 m. D: Richard Quine, MS: George Duning, P: Columbia (Richard

Quine). Alt. Title: Twinkle and Shine.
Performer: Doris Day.

*Be Prepared* W: Richard Quine—
M: Fred Karger / *It Happened to Jane*
WM: Joe Lubin and I.J. Roth / *Twinkle
and Shine* WM: By Dunham.

**622   It Should Happen to You.**
US, 1954, BW, 81 m. D: George
Cukor, MS: Frederick Hollander, P:
Columbia (Fred Kohlmar).

*Let's Fall in Love* (Judy Holliday,
Jack Lemmon) W: Ted Koehler—M:
Harold Arlen.

**623   It's a Great Feeling.** US,
1949, C, 85 m. D: David Butler, MS:
Ray Heindorf, P: Warner (Alex Gottlieb). Orch: Ray Heindorf.

*At the Cafe Rendezvous* (Doris
Day); *Blame My Absent-Minded Heart*
(Doris Day, Dennis Morgan); *Fiddle
Dee Dee* (Quartet); *Give Me a Song with
a Beautiful Melody* (Jack Carson); *It's a
Great Feeling* (Doris Day, Chorus);
*That Was a Big Fat Lie* (Doris Day,
Jack Carson); *There's Nothing Rougher
Than Love* (Doris Day) W: Sammy
Cahn—M: Jule Styne.

**624   It's Always Fair Weather.**
US, 1955, C, 102 m. D: Gene Kelly
and Stanley Donen, MD: Andre
Previn, P: MGM (Arthur Freed). Vo-
cals: Carole Richards for Cyd Charisse;
Jud Conlin for Michael Kidd.

*Baby, You Knock Me Out* (Cyd
Charisse, Chorus) W: Betty Comden
and Adolph Green—M: Andre Previn
/ *Blue Danube* (Gene Kelly, Dan
Dailey, Michael Kidd) W: Betty Com-
den and Adolph Green—M: Johann
Strauss / *I Like Myself* (Gene Kelly);
*March, March* (Gene Kelly, Dan
Dailey, Michael Kidd) W: Betty Com-
den and Adolph Green—M: Andre
Previn / *Music Is Better Than Words*
(Dolores Gray) W: Roger Edens—M:
Andre Previn / *Once Upon a Time*
(Gene Kelly, Dan Dailey, Michael
Kidd); *Situation-Wise* (Dan Dailey);
*Stillman's Gym* (Lou Lubin, Chorus);
*Thanks a Lot, But No Thanks* (Dolores
Gray); *Time for Parting* (Gene Kelly,

Dan Dailey, Michael Kidd) W: Betty
Comden and Adolph Green—M: Andre Previn.

"A delightful musical satire." —
*Variety.*

**625   It's Love Again.** GB, 1936,
BW, 83 m. D: Victor Saville, P: Gaumont (Michael Balcon).

*I Nearly Let Love Go Slipping
Through My Fingers* (Jessie Matthews,
Chorus) WM: Harry M. Woods / *It's
Love Again* (Jessie Matthews); *I've Got
to Dance My Way to Heaven* (Jessie
Matthews, Sonnie Hale, Robert Young,
Chorus) WM: Sam Coslow / *Tony's in
Town* (Male Singers) WM: Harry M.
Woods.

"The score . . . is undistinguished,
with the exception of the theme song
. . . which is tuneful and is excellently
sung by Miss Matthews." —Frank S.
Nugent, *The New York Times.*

**626   It's Only Money.** US, 1962,
BW, 84 m. D: Frank Tashlin, MS:
Walter Scharf, P: Paramount (Paul
Jones).

*Isn't It Romantic?* (Mae Questel)
W: Lorenz Hart—M: Richard Rodgers.

**627   Jacques Brel Is Alive and
Well and Living in Paris.** US, 1975,
C, 98 m. D: Denis Heroux, P: Ameri-
can Film Theatre.

*Alone* (Joe Masiell); *Amsterdam*
(Mort Shuman); *Bachelor's Dance* (Joe
Masiell); *Brussels* (Elly Stone, Mort
Shuman, Joe Masiell); *The Bulls* (Joe
Masiell); *Carousel* (Elly Stone); *The
Desperate Ones* (Elly Stone, Mort Shu-
man, Joe Masiell); *Funeral Tango* (Mort
Shuman); *If We Only Have Love* (Elly
Stone, Mort Shuman, Joe Masiell); *I
Loved* (Elly Stone); *Jackie* (Mort Shu-
man); *The Last Supper* (Elly Stone,
Mort Shuman, Joe Masiell); *Madeleine*
(Shawn Elliot, Judy Lander, Joseph
Neal, Annette Perrone); *Marathon* (Elly
Stone, Mort Shuman, Joe Masiell);
*Marieke* (Elly Stone); *Mathilde* (Mort
Shuman); *Middle Class* (Mort Shuman,
Joe Masiell); *My Childhood* (Elly
Stone); *Ne Me Quitte Pas* (Jacques

Brel); *Next* (Joe Masiell); *Old Folks* (Elly Stone); *Song for Old Lovers* (Elly Stone); *Sons of* . . . (Elly Stone); *The Statue* (Joe Masiell); *The Taxicab* (Mort Shuman); *Timid Frieda* (Elly Stone) Eng. W: Eric Blau and Mort Shuman—French WM: Jacques Brel.

**628  Jailhouse Rock.** US, 1957, BW, 96 m. D: Richard Thorpe, MD: Jeff Alexander, P: MGM (Pandro S. Berman). Performer: Elvis Presley.

*Baby, I Don't Care* WM: Jerry Leiber and Mike Stoller / *Don't Leave Me Now* WM: Aaron Schroeder and Ben Weisman / *I Want to Be Free;* *Jailhouse Rock* WM: Jerry Leiber and Mike Stoller / *One More Day* (Mickey Shaughnessy) WM: Sid Tepper and Roy C. Bennett / *Treat Me Nice* WM: Jerry Leiber and Mike Stoller / *Young and Beautiful* WM: Aaron Schroeder and Abner Silver.

"This time most of his singing can actually be understood." —Howard Thompson, *The New York Times.*

**629  Jam Session.** US, 1944, BW, 77 m. D: Charles Barton, P: Columbia (Irving Briskin). Orch: Louis Armstrong; Duke Ellington; Glen Gray; Teddy Powell; Charlie Barnet; Alvino Rey; Jan Garber.

*Brazil* (Nan Wynn) Eng. W: Bob Russell—M: Ary Barroso / *I Can't Give You Anything But Love, Baby* (Louis Armstrong) W: Dorothy Fields—M: Jimmy McHugh / *I Lost My Sugar in Salt Lake City* (Female Singer) WM: Leon Rene and Johnny Lange / *It Started All Over Again* (The Pied Pipers) W: Bill Carey—M: Carl Fischer / *Murder, He Says* (Female Singer, Chorus) W: Frank Loesser—M: Jimmy McHugh / *St. Louis Blues* (Male Singer) WM: W.C. Handy / *Vict'ry Polka* (Ann Miller, Chorus) W: Sammy Cahn—M: Jule Styne.

**630  The Jazz Singer.** US, 1927, BW, 89 m. D: Alan Crosland, MD: Louis Silvers, P: Warner (Darryl F. Zanuck). Vocal: Joseph Diskay for Warner Oland. Performer: Al Jolson.

The first full-length talking picture released to the public utilized a synchronized sound system known as Vitaphone.

*Blue Skies* WM: Irving Berlin / *Dirty Hands, Dirty Face* W: Edgar Leslie, Grant Clarke and Al Jolson—M: James V. Monaco / *Kol Nidre* (Al Jolson, Warner Oland) WM: Unknown / *Mother of Mine, I Still Have You* W: Grant Clarke—M: Louis Silvers and Al Jolson / *My Gal Sal* (Bobby Gordon) WM: Paul Dresser / *My Mammy* W: Sam M. Lewis and Joe Young—M: Walter Donaldson / *Toot, Toot, Tootsie!* WM: Gus Kahn, Ernie Erdman and Dan Russo / *Waiting for the Robert E. Lee* (Bobby Gordon) W: L. Wolfe Gilbert—M: Lewis F. Muir / *Yahrzeit* (Cantor Joseph Rosenblatt) WM: Unknown.

"The combination of the religious heart interest story and Jolson's singing *Kol Nidre* in a synagog while his father is dying and two *Mammy* lyrics as his mother stands in the wings of the theatre, and later as she sits in the front row, carries abundant power and appeal." —*Variety.*

"Mr. Jolson's persuasive vocal efforts were received with rousing applause. . . . [I]n the expression of song the Vitaphone vitalizes the production enormously." —*The New York Times.*

**631  The Jazz Singer.** US, 1953, C, 107 m. D: Michael Curtiz, P: Warner (Louis F. Edelman). MB: Chorus. Performer: Danny Thomas.

*The Birth of the Blues* W: B.G. De Sylva and Lew Brown—M: Ray Henderson / *Breezin' Along with the Breeze* WM: Haven Gillespie, Seymour Simons and Richard A. Whiting / *Hush-A-Bye* W: Jerry Seelen—M: Sammy Fain / *If I Could Be with You One Hour Tonight* WM: Henry Creamer and Jimmy Johnson / *I Hear the Music Now* (Danny Thomas, Peggy Lee) W: Jerry Seelen—M: Sammy Fain / *I'll String Along with You* W: Al Dubin—M: Harry Warren / *I'm Looking Over a Four Leaf Clover* W: Mort Dixon—M: Harry

M. Woods / *Just One of Those Things* (Peggy Lee) WM: Cole Porter / *Kol Nidre* WM: Unknown—Arr: Norman Luboff / *Living the Life I Love* (Danny Thomas, Peggy Lee) W: Jerry Seelen— M: Sammy Fain / *Lover* (Peggy Lee) W: Lorenz Hart—M: Richard Rodgers / *Oh Moon* W: Jerry Seelen—M: Sammy Fain / *This Is a Very Special Day* (Peggy Lee) WM: Peggy Lee.

"Warner's remake of Al Jolson's 1927 Vitaphone film hit is still sentimental, sometimes overly so. A drama with songs importantly spotted. ... Lee, in her first feature film lead, sparks the song offerings in sock style." —*Variety.*

**632 The Jazz Singer.** US, 1980, C, 115 m. D: Richard Fleischer, MS: Leonard Rosenman, P: Associated Film (Jerry Leider). Performer: Neil Diamond.

*Acapulco* WM: Neil Diamond and Doug Rhone / *Adom Olom* (Chorus) WM: Unknown / *Amazed and Confused* WM: Neil Diamond and Richard Bennett / *America* WM: Neil Diamond / *Hello Again* WM: Neil Diamond and Alan Lindgren / *Hey Louise* WM: Neil Diamond and Gilbert Becaud / *Jerusalem* WM: Neil Diamond / *Kol Nidre* WM: Unknown / *Love on the Rocks; On the Robert E. Lee; Songs of Life; Summerlove; You Baby* WM: Neil Diamond and Gilbert Becaud.

**633 Jennifer.** US, 1953, BW, 73 m. D: Joel Newton, MS: Ernest Gold, P: AA (Berman Swartz).

*Angel Eyes* (Matt Dennis) W: Earl K. Brent—M: Matt Dennis.

**634 Jenny.** US, 1970, C, 88 m. D: George Bloomfield, MS: Michael Small, P: ABC-Palomar/Cinerama (Edgar J. Scherick). Alt. Title: And Jenny Makes Three.

*Queen of Feeling* (Joe Butler) WM: Michael Benedikt and Michael Small / *Waiting* (Nilsson) WM: Harry Nilsson.

**635 Jeremy.** US, 1973, C, 90 m. D: Arthur Barron, MS: Lee Holdridge, P: UA (George Pappas).

*Jeremy* (Glynnis O'Connor) WM: Dorothea Joyce and Lee Holdridge.

**636 The Jerk.** US, 1979, C, 94 m. D: Carl Reiner, MS: Jack Elliott, P: Universal (David V. Picker, William E. McEuen).

*Tonight You Belong to Me* (Steve Martin, Bernadette Peters) W: Billy Rose—M: Lee David.

**637 Jessica.** US-France-Italy, 1962, C, 112 m. D: Jean Negulesco, MS: Mario Mascimbene, P: UA (Jean Negulesco). MB: Chorus. Performer: Maurice Chevalier.

*Fantasia* M: S. Riela / *It Is Better to Love; Jessica* M: Marguerite Monnot / *The Vespa Song* M: Mario Nascimbene / *Will You Remember* M: Marguerite Monnot. W: Dusty Negulesco.

**638 Jesus Christ, Superstar.** US, 1973, C, 103 m. D: Norman Jewison, MD: Andre Previn, P: Universal (Norman Jewison, Robert Stigwood).

*The Arrest* (Ted Neeley, Philip Toubus, Bob Bingham, Kurt Yaghjian, Chorus); *Blood Money* (Carl Anderson, Bob Bingham, Kurt Yaghjian, Chorus); *Could We Start Again, Please?* (Yvonne Elliman, Philip Toubus, Chorus); *The Crucifixion* (Ted Neeley, Chorus); *Damned for All Time* (Carl Anderson, Bob Bingham, Kurt Yaghjian, Chorus); *Everything's Alright* (Yvonne Elliman, Ted Neeley, Carl Anderson, Chorus); *Gethsemane* (Ted Neeley); *Heaven on Their Minds* (Carl Anderson); *Hosanna* (Ted Neeley, Bob Bingham, Chorus); *I Don't Know How to Love Him* (Yvonne Elliman); *Judas's Death* (Carl Anderson, Bob Bingham, Kurt Yaghjian, Chorus); *King Herod's Song* (Josh Mostel); *Last Supper* (Ted Neeley, Carl Anderson, Chorus); *Peter's Denial* (Yvonne Elliman, Philip Toubus, Chorus); *Pilate and Christ* (Barry Dennen, Ted Neeley, Chorus); *Pilate's Dream* (Barry Dennen, Chorus); *Poor Jerusalem* (Ted Neeley); *Simon Zealotes* (Larry T. Marshall, Chorus); *Strange Thing, Mystifying* (Carl Anderson, Ted

Neeley, Chorus); *Superstar* (Carl Anderson, Chorus); *The Temple* (Ted Neeley, Chorus); *Then We Are Decided* (Bob Bingham, Kurt Yaghjian); *This Jesus Must Die* (Bob Bingham, Kurt Yaghjian, Chorus); *Trial Before Pilate* (Barry Dennen, Carl Anderson, Bob Bingham, Chorus); *What's the Buzz?* (Yvonne Elliman, Ted Neeley, Chorus) W: Tim Rice—M: Andrew Lloyd Webber.

"Film version of the 1969 legit stage project ... blares forth with the shallow impact of an inferior imitation of Isaac Hayes." *—Variety.*

**639 The Jewel of the Nile.** US, 1985, C, 104 m. D: Lewis Teague, MS: Jack Nitzsche, P: TCF (Michael Douglas).

*When the Going Gets Tough the Tough Get Going* (Billy Ocean) WM: Wayne Brathwaite, Barry Eastmond, Robert John Lange and Billy Ocean.

**640 Jimi Hendrix.** US, 1973, C, 102 m. D: Joe Boyd, John Head and Gary Weis, P: Warner (Joe Boyd). MB: The Jimi Hendrix Experience; The Band of Gypsies. Performer: Jimi Hendrix.

*Hear My Train A-Comin'* WM: Jimi Hendrix / *Hey Joe* WM: Billy Roberts / *In from the Storm* WM: Jimi Hendrix / *Johnny B. Goode* WM: Chuck Berry / *Like a Rolling Stone* WM: Bob Dylan / *Machine Gun; Purple Haze; Red House* WM: Jimi Hendrix / *Rock Me Baby* WM: B.B. King and Joe Josea / *Wild Thing* WM: Chip Taylor.

**641 Jitterbugs.** US, 1943, BW, 74 m. D: Mal St. Clair, P: TCF (Sol M. Wurtzel). Performer: Vivian Blaine.

*If the Shoe Fits, Wear It; I've Got to See for Myself; The Moon Kissed the Mississippi* WM: Charles Newman and Lew Pollack.

**642 Joe Cocker: Mad Dogs and Englishmen.** GB, 1971, C, 119 m. D: Pierre Adidge, P: MGM (Pierre Adidge, Harry Marks, Robert Abel). Performer: Joe Cocker. GB Title: Mad Dogs and Englishmen.

*Cry Me a River* WM: Arthur Hamilton / *Darling Be Home Soon* WM: John B. Sebastian / *Delta Lady* WM: Leon Russell / *Feelin' Alright* (Joe Cocker, Merry Clayton, Brenda Holloway) WM: Dave Mason / *Give Peace a Chance* WM: John Lennon and Paul McCartney / *Honky Tonk Women* WM: Mick Jagger and Keith Richard / *I've Been Loving You Too Long* WM: Otis Redding and Jerry Butler / *Lawdy Miss Clawdy* WM: Lloyd Price / *Let It Be* (Claudia Linnear) WM: John Lennon and Paul McCartney / *The Letter* WM: Wayne Carson Thompson / *She Came in Through the Bathroom Window* WM: John Lennon and Paul McCartney / *Something* WM: George Harrison / *Space Captain* / *With a Little Help from My Friends* WM: John Lennon and Paul McCartney.

**643 Joey.** US, 1985, C, 97 m. D: Joseph Ellison, P: Rock 'n' Roll/Satori (Joseph Ellison).

*The Boy from New York City* (The Ad-Libs) WM: John Taylor / *Daddy's Home* (The Limelights) WM: James Sheppard and William Miller / *Get a Job* (The Silhouettes) WM: Earl T. Beal, Raymond W. Edwards, William F. Horton and Richard A. Lewis / *I Put a Spell on You* (Screamin' Jay Hawkins) WM: Jay Hawkins / *Little Star* (The Elegants) WM: Vito Picone and Arthur Venosa / *Why Do Fools Fall in Love* (Jimmy Merchant and Herman Santiago of The Teenagers) WM: Morris Levy and Frankie Lymon.

"An intelligent, engaging pic about a youngster who's into the rock 'n' roll music of the 1950s." *—Variety.*

**644 Johnny Angel.** US, 1945, BW, 79 m. D: Edwin L. Marin, MS: Leigh Harline, P: RKO (William L. Pereira).

*Memphis in June* (Hoagy Carmichael) W: Paul Francis Webster—M: Hoagy Carmichael.

**645 Johnny Apollo.** US, 1940, BW, 93 m. D: Henry Hathaway, MD: Alfred Newman, MS: Cyril Mockridge,

P: TCF (Harry Joe Brown). Performer: Dorothy Lamour.

*Dancing for Nickels and Dimes* W: Frank Loesser—M: Lionel Newman / *This Is the Beginning of the End* WM: Mack Gordon / *Your Kiss* W: Frank Loesser—M: Alfred Newman.

**646  Johnny Cash! The Man, His World, His Music.** US, 1969, C, 94 m. D: Robert Elfstrom, P: Continental (Arthur Barron, Evelyn Barron).

*Blue Suede Shoes* (Carl Perkins) WM: Carl Lee Perkins / *Folsom Prison Blues* (Johnny Cash) WM: Johnny Cash / *One Too Many Mornings* (Johnny Cash, Bob Dylan) WM: Bob Dylan / *Ring of Fire* (Johnny Cash) WM: Merle Kilgore and June Carter.

**647  Johnny Concho.** US, 1956, BW, 84 m. D: Don McGuire, MS: Nelson Riddle, P: UA (Frank Sinatra).

*Johnny Concho Theme* (Frank Sinatra) W: Dick Stanford—M: Nelson Riddle.

**648  Johnny Guitar.** US, 1954, C, 110 m. D: Nicholas Ray, MS: Victor Young, P: Republic (Nicholas Ray).

*Johnny Guitar* (Peggy Lee) W: Peggy Lee—M: Victor Young.

**649  The Joker Is Wild.** US, 1957, BW, 123 m. D: Charles Vidor, MS: Walter Scharf, P: Paramount (Samuel Briskin). Performer: Frank Sinatra.

*All the Way* W: Sammy Cahn—M: James Van Heusen / *At Sundown* WM: Walter Donaldson / *I Cried for You* W: Arthur Freed—M: Gus Arnheim and Abe Lyman / *If I Could Be with You One Hour Tonight* WM: Henry Creamer and James P. Johnson / *I Love My Baby* W: Bud Green—M: Harry Warren / *June in January* (Bing Crosby) W: Leo Robin—M: Ralph Rainger / *Naturally* W: Harry Harris—M: from Flatow's "Martha" / *Out of Nowhere* New W: Harry Harris—M: Johnny Green / *Swinging on a Star* New W: Harry Harris—M: James Van Heusen.

**650  Jolson Sings Again.** US,

1949, C, 96 m. D: Henry Levin, MD: George Duning, P: Columbia (Sidney Buchman). Vocals: Al Jolson for Larry Parks. Performer: Larry Parks.

*About a Quarter to Nine* W: Al Dubin—M: Harry Warren / *After You've Gone* W: Henry Creamer—M: Turner Layton / *Anniversary Song* W: Saul Chaplin and Al Jolson—M: J. Ivanovici / *April Showers* W: B.G. De Sylva—M: Louis Silvers / *Baby Face* WM: Benny Davis and Harry Akst / *Back in Your Own Back Yard* WM: Al Jolson, Billy Rose and Dave Dreyer / *California, Here I Come* W: Al Jolson and B.G. De Sylva—M: Joseph Meyer / *Carolina in the Morning* W: Gus Kahn—M: Walter Donaldson / *Chinatown, My Chinatown* W: William Jerome—M: Jean Schwartz / *For Me and My Gal* W: Edgar Leslie and E. Ray Goetz—M: George W. Meyer / *Give My Regards to Broadway* WM: George M. Cohan / *I'm Just Wild About Harry* WM: Noble Sissle and Eubie Blake / *I'm Looking Over a Four Leaf Clover* W: Mort Dixon—M: Harry M. Woods / *I Only Have Eyes for You* W: Al Dubin—M: Harry Warren / *Is It True What They Say About Dixie?* WM: Irving Caesar, Sammy Lerner and Gerald Marks / *Learn to Croon* (Bing Crosby) W: Sam Coslow—M: Arthur Johnston / *Let Me Sing and I'm Happy* WM: Irving Berlin / *Ma Blushin' Rosie* W: Edgar Smith—M: John Stromberg / *My Mammy* W: Sam M. Lewis and Joe Young—M: Walter Donaldson / *Pretty Baby* W: Gus Kahn—M: Tony Jackson and Egbert Van Alstyne / *Rock-a-Bye Your Baby with a Dixie Melody* W: Sam M. Lewis and Joe Young—M: Jean Schwartz / *Sonny Boy* W: Al Jolson, B.G. De Sylva, Lew Brown—M: Ray Henderson / *Swanee* W: Irving Caesar—M: George Gershwin / *Toot, Toot, Tootsie!* WM: Gus Kahn, Ernie Erdman and Dan Russo / *Waiting for the Robert E. Lee* W: L. Wolfe Gilbert—M: Lewis F. Muir / *When the Red, Red Robin Comes Bob, Bob, Bobbin' Along* WM: Harry M. Woods / *You Made Me*

*Love You* W: Joseph McCarthy—M: James V. Monaco.

"The vitality of the Jolson voice is suitably matched in the physical representation provided by Larry Parks." —Thomas M. Pryor, *The New York Times.*

**651 The Jolson Story.** US, 1946, C, 128 m. D: Alfred E. Green, MD: Morris Stoloff, P: Columbia (Sidney Skolsky). Vocals: Al Jolson for Larry Parks; Rudy Wissler for Scotty Beckett.

Jolson appeared onscreen briefly as himself in a long shot, singing *Swanee.*

*About a Quarter to Nine* (Larry Parks, Evelyn Keyes) W: Al Dubin — M: Harry Warren / *After the Ball* (Scotty Beckett) WM: Charles K. Harris / *Anniversary Song* (Larry Parks, Ludwig Donath) W: Saul Chaplin and Al Jolson—M: J. Ivanovici / *April Showers* (Larry Parks) W: B.G. De Sylva— M: Louis Silvers / *Avalon* (Larry Parks) WM: Al Jolson and Vincent Rose / *Ave Maria* (Scotty Beckett, Robert Mitchell Boychoir) W: Sir Walter Scott—M: Franz Schubert / *Blue Bell* (Scotty Beckett) W: Edward Madden and Dolly Morse [Theodora Morse]—M: Theodore F. Morse / *By the Light of the Silvery Moon* (Scotty Beckett) W: Edward Madden—M: Gus Edwards / *California, Here I Come* (Larry Parks, Evelyn Keyes) W: Al Jolson and B.G. De Sylva—M: Joseph Meyer / *Eli Eli* (Scotty Beckett, Ludwig Donath) W: The Bible—M: Probably Jacob Sandler / *Forty-Second Street* (Evelyn Keyes) W: Al Dubin—M: Harry Warren / *I'm Sitting on Top of the World* (Larry Parks) W: Sam M. Lewis and Joe Young—M: Ray Henderson / *I Want a Girl Just Like the Girl That Married Dear Old Dad* (Larry Parks) W: William Dillon—M: Harry von Tilzer / *Let Me Sing and I'm Happy* (Larry Parks) WM: Irving Berlin / *Liza* (Larry Parks, Evelyn Keyes, Chorus) W: Ira Gershwin and Gus Kahn—M: George Gershwin / *Lullaby of Broadway* (Evelyn Keyes) W: Al Dubin—M: Harry Warren / *Ma Blushin' Rosie* (Larry Parks) W: Edgar Smith— M: John Stromberg / *My Mammy* (Larry Parks) W: Sam M. Lewis and Joe Young—M: Walter Donaldson / *On the Banks of the Wabash Far Away* (Scotty Beckett) WM: Paul Dresser / *Rock-a-Bye Your Baby with a Dixie Melody* (Larry Parks) W: Sam M. Lewis and Joe Young—M: Jean Schwartz / *She's a Latin from Manhattan* (Evelyn Keyes, Chorus) W: Al Dubin—M: Harry Warren / *The Spaniard That Blighted My Life* (Larry Parks, Chorus) WM: Billy Merson / *Swanee* (Al Jolson) W: Irving Caesar— M: George Gershwin / *There's a Rainbow 'Round My Shoulder* (Larry Parks) WM: Billy Rose, Al Jolson and Dave Dreyer / *Toot, Toot, Tootsie!* (Larry Parks) WM: Gus Kahn, Ernie Erdman and Dan Russo / *Waiting for the Robert E. Lee* (Larry Parks) W: L. Wolfe Gilbert—M: Lewis F. Muir / *We're in the Money* (Evelyn Keyes) W: Al Dubin—M: Harry Warren / *When the Red, Red Robin Comes Bob, Bob, Bobbin' Along* (Larry Parks) WM: Harry M. Woods / *When You Were Sweet Sixteen* (Scotty Beckett) WM: James Thornton / *You Made Me Love You* (Larry Parks) W: Joseph McCarthy—M: James V. Monaco.

"The real star of the production is that Jolson voice and that Jolson medley." —*Variety.*

**652 Jonathan Livingston Seagull.** US, 1973, C, 120 m. D: Hall Bartlett, P: Paramount (Hall Bartlett). Performer: Neil Diamond.

*Be; Skybird* WM: Neil Diamond.

**653 Journey to the Center of the Earth.** US, 1959, C, 132 m. D: Henry Levin, MS: Bernard Herrmann, P: TCF (Charles Brackett). Performer: Pat Boone.

*My Heart's in the Highlands* W: Sammy Cahn / *My Love Is Like a Red, Red Rose* W: Robert Burns / *Twice as Tall* W: Sammy Cahn—M: James Van Heusen.

**654 Joy of Living.** US, 1938

BW, 90 m. D: Tay Garnett, P: RKO (Felix Young).

*A Heavenly Party* (Irene Dunne, Fuzzy Knight); *Just Let Me Look at You* (Irene Dunne); *What's Good About Good Night?* (Irene Dunne); *You Couldn't Be Cuter* (Irene Dunne, Dorothy Steiner, Estelle Steiner, Douglas Fairbanks, Jr.) W: Dorothy Fields—M: Jerome Kern.

**655  Julie.** US, 1956, BW, 99 m. D: Andrew L. Stone, MS: Leith Stevens, P: MGM (Martin Melcher).

*Julie* (Doris Day) W: Tom Adair—M: Leith Stevens.

**656  The Jungle Princess.** US, 1936, BW, 85 m. D: William Thiele, MD: Boris Morros, P: Paramount (E. Lloyd Sheldon).

*Moonlight and Shadows* (Dorothy Lamour) W: Leo Robin—M: Frederick Hollander.

**657  Jupiter's Darling.** US, 1955, C, 96 m. D: George Sidney, MD: Saul Chaplin, MS: David Rose, P: MGM (George Wells).

*Don't Let This Night Get Away* (Howard Keel, Chorus); *Hannibal's Victory March* (Howard Keel, Chorus); *If This Be Slav'ry* (Gower Champion); *I Have a Dream* (Esther Williams); *I Never Trust a Woman* (Howard Keel); *The Life of an Elephant* (Marge Champion, Gower Champion) W: Harold Adamson—M: Burton Lane.

**658  Just Around the Corner.** US, 1938, BW, 70 m. D: Irving Cummings, MD: Louis Silvers, P: TCF (David Hempstead).

*Brass Buttons and Epaulets* (Bill Robinson); *I Love to Walk in the Rain* (Shirley Temple, Bill Robinson, Chorus); *Just Around the Corner* (Chorus); *This Is a Happy Little Ditty* (Shirley Temple, Joan Davis, Bert Lahr, Bill Robinson) W: Walter Bullock—M: Harold Spina.

**659  Just for You.** US, 1952, C, 104 m. D: Elliott Nugent, MD: Emil Newman, MS: Hugo Friedhofer, P: Paramount (Pat Duggan).

*Call Me Tonight* (Bing Crosby); *Checkin' My Heart* (Jane Wyman); *A Flight of Fancy* (Bing Crosby); *He's Just Crazy for Me* (Jane Wyman); *I'll Si Si Ya in Bahia* (Bing Crosby); *The Live Oak Tree* (Bing Crosby); *The Maiden of Guadalupe* (Bing Crosby, Jane Wyman, Chorus); *On the 10:10 from Ten-Ten-Tennessee* (Bing Crosby); *Zing a Little Zong* (Bing Crosby, Jane Wyman) W: Leo Robin—M: Harry Warren.

**660  Kathy O'.** US, 1958, C, 99 m. D: Jack Sher, MD: Joseph Gershenson, MS: Frank Skinner, P: Universal (Sy Gomberg).

*Kathy O'* (The Diamonds) WM: Charles Tobias, Ray Joseph and Jack Sher.

**661  Keep 'Em Flying.** US, 1941, BW, 86 m. D: Arthur Lubin, P: Universal (Glenn Tryon).

*I'm Getting Sentimental Over You* (Carol Bruce) W: Ned Washington—M: George Bassman / *I'm Looking for the Boy with the Wistful Eyes* (Carol Bruce, Martha Raye, Chorus); *Let's Keep 'Em Flying* (Dick Foran, Carol Bruce, Chorus); *You Don't Know What Love Is* (Carol Bruce) W: Don Raye—M: Gene de Paul.

**662  Kelly and Me.** US, 1957, C, 86 m. D: Robert Z. Leonard, MS: Joseph Gershenson, P: Universal (Robert Arthur).

*Singing a Vagabond Song* (Van Johnson) WM: Sam Messenheimer, Val Burton and Harry Richman.

**663  Kelly's Heroes.** US-Yugoslavia, 1970, C, 145 m. D: Brian G. Hutton, MS: Lalo Schifrin, P: MGM (Gabriel Katzke, Sidney Beckerman).

*All for the Love of Sunshine* (Hank Williams, Jr.) W: Mike Curb—M: Lalo Schifrin and Harley Hatcher / *Burning Bridges* (The Mike Curb Congregation) W: Mike Curb—M: Lalo Schifrin / *Si Tu Me Dis* (Monique Aldebert) W: Gene Lees—M: Lalo Schifrin.

**664  Key Largo.** US, 1948, BW, 101 m. D: John Huston, MS: Max Steiner, P: Warner (Jerry Wald).

*Moanin' Low* (Claire Trevor) W: Howard Dietz—M: Ralph Rainger.

**665  The Kid from Brooklyn.** US, 1946, C, 113 m. D: Norman Z. McLeod, MD: Carmen Dragon, P: RKO (Samuel Goldwyn). Vocals: Dorothy Ellers for Virginia Mayo; Betty Russell for Vera-Ellen.

*Hey! What's Your Name?* (Vera-Ellen, Chorus); *I Love an Old Fashioned Song* (Virginia Mayo, Men); *Josie* (The Goldwyn Girls) W: Sammy Cahn—M: Jule Styne / *Pavlova* (Danny Kaye) WM: Sylvia Fine and Max Liebman / *The Sunflower Song* (The Goldwyn Girls); *You're the Cause of It All* (Virginia Mayo) W: Sammy Cahn—M: Jule Styne.

"Virginia Mayo ... serves as a beautiful foil for Kaye's madcap antics and sings two ballads in acceptable fashion." —*Variety*.

**666  The Kid from Spain.** US, 1932, BW, 96 m. D: Leo McCarey, P: Samuel Goldwyn. MB: The Goldwyn Girls.

Among the Goldwyn Girls at this time were Paulette Goddard, Lucille Ball, Betty Grable and Virginia Bruce.

*The College Song* (Betty Grable); *In the Moonlight* (Eddie Cantor); *Look What You've Done* (Eddie Cantor, Lyda Roberti); *What a Perfect Combination* (Eddie Cantor) W: Bert Kalmar and Irving Caesar—M: Harry Ruby and Harry Akst.

**667  Kid Galahad.** US, 1962, C, 95 m. D: Phil Karlson, MS: Jeff Alexander, P: UA (David Weisbart). Performer: Elvis Presley.

*Home Is Where the Heart Is* WM: Hal David and Sherman Edwards / *I Got Lucky* WM: Dolores Fuller, Fred Wise and Ben Weisman / *King of the Whole Wide World* WM: Ruth Batchelor and Bob Roberts / *Riding the Rainbow; This Is Living* WM: Fred Wise and Ben Weisman / *A Whistlin' Tune* WM: Hal David and Sherman Edwards.

**668  Kid Millions.** US, 1934, BW/C, 90 m. D: Roy Del Ruth, MD: Alfred Newman, P: UA (Samuel Goldwyn). MB: The Goldwyn Girls.

*An Earful of Music* (Ethel Merman); *Ice Cream Fantasy* (Ethel Merman, Eddie Cantor, Warren Hymer) W: Gus Kahn—M: Walter Donaldson / *I Want to Be a Minstrel Man* (Harold Nicholas) W: Harold Adamson—M: Burton Lane / *Mandy* (Eddie Cantor, Ethel Merman, Ann Sothern, The Nicholas Brothers) WM: Irving Berlin / *Okay Toots* (Eddie Cantor); *When My Ship Comes In* (Eddie Cantor) W: Gus Kahn—M: Walter Donaldson / *Your Head on My Shoulder* (Ann Sothern, George Murphy) W: Harold Adamson—M: Burton Lane.

"Do you want a song? Listen to the joyous and healthy voice of Ethel Merman. ... Or to Mr. Cantor himself, in and out of black face." —Andre Sennwald, *The New York Times*.

**669  The Kids Are Alright.** US, 1979, C, 108 m. D: Jeff Stein, P: New World (Bill Curbishly, Tony Klinger). Performers: The Who.

*Anyway Anyhow Anywhere; Baba O'Riley; Happy Jack; I Can See for Miles; I Can't Explain; Join Together; Long Live Rock; The Magic Bus; My Generation; My Generation Blues; Pinball Wizard* WM: Peter Townshend / *Road Runner* WM: Ellas McDaniel / *See Me, Feel Me; Sparks; Tommy, Can You Hear Me; Won't Get Fooled Again* WM: Peter Townshend / *Young Man Blues* WM: Mose Allison.

**670  The Killers.** US, 1946, BW, 105 m. D: Robert Siodmak, MS: Miklos Rozsa, P: Universal (Mark Hellinger). TV Title: A Man Alone.

*The More I Know of Love* (Ava Gardner) W: Jack Brooks—M: Miklos Rozsa.

"The score is an immeasurable aid in furthering suspense." —*Variety*.

**671  A Kind of Loving.** GB, 1962, BW, 112 m. D: John Schlesinger, MS: Ron Grainer, P: Anglo-Amalgamated (Joseph Janni).

*Down by the Riverside* (Alan Bates)
WM: Unknown.

**672  The King and I.** US, 1956,
C, 133 m. D: Walter Lang, MD: Alfred
Newman, P: TCF (Charles Brackett).
Vocals: Marni Nixon for Deborah
Kerr; Reuben Fuentes for Carlos
Rivas.

The Broadway musical opened in
1951 starring Gertrude Lawrence. Yul
Brynner and Terry Saunders repeated
their roles in the film.

*Getting to Know You* (Deborah
Kerr, Chorus); *Hello, Young Lovers*
(Deborah Kerr); *I Have Dreamed* (Rita
Moreno, Carlos Rivas); *I Whistle a
Happy Tune* (Deborah Kerr, Rex
Thompson); *A Puzzlement* (Yul Bryn-
ner); *Shall I Tell You What I Think of
You?* (Deborah Kerr); *Shall We Dance?*
(Deborah Kerr, Yul Brynner); *The
Small House of Uncle Thomas* (Rita
Moreno); *Something Wonderful* (Terry
Saunders); *Song of the King* (Yul Bryn-
ner); *We Kiss in a Shadow* (Rita
Moreno, Carlos Rivas) W: Oscar Ham-
merstein II—M: Richard Rodgers.

"A pictorially exquisite, musically
exciting, and dramatically satisfying
motion picture." —*Variety*.

"Most of the memorable num-
bers are here and are beautifully done."
—Bosley Crowther, *The New York
Times*.

**673  King Creole.** US, 1958,
BW, 116 m. D: Michael Curtiz, MS:
Walter Scharf, P: Paramount (Hal B.
Wallis). MB: The Jordanaires. Per-
former: Elvis Presley.

*As Long as I Have You* WM: Fred
Wise and Ben Weisman / *Banana*
(Liliane Montevecchi) WM: Sid Tep-
per and Roy C. Bennett / *Crawfish*
(Elvis Presley, Kitty White) WM: Fred
Wise and Ben Weisman / *Dixieland
Rock* WM: Aaron Schroeder and
Rachel Frank / *Don't Ask Me Why*
WM: Fred Wise and Ben Weisman /
*Hard Headed Woman* WM: Claude De
Metrius / *King Creole* WM: Jerry Leiber
and Mike Stoller / *Lover Doll* WM: Sid

Wayne and Abner Silver / *New Orleans*
WM: Sid Tepper and Roy C. Bennett
/ *Steadfast, Loyal and True*; *Trouble*
WM: Jerry Leiber and Mike Stoller /
*Turtles, Berries and Gumbo* (Trio) WM:
Al Wood and Kay Twomey / *Young
Dreams* WM: Aaron Schroeder and
Martin Kalmanoff.

"Essentially a musical. . . . Presley
. . . does some very pleasant, soft and
melodious, singing." —*Variety*.

**674  King of Burlesque.** US,
1935, BW, 88 m. D: Sidney Lanfield,
P: TCF (Darryl F. Zanuck, Kenneth
MacGowan).

*I Love to Ride the Horses* (Alice
Faye) W: Jack Yellen—M: Lew Pollack
/ *I'm Shooting High* (Alice Faye, Jack
Oakie, Warner Baxter, Shaw and Lee);
*I've Got My Fingers Crossed* (Alice Faye,
Fats Waller, Dixie Dunbar); *Lovely
Lady* (Kenny Baker); *Spreadin' Rhythm
Around* (Alice Faye, Fats Waller);
*Whose Big Baby Are You?* (Alice Faye)
W: Ted Koehler—M: Jimmy McHugh.

"May be recommended for its
charitable omission of involved chorus
routines, overhead shots of young
women waving feathered fans or the
suggestion that the dance scenes were
made in the Yankee Stadium." —
Frank S. Nugent, *The New York Times*.

**675  The King of Jazz.** US,
1930, C, 101 m. D: John Murray Anderson, MD: Ferde Grofe, P: Universal (Carl Laemmle, Jr.). Orch: Paul
Whiteman.

The Rhythm Boys Trio, signed up
by Whiteman in 1926 and 1927 to sing
with his band, were Bing Crosby,
Harry Barris and Al Rinker.

*A Bench in the Park* (Jeanette Loff,
Stanley Smith, The Brox Sisters, The
Rhythm Boys) W: Jack Yellen—M:
Milton Ager / *Comin' Thro' the Rye* (Fe-
male Singer) W: Robert Burns—M:
Unknown / *Happy Feet* (The Rhythm
Boys) W: Jack Yellen—M: Milton Ager
/ *Has Anyone Seen Our Nell?* (Male
Quartet) / *I Like to Do Things for You*
(Jeanie Lang, Grace Hayes, William

Kent) W: Jack Yellen—M: Milton Ager / *It Happened in Monterey* (Jeanette Loff, John Boles, Nancy Torres) W: Billy Rose—M: Mabel Wayne / *John Peel* (Male Quartet) W: John Woodcock Graves—M: Unknown / *Long Long Ago* (Chorus) WM: Thomas Haynes Bayly / *Mississippi Mud* (The Rhythm Boys) WM: Harry Barris and James Cavanaugh / *Music Hath Charms* (Bing Crosby); *My Bridal Veil* (Laura La Plante, Stanley Smith, Chorus) W: Jack Yellen—M: Milton Ager / *Oh, How I'd Like to Own a Fish Store* (Jack White) / *Ragamuffin Romeo* (Jeanie Lang, George Chiles, Chorus) WM: Harry De Costa and Mabel Wayne / *Santa Lucia* (2 Female Singers) Eng. W: Thomas Oliphant—Ital. WM: Teodoro Cottrau / *Song of the Dawn* (John Boles, Chorus) W: Jack Yellen—M: Milton Ager / *So the Bluebirds and the Blackbirds Got Together* (The Rhythm Boys) W: Billy Moll—M: Harry Barris.

"The millions who never heard the great Paul Whiteman band play George Gershwin's *Rhapsody in Blue* won't hear it here, either. Anderson sees fit to scramble it up with 'production.' It's all busted to pieces." —*Variety.*

**676   King Solomon's Mines.** GB, 1937, BW, 80 m. D: Robert Stevenson, MS: Mischa Spoliansky, P: Gaumont British (Geoffrey Barkas).

*Climbing Up* (Paul Robeson) WM: Eric Maschwitz and Mischa Spoliansky.

**677   The King Steps Out.** US, 1936, BW, 85 m. D: Josef von Sternberg, P: Columbia (William Perlberg). Performer: Grace Moore.

*Learn How to Lose; Madly in Love; Stars in My Eyes; What Shall Remain?* W: Dorothy Fields—M: Fritz Kreisler.

"The libretto was borrowed from an operetta 'Cissy' produced in Vienna a few seasons back. Some of the Kreisler tunes were taken from its score, others from 'Apple Blossom.'" —Frank S. Nugent, *The New York Times.*

**678   Kismet.** US, 1955, C, 113 m. D: Vincente Minnelli, MD: Andre Previn, P: MGM (Arthur Freed).

*And This Is My Beloved* (Howard Keel, Ann Blyth, Vic Damone); *Baubles, Bangles and Beads* (Ann Blyth, Chorus); *Bored* (Dolores Gray); *Fate* (Howard Keel); *Gesticulate* (Howard Keel, Chorus); *Night of My Nights* (Vic Damone, Chorus); *Not Since Ninevah* (Dolores Gray, Chorus); *The Olive Tree* (Howard Keel); *Rahadlakum* (Howard Keel, Dolores Gray, Chorus); *Sands of Time* (Howard Keel); *Stranger in Paradise* (Ann Blyth, Vic Damone) WM: Robert Wright and George "Chet" Forrest.

"Music ... gushes from it ... borrowed from Alexander Borodin's foamy works slightly 'adapted' to modern tempos and fitted with ornamental words." —Bosley Crowther, *The New York Times.*

**679   Kiss Me Deadly.** US, 1955, BW, 105 m. D: Robert Aldrich, MS: Frank DeVol, P: UA (Robert Aldrich).

*Blues from Kiss Me Deadly* (Nat King Cole, Madi Comfort) WM: Frank DeVol.

**680   Kiss Me Kate.** US, 1953, C, 109 m. D: George Sidney, MD: Andre Previn and Saul Chaplin, P: MGM (Jack Cummings).

Based partly on Shakespeare's "Taming of the Shrew," the musical show opened on Broadway on December 30, 1948, with Patricia Morison and Alfred Drake in the leads. In London in 1951, again with Morison, it ran for 501 performances.

*Always True to You in My Fashion* (Ann Miller, Tommy Rall); *Brush Up Your Shakespeare* (Keenan Wynn, James Whitmore); *From This Moment On* (Ann Miller, Tommy Rall, Bobby Van, Bob Fosse, Carol Haney); *I Hate Men* (Kathryn Grayson); *I've Come to Wive It Wealthily in Padua* (Howard Keel); *Kiss Me Kate* (Kathryn Grayson, Howard Keel, Chorus); *So in Love* (Kathryn Grayson, Howard Keel);

*Tom, Dick or Harry* (Ann Miller, Tommy Rall, Bobby Van, Bob Fosse); *Too Darn Hot* (Ann Miller); *We Open in Venice* (Kathryn Grayson, Howard Keel, Ann Miller, Tommy Rall); *Were Thine That Special Face* (Howard Keel); *Where Is the Life That Late I Led?* (Howard Keel); *Why Can't You Behave?* (Ann Miller); *Wunderbar* (Kathryn Grayson, Howard Keel) WM: Cole Porter.

"A really superbly sung affair. . . . It is really Miss Grayson and Mr. Keel tossing off the Porter songs . . . that make[s] for the best things in the show." —Bosley Crowther, *The New York Times.*

**681   Kiss the Boys Goodbye.** US, 1941, BW, 85 m. D: Victor Schertzinger, P: Paramount (William LeBaron).

*I'll Never Let a Day Pass By* (Mary Martin, Don Ameche); *Kiss the Boys Goodbye* (Mary Martin); *Sand in My Shoes* (Connie Boswell); *That's How I Got My Start* (Mary Martin) W: Frank Loesser—M: Victor Schertzinger.

"Effectively showcases the acting and vocal talents of Mary Martin. . . . [The] songs are deftly spotted." — *Variety.*

**682   Kiss Them for Me.** US, 1957, C, 105 m. D: Stanley Donen, MS: Lionel Newman, P: TCF (Jerry Wald).

*Kiss Them for Me* (The McGuire Sisters) W: Carroll Coates—M: Lionel Newman.

**683   Kissin' Cousins.** US, 1964, C, 96 m. D: Gene Nelson, MD: Fred Karger, P: MGM (Sam Katzman). Performer: Elvis Presley.

*Barefoot Ballad* WM: Dolores Fuller and Lee Morris / *Catchin' On Fast* WM: Bill Giant, Bernie Baum and Florence Kaye / *Kissin' Cousins* WM: Fred Wise and Randy Starr / *Once Is Enough* WM: Sid Tepper and Roy C. Bennett / *One Boy, Two Little Girls* WM: Bill Giant, Bernie Baum and Florence Kaye / *Pappy, Won't You Please Come Home* (Glenda Farrell) WM: Hugh Cannon / *Smokey Mountain Boy* WM: Lenore Rosenblatt and Victor Millrose / *Tender Feeling* WM: Bill Giant, Bernie Baum and Florence Kaye.

**684   The Kissing Bandit.** US, 1948, C, 102 m. D: Laslo Benedek, MS: George Stoll, P: MGM (Joe Pasternak).

*If I Steal a Kiss* (Frank Sinatra, Kathryn Grayson) W: Edward Heyman / *I Like You* (Sono Osoto) W: Earl K. Brent and Edward Heyman / *Love Is Where You Find It* (Kathryn Grayson) W: Earl K. Brent / *Senorita* (Frank Sinatra, Kathryn Grayson) W: Edward Heyman / *Siesta* (Frank Sinatra, Chorus); *Tomorrow Means Romance* (Kathryn Grayson) W: Earl K. Brent and Edward Heyman / *What's Wrong with Me?* (Kathryn Grayson, Frank Sinatra) W: Edward Heyman—M: Nacio Herb Brown.

**685   Knickerbocker Holiday.** US, 1944, BW, 85 m. D: Harry Joe Brown, MS: Werner Heymann, P: UA (Harry Joe Brown).

*Hear Ye* (Chester Conklin, Chorus) W: Sammy Cahn—M: Jule Styne / *Holiday* (Johnny "Scat" Davis, Chorus) WM: Theodore Paxton and Nelson Eddy / *Jail Song* (Nelson Eddy) WM: Furman Brown, Nelson Eddy and Kurt Weill / *Love Has Made This Such a Lovely Day* (Nelson Eddy, Constance Dowling, Shelley Winters) W: Sammy Cahn—M: Jule Styne / *The One Indispensable Man* (Charles Coburn, Ernest Cossart) W: Maxwell Anderson—M: Kurt Weill / *One More Smile* (Nelson Eddy, Constance Dowling) W: Sammy Cahn—M: Jule Styne / *September Song* (Charles Coburn) W: Maxwell Anderson—M: Kurt Weill / *Sing Out* (Nelson Eddy, Chorus) WM: Franz Steininger and Furman Brown / *There's Nowhere to Go But Up* (Nelson Eddy, Chorus) W: Maxwell Anderson—M: Kurt Weill / *Zuyder Zee* (Male Quartet) W: Sammy Cahn—M: Jule Styne.

"The music ... is the picture's chief asset." —Paul P. Kennedy, *The New York Times*.

**686 Knock on Wood.** US, 1954, C, 103 m. D: Norman Panama and Melvin Frank, MD: Victor Young, P: Paramount (Norman Panama, Melvin Frank). Performer: Danny Kaye.

*All About You; Knock on Wood; Monahan O'Han* WM: Sylvia Fine.

**687 Kotch.** US, 1971, C, 113 m. D: Jack Lemmon, MS: Marvin Hamlisch, P: ABC (Richard Carter).

*Life Is What You Make It* (Johnny Mathis) W: Johnny Mercer—M: Marvin Hamlisch.

**688 La Bamba.** US, 1987, C, 108 m. D: Luiz Valdez, MS: Carlos Santana and Miles Goodman, P: Columbia (Taylor Hackford, Bill Borden). Vocals: David Hidalgo for Lou Diamond Phillips. Performers: Lou Diamond Phillips; Los Lobos.

Biopic of singing rocker Ritchie Valens, killed at age 18 in the same plane crash that took the lives of Buddy Holly and The Big Bopper (J.P. Richardson).

*Charlena* WM: Herman B. Chaney and Manuel G. Chavez / *Come On, Let's Go* WM: Ritchie Valens / *Crying, Waiting, Hoping* (Marshall Crenshaw) WM: Buddy Holly / *Donna* WM: Ritchie Valens / *Framed* WM: Jerry Leiber and Mike Stoller / *Goodnight My Love* WM: George Motola and John Marascalco / *La Bamba* WM: William Clauson / *Lonely Teardrops* (Howard Huntsberry, Chorus) WM: Berry Gordy, Jr., Gwen Gordy and Tyran Carlo / *Ooh! My Head* WM: Ritchie Valens / *Summertime Blues* (Brian Setzer) WM: Eddie Cochran and Jerry Capehart / *We Belong Together* WM: Sam Weiss, Robert Carr and Johnny Mitchell / *Who Do You Love* (Bo Diddley) WM: Ellas McDaniel.

**689 Labyrinth.** US, 1986, C, 101 m. D: Jim Henson, MS: Trevor Jones, P: Tri-Star (Eric Rattray).

*As the World Falls Down* (David Bowie); *Chilly Down* (David Bowie) WM: David Bowie / *The Goblin Battle* (Trevor Jones); *Hallucination* (Trevor Jones); *Home at Last* (Trevor Jones); *Into the Labyrinth* (Trevor Jones) WM: Trevor Jones / *Magic Dance* (David Bowie) WM: David Bowie / *Sarah* (Trevor Jones); *Thirteen O'Clock* (Trevor Jones) WM: Trevor Jones / *Underground* (David Bowie); *Within You* (David Bowie) WM: David Bowie.

**690 Ladies and Gentlemen, the Rolling Stones.** US, 1975, C, 90 m. D: Rollin Binzer, P: Dragon Aire (Marshall Chess, Rollin Binzer, Bob Fries, Steve Gebhardt). Performers: The Rolling Stones.

*Bitch; Brown Sugar; Gimme Shelter; Jumpin' Jack Flash; Love in Vain; Midnight Rambler; Street Fighting Man; Tumbling Dice* WM: Mick Jagger and Keith Richard.

**691 The Ladies' Man.** US, 1961, C, 106 m. D: Jerry Lewis, MS: Walter Scharf, P: Paramount (Jerry Lewis).

*Don't Go to Paris* (Jerry Lewis, Chorus); *He Doesn't Know* (Pat Stanley) W: Jack Brooks—M: Harry Warren.

**692 Ladies They Talk About.** US, 1933, BW, 68 m. D: Howard Bretherton, P: Warner (Ray Griffith). Alt. Title: Women in Prison.

*If I Could Be with You One Hour Tonight* (Lillian Roth) WM: Henry Creamer and James P. Johnson / *St. Louis Blues* (Etta Moten) WM: W.C. Handy.

**693 Lady, Be Good.** US, 1941, BW, 111 m. D: Norman Z. McLeod, MD: George Stoll, P: MGM (Arthur Freed). Orch: Jimmy Dorsey.

*Fascinating Rhythm* (Connie Russell, The Berry Brothers) W: Ira Gershwin—M: George Gershwin / *The Last Time I Saw Paris* (Ann Sothern) W: Oscar Hammerstein II—M: Jerome Kern / *Oh Lady, Be Good* (Ann Sothern, Robert Young, Red Skelton, Virginia O'Brien, John Carroll, Chorus) W: Ira Gershwin—M: George Gershwin

/ *You'll Never Know* (Ann Sothern, The Berry Brothers) WM: Roger Edens / *Your Words and My Music* (Ann Sothern, Robert Young, Virginia O'Brien, John Carroll) W: Arthur Freed—M: Roger Edens.

"The plot bears no resemblance to the ... original 1924 stage musical. ... The songs in this picture are likewise no relation to the click Gershwin score." — *Variety.*

**694   The Lady Is a Square.** GB, 1958, BW, 99 m. D: Herbert Wilcox, MD: Wally Scott, P: Associated British (Herbert Wilcox, Anna Neagle). Performer: Frankie Vaughan.

*Honey Bunny Baby* WM: Frank Abie / *The Lady Is a Square* WM: Raymond Dutch and John Franz / *Love Is the Sweetest Thing* WM: Ray Noble / *That's My Doll* WM: Dick Glasser and Ann Hall.

**695   Lady of Burlesque.** US, 1943, BW, 91 m. D: William A. Wellman, MS: Arthur Lange, P: UA (Hunt Stromberg). GB Title: Striptease Lady.

*So This Is You* (Frank Fenton); *Take It Off the E-String, Play It on the G-String* (Barbara Stanwyck) W: Sammy Cahn—M: Harry Akst.

**696   Lady on a Train.** US, 1945, BW, 93 m. D: Charles David, MS: Miklos Rozsa, P: Universal (Felix Jackson). Performer: Deanna Durbin.

*Gimme a Little Kiss, Will Ya, Huh?* WM: Roy Turk, Jack Smith and Maceo Pinkard / *Night and Day* WM: Cole Porter / *Pop Goes the Weasel* WM: Charles Twiggs / *Silent Night* W: Joseph Mohr—M: Franz Gruber.

**697   Lady Sings the Blues.** US, 1972, C, 144 m. D: Sidney J. Furie, MD: Gil Askey, MS: Michel Legrand, P: Paramount (Berry Gordy, Jay Weston, James S. White). Performer: Diana Ross.

Based (loosely) on the life of singer Billie Holiday.

*All of Me* WM: Seymour Simons and Gerald Marks / *Don't Explain* W: Arthur Herzog, Jr.—M: Billie Holiday /

*Gimme a Pigfoot* WM: Wesley Wilson / *God Bless the Child* WM: Arthur Herzog, Jr.—M: Billie Holiday / *Good Morning Heartache* WM: Irene Higginbotham, Ervin Drake and Dan Fisher / *I Cried for You* W: Arthur Freed—M: Gus Arnheim and Abe Lyman / *Lady Sings the Blues* WM: Billie Holiday and Herbie Nicholas / *Lover Man* WM: Jimmy Davis, Roger Ramirez and Jimmy Sherman / *The Man I Love* W: Ira Gershwin—M: George Gershwin / *Mean to Me* W: Roy Turk—M: Fred E. Ahlert / *My Man* Eng. W: Channing Pollack—M: Maurice Yvain / *Our Love Is Here to Stay* W: Ira Gershwin—M: George Gershwin / *Strange Fruit* WM: Lewis Allan / *'Tain't Nobody's Bizness If I Do* WM: Porter Grainger, Graham Prince and Clarence Williams / *Them There Eyes* WM: William Tracey, Doris Tauber and Maceo Pinkard / *What a Little Moonlight Can Do* WM: Harry M. Woods / *You've Changed* W: Bill Carey—M: Carl Fischer.

"A talented, very intelligent singer's homage to a jazz style of a sophistication never since matched by anyone." —Vincent Canby, *The New York Times.*

**698   A Lady's Morals.** US, 1930, BW, 75 m. D: Sidney Franklin, P: MGM. Performer: Grace Moore. GB Title: Jenny Lind.

*I Hear Your Voice; Is It Destiny?* W: Clifford Grey—M: Oscar Straus / *Lovely Hours* WM: Carrie Jacobs Bond / *Oh Why?* WM: Arthur Freed, Herbert Stothart and Harry M. Woods / *The Student's Song* W: Clifford Grey—M: Oscar Straus / *Swedish Pastorale* WM: Howard Johnson and Herbert Stothart.

**699   Las Vegas Nights.** US, 1941, BW, 90 m, D: Ralph Murphy, P: Paramount (William LeBaron). Orch: Tommy Dorsey. GB Title: The Gay City.

Frank's first film.

*Dolores* (Frank Sinatra, Bert Wheeler) W: Frank Loesser—M: Louis Alter / *I'll Never Smile Again* (Frank

Sinatra, The Pied Pipers) WM: Ruth Lowe / *I've Gotta Ride* (Phil Regan, Chorus); *Mary, Mary, Quite Contrary* (Constance Moore, Lillian Cornell, Virginia Dale, Bert Wheeler) W: Frank Loesser—M: Burton Lane / *On Miami Shore* (Constance Moore, Lillian Cornell, Virginia Dale, Bert Wheeler, Phil Regan, The Pied Pipers) W: William LeBaron—M: Victor Jacobi.

**700  The Las Vegas Story.** US, 1952, BW, 88 m. D: Robert Stevenson, MS: Constantin Bakaleinikoff, P: RKO (Robert Sparks).

*I Get Along Without You Very Well* (Jane Russell) W: Jane Brown Thompson / *The Monkey Song* (Hoagy Carmichael) W: Hoagy Carmichael / *My Resistance Is Low* (Jane Russell, Hoagy Carmichael) W: Harold Adamson— M: Hoagy Carmichael.

**701  The Last American Hero.** US, 1973, C, 100 m. D: Lamont Johnson, MS: Charles Fox, P: TCF (John Cutts, William Roberts). Alt. Title: Hard Driver.

*I Got a Name* (Jim Croce) W: Norman Gimbel—M: Charles Fox.

**702  The Last of Sheila.** US, 1973, C, 120 m. D: Herbert Ross, MS: Billy Goldenberg, P: Warner (Herbert Ross).

*Friends* (Bette Midler) WM: Mark Klingman and Buzzy Linhart.

**703  The Last Picture Show.** US, 1971, BW, 118 m. D: Peter Bogdanovich, P: Columbia (Stephen J. Friedman).

*Blue Velvet* (Tony Bennett) WM: Bernie Wayne and Lee Morris / *A Bouquet of Roses* (Eddy Arnold) WM: Steve Nelson and Bob Hilliard / *Cold, Cold Heart* (Hank Williams) WM: Hank Williams / *Faded Love* (Hank Williams) / *A Fool Such as I* (Hank Snow) WM: Bill Trader / *Half as Much* (Hank Williams) WM: Curly Williams / *Hey, Good Lookin'* (Hank Williams); *I Can't Help It* (Hank Williams); *Jambalaya* (Hank Williams) WM: Hank Williams / *Kaw-Liga* (Hank Williams) WM:

Fred Rose and Hank Williams / *Lovesick Blues* (Hank Williams) WM: Irving Mills and Clifford Friend / *Mister Snow* (Johnnie Ray) W: Oscar Hammerstein II—M: Richard Rodgers / *Please, Mr. Sun* (Johnnie Ray) W: Sid Frank—M: Ray Getzov / *Rose, Rose, I Love You* (Frankie Laine) W: Wilfred Thomas— M: Based on trad. Chinese melody— Arr: Chris Langdon Carrby / *Slow Poke* (Pee Wee King) WM: Pee Wee King, Redd Stewart and Chilton Price / *Solitaire* (Tony Bennett) W: Renee Borek and Carl Nutter—M: King Guion / *Why Don't You Love Me?* (Hank Williams) WM: Hank Williams / *The Wild Side of Life* (Hank Thompson) WM: William Warren and Arlie Carter / *Wish You Were Here* (Eddie Fisher) WM: Harold Rome / *You Belong to Me* (Jo Stafford) WM: Pee Wee King, Redd Stewart and Chilton Price.

"There is excellent use of many pop tunes of the period and only introduced in a natural manner—a nickel in a jukebox, a car radio, or an early television set." —*Variety*.

**704  The Last Roundup.** US, 1947, BW, 76 m. D: John English, MD: Mischa Bakaleinikoff, P: Columbia (Armand Schaefer). Performer: Gene Autry.

*An Apple for the Teacher* W: Johnny Burke—M: James V. Monaco / *A Hundred and Sixty Acres* WM: David Kapp / *The Last Roundup* WM: Billy Hill / *She'll Be Comin' Round the Mountain* WM: Unknown / *You Can't See the Sun When You're Cryin'* WM: Allan Roberts and Doris Fisher.

**705  Last Summer.** US, 1969, C, 97 m. D: Frank Perry, MS: John Simon, P: AA (Sidney Beckerman, Alfred W. Crown).

*Cordelia* (Buddy Bruno); *Drivin' Daisy* (Cyrus Faryar); *Firehouse Blues* (Bad Kharma Dan and The Bicycle Brothers); *Hal, the Handyman* (John Simon); *Magnetic Mama* (The Electric Meatball); *Safari Mary* (Henry Diltz); *Sonuvagun* (Buddy Bruno); *Temptation,*

*Lust and Laziness* (Aunt Mary's Transcendental Slip and Lurch Band) WM: John Simon.

**706  The Last Sunset.** US, 1961, C, 112 m. D: Robert Aldrich, MS: Ernest Gold, P: Universal (Eugene Frenke, Edward Lewis).

*Pretty Little Girl in the Yellow Dress* (Kirk Douglas) W: Ned Washington—M: Dimitri Tiomkin.

**707  The Last Time I Saw Paris.** US, 1954, C, 116 m. D: Richard Brooks, MS: Conrad Salinger, P: MGM (Jack Cummings). Performer: Odette.

*Alouette* (Chorus) WM: Unknown / *Auld Lang Syne* (Chorus) W: Robert Burns—M: Unknown / *Danse avec Moi* WM: Harold Rome, Francis Lopez and Andre Hornez / *Dream, Dream, Dream* W: Mitchell Parish—M: Jimmy McHugh / *The Last Time I Saw Paris* W: Oscar Hammerstein II—M: Jerome Kern / *Mademoiselle de Paree* (Chorus) Eng. W: Mitchell Parish—M: Paul Durang / *My Heart Sings* WM: Harold Rome and "Jamblan" Henri Herpin.

**708  The Last Tycoon.** US, 1976, C, 125 m. D: Elia Kazan, MS: Maurice Jarre, P: Paramount (Sam Spiegel).

*You Have the Choice* (Jeanne Moreau) WM: Harold Pinter and Maurice Jarre.

**709  The Last Waltz.** US, 1978, C, 117 m. D: Martin Scorsese, P: UA (Robbie Robertson).

Featuring the final concert of The Band, held on Thanksgiving Day of 1976 at Winterland auditorium in San Francisco.

*Baby, Let Me Follow You Down* (Bob Dylan, The Band, Ringo Starr, Ron Wood) WM: Rev. Gary Davis / *Caravan* (Van Morrison) WM: Van Morrison / *Coyote* (Joni Mitchell) WM: Joni Mitchell / *Don't Do It* (The Band) WM: Jaime Robbie Robertson / *Dry Your Eyes* (Neil Diamond) WM: Neil Diamond and Jaime Robbie Robertson / *Evangeline* (Emmylou Harris) WM: Jaime Robbie Robertson / *Forever*

*Young* (Bob Dylan) WM: Bob Dylan / *Further On up the Road* (Eric Clapton) WM: J. Medwick Veasey and Don B. Robey / *Helpless* (Neil Young, Joni Mitchell) WM: Neil Young / *I Don't Believe You* (Bob Dylan); *I Shall Be Released* (Bob Dylan, The Band, Ringo Starr, Ron Wood, Joni Mitchell, Neil Young) WM: Bob Dylan / *It Makes No Difference* (The Band); *The Last Waltz Refrain* (The Band) WM: Jaime Robbie Robertson / *Mannish Boy* (Muddy Waters) WM: Ellas McDaniel, Melvin London and McKinley Morganfield / *Mystery Train* (Paul Butterfield) WM: Sam Phillips and Herman Parker, Jr. / *The Night They Drove Old Dixie Down* (The Band) WM: Jaime Robbie Robertson / *Old Time Religion* (The Band) WM: Unknown / *Ophelia* (The Band); *Shape I'm In* (The Band); *Stagefright* (The Band) WM: Jaime Robbie Robertson / *Such a Night* (Dr. John) WM: Mac Rebennack / *Theme from The Last Waltz* (The Band) WM: Jaime Robbie Robertson / *Turn Up Your Radio* (Van Morrison) WM: Van Morrison / *Up on Cripple Creek* (The Band); *The Weight* (The Staple Singers, The Band) WM: Jaime Robbie Robertson / *Who Do You Love?* (Ronnie Hawkins) WM: Ellas McDaniel.

"A chronicle of one important group very much a part of the music of the late 1960's and 1970's." —*Variety*.

**710  The Late Show.** US, 1977, C, 94 m. D: Robert Benton, MS: Ken Wannberg, P: Warner (Robert Altman).

*What Was* (Bev Kelly) W: Stephen Lehner—M: Ken Wannberg.

**711  The Legend of Billie Jean.** US, 1985, C, 96 m. D: Matthew Robbins, MS: Craig Safan, P: Tri-Star (Jon Peters, Peter Guber).

*Invincible* (Pat Benatar) WM: Holly Knight and Simon Climie.

**712  Les Girls.** US, 1957, C, 114 m. D: George Cukor, P: MGM (Sol C. Siegel). Vocals: Betty Wand for Kay Kendall.

*Ca, C'est L'Amour* (Taina Elg); *Ladies in Waiting* (Kay Kendall, Taina Elg, Mitzi Gaynor); *Les Girls* (Gene Kelly, Kay Kendall, Taina Elg, Mitzi Gaynor); *Why Am I So Gone About That Gal?* (Gene Kelly); *You're Just Too Too* (Gene Kelly, Kay Kendall) WM: Cole Porter.

"An exceptionally tasty musical morsel that is in the best tradition of the Metro studio." — *Variety*.

**713 Let It Be.** GB, 1970, C, 80 m. D: Michael Lindsay-Hogg, P: UA (Neil Aspinall). Performers: The Beatles.

*Across the Universe; Dig It; Don't Let Me Down* WM: John Lennon and Paul McCartney / *For You Blue* WM: George Harrison / *Get Back* WM: John Lennon and Paul McCartney / *Hey Hey Hey Hey* WM: Richard Penniman / *I Dig a Pony* WM: John Lennon and Paul McCartney / *I Me Mine* WM: George Harrison / *I've Got a Feeling* WM: John Lennon and Paul McCartney / *Kansas City* WM: Jerry Leiber and Mike Stoller / *Lawdy Miss Clawdy* WM: Lloyd Price / *Let It Be; The Long and Winding Road; Maxwell's Silver Hammer* WM: John Lennon and Paul McCartney / *Octopus's Garden* WM: Ringo Starr / *Oh! Darling; One After 909* WM: John Lennon and Paul McCartney / *Shake, Rattle and Roll* WM: Charles Calhoun [Jesse Stone] / *Two of Us* WM: John Lennon and Paul McCartney.

"Documents their recording rehearsals and provides a climactic impromptu concert the quartet gives atop their building headquarters in London. ... Some of the tunes are beautiful." —Howard Thompson, *The New York Times*.

**714 Let the Good Times Roll.** US, 1973, C, 99 m. D: Sid Levin and Robert Abel, P: Columbia (Gerald I. Isenberg).

*At the Hop* (Danny and The Juniors) WM: John Madara, Arthur Singer and Dave White / *Blueberry Hill* (Fats Domino) WM: Al Lewis, Larry Stock and Vincent Rose / *Bo Diddley* (Bo Diddley) WM: Ellas McDaniel / *Charlie Brown* (The Coasters) WM: Jerry Leiber and Mike Stoller / *Earth Angel* (The Five Satins) WM: Jesse Belvin / *Everybody Loves a Lover* (The Shirelles) W: Richard Adler—M: Robert Allen / *Good Golly, Miss Molly* (Little Richard) WM: Robert A. Blackwell and John Marascalco / *I'll Be Seeing You* (The Five Satins) W: Irving Kahal—M: Sammy Fain / *I'm a Man* (Bo Diddley) WM: Ellas McDaniel / *In the Still of the Nite* (The Five Satins) WM: Fred Parris / *Johnny B. Goode* (Chuck Berry) WM: Chuck Berry / *Let's Twist Again* (Chubby Checker) WM: Kal Mann and Dave Appell / *Let the Good Times Roll* (Shirley and Lee) WM: Leonard Lee / *Lucille* (Little Richard) WM: Albert Collins and Richard Penniman / *My Blue Heaven* (Fats Domino) W: George Whiting—M: Walter Donaldson / *Poison Ivy* (The Coasters) WM: Jerry Leiber and Mike Stoller / *Pony Time* (Chubby Checker) WM: Don Covay and John Berry / *Reelin' and Rockin'* (Chuck Berry) WM: Chuck Berry / *Rip It Up* (Little Richard) WM: John Marascalco and Robert A. Blackwell / *Rock Around the Clock* (Bill Haley and His Comets) WM: Max C. Freedman and Jimmy De Knight / *Save the Last Dance for Me* (The Five Satins) WM: Doc Pomus and Mort Shuman / *School Day* (Chuck Berry) WM: Chuck Berry / *Shake, Rattle and Roll* (Bill Haley and His Comets) WM: Charles Calhoun [Jesse Stone] / *Sincerely* (The Five Satins) WM: Harvey Fuqua and Alan Freed / *Soldier Boy* (The Shirelles) WM: Florence Green and Luther Dixon / *Sweet Little Sixteen* (Chuck Berry) WM: Chuck Berry / *The Twist* (Chubby Checker) WM: Hank Ballard.

**715 Lethal Weapon.** US, 1987, C, 110 m. D: Richard Donner, P: Warner (Richard Donner, Joel Silver). Performers: Eric Clapton, David Sanborn and Michael Kamen.

*Amanda; Coke Deal; The Desert; Meet Martin Riggs; Mr. Joshua; Nightclub; Roger; They've Got My Daughter; The Weapon* WM: Michael Kamen and Eric Clapton.

**716  Let's Be Happy.** GB, 1957, C, 107 m. D: Henry Levin, MD: Louis Levy, P: Pathe British (Marcel Hellman).

*Hold On to Love* (Tony Martin); *I'm Going to Scotland* (Vera-Ellen, Chorus); *Let's Be Happy* (Vera-Ellen, Tony Martin, Chorus); *The Man from Idaho* (Tony Martin); *One Is a Lonely Number* (Tony Martin) W: Paul Francis Webster—M: Nicholas Brodsky.

"The musical numbers are not only skimpy but also rather trite."— Howard Thompson, *The New York Times.*

**717  Let's Dance.** US, 1950, C, 112 m. D: Norman Z. McLeod, MS: Robert Emmett Dolan, P: Paramount (Robert Fellows).

*Can't Stop Talkin' About Him* (Betty Hutton, Fred Astaire); *The Hyacinth* (Lucile Watson, Fred Astaire); *Jack and the Beanstalk* (Fred Astaire); *Oh Them Dudes* (Betty Hutton, Fred Astaire); *Tunnel of Love* (Betty Hutton, Fred Astaire); *Why Fight the Feeling?* (Betty Hutton) WM: Frank Loesser.

**718  Let's Face It.** US, 1943, BW, 76 m. D: Sidney Lanfield, MD: Robert Emmett Dolan, P: Paramount (Fred Kohlmar).

*Let's Face It* (Dave Willock, Cully Richards, Chorus); *Let's Not Talk About Love* (Betty Hutton) WM: Cole Porter / *Who Did? I Did, Yes I Did* (Bob Hope, Betty Hutton) W: Sammy Cahn—M: Jule Styne.

**719  Let's Make Love.** US, 1960, C, 118 m. D: George Cukor, MD: Lionel Newman and Earl H. Hagen, P: TCF (Jerry Wald).

*Incurably Romantic* (Marilyn Monroe, Bing Crosby, Yves Montand, Frankie Vaughan); *Let's Make Love* (Marilyn Monroe, Yves Montand, Frankie Vaughan) W: Sammy Cahn—M: James Van Heusen / *My Heart Belongs to Daddy* (Marilyn Monroe) WM: Cole Porter / *Sing Me a Song That Sells* (Frankie Vaughan); *Specialization* (Marilyn Monroe, Frankie Vaughan); *You with the Crazy Eyes* (Frankie Vaughan) W: Sammy Cahn —M: James Van Heusen.

**720  Let's Rock!** US, 1958, BW, 79 m. D: Harry Foster, MD: Walter Marx, P: Columbia (Harry Foster). Alt. Title: Keep It Cool.

*All Love Broke Loose* (Wink Martindale) WM: Hal Hackady / *At the Hop* (Danny and The Juniors) WM: John Madara, Arthur Singer and Dave White / *Blast Off* (The Tyrones) WM: Jones / *Casual* (Julius La Rosa) WM: Hal Hackady and Gohman / *Crazy Crazy Party* (Julius La Rosa) WM: Stone and Winley / *Here Comes Love* (Roy Hamilton) WM: Stone / *I'll Be Waiting There for You* (Paul Anka) WM: Paul Anka / *Lonelyville* (Della Reese) WM: Hal Hackady and Marks / *Short Shorts* (The Royal Teens) W: Bob Gaudio and Bill Dalton—M: Bill Crandall and Tom Austin / *There Are Times* (Julius La Rosa); *Two Perfect Strangers* (Julius La Rosa) WM: Hal Hackady and Gohman.

**721  The Life and Times of Judge Roy Bean.** US, 1972, C, 120 m. D: John Huston, MS: Maurice Jarre, P: National General (John Foreman).

*Marmalade, Molasses and Honey* (Andy Williams) W: Alan Bergman and Marilyn Bergman—M: Maurice Jarre / *The Yellow Rose of Texas* (Paul Newman) WM: J.K.—Adapted by: Don George.

**722  Lifeguard.** US, 1976, C, 96 m. D: Daniel Petrie, P: Paramount (Ron Silverman).

*Falling in Love with the Wind* (Carol Carmichael) WM: Dale Menton and Paul Williams.

**723  Light of Day.** US, 1987, C, 107 m. D: Paul Schrader, P: Tri-Star (Rob Cohen, Keith Barish).

*Cleveland Rocks* (Ian Hunter) WM: Ian Hunter / *It's All Coming Down Tonight* (The Barbusters) WM: Frankie Miller and Andy Fraser / *Light of Day* (The Barbusters) WM: Bruce Springsteen / *Only Lonely* (Bon Jovi) WM: Jon Bon Jovi and David Bryan / *Rabbit's Got the Gun* (Joan Jett and The Hunzz) WM: Joan Jett and Kenny Laguna / *Rude Mood* (Michael J. Fox, Michael McKean, Paul Harkins) WM: Stevie Ray Vaughn / *Stay with Me Tonight* (Dave Edmunds) WM: Dave Edmunds and John David / *This Means War* (The Barbusters) WM: Joan Jett, Bob Halligan, Jr. and Kenny Laguna / *Twist It Off* (The Fabulous Thunderbirds) WM: Jimmy L. Vaughn, Ken Wilson, Fran Christina and Preston Hubbard / *You've Got No Place to Go* (Michael J. Fox) WM: Michael J. Fox and Alan Mark Paul.

**724 L'il Abner.** US, 1959, C, 113 m. D: Melvin Frank, MD: Joseph J. Lilley and Nelson Riddle, P: Paramount (Norman Panama).

The Broadway musical of 1956 was based on the popular comic strip by Al Capp.

*The Country's in the Very Best of Hands* (Stubby Kaye, Peter Palmer, Chorus); *Don't That Take the Rag Offen the Bush* (Ted Thurston, Chorus); *If I Had My Druthers* (Peter Palmer, Chorus); *Jubilation T. Cornpone* (Stubby Kaye); *The Matrimonial Stomp* (Stubby Kaye, Chorus); *Namely You* (Peter Palmer, Leslie Parrish); *Otherwise* (Peter Palmer, Leslie Parrish); *Past My Prime* (Leslie Parrish, Stubby Kaye); *Put 'Em Back* (Chorus); *Room Enuf for Us* (Chorus); *A Typical Day* (Stubby Kaye, Peter Palmer, Carmen Alvarez, Bern Hoffman, Leslie Parrish, Joe E. Marks, Billy Hayes, Chorus); *Unnecessary Town* (Peter Palmer, Leslie Parrish, Chorus) W: Johnny Mercer —M: Gene de Paul.

"Filmization . . . is lively, colorful and tuneful, done with smart showmanship in every department. . . . The songs . . . are breezy and amusing." — *Variety.*

**725 Lili.** US, 1953, C, 81 m. D: Charles Walters, MD: Hans Sommer, MS: Bronislau Kaper, P: MGM (Edwin H. Knopf).

*Hi-Lili, Hi-Lo* (Leslie Caron, Mel Ferrer) W: Helen Deutsch—M: Bronislau Kaper.

**726 Lilies of the Field.** US, 1963, BW, 93 m. D: Ralph Nelson, MS: Jerry Goldsmith, P: UA (Ralph Nelson).

*Amen* (Sidney Poitier, Chorus) WM: Unknown.

**727 Lisbon.** US, 1956, C, 90 m. D: Ray Milland, MS: Nelson Riddle, P: Republic (Ray Milland).

*Lisbon Antigua* (Female Singer, Chorus) Eng. W: Harry Dupree— Port. W: Jose Galhardo and Amadeu do Vale—M: Raul Portela.

**728 The Lisbon Story.** GB, 1946, BW, 103 m. D: Paul Stein, P: British National (Louis H. Jackson). Performer: Richard Tauber.

*Never Say Goodbye; Pedro the Fisherman* WM: Harry Parr-Davies and Harold Purcell.

**729 Listen, Darling.** US, 1938, BW, 70 m. D: Edwin L. Marin, MD: George Stoll, MS: George Axt, P: MGM (Jack Cummings). Performer: Judy Garland.

*On the Bumpy Road to Love* WM: Al Hoffman, Al Lewis and Murray Mencher / *Ten Pins in the Sky* W: Joseph McCarthy—M: Milton Ager / *Zing! Went the Strings of My Heart* WM: James F. Hanley.

**730 Lisztomania.** GB, 1975, C, 105 m. D: Ken Russell, MD: John Forsyth, P: Warner (Roy Baird, David Puttnam).

*Excelsior Song* (Paul Nicholas) W: Ken Russell and Rick Wakeman / *Funerailles* (Roger Daltrey) W: Jonathan Benson / *Hell* (Fiona Lewis) / *Love's Dream* (Roger Daltrey) W: Roger Daltrey / *Orpheus Song* (Roger Daltrey); *Peace at Last* (Roger Daltrey)

W: Jonathan Benson and Roger Daltrey. M: Franz Liszt.

**731  Little Boy Lost.** US, 1953,
BW, 95 m. D: George Seaton, MS:
Victor Young, P: Paramount (William
Perlberg). Performer: Bing Crosby.

*A Propos de Rien* W: Johnny
Burke—M: James Van Heusen / *Love Is
Like a Violin* WM: Jimmy Kennedy
and Miarka Laparcerie / *The Magic
Window* W: Johnny Burke—M: James
Van Heusen.

**732  The Little Colonel.** US,
1935, BW/C, 80 m. D: David Butler,
MD: Arthur Lange, P: TCF (B.G. De
Sylva).

*Love's Young Dream* (Evelyn Ven-
able, Shirley Temple) WM: Thomas
Moore.

**733  Little Miss Broadway.** US,
1938, BW, 70 m. D: Irving Cummings,
MD: Louis Silvers, P: TCF (Darryl F.
Zanuck).

*Auld Lang Syne* (Chorus) W: Rob-
ert Burns—M: Unknown / *Be Optimis-
tic* (Shirley Temple, Chorus); *How Can
I Thank You?* (Shirley Temple); *If All
the World Were Paper* (Shirley Temple);
*Little Miss Broadway* (Shirley Temple,
George Murphy, Chorus) W: Walter
Bullock—M: Harold Spina / *Loch Lo-
mond* (Male Quartet) WM: Unknown /
*Swing Me an Old Fashioned Song*
(Shirley Temple, Male Quartet, Female
Quartet); *We Should Be Together*
(Shirley Temple, George Murphy) W:
Walter Bullock—M: Harold Spina /
*When You Were Sweet Sixteen* (Shirley
Temple, Male Quartet) WM: James
Thornton.

"Shirley Temple shows an im-
provement in her tap dancing, her singing and her ability to turn on at will
whatever emotional faucet is demanded
by the script." — *Variety*.

**734  Little Miss Marker.** US,
1934, BW, 80 m. D: Alexander Hall, P:
Paramount (B.P. Schulberg). GB Title: Girl in Pawn.

*The Bowery* (Lynne Overman,
Chorus) W: Charles H. Hoyt—M:

Percy Gaunt / *I'm a Black Sheep Who's
Blue* (Dorothy Dell); *Laugh, You Son-
of-a-Gun* (Shirley Temple, Dorothy
Dell); *Low-Down Lullaby* (Dorothy
Dell) W: Leo Robin—M: Ralph Rain-
ger / *The Sidewalks of New York* (Lynne
Overman, Chorus) WM: James W.
Blake and Charles B. Lawlor.

"Little Shirley Temple . . . is virtually the stellar performer . . . and no
more engaging child has been beheld
on the screen." —Mordaunt Hall, *The
New York Times*.

**735  Little Nellie Kelly.** US,
1940, BW, 100 m. D: Norman Taurog,
MD: George Stoll, P: MGM (Arthur
Freed).

*It's a Great Day for the Irish* (Judy
Garland, Douglas McPhail, Chorus)
WM: Roger Edens / *Nellie Kelly, I Love
You* (Judy Garland, Douglas McPhail,
George Murphy, Charles Winninger,
Chorus) WM: George M. Cohan /
*Pretty Girl Milking Her Cow* (Judy Gar-
land) WM: Adapted by Roger Edens /
*Singin' in the Rain* (Judy Garland) W:
Arthur Freed—M: Nacio Herb Brown.

"A sprinkle of pretty singing of
several songs by Judy Garland. And
that's about all." —Bosley Crowther,
*The New York Times*.

**736  A Little Night Music.** Aus-
tria–West Germany, 1978, C, 124 m.
D: Harold Prince, P: Sascha Film
(Elliott Kastner).

The 1955 Ingmar Bergman movie,
"Smiles of a Summer Night" was the
basis for the 1973 Stephen Sondheim
Broadway musical that ultimately became this motion picture.

*Every Day a Little Death* (Diana
Rigg); *The Glamorous Life* (Chloe
Franks); *It Would Have Been Wonderful*
(Len Cariou, Laurence Guittard);
*Later* (Len Cariou, Lesley-Anne Down,
Christopher Guard); *Night Waltz*
(Elizabeth Taylor, Len Cariou,
Chorus); *Now* (Len Cariou, Lesley-
Anne Down, Christopher Guard);
*Send in the Clowns* (Elizabeth Taylor,
Len Cariou); *Soon* (Len Cariou, Lesley-

Anne Down, Christopher Guard); *A Weekend in the Country* (Chorus); *You Must Meet My Wife* (Elizabeth Taylor, Len Cariou) WM: Stephen Sondheim.

"It should be ebullient and fun. It isn't." —Vincent Canby, *The New York Times*.

**737 The Little Prince.** GB, 1974, C, 88 m. D: Stanley Donen, P: Paramount (Stanley Donen).

*Be Happy* (Donna McKechnie); *Closer and Closer and Closer* (Gene Wilder, Steven Warner); *I'm on Your Side* (Richard Kiley); *I Need Air* (Richard Kiley); *I Never Met a Rose* (Richard Kiley); *It's a Hat* (Richard Kiley, Chorus); *Little Prince* (Richard Kiley, Chorus); *A Snake in the Grass* (Bob Fosse); *Why Is the Desert* (Richard Kiley, Steven Warner); *You're a Child* (Joss Ackland, Steven Warner) W: Alan Jay Lerner—M: Frederick Loewe.

"Alan Jay Lerner's adaptation of the book by Antoine De Saint-Exupery is flat and his lyrics are unmemorable, as are Frederick Loewe's melodies." —*Variety*.

**738 Little Shop of Horrors.** US, 1986, C, 88 m. D: Frank Oz, P: Warner (David Geffen). Vocals: Levi Stubbs for Audrey 2.

*Da-Doo* (Rick Moranis, Michelle Weeks, Tichina Arnold, Tisha Campbell, The Do Wops); *Dentist!* (Steve Martin, Michelle Weeks, Tichina Arnold, Tisha Campbell); *Don't Feed the Plants* (Chorus); *Feed Me* (Audrey 2, Rick Moranis, Michelle Weeks, Tichina Arnold, Tisha Campbell); *Grow for Me* (Michelle Weeks, Tichina Arnold, Tisha Campbell); *Little Shop of Horrors* (Michelle Weeks, Tichina Arnold, Tisha Campbell); *Mean Green Mother from Outer Space* (Audrey 2, Chorus); *The Meek Shall Inherit* (Rick Moranis, Michelle Weeks, Tichina Arnold, Tisha Campbell); *Skid Row* (Michelle Weeks, Tichina Arnold, Tisha Campbell, Ellen Greene, Rick Moranis, Chorus); *Some Fun Now* (Michelle Weeks, Tichina Arnold, Tisha Camp-bell); *Somewhere That's Green* (Ellen Greene); *Suddenly, Seymour* (Rick Moranis, Ellen Greene, Michelle Weeks, Tichina Arnold, Tisha Campbell); *Suppertime* (Audrey 2, Michelle Weeks, Tichina Arnold, Tisha Campbell) W: Howard Ashman—M: Alan Menken.

"Almost nothing is left ... from the 1961 Roger Corman film that inspired the 1982 stage musical." —*Variety*.

**739 Little Women.** US, 1933, BW, 115 m. D: George Cukor, MS: Max Steiner, P: RKO (David O. Selznick, Merian C. Cooper, Kenneth MacGowan).

*Abide with Me* (Katharine Hepburn, Joan Bennett, Jean Parker, Frances Dee, Spring Byington) W: Henry Francis Lyte—M: William Henry Monk / *None But the Lonely Heart* (Paul Lukas) W: Johann Wolfgang von Goethe—M: Peter Ilyich Tchaikovsky / *O Little Town of Bethlehem* (Chorus) W: Phillips Brooks—M: Lewis H. Redner.

**740 Live a Little, Love a Little.** US, 1968, C, 90 m. D: Norman Taurog, MS: Billy Strange, P: MGM (Douglas Laurence). Performer: Elvis Presley.

*Almost in Love* WM: Rick Bonfa and Randy Starr / *Edge of Reality* WM: Bill Giant, Bernie Baum and Florence Kaye / *A Little Less Conversation* WM: Mac Davis and Billy Strange / *Wonderful World* WM: Guy Fletcher and Doug Flett.

**741 Live and Let Die.** GB, 1973, C, 121 m. D: Guy Hamilton, MS: George Martin, P: UA (Albert R. Broccoli, Harry Saltzman).

*Live and Let Die* (Paul McCartney and Wings) WM: Paul McCartney and Linda McCartney.

**742 The Lively Set.** US, 1964, C, 95 m. D: Jack Arnold, MD: Joseph Gershenson, P: Universal (William Alland).

*Boss Barracuda* (The Surfaris) W: Terry Melcher / *Casey Wake Up* (Joanie

Sommers); *If You Love Him* (Joanie Sommers); *The Lively Set* (James Darren) W: Bobby Darin / *Look at Me* (Wink Martindale) W: Randy Newman. M: Bobby Darin.

**743  Living It Up.** US, 1954, C, 95 m. D: Norman Taurog, MD: Walter Scharf, P: Paramount (Paul Jones).

*Champagne and Wedding Cake* (Jerry Lewis); *Ev'ry Street's a Boulevard in Old New York* (Dean Martin, Jerry Lewis, Chorus); *How Do You Speak to an Angel?* (Dean Martin, Jerry Lewis); *Money Burns a Hole in My Pocket* (Dean Martin); *That's What I Like* (Dean Martin); *You're Gonna Dance with Me, Baby* (Sheree North, Jerry Lewis) W: Bob Hilliard—M: Jule Styne.

**744  Lizzie.** US, 1957, BW, 81 m. D: Hugo Haas, MS: Leith Stevens, P: MGM (Jerry Bresler).

*It's Not for Me to Say* (Johnny Mathis) W: Al Stillman—M: Robert Allen.

**745  Lone Star.** US, 1952, BW, 94 m. D: Vincent Sherman, MS: David Buttolph, P: MGM (Z. Wayne Griffin).

*Lovers Were Meant to Cry* (Ava Gardner) WM: Earl K. Brent.

**746  The Long Hot Summer.** US, 1958, C, 117 m. D: Martin Ritt, MS: Alex North, P: TCF (Jerry Wald).

*The Long Hot Summer* (Jimmie Rodgers) W: Sammy Cahn—M: Alex North.

**747  The Longest Day.** US, 1962, BW, 180 m. D: Ken Annakin, Andrew Marton and Bernhard Wicki, P: TCF (Darryl F. Zanuck, Elmo Williams).

*The Longest Day* (Paul Anka) WM: Paul Anka.

**748  Looking for Love.** US, 1964, C, 83 m. D: Don Weis, P: MGM (Joe Pasternak). Performer: Connie Francis.

*Be My Love* W: Sammy Cahn— M: Nicholas Brodszky / *I Can't Believe That You're in Love with Me* W: Clarence Gaskill—M: Jimmy McHugh /

*Let's Have a Party; Looking for Love* W: Stan Vincent—M: Hank Hunter / *This Is My Happiest Moment* W: Ted Murray—M: Benny Davis / *When the Clock Strikes Midnight* W: Stan Vincent—M: Hank Hunter / *Whoever You Are I Love You* W: Peter Udell—M: Gary Geld.

**749  Looking for Mr. Goodbar.** US, 1977, C, 135 m. D: Richard Brooks, MS: Artie Kane, P: Paramount (Freddie Fields).

*Back Stabbers* (The O'Jays) WM: Gene McFadden, John Whitehead and Leon Huff / *Could It Be Magic* (Barry Manilow, Donna Summer, Adrienne Anderson) WM: Barry Manilow and Adrienne Anderson / *Don't Ask to Stay Until Tomorrow* (Marlena Shaw) W: Carol Connors—M: Artie Kane / *Don't Leave Me This Way* (Thelma Houston) WM: Cary Gilbert, Kenny Gamble and Leon Huff / *Love Hangover* (Diana Ross) WM: Marilyn McLeod and Pam Sawyer / *Love to Love You Baby* (Donna Summer) WM: Pete Bellotte, Donna Summer and Giorgio Moroder / *Lowdown* (Boz Scaggs) WM: David Paich and William Scaggs.

**750  Lost Horizon.** US, 1973, C, 143 m. D: Charles Jarrott, P: Columbia (Ross Hunter).

*I Come to You* (Peter Finch, Liv Ullmann); *If I Could Go Back* (Peter Finch); *I Might Frighten Her Away* (Peter Finch, Liv Ullmann); *Living Together, Growing Together* (Chorus); *Lost Horizon* (Shawn Phillips); *Question Me an Answer* (Bobby Van, Chorus); *Reflections* (Sally Kellerman); *Share the Joy* (Olivia Hussey); *The Things I Will Not Miss* (Sally Kellerman, Olivia Hussey); *Where Knowledge Ends* (Liv Ullmann); *The World Is a Circle* (Liv Ullmann, Chorus) W: Hal David—M: Burt Bacharach.

"The form is that of filmed operetta in three acts, superbly mounted." —*Variety.*

**751  Love Affair.** US, 1939, BW, 87 m. D: Leo McCarey, P: RKO (Leo McCarey).

*Sing, My Heart* (Irene Dunne) W: Ted Koehler—M: Harold Arlen / *Wishing* (Irene Dunne, Female Trio) WM: B.G. De Sylva.

**752 Love and Hisses.** US, 1937, BW, 84 m. D: Sidney Lanfield, MS: Louis Silvers, P: TCF (Kenneth MacGowan). Orch: Ben Bernie.

*Be a Good Sport* (The Brewster Twins); *Broadway's Gone Hawaii* (Ruth Terry, The Peters Sisters) W: Mack Gordon—M: Harry Revel / *Darling, Je Vous Aime Beaucoup* (Simone Simon) WM: Anna Sosenko / *I Wanna Be in Winchell's Column* (Dick Baldwin); *Sweet Someone* (Simone Simon) W: Mack Gordon—M: Harry Revel.

**753 Love at First Bite.** US, 1979, C, 96 m. D: Stan Dragoti, MS: Charles Bernstein, P: AIP (Joel Freeman).

*Dancin' Through the Night* (Sydney Barnes) WM: Charles Bernstein, Steven Hines, Joe Long and Robbie Adcock / *Fly by Night* (Pat Hodges) WM: Charles Bernstein, Steven Hines, Joe Long and D. Level / *I Love the Nightlife* (Evelyn "Champagne" King) WM: Alicia Bridges and Susan Hutcheson / *Love Theme* (Yvonne Lewis, Ullanda McCullough, Babi "Dancin" Floyd, Zachary Sanders); *Manhattan* (Yvonne Lewis, Ullanda McCullough, Babi "Dancin" Floyd, Zachary Sanders) WM: Charles Bernstein.

**754 Love Finds Andy Hardy.** US, 1938, BW, 90 m. D: George B. Seitz, MS: David Snell, P: MGM. Performer: Judy Garland.

*In-Between* WM: Roger Edens / *Meet the Beat of My Heart* W: Mack Gordon—M: Harry Revel.

**755 Love Happy.** US, 1949, BW, 91 m. D: David Miller, P: UA (Mary Pickford, Lester Cowan). Performer: Marion Hutton.

*Love Happy; Mama Wants to Know; Willow, Weep for Me* WM: Ann Ronell.

**756 Love Is a Many-Splendored Thing.** US, 1955, C, 102 m. D: Henry King, MS: Alfred Newman, P: TCF (Buddy Adler).

*Love Is a Many-Splendored Thing* (The Four Aces) W: Paul Francis Webster—M: Sammy Fain.

**757 The Love Machine.** US, 1971, C, 108 m. D: Jack Haley, Jr., MS: Artie Butler, P: Columbia (Mike Frankovich). Performer: Dionne Warwick.

*Amanda's Theme* WM: Mark Lindsay and Artie Butler / *He's Movin' On* W: Ruth Batchelor—M: Brian Wells.

**758 Love Me Forever.** US, 1935, BW, 90 m. D: Victor Schertzinger, MD: Louis Silvers, P: Columbia (Max Winslow). GB Title: On Wings of Song. Performer: Grace Moore.

*Funiculi-Funicula* WM: Luigi Denza / *Il Bacio* Ital. W: Aldighieri—M: Luigi Arditi / *Love Me Forever; Whoa* W: Gus Kahn—M: Victor Schertzinger.

**759 Love Me or Leave Me.** US, 1955, C, 122 m. D: Charles Vidor, MD: George Stoll, P: MGM (Joe Pasternak). Performer: Doris Day.

*At Sundown* WM: Walter Donaldson / *Everybody Loves My Baby* WM: Jack Palmer and Spencer Williams / *I'll Never Stop Loving You* W: Sammy Cahn—M: Nicholas Brodszky / *I'm Sitting on Top of the World* (Claude Stroud) W: Sam M. Lewis and Joe Young—M: Ray Henderson / *It All Depends on You* W: B.G. De Sylva and Lew Brown—M: Ray Henderson / *Love Me or Leave Me* W: Gus Kahn—M: Walter Donaldson / *Mean to Me* W: Roy Turk—M: Fred E. Ahlert / *Never Look Back* WM: Chilton Price / *Sam, the Old Accordion Man* WM: Walter Donaldson / *Shaking the Blues Away* WM: Irving Berlin / *Stay on the Right Side, Sister* W: Ted Koehler—M: Rube Bloom / *Ten Cents a Dance* W: Lorenz Hart—M: Richard Rodgers / *You Made Me Love You* W: Joseph McCarthy—M: James V. Monaco.

"It is hard to think of anyone better qualified to do the job of singing Miss [Ruth] Etting's old numbers than the lovely and lyrical Miss Day." —Bosley Crowther, *The New York Times*.

**760 Love Me Tender.** US, 1956, BW, 89 m. D: Robert D. Webb, MS: Lionel Newman, P: TCF (David Weisbart). Performer: Elvis Presley.

Songs used in this film were actually written by Ken Darby, who was Vera Matson's husband and the music director at Fox.

*Let Me; Love Me Tender; Poor Boy; We're Gonna Move* WM: Elvis Presley and Vera Matson.

**761 Love Me Tonight.** US, 1932, BW, 96 m. D: Rouben Mamoulian, MD: Nat W. Finston, P: Paramount (Rouben Mamoulian).

*Isn't It Romantic?* (Maurice Chevalier, Jeanette MacDonald, Bert Roach, Rolfe Sedan, Tyler Brooke, Chorus); *Love Me Tonight* (Maurice Chevalier, Jeanette MacDonald); *Lover* (Jeanette MacDonald); *Mimi* (Maurice Chevalier, C. Aubrey Smith, Charlie Ruggles, Elizabeth Patterson, Ethel Griffies, Blanche Friderici, Charles Butterworth); *The Poor Apache* (Maurice Chevalier); *The Son of a Gun Is Nothing But a Tailor* (C. Aubrey Smith, Elizabeth Patterson, Ethel Griffies, Blanche Friderici, Myrna Loy, Robert Greig, Edgar Norton, Cecil Cunningham, Rita Owin, Mel Calish); *That's the Song of Paree* (Maurice Chevalier, Marion Byron, Gabby Hayes, Chorus); *A Woman Needs Something Like That* (Jeanette MacDonald, Joseph Cawthorn) W: Lorenz Hart—M: Richard Rodgers.

"There are episodes in this production that merited applause and the only reason the audience failed to clap their hands was because they evidently thought they might miss a few words of dialogue or one of the melodious bits of music." —Mordaunt Hall, *The New York Times*.

**762 The Love Parade.** US, 1929, BW, 110 m. D: Ernst Lubitsch, MD: Victor Schertzinger, P: Paramount (Ernst Lubitsch).

*Anything to Please the Queen* (Jeanette MacDonald, Maurice Chevalier); *Champagne* (Lupino Lane, Chorus); *Dream Lover* (Jeanette MacDonald, Chorus); *Let's Be Common* (Lupino Lane, Lillian Roth); *March of the Grenadiers* (Jeanette MacDonald, Chorus); *My Love Parade* (Jeanette MacDonald, Maurice Chevalier); *Nobody's Using It Now* (Maurice Chevalier); *Paris, Stay the Same* (Maurice Chevalier, Lupino Lane); *The Queen Is Always Right* (Lupino Lane, Lillian Roth, Chorus) W: Clifford Grey—M: Victor Schertzinger.

"It can be said that this is the first true screen musical." —*Variety*.

"It is a charming imaginary kingdom satire, interspersed with song." —Mordaunt Hall, *The New York Times*.

**763 Love Thy Neighbor.** US, 1940, BW, 82 m. D: Mark Sandrich, P: Paramount (Mark Sandrich). MB: The Merry Macs.

*Dearest, Darest I?* (Eddie "Rochester" Anderson); *Do You Know Why?* (Mary Martin); *Isn't That Just Like Love?* (Mary Martin) W: Johnny Burke—M: James Van Heusen / *My Heart Belongs to Daddy* (Mary Martin) WM: Cole Porter.

**764 Love with the Proper Stranger.** US, 1963, BW, 100 m. D: Robert Mulligan, MS: Elmer Bernstein, P: Paramount (Alan J. Pakula).

*Love with the Proper Stranger* (Jack Jones) W: Johnny Mercer—M: Elmer Bernstein.

**765 Lovely to Look At.** US, 1952, C, 105 m. D: Mervyn LeRoy, MD: Carmen Dragon, P: MGM (Jack Cummings).

A new version of RKO's 1935 film "Roberta."

*I'll Be Hard to Handle* (Ann Miller, Chorus) W: Bernard Dougall, Oscar Hammerstein II and Dorothy Fields / *I Won't Dance* (Marge Champion, Gower Champion) W: Dorothy Fields and Jimmy McHugh / *Lafayette* (Red

Skelton, Howard Keel, Gower Champion) W: Dorothy Fields / *Lovely to Look At* (Howard Keel, Chorus) W: Dorothy Fields and Jimmy McHugh / *The Most Exciting Night* (Howard Keel) W: Otto Harbach and Dorothy Fields / *Smoke Gets in Your Eyes* (Kathryn Grayson); *The Touch of Your Hand* (Kathryn Grayson, Howard Keel); *Yesterdays* (Kathryn Grayson); *You're Devastating* (Kathryn Grayson, Howard Keel) W: Otto Harbach—M: Jerome Kern.

"The touch of Jerome Kern's hand is still magical." —A.H. Weiler, *The New York Times*.

**766 Lovers and Other Strangers.** US, 1970, C, 106 m. MS: Fred Karlin, P: ABC (David Susskind).

Songwriters Royer and Griffin were also members of the rock group called Bread.

*For All We Know* (Larry Meredith, The Carpenters) W: Robb Wilson [Robb Royer] and Arthur James [Arthur Griffin]—M: Fred Karlin.

**767 Loving You.** US, 1957, C, 101 m. D: Hal Kanter, MS: Walter Scharf, P: Paramount (Hal B. Wallis). MB: The Jordanaires. Performer: Elvis Presley.

*Dancing on a Dare* (Dolores Hart) / *Detour* (Dolores Hart) WM: Paul Westmoreland / *Got a Lot o' Livin' to Do* WM: Aaron Schroeder and Ben Weisman / *Hot Dog* WM: Jerry Leiber and Mike Stoller / *Lonesome Cowboy* WM: Sid Tepper and Roy C. Bennett / *Loving You* WM: Jerry Leiber and Mike Stoller / *Mean Woman Blues* WM: Claude DeMetrius / *Party* WM: Jessie Mae Robinson / *Teddy Bear* WM: Kal Mann and Bernie Lowe / *The Yellow Rose* (Dolores Hart).

"Does Elvis sing? More or less— eight numbers, including the title tune twice." —Howard Thompson, *The New York Times*.

**768 Lucky Lady.** US, 1975, C, 118 m. D: Stanley Donen, MS: Ralph Burns, P: TCF (Michael Gruskoff).

*Ain't Misbehavin'* (Burt Reynolds) W: Andy Razaf—M: Thomas "Fats" Waller and Harry Brooks / *All I Do Is Dream of You* (Vangle Charmichael) W: Arthur Freed—M: Nacio Herb Brown / *Hot Time in the Old Town Tonight* (Bessie Smith) W: Joseph Hayden—M: Theodore M. Metz / *If I Had a Talking Picture of You* (Vangle Charmichael) W: B.G. De Sylva and Lew Brown—M: Ray Henderson / *Lucky Lady* (Liza Minnelli); *While the Getting Is Good* (Liza Minnelli) W: Fred Ebb— M: John Kander / *Young Woman Blues* (Bessie Smith) WM: Bessie Smith.

**769 Lullaby of Broadway.** US, 1951, C, 92 m. D: David Butler, MD: Ray Heindorf, P: Warner (William Jacobs). Performer: Doris Day.

*I Love the Way You Say Goodnight* (Doris Day, Gene Nelson) WM: Eddie Pola and George Wyle / *In a Shanty in Old Shanty Town* W: Joe Young—M: John Siras and Jack Little / *Just One of Those Things* WM: Cole Porter / *Lullaby of Broadway* (Doris Day, Gene Nelson, Chorus) W: Al Dubin—M: Harry Warren / *Please Don't Talk About Me When I'm Gone* W: Sidney Clare— M: Sam H. Stept / *Somebody Loves Me* (Doris Day, Gene Nelson) W: B.G. De Sylva and Ballard MacDonald—M: George Gershwin / *You're Getting to Be a Habit with Me* W: Al Dubin—M: Harry Warren / *Zing! Went the Strings of My Heart* (Gene Nelson) WM: James F. Hanley.

"Most of the tunes are hits of the previous two decades. Day scores with her solo song-and-dance routines." — *Variety*.

**770 Luxury Liner.** US, 1948, C, 98 m. D: Richard Whorf, MD: George Stoll, P: MGM (Joe Pasternak). Orch: Xavier Cugat.

*Alouette* (Jane Powell, Chorus) WM: Unknown / *Come Back to Sorrento* (Lauritz Melchior) WM: Ernesto De Curtis and Claude Aveling / *I've Got You Under My Skin* (Marina Koshetz) WM: Cole Porter / *The Peanut Vendor*

(Jane Powell) Eng. W: Marion Sunshine and L. Wolfe Gilbert—M: Moises Simons / *Spring Came Back to Vienna* (Jane Powell) WM: Janice Torre, Fred Spielman and Fritz Rotter / *Yes! We Have No Bananas* (The Pied Pipers) WM: Frank Silver and Irving Cohn.

**771   Macao.** US, 1952, BW, 80 m. D: Josef von Sternberg, MD: Constantin Bakaleinikoff, MS: Anthony Collins, P: RKO (Alex Gottlieb). Performer: Jane Russell.

*Ocean Breeze* W: Leo Robin—M: Jule Styne / *One for My Baby* W: Johnny Mercer—M: Harold Arlen / *You Kill Me* W: Leo Robin—M: Jule Styne.

**772   McVicar.** GB, 1980, C, 112 m. D: Tom Clegg, MD: Jeff Wayne, P: Crown International (Roy Baird, Bill Curbishley, Roger Daltry). Performer: Roger Daltry.

*Free Me; Just a Dream Away* WM: Russ Ballard / *McVicar; Waiting for a Friend* WM: Billy Nicholls / *White City Lights* WM: Billy Nicholls and Jon Lind / *Without Your Love* WM: Billy Nicholls.

**773   Mad About Music.** US, 1938, BW, 98 m. D: Norman Taurog, MS: Frank Skinner and Charles Previn, P: Universal (Joe Pasternak). MB: Chorus; Cappy Barra's Harmonica Ensemble. Performer: Deanna Durbin.

*Ave Maria* (Deanna Durbin, The Vienna Boys' Choir) W: The Bible—M: Charles Gounod, based on Bach / *Chapel Bells; I Love to Whistle; A Serenade to the Stars* W: Harold Adamson—M: Jimmy McHugh.

**774   The Magic Christian.** GB, 1970, C, 93 m. D: Joseph McGrath, P: Commonwealth United (Denis O'-Dell).

*Carry On to Tomorrow* (Badfinger) WM: Tom Evans and Pete Ham / *Come and Get It* (Badfinger) WM: Paul McCartney / *Mad About the Boy* (Yul Brynner) WM: Noel Coward / *Rock of Ages* (Badfinger) WM: Tom Evans, Pete Ham and Mike Gibbins / *Some-*

*thing in the Air* (Thunderclap Newman) WM: John Keene.

**775   The Magic Garden of Stanley Sweetheart.** US, 1970, C, 117 m. D: Leonard Horn, MS: Jerry Styner, P: MGM (Martin Poll).

*Keep on Keepin' That Man* (Angeline Butler) WM: Dan Penn and Bobby Memmons / *Nobody Knows* (Bill Medley); *Sweet Gingerbread Man* (The Mike Curb Congregation) W: Alan Bergman and Marilyn Bergman—M: Michel Legrand / *Time to Make a Turn* (The Crow) WM: Larry Wiegand / *Water* (Michael Greer) WM: David Lucas.

**776   The Magic of Lassie.** US, 1978, C, 100 m. D: Don Chaffey, MD: Irwin Kostal, P: International Picture Show (Bonita Granville Wrather, William Beaudine, Jr.). Vocals: Debby Boone for Lassie.

*Banjo Song* (Chorus); *Brass Rings and Daydreams* (Lassie, Chorus); *I Can't Say Goodbye* (Chorus); *Nobody's Property* (Chorus); *A Rose Is Not a Rose* (Pat Boone, Alice Faye); *That Hometown Feeling* (James Stewart); *There'll Be Other Friday Nights* (Lassie); *Travelin' Music* (Mickey Rooney); *When You're Loved* (Lassie) WM: Richard M. Sherman and Robert B. Sherman.

**777   Mahogany.** US, 1975, C, 109 m. D: Berry Gordy, Jr., MD: Lee Holdridge, MS: Michael Masser, P: Paramount (Rob Cohen, Jack Ballard).

*Do You Know Where You're Going To?* (Diana Ross) W: Gerry Goffin—M: Michael Masser.

**778   The Main Attraction.** GB, 1962, C, 90 m. D: Daniel Petrie, MD: Muir Mathieson, MS: Andrew Adorian, P: Seven Arts / MGM (John Patrick). Performer: Pat Boone.

*Amore Baciami* WM: C.C. Rossi, C.C. Testoni, Geoffrey Barnes, John Turner and Pat Boone / *Gondoli, Gondola* WM: Renato Carosone and Nisa / *The Main Attraction* WM: Pat Boone and Jeff Cory / *Si, Si, Si* WM: Domenico Modugno and Abel Baer.

**779 Make Mine Laughs.** US, 1949, BW, 64 m. D: Richard Fleischer, P: RKO (George Bilson).

*If You Happen to Find My Heart* (Dennis Day, Anne Shirley) WM: Herb Magidson and Lew Pollack / *Moonlight Over the Islands* (Frances Langford) WM: Mort Greene and Lew Pollack / *Send Back My Love to Me* (Frances Langford) / *Who Killed Vaudeville?* (Joan Davis, Jack Haley) WM: Jack Yellen and Sammy Fain / *You Go Your Way* (Ray Bolger) W: Mort Greene—M: Harry Revel.

**780 Making Love.** US, 1982, C, 113 m. D: Arthur Hiller, MS: Leonard Rosenman, P: TCF (Allen Adler, Daniel Melnick).

*Making Love* (Roberta Flack) WM: Carole Bayer Sager, Burt Bacharach and Bruce Roberts.

**781 Mame.** US, 1974, C, 131 m. D: Gene Saks, MD: Ralph Burns and Billy Byers, P: Warner (Robert Fryer, James Cresson).

Angela Lansbury and Bea Arthur starred in the 1966 Broadway musical version of the Patrick Dennis novel.

*Bosom Buddies* (Lucille Ball, Beatrice Arthur); *Gooch's Song* (Jane Connell); *If He Walked Into My Life* (Lucille Ball); *It's Today* (Lucille Ball, Chorus); *The Letter* (Kirby Furlong, Bruce Davison); *Loving You* (Robert Preston); *Mame* (Robert Preston, Chorus); *The Man in the Moon* (Beatrice Arthur, Chorus); *My Best Girl* (Lucille Ball, Kirby Furlong); *Open a New Window* (Lucille Ball, Kirby Furlong, Chorus); *St. Bridget* (Jane Connell); *We Need a Little Christmas* (Lucille Ball, Chorus) WM: Jerry Herman.

**782 Mammy.** US, 1930, BW/C, 84 m. D: Michael Curtiz, P: Warner (Walter Morosco). MB: Meadows' Merry Minstrels. Performer: Al Jolson.

*Knights of the Road; Let Me Sing and I'm Happy; Looking at You* WM: Irving Berlin / *My Mammy* W: Sam M. Lewis and Joe Young—M: Walter Donaldson / *To My Mammy* WM: Irving Berlin / *Who Paid the Rent for Mrs. Rip Van Winkle?* W: Alfred Bryan—M: Fred Fisher / *Why Do They All Take the Night Boat to Albany?* W: Sam M. Lewis and Joe Young—M: Jean Schwartz / *Yes, We Have No Bananas* [parody] WM: Irving Berlin, Frank Silver and Irving Cohn.

"A lively picture [from the musical 'Mr. Bones'] with Al Jolson singing new and old songs, including among the Irving Berlin new numbers a couple of melodious hits." —*Variety.*

**783 Man About Town.** US, 1939, BW, 85 m. D: Mark Sandrich, MD: Victor Young, P: Paramount (Arthur Hornblow, Jr.). Orch: Matt Malneck.

*Fidgety Joe* (Betty Grable) W: Frank Loesser—M: Matt Malneck / *Strange Enchantment* (Dorothy Lamour); *That Sentimental Sandwich* (Dorothy Lamour, Phil Harris) W: Frank Loesser—M: Frederick Hollander.

**784 Man of La Mancha.** US, 1972, C, 130 m. D: Arthur Hiller, MD: Laurence Rosenthal, P: UA (Arthur Hiller). Vocals: Simon Gilbert for Peter O'Toole.

Richard Kiley played Don Quixote in the original ANTA Theatre production of this musical that opened in 1965 and ran for more than two thousand performances.

*Aldonza* (Sophia Loren, Peter O'Toole); *The Barber's Song* (Gino Conforti); *The Dubbing* (Sophia Loren, Peter O'Toole, Harry Andrews, James Coco); *Dulcinea* (Sophia Loren, Peter O'Toole, Chorus); *Golden Helmet of Mambrino* (Peter O'Toole, James Coco, Gino Conforti); *I'm Only Thinking of Him* (Julia Gregg, Rosalie Crutchley, Ian Richardson); *The Impossible Dream* (Sophia Loren, Peter O'Toole, Julia Gregg, Ian Richardson, Chorus); *I Really Like Him* (James Coco); *It's All the Same* (Sophia Loren, Chorus); *Little Bird, Little Bird* (Chorus); *A Little*

*Gossip* (James Coco); *Man of La Man-cha* (Peter O'Toole, James Coco); *The Psalm* (Ian Richardson) W: Joe Dar-ion—M: Mitch Leigh.

"Loren, no songbird she, does her own warbling, as does Coco." —*Variety*.

**785  Man on Fire.** US, 1957, BW, 95 m. D: Ranald MacDougall, MS: David Raksin, P: MGM (Sol C. Siegel).

*Man on Fire* (The Ames Brothers) W: Paul Francis Webster—M: Sammy Fain.

**786  The Man Who Knew Too Much.** US, 1956, C, 120 m. D: Alfred Hitchcock, MS: Bernard Herrmann, P: Paramount (Alfred Hitchcock).

*Que Sera Sera* (Doris Day) WM: Jay Livingston and Ray Evans.

**787  The Man Who Loved Women.** US, 1983, C, 110 m. D: Blake Edwards, MS: Henry Mancini, P: Columbia (Blake Edwards, Tony Adams).

*Little Boys* (Helen Reddy) W: Alan Bergman and Marilyn Bergman—M: Henry Mancini.

**788  The Man with the Golden Gun.** GB, 1974, C, 125 m. D: Guy Hamilton, MS: John Barry, P: UA (Harry Saltzman, Albert R. Broccoli).

*The Man with the Golden Gun* (Lulu) W: Don Black—M: John Barry.

**789  Man Without a Star.** US, 1955, C, 89 m. D: King Vidor, MD: Joseph Gershenson, P: Universal (Aaron Rosenberg).

*And the Moon Grew Brighter and Brighter* (Kirk Douglas) WM: Lou Singer and Jimmy Kennedy.

**790  Mandalay.** US, 1934, BW, 65 m. D: Michael Curtiz, P: Warner (Robert Presncil).

*When Tomorrow Comes* (Kay Francis) W: Irving Kahal—M: Sammy Fain.

**791  Manhattan Melodrama.** US, 1934, BW, 93 m. D: W.S. Van Dyke II, P: MGM (David O. Selznick).

The song used in this film was an earlier version, with a different lyric, of the classic *Blue Moon*.

*The Bad in Every Man* (Shirley Ross) W: Lorenz Hart—M: Richard Rodgers.

**792  Mannequin.** US, 1937, BW, 95 m. D: Frank Borzage, MS: Edward Ward, P: MGM (Joseph L. Mankiewicz).

*Always and Always* (Joan Crawford) W: Robert Wright and George "Chet" Forrest—M: Edward Ward.

**793  Marjorie Morningstar.** US, 1958, C, 123 m. D: Irving Rapper, MS: Max Steiner, P: Warner (Milton Sperling).

*A Very Precious Love* (Gene Kelly) W: Paul Francis Webster—M: Sammy Fain.

**794  Marked Woman.** US, 1937, BW, 99 m. D: Lloyd Bacon, MD: Leo F. Forbstein, MS: Heinz Roemheld, P: Warner (Louis F. Edelman).

*Mr. and Mrs. Doakes* (Lola Lane) WM: Jack Scholl and M.K. Jerome / *My Silver Dollar Man* (Rosalind Marquis) W: Al Dubin—M: Harry Warren.

**795  The Marriage-Go-Round.** US, 1960, C, 98 m. D: Walter Lang, MS: Dominic Frontiere, P: TCF (Leslie Stevens).

*The Marriage-Go-Round* (Tony Bennett) WM: Alan Bergman, Marilyn Bergman and Lew Spence.

**796  Marriage on the Rocks.** US, 1965, C, 109 m. D: Jack Donohue, MS: Nelson Riddle, P: Warner (William H. Daniels).

*There Was a Sinner Man* (Trini Lopez) WM: Billy Barberis, Bobby Weinstein, Bobby Hart, Trini Lopez and Teddy Randazzo.

**797  Married to the Mob.** US, 1988, C, 103 m. D: Jonathan Demme, MS: David Byrne, P: Orion (Kenneth Utt, Edward Saxon).

*Bizarre Love Triangle* (New Order) WM: New Order / *Devil Does Your Dog Bite* (Tom Tom Club) WM: C. Frantz / *Goodbye Roses* (Q. Lazzarus) WM: W. Garvey / *Jump in the River* (Sinead O'Connor) WM: Sinead O'Connor and

Marco Pirroni / *Liar, Liar* (Debbie Harry) WM: James J. Donna / *Queen of Voodoo* (Voodooist Corporation) WM: W. Barg, S. Albright and S. Breck / *Suspicion of Love* (Chris Isaak) WM: Chris Isaak / *Time Burns* (Ziggy Marley and The Melody Makers) WM: Ziggy Marley / *Too Far Gone* (The Feelies) WM: G. Mercer and B. Million / *You Don't Miss Your Water* (Brian Eno) WM: W. Bell.

**798 Mary Poppins.** US, 1964, C, 140 m. D: Robert Stevenson, MD: Irwin Kostal, P: Buena Vista (Walt Disney).

*Chim Chim Cheree* (Julie Andrews, Dick Van Dyke, Karen Dotrice, Matthew Garber); *Feed the Birds* (Julie Andrews); *Fidelity Fiduciary Bank* (Dick Van Dyke, David Tomlinson); *I Love to Laugh* (Julie Andrews, Dick Van Dyke, Ed Wynn); *Jolly Holiday* (Julie Andrews, Dick Van Dyke, Chorus); *Let's Go Fly a Kite* (Dick Van Dyke, David Tomlinson, Chorus); *The Life I Lead* (Julie Andrews, David Tomlinson); *The Perfect Nanny* (Karen Dotrice, Matthew Garber); *Sister Suffragette* (Glynis Johns); *A Spoonful of Sugar* (Julie Andrews, Dick Van Dyke, Karen Dotrice, Matthew Garber); *Stay Awake* (Julie Andrews); *Step in Time* (Dick Van Dyke, Chorus); *Supercalifragilisticexpialidocious* (Julie Andrews, Dick Van Dyke, Chorus) WM: Richard M. Sherman and Robert B. Sherman.

"A beautiful production, some deliciously animated sequences, some exciting and nimble dancing and a spinning musical score." —Bosley Crowther, *The New York Times.*

**799 M\*A\*S\*H.** US, 1970, C, 116 m. D: Robert Altman, MS: Johnny Mandel, P: TCF (Ingo Preminger, Leon Ericksen).

*M\*A\*S\*H* (Johnny Mandel) W: Michael Altman—M: Johnny Mandel.

**800 The Mating Game.** US, 1959, C, 96 m. D: George Marshall, MS: Jeff Alexander, P: MGM (Philip Barry, Jr.).

*I've Got You Under My Skin* (Debbie Reynolds, Tony Randall) WM: Cole Porter / *The Mating Game* (Debbie Reynolds) W: Lee Adams—M: Charles Strouse.

**801 Maytime.** US, 1937, BW, 132 m. D: Robert Z. Leonard, MD: Herbert Stothart, P: MGM (Hunt Stromberg).

*Carry Me Back to Old Virginny* (Nelson Eddy, Jeanette MacDonald) WM: James A. Bland / *Ham and Eggs* (Nelson Eddy, Chorus) WM: Robert Wright, George "Chet" Forrest and Herbert Stothart / *Now Is the Month of Maying* (Chorus) W: Thomas Morley—M: Unknown / *Santa Lucia* (Nelson Eddy, Jeanette MacDonald, Unbilled Singer) Eng. W: Thomas Oliphant—Ital. WM: Teodoro Cottrau / *Vive l'Opera* (Nelson Eddy, Chorus) WM: Unknown—Adapted by: Robert Wright and George "Chet" Forrest / *Will You Remember?* (Nelson Eddy, Jeanette MacDonald) W: Rida Johnson Young—M: Sigmund Romberg.

"The most entrancing operetta the screen has given us. It establishes Jeanette MacDonald as the possessor of the cinema's loveliest voice ... and it affirms Nelson Eddy's pre-eminence among the baritones of filmdom." —Frank S. Nugent, *The New York Times.*

**802 Medicine Ball Caravan.** US, 1971, C, 90 m. D: Francois Reichenbach, P: Warner (Francois Reichenbach, Tom Donahue). Alt. Title: We Have Come for Your Daughters.

*Act Naturally* (The Youngbloods) WM: Vonie Morrison and Johnny Russell / *Battle of New Orleans* (Doug Kershaw) WM: Jimmy Driftwood / *Black Juju* (Alice Cooper) WM: Dennis Dunaway / *Dreambo* (Sal Valentino) WM: Sal Valentino / *Freakout* (Stoneground) WM: Stoneground / *Free the People* (Delaney and Bonnie) WM: Barbara Keith / *Hippie from Olema* (The Youngbloods) WM: Lowell Levinger / *How Blue Can You Get?* (B.B.

King) WM: Jane Feather and Leonard Feather / *It Takes a Lot to Laugh, It Takes a Train to Cry* (Stoneground) WM: Bob Dylan / *Just a Little Love* (B.B. King) WM: B.B. King / *Louisiana Man* (Doug Kershaw) WM: Doug Kershaw / *Orange Blossom Special* (Doug Kershaw) WM: Ervin T. Rouse.

**803   Meet Danny Wilson.** US, 1952, BW, 86 m. D: Joseph Pevney, MD: Joseph Gershenson, P: Universal (Leonard Goldstein). Performer: Frank Sinatra.

*All of Me* WM: Seymour Simons and Gerald Marks / *A Good Man Is Hard to Find* (Frank Sinatra, Shelley Winters) WM: Eddie Green / *How Deep Is the Ocean?* WM: Irving Berlin / *I've Got a Crush on You* W: Ira Gershwin — M: George Gershwin / *Lonesome Man Blues* WM: Sy Oliver / *She's Funny That Way* W: Richard A. Whiting — M: Neil Moret [Charles N. Daniels] / *That Old Black Magic* W: Johnny Mercer — M: Harold Arlen / *When You're Smiling* WM: Mark Fisher, Joe Goodwin and Larry Shay / *You're a Sweetheart* W: Harold Adamson — M: Jimmy McHugh.

"The songs — there are eight tried and true tunes — are integrated into the proceedings with a minimum of fuss." — A.H. Weiler, *The New York Times.*

**804   Meet Me in Las Vegas.** US, 1956, C, 112 m. D: Roy Rowland, MS: George Stoll and Johnny Green, P: MGM (Joe Pasternak). GB Title: Viva Las Vegas!

*Frankie and Johnny* (Sammy Davis, Jr.) W: Sammy Cahn — M: Unknown — Arr: Johnny Green / *The Gal in the Yaller Shoes* (Dan Dailey, Chorus, Agnes Moorehead); *Hell Hath No Fury* (Frankie Laine); *If You Can Dream* (Lena Horne, The Four Aces); *I Refuse to Rock and Roll* (Cara Williams); *Meet Me in Las Vegas* (The Four Aces); *My Lucky Charm* (Dan Dailey, Jerry Colonna, Mitsuko Sawamura, Chorus) W: Sammy Cahn — M: Nicholas Brodszky.

**805   Meet Me in St. Louis.** US, 1944, C, 113 m. D: Vincente Minnelli, MD: George Stoll, P: MGM (Arthur Freed). Vocals: D. Markas for Mary Astor; Arthur Freed for Leon Ames.

*The Boy Next Door* (Judy Garland); *Have Yourself a Merry Little Christmas* (Judy Garland) WM: Hugh Martin and Ralph Blane / *Meet Me in St. Louis, Louis* (Judy Garland, Joan Carroll, Harry Davenport, Lucille Bremer, Chorus) W: Andrew B. Sterling — M: Kerry Mills / *Over the Bannister* (Judy Garland) WM: Unknown — Arr: Conrad Salinger / *Skip to My Lou* (Judy Garland, Tom Drake, Lucille Bremer, Henry H. Daniels, Jr., Chorus) WM: Unknown — Arr: Hugh Martin and Ralph Blane / *The Trolley Song* (Judy Garland, Chorus) WM: Hugh Martin and Ralph Blane / *Under the Bamboo Tree* (Judy Garland, Margaret O'Brien) WM: Robert Cole and J. Rosamond Johnson / *You and I* (Mary Astor, Leon Ames) W: Arthur Freed — M: Nacio Herb Brown.

"Miss Garland is full of gay exuberance ... and sings ... with a rich voice that grows riper and more expressive in each new film." — Bosley Crowther, *The New York Times.*

**806   Meet the People.** US, 1944, BW, 100 m. D: Charles Riesner, MD: Lennie Hayton, P: MGM (E.Y. Harburg). Orch: Vaughn Monroe.

*I Like to Recognize the Tune* (June Allyson, Vaughn Monroe, Virginia O'Brien, Ziggy Talent, Chorus) W: Lorenz Hart — M: Richard Rodgers / *In Times Like These* (Dick Powell, Lucille Ball, Vaughn Monroe) W: Ralph Freed — M: Sammy Fain / *It's Smart to Be People* (Lucille Ball, Dick Powell, June Allyson, Chorus) W: E.Y. Harburg — M: Burton Lane / *Meet the People* (Dick Powell) W: Ralph Freed — M: Sammy Fain / *Say That We're Sweethearts Again* (Virginia O'Brien) WM: Earl K. Brent / *Schickelgruber* (Spike Jones and His City Slickers) W: Ralph Freed — M: Sammy Fain.

**807 Melba.** GB, 1953, C, 113 m.
D: Lewis Milestone, MD: Muir Mathieson, P: UA (Sam Spiegel). Performer:
Patrice Munsel.

*Ave Maria* Eng. W: The Bible—
French W: Paul Bernard—M: Charles
Gounod / *Is This the Beginning of Love?;
The Melba Waltz* W: Norman Newell—
M: Mischa Spoliansky.

**808 Melvin and Howard.** US,
1980, C, 95 m. D: Jonathan Demme,
MS: Bruce Langhorne, P: Universal
(Art Linson, Don Phillips).

*Bye Bye Blackbird* (Jason Robards)
W: Mort Dixon—M: Ray Henderson.

**809 Merry Andrew.** US, 1958,
C, 103 m. D: Michael Kidd, MD: Nelson Riddle, P: MGM (Sol C. Siegel).
Vocal: Betty Wand for Pier Angeli.

*Chin Up, Stout Fellow* (Danny
Kaye, Robert Coote, Rex Evans);
*Everything Is Ticketty-Boo* (Danny
Kaye, Chorus); *The Pipes of Pan*
(Danny Kaye); *Salud* (Danny Kaye,
Salvatore Baccaloni, Chorus); *The
Square of the Hypotenuse* (Danny Kaye);
*You Can't Always Have What You
Want* (Danny Kaye, Pier Angeli) W:
Johnny Mercer—M: Saul Chaplin.

**810 The Merry Widow.** US,
1934, BW, 99 m. D: Ernst Lubitsch,
MD: Herbert Stothart, P: MGM
(Ernst Lubitsch). MB: Chorus. Performer: Jeanette MacDonald. TV Title:
The Lady Dances.

*Girls, Girls, Girls* (Maurice Chevalier); *If Widows Are Rich; Maxim's*
(Jeanette MacDonald, Maurice Chevalier); *Melody of Laughter; Merry Widow
Waltz* W: Lorenz Hart / *Tonight Will
Teach Me to Forget* W: Gus Kahn / *Vilia*
W: Lorenz Hart. M: Franz Lehar.

"The songs ... have grace and
wit. ... Mr. Chevalier ... has never
been better in voice or charm. Miss
MacDonald is similarly fortunate in
the twin possessions of a captivating
personality and a lyric voice." —Andre
Sennwald, *The New York Times.*

**811 The Merry Widow.** US,
1952, C, 105 m. D: Curtis Bernhardt,

MD: Jay Blackton, P: MGM (Joe Pasternak). Vocals: Trudi Erwin for Lana
Turner.

*Can-Can* (Chorus); *Girls, Girls,
Girls* (Fernando Lamas, Chorus);
*Maxim's* (Fernando Lamas, Richard
Haydn); *Merry Widow Waltz* (Fernando Lamas, Lana Turner, Chorus);
*Night* (Fernando Lamas); *Vilia* (Fernando Lamas, Chorus) W: Paul Francis Webster—M: Franz Lehar.

"Has been mounted in a production that is probably the most colorful
and exquisite it has ever had. ... Some
spirited singing and dancing to the
lyrical old Lehar tunes." —Bosley
Crowther, *The New York Times.*

**812 Mexicali Rose.** US, 1939,
BW, 58 m. D: George Sherman, P: Republic (Harry Grey). Performer: Gene
Autry.

*El Rancho Grande* Eng. W: Bartley
Costello—Span. WM: Silvano R.
Ramos / *Mexicali Rose* W: Helen
Stone—M: Jack B. Tenny / *You're the
Only Star* WM: Gene Autry.

**813 Mexican Hayride.** US,
1948, BW, 77 m. D: Charles Barton, P:
Universal (Robert Arthur).

*Is It Yes or Is It No?* (Luba Malina)
WM: Jack Brooks and Walter Scharf.

**814 Mickey One.** US, 1965,
BW, 93 m. D: Arthur Penn, MS: Eddie
Sauter and Jack Shaindlin, P: Columbia (Arthur Penn).

*I'm Coming Virginia* (Warren
Beatty) W: Will Marion Cook—M:
Donald Heywood.

**815 Midnight Cowboy.** US,
1969, C, 119 m. D: John Schlesinger,
MD: John Barry, P: UA (Jerome Hellman).

*Crossroads of the Stepping Stones*
(Elephants Memory) WM: Michael
Shapiro and Stan Bronstein / *Everybody's Talking* (Harry Nilsson) WM:
Fred Neil / *A Famous Myth* (The
Group) WM: Jeffrey Comanor / *He
Quit Me* (Lesley Miller) WM: Warren
Zevon / *Jungle Jim at the Zoo* (Elephants
Memory) WM: Stan Bronstein, Richard

Sussman and Richard Frank / *Old Man Willow* (Elephants Memory) WM: Stan Bronstein, Michael Shapiro, Myron Yules and Richard Sussman / *Tears and Toys* (The Group) WM: Jeffrey Comanor.

**816  Midnight Express.** GB, 1978, C, 121 m. D: Alan Parker, MS: Giorgio Moroder, P: Columbia (Alan Marshall, David Puttnam).

*Istanbul Blues* (David Castle) WM: David Castle.

**817  A Midsummer Night's Sex Comedy.** US, 1982, C, 88 m. D: Woody Allen, P: Orion (Robert Greenhut).

*The Lord's Prayer* (Jose Ferrer) W: Adapted from the Bible—M: Albert Hay Malotte.

**818  Million Dollar Mermaid.** US, 1952, C, 115 m. D: Mervyn LeRoy, MD: Adolph Deutsch, P: MGM (Arthur Hornblow, Jr.). GB Title: The One-Piece Bathing Suit.

*Let Me Call You Sweetheart* (Chorus) WM: Beth Slater Whitson and Leo Friedman.

**819  Millions in the Air.** US, 1935, BW, 72 m. D: Ray McCarey, P: Paramount (Harold Hurley). Vocal: Bing Crosby for Paul Newlan.

*Crooner's Lullaby* (Paul Newlan) W: Sam Coslow—M: Arthur Johnston / *Laughin' at the Weather Man* (Eleanore Whitney, Robert Cummings) W: Leo Robin—M: Ralph Rainger / *Love Is Just Around the Corner* (Eleanore Whitney, Robert Cummings) W: Leo Robin—M: Lewis E. Gensler / *A Penny in My Pocket* (Wendy Barrie, John Howard) W: Leo Robin—M: Ralph Rainger / *You Tell Her, I S-t-u-t-t-e-r* (Joan Davis) WM: Billy Rose and Cliff Friend.

**820  The Miracle Worker.** US, 1962, BW, 107 m. D: Arthur Penn, MS: Laurence Rosenthal, P: UA (Fred Coe).

*The Miracle Worker* (Anne Bancroft) WM: Arthur Siegel and Don Costa.

"Add to [its] attributes the haunting, often chilling score by Laurence Rosenthal." —*Variety*.

**821  Miss Sadie Thompson.** US, 1953, C, 91 m. D: Curtis Bernhardt, MD: M.W. Stoloff, MS: George Duning, P: Columbia (Jerry Wald). Vocals: Jo Ann Greer for Rita Hayworth. Performer: Rita Hayworth.

*Hear No Evil, See No Evil; The Heat Is On* W: Ned Washington / *A Marine, a Marine, a Marine* (Chorus) W: Allan Roberts / *Native Dance* (Chorus); *Sadie Thompson's Song* W: Ned Washington. M: Lester Lee.

**822  Missing.** US, 1982, C, 122 m. D: Constantine Costa-Gavras, MS: Vangelis, P: Universal (Edward Lewis, Mildred Lewis).

*All or Nothing At All* (Bob Eberly) WM: Jack Lawrence and Arthur Altman.

**823  Mississippi.** US, 1935, BW, 73 m. D: A. Edward Sutherland, P: Paramount (Arthur Hornblow, Jr.). MB: Chorus. Performer: Bing Crosby.

*Down By the River; It's Easy to Remember* W: Lorenz Hart—M: Richard Rodgers / *Little David, Play on Your Harp* (The Cabin Kids) WM: Unknown—Arr: Henry Thacker Burleigh / *Old Folks at Home* (The Cabin Kids) WM: Stephen Collins Foster / *Roll Mississippi* (The Cabin Kids); *Soon* W: Lorenz Hart—M: Richard Rodgers.

**824  Mr. Blandings Builds His Dream House.** US, 1948, BW, 94 m. D: H.C. Potter, MD: Constantin Bakaleinikoff, MS: Leigh Harline, P: RKO (Norman Panama, Melvin Frank).

*Home on the Range* (Cary Grant) WM: Unknown.

**825  Mr. Imperium.** US, 1951, C, 87 m. D: Don Hartman, MS: Bronislau Kaper, P: MGM (Edwin H. Knopf). Vocals: Fran Warren for Lana Turner. GB Title: You Belong to My Heart.

*Andiamo* (Ezio Pinza, Lana Turner); *Let Me Look at You* (Ezio Pinza); *My Love and My Mule* (Ezio Pinza,

Lana Turner) W: Dorothy Fields—M: Harold Arlen / *You Belong to My Heart* (Ezio Pinza, The Guadalajara Trio) Eng. W: Ray Gilbert—Span. WM: Augustin Lara.

**826  Mr. Music.** US, 1950, BW, 113 m. D: Richard Haydn, MS: Joseph J. Lilley and Troy Sanders, P: Paramount (Robert L. Welch). MB: The Merry Macs.

*Accidents Will Happen* (Bing Crosby, Dorothy Kirsten); *And You'll Be Home* (Bing Crosby); *High on the List* (Bing Crosby); *Life Is So Peculiar* (Bing Crosby, Peggy Lee, Groucho Marx); *Milady* (Bing Crosby, Dorothy Kirsten); *Once More the Blue and White* (Bing Crosby, Chorus); *Wouldn't It Be Funny?* (Bing Crosby) W: Johnny Burke—M: James Van Heusen.

"One of the nicest sets of new songs that Jimmy Van Heusen and Johnny Burke have ever turned out." —Bosley Crowther, *The New York Times.*

**827  Moment by Moment.** US, 1978, C, 102 m. D: Jane Wagner, MS: Lee Holdridge, P: Universal (Robert Stigwood).

*For You and I* (10CC) WM: Eric Stewart and Graham Gouldman / *The Lady Wants to Know* (Michael Franks) WM: Michael Franks / *Moment by Moment* (Yvonne Elliman) W: Molly Ann Leiken—M: Lee Holdridge / *Sometimes When We Touch* (Dan Hill) W: Dan Hill—M: Barry Mann / *You Know I Love You* (Charles Lloyd); *Your Heart Never Lies* (Charles Lloyd) WM: Charles Lloyd.

**828  Moment to Moment.** US, 1966, C, 108 m. D: Mervyn LeRoy, MS: Henry Mancini, P: Universal (Mervyn LeRoy).

*Moment to Moment* (Chorus) W: Johnny Mercer—M: Henry Mancini.

**829  Mona Lisa.** GB, 1986, C, 104 m. D: Neil Jordan, MS: Michael Kamen, P: Handmade (Stephen Wooley, Patrick Cassavetti). Performer: Nat King Cole.

*Mona Lisa* W: Ray Evans—M: Jay Livingston / *When I Fall in Love* W: Edward Heyman—M: Victor Young.

**830  Monkey Business.** US, 1931, BW, 77 m. D: Norman Z. McLeod, P: Paramount (Herman J. Mankiewicz). Performers: The Four Marx Brothers.

*Ho Hum* W: Edward Heyman—M: Dana Suesse / *Sweet Adeline* W: Richard H. Gerrard—M: Henry W. Armstrong / *You Brought a New Kind of Love to Me* (Voice of Maurice Chevalier) WM: Sammy Fain, Irving Kahal and Pierre Norman.

**831  The Monkey's Uncle.** US, 1965, C, 87 m. D: Robert Stevenson, P: Buena Vista (Walt Disney, Ron Miller).

*Monkey's Uncle* (Annette Funicello, The Beach Boys) WM: Richard M. Sherman and Robert B. Sherman.

**832  Monte Carlo.** US, 1930, BW, 90 m. D: Ernst Lubitsch, MD: W. Franke Harling, P: Paramount (Ernst Lubitsch). MB: Chorus. Performers: Jeanette MacDonald and Jack Buchanan.

*Always in All Ways; Beyond the Blue Horizon; Give Me a Moment Please; She'll Love Me and Like It* (Claud Allister); *Trimmin' the Women* (Jack Buchanan, Tyler Brooke, John Roche); *Whatever It Is, It's Grand* W: Leo Robin—M: Richard A. Whiting and W. Franke Harling.

"Film producers have lately been persuaded that singing pictures are amiss, but they had not witnessed this brilliant piece of work." —Mordaunt Hall, *The New York Times.*

**833  Monte Walsh.** US, 1970, C, 106 m. D: William Fraker, MS: John Barry, P: Cinema Center/National General (Hal Landers, Bobby Roberts).

*The Good Times Are Coming* (Mama Cass) W: Hal David—M: John Barry.

**834  Moon Over Burma.** US, 1940, BW, 76 m. D: Louis King, MS:

Victor Young, P: Paramount (Anthony Veiller). Performer: Dorothy Lamour.

*Mexican Magic* W: Frank Loesser—M: Harry Revel / *Moon Over Burma* W: Frank Loesser—M: Frederick Hollander.

**835  Moon Over Miami.** US, 1941, C, 91 m. D: Walter Lang, MD: Alfred Newman, P: TCF (Harry Joe Brown).

*Is That Good?* (Jack Haley, Charlotte Greenwood); *I've Got You All to Myself* (Don Ameche); *The Kindergarten Conga* (Betty Grable, Chorus); *Loveliness and Love* (Don Ameche, Betty Grable, Chorus); *Oh Me, Oh Mi-ami* (Betty Grable, Carole Landis, Charlotte Greenwood, Chorus); *Solitary Seminole* (Chorus); *What Can I Do for You?* (Betty Grable, Carole Landis); *You Started Something* (Don Ameche, Betty Grable, Carole Landis, Robert Cummings) W: Leo Robin—M: Ralph Rainger.

**836  Moon Over Parador.** US, 1988, C, 105 m. D: Paul Mazursky, MS: Maurice Jarre, P: Universal (Paul Mazursky). Performer: Sammy Davis, Jr.

*Begin the Beguine* WM: Cole Porter / *Besame Mucho* Eng. W: Sunny Skylar—Span. WM: Consuelo Velasquez.

**837  Moonraker.** GB, 1979, C, 126 m. D: Lewis Gilbert, MS: John Barry, P: UA (Albert R. Broccoli).

*Moonraker* (Shirley Bassey) W: Hal David—M: John Barry.

**838  Moonstruck.** US, 1988, C, 102 m. D: Norman Jewison, MS: Dick Hyman, P: MGM (Patrick Palmer, Norman Jewison).

*It Must Be Him* (Vikki Carr) WM: Gilbert Becaud and Maurice Vidalin / *That's Amore* (Dean Martin) W: Jack Brooks—M: Harry Warren.

**839  More American Graffiti (Purple Haze).** US, 1979, C, 111 m. D: B.W.L. Norton, MS: Gene Finley, P: Universal (Howard Kazanjian).

*The Ballad of the Green Berets* (Barry Sadler) WM: Barry Sadler and Robin Moore / *Beechwood 4-5789* (The Marvelettes) WM: William Stevenson, George Gordy and Marvin Gaye / *Cool Jerk* (The Capitols) WM: Donald Storball / *Dead Man's Curve* (Jan and Dean) WM: Roger Christian, Jan Berry, Artie Kornfeld and Brian Wilson / *Fingertips* (Little Stevie Wonder) WM: Henry Crosby and Clarence Paul / *Good Lovin'* (The Young Rascals) WM: Rudy Clark and Arthur Resnick / *Hang On Sloopy* (The McCoys) WM: Bert Russell and Wes Farrell / *Heat Wave* (Martha and The Vandellas) WM: Eddie Holland, Lamont Dozier and Brian Holland / *I-Feel-Like-I'm-Fixin'-to-Die Rag* (Country Joe and The Fish) WM: Joe McDonald / *I'm a Man* (Doug Sahm) / *Incense and Peppermints* (The Strawberry Alarm Clock) WM: John Carter and Tim Gilbert / *Just Like a Woman* (Bob Dylan) WM: Bob Dylan / *Light My Fire* (The Doors) WM: Jim Morrison, John Densmore, Robert Krieger and Raymond Manzarek / *Like a Rolling Stone* (Bob Dylan) WM: Bob Dylan / *Mr. Lonely* (Bobby Vinton) WM: Bobby Vinton and Gene Allan / *My Boyfriend's Back* (The Angels) WM: Robert Feldman, Gerald Goldstein and Richard Gottehrer / *My Guy* (Mary Wells) WM: William "Smokey" Robinson / *96 Tears* (The Mysterians) WM: Rudy Martinez / *Our Day Will Come* (Ruby and The Romantics) W: Mort Garson—M: Bob Hilliard / *The Race Is On* (Doug Sahm) / *Reflections* (The Supremes) WM: Eddie Holland, Lamont Dozier and Brian Holland / *Respect* (Aretha Franklin) WM: Otis Redding / *Season of the Witch* (Donovan) WM: Donovan / *She's Not There* (The Zombies) WM: Rod Argent / *Since I Fell for You* (Lenny Welch) WM: Buddy Johnson / *The Sounds of Silence* (Simon and Garfunkel) WM: Paul Simon / *Stop! in the Name of Love* (The Supremes) WM: Eddie Holland, Lamont Dozier and Brian Holland / *Strange Brew* (Donovan) / *Tighten Up Your Wig* (Steppenwolf) / *Turn! Turn!*

*Turn!* (The Byrds) WM: Pete Seeger / *What Kind of Fool Do You Think I Am?* (The Tams) WM: Ray Whitley / *When a Man Loves a Woman* (Percy Sledge) WM: Andrew Wright and Calvin Lewis / *Where Did Our Love Go?* (The Supremes) WM: Eddie Holland, Lamont Dozier and Brian Holland / *Wooly Bully* (Sam the Sham and The Pharaohs) WM: Domingo Samudio / *You Really Got a Hold on Me* (Smokey Robinson and The Miracles) WM: William "Smokey" Robinson / *Your Precious Love* (Marvin Gaye and Tammi Terrell) WM: Valerie Simpson and Nicholas Ashford / *You Were On My Mind* (The We Five) WM: Sylvia Fricker.

**840  Morocco.** US, 1930, BW, 92 m. D: Josef von Sternberg, MS: Karl Hajos, P: Paramount (Hector Turnbull). Performer: Marlene Dietrich.

*Give Me the Man; What Am I Bid for My Apples?* W: Leo Robin — M: Karl Hajos / *When Love Is Dead* WM: Millandy and Cremieux.

**841  Mother Wore Tights.** US, 1947, C, 107 m. D: Walter Lang, MD: Alfred Newman, P: TCF (Lamar Trotti).

*Burlington Bertie from Bow* (Betty Grable, Dan Dailey) WM: William Hargreaves / *Fare-thee-well, Dear Alma Mater* (Chorus); *Kokomo, Indiana* (Betty Grable, Dan Dailey); *Rolling Down to Bowling Green* (Betty Grable, Dan Dailey) W: Mack Gordon — M: Josef Myrow / *Stumbling* (Mona Freeman, Lee Patrick, Chick Chandler) WM: Zez Confrey / *Swingin' Down the Lane* (Mona Freeman, Chorus) W: Gus Kahn — M: Isham Jones / *There's Nothing Like a Song* (Betty Grable, Dan Dailey); *This Is My Favorite City* (Betty Grable, Dan Dailey) W: Mack Gordon — M: Josef Myrow / *Tra-la-la* (Betty Grable, Dan Dailey, Mona Freeman) W: Mack Gordon — M: Harry Warren / *You Do* (Betty Grable, Dan Dailey, Mona Freeman) W: Mack Gordon — M: Josef Myrow.

"Musical is severely limited by its long and mediocre score of tunes." — *Variety.*

**842  Moulin Rouge.** US, 1934, BW, 69 m. D: Sidney Lanfield, MD: Alfred Newman, P: TCF (Darryl F. Zanuck).

*The Boulevard of Broken Dreams* (Constance Bennett, Russ Columbo, The Boswell Sisters); *Coffee in the Morning* (Constance Bennett, Russ Columbo, The Boswell Sisters); *Song of Surrender* (Tullio Carminati, The Boswell Sisters) W: Al Dubin — M: Harry Warren.

**843  Moulin Rouge.** GB, 1952, C, 123 m. D: John Huston, MS: Georges Auric, P: Romulus (Jack Clayton). Vocal: Muriel Smith for Zsa Zsa Gabor.

*The Song from Moulin Rouge* (Zsa Zsa Gabor) W: William Engvick — M: Georges Auric.

**844  Move.** US, 1970, C, 90 m. D: Stuart Rosenberg, P: TCF (Pandro S. Berman).

*Move* (Larry Marks) W: Alan Bergman and Marilyn Bergman — M: Marvin Hamlisch.

**845  Move Over, Darling.** US, 1963, C, 103 m. D: Michael Gordon, MS: Lionel Newman, P: TCF (Aaron Rosenberg, Martin Melcher). Performer: Doris Day.

*Move Over, Darling* WM: Joe Lubin, Hal Kanter and Terry Melcher / *Twinkle Lullaby* WM: Joe Lubin.

**846  Mrs. Brown, You've Got a Lovely Daughter.** GB, 1968, C, 110 m. D: Saul Swimmer, P: MGM (Allen Klein). Performers: Herman's Hermits.

*Daisy Chain* WM: Peter Noone, Keith Hopwood, Derek Leckenby and Karl Green / *Holiday Inn* WM: Geoff Stephens / *I'm into Something Good* WM: Gerry Goffin and Carole King / *It's Nice to Be Out in the Morning; Lemon and Lime* WM: Graham Gouldman / *The Most Beautiful Thing in My Life* WM: Kenny Young / *Mrs. Brown, You've Got a Lovely Daughter* WM: Trevor Peacock / *Ooh She's Done It*

Again WM: Graham Gouldman /
*There's a Kind of Hush* WM: Les Reed
and Geoff Stephens / *The World Is for
the Young* WM: Graham Gouldman.

**847  Murder at the Vanities.**
US, 1934, BW, 89 m. D: Mitchell Lei-
sen, P: Paramount (E. Lloyd Sheldon).
Orch: Duke Ellington.

*Cocktails for Two* (Carl Brisson,
Chorus); *Ebony Rhapsody* (Kitty Car-
lisle, Gertrude Michael, Carl Brisson);
*Live and Love Tonight* (Kitty Carlisle,
Gertrude Michael, Carl Brisson); *Mari-
juana* (Gertrude Michael); *My Lovely
One* (Chorus); *Where Do They Come
From?* (Kitty Carlisle, Chorus) W: Sam
Coslow—M: Arthur Johnston.

"It's a backstage musical but
different." — *Variety.*

**848  Murphy's Romance.** US,
1985, C, 107 m. D: Martin Ritt, MS:
Carole King, P: Columbia (Laura Zis-
kin).

*Murphy's Romance* (Carole King)
WM: Carole King.

**849  Muscle Beach Party.** US,
1964, C, 94 m. D: William Asher, P:
AIP (James H. Nicholson, Robert Dillon).

*A Boy Needs a Girl* (Frankie Ava-
lon); *A Girl Needs a Boy* (Annette Funi-
cello); *Happy Street* (Little Stevie
Wonder) WM: Jerry Styner and Guy
Hemric / *Muscle Beach Party* (Dick
Dale and The Deltones); *Muscle Bustle*
(Donna Love); *My First Love* (Dick
Dale and The Deltones); *Runnin' Wild*
(Frankie Avalon); *Surfer's Holiday*
(Annette Funicello, Frankie Avalon)
WM: Roger Christian, Gary Usher and
Brian Wilson.

**850  Music for Millions.** US,
1944, BW, 120 m. D: Henry Koster,
MD: George Stoll, P: MGM (Joe Pasternak).

*At Sundown* (Marsha Hunt) WM:
Walter Donaldson / *Toscanini, Iturbi
and Me* (Jimmy Durante) WM: Walter
Bullock and Harold Spina / *Umbriago*
(Jimmy Durante) W: Irving Caesar—
M: Jimmy Durante.

**851  Music in the Air.** US,
1934, BW, 85 m. D: Joe May, MD:
Louis De Francesco, P: Fox (Erich
Pommer). Vocals: Betty Hiestand for
June Lang; James O'Brien for Douglass
Montgomery.

*I Am So Eager* (Gloria Swanson,
June Lang, John Boles, Chorus); *I'm
Alone* (Gloria Swanson); *I've Told
Every Little Star* (Gloria Swanson, June
Lang, Douglass Montgomery, John
Boles, Chorus); *One More Dance*
(Gloria Swanson, John Boles); *There's
a Hill Beyond a Hill* (Chorus); *We Be-
long Together* (Gloria Swanson, John
Boles, June Lang, Douglass Mont-
gomery, Chorus) W: Oscar Hammer-
stein II—M: Jerome Kern.

"Sends out in a high-hearted cavalcade all the gay, tender and superbly
romantic lyrics which warmed the flinty
heart of Broadway back in the Winter
of '32." —Andre Sennwald, *The New
York Times.*

**852  The Music Man.** US, 1962,
C, 151 m. D: Morton Da Costa, MD:
Ray Heindorf, P: Warner (Morton Da
Costa).

The 1957 Broadway musical starred
Robert Preston and Barbara Cook.
The Buffalo Bills, a quartet consisting
of Jacey Squires, Olin Britt, Ewart
Dunlap and Oliver Hix, repeated their
stage performances for the screen.

*Being in Love* (Shirley Jones); *Gary,
Indiana* (Robert Preston, Ronny How-
ard); *Goodnight My Someone* (Shirley
Jones, Robert Preston); *Iowa Stubborn*
(Chorus); *Lida Rose* (Shirley Jones,
The Buffalo Bills); *Marian the Librar-
ian* (Robert Preston); *Piano Lesson*
(Shirley Jones, Pert Kelton); *Pick-a-
Little, Talk-a-Little* (Hermione Gingold,
Chorus); *Rock Island* (Chorus); *The
Sadder-But-Wiser Girl* (Robert Preston);
*Seventy-Six Trombones* (Shirley Jones,
Robert Preston, Chorus); *Shipoopi*
(Buddy Hackett, Chorus); *Sincere*
(The Buffalo Bills); *Till There Was You*
(Shirley Jones, Robert Preston); *Trouble*
(Robert Preston, Chorus); *Wells Fargo*

Wagon (Chorus); *Will I Ever Tell You?* (Shirley Jones, The Buffalo Bills) WM: Meredith Willson.

"Warners might have secured bigger screen names but it is impossible to imagine any of them matching Preston's authority, backed by 883 stage performances." — *Variety*.

**853 Mutiny on the Bounty.** US, 1962, C, 179 m. D: Lewis Milestone, MD: Robert Armbruster, MS: Bronislau Kaper, P: MGM (Aaron Rosenberg).

*Follow Me* (Chorus) W: Paul Francis Webster—M: Bronislau Kaper.

**854 My Dream Is Yours.** US, 1949, C, 101 m. D: Michael Curtiz, MD: Ray Heindorf, P: Warner (Michael Curtiz). Orch: Frankie Carle. Performer: Doris Day.

*Canadian Capers* WM: Gus Chandler, Bert White and Henry Cohen / *Freddie, Get Ready* (Doris Day, Jack Carson) W: Ralph Blane / *I'll String Along with You* W: Al Dubin / *Love Finds a Way* (Lee Bowman, Chorus); *My Dream Is Yours* (Doris Day, Lee Bowman) W: Ralph Blane / *Nagasaki* W: Mort Dixon / *Someone Like You; Tick, Tick, Tick* W: Ralph Blane / *With Plenty of Money and You* W: Al Dubin / *You Must Have Been a Beautiful Baby* W: Johnny Mercer. M: Harry Warren.

"Doris Day fills the sound track with songs ... but they are routine melodies for the most part. And Lee Bowman sings some dreary, toneless things." — Thomas M. Pryor, *The New York Times*.

**855 My Fair Lady.** US, 1964, C, 170 m. D: George Cukor, MD: Andre Previn, P: Warner (Jack L. Warner). Vocals: Marni Nixon for Audrey Hepburn; Bill Shirley for Jeremy Brett.

*Ascot Gavotte* (Chorus); *Get Me to the Church on Time* (Stanley Holloway, Chorus); *A Hymn to Him* (Rex Harrison, Wilfred Hyde-White); *I Could Have Danced All Night* (Audrey Hep-

burn); *I'm an Ordinary Man* (Rex Harrison); *I've Grown Accustomed to Her Face* (Rex Harrison); *Just You Wait* (Audrey Hepburn); *On the Street Where You Live* (Jeremy Brett); *The Rain in Spain* (Audrey Hepburn, Rex Harrison, Wilfred Hyde-White); *Show Me* (Audrey Hepburn, Jeremy Brett); *Why Can't the English?* (Rex Harrison); *With a Little Bit of Luck* (Stanley Holloway, John Alderson, John McLiam, Chorus); *Without You* (Audrey Hepburn); *Wouldn't It Be Loverly?* (Audrey Hepburn, Chorus); *You Did It* (Rex Harrison, Wilfred Hyde-White) W: Alan Jay Lerner—M: Frederick Loewe.

"A stunningly effective screen treatment. ... A certain amount of new music ... and added lyrics ... are part of the adjustment to the cinematic medium. But it is the original stage score which stands out." — *Variety*.

"The structure and, indeed, the very words of the musical play as it was performed on Broadway for six and a half years are preserved. And every piece of music of the original score is used." —Bosley Crowther, *The New York Times*.

**856 My Favorite Brunette.** US, 1947, BW, 87 m. D: Elliott Nugent, MS: Robert Emmett Dolan, P: Paramount (Daniel Dare).

*Beside You* (Bob Hope, Dorothy Lamour) WM: Jay Livingston and Ray Evans.

**857 My Favorite Spy.** US, 1942, BW, 86 m. D: Tay Garnett, MD: Constantin Bakaleinikoff, P: RKO (Harold Lloyd). Orch: Kay Kyser. Performer: Kay Kyser.

*Got the Moon in My Pocket*; *Just Plain Lonesome* W: Johnny Burke—M: James Van Heusen.

**858 My Favorite Spy.** US, 1951, BW, 93 m. D: Norman Z. McLeod, MS: Victor Young, P: Paramount (Paul Jones).

*I Wind Up Taking a Fall* (Bob Hope) W: Johnny Mercer—M: Robert Emmett Dolan / *Just a Moment More*

(Hedy Lamarr) WM: Jay Livingston and Ray Evans.

**859 My Favorite Year.** US, 1982, C, 92 m. D: Richard Benjamin, MS: Ralph Burns, P: MGM/UA (Michael Gruskoff).

*How High the Moon* (Les Paul and Mary Ford) W: Nancy Hamilton—M: Morgan Lewis / *Star Dust* (Nat King Cole) W: Mitchell Parish—M: Hoagy Carmichael.

**860 My Foolish Heart.** US, 1949, BW, 98 m. D: Mark Robson, MD: Emil Newman, MS: Victor Young, P: RKO (Samuel Goldwyn).

*My Foolish Heart* (Susan Hayward) W: Ned Washington—M: Victor Young.

**861 My Friend Irma.** US, 1949, BW, 103 m. D: George Marshall, MS: Roy Webb, P: Paramount (Hal B. Wallis). Performer: Dean Martin.

*The Donkey Serenade* (Dean Martin, Jerry Lewis) W: Robert Wright and George "Chet" Forrest—M: Rudolf Friml and Herbert Stothart / *Here's to Love; Just for Fun; My Own, My Only, My All* WM: Jay Livingston and Ray Evans.

**862 My Friend Irma Goes West.** US, 1950, BW, 90 m. D: Hal Walker, MS: Leigh Harline, P: Paramount (Hal B. Wallis). Performer: Dean Martin.

*Baby, Obey Me; Fiddle and Gittar Band; I'll Always Love You* (Dean Martin, Corinne Calvet); *Querida Mia* WM: Jay Livingston and Ray Evans.

**863 My Man.** US, 1928, BW, 85 m. D: Archie Mayo, P: Warner. Performer: Fanny Brice.

Miss Brice's first screen appearance.

*I'd Rather Be Blue Over You* W: Billy Rose—M: Fred Fisher / *If You Want the Rainbow* W: Billy Rose and Mort Dixon—M: Oscar Levant / *I'm an Indian* W: Blanche Merrill—M: Leo Edwards / *I Was a Flora Dora Baby* WM: Harry Carroll and Ballard MacDonald / *My Man* Eng. W: Channing

Pollock—M: Maurice Yvain / *Second Hand Rose* W: Grant Clarke—M: James F. Hanley.

"It is all ... singularly low-brow, relieved by Miss Brice's own melodies and recitations." —Mordaunt Hall, *The New York Times*.

**864 My Sister Eileen.** US, 1955, C, 108 m. D: Richard Quine, MD: Morris Stoloff, MS: George Duning, P: Columbia (Fred Kohlmar).

*As Soon As They See Eileen* (Betty Garrett); *Atmosphere* (Chorus); *Give Me a Band and My Baby* (Janet Leigh, Betty Garrett, Bob Fosse, Tommy Rall); *I'm Great But No One Knows It* (Janet Leigh, Betty Garrett, Kurt Kasznar, Dick York); *It's Bigger Than You and Me* (Jack Lemmon); *There's Nothing Like Love* (Janet Leigh, Betty Garrett, Bob Fosse) W: Leo Robin—M: Jule Styne.

"Mr. Styne and Mr. Robin have dished up some apt and lively songs." —Bosley Crowther, *The New York Times*.

**865 My Wild Irish Rose.** US, 1947, C, 101 m. D: David Butler, MD: Leo F. Forbstein, MS: Ray Heindorf and Max Steiner, P: Warner (William Jacobs). MB: Chorus. Performer: Dennis Morgan.

*By the Light of the Silvery Moon* W: Edward Madden—M: Gus Edwards / *Come Down, Ma Evenin' Star* (Andrea King) W: Robert B. Smith—M: John Stromberg / *Dear Old Donegal* WM: Steve Graham / *Hush-A-Bye* W: Ted Koehler—M: M.K. Jerome / *In the Evening By the Moonlight* (Ben Blue) WM: James A. Bland / *A Little Bit of Heaven* W: J. Keirn Brennan—M: Ernest R. Ball / *Miss Lindy Lou* (Dennis Morgan, Ben Blue) W: Ted Koehler—M: M.K. Jerome / *Mother Machree* W: Rida Johnson Young—M: Chauncey Olcott and Ernest R. Ball / *My Nellie's Blue Eyes* WM: William J. Scanlan / *My Wild Irish Rose* WM: Chauncey Olcott / *The Natchez and the Robert E. Lee* (Chorus) W: Ted Koehler—M: M.K.

Jerome / *One Little, Sweet Little Girl* WM: Dan Sullivan / *There's Room in My Heart for Them All* W: Ted Koehler—M: M.K. Jerome / *Wait Till the Sun Shines, Nellie* W: Andrew B. Sterling—M: Harry von Tilzer / *When Irish Eyes Are Smiling* W: Chauncey Olcott and George Graff, Jr.—M: Ernest R. Ball / *Will You Love Me in December?* W: James J. Walker—M: Ernest R. Ball / *You Tell Me Your Dream* WM: Neil Moret [Charles N. Daniels], Jay Blackton, Albert H. Brown and Seymour Rice.

"There is one thing that can be said about 'My Wild Irish Rose'; it contains in its score an impressive number of songs, Irish and otherwise. And thanks be to the merciful saints, Mr. Morgan gets to sing Mr. Olcott's favorite song only once!" —Thomas M. Pryor, *The New York Times*.

**866  The Naked Gun: From the Files of Police Squad.** US, 1988, C, 85 m. D: David Zucker, MS: Ira Newborn, P: Paramount (Robert K. Weiss).

*I Love L.A.* (Randy Newman) WM: Randy Newman / *I'm Into Something Good* (Peter Noone) WM: Gerry Goffin and Carole King / *Louie Louie* (Rice University Marching Owl Band) WM: Richard Berry.

**867  Nana.** US, 1934, BW, 89 m. D: Dorothy Arzner, MS: Alfred Newman, P: UA (Samuel Goldwyn). GB Title: Lady of the Boulevards.

*That's Love* (Anna Sten) W: Lorenz Hart—M: Richard Rodgers.

**868  Nancy Goes to Rio.** US, 1950, C, 99 m. D: Robert Z. Leonard, MS: George Stoll, P: MGM (Joe Pasternak). MB: Bando da Lua.

*Cha Bomm Pa Pa* (Carmen Miranda) WM: Ray Gilbert / *Love Is Like This* (Jane Powell, Chorus) WM: Vianna and Ray Gilbert / *Magic Is the Moonlight* (Jane Powell, Ann Sothern) Eng. W: Charles Pasquale—Span. WM: Maria Grever / *Nancy Goes to Rio* (Scotty Beckett) W: Earl K. Brent—M:

George Stoll / *Shine on Harvest Moon* (Jane Powell, Ann Sothern, Louis Calhern) WM: Jack Norworth and Nora Bayes / *Time and Time Again* (Jane Powell) W: Earl K. Brent—M: Fred Spielman / *Yipsee-i-o* (Carmen Miranda) WM: Ray Gilbert.

"A few nice songs . . . and an eye-filling MGM production are the only ingredients worth mentioning." —*The New York Times*.

**869  Nashville.** US, 1975, C, 159 m. D: Robert Altman, MD: Richard Baskin, P: Paramount (Jerry Weintraub, Robert Altman, Martin Starger).

*Bluebird* (Timothy Brown); *Down to the River* (Sheila Bailey, Patti Bryant); *Dues* (Ronee Blakely) WM: Ronee Blakely / *For the Sake of the Children* (Henry Gibson, Chorus) WM: Richard Baskin and Richard Reicheg / *The Heart of a Gentle Woman* (Dave Peel) WM: Dave Peel / *Honey, Won't You Let Me Try Again?* (Keith Carradine) WM: Keith Carradine / *I Don't Know If I Found It in You* (Karen Black) WM: Karen Black / *I'm Easy* (Keith Carradine) WM: Keith Carradine / *I Never Get Enough* (Gwen Welles) WM: Richard Baskin and Ben Raleigh / *It Don't Worry Me* (Barbara Harris, Keith Carradine, Chorus) WM: Keith Carradine / *Keep a-Goin'* (Henry Gibson) WM: Henry Gibson and Richard Baskin / *Let Me Be the One* (Gwen Welles) WM: Richard Baskin / *Memphis* (Karen Black) WM: Karen Black / *My Baby's Cookin' in Another Man's Pan* (Jonnie Barnett) WM: Jonnie Barnett / *My Idaho Home* (Ronee Blakely) WM: Ronee Blakely / *Old Man Mississippi* (Misty Mountain Boys) WM: Juan Grizzle / *One, I Love You* (Ronee Blakely, Henry Gibson, Gwen Welles) WM: Richard Baskin / *Rolling Stone* (Karen Black) WM: Karen Black / *Since You've Gone* (Keith Carradine, Allan Nicholls, Cristina Raines) WM: Gary Busey / *Tapedeck in His Tractor* (Ronee Blakely) WM: Ronee Blakely / *There's Trouble in the U.S.A.* (Unbilled

Singer) WM: Arlene Barnett / *Two Hundred Years* (Henry Gibson, Chorus) WM: Henry Gibson and Richard Baskin / *Yes I Do* (Lily Tomlin, Chorus) WM: Lily Tomlin and Richard Baskin.

"One of the most ambitious, and more artistically, successful, 'backstage' musical dramas." — *Variety*.

**870  National Lampoon's Animal House.** US, 1978, C, 109 m. D: John Landis, MS: Elmer Bernstein, P: Universal (Matty Simmons, Ivan Reitman).

*Animal House* (Stephen Bishop); *Dream Girl* (Stephen Bishop) WM: Stephen Bishop / *Hey Paula* (Paul and Paula) WM: Ray Hildebrand / *Let's Dance* (Chris Montez) WM: Jim Lee / *Louie Louie* (The Kingsmen) WM: Richard Berry / *Money* (John Belushi) WM: Berry Gordy, Jr. and Janie Bradford / *Shout* (Otis Day and The Knights) WM: O'Kelly Isley, Ronald Isley and Rudolph Isley / *Tossin' and Turnin'* (Bobby Lewis) WM: Malou Rene and Ritchie Adams / *Twistin' the Night Away* (Sam Cooke) WM: Sam Cooke / *Who's Sorry Now?* (Connie Francis) WM: Bert Kalmar, Harry Ruby and Ted Snyder / *Wonderful World* (Sam Cooke) WM: Barbara Campbell, Lou Adler and Herb Alpert.

**871  Naughty But Nice.** US, 1939, BW, 90 m. D: Ray Enright, MD: Leo F. Forbstein, P: Warner (Sam Bischoff).

*Corn Pickin'* (Ann Sheridan); *Hooray for Spinach* (Ann Sheridan); *I'm Happy About the Whole Thing* (Dick Powell, Gale Page); *In a Moment of Weakness* (Ann Sheridan, Gale Page) W: Johnny Mercer—M: Harry Warren.

**872  Naughty Marietta.** US, 1935, BW, 106 m. D: W.S. Van Dyke II, MD: Herbert Stothart, P: MGM (Hunt Stromberg).

*Ah, Sweet Mystery of Life* (Jeanette MacDonald, Nelson Eddy) W: Rida Johnson Young / *Antoinette and Anatole* (Charles Bruins, Chorus); *Chansonette* (Jeanette MacDonald, Chorus) W: Gus Kahn / *I'm Falling in Love with Someone* (Nelson Eddy); *Italian Street Song* (Jeanette MacDonald, Nelson Eddy, Zarubi Elmassian, Chorus); *'Neath the Southern Moon* (Nelson Eddy) W: Rida Johnson Young / *The Owl and the Bob Cat* (Nelson Eddy, Chorus); *Prayer* (Delos Jewkes, Jeanette MacDonald, Chorus); *Ship Ahoy* (Jeanette MacDonald, Akim Tamiroff, Chorus) W: Gus Kahn / *Tramp, Tramp, Tramp* (Nelson Eddy, Chorus) W: Rida Johnson Young and Gus Kahn. M: Victor Herbert.

"An adaptation of the Victor Herbert operetta. . . . Much of the original score, plus a couple of added tunes [lyrics by Gus Kahn] is included. . . . MacDonald sings particularly well. . . . Picture marks the full-length debut of Eddy who reveals a splendid and powerful baritone with the distinct asset for the camera of not being breathy." — *Variety*.

**873  Neighbors.** US, 1981, C, 94 m. D: John G. Avildsen, MS: Bill Conti, P: Columbia (Richard D. Zanuck, David Brown).

*Hello, I Love You* (The Doors) WM: Robert Krieger, Jim Morrison, John Densmore and Raymond Manzarek / *Stayin' Alive* (The Bee Gees) WM: Barry Gibb, Maurice Gibb and Robin Gibb.

**874  Neptune's Daughter.** US, 1949, C, 93 m. D: Edward Buzzell, MD: George Stoll, P: MGM (Jack Cummings). Orch: Xavier Cugat.

*Baby, It's Cold Outside* (Esther Williams, Ricardo Montalban, Betty Garrett, Red Skelton); *I Love Those Men* (Betty Garrett); *My Heart Beats Faster* (Ricardo Montalban) WM: Frank Loesser.

"Combines comedy, songs and dances into an amusing froth." — *Variety*.

**875  Never a Dull Moment.** US, 1943, BW, 60 m. D: Edward Lilley, P: Universal (Howard Benedict).

*My Blue Heaven* (Frances Langford) W: George Whiting—M: Walter

Donaldson / *Sleepy Time Gal* (Frances Langford) W: Joseph R. Alden and Raymond B. Egan—M: Ange Lorenzo and Richard A. Whiting / *Yakimboomba* (The Ritz Brothers) WM: Eddie Cherkose, David Rose and Jacques Press.

**876 Never a Dull Moment.** US, 1950, BW, 89 m. D: George Marshall, MS: Frederick Hollander, P: RKO (Harriet Parsons). Performer: Irene Dunne.

*The Man with the Big Felt Hat; Once You Find Your Guy; Sagebrush Lullaby* WM: Kay Swift.

**877 Never Give a Sucker an Even Break.** US, 1941, BW, 71 m. D: Edward Cline, MS: Frank Skinner, P: Universal. GB Title: What a Man.

*Dark Eyes* (Gloria Jean) WM: Based on Russian Folk Song *Otchi Tchorniya*—Arr: Harry Horlick and Gregory Stone.

**878 Never Say Goodbye.** US, 1946, BW, 97 m. D: James V. Kern, MS: Frederick Hollander, P: Warner (William Jacobs).

*Remember Me* (Eleanor Parker, Errol Flynn) W: Al Dubin—M: Harry Warren.

**879 Never Say Never Again.** US, 1983, C, 137 m. D: Irvin Kershner, MS: Michel Legrand, P: Warner (Jack Schwartzman).

*Never Say Never Again* (Lani Hall) W: Alan Bergman and Marilyn Bergman—M: Michel Legrand.

**880 Never Too Late.** US, 1965, C, 105 m. D: Bud Yorkin, MS: David Rose, P: Warner (Norman Lear).

*Never Too Late* (Vic Damone) WM: Ray Evans, Jay Livingston and David Rose.

**881 New Faces.** US, 1954, C, 99 m. D: Harry Horner, MS: Raoul Kraushaar, P: TCF (Leonard Sillman, Edward L. Alperson, Berman Swartz).

*Bal, Petit Bal* (Eartha Kitt, Robert Clary) WM: F. Lemarque / *Boston Beguine* (Alice Ghostley) WM: Sheldon M. Harnick / *C'est Si Bon* (Eartha Kitt) Eng. W: Jerry Seelan—Fr. WM: Andre Hornez and Henri Betti / *Guess Who I Saw Today?* (June Carroll) W: Elisse Boyd—M: Murray Grand / *I'm in Love with Miss Logan* (Robert Clary) WM: Ronny Graham / *Lizzie Borden* (Paul Lynde, Chorus) WM: Michael Brown / *Lucky Pierre* (Robert Clary) WM: Ronny Graham / *Monotonous* (Eartha Kitt); *Penny Candy* (June Carroll) WM: Arthur Siegel and June Carroll / *Santa Baby* (Eartha Kitt) WM: Joan Javits, Phil Springer and Tony Springer / *Time for Tea* (Alice Ghostley, June Carroll) / *Uska Dara* (Eartha Kitt) WM: Stella Lee.

**882 A New Kind of Love.** US, 1963, C, 110 m. D: Melville Shavelson, MS: Leith Stevens, P: Paramount (Melville Shavelson).

*In the Park in Paree* (Maurice Chevalier) W: Leo Robin—M: Ralph Rainger / *Louise* (Maurice Chevalier) W: Leo Robin—M: Richard A. Whiting / *Mimi* (Maurice Chevalier) W: Lorenz Hart—M: Richard Rodgers / *You Brought a New Kind of Love to Me* (Frank Sinatra) WM: Sammy Fain, Irving Kahal and Pierre Norman.

**883 New Moon.** US, 1930, BW, 78 m. D: Jack Conway, MD: Herbert Stothart, P: MGM.

*Farmer's Daughter* (Grace Moore, Lawrence Tibbett, Roland Young, Emily Fitzroy) M: Herbert Stothart / *Lover, Come Back to Me* (Grace Moore, Lawrence Tibbett, Roland Young, Adolph Menjou); *One Kiss* (Grace Moore); *Softly, As in a Morning Sunrise* (Lawrence Tibbett); *Soldiers' Chorus* (Chorus); *Stouthearted Men* (Lawrence Tibbett, Chorus); *Wanting You* (Grace Moore, Lawrence Tibbett) M: Sigmund Romberg / *What Is Your Price, Madame?* (Lawrence Tibbett, Adolph Menjou) M: Herbert Stothart. W: Oscar Hammerstein II.

**884 New Moon.** US, 1940, BW, 105 m. D: Robert Z. Leonard, MD: Herbert Stothart, P: MGM (Robert Z. Leonard).

*Dance Your Cares Away* (Chorus) W: Unknown—M: Sigmund Romberg / *Lover, Come Back to Me* (Jeanette MacDonald, Nelson Eddy); *Marianne* (Jeanette MacDonald, Nelson Eddy) W: Oscar Hammerstein II—M: Sigmund Romberg / *The Marseillaise* (Chorus) WM: Claude Rouget de Lisle / *No More Weeping* (Chorus) WM: Unknown / *One Kiss* (Jeanette MacDonald) W: Oscar Hammerstein II—M: Sigmund Romberg / *Shoes* (Nelson Eddy) W: Unknown—M: Sigmund Romberg / *Softly, As in a Morning Sunrise* (Nelson Eddy); *Stouthearted Men* (Nelson Eddy, Chorus); *Stranger in Paree* (Jeanette MacDonald) W: Oscar Hammerstein II—M: Sigmund Romberg / *Troubles of the World* (Chorus); *Wailing* (Chorus) WM: Unknown / *Wanting You* (Jeanette MacDonald, Nelson Eddy) W: Oscar Hammerstein II—M: Sigmund Romberg.

**885 New Orleans.** US, 1947, BW, 89 m. D: Arthur Lubin, MD: Nathaniel Finston, P: UA (Jules Levey). Orch: Woody Herman; Louis Armstrong and His All-Stars.

A little background about the song *Farewell to Storyville*. Famous as the redlight district of the port city of New Orleans, Storyville's bordellos were shut down by the U.S. Navy in wartime 1917 in response to public moral indignation. Looking for work, musicians scattered to other cities like Chicago, New York and Los Angeles.

*Basin Street Blues* (Louis Armstrong) WM: Spencer Williams / *The Blues Are Brewin'* (Billie Holiday, Louis Armstrong) W: Eddie DeLange—M: Louis Alter / *Dippermouth Blues* (Louis Armstrong) W: Walter Melrose—M: Joe "King" Oliver / *Do You Know What It Means to Miss New Orleans* (Billie Holiday, Louis Armstrong, Dorothy Patrick) W: Eddie DeLange—M: Louis Alter / *Farewell to Storyville* (Billie Holiday) WM: Spencer Williams and Clarence Williams / *Maryland, My Maryland* (Louis Armstrong) W: James

Ryder Randall—M: Walter de Mapes / *New Orleans Stomp* (Dorothy Patrick) WM: Joe "King" Oliver / *West End Blues* (Louis Armstrong) W: Clarence Williams—M: Joe "King" Oliver / *Where the Blues Were Born in New Orleans* (Louis Armstrong) W: Cliff Dixon—M: Bob Carleton.

**886 New York, New York.** US, 1977, C, 153 m. D: Martin Scorsese, MD: Ralph Burns, P: UA (Robert Chartoff, Irwin Winkler). Performer: Liza Minnelli.

Cut from the original release, then reinserted in 1981, was a musical performance by Liza Minnelli and Larry Kert called *Happy Endings* written by Kander and Ebb.

*Blue Moon* (Mary Kay Place, Robert De Niro) W: Lorenz Hart—M: Richard Rodgers / *But the World Goes 'Round* W: Fred Ebb—M: John Kander / *Do Nothin' Till You Hear from Me* (Mary Kay Place) W: Bob Russell—M: Duke Ellington / *Honeysuckle Rose* (Diahnne Abbott) W: Andy Razaf—M: Thomas "Fats" Waller / *Just You, Just Me* W: Raymond Klages—M: Jesse Greer / *The Man I Love* W: Ira Gershwin—M: George Gershwin / *New York, New York* W: Fred Ebb—M: John Kander / *Once in a While* W: Bud Green—M: Michael Edwards / *Taking a Chance on Love* W: John Latouche and Ted Fetter—M: Vernon Duke / *You Are My Lucky Star* W: Arthur Freed—M: Nacio Herb Brown / *You Brought a New Kind of Love to Me* WM: Sammy Fain, Irving Kahal and Pierre Norman.

"In a final burst from Old Hollywood, Minnelli tears into the title song and it's a wowser." —*Variety.*

**887 Niagara.** US, 1953, C, 89 m. D: Henry Hathaway, MS: Sol Kaplan, P: TCF (Charles Brackett).

*Hold Me—Hold Me—Hold Me* (Marilyn Monroe) W: Betty Comden and Adolph Green—M: Jule Styne.

**888 Nice Girl?** US, 1941, BW, 95 m. D: William A. Seiter, MD:

Charles Previn, P: Universal (Joe Pasternak). Performer: Deanna Durbin.

*Beneath the Lights of Home* W: Bernie Grossman—M: Walter Jurmann / *Love at Last* W: Eddie Cherkose—M: Jacques Press / *Old Folks at Home* WM: Stephen Collins Foster / *Perhaps* W: Aldo Franchetti—M: Andreas De Segurola / *Thank You, America* W: Bernie Grossman—M: Walter Jurmann.

**889  Night and Day.** US, 1946, C, 128 m. D: Michael Curtiz, MD: Ray Heindorf, P: Warner (Arthur Schwartz).

Hollywood-style biopic of songwriter-composer Cole Porter.

*Begin the Beguine* (Carlos Ramirez, Chorus); *Bulldog, Bulldog* (Chorus); *Do I Love You?* (Ginny Simms); *Don't Fence Me In* (Roy Rogers); *Easy to Love* (Chorus); *I Get a Kick Out of You* (Ginny Simms); *I'm in Love Again* (Jane Wyman); *I'm Unlucky at Gambling* (Eve Arden); *In the Still of the Night* (Dorothy Malone, Cary Grant, Chorus); *I've Got You Under My Skin* (Ginny Simms) WM: Cole Porter / *I Wonder What's Become of Sally* (Ginny Simms) W: Jack Yellen—M: Milton Ager / *Just One of Those Things* (Ginny Simms, Chorus); *Let's Do It* (Jane Wyman); *Miss Otis Regrets* (Monty Woolley); *My Heart Belongs to Daddy* (Mary Martin); *Night and Day* (Cary Grant, Alexis Smith, Chorus); *Old Fashioned Garden* (Cary Grant); *Rosalie* (Chorus); *What Is This Thing Called Love?* (Ginny Simms); *You Do Something to Me* (Jane Wyman, Chorus); *You're the Top* (Ginny Simms, Cary Grant); *You've Got That Thing* (Chorus) WM: Cole Porter.

**890  A Night at the Opera.** US, 1935, BW, 92 m. D: Sam Wood, MD: Herbert Stothart, P: MGM (Irving Thalberg).

*Alone* (Kitty Carlisle, Allan Jones) W: Arthur Freed—M: Nacio Herb Brown / *Cosi Cosa* (Kitty Carlisle, Allan Jones) W: Ned Washington—M: Bronislau Kaper and Walter Jurmann.

**891  A Night in Casablanca.** US, 1946, BW, 85 m. D: Archie Mayo, MS: Werner Janssen, P: UA (David L. Loew).

*Who's Sorry Now* (Lisette Verea, Chorus) WM: Bert Kalmar, Harry Ruby and Ted Snyder.

**892  The Night of the Iguana.** US, 1964, BW, 118 m. D: John Huston, MS: Benjamin Frankel, P: MGM (Ray Stark).

*Happy Days Are Here Again* (Chorus) W: Jack Yellen—M: Milton Ager.

**893  Night Shift.** US, 1982, C, 105 m. D: Ron Howard, MS: Burt Bacharach, P: Warner (Brian Grazer).

*That's What Friends Are For* (Rod Stewart) W: Carole Bayer Sager—M: Burt Bacharach.

**894  The Night They Raided Minsky's.** US, 1968, C, 99 m. D: William Friedkin, P: UA (Norman Lear). GB Title: The Night They Invented Striptease.

*The Night They Raided Minsky's* (Rudy Vallee); *Perfect Gentlemen* (Jason Robards, Norman Wisdom); *Take 10 Terrific Girls* (Rudy Vallee, Dexter Maitland, Chorus); *You Rat You* (Lillian Heyman) W: Lee Adams—M: Charles Strouse.

**895  A Nightmare on Elm Street 4: The Dream Master.** US, 1988, C, 92 m. D: Renny Harlin, P: New Line (Robert Shaye, Rachel Talalay).

*Angel* (Love Hate) WM: Skid Rose / *Back to the Wall* (Divinyls) WM: C. Amphlett, R. Feldman and M. McEntree / *Don't Be Afraid of Your Dreams* (Go West) WM: M. Piccirillo / *Love Kills* (Vinnie Vincent Invasion) WM: Vinnie Vincent / *My Way or the Highway* (Jimmy Davis and Junction) W: Jimmy Davis, J. Scott and T. Burroughs / *Resurrection* (Craig Safan) WM: Craig Safan / *Rip Her to Shreds* (Blondie) WM: Debbie Harry and C. Stein / *Standing Over You* (The Angels from Angel City) WM: Brewster and

Eccles / *Therapist* (Vigil) WM: Vigil / *Under the Night Stars* (Sea Hags) WM: Yocom and Schlosshardt.

**896   Nine and a Half Weeks.** US, 1986, C, 113 m. D: Adrian Lyne, MS: Jack Nitzsche, P: MGM (Anthony Rufus Isaacs, Zalman King).

*The Best Is Yet to Come* (Luba) WM: T. Britten and G. Lyle / *Black on Black* (Dalbello) WM: Dalbello / *Bread and Butter* (Devo) WM: Larry Parks and Jay Turnbow / *Cannes* (Stewart Copeland) WM: Stewart Copeland / *Eurasian Eyes* (Corey Hart) WM: Corey Hart / *I Do What I Do* (John Taylor, Johnathan Elias, B.J. Nelson, Michael Des Barres, Dalbello, Michael Brecker) WM: John Taylor, Michael Des Barres and Johnathan Elias / *Let It Go* (Luba) WM: Luba / *Slave to Love* (Bryan Ferry) WM: Bryan Ferry / *This City Never Sleeps* (Eurythmics) WM: Annie Lennox and Dave A. Stewart / *You Can Leave Your Hat On* (Joe Cocker) WM: Randy Newman.

**897   9 to 5.** US, 1980, C, 110 m. D: Colin Higgins, MS: Charles Fox, P: TCF (Bruce Gilbert).

*9 to 5* (Dolly Parton) WM: Dolly Parton.

**898   1941.** US, 1979, C, 118 m. D: Steven Spielberg, MS: John Williams, P: Columbia/Universal (Buzz Feitshans). Performers: The Andrews Sisters.

*Daddy* WM: Bobby Troup / *Down By the O-Hi-O* WM: Abe Olman and Jack Yellen.

**899   No Nukes.** US, 1980, C, 103 m. D: Julian Schlossberg, Danny Goldberg and Anthony Potenza, P: Warner (Julian Schlossberg, Danny Goldberg). Alt. Title: The Muse Concert: No Nukes.

*Barrels of Pain* (Graham Nash) / *Before the Deluge* (Jackson Browne) WM: Jackson Browne / *Devil with the Blue Dress On* (Bruce Springsteen) WM: Frederick Long and William Stevenson / *Get Together* (Jessie Colin Young) WM: Chester Powers / *Little Sister* (Ry Cooder) WM: Doc Pomus and Mort Shuman / *Lotta Love* (Nicolette Larson) WM: Neil Young / *Mockingbird* (James Taylor, Carly Simon) WM: Inez Foxx and Charlie Foxx / *Our House* (Graham Nash) WM: Graham Nash / *Power* (The Doobie Brothers, John Hall, James Taylor) WM: John J. Hall and Johanna Hall / *Quarter to Three* (Bruce Springsteen) WM: Frank Guida, Joe Royster, Gene Barge and Gary Anderson / *The River* (Bruce Springsteen) WM: Bruce Springsteen / *Runaway* (Bonnie Raitt) W: Del Shannon [Charles Westover] — M: Max Crook / *Running on Empty* (Jackson Browne) WM: Jackson Browne / *Stand and Fight* (James Taylor) / *Stay* (Bruce Springsteen, Jackson Browne) WM: Maurice Williams / *Suite: Judy Blue Eyes* (Crosby, Stills and Nash) WM: Stephen Stills / *Takin' It to the Streets* (The Doobie Brothers, Jackson Browne, Nicolette Larson, Graham Nash, Bonnie Raitt, Carly Simon, James Taylor, Phoebe Snow) WM: Michael McDonald / *Teach Your Children* (Crosby, Stills, Nash and Young) WM: Graham Nash / *Thunder Road* (Bruce Springsteen) / *The Times They Are A-Changin'* (Graham Nash, John Hall, Carly Simon, James Taylor) WM: Bob Dylan / *We Almost Lost Detroit* (Gil Scott-Heron) WM: Gil Scott-Heron / *What a Fool Believes* (The Doobie Brothers) WM: Kenny Loggins and Michael McDonald / *Your Smiling Face* (James Taylor) WM: James Taylor.

"The music ... is sturdier than its politics." — Janet Maslin, *The New York Times.*

**900   No Tree in the Street.** GB, 1958, BW, 108 m. D: J. Lee Thompson, MS: Laurie Johnson, P: Associated British (Frank Godwin). GB Title: No Trees in the Street.

*Liza Johnson* (Stanley Holloway) WM: George Le Brunn and Edgar Bateman.

**901   Nora Prentiss.** US, 1947,

BW, 111 m. D: Vincent Sherman, MS: Franz Waxman, P: Warner (William Jacobs).

*Who Cares What People Say?* (Ann Sheridan, Kent Smith) W: Jack Scholl—M: M.K. Jerome.

**902 Norma Rae.** US, 1979, C, 113 m. D: Martin Ritt, MS: David Shire, P: TCF (Tamara Asseyev, Alex Rose).

*It Goes Like It Goes* (Jennifer Warnes) W: Norman Gimbel—M: David Shire.

**903 North to Alaska.** US, 1960, C, 122 m. D: Henry Hathaway, MS: Lionel Newman, P: TCF (Henry Hathaway).

*If You Knew* (Fabian) WM: Russell Faith, Robert P. Marcucci and Peter De Angelis / *North to Alaska* (Johnny Horton) WM: Mike Phillips.

**904 Northwest Outpost.** US, 1947, BW, 91 m. D: Allan Dwan, MD: Robert Armbruster, P: Republic (Allan Dwan). MB: The American GI Chorus. GB Title: End of the Rainbow.

*Love Is the Time* (Ilona Massey); *Nearer and Dearer* (Nelson Eddy, Ilona Massey); *One More Mile to Go* (Nelson Eddy); *Raindrops on a Drum* (Nelson Eddy, Ilona Massey) W: Edward Heyman—M: Rudolf Friml / *Russian Easter Hymn* (Nelson Eddy) WM: Unknown / *Tell Me with Your Eyes* (Ilona Massey, Hugo Haas); *Weary* (Chorus) W: Edward Heyman—M: Rudolf Friml.

**905 Norwood.** US, 1970, C, 96 m. D: Jack Haley, Jr., MD: Al De Lory, P: Paramount (Hal B. Wallis). Performer: Glen Campbell.

*Down Home; Everything a Man Could Ever Need; I'll Paint You a Song* WM: Mac Davis / *Marie* WM: Mitchell Torok and Ramona Redd / *Norwood* WM: Mac Davis / *Ol' Norwood's Comin' Home* WM: Mitchell Torok and Ramona Redd / *The Repo Man* WM: Mac Davis.

**906 Nothing but a Man.** US,

1964, BW, 92 m. D: Michael Roemer, P: Cinema V (Robert Young, Michael Roemer, Robert Rubin).

*Bye Bye Baby* (Mary Wells) WM: Mary Wells / *Fingertips* (Little Stevie Wonder) WM: Henry Crosby and Clarence Paul / *Heat Wave* (Martha and The Vandellas) WM: Eddie Holland, Lamont Dozier and Brian Holland / *I'll Try Something New* (Smokey Robinson and The Miracles) WM: William "Smokey" Robinson / *Mickey's Monkey* (Smokey Robinson and The Miracles) WM: Eddie Holland, Lamont Dozier and Brian Holland / *This Is When I Need You Most* (Martha and The Vandellas) / *Way Over There* (Smokey Robinson and The Miracles); *You Really Got a Hold on Me* (Smokey Robinson and The Miracles) WM: William "Smokey" Robinson.

**907 Nothing in Common.** US, 1986, C, 118 m. D: Garry Marshall, MS: Patrick Leonard, P: Tri-Star (Alexandra Rose).

*Burning of the Heart* (Richard Marx); *If It Wasn't Love* (Carly Simon) WM: Patrick Leonard and Kathy Wakefield / *Loving Stranger* (Christopher Cross) WM: Patrick Leonard, Christopher Cross and John Bettis / *No One's Gonna Love You* (Real to Reel) WM: Billy Smith, Marquis Dair, Leon F. Sylvers III and Dominic Leslie / *Nothing in Common* (The Thompson Twins) WM: Tom Bailey and Alannah Currie / *Over the Weekend* (Nick Heyward) WM: Nick Heyward / *Seven Summers* (Cruzados) WM: Tito Larriva / *Until You Say You Love Me* (Aretha Franklin) WM: Narada Michael Walden and Preston Glass.

**908 Now and Forever.** US, 1934, BW, 81 m. D: Henry Hathaway, P: Paramount (Louis D. Lighton).

*The World Owes Me a Living* (Shirley Temple) WM: Larry Morey and Leigh Harline.

**909 The Nutty Professor.** US, 1963, C, 107 m. D: Jerry Lewis, MS: Walter Scharf, P: Paramount (Ernest

D. Glucksman). Orch: Les Brown and His Band of Renown.

*That Old Black Magic* (Jerry Lewis) W: Johnny Mercer—M: Harold Arlen.

**910  O Lucky Man!** GB, 1973, C, 174 m. D: Lindsay Anderson, MS: Alan Price, P: Warner (Michael Medwin, Lindsay Anderson). Performer: Alan Price.

*Changes; Justice; Look Over Your Shoulder; My Home Town; O Lucky Man; Poor People; Sell Sell* W: Alan Price.

"The music and songs . . . add by underlining and counterpointing the action." —*Variety.*

**911  Ocean's Eleven.** US, 1960, C, 127 m. D: Lewis Milestone, MS: Nelson Riddle, P: Warner (Lewis Milestone).

*Ain't That a Kick in the Head?* (Dean Martin); *Ee-O Eleven* (Sammy Davis, Jr.) W: Sammy Cahn—M: James Van Heusen.

**912  Octopussy.** GB, 1983, C, 130 m. D: John Glen, MS: John Barry, P: UA (Albert R. Broccoli).

*All Time High* (Rita Coolidge) W: Tim Rice—M: John Barry.

**913  The Odessa File.** GB-Germany, 1974, C, 128 m. D: Ronald Neame, MS: Andrew Lloyd Webber, P: Columbia (John Woolf).

*Christmas Dream* (Perry Como, The London Boy Singers) W: Tim Rice—M: Andrew Lloyd Webber.

**914  An Officer and a Gentleman.** US, 1982, C, 125 m. D: Taylor Hackford, MS: Jack Nitzsche, P: Paramount (Martin Elfand).

*Hungry for Your Love* (Van Morrison) WM: Van Morrison / *An Officer and a Gentleman* (Lee Ritenour) WM: Lee Ritenour, Jack Nitzsche and Buffy Sainte-Marie / *Treat Me Right* (Pat Benatar) WM: Pat Benatar and Doug Lubahn / *Tunnel of Love* (Dire Straits) WM: Mark Knopfler / *Tush* (ZZ Top) WM: Billy Gibbons, Joe Hill and Frank Beard / *Up Where We Belong* (Joe Cocker, Jennifer Warnes) WM: Jack Nitzsche, Will Jennings and Buffy Sainte-Marie.

**915  Oh! What a Lovely War.** GB, 1969, C, 139 m. D: Richard Attenborough, MD: Alfred Ralston, P: Paramount (Brian Duffy, Richard Attenborough).

*Adieu la Vie* (Pia Colombo) WM: Sablon / *Belgium Put the Kaibosh on the Kaiser* (Jean Pierre Cassel, Chorus) WM: Ellerton / *The Bells of Hell* (Chorus) / *Christmas Day in the Cookhouse* (Ben Howard) / *Comrades* (Joe Melia) WM: Felix McGlennon and Tom Costello / *Far, Far from Wipers* (Richard Howard) WM: Bingham and Greene / *Goodbye-ee* (Joe Melia, Corin Redgrave) W: Bert Lee—M: R.P. Weston / *Hush! Here Comes a Whizzbang* (Chorus) WM: R.P. Weston, Barnes and Maurice Scott / *I Do Like to Be Beside the Seaside* (Michael Redgrave, Chorus) WM: John A. Glover-Kind / *I'll Make a Man of You* (Maggie Smith, Chorus) W: Arthur Wimperis—M: Herman Finck / *I Want to Go Home* (Chorus) / *Keep the Home Fires Burning* (Joanne Brown) W: Lena Guilbert-Ford—M: Ivor Novello / *Oh! It's a Lovely War* (Chorus) W: Maurice Scott—M: J.P. Long / *Over There* (Chorus) WM: George M. Cohan / *Pack Up Your Troubles in Your Old Kit Bag* (Chorus) W: George Asaf—M: Felix Powell / *Send for the Boys of the Girls' Brigade* (Richard Howard) / *Silent Night* (Chorus) W: Joseph Mohr—M: Franz Gruber / *There's a Long, Long Trail* (Chorus) W: Stoddard King—M: Zo Elliott / *They Didn't Believe Me* (Chorus) W: Herbert Reynolds [Michael E. Rourke]—M: Jerome Kern / *They Were Only Playing Leapfrog* (Chorus) WM: Unknown / *When This Bloody War Is Over* (Maurice Arthur, Chorus) W: Charles Carroll Sawyer—M: Henry Tucker / *Your King and Country Want You* (Penny Allen) WM: Paul Rubens.

"A satire on war in which the songs are an integral part of the message." —*Variety.*

**916  Oklahoma!** US, 1955, C, 145 m. D: Fred Zinnemann, MD: Jay Blackton, P: Magna (Arthur Hornblow, Jr.).

This landmark musical opened on Broadway in March 1943 and ran for more than two thousand performances.

*All 'er Nothing* (Gloria Grahame, Gene Nelson); *The Farmer and the Cowman* (Gloria Grahame, Gene Nelson, Gordon MacRae, Charlotte Greenwood, J.C. Flippen, James Whitmore, Chorus); *I Caint Say No* (Gloria Grahame); *Kansas City* (Gene Nelson, Charlotte Greenwood, Chorus); *Many a New Day* (Shirley Jones, Chorus); *Oh, What a Beautiful Mornin'* (Gordon MacRae); *Oklahoma!* (Shirley Jones, Gordon MacRae, James Whitmore, Gene Nelson, J.C. Flippen, Charlotte Greenwood, Chorus); *Out of My Dreams* (Shirley Jones, Chorus); *People Will Say We're in Love* (Shirley Jones, Gordon MacRae); *Pore Jud Is Daid* (Gordon MacRae, Rod Steiger); *Surrey with the Fringe on Top* (Shirley Jones, Gordon MacRae, Charlotte Greenwood) W: Oscar Hammerstein II—M: Richard Rodgers.

"The tunes ring out with undiminished delight." —*Variety*.

**917  Oklahoma Crude.** US, 1973, C, 108 m. D: Stanley Kramer, MS: Henry Mancini, P: Columbia (Stanley Kramer).

*Send a Little Love My Way* (Anne Murray) W: Hal David—M: Henry Mancini.

**918  The Oklahoma Kid.** US, 1939, BW, 85 m. D: Lloyd Bacon, MS: Max Steiner, P: Warner (Sam Bischoff). Performer: James Cagney.

Ms. Crockett, a relative of Davy's, wrote her classic lullaby when she was fifteen.

*I Don't Want to Play in Your Yard* W: Philip Wingate—M: H.W. Petrie / *Rock-a-Bye Baby* WM: Effie I. Canning [Effie I. Crockett].

**919  Old Man Rhythm.** US, 1935, BW, 75 m. D: Edward Ludwig, P: RKO (Zion Myers). Performer: Johnny Mercer.

*Boys Will Be Boys; Comes the Revolution, Baby; I Never Saw a Better Night; Old Man Rhythm* (Grace Bradley, George Barbier); *There's Nothing Like a College Education; When You Are in My Arms* (Grace Bradley, Charles "Buddy" Rogers) W: Johnny Mercer—M: Lewis E. Gensler.

**920  The Old West.** US, 1952, BW, 61 m. D: George Archainbaud, P: Columbia (Armand Schaefer). Performer: Gene Autry.

*Music By the Angels; Somebody Bigger Than You and I* WM: Johnny Lange, Hy Heath and Sonny Burke.

**921  Oliver!** GB, 1968, C, 153 m. D: Carol Reed, MD: John Green, P: Columbia (John Woolf).

*As Long As He Needs Me* (Shani Wallis); *Be Back Soon* (Ron Moody, Chorus); *Boy for Sale* (Harry Secombe); *Consider Yourself* (Jack Wild, Mark Lester, Chorus); *Food, Glorious Food* (Mark Lester, Chorus); *I'd Do Anything* (Jack Wild, Mark Lester, Shani Wallis, Sheila White, Ron Moody, Chorus); *It's a Fine Life* (Shani Wallis, Sheila White, Chorus); *Oliver!* (Harry Secombe, Peggy Mount, Chorus); *Oom-Pah-Pah* (Shani Wallis, Chorus); *Reviewing the Situation* (Ron Moody); *Where Is Love?* (Mark Lester); *Who Will Buy?* (Mark Lester, Chorus); *You've Got to Pick a Pocket or Two* (Ron Moody) WM: Lionel Bart.

"This $10 million pic is a bright, shiny, heartwarming musical, packed with songs and lively production high spots. Lionel Bart's [1960] stage musical hit is adroitly opened out by director Carol Reed." —*Variety*.

**922  On a Clear Day You Can See Forever.** US, 1970, C, 129 m. D: Vincente Minnelli, MD: Nelson Riddle, P: Paramount (Howard W. Koch). Performer: Barbra Streisand.

*Come Back to Me* (Yves Montand); *Go to Sleep; He Isn't You; Hurry! It's*

*Lovely Up Here; Love with All the Trimmings; Melinda* (Yves Montand); *On a Clear Day* (Barbra Streisand, Yves Montand, Chorus); *What Did I Have That I Don't Have?* W: Alan Jay Lerner—M: Burton Lane.

**923  On Her Majesty's Secret Service.** GB, 1969, C, 140 m. D: Peter Hunt, MS: John Barry, P: UA (Harry Saltzman, Albert R. Broccoli).

*We Have All the Time in the World* (Louis Armstrong) W: Hal David—M: John Barry.

**924  On Moonlight Bay.** US, 1951, C, 95 m. D: Roy Del Ruth, MD: Ray Heindorf, P: Warner (William Jacobs).

*Christmas Story* (Doris Day, Chorus) WM: Pauline Walsh / *Cuddle Up a Little Closer* (Doris Day, Gordon MacRae); *Every Little Movement Has a Meaning of Its Own* (Doris Day, Jack Smith) W: Otto Harbach—M: Karl Hoschna / *I'm Forever Blowing Bubbles* (Doris Day, Jack Smith) W: Jaan Kenbrovin [James Kendis, James Brockman and Nat Vincent]—M: John W. Kellette / *Love Ya* (Doris Day, Jack Smith) W: Charles Tobias—M: Peter De Rose / *Moonlight Bay* (Doris Day, Chorus) W: Edward Madden—M: Percy Wenrich / *Tell Me* (Doris Day) W: J. Will Callahan—M: Max Kortlander / *Till We Meet Again* (Doris Day, Gordon MacRae) W: Raymond B. Egan—M: Richard A. Whiting.

**925  On the Avenue.** US, 1937, BW, 89 m. D: Roy Del Ruth, MD: Arthur Lange, P: TCF (Gene Markey).

*The Girl on the Police Gazette* (Dick Powell, Chorus); *He Ain't Got Rhythm* (Alice Faye, The Ritz Brothers, Chorus); *I've Got My Love to Keep Me Warm* (Alice Faye, Dick Powell); *Slumming on Park Avenue* (Alice Faye, The Ritz Brothers, Chorus); *This Year's Kisses* (Alice Faye); *You're Laughing at Me* (Dick Powell) WM: Irving Berlin.

"In the better, but not the best, Berlin tradition." —Frank S. Nugent, *The New York Times.*

**926  On the Double.** US, 1961, C, 92 m. D: Melville Shavelson, MS: Leith Stevens, P: Paramount (Jack Rose). Performer: Danny Kaye.

*Cocktails for Two* W: Sam Coslow—M: Arthur Johnston / *Darlin' Meggie; The Mackensie Hielanders; On the Double* WM: Sylvia Fine.

**927  On the Riviera.** US, 1951, C, 90 m. D: Walter Lang, MS: Alfred Newman, P: TCF (Sol C. Siegel). Performer: Danny Kaye.

*Ballin' the Jack* W: Jim Burris—M: Chris Smith / *Happy Ending; On the Riviera; Popo the Puppet; Rhythm of a New Romance* WM: Sylvia Fine.

**928  On the Town.** US, 1949, C, 98 m. D: Gene Kelly and Stanley Donen, MD: Lennie Hayton and Roger Edens, P: MGM (Arthur Freed).

Originally based on Jerome Robbins ballet "Fancy Free." The cast of the 1944 Broadway musical included Nancy Walker and Alice Pearce as well as Betty Comden and Adolph Green who wrote the book and lyrics. Roger Edens added new tunes for the film.

*Come Up to My Place* (Betty Garrett, Frank Sinatra) M: Leonard Bernstein / *Count on Me* (Frank Sinatra, Gene Kelly, Jules Munshin, Ann Miller, Betty Garrett, Alice Pearce) M: Roger Edens / *I Feel Like I'm Not Out of Bed Yet* (Bern Hoffman) M: Leonard Bernstein / *Main Street* (Gene Kelly) M: Roger Edens / *New York, New York* (Frank Sinatra, Gene Kelly, Jules Munshin) M: Leonard Bernstein / *On the Town* (Frank Sinatra, Gene Kelly, Jules Munshin, Ann Miller, Betty Garrett, Vera-Ellen); *Prehistoric Man* (Ann Miller, Gene Kelly, Frank Sinatra, Jules Munshin, Betty Garrett); *You're Awful* (Frank Sinatra, Betty Garrett) M: Roger Edens. W: Betty Comden and Adolph Green.

"The whole thing precipitately moves, with song, dance, comedy and romance ingeniously interwoven and performed." —Bosley Crowther, *The New York Times.*

**929 On with the Show.** US, 1929, C, 101 m. D: Alan Crosland, MD: Louis Silvers, P: Warner (Darryl F. Zanuck). Vocals: Josephine Houston for Betty Compson and Sally O'Neil.

*Am I Blue?* (Ethel Waters, Harmony Four Quartet); *Birmingham Bertha* (Ethel Waters); *Don't It Mean a Thing to You?* (Josephine Houston, Arthur Lake); *In the Land of Let's Pretend* (Mildred Carroll, Chorus); *Let Me Have My Dreams* (Betty Compson, Sally O'Neil); *Lift the Juleps to Your Two Lips* (Josephine Houston, Henry Fink, Chorus); *Wedding Day* (Josephine Houston, Henry Fink, Arthur Lake, Chorus); *Welcome Home* (Henry Fink, Chorus) W: Grant Clarke—M: Harry Akst.

**930 Once Is Not Enough.** US, 1974, 122 m. D: Guy Green, MS: Henry Mancini, P: Paramount (Howard W. Koch). Alt. Title: Jacqueline Susann's Once Is Not Enough.

*All the Way* (Frank Sinatra) W: Sammy Cahn—M: James Van Heusen.

**931 The One and Only.** US, 1978, C, 98 m. D: Carl Reiner, MS: Patrick Williams, P: Paramount (Steve Gordon, David V. Picker).

*Getting to Know You* (Henry Winkler) W: Oscar Hammerstein II—M: Richard Rodgers / *The One and Only* (Kasey Ciszk) W: Alan Bergman and Marilyn Bergman—M: Patrick Williams.

**932 The One and Only, Genuine, Original Family Band.** US, 1968, C, 117 m. D: Michael O'Herlihy, MD: Jack Elliott, P: Walt Disney (Bill Anderson).

*'Bout Time* (John Davidson, Lesley Ann Warren); *Dakota* (John Davidson, Chorus); *Drummin' Drummin' Drummin'* (Walter Brennan, Jon Walmsley, Pamelyn Ferdin, Bobby Riha, Smitty Wordes, Heidi Rook, Chorus); *The Happiest Girl Alive* (Lesley Ann Warren); *Let's Put It Over with Grover* (Walter Brennan, Buddy Ebsen, Lesley Ann Warren, Janet Blair, Chorus); *Oh, Benjamin Harrison* (Buddy Ebsen, John Davidson, Steve Harmon, Wally Cox, Richard Deacon, John Craig); *The One and Only, Genuine, Original Family Band* (Walter Brennan, Buddy Ebsen, Lesley Ann Warren, Janet Blair, Chorus); *Ten Feet Off the Ground* (Buddy Ebsen, Lesley Ann Warren, Janet Blair, Chorus); *West o' the Wide Missouri* (Buddy Ebsen, Lesley Ann Warren, Janet Blair, Debbie Smith, Kurt Russell, Bobby Riha, Goldie Hawn, Steve Harmon, Chorus) WM: Richard M. Sherman and Robert B. Sherman.

**933 One Hour with You.** US, 1932, BW, 80 m. D: Ernst Lubitsch and George Cukor, MD: Nat W. Finston, P: Paramount (Ernst Lubitsch).

*Oh, That Mitzi!* (Maurice Chevalier) W: Leo Robin—M: Oscar Straus / *One Hour with You* (Maurice Chevalier, Jeanette MacDonald, Charles Ruggles, Donald Novis, Genevieve Tobin); *Three Times a Day* (Maurice Chevalier, Genevieve Tobin) W: Leo Robin—M: Richard A. Whiting / *We Will Always Be Sweethearts* (Maurice Chevalier, Jeanette MacDonald); *What a Little Thing Like a Wedding Ring Can Do* (Maurice Chevalier, Jeanette MacDonald) W: Leo Robin—M: Oscar Straus / *What Would You Do?* (Maurice Chevalier) W: Leo Robin—M: Richard A. Whiting.

"Jeanette MacDonald is a superb vis-a-vis for the star, intelligently getting her song lyrics over in a quiet, chatty manner." — *Variety*.

**934 One Hundred Men and a Girl.** US, 1937, BW, 84 m. D: Henry Koster, MD: Charles Previn, P: Universal (Joe Pasternak, Charles R. Rogers). Performer: Deanna Durbin.

*A Heart That's Free* W: Thomas T. Railey—M: Alfred G. Robyn / *It's Raining Sunbeams* W: Sam Coslow—M: Frederick Hollander.

**935 One Minute to Zero.** US, 1952, BW, 105 m. D: Tay Garnett,

MD: Constantin Bakaleinikoff, P: RKO (Edmund Grainger).

*Tell Me, Golden Moon* (Robert Mitchum, Ann Blyth) WM: Norman Bennett and Nobuyuki Takeoda.

**936 One Night in the Tropics.** US, 1940, BW, 82 m. D: A. Edward Sutherland, MD: Charles Previn, P: Universal (Leonard Spiegelgass).

*Remind Me* (Peggy Moran, Allan Jones); *You and Your Kiss* (Allan Jones) W: Dorothy Fields / *Your Dream* (Allan Jones, Nancy Kelly) W: Otto Harbach and Oscar Hammerstein II. M: Jerome Kern.

**937 One Night of Love.** US, 1934, BW, 80 m. D: Victor Schertzinger, MD: Pietro Cimini, MS: Louis Silvers, P: Columbia (Everett Riskin). Performer: Grace Moore.

*Ciribiribin* W: Rudolf Thaler — M: Alberto Pestalozza / *Indian Love Call* W: Otto Harbach and Oscar Hammerstein II — M: Rudolf Friml / *One Night of Love* W: Gus Kahn — M: Victor Schertzinger / *'Tis the Last Rose of Summer* W: Thomas Moore — M: Richard Alfred Milliken.

**938 One on One.** US, 1977, C, 98 m. D: Lamont Johnson, P: Warner (Martin Hornstein). Performers: Seals and Crofts.

*The Basketball Game; Flyin'; Hustle; It'll Be All Right; Janet's Theme; John Wayne; Love Conquers All; My Fair Share; The Party; Picnic; Reflections; This Day Belongs to Me; Time Out* W: Paul Williams — M: Charles Fox.

**939 One Touch of Venus.** US, 1948, BW, 81 m. D: William A. Seiter, MD: Leo Arnaud, P: Universal (Lester Cowan). Vocals: Eileen Wilson for Ava Gardner.

*My Heart Is Showing* (Ava Gardner, Olga San Juan, Dick Haymes, Robert Walker, Chorus) W: Ann Ronell / *Speak Low* (Ava Gardner, Dick Haymes) W: Ogden Nash / *That's Him* (Ava Gardner, Olga San Juan, Eve Arden) W: Ogden Nash and Ann Ronell / *The Trouble with Women* (Chorus)

W: Ogden Nash. M: Kurt Weill.

**940 One-Trick Pony.** US, 1980, C, 98 m. D: Robert M. Young, MS: Paul Simon, P: Warner (Michael Tannen, Michael Hausman). Performer: Paul Simon.

*Ace in the Hole* WM: Paul Simon / *Do You Believe in Magic?* (The Lovin' Spoonful) WM: John B. Sebastian / *God Bless the Absentee; How the Heart Approaches What It Yearns; Jonah; Late in the Evening; Long Long Day; Nobody; Oh Marion; One-Trick Pony* WM: Paul Simon / *Rock Lobster* (The B-52's) WM: Fred Schneider and Ricky Wilson / *Soul Man* (Sam and Dave) WM: Isaac Hayes and David Porter / *That's Why God Made the Movies* WM: Paul Simon.

**941 One Way Passage.** US, 1932, BW, 69 m. D: Tay Garnett, P: Warner (Hal B. Wallis).

*Where Was I?* (Heinie Conklin) W: Al Dubin — M: W. Franke Harling.

**942 Only When I Laugh.** US, 1981, C, 120 m. D: Glenn Jordan, MS: David Shire, P: Columbia (Roger M. Rothstein, Neil Simon). GB Title: It Hurts Only When I Laugh.

*I Guess I'll Have to Change My Plan* (Kristy McNicol, Marsha Mason) W: Howard Dietz — M: Arthur Schwartz.

**943 Operator 13.** US, 1934, BW, 86 m. D: Richard Boleslavsky, MS: William Axt, P: MGM (Lucien Hubbard). GB Title: Spy 13.

*Jungle Fever* (The Four Mills Brothers) W: Howard Dietz — M: Walter Donaldson / *Once in a Lifetime* (Marion Davies); *Sleepy Head* (The Four Mills Brothers) W: Gus Kahn — M: Walter Donaldson.

**944 Orchestra Wives.** US, 1942, BW, 98 m. D: Archie Mayo, MD: Alfred Newman, P: TCF (William LeBaron). Orch: Glenn Miller. MB: The Modernaires. Vocals: Pat Friday for Lynn Bari.

*At Last* (Ray Eberle, Lynn Bari); *I've Got a Gal in Kalamazoo* (Tex Beneke, Marion Hutton); *People Like You and Me* (Tex Beneke, Marion

Hutton, Ray Eberle); *Serenade in Blue* (Ray Eberle, Lynn Bari); *That's Sabotage* (Marion Hutton) W: Mack Gordon—M: Harry Warren.

**945 The Other Side of the Mountain.** US, 1975, C, 101 m. D: Larry Peerce, MS: Charles Fox, P: Universal (Edward S. Feldman). GB Title: A Window to the Sky.

*Richard's Window* (Olivia Newton-John) W: Norman Gimbel—M: Charles Fox.

**946 The Other Side of the Mountain, Part Two.** US, 1978, C, 100 m. D: Larry Peerce, MS: Lee Holdridge, P: Universal (Edward S. Feldman).

*The Other Side of the Mountain, Part Two* (Merrily Webber) W: Molly Ann Leikin—M: Lee Holdridge.

**947 Out of Africa.** US-GB, 1985, C, 161 m. D: Sydney Pollack, MS: John Barry, P: Universal (Sydney Pollack).

*The Music of Goodbye* (Melissa Manchester, Al Jarreau) W: Alan Bergman and Marilyn Bergman—M: John Barry.

**948 Out of This World.** US, 1945, BW, 96 m. D: Hal Walker, MS: Victor Young, P: Paramount (Sam Coslow). Vocals: Bing Crosby for Eddie Bracken.

*All I Do Is Beat That Golden Drum* (Cass Daley) WM: Sam Coslow / *I'd Rather Be Me* (Eddie Bracken) WM: Sam Coslow, Eddie Cherkose and Felix Bernard / *June Comes Around Every Year* (Eddie Bracken); *Out of This World* (Eddie Bracken) W: Johnny Mercer—M: Harold Arlen / *A Sailor with an Eight Hour Pass* (Cass Daley) WM: Ben Raleigh and Bernie Wayne.

**949 Pagan Love Song.** US, 1950, C, 76 m. D: Robert Alton, MD: Adolph Deutsch, P: MGM (Arthur Freed).

Esther Williams sang her own songs here rather than being dubbed as she usually was.

*Etiquette* (Howard Keel, Children); *The House of Singing Bamboo* (Howard Keel, Chorus) M: Harry Warren / *Pagan Love Song* (Howard Keel, Chorus) M: Nacio Herb Brown / *The Sea of the Moon* (Esther Williams); *Singing in the Sun* (Howard Keel, Esther Williams, Chorus); *Why Is Love So Crazy?* (Howard Keel) M: Harry Warren. W: Arthur Freed.

**950 Page Miss Glory.** US, 1935, BW, 90 m. D: Mervyn LeRoy, MD: Leo F. Forbstein, P: Warner/Cosmopolitan (Robert Lord).

*Page Miss Glory* (Dick Powell, Marion Davies) W: Al Dubin—M: Harry Warren.

"Dick Powell ... is well nigh wasted, virtually dragged in for his ... title song duet with the star." —*Variety*.

**951 Paint Your Wagon.** US, 1969, C, 166 m. D: Joshua Logan, MD: Nelson Riddle, P: Paramount (Tom Shaw, Alan Jay Lerner). MB: The Nitty Gritty Dirt Band. Vocals: Anita Gordon for Jean Seberg.

*Best Things* (Lee Marvin, Clint Eastwood, Chorus); *The First Thing You Know* (Lee Marvin); *Gold Fever* (Clint Eastwood, Chorus); *The Gospel of No Name City* (Alan Dexter) M: Andre Previn / *Hand Me Down That Can o' Beans* (Lee Marvin, Chorus); *I'm on My Way* (Chorus); *I Still See Elisa* (Clint Eastwood); *I Talk to the Trees* (Clint Eastwood) M: Frederick Loewe / *A Million Miles Away Behind the Door* (Jean Seberg) M: Andre Previn / *There's a Coach Comin' In* (Harve Presnell, Chorus); *They Call the Wind Maria* (Harve Presnell, Chorus); *Wand'rin Star* (Lee Marvin, Chorus); *Whoop-Ti-Ay!* (Chorus) M: Frederick Loewe. W: Alan Jay Lerner.

"What the $17 million-plus film (from the 1951 Lerner-Loewe Broadway musical) lacks in a skimpy story line it makes up in the music and expert choreography. There are no obvious 'musical numbers.' All the songs, save one or two, work neatly, quietly and well into the script." —*Variety*.

**952   Painting the Clouds with Sunshine.** US, 1951, C, 87 m. D: David Butler, P: Warner (William Jacobs).

*The Birth of the Blues* (Lucille Norman) W: B.G. De Sylva and Lew Brown—M: Ray Henderson / *Jealousy* (Lucille Norman) W: Vera Bloom—M: Jacob Gade / *Man Is a Necessary Evil* (Female Trio) W: Jack Elliott—M: Sonny Burke / *Painting the Clouds with Sunshine* (Dennis Morgan, Lucille Norman, Chorus); *Tip Toe Through the Tulips with Me* (Gene Nelson, Lucille Norman, Virginia Mayo, Virginia Gibson) W: Al Dubin—M: Joe Burke / *Vienna Dreams* (Lucille Norman) W: Irving Caesar—M: Rudolf Siencynski / *We're in the Money* (Dennis Morgan, Chorus) W: Al Dubin—M: Harry Warren / *With a Song in My Heart* (Dennis Morgan, Lucille Norman) W: Lorenz Hart—M: Richard Rodgers / *You're My Everything* (Dennis Morgan) W: Mort Dixon and Joe Young—M: Harry Warren.

**953   The Pajama Game.** US, 1957, C, 101 m. D: George Abbott and Stanley Donen, MD: Ray Heindorf, P: Warner (George Abbott, Stanley Donen).

*Hernando's Hideaway* (Carol Haney, Chorus); *Hey There* (Doris Day, John Raitt); *I'll Never Be Jealous Again* (Eddie Foy, Jr., Reta Shaw); *I'm Not at All in Love* (Doris Day, Barbara Nichols, Thelma Pelish, Chorus); *Once-a-Year Day* (Doris Day, John Raitt, Chorus); *The Pajama Game* (Eddie Foy, Jr.); *Racing with the Clock* (Eddie Foy, Jr., Chorus); *Seven and a Half Cents* (Doris Day, Barbara Nichols, Jack Straw, Chorus); *Small Talk* (Doris Day, John Raitt); *Steam Heat* (Carol Haney, Buzz Miller, Kenneth Le Roy); *There Once Was a Man* (Doris Day, John Raitt) WM: Richard Adler and Jerry Ross.

"It's as good as it was on the stage [1954], which was quite good enough." —Bosley Crowther, *The New York Times*.

"Carol Haney, recreating her soubret role opposite Eddie Foy, Jr. (also of the original stage cast) whams with *Steam Heat*." —*Variety*.

**954   Pajama Party.** US, 1964, C, 85 m. D: Don Weis, MS: Les Baxter, P: AIP (James H. Nicolson, Samuel Z. Arkoff). MB: The Nooney Rickett Four. Performer: Annette Funicello.

*Among the Young; It's That Kind of Day; Pajama Party; Stuffed Animal; There Has to Be a Reason; Where Did I Go Wrong?* (Dorothy Lamour) WM: Jerry Styner and Guy Hemric.

**955   Pal Joey.** US, 1957, C, 111 m. D: George Sidney, MD: Morris Stoloff, P: Columbia (Fred Kohlmar). Vocals: Jo Ann Greer for Rita Hayworth; Trudi Erwin for Kim Novak.

Gene Kelly had his first leading role in the 1940 Broadway production. The show was revived in 1952.

*Bewitched* (Rita Hayworth, Frank Sinatra); *Great Big Town* (Chorus); *I Could Write a Book* (Frank Sinatra, Chorus); *I Didn't Know What Time It Was* (Frank Sinatra); *The Lady Is a Tramp* (Frank Sinatra); *My Funny Valentine* (Kim Novak); *That Terrific Rainbow* (Kim Novak, Chorus); *There's a Small Hotel* (Frank Sinatra); *What Do I Care for a Dame* (Frank Sinatra, Chorus); *Zip* (Rita Hayworth) W: Lorenz Hart—M: Richard Rodgers.

"Standout of the score is *Lady Is a Tramp*. It's a wham arrangement and Sinatra gives it powerhouse delivery." —*Variety*.

"The purist might . . . note that several songs from the original score have been dropped in favor of tunes from other Rodgers-Hart hit musicals. . . . this does not constitute short-changing the public." —A.H. Weiler, *The New York Times*.

**956   The Paleface.** US, 1948, C, 91 m. D: Norman Z. McLeod, MS: Victor Young, P: Paramount (Robert L. Welch).

*Buttons and Bows* (Bob Hope, Jane

Russell) WM: Jay Livingston and Ray Evans / *Get a Man!* (Iris Adrian, Chorus) WM: Joseph J. Lilley / *Meetcha 'Round the Corner* (Iris Adrian) WM: Jay Livingston and Ray Evans.

**957 The Palm Beach Story.** US, 1942, BW, 90 m. D: Preston Sturges, MD: Victor Young, P: Paramount (Paul Jones).

*Goodnight Sweetheart* (Rudy Vallee) WM: Ray Noble, James Campbell, Reginald Connelly and Rudy Vallee.

**958 Palm Springs.** US, 1936, BW, 74 m. D: Aubrey Scotto, MD: Boris Morros, P: Paramount (Walter Wanger). GB Title: Palm Springs Affair. Performer: Frances Langford.

*The Hills of Old Wyomin'* (Frances Langford, Smith Ballew); *I Don't Want to Make History* W: Leo Robin—M: Ralph Rainger / *I'm in the Mood for Love* W: Dorothy Fields—M: Jimmy McHugh / *Will I Ever Know?* WM: Mack Gordon and Harry Revel.

**959 Palm Springs Weekend.** US, 1963, C, 100 m. D: Norman Taurog, MS: Frank Perkins, P: Warner (Michael Hoey).

*Bye Bye Blackbird* (Ty Hardin, Jerry Van Dyke) W: Mort Dixon—M: Ray Henderson / *Go, Go-Devil* (Chorus) / *A Little Bit o' Give* (Robert Conrad, Chorus) W: Vincent Castle—M: Bodie Chandler / *Live Young* (Troy Donahue, Chorus) W: Larry Kusik—M: Paul Evans / *Ox-Driver* (Modern Folk Quartet) WM: Unknown / *Shilly-Shally* (Chorus) / *What Will I Tell Him* (Connie Stevens) WM: Barry De Vorzon and Bodie Chandler.

**960 Palmy Days.** US, 1931, BW, 77 m. D: A. Edward Sutherland, MD: Alfred Newman, P: UA (Samuel Goldwyn). MB: The Goldwyn Girls.

*Bend Down, Sister* (Charlotte Greenwood, Charles Middleton, George Raft, Walter Catlett) W: Ballard MacDonald and Dave Silverstein—M: Con Conrad / *Dunk Dunk Dunk* (The Goldwyn Girls); *Goose Pimples* (Charlotte Greenwood) W: Ballard MacDonald

—M: Con Conrad / *My Honey Said Yes, Yes* (Eddie Cantor, Charlotte Greenwood) WM: Cliff Friend / *There's Nothing Too Good for My Baby* (Eddie Cantor) W: Benny Davis—M: Harry Akst.

**961 Panama Hattie.** US, 1942, BW, 79 m. D: Norman Z. McLeod, MD: George Stoll, P: MGM (Arthur Freed).

*Did I Get Stinkin' at the Savoy* (Virginia O'Brien) W: E.Y. Harburg—M: Walter Donaldson / *Fresh As a Daisy* (Virginia O'Brien); *I've Still Got My Health* (Ann Sothern); *Just One of Those Things* (Lena Horne); *Let's Be Buddies* (Ann Sothern, Jackie Horner); *Make It Another Old Fashioned Please* (Ann Sothern) WM: Cole Porter / *The Son of a Gun Who Picks on Uncle Sam* (Chorus) W: E.Y. Harburg—M: Burton Lane / *The Sping* (Lena Horne, The Bernard Brothers) WM: Phil Moore and J. Le Gon.

**962 Pandora and the Flying Dutchman.** GB, 1951, C, 123 m. D: Albert Lewin, MS: Alan Rawsthorne, P: MGM (Albert Lewin, Joseph Kaufman). Performer: Ava Gardner.

*How Am I to Know?* W: Dorothy Parker—M: Jack King / *You're Driving Me Crazy* WM: Walter Donaldson.

**963 Papa's Delicate Condition.** US, 1963, C, 98 m. D: George Marshall, MS: Joseph J. Lilley, P: Paramount (Jack Rose).

*Bill Bailey, Won't You Please Come Home?* (Glynis Johns) WM: Hugh Cannon / *Call Me Irresponsible* (Jackie Gleason) W: Sammy Cahn—M: James Van Heusen.

**964 Paper Tiger.** GB, 1976, C, 99 m. D: Ken Annakin, MS: Roy Budd, P: Maclean (Euan Lloyd).

*My Little Friend* (Roy Coniff Singers) W: Sammy Cahn—M: Roy Budd.

**965 Paradise Alley.** US, 1978, C, 109 m. D: Sylvester Stallone, MS: Bill Conti, P: Universal (John F. Roach, Ronald A. Suppa).

*Angel Voice* (Frank Stallone, Jr.) WM: Frank Stallone, Jr. / *Annie's Back in Town* (Tom Waits); *Paradise Alley* (Tom Waits) WM: Tom Waits / *Please Be Someone to Me* (Frank Stallone, Jr.) WM: Frank Stallone, Jr. / *Too Close to Paradise* (Sylvester Stallone) W: Bruce Roberts and Carole Bayer Sager—M: Bill Conti.

**966 Paradise, Hawaiian Style.** US, 1966, C, 91 m. D: Michael Moore, MD: Joseph J. Lilley, P: Paramount (Hal B. Wallis). MB: The Jordanaires. Performer: Elvis Presley.

*Bill Bailey, Won't You Please Come Home* (Donna Butterworth) WM: Hugh Cannon / *Datin'* (Elvis Presley, Donna Butterworth) WM: Fred Wise and Randy Starr / *A Dog's Life* WM: Sid Wayne and Ben Weisman / *Drums of the Islands* WM: Sid Tepper and Roy C. Bennett / *House of Sand; Paradise, Hawaiian Style; Queenie Wahine's Papaya* (Elvis Presley, Donna Butterworth); *Scratch My Back* (Elvis Presley, Marianna Hill); *Stop Where You Are; This Is My Heaven* WM: Bill Giant, Bernie Baum and Florence Kaye.

**967 Paramount on Parade.** US, 1930, BW/C, 102 m. D: Dorothy Arzner, Otto Brower, Edmund Goulding, Victor Heerman, Edwin H. Knopf, Rowland V. Lee, Ernst Lubitsch, Lother Mendes, Victor Schertzinger, A. Edward Sutherland and Frank Tuttle. P: Paramount (Elsie Janis). Orch: Abe Lyman.

*All I Want Is Just One Girl* (Maurice Chevalier, Mitzi Green) W: Leo Robin—M: Richard A. Whiting / *Anytime's the Time to Fall in Love* (Lillian Roth, Charles "Buddy" Rogers, Chorus) W: Elsie Janis—M: Jack King / *Come Back to Sorrento* (Nino Martini) WM: Ernesto De Curtis and Claude Aveling / *Dancing to Save Your Sole* (Nancy Carroll); *I'm in Training for You* (Jack Oakie, Zelma O'Neal) W: L. Wolfe Gilbert—M: Abel Baer / *I'm Isadore the Toreador* (Kay Francis, Harry Green) WM: David Franklin / *I'm True to the Navy Now* (Clara Bow, Jack Oakie, Chorus) W: Elsie Janis—M: Jack King / *Let's Drink to the Girl of My Dreams* (Virginia Bruce, Mary Brian, Joan Peers, Fay Wray, Gary Cooper, Richard Arlen, Jean Arthur, James Hall, Phillips Holmes, David Newell) W: L. Wolfe Gilbert—M: Abel Baer / *My Marine* (Ruth Chatterton, Fredric March, Stuart Erwin) W: Raymond B. Egan—M: Richard A. Whiting / *Nichavo* (Dennis King) WM: Mme Mana-Zucca and Helen Jerome / *Sweepin' the Clouds Away* (Maurice Chevalier, Chorus) WM: Sam Coslow / *We're the Masters of Ceremony* (Jack Oakie, Leon Errol, Skeets Gallagher) WM: Ballard MacDonald and Dave Dreyer / *What Did Cleopatra Say?* (Helen Kane) W: Elsie Janis—M: Jack King.

"Even with all the competition Maurice Chevalier comes through in first place." —*Variety.*

**968 Pardners.** US, 1956, C, 90 m. D: Norman Taurog, P: Paramount (Paul Jones).

*Buckskin Beauty* (Jerry Lewis); *Me 'n' You 'n' the Moon* (Dean Martin); *Pardners* (Dean Martin, Jerry Lewis); *The Wind, the Wind* (Dean Martin) W: Sammy Cahn—M: James Van Heusen.

"Contrived sound and fury and some songs that are pleasant but hardly memorable." —A.H. Weiler, *The New York Times.*

**969 The Parent Trap.** US, 1961, C, 124 m. D: David Swift, MS: Paul Smith, P: Walt Disney (George Golitzen).

*For Now For Always* (Maureen O'Hara, Chorus); *Let's Get Together* (Hayley Mills); *The Parent Trap* (Tommy Sands, Annette Funicello); *Whistling at the Boys* (Chorus) WM: Richard M. Sherman and Robert B. Sherman.

**970 Paris Holiday.** US, 1958, C, 100 m. D: Gerd Oswald, MS: Joseph J. Lilley, P: UA (Bob Hope). Performer: Bob Hope.

*April in Paris* W: E.Y. Harburg— M: Vernon Duke / *The Last Time I Saw Paris* W: Oscar Hammerstein II—M: Jerome Kern / *Nothing in Common* (Bing Crosby, Bob Hope) W: Sammy Cahn—M: James Van Heusen.

**971 Paris Honeymoon.** US, 1939, BW, 92 m. D: Frank Tuttle, P: Paramount (Harlan Thompson).

*The Funny Old Hills* (Bing Crosby, Edward Everett Horton) W: Leo Robin—M: Ralph Rainger / *I Ain't Got Nobody* (Bing Crosby) W: Roger Graham—M: Spencer Williams and Dave Peyton / *I Have Eyes* (Bing Crosby, Shirley Ross, Franciska Gaal); *Joobalai* (Bing Crosby, Franciska Gaal, Chorus); *You're a Sweet Little Headache* (Bing Crosby) W: Leo Robin—M: Ralph Rainger.

**972 Partners.** US, 1982, C, 98 m. D: James Burrows, MS: Georges Delerue, P: Paramount (Aaron Russo).

*Call Me* (Blondie) WM: Deborah Harry and Giorgio Moroder.

**973 Pat Garrett and Billy the Kid.** US, 1973, C, 106 m. D: Sam Peckinpah, MS: Bob Dylan, P: MGM (Gordon Carroll). Performer: Bob Dylan.

*Billy; Knockin' on Heaven's Door* WM: Bob Dylan.

**974 A Patch of Blue.** US, 1965, 105 m. BW, D: Guy Green, MS: Jerry Goldsmith, P: MGM (Pandro S. Berman).

*Over the Rainbow* (Elizabeth Hartman) W: E.Y. Harburg—M: Harold Arlen.

**975 The Patsy.** US, 1964, C, 101 m. D: Jerry Lewis, MS: David Raksin, P: Paramount (Ernest D. Glucksman).

*I Lost My Heart in a Drive-In Movie* (Jerry Lewis) WM: Jack Brooks and David Raksin.

**976 Peggy Sue Got Married.** US, 1986, C, 104 m. D: Francis Coppola, MS: John Barry, P: Tri-Star (Paul R. Gurian).

*He Don't Love You* (Nicolas Cage, Pride and Joy) WM: Curtis Mayfield, Calvin Carter and Jerry Butler / *I Wonder Why* (Dion and The Belmonts) W: Ricardo Weeks—M: Melvin Anderson / *Peggy Sue* (Buddy Holly) WM: Buddy Holly, Norman Petty and Jerry Allison / *A Teenager in Love* (Dion and The Belmonts) WM: Doc Pomus and Mort Shuman.

**977 Pennies from Heaven.** US, 1936, BW, 81 m. D: Norman Z. McLeod, MD: George Stoll, P: Columbia (Emmanuel Cohen). Orch: Louis Armstrong. Performer: Bing Crosby.

*Let's Call a Heart a Heart; One, Two, Button Your Shoe; Pennies from Heaven; Skeleton in the Closet* (Bing Crosby, Louis Armstrong); *So Do I* W: Johnny Burke—M: Arthur Johnston.

**978 Pennies from Heaven.** US, 1981, C, 107 m. D: Herbert Ross, MD: Marvin Hamlisch and Billy May, P: MGM (Nora Kaye, Herbert Ross).

*The Clouds Will Soon Roll By* (Elsie Carlisle, Ambrose and His Orch.) WM: Harry M. Woods and George Brown / *Did You Ever See a Dream Walking?* (Bing Crosby) W: Mack Gordon—M: Harry Revel / *I'll Never Have to Dream Again* (Connie Boswell) W: Charles Newman—M: Isham Jones / *It's a Sin to Tell a Lie* (Dolly Dawn, George Hall and His Orch.) WM: Billy Mayhew / *I Want to Be Bad* (Helen Kane) W: B.G. De Sylva and Lew Brown—M: Ray Henderson / *Let's Face the Music and Dance* (Fred Astaire) WM: Irving Berlin / *Let's Misbehave* (Irving Aaronson and His Commanders) WM: Cole Porter / *Let's Put Out the Lights and Go to Sleep* (Rudy Vallee and His Connecticut Yankees) WM: Herman Hupfeld / *Life Is Just a Bowl of Cherries* (Walt Harrah, Gene Merlino, Vern Rowe, Robert Tebow, Al Vescoro) W: Lew Brown—M: Ray Henderson / *Love Is Good for Anything That Ails You* (Phyllis Robbins, Orlando and His Orch.) WM: Cliff Friend and Matt Malneck / *Pennies from Heaven* (Arthur Tracy) W: Johnny

Burke—M: Arthur Johnston / *Yes, Yes* (Sam Browne and The Carlyle Cousins) WM: Cliff Friend and Con Conrad.

"Worked into this lugubrious, neo-Brechtian tragedy are more than a dozen musical numbers of grave opulence." —*Variety*.

"All of the musical numbers are good, and a couple are great, reflecting the interests of Mr. Ross and Nora Kaye, his co-producer (and wife)." —Vincent Canby, *The New York Times*.

**979  Pepe.** US, 1960, C, 195 m. D: George Sidney, MD: Johnny Green, P: Columbia (George Sidney).

*The Faraway Part of Town* (Judy Garland) W: Dory Langdon [Dory Previn]—M: Andre Previn / *Hooray for Hollywood* (Sammy Davis, Jr.) W: Johnny Mercer—M: Richard A. Whiting / *Let's Fall in Love* (Bing Crosby) W: Ted Koehler—M: Harold Arlen / *Lovely Day* (Shirley Jones) W: Dory Langdon—M: Maria Teresa Lara / *Mimi* (Maurice Chevalier) W: Lorenz Hart—M: Richard Rodgers / *Pennies from Heaven* (Bing Crosby) W: Johnny Burke—M: Arthur Johnston / *Pepe* (Shirley Jones, Cantinflas, Chorus) W: Dory Langdon—M: Hans Wittstatt / *September Song* (Maurice Chevalier) W: Maxwell Anderson—M: Kurt Weill / *South of the Border* (Bing Crosby, Cantinflas) WM: Jimmy Kennedy and Michael Carr / *That's How It Went, All Right* (Bobby Darin, Shirley Jones, Michael Callan, Matt Mattox) W: Dory Langdon—M: Andre Previn.

**980  Perfect Understanding.** GB, 1933, BW, 80 m. D: Cyril Gardner, MS: Henry Sullivan, P: UA (Gloria Swanson).

*Ich Liebe Dich, My Dear* (Gloria Swanson) WM: Jack Hart and Tom Blight.

**981  The Perils of Pauline.** US, 1947, C, 96 m. D: George Marshall, MD: Robert Emmett Dolan, P: Paramount (Sol C. Siegel). Performer: Betty Hutton.

*I Wish I Didn't Love You So* WM: Frank Loesser / *Poor Pauline* W: Charles McCarron—M: Raymond Walker / *Poppa, Don't Preach to Me; Rumble, Rumble, Rumble; The Sewing Machine;* WM: Frank Loesser.

**982  Permanent Record.** US, 1988, C, 91 m. D: Marisa Silver, P: Paramount (Frank Mancuso, Jr.).

*All Day and All of the Night* (The Stranglers) WM: Ray Davies / *Baby the Trans* (Joe Strummer and The Latino Rockabilly War) WM: Joe Strummer / *'Cause I Said So* (The Godfathers) WM: The Godfathers / *Nefertiti Rock* (Joe Strummer and The Latino Rockabilly War); *Nothin' Bout Nothin'* (Joe Strummer and The Latino Rockabilly War) WM: Joe Strummer / *Something Happened* (Lou Reed) WM: J. Reed / *Trash City* (Joe Strummer and The Latino Rockabilly War) WM: Joe Strummer / *Waiting on Love* (Bodeans) WM: K. Neumann and S. Llanas / *Wishing on Another Lucky Star* (J.D. Souther) WM: John David Souther.

**983  Pete Kelly's Blues.** US, 1955, C, 95 m. D: Jack Webb, P: Warner (Jack Webb). Performer: Peggy Lee.

*Bye Bye Blackbird* W: Mort Dixon—M: Ray Henderson / *Ella Hums the Blues* (Ella Fitzgerald) M: Ray Heindorf / *Hard Hearted Hannah* (Ella Fitzgerald) WM: Jack Yellen, Milton Ager, Bob Bigelow and Charles Bates / *He Needs Me* WM: Arthur Hamilton / *I'm Gonna Meet My Sweetie Now* W: Benny Davis—M: Jesse Green / *I Never Knew That Roses Grew* W: Gus Kahn—M: Ted Fiorito / *Oh! Didn't He Ramble* WM: Bob Cole and J. Rosamond Johnson [composite pseudonym, Will Handy] / *Pete Kelly's Blues* (Ella Fitzgerald) W: Sammy Cahn—M: Ray Heindorf / *Sing a Rainbow* WM: Arthur Hamilton / *Somebody Loves Me* W: B.G. De Sylva and Ballard MacDonald—M: George Gershwin / *Sugar* W: Sidney Mitchell and Edna Alexander—M: Maceo Pinkard / *What Can I Say*

*After I Say I'm Sorry?* WM: Abe Lyman and Walter Donaldson.

"Jazz addicts . . . may have a special interest in the musical frame." —*Variety.*

**984 Pete's Dragon.** US, 1977, C, 134 m. D: Don Chaffey, MD: Irwin Kostal, P: Walt Disney (Ron Miller, Jerome Courtland).

*Bill of Sale* (Helen Reddy, Shelley Winters, Charles Tyner, Gary Morgan, Jeff Conaway); *Boo Bop Bopbop Bop* (Sean Marshall, Charlie Callas); *Brazzle Dazzle Day* (Helen Reddy, Mickey Rooney, Sean Marshall); *Candle on the Water* (Helen Reddy); *Every Little Piece* (Red Buttons, Jim Dale); *The Happiest Home in These Hills* (Shelley Winters, Charles Tyner, Gary Morgan, Jeff Conaway); *I Saw a Dragon* (Helen Reddy, Mickey Rooney, Chorus); *It's Not Easy* (Helen Reddy, Sean Marshall); *Passamashloddy* (Jim Dale, Red Buttons, Chorus); *There's Room for Everyone* (Helen Reddy, Sean Marshall) WM: Joel Hirschhorn and Al Kasha.

**985 Phantom of the Opera.** US, 1943, C, 92 m. D: Arthur Lubin, MS: Edward Ward, P: Universal (George Waggner).

*Lullaby of the Bells* (Susanna Foster, Nelson Eddy) W: George Waggner —M: Edward Ward.

**986 The Philadelphia Story.** US, 1940, BW, 112 m. D: George Cukor, MS: Franz Waxman, P: MGM (Joseph L. Mankiewicz).

*Lydia, the Tattooed Lady* (Virginia Weidler); *Over the Rainbow* (James Stewart) W: E.Y. Harburg—M: Harold Arlen.

**987 Phone Call from a Stranger.** US, 1952, BW, 96 m. D: Jean Negulesco, MS: Franz Waxman, P: TCF (Nunnally Johnson).

*Again* (Warren Stevens) W: Dorcas Cochran—M: Lionel Newman.

**988 Picnic.** US, 1955, C, 115 m. D: Joshua Logan, MS: George Duning, P: Columbia (Fred Kohlmar).

*Ain't She Sweet?* (Chorus) W: Jack Yellen—M: Milton Ager / *Old MacDonald Had a Farm* (William Holden, Susan Strasberg) WM: Unknown.

**989 The Picture of Dorian Gray.** US, 1945, BW/C, 110 m. D: Albert Lewin, MS: Herbert Stothart, P: MGM (Pandro S. Berman).

*Little Yellow Bird* (Angela Lansbury) WM: C.W. Murphy and William Hargreaves.

**990 Pigskin Parade.** US, 1936, BW, 93 m. D: David Butler, MD: David Buttolph, P: TCF (Bogart Rogers). GB Title: Harmony Parade.

*Balboa* (Judy Garland, Betty Grable, Johnny Downs, Jack Haley, Patsy Kelly, The Yacht Club Boys); *Hold That Bulldog* (Chorus); *It's Love I'm After* (Judy Garland); *Texas Tornado* (Judy Garland) W: Sidney D. Mitchell—M: Lew Pollack / *We'd Rather Be in College* (The Yacht Club Boys) / *Woo! Woo!* (The Yacht Club Boys) / *You Do the Darndest Things, Baby* (Jack Haley, Arline Judge); *You're Slightly Terrific* (Tony Martin, Dixie Dunbar) W: Sidney D. Mitchell—M: Lew Pollack.

"Anthony Martin and young Judy Garland do well by . . . Pollack-Mitchell tunes." —Frank S. Nugent, *The New York Times.*

**991 Pillow Talk.** US, 1959, C, 105 m. D: Michael Gordon, MD: Joseph Gershenson, MS: Frank DeVol, P: Universal (Ross Hunter, Martin Melcher).

*Inspiration* (Doris Day) W: Joe Lubin—M: I.J. Roth / *Pillow Talk* (Doris Day, Rock Hudson) WM: Buddy Pepper and Inez James / *Possess Me* (Doris Day) W: Joe Lubin—M: I.J. Roth / *Roly Poly* (Doris Day, Rock Hudson, Perry Blackwell) WM: Elsa Doran and Sol Lake / *You Lied* (Perry Blackwell) W: Joe Lubin—M: I.J. Roth.

**992 Pillow to Post.** US, 1945, BW, 92 m. D: Vincent Sherman, MD: Leo F. Forbstein, MS: Frederick Hollander, P: Warner (Alex Gottlieb). Orch: Louis Armstrong.

*Whatcha Say* (Louis Armstrong) W: Ted Koehler—M: Burton Lane.

**993  Pin-Up Girl.** US, 1944, C, 83 m. D: H. Bruce Humberstone, MD: Emil Newman and Charles Henderson, P: TCF (William LeBaron). Orch: Charles Spivak.

*Don't Carry Tales Out of School* (Betty Grable, Chorus); *Once Too Often* (Betty Grable); *Red Robins, Bob Whites and Blue Birds* (Martha Raye, Chorus); *Story of the Very Merry Widow* (Betty Grable, Chorus); *Time Alone Will Tell* (Quartet); *Yankee Doodle Hayride* (Martha Raye); *You're My Little Pin-Up Girl* (Betty Grable, Chorus) W: Mack Gordon—M: James V. Monaco.

**994  The Pink Panther.** US, 1964, C, 113 m. D: Blake Edwards, MS: Henry Mancini, P: UA (Martin Jurow).

*It Had Better Be Tonight* (Fran Jeffries) WM: Johnny Mercer, Henry Mancini and Franco Migliacci.

**995  The Pink Panther Strikes Again.** GB, 1976, C, 103 m. D: Blake Edwards, MS: Henry Mancini, P: UA (Blake Edwards).

*Come to Me* (Tom Jones, Peter Sellers) W: Don Black—M: Henry Mancini.

**996  The Pirate.** US, 1948, C, 102 m. D: Vincente Minnelli, MD: Lennie Hayton, P: MGM (Arthur Freed).

*Be a Clown* (Judy Garland, Gene Kelly); *Love of My Life* (Judy Garland); *Mack the Black* (Judy Garland, Chorus); *Nina* (Gene Kelly); *You Can Do No Wrong* (Judy Garland) WM: Cole Porter.

"It's an eye and ear treat of light musical entertainment, garbing its amusing antics, catchy songs and able terping in brilliant color." — *Variety.*

"A dazzling, spectacular extravaganza. ... Miss Garland teams nicely with Mr. Kelly, singing or dancing. ... the finale is a lively roughhouse session

of clowning set to the tune of *Be a Clown,* easily the best of Cole Porter's several songs." —Thomas M. Pryor, *The New York Times.*

**997  Platoon.** US, 1986, C, 120 m. D: Oliver Stone, MS: Georges Delerue, P: Hemdale (Arnold Kopelson).

*Groovin'* (The Young Rascals) WM: Feliz Cavaliere and Eddie Brigati / *Hello, I Love You* (The Doors) WM: Robert Krieger, James Morrison, John Densmore and Raymond Manzarek / *Okie from Muskogee* (Merle Haggard) / *Respect* (Aretha Franklin) WM: Otis Redding / *Sittin' on the Dock of the Bay* (Otis Redding) WM: Otis Redding and Steve Cropper / *The Tracks of My Tears* (Smokey Robinson) WM: Warren Moore, William "Smokey" Robinson and Marvin Tarpin / *When a Man Loves a Woman* (Percy Sledge) WM: Calvin Lewis and Andrew Wright / *White Rabbit* (Jefferson Airplane) WM: Grace Slick.

**998  Play Misty for Me.** US, 1971, C, 102 m. D: Clint Eastwood, MS: Dee Barton, P: Universal (Robert Daley).

*The First Time Ever I Saw Your Face* (Roberta Flack) WM: Ewan MacColl.

**999  Please Don't Eat the Daisies.** US, 1960, C, 111 m. D: Charles Walters, MS: David Rose, P: MGM (Joe Pasternak). Performer: Doris Day.

*Any Way the Wind Blows* W: By Dunham—M: Marilyn Hooven and Joe Hooven / *Please Don't Eat the Daisies* WM: Joe Lubin / *Que Sera, Sera* WM: Jay Livingston and Ray Evans.

**1000  The Pleasure Seekers.** US, 1964, C, 107 m. D: Jean Negulesco, MS: Lionel Newman, P: TCF (David Weisbart). Performer: Ann-Margret.

*Everything Makes Music When You're in Love; Next Time; The Pleasure Seekers; Something to Think About* W: Sammy Cahn—M: James Van Heusen.

**1001  Pocketful of Miracles.**

US, 1961, C, 136 m. D: Frank Capra, MS: Walter Scharf, P: UA (Frank Capra).

*Pocketful of Miracles* (Frank Sinatra) W: Sammy Cahn—M: James Van Heusen.

**1002 Pointed Heels.** US, 1929, BW/C, 61 m. D: A. Edward Sutherland, P: Paramount.

*Ain'tcha?* (Helen Kane) WM: Mack Gordon and Max Rich / *I Have to Have You* (Helen Kane, Skeets Gallagher) W: Leo Robin—M: Richard A. Whiting.

**1003 Pollyanna.** US, 1960, C, 134 m. D: David Swift, MS: Paul Smith, P: Walt Disney (George Golitzen).

*America, the Beautiful* (Hayley Mills, Chorus) W: Katherine Lee Bates—M: Samuel A. Ward / *Pollyanna* (Chorus) W: Gil George—M: Paul Smith / *Pollyanna's Song* (Hayley Mills) W: David Swift—M: Paul Smith.

**1004 Poor Little Rich Girl.** US, 1936, BW, 72 m. D: Irving Cummings, MD: Louis Silvers, P: TCF (Darryl F. Zanuck, B.G. De Sylva).

*But Definitely* (Shirley Temple, Alice Faye, Jack Haley); *Buy a Bar of Barry's* (Shirley Temple, Chorus); *Military Man* (Shirley Temple, Alice Faye, Jack Haley, Chorus); *Oh, My Goodness!* (Shirley Temple); *Wash Your Necks with a Cake of Peck's* (Shirley Temple); *When I'm with You* (Shirley Temple, Tony Martin, Alice Faye); *You Gotta Eat Your Spinach, Baby* (Shirley Temple, Alice Faye, Jack Haley) W: Mack Gordon—M: Harry Revel.

"Miss Temple, as someone has said, never looked lovelier. Her voice has begun to take on torch-singer and crooner qualities." —Frank S. Nugent, *The New York Times*.

**1005 Popeye.** US, 1980, C, 118 m. D: Robert Altman, MD: Van Dyke Parks, P: Walt Disney/Paramount (Robert Evans).

*Blow Me Down* (Robin Williams, Chorus); *Din'we* (Robert Fortier); *He Needs Me* (Shelley Duvall); *He's Large* (Shelley Duvall, Chorus); *I'm Mean* (Paul L. Smith, Chorus) WM: Harry Nilsson / *I'm Popeye the Sailor Man* (Robin Williams, Chorus) WM: Sam Lerner / *It's Not Easy Being Me* (Ray Walston, Paul L. Smith); *I Yam What I Yam* (Robin Williams, Chorus); *Kids* (Ray Walston); *Sailin'* (Robin Williams, Shelley Duvall); *Swee'pea's Lullaby* (Robin Williams); *Sweethaven* (Chorus) WM: Harry Nilsson.

**1006 Poppy.** US, 1936, BW, 75 m. D: A. Edward Sutherland, MS: Frederick Hollander, P: Paramount (Paul Jones).

*Rendezvous with a Dream* (Rochelle Hudson) W: Leo Robin—M: Ralph Rainger.

**1007 Porgy and Bess.** US, 1959, C, 138 m. D: Otto Preminger, MD: Andre Previn and Ken Darby, P: Columbia (Samuel Goldwyn). Vocals: Robert McFerrin for Sidney Poitier; Adele Addison for Dorothy Dandridge; Loulie Jean Norman for Diahann Carroll; Inez Matthews for Ruth Attaway.

*Bess, Oh Where's My Bess?* (Sidney Poitier); *Bess, You Is My Woman Now* (Sidney Poitier, Dorothy Dandridge); *Crab Man's Call* (Vince Townsend, Jr.); *The Crap Game* (Diahann Carroll, Joel Fluellen, Chorus); *De Police Put Me In* (Clarence Muse); *Gone, Gone, Gone* (Leslie Scott, Chorus); *Good Mornin', Sistuh* (Chorus); *Honey Man's Call* (Clarence Muse); *I Ain't Got No Shame* (Chorus); *I Got Plenty o' Nuttin'* (Sidney Poitier, Chorus); *I Loves You, Porgy* (Sidney Poitier, Dorothy Dandridge); *I'm on My Way* (Sidney Poitier, Chorus); *It Ain't Necessarily So* (Sammy Davis, Jr., Chorus); *It Takes a Long Pull to Get There* (Leslie Scott, Chorus); *My Man's Gone Now* (Ruth Attaway, Chorus); *Oh, I Can't Sit Down* (Pearl Bailey, Sammy Davis, Jr., Chorus); *Porgy's Prayer* (Sidney Poitier); *A Red Headed Woman Makes a Choo Choo Jump Its Track* (Brock

Peters, Chorus); *Strawberry Woman's Call* (Helen Thigpen); *Summertime* (Diahann Carroll, Chorus); *There's a Boat Dat's Leavin' Soon for New York* (Sammy Davis, Jr.); *They Pass By Singing* (Sidney Poitier); *Time and Time Again* (Ruth Attaway); *The Train Is at the Station* (Dorothy Dandridge, Chorus); *What You Want with Bess?* (Dorothy Dandridge, Brock Peters); *A Woman Is a Sometime Thing* (Leslie Scott, Diahann Carroll, Sammy Davis, Jr., Earl Jackson); *Yo' Mammy's Gone* (Earl Jackson) W: Ira Gershwin and Du Bose Heyward—M: George Gershwin.

"Some liberties with the arrangements, in the de-operatizing direction, may irritate loyal followers of Gershwin who notice such matters." *— Variety.*

"Under Andre Previn's direction, the score is magnificently played and sung." —Bosley Crowther, *The New York Times.*

**1008   The Poseidon Adventure.** US, 1972, C, 117 m. D: Ronald Neame, MS: John Williams, P: TCF (Irwin Allen). Vocal: Renee Armand for Carol Lynley.

*The Morning After* (Carol Lynley) WM: Joel Hirschhorn and Al Kasha.

**1009   Possessed.** US, 1931, BW, 72 m. D: Clarence Brown, P: MGM.

*How Long Will It Last?* (Joan Crawford) W: Max Lief—M: Joseph Meyer.

**1010   Presenting Lily Mars.** US, 1943, BW, 104 m. D: Norman Taurog, MD: George Stoll, P: MGM (Joe Pasternak). Orch: Tommy Dorsey; Bob Crosby and His Bob Cats.

*Broadway Rhythm* (Judy Garland) W: Arthur Freed—M: Nacio Herb Brown / *Every Little Movement Has a Meaning of Its Own* (Judy Garland, Connie Gilchrist) W: Otto Harbach—M: Karl Hoschna / *Is It Love?* (Marta Eggerth); *Love Is Everywhere* (Chorus); *A Russian Rhapsody* (Marta Eggerth); *Think of Me* (Bob Crosby, Chorus) W: Paul Francis Webster—Walter Jurmann / *Three O'Clock in the Morning* (Judy Garland) W: Dorothy Terriss [Theodora Morse]—M: Julian Robledo / *Tom, Tom the Piper's Son* (Judy Garland) W: E.Y. Harburg—M: Burton Lane / *When I Look at You* (Judy Garland, Marta Eggerth) W: Paul Francis Webster—M: Walter Jurmann / *Where There's Music* (Judy Garland, Chorus) WM: Roger Edens.

**1011   Pretty in Pink.** US, 1986, C, 96 m. D: Howard Deutch, MS: Michael Gore, P: Paramount (Lauren Shuler). Vocal: Otis Redding for Jon Cryer.

*Bring on the Dancing Horses* (Echo and The Bunnymen) WM: Sargeant, McCulloch, Pattinson and DeFreitas / *Do Wot You Do* (INXS) WM: Michael Hutchence and Andrew Ferriss / *Get to Know Ya* (Jesse Johnson) WM: Jesse Johnson / *If You Leave* (Orchestral Manoeuvres in the Dark) WM: Paul Humphreys, Andrew McCluskey, Malcolm Holmes and Martin Cooper / *Left of Center* (Suzanne Vega) WM: Suzanne Vega / *Please Please Please Let Me Get What I Want* (The Smiths) WM: Morrissey and Johnny Marr / *Pretty in Pink* (The Psychedelic Furs) WM: Roger Morris, John Ashton, Duncan Kilburn, Vincent Ely, Richard Butler and Tim Butler / *Round, Round* (Belouis Some) WM: Neville Keighley / *Shell-Shock* (New Order) WM: New Order and John Robie / *Try a Little Tenderness* (Jon Cryer) WM: Harry M. Woods, Jimmy Campbell and Reg Connelly / *Wouldn't It Be Good* (Danny Hutton Hitters) WM: Nik Kershaw.

**1012   The Pride of the Yankees.** US, 1942, BW, 127 m. D: Sam Wood, MS: Leigh Harline, P: RKO (Samuel Goldwyn). Orch: Ray Noble.

*Always* (Betty Avery) WM: Irving Berlin.

**1013   The Prime of Miss Jean Brodie.** GB, 1969, C, 116 m. D: Ronald Neame, MD: Arthur Greenslade, MS: Rod McKuen, P: TCF (Robert Fryer, James Gesson).

*Jean* (Rod McKuen) WM: Rod McKuen.

**1014 Princess Charming.** GB, 1934, BW, 78 m. D: Maurice Elvey, MD: Louis Levy, P: Gainsborough/ Gaumont British (Michael Balcon). Performer: Evelyn Laye. Alt. Title: The Escape of Princess Charming.

*Love Is a Song; Near and Yet So Far; The Princess's Awakening* W: Max Kester—M: Ray Noble.

**1015 Private Buckaroo.** US, 1942, BW, 68 m. D: Edward Cline, P: Universal (Ken Goldsmith). Orch: Harry James and His Music Makers. Performers: The Andrews Sisters.

*Don't Sit Under the Apple Tree* W: Charles Tobias and Lew Brown—M: Sam H. Stept / *I Love the South* (Joe E. Lewis) / *Johnny Get Your Gun Again* WM: Don Raye and Gene de Paul / *Nobody Knows the Trouble I've Seen* (Dick Foran, Female Singer) WM: Unknown / *Private Buckaroo* (Dick Foran) WM: Charles Newman and Allie Wrubel / *Six Jerks in a Jeep* WM: Sid Robin / *That's the Moon My Son* WM: Art Kassel, Sammy Gallop and Norman Litman / *Three Little Sisters* WM: Irving Taylor and Vic Mizzy / *You Made Me Love You* (Helen Forrest) W: Joseph McCarthy—M: James V. Monaco.

**1016 Private Lessons.** US, 1981, C, 87 m. D: Alan Myerson, P: Universal (R. Ben Efraim).

*Doc* (Earl Klugh) WM: Earl Klugh / *Fantasy* (Earth, Wind and Fire) WM: Maurice White, Verdine White and Eddie de Barrio / *Hot Legs* (Rod Stewart) WM: Rod Stewart / *I Don't Want to Talk About It* (Crazy Horse) WM: Danny Whitten / *I Need a Lover* (John Cougar) WM: John Cougar Mellencamp / *Just When I Needed You the Most* (Randy Vanwarmer) WM: Randy Vanwarmer / *Lost in Love* (Air Supply) WM: Graham Russell / *Spanish Night* (Earl Klugh) WM: Earl Klugh / *That's the Reason* (Willie Nile) WM: Willie Nile / *Tonight's the Night* (Rod Stewart) WM: Rod Stewart.

**1017 Privilege.** GB, 1967, C, 103 m. D: Peter Watkins, MD: Mike Leander, P: Universal (John Heyman).

*Free Me* (Paul Jones, Chorus); *I've Been a Bad Bad Boy* (Paul Jones, Chorus); *Jerusalem* (George Bean) W: Mark London—M: Mike Leander / *Onward Christian Soldiers* (George Bean, Chorus) W: Sabine Baring—M: Sir Arthur Sullivan / *Privilege* (Paul Jones, Chorus) W: Mark London—M: Mike Leander.

**1018 The Producers.** US, 1968, C, 88 m. D: Mel Brooks, MS: John Morris, P: MGM (Sidney Glazier).

*Love Power* (Dick Shawn) W: Herb Hartig—M: Norman Blagman / *Prisoners of Love* (Chorus); *Springtime for Hitler* (Mel Brooks, Chorus) WM: Mel Brooks.

**1019 The Promise.** US, 1979, C, 98 m. D: Gilbert Cates, MS: David Shire, P: Universal (Fred Weintraub, Paul Heller).

*I'll Never Say Goodbye* (Melissa Manchester) W: Alan Bergman and Marilyn Bergman—M: David Shire.

**1020 Psych-Out.** US, 1968, C, 82 m. D: Richard Rush, P: AIP (Dick Clark).

*Ashbury Wednesday* (Boenzee Cryque) WM: Rusty Young, Mitchell Mitchell, Joe E. Neddo, George Grantham and S. Bush / *Beads of Innocence* (The Storybook) WM: Harlene Stein and Ronald Stein / *Incense and Peppermints* (The Strawberry Alarm Clock) WM: John Carter and Tim Gilbert / *The Love Children* (The Storybook) WM: Ronald Stein / *The Pretty Song* (The Storybook) WM: The Strawberry Alarm Clock / *Psych-Out* (The Storybook); *Psych-Out Sanitorium* (The Storybook) WM: Ronald Stein / *Pushin' Too Hard* (The Seeds) WM: Sky Saxon / *Rainy Day Mushroom Pillow* (The Strawberry Alarm Clock) WM: Steven Bartek and George Bunnell, Jr. / *Two Fingers Pointing on You* (The Seeds) WM: Sky Saxon / *The World's on Fire* (The Strawberry Alarm Clock) WM: The Strawberry Alarm Clock.

**1021  Pursuit to Algiers.** US, 1945, BW, 65 m. D: Roy William Neill, MD: Edgar Fairchild, P: Universal (Roy William Neill).

*Loch Lomond* (Nigel Bruce) WM: Unknown.

**1022  Puttin' on the Ritz.** US, 1930, BW/C, 88 m. D: Edward Sloman, P: UA (John Considine, Jr.). Performer: Harry Richman.

*Puttin' on the Ritz* WM: Irving Berlin / *Singing a Vagabond Song* WM: Sam Messenheimer, Val Burton and Harry Richman / *There's Danger in Your Eyes, Cherie!* W: Jack Meskill—M: Pete Wendling / *With You* WM: Irving Berlin.

**1023  Quadrophenia.**     GB, 1979, C, 115 m. D: Franc Roddam, P: World-Northall (Roy Baird, Bill Curbishley).

*Baby Love* (The Supremes) WM: Eddie Holland, Lamont Dozier and Brian Holland / *Bell Boy* (The Who) WM: Peter Townshend / *Be My Baby* (The Ronettes) WM: Jeff Barry, Ellie Greenwich and Phil Spector / *Cut My Hair* (The Who) WM: Peter Townshend / *Da Doo Ron Ron* (The Crystals) WM: Jeff Barry, Ellie Greenwich and Phil Spector / *Doctor Jimmy* (The Who); *Five Fifteen* (The Who); *Helpless Dancer* (The Who) WM: Peter Townshend / *He's So Fine* (The Chiffons) WM: Ronnie Mack / *Hi-Heel Sneakers* (Cross Section) WM: Robert Higgenbotham / *I Am the Sea* (The Who); *I'm One* (The Who); *I've Had Enough* (The Who) WM: Peter Townshend / *Louie Louie* (The Kingsmen) WM: Richard Berry / *Love, Reign O'er Me* (The Who) WM: Peter Townshend / *Night Train* (James Brown) W: Oscar Washington and Lewis C. Simkins—M: Jimmy Forrest / *The Punk and the Godfather* (The Who); *Quadrophenia* (The Who); *The Real Me* (The Who) WM: Peter Townshend / *Rhythm of the Rain* (The Cascades) WM: John Gummoe / *Sea and Sand* (The Who) WM: Peter Townshend / *The Wah Watusi* (The

Orlons) WM: Dave Appell and Kal Mann / *Zoot Suit* (High Numbers).

**1024  R.P.M.** US, 1970, C, 97 m. D: Stanley Kramer, MS: Barry De Vorzon, P: Columbia (Stanley Kramer).

*Stop! I Don't Wanna Hear It Anymore* (Melanie) WM: Perry Botkin, Jr., Barry De Vorzon and Melanie Safka.

**1025  Rachel and the Stranger.** US, 1948, BW, 79 m. D: Norman Foster, MD: Constantin Bakaleinikoff, P: RKO (Richard H. Berger).

*Foolish Pride* (Robert Mitchum); *Just Like Me* (Robert Mitchum, Gary Gray); *O-He-O-Hi-O-Ho* (Robert Mitchum); *Summer Song* (Loretta Young, Robert Mitchum); *Tall Dark Stranger* (Loretta Young, Robert Mitchum) W: Waldo Salt—M: Roy Webb.

**1026  The Racket.** US, 1951, BW, 88 m. D: John Cromwell, MS: Constantin Bakaleinikoff, P: RKO (Edmund Grainger).

*A Lovely Way to Spend an Evening* (Lizabeth Scott) W: Harold Adamson—M: Jimmy McHugh.

**1027  Radio Days.** US, 1987, C, 88 m. D: Woody Allen, MS: Dick Hyman, P: Orion (Robert Greenhut).

*The Donkey Serenade* (Allan Jones) W: Robert Wright and George "Chet" Forrest—M: Rudolf Friml and Herbert Stothart / *Good-bye* (Helen Ward) WM: Gordon Jenkins / *Remember Pearl Harbor* (Sammy Kaye) WM: Don Reid and Sammy Kaye / *South American Way* (Carmen Miranda) W: Al Dubin—M: Jimmy McHugh / *You and I* (Frank Sinatra) WM: Meredith Willson.

**1028  Raging Bull.** US, 1980, BW/C, 128 m. D: Martin Scorsese, P: UA (Robert Chartoff, Irwin Winkler).

*Bye Bye Baby* (Marilyn Monroe) W: Leo Robin—M: Jule Styne / *Cow-Cow Boogie* (Ella Fitzgerald and The Ink Spots) WM: Don Raye, Gene de Paul and Benny Carter / *Prisoner of Love* (Russ Columbo, Perry Como) W: Leo Robin—M: Russ Columbo and Clarence Gaskill / *That's My Desire*

(Frankie Laine) WM: Carroll Loveday and Helmy Kresa.

**1029  Rain Man.** US, 1988, C, 140 m. D: Barry Levinson, MS: Hans Zimmer, P: UA (Mark Johnson).

*At Last* (Etta James) W: Mack Gordon—M: Harry Warren / *Beyond the Blue Horizon* (Lou Christie) W: Leo Robin—M: Richard A. Whiting and W. Franke Harling / *Dry Bones* (The Delta Rhythm Boys) W: James Weldon Johnson—M: J. Rosamund Johnson / *Iko-Iko* (The Belle Stars) WM: Marylin Jones, Sharon Jones, Joe Jones and Jessie Thomas / *Lonely Avenue* (Ian Gillian and Roger Glover) WM: Doc Pomus / *Nathan Jones* (Bananarama) WM: Leonard Caston and Kathy Wakefield / *Scatterlings of Africa* (Johnny Clegg and Savuka) WM: Johnny Clegg / *Star Dust* (Rob Wasserman, Aaron Neville) W: Mitchell Parish—M: Hoagy Carmichael.

**1030  Rainbow 'Round My Shoulder.** US, 1952, C, 78 m. D: Richard Quine, MD: George Duning, P: Columbia (Jonie Taps). Performer: Frankie Laine.

*Bye Bye Blackbird* W: Mort Dixon—M: Ray Henderson / *Girl in the Wood* WM: Terry Gilkyson, Neal Gilkyson and Stuart Gilkyson / *She's Funny That Way* (Frankie Laine, Billy Daniels) WM: Richard A. Whiting and Neil Moret [Charles N. Daniels] / *There's a Rainbow 'Round My Shoulder* WM: Billy Rose, Al Jolson and Dave Dreyer / *Wonderful, Wasn't It?* W: Hal David—M: Don Rodney / *Wrap Your Troubles in Dreams* W: Ted Koehler and Billy Moll—M: Harry Barris.

**1031  The Rainmakers.** US, 1935, BW, 79 m. D: Fred Guiol, MD: Roy Webb, P: RKO (Lee Marcus).

*Isn't Love the Grandest Thing?* (Bert Wheeler, Dorothy Lee) W: Jack Scholl—M: Louis Alter.

**1032  Raintree County.** US, 1957, C, 168 m. D: Edward Dmytryk, MS: Johnny Green, P: MGM (David Lewis).

*The Song of Raintree County* (Nat King Cole) W: Paul Francis Webster—M: Johnny Green.

**1033  Reaching for the Moon.** US, 1931, BW, 91 m. D: Edmund Goulding, P: UA (Douglas Fairbanks).

*When the Folks High-up Do the Mean Low-down* (Bebe Daniels, Bing Crosby) WM: Irving Berlin.

**1034  Rebecca of Sunnybrook Farm.** US, 1938, BW, 80 m. D: Allan Dwan, MS: Arthur Lange, P: TCF (Raymond Griffith). MB: Raymond Scott Quintet. Performer: Shirley Temple.

*Alone with You* W: Sidney D. Mitchell—M: Lew Pollack / *Animal Crackers in My Soup* W: Ted Koehler and Irving Caesar—M: Ray Henderson / *Au Revoir* W: Sidney D. Mitchell—M: Lew Pollack / *Come and Get Your Happiness* W: Jack Yellen—M: Samuel Pokrass / *Crackly Corn Flakes; Happy Ending* W: Sidney D. Mitchell—M: Lew Pollack / *An Old Straw Hat* W: Mack Gordon—M: Harry Revel / *On The Good Ship Lollipop* W: Sidney Clare—M: Richard A. Whiting / *Parade of the Wooden Soldiers* (Shirley Temple, Bill Robinson) WM: Sidney D. Mitchell, Lew Pollack and Raymond Scott / *When I'm with You* W: Mack Gordon—M: Harry Revel.

**1035  Red Garters.** US, 1954, C, 91 m. D: George Marshall, MS: Joseph J. Lilley, P: Paramount (Pat Duggan).

*Bad News* (Rosemary Clooney); *Brave Man* (Rosemary Clooney, Chorus); *A Dime and a Dollar* (Guy Mitchell, Chorus); *Good Intentions* (Rosemary Clooney); *Lady Killer* (Rosemary Clooney); *Man and Woman* (Rosemary Clooney, Guy Mitchell); *Meet a Happy Guy* (Guy Mitchell); *Red Garters* (Rosemary Clooney, Chorus); *This Is Greater Than I Thought* (Joanne Gilbert); *Vaquero* (Guy Mitchell) WM: Jay Livingston and Ray Evans.

"The only trouble with this photographed musical comedy is that it lacks a good story and first-class songs." — Bosley Crowther, *The New York Times.*

**1036   Red, Hot, and Blue.** US, 1949, BW, 84 m. D: John Farrow, P: Paramount (Robert Fellows). Performer: Betty Hutton.

*Hamlet; I Wake Up in the Morning Feeling Fine; Now That I Need You; That's Loyalty* WM: Frank Loesser.

**1037   Red Salute.** US, 1935, BW, 78 m. D: Sidney Lanfield, P: UA (Edward Small). GB Title: Arms and the Girl. Alt. Title: Runaway Daughter. TV Title: Her Enlisted Man.

*I Wonder Who's Kissing Her Now* (Cliff Edwards) W: Will M. Hough and Frank R. Adams—M: Joseph E. Howard and Harold Orlob.

**1038   Red Sky at Morning.** US, 1970, C, 112 m. D: James Goldstone, MS: Billy Goldenberg, P: Universal (Hal B. Wallis).

*Don't Sit Under the Apple Tree* (The Andrews Sisters) W: Charles Tobias and Lew Brown—M: Sam H. Stept / *Oh Johnny, Oh Johnny, Oh!* (Miriam Gulager) W: Ed Rose—M: Abe Olman / *Paper Doll* (The Mills Brothers) WM: Johnny S. Black.

**1039   Remains to Be Seen.** US, 1953, BW, 89 m. D: Don Weis, MD: Jeff Alexander, P: MGM (Arthur Hornblow, Jr.).

*Taking a Chance on Love* (Dorothy Dandridge) W: John Latouche and Ted Fetter—M: Vernon Duke / *Toot, Toot, Tootsie!* (June Allyson, Van Johnson) WM: Gus Kahn, Ernie Erdman and Dan Russo.

**1040   Renaldo and Clara.** US, 1978, C, 292 m [later cut to 122 m]. D: Bob Dylan, P: Lombard Street Films (Mel Howard, Jack Baran).

*Ballad in Plain D* (Gordon Lightfoot) WM: Bob Dylan / *Catfish* (Rob Stoner) WM: Bob Dylan and Jacques Levy / *Chestnut Mare* (Roger McGuinn) WM: Roger McGuinn / *Cucurrucucu Paloma* (Mama Maria Frasca) WM: Thomas Mendez / *Diamonds and Rust* (Joan Baez) WM: Joan Baez / *Eight Miles High* (Roger McGuinn) WM: Gene Clark, David Crosby and Jim McGuinn / *Fast Speaking Woman* (Anne Waldman) / *God and Mama* (Mama Maria Frasca) / *A Hard Rain's A-Gonna Fall* (Bob Dylan) WM: Bob Dylan / *Hollywood Waltz* (The Eagles) / *The House of the Rising Sun* (Bob Dylan) WM: Unknown—Arr: Bob Dylan / *Hurricane* (Bob Dylan) WM: Bob Dylan and Jacques Levy / *If You See Her Say Hello* (Bob Dylan) WM: Bob Dylan / *In the Morning* (Hal Frazier) / *In the Pines* (Leadbelly) / *Isis* (Bob Dylan) WM: Bob Dylan and Jacques Levy / *It Ain't Me, Babe* (Bob Dylan); *It Takes a Lot to Laugh, It Takes a Train to Cry* (Bob Dylan); *I Want You* (Bob Dylan); *Just Like a Woman* (Bob Dylan, Ronee Blakely) WM: Bob Dylan / *Kaw-Liga* (Bob Dylan) WM: Fred Rose and Hank Williams / *Knockin' on Heaven's Door* (Bob Dylan, Ronee Blakely, Joan Baez) WM: Bob Dylan / *Little Moses* (Bob Dylan) / *Mama's Lament* (Mama Maria Frasca) / *Mule Skinner Blues* (Jack Elliot) WM: Jimmie Rodgers and George Vaughn / *Need a New Sun Rising* (Ronee Blakely) WM: Ronee Blakely / *One More Cup of Coffee* (Bob Dylan); *One Too Many Mornings* (Bob Dylan); *Patty's Gone to Laredo* (Bob Dylan) WM: Bob Dylan / *People, Get Ready* (Bob Dylan) WM: Curtis Mayfield / *Romance in Durango* (Bob Dylan) WM: Bob Dylan and Jacques Levy / *Sad Eyed Lady of the Lowlands* (Bob Dylan) WM: Bob Dylan / *Salt Pork West Virginia* (Jack Elliot) WM: Jack Elliot / *Sara* (Bob Dylan); *She Belongs to Me* (Bob Dylan) WM: Bob Dylan / *Suzanne* (Joan Baez) WM: Leonard Cohen / *Tangled Up in Blue* (Bob Dylan) WM: Bob Dylan / *Time of the Preacher* (Willie Nelson) WM: Willie Nelson / *What Will You Do When Jesus Comes?* (Bob Dylan); *When I Paint My Masterpiece* (Bob Dylan) WM: Bob Dylan.

**1041   Return to Peyton Place.** US, 1961, C, 122 m. D: Jose Ferrer, MD: Leonid Raab, MS: Franz Waxman, P: TCF (Jerry Wald).

The Wonderful Season of Love (Rosemary Clooney) W: Paul Francis Webster—M: Franz Waxman.

**1042 Reveille with Beverly.** US, 1943, BW, 78 m. D: Charles Barton, MD: Morris Stoloff, P: Columbia (Sam White). Orch: Count Basie; Duke Ellington; Freddie Slack; Bob Crosby.

Cow-Cow Boogie (Ella Mae Morse) WM: Don Raye, Gene de Paul and Benny Carter / Night and Day (Frank Sinatra) WM: Cole Porter / Take the "A" Train (Female Singer) WM: Billy Strayhorn / Thumbs Up and V for Victory (Ann Miller, Chorus).

"A cheerless series of musical numbers strung together with a tired little story." —Theodore Strauss, The New York Times.

**1043 Rhapsody in Blue.** US, 1945, BW, 139 m. D: Irving Rapper, MD: Ray Heindorf, P: Warner (Jesse L. Lasky). Orch: Paul Whiteman. Vocals: Louanne Hogan for Joan Leslie; Bill Days for Mark Stevens.

Delishious (Joan Leslie) W: Ira Gershwin / I'll Build a Stairway to Paradise (Chorus) W: B.G. De Sylva and Ira Gershwin / Love Walked In (Mark Stevens); Oh Lady, Be Good (Joan Leslie) W: Ira Gershwin / Somebody Loves Me (Tom Patricola) W: B.G. De Sylva and Ballard MacDonald / Summertime (Anne Brown) W: Du Bose Heyward / Swanee (Al Jolson) W: Irving Caesar / S'Wonderful (Joan Leslie, Chorus) W: Ira Gershwin. M: George Gershwin.

"Throughout, the brilliant music of Mr. Gershwin is spotted abundantly, and that is the best—in fact, the only—intrinsically right thing in the film." —Bosley Crowther, The New York Times.

**1044 Rhythm on the River.** US, 1940, BW, 92 m. D: Victor Schertzinger, MS: Victor Young, P: Paramount (William LeBaron).

Ain't It a Shame About Mame? (Mary Martin) W: Johnny Burke—M: James V. Monaco / I Don't Want to Cry Anymore (Mary Martin) WM: Victor Schertzinger / Only Forever (Bing Crosby, Mary Martin); Rhythm on the River (Bing Crosby); That's for Me (Bing Crosby, Mary Martin); When the Moon Comes Over Madison Square (Bing Crosby) W: Johnny Burke—M: James V. Monaco.

"One of the most likeable musical pictures of the season." —Bosley Crowther, The New York Times.

**1045 Rich and Famous.** US, 1981, C, 117 m. D: George Cukor, MS: Georges Delerue, P: MGM (William Allyn).

On the Sunny Side of the Street (Willie Nelson) W: Dorothy Fields—Jimmy McHugh.

**1046 Rich, Young and Pretty.** US, 1951, C, 95 m. D: Norman Taurog, MD: David Rose, P: MGM (Joe Pasternak).

Dark Is the Night (Jane Powell) W: Sammy Cahn—M: Nicholas Brodszky / Deep in the Heart of Texas (Wendell Corey) W: June Hershey—M: Don Swander / How Do You Like Your Eggs in the Morning? (Jane Powell, Vic Damone, The Four Freshmen); I Can See You (Jane Powell, Vic Damone); L'Amour Toujours (Danielle Darrieux) W: Sammy Cahn—M: Nicholas Brodszky / The Old Piano Roll Blues (Jane Powell, Vic Damone) WM: Cy Coben / Paris (Fernando Lamas) W: Sammy Cahn—M: Nicholas Brodszky / There's Danger in Your Eyes, Cherie! (Danielle Darrieux) W: Jack Meskill—M: Pete Wendling / We Never Talk Much (Jane Powell, Vic Damone, Fernando Lamas, Danielle Darrieux, Chorus); Wonder Why (Jane Powell, Vic Damone) W: Sammy Cahn—M: Nicholas Brodszky.

"Boasts quite a few lilting numbers. ... The vocalists ... give the numbers top treatment." —A.H. Weiler, The New York Times.

**1047 Ride 'Em Cowboy.** US, 1942, BW, 86 m. D: Arthur Lubin, MD: Charles Previn, MS: Frank Skinner, P: Universal (Alex Gottlieb).

Orch: The Buckaroos Band. MB: The Ranger Chorus of Forty.

*A-Tisket, A- Tasket* (Ella Fitzgerald) WM: Ella Fitzgerald and Al Feldman [Van Alexander] / *Beside the Rio Tonto* (The Merry Macs) W: Don Raye —M: Gene de Paul / *I'll Remember April* (Dick Foran) W: Don Raye and Patricia Johnston—M: Gene de Paul / *Rockin' 'n' Reelin'* (Ella Fitzgerald, The Merry Macs); *Wake Up Jacob* (The Merry Macs) W: Don Raye—M: Gene de Paul.

"Hits high spots with Abbott and Costello, but it does have a lot of interruptions." —Theodore Strauss, *The New York Times*.

**1048  Riding High.** US, 1950, BW, 112 m. D: Frank Capra, MD: Victor Young, P: Paramount (Frank Capra). Performer: Bing Crosby.

*The Horse Told Me; Someplace on Anywhere Road; Sunshine Cake* (Bing Crosby, Coleen Gray, Clarence Muse); *Sure Thing* W: Johnny Burke—M: James Van Heusen.

**1049  Riff-Raff.** US, 1935, BW, 89 m. D: J. Walter Ruben, MS: Edward Ward, P: MGM (Irving Thalberg).

*You Are My Lucky Star* (Jean Harlow, Chorus) W: Arthur Freed—M: Nacio Herb Brown.

**1050  Ring-a-Ding Rhythm.** GB, 1962, BW, 73 m. D: Richard Lester, P: Columbia (Milton Subotsky). GB Title: It's Trad, Dad.

*Another Tear Falls* (Gene McDaniels) W: Hal David—M: Burt Bacharach / *Beale Street Blues* (Kenny Ball) WM: W.C. Handy / *Double Trouble* (The Brooks Brothers) WM: Geoff Brook and Ricky Brook / *Down By the Riverside* (Ottilie Patterson) WM: Chris Barber / *Dream Away Romance* (The Temperance Seven) WM: Paul McDowell and Clifford Beven / *Everybody Loves My Baby* (The Temperance Seven) WM: Jack Palmer and Spencer Williams / *Let's Talk About Love* (Helen Shapiro) WM: Norrie Paramor and Bunny Lewis / *Lonely City* (John Leyton) WM: Geoffrey Goddard / *Lose Your Inhibition Twist* (Chubby Checker) WM: Kal Mann and Dave Appell / *My Maryland* (Lightfoot) WM Arr: Terry Lightfoot / *Nineteen-Nineteen March* (Kenny Ball) WM: Norrie Paramor and Milton Subotsky / *Rainbows* (Craig Douglas); *Ring-a- Ding* (Helen Shapiro) WM: Norrie Paramor and Bunny Lewis / *Seven Day Weekend* (Gary "US" Bonds) WM: Doc Pomus and Mort Shuman / *Sometime Yesterday* (Helen Shapiro) WM: Clive Westlake / *Space Ship to Mars* (Gene Vincent and Sounds Incorporated); *Tavern in the Town* (Terry Lightfoot) WM: Norrie Paramor and Milton Subotsky / *What Am I to Do?* (The Paris Sisters); *You Never Talk About Me* (Del Shannon) WM: Doc Pomus and Mort Shuman.

**1051  Rio Bravo.** US, 1959, C, 141 m. D: Howard Hawks, MS: Dimitri Tiomkin, P: Warner (Howard Hawks).

*Cindy* (Ricky Nelson) WM: Unknown / *My Rifle, My Pony and Me* (Dean Martin, Ricky Nelson); *Rio Bravo* (Dean Martin) W: Paul Francis Webster—M: Dimitri Tiomkin.

**1052  Rio Grande.** US, 1950, BW, 105 m. D: John Ford, MS: Victor Young, P: Republic (John Ford, Merian C. Cooper). Performers: The Sons of the Pioneers.

*Aha, San Antone* WM: Dale Evans / *The Cattle Call* WM: Tex Owens / *Footsore Cavalry* WM: Stan Jones / *I'll Take You Home Again, Kathleen* WM: Thomas Westendorf / *My Gal Is Purple; Yellow Stripes* WM: Stan Jones / *You're in the Army Now* W: Tell Taylor and Ole Olsen—M: Isham Jones.

**1053  Rio Rita.** US, 1929, BW/C, 140 m. D: Luther Reed, MD: Victor Baravalle, MS: Harry Tierney, P: RKO (William LeBaron).

RKO's first musical began life as a hit Broadway musical comedy in 1927, produced by Florenz Ziegfeld.

*Are You There?* (Dorothy Lee, Bert Wheeler); *Espanola* (Robert Woolsey, Chorus); *If You're in Love, You'll Waltz*

(Bebe Daniels); *Jumping Bean* (Dorothy Lee, Chorus); *The Kinkajou* (Dorothy Lee, Chorus); *Out on the Loose* (Bert Wheeler, Chorus); *Over the Boundary Line* (Chorus); *Poor Fool* (Bebe Daniels); *The Rangers' Song* (John Boles, Chorus); *Rio Rita* (Bebe Daniels, John Boles); *River Song* (Bebe Daniels); *Siesta Time* (Chorus); *The Spanish Shawl* (Eva Rosita); *Sweethearts* (Bebe Daniels); *Sweetheart, We Need Each Other* (Dorothy Lee, Bert Wheeler); *You're Always in My Arms* (Bebe Daniels, John Boles) W: Joseph McCarthy —M: Harry Tierney.

"The tuneful melodies that were sung on the stage by J. Harold Murray as the redoubtable Captain Jim are rendered admirably by John Boles. Bebe Daniels acts the dark-eyed Rio Rita and her singing, while not up to the standard set by Ethlin Terry in the stage version, is a surprise." —Mordaunt Hall, *The New York Times*.

**1054 Rio Rita.** US, 1942, BW, 91 m. D: S. Sylvan Simon, MS: Herbert Stothart, P: MGM (Pandro S. Berman).

*Long Before You Came Along* (Kathryn Grayson, John Carroll) W: E.Y. Harburg—M: Harold Arlen / *The Rangers' Song* (Kathryn Grayson, John Carroll, Chorus); *Rio Rita* (John Carroll) W: Joseph McCarthy—M: Harry Tierney.

"So far as the oft-filmed version of the former Ziegfeld stage musical is concerned, Metro uses but the original title song and the *Rangers* number." —*Variety*.

"A musical-comedy plot is worth only as many gags, songs and nonsensical merriment that you can pack into it. So perhaps it's just as well that Abbott and Costello, those lunatic tumbleweeds, should take almost complete charge. ... Kathryn Grayson warbles tunes like an angel who's been paying strict attention to her upper registers." —Theodore Strauss, *The New York Times*.

**1055 The Ritz.** US, 1976, C, 91 m. D: Richard Lester, MS: Ken Thorne, P: Warner (Denis O'Dell).

*Everything's Coming Up Roses* (Rita Moreno) W: Stephen Sondheim—M: Jule Styne / *Liberated Man* (C.T. Wilkinson) WM: Ken Thorne and Peter Outter / *The Three Caballeros* (Jack Weston, F. Murray Abraham, Paul B. Price) WM: Manuel Esperton and Ray Gilbert.

**1056 River of No Return.** US, 1954, C, 91 m. D: Otto Preminger, MD: Lionel Newman, MS: Cyril Mockridge, P: TCF (Stanley Rubin). Performer: Marilyn Monroe.

*Bye Bye Blackbird* W: Mort Dixon—M: Ray Henderson / *I'm Gonna File My Claim; One Silver Dollar; River of No Return* W: Ken Darby —M: Lionel Newman.

**1057 Road House.** US, 1948, BW, 95 m. D: Jean Negulesco, MS: Cyril Mockridge, P: TCF (Edward Chodorov). Performer: Ida Lupino.

*Again* W: Dorcas Cochran—M: Lionel Newman / *One for My Baby* W: Johnny Mercer—M: Harold Arlen / *There'll Be Some Changes Made* W: Billy Higgins—M: W. Benton Overstreet.

"Her singing of three low-down numbers is convincing." —A.H. Weiler, *The New York Times*.

**1058 Road to Bali.** US, 1952, C, 90 m. D: Hal Walker, MD: Joseph J. Lilley, P: Paramount (Harry Tugend).

*Chicago Style* (Bob Hope, Bing Crosby); *Hoot Mon* (Bob Hope, Bing Crosby); *Merry Go Runaround* (Bob Hope, Bing Crosby, Dorothy Lamour); *Moonflowers* (Dorothy Lamour); *To See You* (Bing Crosby) W: Johnny Burke—James Van Heusen.

**1059 The Road to Hong Kong.** GB, 1962, BW, 91 m. D: Norman Panama and Melvin Frank, P: UA (Norman Panama, Melvin Frank).

*Let's Not Be Sensible* (Bing Crosby, Joan Collins); *The Road to Hong Kong* (Bing Crosby, Bob Hope, Joan Collins);

*Teamwork* (Bing Crosby, Bob Hope, Joan Collins); *Warmer Than a Whisper* (Dorothy Lamour) W: Sammy Cahn—M: James Van Heusen.

**1060 Road to Morocco.** US, 1942, BW, 83 m. D: David Butler, P: Paramount (Paul Jones).

*Ain't Got a Dime to My Name* (Bing Crosby); *Constantly* (Bing Crosby, Dorothy Lamour); *Moonlight Becomes You* (Bing Crosby, Bob Hope, Dorothy Lamour); *Road to Morocco* (Bing Crosby, Bob Hope) W: Johnny Burke—M: James Van Heusen.

**1061 Road to Rio.** US, 1947, BW, 100 m. D: Norman Z. McLeod, MD: Robert Emmett Dolan, P: Paramount (Daniel Dare).

*Apalachicola, Fla.* (Bing Crosby, Bob Hope, The Andrews Sisters); *But Beautiful* (Bing Crosby); *Experience* (Bing Crosby, Dorothy Lamour); *You Don't Have to Know the Language* (Bing Crosby, The Andrews Sisters) W: Johnny Burke—M: James Van Heusen.

**1062 Road to Singapore.** US, 1940, BW, 84 m. D: Victor Schertzinger, MD: Victor Young, P: Paramount (Harlan Thompson).

*Captain Custard* (Bing Crosby, Bob Hope) M: Victor Schertzinger / *Kaigoon* (Chorus) M: James V. Monaco / *The Moon and the Willow Tree* (Dorothy Lamour) M: Victor Schertzinger / *Sweet Potato Piper* (Bing Crosby, Bob Hope, Dorothy Lamour); *Too Romantic* (Bing Crosby, Dorothy Lamour) M: James V. Monaco. W: Johnny Burke.

**1063 Road to Utopia.** US, 1945, BW, 90 m. D: Hal Walker, MS: Leigh Harline, P: Paramount (Paul Jones).

*Good-Time Charley* (Bing Crosby, Bob Hope); *It's Anybody's Spring* (Bing Crosby); *Personality* (Dorothy Lamour); *Put It There, Pal* (Bing Crosby, Bob Hope); *Sunday, Monday, or Always* (Bing Crosby); *Welcome to My Dream* (Bing Crosby); *Would You*

(Dorothy Lamour) W: Johnny Burke—M: James Van Heusen.

**1064 Road to Zanzibar.** US, 1941, BW, 92 m. D: Victor Schertzinger, MS: Victor Young, P: Paramount (Paul Jones). Performer: Bing Crosby.

*Birds of a Feather; It's Always You; On the Road to Zanzibar* (Bing Crosby, Bob Hope); *You Lucky People You; You're Dangerous* (Dorothy Lamour) W: Johnny Burke—M: James Van Heusen.

**1065 Roberta.** US, 1935, BW/C, 85 m. D: William A. Seiter, MD: Max Steiner, P: RKO (Pandro S. Berman).

*Fashion Show* (Fred Astaire) W: Dorothy Fields—M: Jerome Kern / *I'll Be Hard to Handle* (Ginger Rogers) W: Bernard Dougall—M: Jerome Kern / *Indiana* (Chorus) W: Ballard MacDonald—M: James F. Hanley / *I Won't Dance* (Fred Astaire, Ginger Rogers) W: Otto Harbach, Oscar Hammerstein II and Dorothy Fields—M: Jerome Kern / *Let's Begin* (Fred Astaire, Candy Candido) W: Otto Harbach—M: Jerome Kern / *Lovely to Look At* (Irene Dunne, Fred Astaire, Ginger Rogers, Chorus) W: Otto Harbach, Dorothy Fields and Jimmy McHugh—M: Jerome Kern / *Russian Song* (Irene Dunne) WM: Unknown / *Smoke Gets in Your Eyes* (Irene Dunne); *Yesterdays* (Irene Dunne) W: Otto Harbach—M: Jerome Kern.

"Jerome Kern's songs, some of them borrowed from the stage edition and others composed for the occasion, are distinguished both for their literacy and their romantic wit." —Andre Sennwald, *The New York Times.*

**1066 Robin and the Seven Hoods.** US, 1964, C, 103 m. D: Gordon Douglas, MS: Nelson Riddle, P: Warner (Howard W. Koch).

*All for One and One for All* (Peter Falk, Chorus); *Any Man Who Loves His Mother* (Dean Martin, Male Quartet); *Bang! Bang!* (Sammy Davis, Jr.); *Charlotte Couldn't Charleston* (Chorus); *Don't Be a Do-Badder* (Bing Crosby,

Frank Sinatra, Dean Martin, Sammy Davis, Jr., Chorus); *Give Praise! Give Praise! Give Praise!* (Chorus); *I Like to Lead When I Dance* (Frank Sinatra); *Mister Booze* (Bing Crosby, Frank Sinatra, Dean Martin, Sammy Davis, Jr., Chorus); *My Kind of Town* (Frank Sinatra); *Style* (Bing Crosby, Frank Sinatra, Dean Martin) W: Sammy Cahn —M: James Van Heusen.

**1067 Rock-a-Bye Baby.** US, 1958, C, 103 m. D: Frank Tashlin, MS: Walter Scharf, P: Paramount (Jerry Lewis).

*Dormi, Dormi, Dormi* (Jerry Lewis, Salvatore Baccaloni); *The Land of La-La-La* (Jerry Lewis, Gary Lewis); *Love Is a Lonely Thing* (Jerry Lewis); *Rock-a-Bye Baby* (Jerry Lewis); *The White Virgin of the Nile* (Marilyn Maxwell); *Why Can't He Care for Me?* (Connie Stevens) W: Sammy Cahn—M: Harry Warren.

**1068 Rock All Night.** US, 1957, BW, 65 m. D: Roger Corman, P: AIP (Roger Corman). Vocals: Nora Hayes for Abby Dalton.

*The Great Pretender* (Abby Dalton) WM: Buck Ram / *He's Mine* (The Platters) WM: Zola Taylor, Paul Robi and Miles / *I Guess I Won't Hang Around Here Anymore* (Abby Dalton) WM: Buck Ram / *I'm Sorry* (The Platters) WM: Tinturin and White / *I Wanna Rock Now* (The Blockbusters) / *Rock All Night* (The Blockbusters); *Rock and Roll Guitar* (The Blockbusters) WM: Buck Ram.

**1069 Rocky.** US, 1976, C, 119 m. D: John G. Avildsen, MS: Bill Conti, P: UA (Irwin Winkler).

*Gonna Fly Now* (De Etta Little, Nelson Pigford) WM: Ayn Robbins, Bill Conti and Carol Connors / *Take Me Back* (Valentine) WM: Frank Stallone, Jr. / *You Take My Heart Away* (De Etta Little, Nelson Pigford) WM: Ayn Robbins, Bill Conti and Carol Connors.

**1070 Rocky III.** US, 1982, C, 99 m. D: Sylvester Stallone, MS: Bill

Conti, P: MGM/UA (Irwin Winkler, Robert Chartoff).

*Eye of the Tiger* (Survivor) WM: Frank Sullivan and Jim Peterik.

**1071 The Rocky Horror Picture Show.** GB, 1975, C, 95 m. D: Jim Sharman, MD: Richard Hartley, P: TCF (Lou Adler, Michael White).

*Dammit Janet* (Susan Sarandon, Barry Bostwick, Chorus); *Eddie* (Jonathan Adams, Chorus); *Fanfare—Don't Dream It* (Tim Curry, Chorus); *Floor Show* (Susan Sarandon, Barry Bostwick, Little Nell, Peter Hinwood); *Hot Patootie—Bless My Soul* (Meatloaf, Chorus); *I Can Make You a Man* (Tim Curry, Chorus); *I'm Going Home* (Tim Curry, Chorus); *Over at the Frankenstein Place* (Susan Sarandon, Barry Bostwick, Richard O'Brien, Chorus); *Science Fiction* (Richard O'Brien, Chorus); *Super Heroes* (Susan Sarandon, Barry Bostwick, Chorus); *Sweet Transvestite* (Tim Curry, Chorus); *The Time Warp* (Richard O'Brien, Little Nell, Patricia Quinn, Charles Gray, Chorus); *Toucha, Toucha, Touch Me* (Susan Sarandon, Chorus); *Wild and Untamed Thing* (Tim Curry, Richard O'Brien, Chorus) WM: Richard O'Brien.

"Adapted from a rock stage musical of same title. ... The sparkle's gone." —*Variety.*

**1072 The Rogue Song.** US, 1930, C, 115 m. D: Lionel Barrymore and Hal Roach, MS: Dimitri Tiomkin, P: MGM (Lionel Barrymore). Performer: Lawrence Tibbett.

Tibbett's screen debut was an adaptation of Franz Lehar's 1912 operetta 'Gypsy Love.' No print of this film has survived.

*Love Comes Like a Bird on the Wing* (Lawrence Tibbett, Catherine Dale Owen, Judith Vosselli, Chorus) M: Franz Lehar / *Once in the Georgian Hills; The Rogue Song* (Lawrence Tibbett, Stan Laurel, Oliver Hardy, Chorus); *Song of the Shirt; When I'm Looking at You* M: Herbert Stothart / *The White Dove* (Lawrence Tibbett,

Catherine Dale Owen) M: Franz Lehar. W: Clifford Grey.

"When Mr. Tibbett sings, one cares not why, for the story, such as it is, takes second place in this film. . . . When his voice swells from the screen one forgets . . . that the singer himself is not on the stage. Never before have a singer's efforts on the screen been applauded so genuinely." —Mordaunt Hall, *The New York Times.*

**1073  Roman Scandals.** US, 1933, BW, 92 m. D: Frank Tuttle and Busby Berkeley, MD: Alfred Newman, P: UA (Samuel Goldwyn). MB: The Goldwyn Girls. Performer: Eddie Cantor.

*Build a Little Home; Keep Young and Beautiful* (Eddie Cantor, Billy Barty); *No More Love* (Ruth Etting) W: Al Dubin—M: Harry Warren / *Put a Tax on Love* W: Al Dubin and L. Wolfe Gilbert—M: Harry Warren / *Rome Wasn't Built in a Day* W: Al Dubin—M: Harry Warren.

"Mr. Cantor . . . is exceptionally good in the episodes in which he sings." —Mordaunt Hall, *The New York Times.*

**1074  Romance on the High Seas.** US, 1948, C, 99 m. D: Michael Curtiz, MD: Ray Heindorf, P: Warner (Alex Gottlieb). MB: The Page Cavanaugh Trio. Performer: Doris Day. GB Title: It's Magic.

One of Les Brown's band singers in the 1940's, this was Doris Day's first film. The hit song *It's Magic* was her third million-selling record and helped propel her to international stardom.

*I'm in Love; It's Magic; It's You or No One; Put 'Em in a Box; Run, Run, Run* (Jack Carson); *The Tourist Trade* (Sir Lancelot, Avon Long) W: Sammy Cahn—M: Jule Styne.

"Maybe this bouncy young lady . . . has ability and personality. But as shown in this picture . . . she has no more than a vigorous disposition which hits the screen with a thud." —Bosley Crowther, *The New York Times.*

**1075  Rome Adventure.** US, 1962, C, 119 m. D: Delmer Daves, MS: Max Steiner, P: Warner (Delmer Daves). GB Title: Lovers Must Learn.

*Al Di La* (Emilio Pericoli) Eng. W: Ervin Drake—Ital. W: Mogo—M: Carlo Donida.

**1076  Room Service.** US, 1938, BW, 78 m. D: William A. Seiter, MS: Roy Webb, P: RKO (Pandro S. Berman).

*Swing Low, Sweet Chariot* (Groucho Marx, Chico Marx, Cliff Dunstan, Donald McBride, Chorus) WM: Unknown—Arr: Henry Thacker Burleigh.

**1077  Rosalie.** US, 1937, BW, 122 m. D: W.S. Van Dyke II, MD: Herbert Stothart, P: MGM (William Anthony McGuire). Vocal: Camille Sorey for Lois Clements.

*Anchors Aweigh* (Nelson Eddy, Chorus) W: Alfred Hart Miles and Royal Lovell—M: Charles A. Zimmerman / *The Caissons Go Rolling Along* (Nelson Eddy, Chorus) WM: Edmund Gruber / *In the Still of the Night* (Nelson Eddy); *I've a Strange New Rhythm in My Heart* (Eleanor Powell) WM: Cole Porter / *On, Brave Old Army Team* (Nelson Eddy) WM: Philip Equer / *Rosalie* (Nelson Eddy, Chorus); *Spring Love Is in the Air* (Ilona Massey); *To Love or Not to Love* (Nelson Eddy, Ray Bolger, Chorus); *Who Knows?* (Nelson Eddy, Lois Clements); *Why Should I Care?* (Frank Morgan and Dummy) WM: Cole Porter.

**1078  The Rose.** US, 1979, C, 134 m. D: Mark Rydell, MD: Paul A. Rothchild, P: TCF (Marvin Worth, Aaron Russo). Performer: Bette Midler.

*Fire Down Below* (Bette Midler, Michael Green, Claude Sacha, Michael St. Laurent, Sylvester and Pearl White) WM: Bob Seger / *Keep on Rockin'* WM: John Carter and Sam Hagar / *Let Me Call You Sweetheart* WM: Beth Slater Whitson and Leo Friedman / *Love Me with a Feeling* WM: Hudson Whittaker

/ *Midnight in Memphis* WM: Tony Johnson / *The Rose* WM: Amanda McBroom / *Sold My Soul to Rock 'n' Roll* WM: Gene Pistilli / *Stay with Me* WM: Jerry Ragovoy and George Weiss / *When a Man Loves a Woman* WM: Andrew Wright and Calvin Lewis / *Whose Side Are You On?* WM: Charley Williams and Kenny Hopkins.

"An ultra-realistic look at the infusion of money, sex, drugs and booze into the simple process of singing a song, a chore Midler does faultlessly in several excellent concert sequences." — *Variety.*

**1079 Rose Marie.** US, 1936, BW, 110 m. D: W. S. Van Dyke II, MD: Herbert Stothart, P: MGM (Hunt Stromberg). TV Title: Indian Love Call.

*Dinah* (Jeanette MacDonald) W: Sam M. Lewis and Joe Young—M: Harry Akst / *Indian Love Call* (Jeanette MacDonald, Nelson Eddy) W: Otto Harbach and Oscar Hammerstein II—M: Rudolf Friml / *Just for You* (Nelson Eddy) W: Gus Kahn—M: Rudolf Friml and Herbert Stothart / *The Mounties* (Nelson Eddy) W: Otto Harbach and Oscar Hammerstein II—M: Rudolf Friml and Herbert Stothart / *Pardon Me, Madame* (Jeanette MacDonald, Chorus) W: Gus Kahn—M: Herbert Stothart / *Rose Marie* (Nelson Eddy) W: Otto Harbach and Oscar Hammerstein II—M: Rudolf Friml / *Some of These Days* (Jeanette MacDonald, Gilda Gray) WM: Shelton Brooks / *Totem Tom-Tom* (Chorus) W: Otto Harbach and Oscar Hammerstein II—M: Rudolf Friml and Herbert Stothart.

"A lyric recording of the Rudolf Friml—Herbert Stothart score that distinguished the operetta when first it played to Broadway in 1924." —Frank S. Nugent, *The New York Times.*

**1080 Rose Marie.** US, 1954, C, 115 m. D: Mervyn LeRoy, MD: George Stoll, P: MGM (Mervyn LeRoy).

*Alouette* (Chorus) WM: Unknown / *Free to Be Free* (Ann Blyth); *I Have the Love* (Ann Blyth, Fernando Lamas) W: Paul Francis Webster—M: Rudolf Friml / *I'm a Mountie Who Never Got His Man* (Bert Lahr) W: Herbert Baker—M: George Stoll / *Indian Love Call* (Ann Blyth, Fernando Lamas) W: Otto Harbach and Oscar Hammerstein II—M: Rudolf Friml / *The Mounties* (Howard Keel, Chorus) W: Otto Harbach and Oscar Hammerstein II—M: Rudolf Friml and Herbert Stothart / *The Right Place for a Girl* (Howard Keel) W: Paul Francis Webster—M: Rudolf Friml / *Rose Marie* (Howard Keel) W: Otto Harbach and Oscar Hammerstein II—M: Rudolf Friml.

"The scenery and songs are its salvation. . . . Mr. Keel booms the loudest and the longest with the memorable *Rose Marie,* but Miss Blyth and Mr. Lamas carry the farthest with the echoing *Indian Love Call.*" —Bosley Crowther, *The New York Times.*

**1081 Rose of Washington Square.** US, 1939, BW, 86 m. D: Gregory Ratoff, MD: Louis Silvers, P: TCF (Darryl F. Zanuck). Orch: Louis Prima.

*California, Here I Come* (Al Jolson) W: Al Jolson and B.G. De Sylva—M: Joseph Meyer / *I'm Just Wild About Harry* (Alice Faye) WM: Noble Sissle and Eubie Blake / *I'm Sorry I Made You Cry* (Alice Faye) WM: N.J. Clesi / *I Never Knew Heaven Could Speak* (Alice Faye) WM: Mack Gordon and Harry Revel / *My Mammy* (Al Jolson) W: Sam M. Lewis and Joe Young—M: Walter Donaldson / *My Man* (Alice Faye) Eng. W: Channing Pollock—M: Maurice Yvain / *Pretty Baby* (Al Jolson) W: Gus Kahn—M: Tony Jackson and Egbert Van Alstyne / *Rock-a-Bye Your Baby with a Dixie Melody* (Al Jolson) W: Sam M. Lewis and Joe Young—M: Jean Schwartz / *Rose of Washington Square* (Alice Faye) W: Ballard MacDonald—M: James F. Hanley / *Toot, Toot, Tootsie!* (Al Jolson) WM: Gus Kahn, Ernie Erdman and Dan Russo /

*The Vamp* (Alice Faye, Chorus) WM: Byron Gay.

**1082   Roustabout.** US, 1964, C, 101 m. D: John Rich, MS: Joseph J. Lilley, P: Paramount (Hal B. Wallis). MB: The Jordanaires. Performer: Elvis Presley.

*Big Love, Big Heartache* WM: Dolores Fuller, Lee Morris and Sonny Hendrix / *Carny Town* WM: Fred Wise and Randy Starr / *Hard Knocks* WM: Joy Byers / *It's a Wonderful World* WM: Sid Tepper and Roy C. Bennett / *It's Carnival Time* WM: Ben Weisman and Sid Wayne / *Little Egypt* WM: Jerry Leiber and Mike Stoller / *One-Track Heart; Poison Ivy League; Roustabout* WM: Bill Giant, Bernie Baum and Florence Kaye / *There's a Brand New Day on the Horizon* WM: Joy Byers / *Wheels on My Heels* WM: Sid Tepper and Roy C. Bennett.

**1083   Royal Wedding.** US, 1951, C, 93 m. D: Stanley Donen, MD: Johnny Green, P: MGM (Arthur Freed). GB Title: Wedding Bells.

*Every Night at Seven* (Fred Astaire, Chorus); *The Happiest Day of My Life* (Jane Powell); *How Could You Believe Me When I Said I Love You When You Know I've Been a Liar All My Life* (Jane Powell, Fred Astaire); *I Left My Hat in Haiti* (Fred Astaire, Chorus); *Open Your Eyes* (Jane Powell); *Too Late Now* (Jane Powell); *What a Lovely Day for a Wedding* (Keenan Wynn, Chorus); *You're All the World to Me* (Fred Astaire) W: Alan Jay Lerner—M: Burton Lane.

"The best that we can say is that it has one swell number in it, built on the world's longest-titled song." —Bosley Crowther, *The New York Times*.

"This is an engaging concoction of songs and dances in a standard musical framework." —*Variety*.

**1084   The Ruling Class.** GB, 1972, C, 154 m. D: Peter Medak, MS: John Cameron, P: Keep Films (Jules Buck, Jack Hawkins).

*Dry Bones* (Peter O'Toole) W:

James Weldon Johnson—M: J. Rosamund Johnson / *My Blue Heaven* (Peter O'Toole, Carolyn Seymour) W: George Whiting—M: Walter Donaldson.

**1085   Sabrina.** US, 1954, BW, 113 m. D: Billy Wilder, MS: Frederick Hollander, P: Paramount (Billy Wilder). GB Title: Sabrina Fair.

*La Vie en Rose* (Audrey Hepburn) Eng. W: Mack David—Fr. W: Edith Piaf—M: R.S. Louiguy.

**1086   Saddle the Wind.** US, 1958, C, 84 m. D: Robert Parrish, MS: Jeff Alexander, P: MGM (Armand Deutsch).

*Saddle the Wind* (Julie London) WM: Jay Livingston and Ray Evans.

**1087   Sadie McKee.** US, 1934, BW, 90 m. D: Clarence Brown, P: MGM (Lawrence Weingarten).

*After You've Gone* (Gene Austin, Candy Candido, Coco) W: Henry Creamer—M: Turner Layton / *All I Do Is Dream of You* (Gene Raymond); *Please Make Me Care* (Esther Ralston) W: Arthur Freed—M: Nacio Herb Brown.

**1088   A Safe Place.** US, 1971, C, 94 m. D: Henry Jaglom, P: Columbia (Bert Schneider).

*As Time Goes By* (Dooley Wilson) WM: Herman Hupfeld / *I'm Old Fashioned* (Fred Astaire) W: Johnny Mercer—M: Jerome Kern / *It's a Big, Wide Wonderful World* (Buddy Clark) WM: John Rox / *La Mer* (Charles Trenet) WM: Charles Trenet / *Lavender Blue* (Vera Lynn) W: Larry Morey—M: Eliot Daniel / *La Vie en Rose* (Edith Piaf) Fr. W: Edith Piaf—M: R.S. Louiguy / *Passing By* (Buddy Clark) / *Someone to Watch Over Me* (Dinah Shore) W: Ira Gershwin—M: George Gershwin / *Something to Remember You By* (Helen Forrest) W: Howard Dietz—M: Arthur Schwartz / *Vous Qui Passer Sans Me Voir* (Charles Trenet) WM: Charles Trenet.

**1089   St. Louis Blues.** US, 1939, BW, 87 m. D: Raoul Walsh, P: Paramount (Jeff Lazarus). MB: The Hall

Johnson Choir. TV Title: Best of the Blues.

*Blue Nightfall* (Dorothy Lamour) W: Frank Loesser—M: Burton Lane / *Dark Eyes* (Maxine Sullivan) WM: Russian Folk Song—Arr: Harry Horlick and Gregory Stone / *I Go for That* (Dorothy Lamour) W: Frank Loesser —M: Matt Malneck / *Junior* (Dorothy Lamour) W: Frank Loesser—M: Burton Lane / *Kinda Lonesome* (Maxine Sullivan) WM: Leo Robin, Sam Coslow and Hoagy Carmichael / *Let's Dream in the Moonlight* (Dorothy Lamour) WM: Raoul Walsh and Matt Malneck / *Loch Lomond* (Maxine Sullivan) WM: Unknown / *St. Louis Blues* (Dorothy Lamour) WM: W.C. Handy.

**1090 Sally, Irene and Mary.** US, 1938, BW, 72 m. D: William A. Seiter, MD: Arthur Lange, P: TCF (Gene Markey). MB: The Raymond Scott Quintet.

*Got My Mind on Music* (Alice Faye, Joan Davis, Marjorie Weaver) W: Mack Gordon—M: Harry Revel / *Half Moon on the Hudson* (Alice Faye, Joan Davis, Marjorie Weaver, The Brian Sisters); *Help Wanted* (Joan Davis) W: Walter Bullock—M: Harold Spina / *Hot Patatta* (Jimmy Durante) WM: Jimmy Durante / *I Could Use a Dream* (Alice Faye, Tony Martin) W: Walter Bullock—M: Harold Spina / *Sweet As a Song* (Tony Martin) W: Mack Gordon—M: Harry Revel / *This Is Where I Came In* (Alice Faye, Tony Martin); *Who Stole the Jam?* (Alice Faye, Joan Davis, The Brian Sisters) W: Walter Bullock—M: Harold Spina.

"It's the vocal prowess of Tony Martin and Alice Faye, Mr. and Mrs. in private life and the romance interest here, that does much to sustain the interest." *—Variety.*

**1091 Salsa.** US, 1988, C, 97 m. D: Boaz Davidson, P: Cannon (Menahem Golan, Yoram Globus).

*Cali Pachanguero* (Grupo Niche) WM: Jairo Vorela and George Sigara /

*Chicos Y Chicas* (Mavis Vegas Davis) WM: Bob Esty and Michele Aller / *Good Lovin'* (Kenny Ortega) WM: Arthur Resnick and Rudy Clark / *I Know* (Marisela, The Edwin Hawkins Singers) WM: Barbara George / *Margarita* (Wilkins) WM: Wilkins Velez, Michael Sembello and Randy Waldman / *Oye Como Va* (Tito Puente) WM: Tito Puente / *Puerto Rico* (Bobby Caldwell plus others) WM: Wilkins Velez, Michael Sembello, Randy Waldman and Bobby Caldwell / *Spanish Harlem* (Ben E. King) WM: Jerry Leiber and Phil Spector / *Under My Skin* (Robby Rosa) WM: Michael Sembello and Randy Waldman / *Your Love* (Laura Branigan) WM: David Friedman.

**1092 Same Time, Next Year.** US, 1978, C, 117 m. D: Robert Mulligan, MS: Marvin Hamlisch, P: Universal (Walter Mirisch, Morton Gottlieb).

*The Last Time I Felt Like This* (Johnny Mathis, Jane Oliver) W: Alan Bergman and Marilyn Bergman—M: Marvin Hamlisch.

**1093 San Antonio.** US, 1945, C, 111 m. D: David Butler, MS: Max Steiner, P: Warner (Robert Buckner). Performer: Alexis Smith.

*Put Your Little Foot Right Out* WM: Larry Spier / *Some Sunday Morning* W: Ted Koehler—M.K. Jerome and Ray Heindorf / *Somewhere in Monterey* WM: Charles Kisco and Jack Scholl.

**1094 San Francisco.** US, 1936, BW, 117 m. D: W.S. Van Dyke II, MD: Herbert Stothart, P: MGM (John Emerson, Bernard Hyman). MB: Long Beach Boys' Choir. Performer: Jeanette MacDonald.

*Battle Hymn of the Republic* W: Julia Ward Howe—M: William Steffe / *Happy New Year* (Shirley Ross) W: Gus Kahn—M: Bronislau Kaper and Walter Jurmann / *A Heart That's Free* W: Thomas T. Railey—M: Alfred G. Robyn / *The Holy City* W: Frederick Edward Weatherly—M: Stephen Adams [Michael Maybrick] / *Nearer,*

*My God, to Thee* W: Sarah Adams—M: Lowell Mason / *Philippine Dance* (Male Trio) WM: Bob Carleton / *San Francisco* (Jeanette MacDonald, Shirley Ross, Ted Healy) W: Gus Kahn—M: Bronislau Kaper and Walter Jurmann / *Would You?* W: Arthur Freed—M: Nacio Herb Brown.

"Entrancing musical sequences arranged for the lyric soprano of Jeanette MacDonald." —Frank S. Nugent, *The New York Times.*

**1095   San Quentin.** US, 1937, BW, 70 m. D: Lloyd Bacon, MD: Joseph Nussbaum and Ray Heindorf, MS: Heinz Roemheld and David Raksin, P: Warner (Sam Bischoff).

*How Could You?* (Ann Sheridan) W: Al Dubin—M: Harry Warren.

**1096   Sanders of the River.** GB, 1935, BW, 98 m. D: Zoltan Korda, P: UA (Alexander Korda). Performer: Paul Robeson. Alt. Title: Bosambo.

*The Canoe Song; Congo Lullabye* (Nina Mae McKinney, Paul Robeson, Chorus); *The Killing Song; Love Song* W: Arthur Wimperis—M: Mischa Spoliansky.

**1097   The Sandpiper.** US, 1965, C, 116 m. D: Vincente Minnelli, MS: Johnny Mandel, P: MGM (Martin Ransohoff).

*The Shadow of Your Smile* (Chorus) W: Paul Francis Webster—M: Johnny Mandel.

**1098   Saratoga.** US, 1937, BW, 94 m. D: Jack Conway, MS: Edward Ward, P: MGM (Bernard H. Hyman, John Emerson).

Jean Harlow died while she was making this film.

*The Horse with the Dreamy Eyes* (Clark Gable, Jean Harlow, Cliff Edwards, Hattie McDaniel, Una Merkel) W: Robert Wright and George "Chet" Forrest—M: Walter Donaldson.

**1099   Saturday Night Fever.** US, 1977, C, 118 m. D: John Badham, MD: David Shire, P: Paramount (Robert Stigwood).

*Boogie Shoes* (KC and The Sunshine Band) WM: Harry Casey and Richard Finch / *Calypso Breakdown* (Ralph MacDonald) WM: Ronald Bell / *Disco Duck* (Rick Dees) WM: Rick Dees / *Disco Inferno* (The Trammps) WM: Leo Green and Ron Kersey / *How Deep Is Your Love?* (The Bee Gees); *If I Can't Have You* (Yvonne Elliman); *Jive Talkin'* (The Bee Gees); *K. Jee* (M.F.S.B.); *More Than a Woman* (Tavares); *Night Fever* (The Bee Gees); *Stayin' Alive* (The Bee Gees); *You Should Be Dancing* (The Bee Gees) WM: Barry Gibb, Maurice Gibb and Robin Gibb.

"Between original music by Barry, Robin and Maurice Gibb plus David Shire, and familiar Platter hits, the film usually has some rhythm going on in the background." —*Variety.*

**1100   Say It in French.** US, 1938, BW, 70 m. D: Andrew L. Stone, MD: Borris Morros, P: Paramount (Andrew L. Stone).

*April in My Heart* (Olympe Bradna) WM: Helen Meinard and Hoagy Carmichael.

**1101   Say It with Songs.** US, 1929, BW, 89 m. D: Lloyd Bacon, P: Warner. Performer: Al Jolson.

*Back in Your Own Back Yard* WM: Al Jolson, Billy Rose and Dave Dreyer / *I'm in Seventh Heaven* WM: Al Jolson, B.G. De Sylva, Lew Brown and Ray Henderson / *I'm Ka-razy for You* WM: Al Jolson, Billy Rose and Dave Dreyer / *Little Pal* WM: B.G. De Sylva, Lew Brown and Ray Henderson / *One Sweet Kiss* WM: Dave Dreyer and Al Jolson / *Used to You; Why Can't You?* WM: B.G. De Sylva, Lew Brown and Ray Henderson.

**1102   Say One for Me.** US, 1959, C, 119 m. D: Frank Tashlin, MD: Lionel Newman, P: TCF (Frank Tashlin). Vocal: Rosemary June for Judy Harriet.

*Chico's Choo-Choo* (Debbie Reynolds, Robert Wagner, Chorus); *The Girl Most Likely to Succeed* (Debbie Reynolds, Robert Wagner); *I Couldn't*

*Care Less* (Bing Crosby); *The Night That Rock and Roll Died, Almost* (Judy Harriet); *Say One for Me* (Bing Crosby, Debbie Reynolds); *The Secret of Christmas* (Bing Crosby, Chorus); *You Can't Love 'Em All* (Debbie Reynolds, Robert Wagner) W: Sammy Cahn—M: James Van Heusen.

**1103 Scared Stiff.** US, 1953, BW, 108 m. D: George Marshall, MD: Joseph J. Lilley, P: Paramount (Hal B. Wallis).

*I Don't Care If the Sun Don't Shine* (Dean Martin, Chorus) WM: Mack David / *Mama Yo Quiero* (Jerry Lewis with voice of Carmen Miranda) Eng. W: Al Stillman—Span. WM: Jararaca Paiva and Vincente Paiva / *San Domingo* (Dean Martin, Jerry Lewis, Carmen Miranda); *Song of the Enchilada Man* (Dean Martin, Jerry Lewis, Carmen Miranda); *When Someone Wonderful Thinks You're Wonderful* (Dean Martin) WM: Mack David and Jerry Livingston / *You Hit the Spot* (Dean Martin, Chorus) W: Mack Gordon— M: Harry Revel.

**1104 The Scarlet Hour.** US, 1955, BW, 95 m. D: Michael Curtiz, MS: Leith Stevens, P: Paramount (Michael Curtiz).

*Never Let Me Go* (Nat King Cole) WM: Jay Livingston and Ray Evans.

**1105 School Daze.** US, 1988, C, 114 m. D: Spike Lee, P: Columbia (Spike Lee, Monty Ross, Loretha C. Jones).

*Be Alone Tonight* (The Rays) WM: Raymond Jones / *Be One* (Phyllis Hyman) WM: Bill Lee / *Da'Butt* (E.U.) WM: Marcus Miller and Mark Stevens / *I Can Only Be Me* (Keith John) WM: Stevie Wonder / *I'm Building Me a Home* (The Morehouse College Glee Club) WM: Uzee Brown / *One Little Acorn* (Kenny Barron and Terrence Blanchard) WM: Bill Lee / *Perfect Match* (Tech and The EFFX) WM: Lenny White and Tina Harris / *Straight and Happy* (Jigaboos and Wannabees Chorus) WM: Bill Lee / *We've Already*

*Said Goodbye* (Pieces of a Dream) WM: Raymond Jones.

**1106 Scrooge.** GB, 1970, C, 118 m. D: Ronald Neame, MD: Ian Fraser, P: Cinema Center (Robert H. Solo).

*The Beautiful Day* (Richard Beaumont); *A Christmas Carol* (Albert Finney, Chorus); *Christmas Children* (David Collings, Richard Beaumont, Karen Scargill); *December the 25th* (Laurence Naismith, Chorus); *Father Christmas* (Children); *Happiness* (Suzanne Neve, Albert Finney); *I Hate People* (Albert Finney); *I Like Life* (Kenneth More, Albert Finney); *I'll Begin Again* (Albert Finney); *See the Phantoms* (Alec Guinness, Chorus); *Thank You Very Much* (Albert Finney, Anton Rodgers, Chorus); *You . . . You* (Albert Finney) WM: Leslie Bricusse.

**1107 Seaside Swingers.** GB, 1965, C, 94 m. D: James Hill, P: Embassy (Maurice J. Wilson, Ronald J. Kahn). GB Title: Every Day's a Holiday.

*All I Want Is You* (John Leyton); *A Boy Needs a Girl* (John Leyton, Grazina Frame) WM: Kenny Lynch and Clive Westlake / *Crazy Horse Saloon* (John Leyton) W: Jackie Rae—M: Tony Osborne / *Don't Do That to Me* (Freddie and The Dreamers) WM: Freddie Garrity / *What's Cookin'* (Freddie and The Dreamers) W: Jackie Rae—M: Tony Osborne.

**1108 Second Chorus.** US, 1940, BW, 83 m. D: Henry C. Potter, MS: Artie Shaw, P: Paramount (Boris Morros). Orch: Artie Shaw. Performer: Fred Astaire.

*I Ain't Hep to That Step But I'll Dig It* (Fred Astaire, Paulette Goddard, Chorus) M: Hal Borne / *Love of My Life* M: Artie Shaw / *Poor Mr. Chisholm* M: Bernie Hanighen. W: Johnny Mercer.

**1109 Second Fiddle.** US, 1939, BW, 86 m. D: Sidney Lanfield, MD: Louis Silvers, P: TCF (Gene Markey).

*Back to Back* (Mary Healy); *I'm*

*Sorry for Myself* (Mary Healy, Rudy Vallee); *I Poured My Heart into a Song* (Mary Healy, Tyrone Power, Rudy Vallee); *An Old Fashioned Tune Is Always New* (Rudy Vallee); *The Song of the Metronome* (Sonja Henie, Rudy Vallee, The Brian Sisters, Chorus); *When Winter Comes* (Rudy Vallee) WM: Irving Berlin.

"An indifferent Berlin score. . . . Rudy Vallee and Mary Healy do their best." —Frank S. Nugent, *The New York Times*.

**1110   The Secret Life of Walter Mitty.** US, 1947, C, 105 m. D: Norman Z. McLeod, MD: Emil Newman, MS: David Raksin, P: RKO (Samuel Goldwyn). Performer: Danny Kaye.

*Anatole; Symphony for Unstrung Tongue* WM: Sylvia Fine.

**1111   See Here, Private Hargrove.** US, 1944, BW, 100 m. D: Wesley Ruggles, MS: David Snell, P: MGM (George Haight).

*In My Arms* (Bob Crosby) W: Frank Loesser—M: Ted Grouya.

**1112   Send Me No Flowers.** US, 1964, C, 100 m. D: Norman Jewison, MD: Joseph Gershenson, MS: Frank DeVol, P: Universal (Harry Keller).

*Send Me No Flowers* (Doris Day) W: Hal David—M: Burt Bacharach.

**1113   Separate Tables.** US, 1958, BW, 99 m. D: Delbert Mann, MS: David Raksin, P: UA (Harold Hecht).

*Separate Tables* (Vic Damone) W: Harold Adamson—M: Harry Warren.

**1114   September Affair.** US, 1950, BW, 104 m. D: William Dieterle, MS: Victor Young, P: Paramount (Hal B. Wallis).

Maxwell Anderson and Kurt Weill wrote the memorable *September Song* for Walter Huston to sing in his role of Peter Stuyvesant in the less than successful Broadway musical of 1938 called 'Knickerbocker Holiday.' Charles Coburn sang it in the 1944 film version.

*September Song* (Walter Huston) W: Maxwell Anderson—M: Kurt Weill.

**1115   Serenade.** US, 1956, C, 121 m. D: Anthony Mann, MD: Ray Heindorf, P: Warner (Henry Blanke). Performer: Mario Lanza.

*Ave Maria* W: Sir Walter Scott— M: Franz Schubert / *My Destiny; Serenade* W: Sammy Cahn—M: Nicholas Brodszky.

**1116   Sgt. Pepper's Lonely Hearts Club Band.** US, 1978, C, 111 m. D: Michael Schultz, MD: George Martin, P: Universal (Robert Stigwood).

*Because* (Alice Cooper, The Bee Gees); *Being for the Benefit of Mr. Kite* (The Bee Gees, George Burns, Peter Frampton); *Carry That Weight* (The Bee Gees); *Come Together* (Aerosmith); *A Day in the Life* (The Bee Gees); *Fixing a Hole* (George Burns); *Get Back* (Billy Preston); *Getting Better* (The Bee Gees, Peter Frampton); *Golden Slumbers* (Peter Frampton); *Good Morning, Good Morning* (The Bee Gees, Peter Frampton, Paul Nicholas); *Got to Get You Into My Life* (Earth, Wind and Fire) WM: John Lennon and Paul McCartney / *Here Comes the Sun* (Sandy Farina) WM: George Harrison / *I Want You* (The Bee Gees, Paul Nicholas, Donald Pleasance, Stargard, Diane Steinberg); *The Long and Winding Road* (Peter Frampton); *Lucy in the Sky with Diamonds* (Stargard, Diane Steinberg); *Maxwell's Silver Hammer* (Steve Martin, Chorus); *Mean Mr. Mustard* (Frankie Howerd); *Nowhere Man* (The Bee Gees); *Oh! Darling* (Robin Gibb); *Polythene Pam* (The Bee Gees); *Sgt. Pepper's Lonely Hearts Club Band* The Bee Gees, Peter Frampton, Paul Nicholas, Chorus); *She Came in Through the Bathroom Window* (The Bee Gees, Peter Frampton); *She's Leaving Home* (The Bee Gees, Jay MacIntosh, John Wheeler); *Strawberry Fields Forever* (Sandy Farina); *When I'm Sixty-Four* (Frankie Howerd, Sandy Farina); *With a Little Help from My Friends* (The Bee Gees, Peter Frampton); *You Never Give Me Your Money* (Paul Nicholas, Diane

Steinberg) WM: John Lennon and Paul McCartney.

**1117 Seven Brides for Seven Brothers.** US, 1954, C, 103 m. D: Stanley Donen, MD: Adolph Deutsch, P: MGM (Jack Cummings). Vocals: Bill Lee for Matt Mattox.

*Bless Yore Beautiful Hide* (Howard Keel); *Goin' Co'tin'* (Jane Powell, Chorus); *June Bride* (Virginia Gibson, Chorus); *Lonesome Polecat* (Matt Mattox, Russ Tamblyn, Tommy Rall, Jeff Richards, Marc Platt, Jacques D'Amboise); *Sobbin' Women* (Howard Keel, Chorus); *Spring, Spring, Spring* (Chorus); *When You're in Love* (Jane Powell, Howard Keel); *Wonderful, Wonderful Day* (Jane Powell) W: Johnny Mercer—M: Gene de Paul.

"This is a happy, hand-clapping, foot-stomping country type of musical with all the slickness of a Broadway show. . . . Howard Keel's robust baritone and Jane Powell's lilting soprano make their songs extremely listenable." —*Variety.*

**1118 The Seven Hills of Rome.** US-Italy, 1958, C, 104 m. D: Roy Rowland, MD: George Stoll, P: MGM (Lester Welch). Performer: Mario Lanza.

*Arrivederci Roma* (Mario Lanza, Luisa Di Meo) WM: Carl Sigman and Renato Rascel / *Come Dance with Me* W: George Blake—M: Dick Leibert / *Jezebel* WM: Wayne Shanklin / *Lolita* WM: Buzzi-Peccia / *Memories Are Made of This* WM: Terry Gilkyson, Richard Dehr and Frank Miller / *The Seven Hills of Rome* W: Paul Francis Webster—M: Johnny Green / *Temptation* W: Arthur Freed—M: Nacio Herb Brown.

**1119 The Seven Little Foys.** US, 1955, C, 95 m. D: Melville Shavelson, MD: Joseph J. Lilley, P: Paramount (Jack Rose). Vocal: Viola Vonn for Milly Vitale. Performers: Bob Hope; 7 Children [Jimmy Baird, Linda Bennett, Paul De Rolf, Tommy Duran, Lee Erickson, Billy Gray, Lydia Reed].

*Chinatown, My Chinatown* W: William Jerome—M: Jean Schwartz / *I'm the Greatest Father of Them All* WM: William Jerome, Eddie Foy and Joseph J. Lilley / *I'm Tired* W: William Jerome—M: Jean Schwartz / *Mary's a Grand Old Name* (James Cagney, Bob Hope) WM: George M. Cohan / *Nobody* (Bob Hope, Milly Vitale) W: Alex Rogers—M: Bert Williams / *Row, Row, Row* W: William Jerome—M: James V. Monaco / *The Yankee Doodle Boy* (James Cagney, Bob Hope) WM: George M. Cohan.

**1120 Seven Sinners.** US, 1940, BW, 87 m. D: Tay Garnett, MD: Charles Previn, MS: Frank Skinner, P: Universal (Joe Pasternak). Performer: Marlene Dietrich. GB Title: Cafe of the Seven Sinners.

*I Can't Give You Anything But Love, Baby* W: Dorothy Fields—M: Jimmy McHugh / *I Fall Overboard; I've Been in Love Before; The Man's in the Navy* W: Frank Loesser—M: Frederick Hollander.

"She sings . . . in her . . . husky, smoke-seared voice." —Bosley Crowther, *The New York Times.*

**1121 1776.** US, 1972, C, 141 m. D: Peter H. Hunt, MD: Ray Heindorf, P: Columbia (Jack L. Warner).

*But, Mr. Adams* (William Daniels, Howard Da Silva, Rex Robbins, John Myhers); *The Egg* (William Daniels, Howard Da Silva, Ken Howard); *He Plays the Violin* (Blythe Danner, William Daniels, Howard Da Silva); *Is Anybody There?* (William Daniels); *The Lees of Old Virginia* (William Daniels, Howard Da Silva, Ronald Holgate); *Molasses to Rum* (John Cullum); *Momma Look Sharp* (Stephen Nathan, William Duell, Mark Montgomery); *Piddle, Twiddle and Resolve* (William Daniels); *Sit Down, John* (William Daniels, Chorus); *Till Then* (William Daniels, Virginia Vestoff); *Yours, Yours, Yours* (William Daniels, Virginia Vestoff) WM: Sherman Edwards.

**1122 Seventh Heaven.** US, 1937, BW, 102 m. D: Henry King, MS: Louis Silvers, P: TCF (Raymond Griffith).

*Seventh Heaven* (Chorus) W: Sidney D. Mitchell—M: Lew Pollack.

**1123 Shaft.** US, 1971, C, 100 m. D: Gordon Parks, MS: Isaac Hayes, P: MGM (Joel Freeman).

*Theme from Shaft* (Isaac Hayes, The Bar-Kays and Movement) WM: Isaac Hayes.

**1124 Shaft in Africa.** US, 1973, C, 112 m. D: John Guillermin, MS: Johnny Pate, P: MGM (Roger Lewis).

*Are You Man Enough?* (The Four Tops) WM: Dennis Lambert and Brian Potter.

**1125 The Shaggy D.A.** US, 1976, C, 91 m. D: Robert Stevenson, MS: Buddy Baker, P: Walt Disney (Ron Miller).

*The Shaggy D.A.* (Dean Jones) WM: Norman Buddy Baker.

**1126 Shake, Rattle and Rock!** US, 1956, BW, 78 m. D: Edward L. Cahn, MS: Alexander Courage, P: AIP (James H. Nicholson).

*Ain't That a Shame* (Fats Domino) WM: Antoine "Fats" Domino and Dave Bartholomew / *Feelin' Happy* (Joe Turner) WM: Joe Turner / *Honey Chile* (Fats Domino); *I'm in Love Again* (Fats Domino) WM: Antoine "Fats" Domino and Dave Bartholomew / *Lipstick, Powder and Paint* (Joe Turner) WM: Joe Turner / *Rockin' on Saturday Night* (Annita Ray, Tommy Charles) WM: George Matola and Johnny Lehman / *Sweet Love on My Mind* (Annita Ray, Tommy Charles).

**1127 Shall We Dance.** US, 1937, BW, 116 m. D: Mark Sandrich, MD: Nathaniel Shilkret, P: RKO (Pandro S. Berman).

*They Can't Take That Away from Me* was the only Gershwin song ever nominated for an Academy Award. It lost to *Sweet Leilani* by Harry Owens.

*Beginner's Luck* (Fred Astaire); *Let's Call the Whole Thing Off* (Fred Astaire, Ginger Rogers); *Shall We Dance* (Fred Astaire); *Slap That Bass* (Fred Astaire, Unbilled Singers); *They All Laughed* (Fred Astaire, Ginger Rogers); *They Can't Take That Away from Me* (Fred Astaire) W: Ira Gershwin—M: George Gershwin.

"A zestful, prancing, sophisticated musical show. It has a grand score." — Frank Nugent, *The New York Times*.

"All six songs . . . have been nicely spotted with no attempt to overplay any of them. Nor is there a bad ditty in the batch." — *Variety*.

**1128 Shampoo.** US, 1975, C, 110 m. D: Hal Ashby, MS: Paul Simon, P: Columbia (Warren Beatty).

*Strawberry Fields Forever* (The Beatles) WM: John Lennon and Paul McCartney / *Wouldn't It Be Nice* (The Beach Boys) WM: Tony Asher and Brian Wilson.

**1129 She Done Him Wrong.** US, 1933, BW, 66 m. D: Lowell Sherman, P: Paramount (William LeBaron). Performer: Mae West.

*Easy Rider* WM: Shelton Brooks / *Frankie and Johnny* WM: Unknown / *A Guy What Takes His Time* WM: Ralph Rainger / *Silver Threads Among the Gold* W: Eben E. Rexford—M: Hart Pease Danks.

**1130 She Loves Me Not.** US, 1934, BW, 83 m. D: Elliott Nugent, P: Paramount (Benjamin Glazer).

*After All, You're All I'm After* (Bing Crosby) W: Edward Heyman—M: Arthur Schwartz / *I'm Hummin'— I'm Whistlin'— I'm Singin'* (Bing Crosby) W: Mack Gordon—M: Harry Revel / *Love in Bloom* (Bing Crosby, Kitty Carlisle) W: Leo Robin—M: Ralph Rainger / *Put a Little Rhythm in Everything You Do* (Miriam Hopkins); *Straight from the Shoulder* (Bing Crosby, Kitty Carlisle) W: Mack Gordon—M: Harry Revel.

**1131 She's Having a Baby.** US, 1988, C, 106 m. D: John Hughes, P: Paramount (John Hughes).

*Apron Strings* (Everything But the

Girl) WM: Ben Wat and Tracey Thorn / *Crazy Love* (Bryan Ferry) WM: Van Morrison / *Desire* (Gene Loves Jezebel) WM: Jay Aston / *Full of Love* (Dr. Calculus) WM: Stephen Duffy / *Happy Families* (XTC) WM: Andy Partridge / *Haunted When the Minutes Drag* (Love and Rockets) WM: David J., Daniel Ash and Kevin Haskins / *It's All in the Game* (Carmel) WM: Carl Sigman and Charles G. Dawes / *She's Having a Baby* (Dave Wakeling) WM: Dave Wakeling and Ian Ritchie / *This Woman's Work* (Kate Bush) WM: Kate Bush / *You Just Haven't Earned It Yet Baby* (Kirsty MacColl) WM: Steven Morrissey and Johnny Marr.

"The pop-music soundtrack . . . is as lighthearted as the comedy is leaden." —Janet Maslin, *The New York Times.*

**1132  Ship Ahoy.** US, 1942, BW, 95 m. D: Edward Buzzell, MD: George Stoll, P: MGM (Jack Cummings). Orch: Tommy Dorsey. MB: The Pied Pipers.

In 1939, eight Pied Pipers joined the Tommy Dorsey band. Dorsey cut this number to four: Jo Stafford, John Huddleston, Chuck Lowry and Allen Storr.

*I'll Take Tallulah* (Eleanor Powell, Red Skelton, Bert Lahr) W: E.Y. Harburg—M: Burton Lane / *Last Call for Love* (Frank Sinatra, Connie Haines) WM: E.Y. Harburg, Margery Cummings and Burton Lane / *Moonlight Bay* (Frank Sinatra) W: Edward Madden—M: Percy Wenrich / *Poor You* (Frank Sinatra, Virginia O'Brien, Red Skelton) W: E.Y. Harburg—M: Burton Lane.

"Metro has provided a moderate and tuneful little cruise." —Bosley Crowther, *The New York Times.*

**1133  Shipmates Forever.** US, 1935, BW, 124 m. D: Frank Borzage, P: Warner/First National. Performer: Dick Powell.

*Abdul Abulbul Amir* WM: Frank Crumit / *Don't Give Up the Ship; I'd Love to Take Orders from You* (Dick Powell, Ruby Keeler); *I'd Rather Listen to Your Eyes* W: Al Dubin—M: Harry Warren.

**1134  Shipyard Sally.** GB, 1939, BW, 79 m. D: Monty Banks, MD: Louis Levy, P: TCF (Robert T. Kane). Performer: Gracie Fields.

*Danny Boy* WM: Frederick Edward Weatherly / *Grandfather's Bagpipes* WM: Will Haines and Jimmy Harper / *I've Got the Jitterbugs* / *Wish Me Luck As You Wave Me Goodbye* WM: Harry Parr-Davies and Phil Park.

**1135  The Shocking Miss Pilgrim.** US, 1947, C, 85 m. D: George Seaton, MD: Alfred Newman, P: TCF (William Perlberg).

For this movie, Ira Gershwin put lyrics to unpublished music left by his brother George at his death ten years earlier.

*Aren't You Kind of Glad We Did?* (Betty Grable, Dick Haymes); *The Back Bay Polka* (Betty Grable, Elizabeth Patterson, Allyn Joslyn, Charles Kemper, Lillian Bronson, Arthur Shields); *Changing My Tune* (Betty Grable); *For You, For Me, For Evermore* (Betty Grable, Dick Haymes); *One, Two, Three* (Dick Haymes, Chorus); *Stand Up and Fight* (Chorus); *Sweet Packard* (Chorus); *Waltzing Is Better Sitting Down* (Betty Grable, Dick Haymes) W: Ira Gershwin—M: George Gershwin.

"The bulk of the music is as sticky as toothpaste being squeezed out of a tube." —Bosley Crowther, *The New York Times.*

**1136  Shoot the Moon.** US, 1982, C, 123 m. D: Alan Parker, P: MGM (Alan Marshall).

*All I Have to Do Is Dream* (Juice Newton) WM: Boudleaux Bryant.

**1137  Show Boat.** US, 1936, BW, 113 m. D: James Whale, MD: Victor Baravalle, P: Universal (Carl Laemmle, Jr.).

*After the Ball* (Irene Dunne, Chorus) WM: Charles K. Harris / *Bill* (Helen Morgan) W: P.G. Wodehouse and Oscar Hammerstein II—M: Jerome Kern / *Can't Help Lovin' Dat Man* (Helen Morgan, Irene Dunne, Hattie McDaniel, Paul Robeson, Chorus); *Cotton Blossom* (Chorus); *Gallivantin' Around* (Irene Dunne) W: Oscar Hammerstein II—M: Jerome Kern / *Goodbye, My Lady Love* (Queenie Smith, Sammy White) WM: Joseph E. Howard / *I Have the Room Above* (Irene Dunne, Allan Jones); *I Still Suits Me* (Hattie McDaniel, Paul Robeson); *Ol' Man River* (Paul Robeson, Chorus); *Only Make Believe* (Irene Dunne, Allan Jones); *Where's the Mate for Me?* (Allan Jones); *You Are Love* (Irene Dunne, Allan Jones) W: Oscar Hammerstein II—M: Jerome Kern.

"'Show Boat,' Universal's second talkerized version, is a smash filmusical. . . . Robeson's *Ol' Man River* is perhaps the single song highlight." —*Variety*.

"There are melodies that are timeless and voices that should be, and Universal's 'Show Boat' has them both." —Frank S. Nugent, *The New York Times*.

**1138   Show Boat.** US, 1951, C, 107 m. D: George Sidney, MD: Adolph Deutsch, P: MGM (Arthur Freed). Vocals: Annette Warren for Ava Gardner.

*After the Ball* (Kathryn Grayson, Chorus) WM: Charles K. Harris / *Bill* (Ava Gardner) W: P.G. Wodehouse and Oscar Hammerstein II—M: Jerome Kern / *Can't Help Lovin' Dat Man* (Kathryn Grayson, Ava Gardner); *Cotton Blossom* (Chorus); *I Might Fall Back on You* (Marge and Gower Champion); *Life Upon the Wicked Stage* (Marge and Gower Champion); *Ol' Man River* (William Warfield); *Only Make Believe* (Kathryn Grayson, Howard Keel); *Where's the Mate for Me?* (Howard Keel); *Why Do I Love You?* (Kathryn Grayson, Howard Keel); *You Are Love* (Kathryn Grayson, Howard Keel) W: Oscar Hammerstein II—M: Jerome Kern.

"'Show Boat' has never reached the screen . . . in anything like the visual splendor and richness of musical score as are tastefully brought together in this brilliant re-creation of the show." —Bosley Crowther, *The New York Times*.

**1139   Show Business.** US, 1944, BW, 92 m. D: Edwin L. Marin, MD: Constantin Bakaleinikoff, MS: George Duning, P: RKO (Eddie Cantor).

*Alabamy Bound* (Eddie Cantor) W: B.G. De Sylva and Bud Green—M: Ray Henderson / *The Curse of an Aching Heart* (Eddie Cantor) W: Henry Fink—M: Al Piantadosi / *The Daughter of Rosie O'Grady* (Pat Rooney) W: Monty C. Brice—M: Walter Donaldson / *Dinah* (Eddie Cantor, George Murphy, Constance Moore, Joan Davis) W: Sam M. Lewis and Joe Young—M: Harry Akst / *I Don't Want to Get Well* (Eddie Cantor, George Murphy) W: Howard Johnson and Harry Pease—M: Harry Jentes / *It Had to Be You* (Eddie Cantor, George Murphy, Constance Moore) W: Gus Kahn—M: Isham Jones / *I Want a Girl Just Like the Girl That Married Dear Old Dad* (Eddie Cantor, George Murphy, Constance Moore, Joan Davis) W: William Dillon—M: Harry von Tilzer / *Makin' Whoopee* (Eddie Cantor) W: Gus Kahn—M: Walter Donaldson / *They're Wearing 'Em Higher in Hawaii* (Eddie Cantor, George Murphy) W: Joe Goodwin—M: Halsey K. Mohr / *While Strolling Through the Park One Day* (Eddie Cantor, George Murphy, Constance Moore, Joan Davis) WM: Ed Haley and Robert A. Keiser / *You May Not Remember* (Nancy Kelly) WM: George Jessel and Ben Oakland.

**1140   The Show of Shows.** US, 1929, BW/C, 128 m. D: John G. Adolfi, P: Warner (Darryl F. Zanuck). Orch: Ted Lewis.

*If I Could Learn to Love* (Georges Carpentier, Alice White, Patsy Ruth Miller) W: Herman Ruby—M: M.K. Jerome / *Just an Hour of Love* (Irene Bordoni) W: Alfred Bryan—M: Edward

Ward / *Lady Luck* (Alexander Gray, Chorus) WM: Ray Perkins / *Li-Po-Li* (Nick Lucas, Myrna Loy) W: Alfred Bryan—M: Edward Ward / *The Only Song I Know* (Nick Lucas) W: J. Keirn Brennan—M: Ray Perkins / *Pingo Pongo* (Winnie Lightner) W: Al Dubin—M: Joe Burke / *Rock-a-Bye Your Baby with a Dixie Melody* (Sid Silvers) W: Sam M. Lewis and Joe Young—M: Jean Schwartz / *Singin' in the Bathtub* (Winnie Lightner) WM: Herb Magidson, Ned Washington and Michael H. Cleary / *Your Love Is All That I Crave* (Frank Fay) WM: Al Dubin, Perry Bradford and James P. Johnson / *Your Mother and Mine* (Beatrice Lillie, Frank Fay, Louise Fazenda, Lloyd Hamilton) W: Joe Goodwin—M: Gus Edwards / *You Were Meant for Me* (Winnie Lightner, Bull Montana) W: Arthur Freed—M: Nacio Herb Brown.

**1141 Sign O' the Times.** US, 1987, C, 85 m. D: Prince, P: Cineplex Odeon (Robert Cavallo, Joseph Ruffalo, Steven Fargnoli). Performer: Prince.

*Adore; The Ballad of Dorothy Parker; The Cross; Forever in My Life; Hot Thing; Housequake; If I Could Take the Place of Your Man; If I Was Your Girlfriend; It* WM: Prince Rogers Nelson / *It's Gonna Be a Beautiful Night* WM: Prince Rogers Nelson, Dr. Fink and Eric Leeds / *Play in the Sunshine; Sign O' the Times* WM: Prince Rogers Nelson / *Slow Love* WM: Prince Rogers Nelson and Carol Davis / *Starfish and Coffee* WM: Prince Rogers Nelson and Susannah / *Strange Relationship; U Got the Look* (Sheena Easton, Prince) WM: Prince Rogers Nelson.

**1142 The Silencers.** US, 1966, C, 102 m. D: Phil Karlson, MS: Elmer Bernstein, P: Columbia (Irving Allen). Performer: Dean Martin.

*Empty Saddles; The Glory of Love* WM: Billy Hill / *If You Knew Susie* WM: B.G. De Sylva and Joseph Meyer / *The Last Roundup* WM: Billy Hill / *On the Sunny Side of the Street* W: Dorothy Fields—M: Jimmy McHugh / *Red Sails*

*in the Sunset* W: Jimmy Kennedy—M: Hugh Williams / *Side By Side* WM: Harry M. Woods / *The Silencers* (Cyd Charisse, Dean Martin, Vicci Carr) W: Mack David—M: Elmer Bernstein / *South of the Border* WM: Jimmy Kennedy and Michael Carr.

**1143 Silent Running.** US, 1971, C, 89 m. D: Douglas Trumbull, MS: Peter Schickele, P: Universal (Michel Gruskoff, Douglas Trumbull). Performer: Joan Baez.

*Rejoice in the Sun; Silent Running* W: Diane Lampert—M: Peter Schickele.

**1144 Silk Stockings.** US, 1957, C, 117 m. D: Rouben Mamoulian, MD: Andre Previn, P: MGM (Arthur Freed). Vocals: Carol Richards for Cyd Charisse.

*All of You* (Fred Astaire); *Fated to Be Mated* (Fred Astaire, Cyd Charisse); *It's a Chemical Reaction, That's All* (Fred Astaire, Cyd Charisse); *Josephine* (Janis Paige); *Paris Loves Lovers* (Fred Astaire, Cyd Charisse); *Red Blues* (Chorus); *The Ritz Roll and Rock* (Fred Astaire); *Satin and Silk* (Janis Paige); *Siberia* (Peter Lorre, Joseph Buloff, Jules Munshin); *Stereophonic Sound* (Fred Astaire, Janis Paige); *Too Bad* (Peter Lorre, Joseph Buloff, Jules Munshin, Fred Astaire); *Without Love* (Fred Astaire, Cyd Charisse) WM: Cole Porter.

"A top-grade musical version of Metro's 1939 'Ninotchka'." —*Variety.*

"An all-round refreshing show. ... The songs are the ones from the stage [1955], those wonderful Cole Porter ditties." —Bosley Crowther, *The New York Times.*

**1145 Sing and Be Happy.** US, 1937, BW, 67 m. D: James Tinling, MD: Samuel Kaylin, P: TCF (Milton H. Feld). Performer: Tony Martin.

*Sing and Be Happy; Travelin' Light; What a Beautiful Beginning* W: Sidney Clare—M: Harry Akst.

**1146 Sing As We Go.** GB, 1934, BW, 80 m. D: Basil Dean, P:

ATP (Basil Dean). Performer: Gracie Fields.

*In My Little Bottom Drawer* WM: Will Haines, Jimmy Harper and Maurice Beresford / *Sing As We Go* WM: Harry Parr-Davies and Gracie Fields.

**1147  Sing, Baby, Sing.** US, 1936, BW, 87 m. D: Sidney Lanfield, MD: Louis Silvers, P: TCF (Darryl F. Zanuck).

*Love Will Tell* (Alice Faye) W: Jack Yellen—M: Lew Pollack / *The Music Goes 'Round and 'Round* (The Ritz Brothers) W: Red Hodgson—M: Edward Farley and Michael Riley / *Sing, Baby, Sing* (Alice Faye) W: Jack Yellen—M: Lew Pollack / *Singing a Vagabond Song* (The Ritz Brothers) WM: Sam Messenheimer, Val Burton and Harry Richman / *When Did You Leave Heaven?* (Tony Martin) W: Walter Bullock—M: Richard A. Whiting / *When My Baby Smiles at Me* (The Ritz Brothers) W: Andrew B. Sterling and Ted Lewis—M: Bill Munro / *You Turned the Tables on Me* (Alice Faye) W: Sidney D. Mitchell—M: Louis Alter.

"The songs . . . are fairly well-known by this time, courtesy of the radio companies, but . . . Alice Faye sings them well." —Frank S. Nugent, *The New York Times.*

**1148  Sing, Boy, Sing.** US, 1958, BW, 90 m. D: Henry Ephron, MS: Lionel Newman, P: TCF (Henry Ephron). Performer: Tommy Sands.

*A Bundle of Dreams* WM: Homer Escamilla and Billy Strange / *Crazy 'Cause I Love You* WM: Spade Cooley / *I'm Gonna Walk and Talk with My Lord* WM: Martha Carson / *Just a Little Bit More* WM: Rose Marie McCoy and Charles Singleton / *People in Love* W: Leven—M: Lionel Newman / *Rock of Ages* WM: Unknown / *Sing, Boy, Sing* WM: Tommy Sands and Rod McKuen / *Soda-Pop Pop* WM: Betty and Darla Daret / *Teen Age Crush* WM: Audrey Allison and Joe Allison / *That's All I Want from You* WM: M. Rotha / *Who*

*Baby* WM: Jeanne Carroll and Billy Olofson / *Would I Love You* W: Bob Russell—M: Harold Spina / *Your Daddy Wants to Do Right* WM: Tommy Sands.

"He sings a fine, quiet *Rock of Ages* near the end . . . the slower ballads are nice and mellow." —Howard Thompson, *The New York Times.*

**1149  Sing Me a Love Song.** US, 1936, BW, 78 m. D: Ray Enright, MD: Leo F. Forbstein, P: Warner/First National (Sam Bischoff). Performer: James Melton. GB Title: Come Up Smiling.

*The Little House That Love Built; Summer Night; That's the Least You Can Do for the Lady* W: Al Dubin—M: Harry Warren / *Your Eyes Have Told Me So* W: Gus Kahn and Egbert Van Alstyne—M: Walter Blaufuss.

**1150  Sing, You Sinners.** US, 1938, BW, 88 m. D: Wesley Ruggles, MD: Boris Morros, P: Paramount (Wesley Ruggles).

*Don't Let That Moon Get Away* (Bing Crosby); *I've Got a Pocketful of Dreams* (Bing Crosby, Fred MacMurray, Donald O'Connor); *Laugh and Call It Love* (Bing Crosby) W: Johnny Burke—M: James V. Monaco / *Small Fry* (Bing Crosby, Fred MacMurray, Donald O'Connor) W: Frank Loesser—M: Hoagy Carmichael / *Where Is Central Park?* (Bing Crosby, Fred MacMurray, Donald O'Connor) W: Johnny Burke—M: James V. Monaco.

**1151  Singin' in the Rain.** US, 1952, C, 102 m. D: Gene Kelly and Stanley Donen, MD: Lennie Hayton, P: MGM (Arthur Freed).

*All I Do Is Dream of You* (Debbie Reynolds, Gene Kelly); *Beautiful Girl* (Jimmy Thompson, Chorus); *The Broadway Melody* (Gene Kelly); *Broadway Rhythm* (Gene Kelly, Chorus) W: Arthur Freed—M: Nacio Herb Brown / *Fit As a Fiddle* (Gene Kelly, Donald O'Connor) W: Arthur Freed—M: Al Hoffman and Al Goodhart / *Good Morning* (Debbie Reynolds, Gene Kelly,

Donald O'Connor); *I've Got a Feelin' You're Foolin'* (Chorus); *Make 'Em Laugh* (Donald O'Connor) W: Arthur Freed—M: Nacio Herb Brown / *Moses* (Gene Kelly, Donald O'Connor) WM: Betty Comden, Adolph Green and Roger Edens / *Should I?* (Wilson Wood); *Singin' in the Rain* (Debbie Reynolds, Gene Kelly, Donald O'Connor); *The Wedding of the Painted Doll* (Chorus); *Would You?* (Debbie Reynolds [Voice of Betty Royce]); *You Are My Lucky Star* (Debbie Reynolds, Gene Kelly); *You Were Meant for Me* (Gene Kelly) W: Arthur Freed M: Nacio Herb Brown.

"O'Connor has the film's highspot with a solo number, *Make 'Em Laugh.*" — *Variety.*

"A lot of room is made for singing and dancing in the liveliest Kelly-cum-all style. . . . But by far his most captivating number is done to the title song—a beautifully soggy tapdance performed in the splashing rain." — Bosley Crowther, *The New York Times.*

**1152 The Singing Fool.** US, 1928, BW, 110 m. D: Lloyd Bacon, P: Warner (Darryl F. Zanuck). Performer: Al Jolson.

*Golden Gate* WM: Billy Rose, Dave Dreyer, Al Jolson and Joseph Meyer / *I'm Sitting on Top of the World* W: Sam M. Lewis and Joe Young—M: Ray Henderson / *It All Depends on You* W: B.G. De Sylva and Lew Brown—M: Ray Henderson / *Keep Smiling at Trouble* W: Al Jolson and B.G. De Sylva—M: Lewis E. Gensler / *Sonny Boy* W: Al Jolson, B.G. De Sylva and Lew Brown—M: Ray Henderson / *The Spaniard That Blighted My Life* WM: Billy Merson / *There's a Rainbow 'Round My Shoulder* WM: Billy Rose, Dave Dreyer and Al Jolson.

"Al Jolson sat in a comfortable seat in the Winter Garden last night and watched his shadow work on the screen in the same theatre where he had so often won the hearts of the audience by his songs from the stage. . . . and like others realized that this audible picture was a capital entertainment. The price for orchestra seats for this first performance was $11. The tickets were of gilded cardboard with a drawing of Mr. Jolson as he is and then in black face." —Mordaunt Hall, *The New York Times.*

**1153 The Singing Kid.** US, 1936, BW, 85 m. D: William Keighley, MD: Leo F. Forbstein, P: Warner (Robert Lord). Orch: Cab Calloway. MB: The Four Yacht Club Boys. Performer: Al Jolson.

Jolson's last starring role in a film.

*About a Quarter to Nine* W: Al Dubin—M: Harry Warren / *April Showers* W: B.G. De Sylva—M: Louis Silvers / *California, Here I Come* W: Al Jolson and B.G. De Sylva—M: Joseph Meyer / *Here's Looking at You; I Love to Sing-A* (Al Jolson, Cab Calloway) W: E.Y. Harburg—M: Harold Arlen / *My Mammy* W: Sam M. Lewis and Joe Young—M: Walter Donaldson / *Save Me, Sister* (Al Jolson, Cab Calloway, Wini Shaw) W: E.Y. Harburg—M: Harold Arlen / *Sonny Boy* W: Al Jolson, B.G. De Sylva and Lew Brown—M: Ray Henderson / *Swanee* W: Irving Caesar—M: George Gershwin / *Who's the Swingin'est Man in Town? / You're the Cure for What Ails Me* (Al Jolson, Sybil Jason, Edward Everett Horton, Allen Jenkins) W: E.Y. Harburg —M: Harold Arlen.

**1154 The Singing Marine.** US, 1937, BW, 107 m. D: Ray Enright, P: Warner (Louis F. Edelman). Performer: Dick Powell.

*'Cause My Baby Says It's So; I Know Now* (Dick Powell, Doris Weston); *The Lady Who Couldn't Be Kissed* (Lee Dixon) W: Al Dubin / *Night Over Shanghai* W: Johnny Mercer / *The Song of the Marines; You Can't Run Away from Love Tonight* W: Al Dubin. M: Harry Warren.

**1155 The Singing Nun.** US, 1966, C, 98 m. D: Henry Koster, MD: Harry Sukman, P: MGM (Jon Beck). MB: Chorus. Performer: Debbie Reynolds.

*Alleluia; Avec Toi; Beyond the Stars; Brother John; Dominique; It's a Miracle; Je Voudrais; Mets Ton Joli Jupon; A Pied Piper's Song; Raindrops; Sister Adele* WM: Randy Sparks and Soeur Sourire.

"Debbie Reynolds expertly warbles ... to her own guitar accompaniment." *—Variety*.

**1156   Situation Hopeless—But Not Serious.** US, 1965, BW, 97 m. D: Gottfried Reinhardt, MS: Harold Byrne, P: Paramount (Gottfried Reinhardt).

*Wooden Heart* (Robert Redford) WM: Fred Wise, Ben Weisman, Kay Twomey and Berthold Kaempfert.

**1157   Skatetown, U.S.A..** US, 1979, C, 98 m. D: William A. Levey, P: Columbia (William A. Levey, Lorin Dreyfuss).

*Boogie Nights* (Heat Wave) WM: Rod Temperton / *Boogie Wonderland* (Earth, Wind and Fire, with The Emotions) W: Allee Willis—M: Jonathan Lind / *Born to Be Alive* (Patrick Hernandez) WM: Patrick Hernandez / *Feelin' Alright* (Dave Mason); *I Fell in Love* (Dave Mason) WM: Dave Mason / *Perfect Dancer* (Marilyn McCoo, Billy Davis, Jr.) WM: Dennis Lambert and Brian Potter / *Roller Girl* (John Sebastian) WM: John B. Sebastian / *Shake Your Body* (The Jacksons) WM: Michael Jackson and Stephen Jackson / *Skatetown, USA* (Dave Mason) WM: Dave Mason and B. Cooper / *Under My Thumb* (Hounds) WM: Mick Jagger and Keith Richard.

**1158   Ski Party.** US, 1965, C, 90 m. D: Alan Rafkin, MS: Gary Usher, P: AIP (Gene Corman).

*The Gasser* (The Hondells) / *I Got You* (James Brown and The Famous Flames) WM: James Brown / *Lots Lots More* (Frankie Avalon) WM: Ritchie Adams and Larry Kusik / *Painting the Town* (Frankie Avalon) WM: Bob Gaudio / *Ski Party* (The Hondells) WM: Gary Usher and Roger Christian / *Sunshine, Lollipops and Rainbows*

(Lesley Gore) W: Howard Liebling— M: Marvin Hamlisch / *We'll Never Change Them* (Deborah Walley) WM: Guy Hemric and Jerry Styner.

**1159   Skirts Ahoy.** US, 1952, C, 109 m. D: Sidney Lanfield, MD: George Stoll, P: MGM (Joe Pasternak). MB: The De Marco Sisters.

*Glad to Have You Aboard* (Esther Williams); *Hold Me Close to You* (Billy Eckstine) W: Ralph Blane—M: Harry Warren / *Oh, By Jingo, Oh By Gee* (Debbie Reynolds, Bobby Van) WM: Lew Brown and Albert von Tilzer / *What Good Is a Gal Without a Guy?* (Esther Williams, Joan Evans, Vivian Blaine); *What Makes a Wave?* (Esther Williams) W: Ralph Blane—M: Harry Warren.

**1160   The Sky's the Limit.** US, 1943, BW, 89 m. D: Edward H. Griffith, MD: Leo F. Forbstein, MS: Leigh Harline, P: RKO (David Hempstead). Vocals: Sally Sweetland for Joan Leslie.

*A Lot in Common with You* (Fred Astaire, Joan Leslie); *My Shining Hour* (Fred Astaire, Joan Leslie); *One for My Baby* (Fred Astaire) W: Johnny Mercer —M: Harold Arlen.

"RKO has done little to pad it with presentable dances and songs." —Bosley Crowther, *The New York Times*.

**1161   Slap Shot.** US, 1977, C, 122 m. D: George Roy Hill, MD: Elmer Bernstein, P: Universal (Robert J. Wunsch, Stephen Friedman).

*Rhiannon* (Fleetwood Mac) WM: Stevie Nicks / *Right Back Where We Started From* (Maxine Nightingale) WM: Pierre Tubbs and Vincent Edwards / *Say You Love Me* (Fleetwood Mac) WM: Christine McVie / *Sorry Seems to Be the Hardest Word* (Elton John) WM: Elton John and Bernie Taupin / *You Make Me Feel Like Dancing* (Leo Sayer) WM: Leo Sayer and Vini Poncia.

**1162   Sleepytime Gal.** US, 1942, BW, 84 m. D: Albert S. Rogell, MD: Cy Feuer, P: Republic (Albert J.

Cohen). Orch: Skinnay Ennis. Performer: Judy Canova.

*Barrelhouse Bessie from Basin Street; I Don't Want Nobody At All* W: Herb Magidson—M: Jule Styne / *Sleepytime Gal* W: Joseph R. Alden and Raymond B. Egan—M: Ange Lorenzo and Richard A. Whiting / *When the Cat's Away* W: Herb Magidson—M: Jule Styne.

**1163  Slightly Honorable.** US, 1940, BW, 83 m. D: Tay Garnett, MS: Werner Janssen, P: UA (Tay Garnett).

*We've Got Love* (Ruth Terry) W: George R. Brown—M: Jule Styne.

**1164  The Slipper and the Rose.** GB, 1976, C, 128 m. D: Bryan Forbes, MD: Angela Morley, P: Universal (David Frost, Stuart Lyons).

*A Bride Finding Ball* (Richard Chamberlain, Julian Orchard); *Once I Was Loved* (Gemma Craven); *Position and Positioning* (Christopher Gable, John Turner, Chorus); *Protocoligorically Correct* (Michael Hordern, Kenneth More, Peter Graves, Chorus); *Secret Kingdom* (Richard Chamberlain, Gemma Craven); *The Slipper and the Rose Waltz* (Richard Chamberlain, Gemma Craven); *Suddenly It Happens* (Annette Crosbie, Gemma Craven, Chorus); *Tell Him Anything* (Gemma Craven); *What a Comforting Thing to Know* (Richard Chamberlain, Christopher Gable); *Why Can't I Be Two People?* (Richard Chamberlain) WM: Richard M. Sherman and Robert B. Sherman.

**1165  Slow Dancing in the Big City.** US, 1978, C, 101 m. D: John G. Avildsen, MS: Bill Conti, P: UA (Michael Levee, John G. Avildsen).

*I Feel the Earth Move* (Carole King) WM: Carole King.

**1166  Small Town Girl.** US, 1953, C, 93 m. D: Leslie Kardos, MD: Andre Previn, P: MGM (Joe Pasternak).

*The Fellow I'd Follow* (Jane Powell); *Fine Fine Fine* (Jane Powell, Bobby Van); *I've Gotta Hear That Beat* (Ann Miller); *The Lullaby of the Lord* (Jane Powell, Chorus); *My Flaming Heart* (Nat King Cole); *My Gaucho* (Chorus); *Small Towns Are Smile Towns* (Jane Powell); *Take Me to Broadway* (Bobby Van) W: Leo Robin—M: Nicholas Brodszky.

"It is the spotlighting of young Bobby Van in a song-dance-comedy spot that impresses the most." —*Variety*.

**1167  Smash-Up—The Story of a Woman.** US, 1947, BW, 103 m. D: Stuart Heisler, MS: Daniele Amfitheatrof, P: Universal (Walter Wanger). Vocals: Peg LaCentra for Susan Hayward; Hal Derwin for Lee Bowman. GB Title: A Woman Destroyed.

*Hush-a-Bye Island* (Susan Hayward, Lee Bowman); *I Miss That Feeling* (Susan Hayward); *Life Can Be Beautiful* (Susan Hayward, Eddie Albert) W: Harold Adamson—M: Jimmy McHugh.

**1168  Smilin' Through.** US, 1941, C, 100 m. D: Frank Borzage, MS: Herbert Stothart, P: MGM (Victor Saville). MB: Chorus. Performer: Jeanette MacDonald.

The first version was a silent starring Norma Talmadge in 1922, followed by a Norma Shearer talkie ten years later.

*Drink to Me Only with Thine Eyes* W: Ben Jonson—M: Unknown, possibly Colonel R. Mellish / *The Kerry Dance* (Jeanette MacDonald, Jackie Horner) W: James Lyman Molloy—M: Unknown / *Land of Hope and Glory* W: Arthur C. Benson—M: Edward Elgar / *A Little Love, a Little Kiss* Eng. W: Adrian Ross—Fr. W: Nilson Fysher—M: Lao Silesu / *Smilin' Through* WM: Arthur A. Penn / *There's a Long, Long Trail* W: Stoddard King—M: Zo Elliott.

"Metro-Goldwyn-Mayer has tapped Jeanette MacDonald for the lead, adorned all with songs and Technicolor and brought the old love story forth in a gaudy but stiff-jointed version." —Bosley Crowther, *The New York Times*.

**1169   The Smiling Lieutenant.**
US, 1931, BW, 89 m. D: Ernst Lubitsch, P: Paramount (Ernst Lubitsch).
*Breakfast Table Love* (Claudette Colbert, Maurice Chevalier); *Jazz Up Your Lingerie* (Claudette Colbert, Miriam Hopkins); *Live for Today* (Claudette Colbert, Maurice Chevalier); *One More Hour of Love* (Maurice Chevalier); *Toujours L'Amour in the Army* (Maurice Chevalier); *While Hearts Are Singing* (Claudette Colbert) W: Clifford Grey—M: Oscar Straus.
"Wit and melody swing through Maurice Chevalier's latest picture. . . . None other than Oscar Straus is responsible for the charming musical compositions." —Mordaunt Hall, *The New York Times.*

**1170   Smokey and the Bandit.**
US, 1977, C, 96 m. D: Hal Needham, P: Universal (Mort Engleberg). Performer: Jerry Reed.
*The Bandit* WM: Dick Feller / *East Bound and Down* WM: Dick Feller and Jerry Reed / *The Legend* WM: Jerry Reed.

**1171   So This Is Love.** US, 1953, C, 101 m. D: Gordon Douglas, MD: Ray Heindorf, MS: Max Steiner, P: Warner (Henry Blanke). Performer: Kathryn Grayson. GB Title: The Grace Moore Story.
*Ciribiribin* WM: Jack Lawrence, Harry James and Alberto Pestalozza / *I Wish I Could Shimmy Like My Sister Kate* WM: Armand J. Piron and Peter Bocage / *The Kiss Waltz* / *Oh Me! Oh My!* W: Arthur Francis [Ira Gershwin] —M: Vincent Youmans / *Remember* WM: Irving Berlin / *Time on My Hands* W: Harold Adamson and Mack Gordon—M: Vincent Youmans.

**1172   So This Is Paris.** US, 1954, C, 96 m. D: Richard Quine, MD: Joseph Gershenson, P: Universal (Albert J. Cohen).
*A Dame's a Dame* (Tony Curtis, Gene Nelson, Paul Gilbert) WM: Phil Moody and Pony Sherrell / *I Can't Give You Anything But Love, Baby* (Gloria De Haven) W: Dorothy Fields—M: Jimmy McHugh / *If You Were There* (Gloria De Haven, Gene Nelson); *Looking for Someone to Love* (Gene Nelson); *So This Is Paris* (Chorus); *Two of Us* (Gloria De Haven, Tony Curtis); *Wait Till Paris Sees Us* (Tony Curtis, Gene Nelson, Paul Gilbert) WM: Phil Moody and Pony Sherrell.

**1173   Society Lawyer.** US, 1939, BW, 77 m. D: Edwin L. Marin, P: MGM (John W. Considine, Jr.).
*The Honorable Mr. So and So* (Virginia Bruce) WM: Sam Coslow.

**1174   Some Came Running.**
US, 1958, C, 136 m. D: Vincente Minnelli, MS: Elmer Bernstein, P: MGM (Sol C. Siegel).
*After You've Gone* (Shirley MacLaine) W: Henry Creamer—M: Turner Layton / *To Love and Be Loved* (Frank Sinatra) W: Sammy Cahn—M: James Van Heusen.

**1175   Some Like It Hot.** US, 1959, BW, 119 m. D: Billy Wilder, MS: Adolph Deutsch, P: UA (Billy Wilder). Performer: Marilyn Monroe.
*By the Beautiful Sea* (Chorus) W: Harold Atteridge—M: Harry Carroll / *Down Among the Sheltering Palms* (Chorus) W: James Brockman—M: Abe Olman / *I'm Thru with Love* W: Gus Kahn—M: Matt Malneck and Fud Livingston / *I Wanna Be Loved By You* W: Bert Kalmar—M: Herbert Stothart and Harry Ruby / *Runnin' Wild!* W: Joe Grey and Leo Wood—M: A. Harrington Gibbs.

**1176   Somebody Killed Her Husband.** US, 1978, C, 97 m. D: Lamont Johnson, MS: Alex North, P: Columbia (Martin Poll).
*Love Keeps Getting Stronger Every Day* (Neil Sedaka) W: Howard Greenfield—M: Neil Sedaka.

**1177   Somebody Loves Me.**
US, 1952, C, 97 m. D: Irving S. Brecher, MD: Emil Newman, P: Paramount (William Perlberg, George Seaton). Vocals: Pat Morgan for Ralph Meeker.

*Dixie Dreams* (Betty Hutton) WM: Arthur Johnston, George W. Meyer, Grant Clarke and Roy Turk / *Honey Oh My Honey* (Adele Jergens) WM: Jay Livingston and Ray Evans / *I Can't Tell Why I Love You* (Betty Hutton) W: Will Cobb—M: Gus Edwards / *I Cried for You* (Ralph Meeker) W: Arthur Freed—M: Gus Arnheim and Abe Lyman / *Jealous* (Betty Hutton, Ralph Meeker) W: Tommy Malie and Dick Finch—M: Jack Little / *June Night* (Betty Hutton, Ralph Meeker) WM: Cliff Friend and Abel Baer / *Love Him* (Betty Hutton, Ralph Meeker) WM: Jay Livingston and Ray Evans / *On San Francisco Bay* (Betty Hutton) W: Vincent Bryan—M: Gertrude Hoffman / *Rose Room* (Betty Hutton, Ralph Meeker) WM: Harry Williams and Art Hickman / *Smiles* (Betty Hutton, Chorus) W: J. Will Callahan—M: Lee G. Roberts / *Somebody Loves Me* (Betty Hutton, Ralph Meeker) W: B.G. De Sylva and Ballard MacDonald—M: George Gershwin / *Teasing Rag* (Betty Hutton) WM: Joe Jordan / *Thanks to You* (Ralph Meeker) WM: Jay Livingston and Ray Evans / *Toddling the Todalo* (Betty Hutton, Adele Jergens) WM: E. Ray Goetz and A. Baldwin Sloane / *The Wang Wang Blues* (Henry Slate, Sid Tomack) W: Gus Mueller and Buster Johnson—M: Henry Busse / *'Way Down Yonder in New Orleans* (Betty Hutton, Chorus) W: Henry Creamer—M: Turner Layton.

"Aside from a wealth of noted old tunes, a couple of new ditties and the obvious talents of the ebullient Betty Hutton ... 'Somebody Loves Me' leaves one with the disturbing yen to ask, 'I wonder why'." —A.H. Weiler, *The New York Times.*

**1178 Somebody Up There Likes Me.** US, 1956, BW, 113 m. D: Robert Wise, P: MGM (Charles Schnee).

*Somebody Up There Likes Me* (Perry Como) W: Sammy Cahn—M: Bronislau Kaper.

**1179 Something for the Boys.** US, 1944, C, 85 m. D: Lewis Seiler, P: TCF (Irving Starr).

*Boom Brachee* (Carmen Miranda); *In the Middle of Nowhere* (Perry Como); *I Wish We Didn't Have to Say Goodnight* (Perry Como, Vivian Blaine); *Samba Boogie* (Carmen Miranda) W: Harold Adamson—M: Jimmy McHugh / *Something for the Boys* (Vivian Blaine) WM: Cole Porter / *Wouldn't It Be Nice?* (Perry Como, Vivian Blaine, Michael O'Shea) W: Harold Adamson—M: Jimmy McHugh.

**1180 Something in the Wind.** US, 1947, BW, 89 m. D: Irving Pichel, P: Universal (Joseph Sistrom). Performer: Deanna Durbin.

*Happy Go Lucky and Free; It's Only Love; Something in the Wind; The Turntable Song; You Wanna Keep Your Baby Lookin' Right* W: Leo Robin—M: Johnny Green.

**1181 Sometimes a Great Notion.** US, 1971, C, 114 m. D: Paul Newman, MS: Henry Mancini, P: Universal (John C. Foreman). GB Title: Never Give an Inch.

*All His Children* (Charlie Pride) W: Alan Bergman and Marilyn Bergman—M: Henry Mancini.

**1182 Son of Paleface.** US, 1952, C, 95 m. D: Frank Tashlin, MS: Lyn Murray, P: Paramount (Robert L. Welch).

*Am I in Love?* (Jane Russell, Bob Hope) WM: Jack Brooks / *Buttons and Bows* (Jane Russell, Bob Hope, Roy Rogers); *California Rose* (Roy Rogers) WM: Jay Livingston and Ray Evans / *Four Legged Friend* (Roy Rogers); *There's a Cloud in My Valley of Sunshine* (Roy Rogers) WM: Jack Hope, Jack Brooks and Lyle Morraine / *What a Dirty Shame* (Chorus); *Wing-Ding Tonight* (Jane Russell, Bob Hope) WM: Jay Livingston and Ray Evans.

"A generous set of new songs." — Bosley Crowther, *The New York Times.*

**1183 Song o' My Heart.** US, 1930, BW, 85 m. D: Frank Borzage, P:

Fox. Performer: John McCormack.

*A Fair Story By the Fireside* WM: Charles Glover and C. Mordaunt Spencer / *I Feel You Near Me* WM: Charles Glover, William Kernell and James F. Hanley / *I Hear You Calling Me* WM: Harold Herford and Charles Marshall / *Just for a Day; Kitty My Love* WM: Charles Glover and C. Mordaunt Spencer / *Little Boy Blue* W: Eugene Field—M: Ethelbert Nevin / *Paddy Me Lad* WM: Albert Hay Malotte / *A Pair of Blue Eyes* WM: Charles Glover, William Kernell and James F. Hanley / *The Rose of Tralee* WM: Charles Glover and C. Mordaunt Spencer / *Song o' My Heart* WM: Charles Glover, William Kernell and James F. Hanley / *Then You'll Remember Me* WM: Alfred Burns and William Michael Balfe.

**1184  Song of Freedom.** GB, 1936, BW, 80 m. D: J. Elder Wills, P: Hammer (J. Fraser Passmore). Performer: Paul Robeson.

*The Black Emperor; Lonely Road; Sleepy River* (Paul Robeson, Elizabeth Welch, Chorus); *Song of Freedom* W: Henrik Ege—M: Eric Ansell.

**1185  Song of Norway.** US, 1970, C, 142 m. D: Andrew L. Stone, MD: Roland Shaw, P: ABC (Andrew L. Stone, Virginia Stone).

With music adapted from melodies by Edvard Grieg. The original production of the life of this composer was presented by the Los Angeles and San Francisco Civic Light Opera Company in July, 1944, and then moved to Broadway in August.

*At Christmastime* (Harry Secombe, Elizabeth Larner, Toralv Maurstad, Florence Henderson, Chorus); *Be a Boy Again* (Frank Porretta); *Freddy and His Fiddle* (Chorus); *Hill of Dreams* (Toralv Maurstad, Florence Henderson, Frank Porretta); *Hymn of Betrothal* (Chorus); *I Love You* (Florence Henderson); *Life of a Wife of a Sailor* (Chorus); *The Little House* (Florence Henderson); *Midsummer's Eve—Hand in Hand* (Chorus); *A Rhyme and a Reason* (Florence Hender-

son, Children); *Ribbons and Wrappings* (Harry Secombe, Toralv Maurstad, Florence Henderson, Elizabeth Larner, Chorus); *The Solitary Wanderer* (Florence Henderson) WM: Robert Wright and George "Chet" Forrest / *Solvejg's Song* (Chorus) WM: R. Nordraak and B. Bjorson / *The Song of Norway* (Frank Porretta); *Strange Music* (Toralv Maurstad); *Three There Were* (Frank Porretta); *When We Wed* (Chorus); *Wrong to Dream* (Florence Henderson) WM: Robert Wright and George "Chet" Forrest.

**1186  Song of Songs.** US, 1933, BW, 90 m. D: Rouben Mamoulian, MD: Nathaniel W. Finston, MS: Karl Hajos and Milien Rodern, P: Paramount (Rouben Mamoulian). Performer: Marlene Dietrich.

*Heidenroslein* WM: Franz Schubert / *Jonny* W: Edward Heyman—M: Frederick Hollander.

**1187  Song of Surrender.** US, 1949, BW, 93 m. D: Mitchell Leisen, MS: Victor Young, P: Paramount (Richard Maibaum).

*Song of Surrender* (Buddy Clark) WM: Jay Livingston, Ray Evans and Victor Young.

**1188  Song of the Islands.** US, 1942, C, 75 m. D: Walter Lang, MD: Alfred Newman, P: TCF (William LeBaron). Orch: Harry Owens and His Royal Hawaiians.

*Blue Shadows and White Gardenias* (Betty Grable) W: Mack Gordon—M: Harry Owens / *Cockeyed Mayor of Kaunakakai* (Hilo Hattie) WM: Al Stillman and R. Alex Anderson / *Down on Ami Ami Oni Oni Isle* (Betty Grable, Hilo Hattie, Chorus) W: Mack Gordon—M: Harry Owens / *Hawaiian War Chant* (Chorus) Eng. W: Ralph Freed—M: Johnny Noble and Prince Leleiohaku / *Home on the Range* (Jack Oakie) WM: Unknown / *Maluna Malolo Mawaena* (Betty Grable, Hilo Hattie, Thomas Mitchell, Chorus); *O'Brien Has Gone Hawaiian* (Betty Grable); *Sing Me a Song of the Islands* (Betty

Grable, Hilo Hattie, Chorus); *What's Buzzin' Cousin* (Jack Oakie) W: Mack Gordon—M: Harry Owens.

"A spontaneous and breezy mixture of comedy, song, dance and romance—set in Hawaiian atmosphere." —*Variety*.

**1189   Song of the Open Road.** US, 1944, BW, 93 m. D: S. Sylvan Simon, MD: Charles Previn, P: UA (Charles R. Rogers). Orch: Sammy Kaye. Performer: Jane Powell.

*Hawaiian War Chant* (Chorus) Eng. W: Ralph Freed—M: Johnny Noble and Prince Leleiohaku / *Here It Is Monday* (Jane Powell, Edgar Bergen, Chorus); *I'm Having Fun in the Sun; Rollin' Down the Road; Too Much in Love* W: Kim Gannon—M: Walter Kent.

**1190   Song of the South.** US, 1946, C, 94 m. D: Wilfred Jackson and Harve Foster, P: Walt Disney (Perce Pearce).

*Everybody Has a Laughing Place* (Nicodemus Stewart, Johnny Lee) W: Ray Gilbert—M: Allie Wrubel / *How Do You Do?* (James Baskett, Johnny Lee) WM: Robert MacGimsey / *Let the Rain Pour Down* (Chorus) W: Ken Darby—M: Foster Carling / *Song of the South* (Chorus) W: Sam Coslow—M: Arthur Johnston / *Sooner or Later* (Hattie McDaniel) W: Ray Gilbert—M: Charles Wolcott / *Uncle Remus Said* (Chorus) WM: Johnny Lange, Hy Heath and Eliot Daniel / *Who Wants to Live Like That?* (James Baskett) W: Ken Darby—M: Foster Carling / *Zip-A-Dee-Doo-Dah* (James Baskett, Luana Patten, Bobby Driscoll, Chorus) W: Ray Gilbert—M: Allie Wrubel.

**1191   Song of the Thin Man.** US, 1947, BW, 86 m. D: Eddie Buzzell, MS: David Snell, P: MGM (Nat Perrin).

*You're Not So Easy to Forget* (Gloria Grahame) WM: Herb Magidson and Ben Oakland.

**1192   The Song Remains the Same.** US, 1976, C, 136 m. D: Peter Clifton and Joe Massot, P: Columbia (Peter Grant). Performers: Led Zeppelin.

*Celebration Day* WM: John Paul Jones, James Page and Robert Plant / *Dazed and Confused* WM: James Page / *Moby Dick* WM: John Bonham, John Paul Jones and James Page / *No Quarter* WM: John Paul Jones, James Page and Robert Plant / *Rain Song* WM: James Page and Robert Plant / *Rock and Roll* WM: John Bonham, John Paul Jones, James Page and Robert Plant / *The Song Remains the Same; Stairway to Heaven* WM: James Page and Robert Plant / *Whole Lotta Love* WM: John Bonham, John Paul Jones, James Page and Robert Plant.

**1193   Sons O' Guns.** US, 1936, BW, 82 m. D: Lloyd Bacon, MD: Leo F. Forbstein, P: Warner (Harry Joe Brown).

*For a Buck and a Quarter a Day* (Joe E. Brown); *In the Arms of an Army Man* (Wini Shaw) W: Al Dubin—M: Harry Warren.

**1194   The Sound of Music.** US, 1965, C, 174 m. D: Robert Wise, MD: Irwin Kostal, P: TCF (Robert Wise). Vocals: Bill Lee for Christoper Plummer; Margery McKay for Peggy Wood.

The stage musical, starring Mary Martin and Theodore Bikel, opened on Broadway in November, 1959. *Edelweiss* was the last song written by Oscar Hammerstein before his death in 1960.

*Climb Every Mountain* (Peggy Wood, Chorus); *Do-Re-Mi* (Julie Andrews, Children); *Edelweiss* (Christopher Plummer, Julie Andrews, Children) W: Oscar Hammerstein II—M: Richard Rodgers / *I Have Confidence in Me* (Julie Andrews) WM: Richard Rodgers / *The Lonely Goatherd* (Julie Andrews, Children); *Maria* (Anna Lee, Marni Nixon, Portia Nelson, Evadne Baker); *My Favorite Things* (Julie Andrews, Children); *Preludium* (Chorus); *Sixteen Going on Seventeen* (Charmian Carr, Daniel Truhitte); *So Long, Farewell* (Children) W: Oscar Hammerstein

II—M: Richard Rodgers / *Something Good* (Julie Andrews, Christopher Plummer) WM: Richard Rodgers / *The Sound of Music* (Julie Andrews, Christopher Plummer, Children) W: Oscar Hammerstein II—M: Richard Rodgers.

"A warmly-pulsating, captivating drama set to the most imaginative use of the lilting R-H tunes." —*Variety*.

"Miss Andrews, with her air of radiant vigor . . . and her ability to make her dialog as vivid and appealing as she makes her songs, brings a nice sort of Mary Poppins logic and authority to this role." —Bosley Crowther, *The New York Times*.

**1195  Soup for One.** US, 1982, C, 87 m. D: Jonathan Kaufer, P: Warner (Marvin Worth).

*Dream Girl* (Teddy Pendergrass); *I Want Your Love* (Chic); *I Work for a Livin'* (Fonzi Thornton) WM: Bernard Edwards and Nile Rodgers / *Jump, Jump* (Deborah Harry) WM: Deborah Harry and Chris Stein / *Let's Go on Vacation* (Sister Sledge); *Soup for One* (Chic); *Tavern on the Green* (Chic) WM: Bernard Edwards and Nile Rodgers.

**1196  South Pacific.** US, 1958, C, 171 m. D: Joshua Logan, MD: Alfred Newman, P: TCF (Buddy Adler). Vocals: Muriel Smith for Juanita Hall; Giorgio Tozzi for Rossano Brazzi; Bill Lee for John Kerr; Marie Greene for Candace Lee; Betty Wand for Warren Hsieh.

Mary Martin originated the role of Nellie Forbush opposite Ezio Pinza as Emile de Becque in the stage version which opened on Broadway on April 7, 1949.

*Bali Ha'i* (Juanita Hall); *Bloody Mary* (Chorus); *A Cockeyed Optimist* (Mitzi Gaynor); *Dites-Moi* (Mitzi Gaynor, Candace Lee, Warren Hsieh); *Happy Talk* (Juanita Hall); *Honey Bun* (Mitzi Gaynor, Ray Walston); *I'm Gonna Wash That Man Right Outa My Hair* (Mitzi Gaynor); *I'm in Love with a Wonderful Guy* (Mitzi Gaynor); *My Girl Back Home* (Mitzi Gaynor, John Kerr); *Some Enchanted Evening* (Rossano Brazzi, Mitzi Gaynor); *There Is Nothin' Like a Dame* (Ray Walston, Chorus); *This Nearly Was Mine* (Rossano Brazzi); *Twin Soliloquies* (Mitzi Gaynor, Rossano Brazzi); *Younger Than Springtime* (John Kerr); *You've Got to Be Carefully Taught* (John Kerr) W: Oscar Hammerstein II—M: Richard Rodgers.

"It's a surefire score. It's probably the greatest galaxy of popular favorites from a single show in the history of musical comedy." —*Variety*.

"One good song, *My Girl Back Home*, is added to the beautiful but loudly played score." —Bosley Crowther, *The New York Times*.

**1197  Sparkle.** US, 1976, C, 100 m. D: Sam O'Steen, P: Warner (Howard Rosenman). Performers: Irene Cara; Lonette McKee.

*Hooked on Your Love; Jump; Look Into Your Heart; Rock with Me; Something He Can Feel; Sparkle* WM: Curtis Mayfield.

**1198  Speak Easily.** US, 1932, BW, 82 m. D: Edward Sedgwick, P: MGM (Lawrence Weingarten).

*Singin' in the Rain* (Jimmy Durante) W: Arthur Freed—M: Nacio Herb Brown.

**1199  Speedway.** US, 1968, C, 94 m. D: Norman Taurog, MS: Jeff Alexander, P: MGM (Douglas Laurence). MB: The Jordanaires. Performer: Elvis Presley.

*He's Your Uncle, Not Your Dad* WM: Sid Wayne and Ben Weisman / *Let Yourself Go* WM: Joy Byers / *Speedway* WM: Mel Glazer and Stephen Schlaks / *There Ain't Nothing Like a Song* (Elvis Presley, Nancy Sinatra) WM: Joy Byers and William Johnston / *Who Are You* WM: Sid Wayne and Ben Weisman / *Your Groovy Self* (Nancy Sinatra) WM: Lee Hazelwood / *Your Time Hasn't Come Yet, Baby* WM: Joel Hirschhorn and Al Kasha.

**1200 Spies Like Us.** US, 1985, C, 109 m. D: John Landis, P: Warner (Brian Grazer, George Folsey, Jr.).

*Spies Like Us* (Paul McCartney) WM: Paul McCartney.

**1201 Spinout.** US, 1966, C, 90 m. D: Norman Taurog, MD: George Stoll, P: MGM (Joe Pasternak). MB: The Jordanaires. Performer: Elvis Presley. GB Title: California Holiday.

*Adam and Evil* WM: Randy Starr and Fred Wise / *All That I Am; Am I Ready* WM: Sid Tepper and Roy C. Bennett / *Beach Shack* WM: Bill Giant, Bernie Baum and Florence Kaye / *I'll Be Back* WM: Sid Wayne and Ben Weisman / *Never Say Yes* WM: Doc Pomus and Mort Shuman / *Smorgasbord* WM: Sid Tepper and Roy C. Bennett / *Spinout* WM: Sid Wayne, Ben Weisman and Dolores Fuller / *Stop, Look and Listen* WM: Joy Byers.

**1202 Spring Parade.** US, 1940, BW, 89 m. D: Henry Koster, MD: Charles Previn, MS: Robert Stolz, P: Universal (Joe Pasternak). Performer: Deanna Durbin.

*Blue Danube Dream* M: Johann Strauss II / *In a Spring Parade* M: Charles Previn / *It's Foolish But It's Fun; Waltzing in the Clouds; When April Sings* M: Robert Stolz. W: Gus Kahn.

"Miss Durban has . . . never been in better voice . . . she has much tuneful delight with a group of new songs." —Bosley Crowther, *The New York Times.*

**1203 Springtime in the Rockies.** US, 1942, C, 91 m. D: Irving Cummings, MS: Alfred Newman, P: TCF (William LeBaron). Orch: Harry James; Bando da Lua.

*Chattanooga Choo Choo* (Carmen Miranda); *I Had the Craziest Dream* (Helen Forrest); *I Like to Be Loved By You* (Carmen Miranda); *Pan American Jubilee* (Betty Grable, John Payne, Chorus); *Run, Little Raindrop, Run* (Betty Grable, John Payne, Chorus) W: Mack Gordon—M: Harry Warren / *Tic Tac Do Meu Coracao* (Carmen

Miranda) WM: Alcyr Peres Vermelho and Walfrido Silva.

**1204 The Spy Who Loved Me.** GB, 1977, C, 125 m. D: Lewis Gilbert, MS: Marvin Hamlisch, P: UA (Albert R. Broccoli).

*Nobody Does It Better* (Carly Simon) W: Carole Bayer Sager—M: Marvin Hamlisch.

**1205 Stablemates.** US, 1938, BW, 89 m. D: Sam Wood, MS: Edward Ward, P: MGM (Harry Rapf). Performer: Wallace Beery.

*That's How I Need You* W: Joe McCarthy and Joe Goodwin—M: Al Piantadosi / *When You Wore a Tulip* W: Jack Mahoney—M: Percy Wenrich.

**1206 Stage Door Canteen.** US, 1943, BW, 132 m. D: Frank Borzage, MD: Constantin Bakaleinikoff, MS: Freddie Rich, P: UA (Sol Lesser). Orch: Benny Goodman; Count Basie; Xavier Cugat; Guy Lombardo; Kay Kyser; Freddy Martin.

*Auld Lang Syne* (Chorus) W: Robert Burns—M: Unknown / *Don't Worry Island* (Male Trio) W: Al Dubin—M: James V. Monaco / *The Girl I Love to Leave Behind* (Ray Bolger) W: Lorenz Hart—M: Richard Rodgers / *Goodnight Sweetheart* (Kenny Baker) WM: Ray Noble, James Campbell, Reginald Connelly and Rudy Vallee / *The Lord's Prayer* (Gracie Fields) W: Adapted from The Bible—M: Albert Hay Malotte / *The Machine Gun Song* (Gracie Fields) W: Al Dubin—M: James V. Monaco / *Marching Through Berlin* (Ethel Merman) WM: Bob Reed and Harry Miller / *The Marines' Hymn* (Chorus) W: Unknown, possibly Henry C. Davis—M: Jacques Offenbach / *Quicksands* (Ethel Waters); *A Rookie and His Rhythm* (Harry Babbitt, Sully Mason, Trudi Erwin); *She's a Bombshell from Brooklyn* (Lina Romay, Chorus); *We Mustn't Say Goodbye* (Lanny Ross) W: Al Dubin—M: James V. Monaco / *Why Don't You Do Right* (Peggy Lee) WM: Joe McCoy.

"A sock filmusical of great stature." — *Variety*.

**1207 Stage Fright.** GB, 1950, BW, 110 m. D: Alfred Hitchcock, MS: Leighton Lucas, P: Warner (Alfred Hitchcock). Performer: Marlene Dietrich.

*La Vie en Rose* W: Edith Piaf — M: R.S. Louiguy / *The Laziest Gal in Town* WM: Cole Porter.

**1208 Stand by Me.** US, 1986, C, 87 m. D: Rob Reiner, MS: Jack Nitzsche, P: Columbia (Bruce A. Evans, Raynold Gideon, Andrew Scheinman).

*Come Go with Me* (The Del Vikings) WM: Clarence E. Quick / *Everyday* (Buddy Holly) WM: Buddy Holly [Charles Hardin] and Norman Petty / *Get a Job* (The Silhouettes) WM: Earl T. Beal, Raymond W. Edwards, William F. Horton and Richard A. Lewis / *Great Balls of Fire* (Jerry Lee Lewis) WM: Jack Hammer and Otis Blackwell / *Let the Good Times Roll* (Shirley and Lee) WM: Leonard Lee / *Lollipop* (The Chordettes) WM: Beverly Ross and Julius Dixon / *Mr. Lee* (The Bobbettes) WM: Heather Dixon, Helen Gathers, Emma Ruth Pought, Laura Webb and Jannie Pought / *Stand by Me* (Ben E. King) WM: Ben E. King, Jerry Leiber and Mike Stoller / *Whispering Bells* (The Del Vikings) WM: F. Lowry and Clarence E. Quick / *Yakety Yak* (The Coasters) WM: Jerry Leiber and Mike Stoller.

**1209 Stand Up and Cheer.** US, 1934, BW, 69 m. D: Hamilton MacFadden, MD: Arthur Lange, P: Fox (Winfield Sheehan).

*Baby, Take a Bow* (Shirley Temple, James Dunn, Chorus); *Broadway's Gone Hill Billy* (Sylvia Froos, The Randall Sisters, Chorus); *I'm Laughin'* (Dick Foran, Tess Gardella, Aggie Herring, Si Jenks, Chorus) WM: Lew Brown and Jay Gorney / *Stand Up and Cheer* (Dick Foran) WM: Lew Brown and Harry Akst / *This Is Our Last Night Together* (John Boles, Sylvia Froos, Chorus); *We're Out of the Red* (Dick Foran, Chorus) WM: Lew Brown and Jay Gorney.

"With its adroit travesty on politics, its pleasant tunes and its effervescent quality ... often comes close to a conception of what a modern Gilbert and Sullivan opus might be." — Mordaunt Hall, *The New York Times*.

**1210 Star!** US, 1968, C, 175 m. [later 120 m.] D: Robert Wise, MD: Lennie Hayton, P: TCF (Saul Chaplin). Title of Shortened Version: Those Were the Days.

*Burlington Bertie from Bow* (Julie Andrews) WM: William Hargreaves / *Dear Little Boy* (Julie Andrews, Daniel Massey); *Do, Do, Do* (Julie Andrews) W: Ira Gershwin — M: George Gershwin / *Forbidden Fruit* (Daniel Massey); *Has Anybody Seen Our Ship?* (Julie Andrews, Daniel Massey) WM: Noel Coward / *In My Garden of Joy* (Chorus) WM: Saul Chaplin / *Jenny* (Julie Andrews) W: Ira Gershwin — M: Kurt Weill / *Limehouse Blues* (Julie Andrews, Chorus) W: Douglas Furber — M: Philip Braham / *My Ship* (Julie Andrews) W: Ira Gershwin — M: Kurt Weill / *'N' Everything* (Garrett Lewis) WM: B.G. De Sylva, Gus Kahn and Al Jolson / *Oh, It's a Lovely War* (Julie Andrews, Chorus) W: Maurice Scott — M: J.P. Long / *Parisian Pierrot* (Julie Andrews, Daniel Massey) WM: Noel Coward / *The Physician* (Julie Andrews, Chorus) WM: Cole Porter / *Piccadilly* (Julie Andrews, Bruce Forsyth, Beryl Reid) WM: Walter Williams, Bruce Seiver and Paul Morand / *Someday I'll Find You* (Julie Andrews) WM: Noel Coward / *Someone to Watch Over Me* (Julie Andrews) W: Ira Gershwin — M: George Gershwin / *Star!* (Julie Andrews) W: Sammy Cahn — M: James Van Heusen.

"The 17 musical numbers are staged in polished fashion." — *Variety*.

**1211 Star Dust.** US, 1940, BW, 85 m. D: Walter Lang, MS: David Buttolph, P: TCF (Kenneth MacGowan).

*Don't Let It Get You Down* (Charlotte Greenwood, Mary Healy); *Secrets in the Moonlight* (John Payne) WM: Mack Gordon / *Star Dust* (Mary Healy) W: Mitchell Parish—M: Hoagy Carmichael.

**1212   A Star Is Born.** US, 1954, C, 154 [or 181] m. D: George Cukor, MD: Ray Heindorf, P: Warner (Sidney Luft). Performer: Judy Garland.

*Black Bottom* W: B.G. De Sylva and Lew Brown—M: Ray Henderson / *Born in a Trunk* W: Leonard Gershe—M: Roger Edens / *Gotta Have Me Go with You* (Judy Garland, Don McKabe, Jack Harmon); *Here's What I'm Here For* W: Ira Gershwin—M: Harold Arlen / *I'll Get By* W: Roy Turk—M: Fred E. Ahlert / *It's a New World; Lose That Long Face; The Man That Got Away* W: Ira Gershwin—M: Harold Arlen / *My Melancholy Baby* W: George A. Norton —M: Ernie Burnett / *The Peanut Vendor* W: Marion Sunshine and L. Wolfe Gilbert—M: Moises Simons / *Someone At Last* W: Ira Gershwin—M: Harold Arlen / *Swanee* W: Irving Caesar—M: George Gershwin / *You Took Advantage of Me* W: Lorenz Hart—M: Richard Rodgers.

"There is the muchness of music that runs from a fine, haunting torchsong, at the outset, *The Man That Got Away*, to a mammoth extensive production number recounting the career of a singer. It is called *Born in a Trunk*. Miss Garland is excellent in all things." —Bosley Crowther, *The New York Times*.

**1213   A Star Is Born.** US, 1976, C, 140 m. D: Frank Pierson, MD: Paul Williams, P: Warner (Jon Peters, Barbra Streisand).

*Crippled Crow* (Kris Kristofferson) WM: Donna Weiss / *Evergreen* (Barbra Streisand, Kris Kristofferson) W: Paul Williams—M: Barbra Streisand / *Everything* (Barbra Streisand) WM: Paul Williams and Rupert Holmes / *I Believe in Love* (Barbra Streisand, Vanetta Fields, Clydie King) W: Marilyn Berg-

man and Alan Bergman—M: Kenny Loggins / *Lost Inside of You* (Barbra Streisand, Kris Kristofferson) WM: Leon Russell and Barbra Streisand / *Queen Bee* (Barbra Streisand, Vanetta Fields, Clydie King) WM: Rupert Holmes / *Watch Closely Now* (Barbra Streisand, Kris Kristofferson); *With One More Look at You* (Barbra Streisand, Kris Kristofferson); *The Woman in the Moon* (Barbra Streisand) WM: Kenny Ascher and Paul Williams.

"As long as this 'A Star Is Born' attends to music, it is not at all bad." — Vincent Canby, *The New York Times*.

**1214   The Star Maker.** US, 1939, BW, 94 m. D: Roy Del Ruth, P: Paramount (Charles R. Rogers). Performer: Bing Crosby.

*An Apple for the Teacher* (Bing Crosby, Linda Ware); *Go Fly a Kite* W: Johnny Burke—M: James V. Monaco / *If I Was a Millionaire* WM: Will Cobb and Gus Edwards / *Jimmy Valentine* WM: Edward Madden and Gus Edwards / *A Man and His Dream* W: Johnny Burke—M: James V. Monaco / *School Days* (Chorus) WM: Will Cobb and Gus Edwards / *Still the Bluebird Sings* W: Johnny Burke—M: James V. Monaco / *Sunbonnet Sue* WM: Will Cobb and Gus Edwards.

**1215   Star Spangled Rhythm.** US, 1942, BW, 99 m. D: George Marshall, MD: Robert Emmett Dolan, P: Paramount (Joseph Sistrom). Vocals: Martha Mears for Veronica Lake.

*Hit the Road to Dreamland* (Mary Martin, Dick Powell, The Golden Gate Quartet); *I'm Doin' It for Defense* (Betty Hutton); *Old Glory* (Bing Crosby, Chorus); *On the Swing Shift* (Dona Drake [Rita Rio], Marjorie Reynolds, Betty Rhodes); *Sharp as a Tack* (Eddie "Rochester" Anderson); *A Sweater, a Sarong, and a Peek-a-Boo Bang* (Paulette Goddard, Dorothy Lamour, Veronica Lake, Arthur Treacher, Walter Catlett, Sterling Holloway); *That Old Black Magic* (Johnny Johnston) W: Johnny Mercer—M: Harold Arlen.

**1216　Stardust.** GB, 1975, C, 111 m. D: Michael Apted, MD: Dave Edmunds and David Puttnam, P: Columbia (David Puttnam, Sanford Lieberson).

Edmunds' Stray Cats were Paul Nicholas and David Essex.

*All Along the Watchtower* (Jimi Hendrix) WM: Bob Dylan / *Americana Stray Cat Blues* (David Essex) / *Baby, I'm Yours* (Barbara Lewis) WM: Van McCoy / *Baby Love* (The Supremes) WM: Eddie Holland, Lamont Dozier and Brian Holland / *Carrie-Anne* (The Hollies) WM: Allan Clarke, Graham Nash and Tony Hicks / *Da Doo Ron Ron* (Dave Edmunds and The Electricians) WM: Jeff Barry, Ellie Greenwich and Phil Spector / *Dancing in the Street* (Martha and The Vandellas) WM: William Stevenson and Marvin Gaye / *Dea Sancta* (David Essex) / *Dizzy* (Tommy Roe) WM: Tommy Roe and Freddy Weller / *Don't Let the Sun Catch You Crying* (Gerry and The Pacemakers) WM: Gerry Marsden / *Do Wah Diddy Diddy* (Manfred Mann) WM: Jeff Barry and Ellie Greenwich / *Do You Want to Know a Secret?* (Billy J. Kramer and The Dakotas) WM: John Lennon and Paul McCartney / *Dream Lover* (Bobby Darin) WM: Bobby Darin / *Eve of Destruction* (Barry McGuire) WM: P.F. Sloan and Steve Barri / *Happy Birthday, Sweet Sixteen* (Neil Sedaka) WM: Neil Sedaka and Howard Greenfield / *Hats Off to Larry* (Del Shannon) WM: Del Shannon / *The House of the Rising Sun* (The Animals) WM: Alan Price / *I've Gotta Get a Message to You* (The Bee Gees) WM: Barry Gibb, Robin Gibb and Maurice Gibb / *Layla* (Derek and The Dominoes) WM: Eric Clapton and James Beck Gordon / *Let It Be Me* (Dave Edmunds and The Stray Cats) / *The Letter* (The Boxtops) WM: Wayne Carson Thompson / *Make Me Good* (Dave Edmunds and The Stray Cats) / *Matthew and Son* (Cat Stevens) WM: Cat Stevens / *Monday, Monday* (The Mamas and The Papas) WM: John E.A. Phillips / *My Generation* (The Who) WM: Peter Townshend / *One Fine Day* (The Chiffons) WM: Gerry Goffin and Carole King / *She's Not There* (The Zombies) WM: Rod Argent / *A Shot of Rhythm and Blues* (Dave Edmunds and The Stray Cats) WM: Terry Thompson / *Some Other Guy* (Dave Edmunds and The Stray Cats) WM: Richard Barrett, Elmo Glick and Mike Stoller / *Star Dust* (David Essex) W: Mitchell Parish —M: Hoagy Carmichael / *Summer in the City* (The Lovin' Spoonful) WM: John B. Sebastian, Steve Boone and Mark Sebastian / *Take It Away* (David Essex) / *Up on the Roof* (The Drifters) WM: Gerry Goffin and Carole King / *Uptight* (Stevie Wonder) WM: Stevie Wonder, Sylvia Moy and Henry Cosby / *What Becomes of the Broken Hearted?* (Jimmy Ruffin) WM: James Dean, Paul Riser and William Weatherspoon / *When Will I Be Loved?* (Dave Edmunds and The Stray Cats) / *White Rabbit* (Jefferson Airplane) WM: Grace Slick / *A Whiter Shade of Pale* (Procol Harum) WM: Gary Brooker and Keith Reid / *With a Little Help from My Friends* (Joe Cocker) WM: John Lennon and Paul McCartney / *You Kept Me Waiting* (David Essex) / *You've Got Your Troubles* (The Fortunes) WM: Roger Greenaway and Roger Cook / *You've Lost That Lovin' Feelin'* (The Righteous Brothers) WM: Phil Spector, Barry Mann and Cynthia Weil.

"Details the loves, joys and tribulations . . . of the music scene glimpsed from the lowest beginnings to number one position in the global charts." — *Variety*.

**1217　Starlift.** US, 1951, BW, 103 m. D: Roy Del Ruth, MD: Ray Heindorf, P: Warner (Robert Arthur).

Operation Starlift was a project intended to bring movie stars to San Francisco to entertain troops headed for Korea. The idea did not survive the planning stage.

*Good Green Acres of Home* (Gordon

MacRae, Chorus) W: Irving Kahal—
M: Sammy Fain / *I May Be Wrong But
I Think You're Wonderful* (Jane Wyman)
W: Harry Ruskin—M: Henry Sullivan
/ *It's Magic* (Gene Nelson, Janice Rule,
Chorus) W: Sammy Cahn—M: Jule
Styne / *Liza* (Patrice Wymore) W: Ira
Gershwin and Gus Kahn—M: George
Gershwin / *Look Out Stranger, I'm a
Texas Ranger* (Gary Cooper, Phil Harris, Virginia Gibson, Frank Lovejoy)
WM: Ruby Ralesin and Phil Harris /
*S'Wonderful* (Doris Day) W: Ira Gershwin—M: George Gershwin / *What Is
This Thing Called Love?* (Lucille Norman, Gordon MacRae); *You Do Something to Me* (Doris Day) WM: Cole
Porter / *You Oughta Be in Pictures*
(Doris Day) W: Edward Heyman—M:
Dana Suesse / *You're Gonna Lose Your
Gal* (Doris Day, Gordon MacRae) W:
Joe Young—M: James V. Monaco.

**1218 The Stars Are Singing.**
US, 1953, C, 99 m. D: Norman Taurog, MD: Victor Young, P: Paramount
(Irving Asher).

*Because* (Lauritz Melchior) W:
Edward Teschemacher—M: Guy
d'Hardelot / *Come On-a My House*
(Rosemary Clooney) WM: William
Saroyan and Ross Bagdasarian / *Feed
Fido Some Rruff* (Rosemary Clooney,
Anna Maria Alberghetti); *Haven't Got
a Worry to My Name* (Rosemary
Clooney); *I Do I Do I Do* (Rosemary
Clooney); *Lovely Weather for Ducks*
(Rosemary Clooney); *My Heart Is Home*
(Anna Maria Alberghetti, Lauritz Melchior); *My Kind of Day* (Anna Maria
Alberghetti) WM: Jay Livingston and
Ray Evans.

**1219 Starting Over.** US, 1979,
C, 106 m. D: Alan J. Pakula, MS: Marvin Hamlisch, P: Paramount (Alan J.
Pakula, James L. Brooks).

*Better Than Ever* (Candice Bergen,
Stephanie Mills) W: Carole Bayer
Sager—M: Marvin Hamlisch.

**1220 State Fair.** US, 1945, C,
100 m. D: Walter Lang, MD: Alfred
Newman and Charles Henderson, P:

TCF (William Perlberg). Vocals: Louanne Hogan for Jeanne Crain.

The only Rodgers and Hammerstein score ever written directly for a
film, this was a musical version of a
1933 nonmusical starring Will Rogers
and Janet Gaynor.

*All I Owe Ioway* (Vivian Blaine,
William Marshall, Fay Bainter, Donald
Meek, Charles Winninger, Chorus);
*Isn't It Kinda Fun?* (Vivian Blaine, Dick
Haymes); *It Might As Well Be Spring*
(Jeanne Crain); *It's a Grand Night for
Singing* (Jeanne Crain, Vivian Blaine,
Dick Haymes, William Marshall, Dana
Andrews, Chorus); *Our State Fair* (Fay
Bainter, Percy Kilbride, Charles Winninger); *That's for Me* (Jeanne Crain,
Dana Andrews, Vivian Blaine, Dick
Haymes) W: Oscar Hammerstein II—
M: Richard Rodgers.

"The tunes are whammo from
both lyrical and melody content." —
*Variety.*

"This song version of the old Will
Rogers talking-film is no more than an
average screen musical, with a nice
bucolic flavor here and there." —Bosley
Crowther, *The New York Times.*

**1221 State Fair.** US, 1962, C,
118 m. D: Jose Ferrer, MD: Alfred
Newman, P: TCF (Charles Brackett).
Vocals: Anita Gordon for Pamela
Tiffin.

Richard Rodgers wrote both words
and music for five new songs, to be
combined with five by Rodgers and
Hammerstein from the previous version of the film.

*Isn't It Kinda Fun?* (Ann-Margret,
David Street); *It Might As Well Be
Spring* (Pamela Tiffin); *It's a Grand
Night for Singing* (Pat Boone, Pamela
Tiffin, Bobby Darin, Bob Smart,
Chorus) W: Oscar Hammerstein II—
M: Richard Rodgers / *It's the Little
Things in Texas* (Tom Ewell, Alice
Faye, Children); *More Than Just a
Friend* (Tom Ewell); *Never Say "No"*
(Alice Faye) WM: Richard Rodgers /
*Our State Fair* (Pat Boone, Alice Faye,

Tom Ewell, Chorus); *That's for Me* (Pat Boone) W: Oscar Hammerstein II— M: Richard Rodgers / *This Isn't Heaven* (Bobby Darin); *Willing and Eager* (Pat Boone, Ann-Margret) WM: Richard Rodgers.

"The old songs are still charming, but they are not rendered with quite the zest and feeling of the 1945 cast." — *Variety*.

**1222   Stay Away, Joe.** US, 1968, C, 102 m. D: Peter Tewksbury, MS: Jack Marshall, P: MGM (Douglas Laurence). MB: The Jordanaires. Performer: Elvis Presley.

*All I Needed Was the Rain; Dominick* WM: Ben Weisman and Sid Wayne / *Stay Away* WM: Sid Tepper and Roy C. Bennett / *Stay Away, Joe* WM: Ben Weisman and Sid Wayne.

**1223   Stealing Home.** US, 1988, C, 98 m. D: Steven Kampmann, P: (Thom Mount, Hank Moonjean).

*All I Have to Do Is Dream* (The Everly Brothers) WM: Boudleaux Bryant / *And When She Danced* (Marilyn Martin, David Foster) WM: David Foster and Linda Thompson-Jenner / *Baby, It's You* (The Shirelles) WM: Mack David, Burt Bacharach and Barney Williams / *Bo Diddley* (Bo Diddley) WM: Ellas McDaniel / *Home Movies* (David Foster); *Katie's Theme* (David Foster) WM: David Foster / *Poison Ivy* (The Nylons) WM: Jerry Leiber and Mike Stoller / *Sherry* (The Four Seasons) WM: Bob Gaudio / *Stealing Home* (David Foster) WM: David Foster.

**1224   The Steel Trap.** US, 1952, BW, 85 m. D: Andrew L. Stone, MS: Dimitri Tiomkin, P: TCF (Bert E. Friedlob).

*So Much to Me* (Helen Humes) W: Stan Jones—M: Dimitri Tiomkin.

**1225   Steelyard Blues.** US, 1973, C, 93 m. D: Alan Myerson, P: Warner (Tony Bill, Michael Phillips, Julia Phillips). Performers: Paul Butterfield, Mike Bloomfield, Nick Gravenites, Maria Muldaur, John Kahn,

Chris Parker, Merle Saunders and Annie Sampson. TV Title: The Final Crash.

*Being Different Has Never Been a Crime; Brand New Family; Common Ground; Here I Come, There She Goes; Make the Headlines; Poachin'; Swing with It; They're Letting Me Drive Again; Woman's Love* WM: Mike Bloomfield and Nick Gravenites.

**1226   Step Lively.** US, 1944, BW, 88 m. D: Tim Whelan, MD: Constantin Bakaleinikoff, P: RKO (Robert Fellows).

*And Then You Kissed Me* (Frank Sinatra); *Ask the Madame* (George Murphy, Gloria De Haven, Chorus); *As Long As There's Music* (Frank Sinatra); *Come Out, Come Out, Wherever You Are* (Frank Sinatra, Gloria De Haven); *Some Other Time* (Frank Sinatra, Gloria De Haven); *Where Does Love Begin* (Frank Sinatra, Gloria De Haven, George Murphy, Anne Jeffreys, Chorus); *Why Must There Be an Opening Song?* (Anne Jeffreys) W: Sammy Cahn—M: Jule Styne.

"Frankie moans enough music to throw his bobby-socks fans into fits." —Bosley Crowther, *The New York Times*.

**1227   The Sterile Cuckoo.** US, 1969, C, 107 m. D: Alan J. Pakula, MS: Fred Karlin, P: Paramount (Alan J. Pakula). GB Title: Pookie.

*Come Saturday Morning* (The Sandpipers) W: Dory Previn—M: Fred Karlin.

**1228   The Stooge.** US, 1953, BW, 100 m. D: Norman Taurog, MD: Joseph J. Lilley, P: Paramount (Hal B. Wallis). Performer: Dean Martin.

*A Girl Named Mary and a Boy Named Bill* (Dean Martin, Polly Bergen) W: Mack David—M: Jerry Livingston / *I'm Yours* W: E.Y. Harburg— M: Johnny Green / *Just One More Chance* W: Sam Coslow—M: Arthur Johnston / *Louise* (Dean Martin, Jerry Lewis) W: Leo Robin—M: Richard A. Whiting / *Who's Your Little Whoo-Zis?*

W: Walter Hirsch—M: Al Goering and Ben Bernie / *With My Eyes Wide Open I'm Dreaming* W: Mack Gordon—M: Harry Revel.

**1229  Stop the World—I Want to Get Off.** GB, 1966, 98 m. D: Philip Saville, MD: Al Ham, P: Warner (Bill Sargent).

*Glorious Russian* (Millicent Martin); *Gonna Build a Mountain* (Tony Tanner) WM: Leslie Bricusse and Anthony Newley / *I Believed It All* (Chorus) WM: Al Ham / *I Wanna Be Rich* (Tony Tanner, Chorus); *Lumbered* (Millicent Martin, Tony Tanner); *Malinki Meilchick* (Millicent Martin, Tony Tanner); *Mumbo Jumbo* (Tony Tanner); *Once in a Lifetime* (Tony Tanner); *Someone Nice Like You* (Millicent Martin, Tony Tanner); *Typically English* (Millicent Martin, Tony Tanner); *Typically Japanese* (Millicent Martin); *What Kind of Fool Am I?* (Tony Tanner) WM: Leslie Bricusse and Anthony Newley.

**1230  The Stork Club.** US, 1945, BW, 98 m. D: Hal Walker, MD: Robert Emmett Dolan, P: Paramount (B.G. De Sylva).

*Doctor, Lawyer, Indian Chief* (Betty Hutton) W: Paul Francis Webster—M: Hoagy Carmichael / *If I Had a Dozen Hearts* (Betty Hutton, Andy Russell) W: Paul Francis Webster—M: Harry Revel / *Love Me* (Andy Russell) W: Sammy Cahn—M: Jule Styne / *A Square in a Social Circle* (Betty Hutton) WM: Jay Livingston and Ray Evans.

**1231  Stormy Weather.** US, 1943, BW, 77 m. D: Andrew L. Stone, MD: Benny Carter, P: TCF (William LeBaron). Orch: Cab Calloway.

*Ain't Misbehavin'* (Ada Brown, Fats Waller) W: Andy Razaf—M: Thomas "Fats" Waller and Harry Brooks / *Diga Diga Doo* (Lena Horne, Chorus) W: Dorothy Fields—M: Jimmy McHugh / *Geechee Joe* (Cab Calloway) WM: Cab Calloway, Jack Palmer and Andy Gibson / *I Can't Give You Anything But Love, Baby* (Lena Horne, Bill Robinson) W: Dorothy Fields—M: Jimmy McHugh / *I Lost My Sugar in Salt Lake City* (Mae E. Johnson) WM: Leon Rene and Johnny Lange / *My, My, Ain't That Somethin'?* (Lena Horne, Bill Robinson) WM: Harry Tobias and Pinky Tomlin / *Nobody's Sweetheart* (Ernest Whitman) WM: Gus Kahn, Ernie Erdman, Billy Meyers and Elmer Schoebel / *Stormy Weather* (Lena Horne, Bill Robinson) W: Ted Koehler—M: Harold Arlen / *That Ain't Right* (Ada Brown, Fats Waller) WM: Irving Mills and Nat King Cole / *There's No Two Ways About Love* (Lena Horne, Bill Robinson) W: Ted Koehler—M: James P. Johnson and Irving Mills.

"Musically . . . it is a joy to the ear." —Thomas M. Pryor, *The New York Times.*

**1232  The Story of Vernon and Irene Castle.** US, 1939, BW, 93 m. D: Henry C. Potter, MS: Victor Baravelle, P: RKO (George Haight, Pandro S. Berman).

*By the Beautiful Sea* (Chorus) W: Harold Atteridge—M: Harry Carroll / *Chicago* (Chorus) WM: Fred Fisher / *Come Josephine, in My Flying Machine* (Chorus) W: Alfred Bryan—M: Fred Fisher / *Cuddle Up a Little Closer* (Chorus) W: Otto Harbach—M: Karl Hoschna / *The Darktown Strutters' Ball* (French Singer) Fr. W: Elsie Janis—Eng. WM: Shelton Brooks / *The Glow Worm* (Chorus) Eng. W: Lilla Cayley Robinson—Ger. WM: Paul Lincke / *Hello, Frisco!* (Chorus) W: Gene Buck—M: Louis A. Hirsch / *Hello, Hello, Who's Your Lady Friend* (Fred Astaire, Chorus) WM: Worton David, Bert Lee and Harry Fragson / *It's a Long Way to Tipperary* (Chorus) WM: Jack Judge and Harry Williams / *Oh, You Beautiful Doll* (Chorus) W: A. Seymour Brown—M: Nat D. Ayer / *Only When You're in My Arms* (Fred Astaire) W: Harry Ruby and Bert Kalmar—M: Con Conrad / *Row, Row, Row* (Chorus) W: William Jerome—M: James V. Monaco / *Take*

*Me Back to New York Town* (Chorus) W: Andrew B. Sterling—M: Harry von Tilzer / *Way Down Yonder in New Orleans* (Chorus) W: Henry Creamer—M: Turner Layton / *The Yama Yama Man* (Ginger Rogers) W: George Collin Davis—M: Karl Hoschna.

**1233   Stowaway.** US, 1936, BW, 86 m. D: William A. Seiter, MD: Louis Silvers, P: TCF (B.G. De Sylva).

*Goodnight, My Love* (Shirley Temple, Alice Faye); *I Wanna Go to the Zoo* (Shirley Temple); *One Never Knows, Does One?* (Alice Faye) WM: Mack Gordon and Harry Revel / *Please* (Chinese Singer) W: Leo Robin—M: Ralph Rainger / *That's What I Want for Christmas* (Shirley Temple) W: Irving Caesar —M: Gerald Marks / *You Gotta S-M-I-L-E to Be H-A-Double-P-Y* (Shirley Temple) WM: Mack Gordon and Harry Revel.

**1234   The Strawberry Blonde.** US, 1941, BW, 97 m. D: Raoul Walsh, MS: Heinz Roemheld, P: Warner (William Cagney).

*The Band Played On* (James Cagney, Rita Hayworth) W: John Palmer—M: Charles Ward / *Bill Bailey, Won't You Please Come Home* (Chorus) WM: Hugh Cannon / *In the Evening By the Moonlight* (Chorus) WM: James A. Bland / *Love Me and the World Is Mine* (Quartet) W: Dave Reed, Jr.—M: Ernest R. Ball / *Meet Me in St. Louis, Louis* (Lucille Fairbanks) W: Andrew B. Sterling—M: Kerry Mills / *Wait Till the Sun Shines, Nellie* (Chorus) W: Andrew B. Sterling—M: Harry von Tilzer.

**1235   The Strawberry Statement.** US, 1970, C, 103 m. D: Stuart Hagmann, MS: Ian Freebairn-Smith, P: MGM (Irwin Winkler, Robert Chartoff).

*Circle Game* (Buffy Sainte-Marie) WM: Joni Mitchell / *Down By the River* (Neil Young); *Helpless* (Crosby, Stills, Nash and Young); *The Loner* (Neil Young) WM: Neil Young / *Long Time Gone* (Crosby, Stills, Nash and Young) WM: David Crosby / *Our House*

(Crosby, Stills, Nash and Young) WM: Graham Nash / *Something in the Air* (Thunderclap Newman) WM: John Keene / *Suite Judy Blue Eyes* (Crosby, Stills, Nash and Young) WM: Stephen Stills.

**1236   Street Girl.** US, 1929, BW, 91 m. D: Wesley Ruggles, MD: Victor Baravelle, P: Radio Pictures (William LeBaron). Orch: Gus Arnheim and His Cocoanut Grove Ambassadors. MB: The Radio Pictures Beauty Chorus; Raymond Maurel and The Cimini Male Chorus.

*Broken Up Tune* (Doris Eaton); *Lovable and Sweet* (Jack Oakie, John Harron, Ned Sparks); *My Dream Memory* (Betty Compson) W: Sidney Clare—M: Oscar Levant.

**1237   Strictly Dishonorable.** US, 1951, BW, 86 m. D: Melvin Frank, MS: Lennie Hayton, P: MGM (Melvin Frank, Norman Panama).

*Everything I Have Is Yours* (Ezio Pinza) W: Harold Adamson—M: Burton Lane.

**1238   Strike Me Pink.** US, 1936, BW, 100 m. D: Norman Taurog, MD: Alfred Newman, P: UA (Samuel Goldwyn). MB: The 1936 Goldwyn Girls.

*Calabash Pipe* (Ethel Merman, Eddie Cantor); *First You Have Me High* (Ethel Merman); *The Lady Dances* (Rita Rio [later Dona Drake], Eddie Cantor); *Shake It Off with Rhythm* (Ethel Merman) W: Lew Brown—M: Harold Arlen.

**1239   Strike Up the Band.** US, 1940, BW, 120 m. D: Busby Berkeley, P: MGM (Arthur Freed). Orch: Paul Whiteman. MB: Six Hits and A Miss. Performers: Judy Garland and Mickey Rooney.

*Do the Conga; Drummer Boy* (Judy Garland); *Nell of New Rochelle; Nobody* (Judy Garland) WM: Roger Edens / *Our Love Affair* W: Arthur Freed—M: Roger Edens / *Strike Up the Band* W: Ira Gershwin—M: George Gershwin.

"As they say in Hollywood, this show has everything—music, laughter, tears, etc. etc. As usual, everything is a little too much." —Theodore Strauss, *The New York Times*.

**1240 The Strip.** US, 1951, BW, 85 m. D: Leslie Kardos, MS: George Stoll, P: MGM (Joe Pasternak). Orch: Louis Armstrong; Earl Hines; Jack Teagarden.

*Ain't Misbehavin'* (Mickey Rooney, Louis Armstrong) W: Andy Razaf—M: Thomas "Fats" Waller and Harry Brooks / *Basin Street Blues* (Louis Armstrong) WM: Spencer Williams / *Don't Blame Me* (Vic Damone) W: Dorothy Fields—M: Jimmy McHugh / *A Kiss to Build a Dream On* (Kay Brown, Louis Armstrong) W: Bert Kalmar and Oscar Hammerstein II—M: Harry Ruby / *La Bota* (Monica Lewis) WM: Haven Gillespie II and Charles Wolcott / *Rose Room* (Louis Armstrong) WM: Harry Williams and Art Hickman / *Shadrach* (Louis Armstrong) WM: Robert Mac-Gimsey.

**1241 Stripes.** US, 1981, C, 105 m. D: Ivan Reitman, MS: Elmer Bernstein, P: Columbia (Ivan Reitman, Dan Goldberg).

*Do Wah Diddy Diddy* (Bill Murray, Harold Ramis) WM: Jeff Barry and Ellie Greenwich / *The Rubberband Man* (The Spinners) WM: Thom Bell and Linda Creed.

**1242 The Stripper.** US, 1963, BW, 95 m. D: Franklin J. Schaffner, MS: Jerry Goldsmith, P: TCF (Jerry Wald). GB Title: The Woman of Summer.

*Something's Gotta Give* (Joanne Woodward) WM: Johnny Mercer.

"Jerry Goldsmith's score has sparkle and character, and is obtrusive in a constructive manner—when a musical lift is needed to enliven the going." —*Variety*.

**1243 The Student Prince.** US, 1954, C, 107 m. D: Richard Thorpe, MD: George Stoll, P: MGM (Joe Pasternak). MB: Chorus. Vocals: Mario Lanza for Edmund Purdom. Performer: Edmund Purdom.

*Beloved* W: Paul Francis Webster —M: Nicholas Brodszky / *Deep in My Heart, Dear* (Ann Blyth, Edmund Purdom); *Drinking Song* W: Dorothy Donnelly—M: Sigmund Romberg / *Gaudeamus Igitur* WM: Unknown / *Golden Days* W: Dorothy Donnelly— M: Sigmund Romberg / *I'll Walk with God* W: Paul Francis Webster—M: Nicholas Brodszky / *Serenade; Students' Marching Song* (Ann Blyth) W: Dorothy Donnelly—M: Sigmund Romberg / *Summertime in Heidelberg* (Ann Blyth, Edmund Purdom) W: Paul Francis Webster—M: Nicholas Brodszky.

"A cheerful and thoroughly uninhibited outpouring of synthetic German schmaltz, as bubbly as boiling maple syrup." —Bosley Crowther, *The New York Times*.

**1244 Student Tour.** US, 1934, BW, 87 m. D: Charles F. Reisner, MD: Jack Virgil, P: MGM (Monta Bell).

*The Carlo* (Nelson Eddy); *Fight 'Em* (Maxine Doyle, Chorus); *From Now On* (Maxine Doyle) W: Arthur Freed—M: Nacio Herb Brown / *I Just Say It with Music* (Jimmy Durante) WM: Jimmy Durante / *A New Moon Is Over My Shoulder* (Phil Regan, Maxine Doyle, Chorus); *The Snake Dance* (Florine McKinney, Chorus) W: Arthur Freed—M: Nacio Herb Brown.

**1245 Summer Holiday.** US, 1948, C, 92 m. D: Rouben Mamoulian, MD: Lennie Hayton, P: MGM (Arthur Freed).

A musical remake of Eugene O'Neill's play, 'Ah Wilderness.'

*Afraid to Fall in Love* (Mickey Rooney, Gloria De Haven); *All Hail to Danville High* (Chorus); *Independence Day* (Selena Royle, Agnes Moorehead, Walter Huston, Frank Morgan, Chorus); *Our Home Town* (Mickey Rooney, Gloria De Haven, Selena Royle, Agnes Moorehead, Walter Huston, Frank Morgan, Butch Jenkins, Shirley Johns, Michael Kirby); *The Stanley Steamer* (Mickey Rooney,

Gloria De Haven, Selena Royle, Agnes Moorehead, Walter Huston, Butch Jenkins, Shirley Johns); *Weary Blues* (Marilyn Maxwell); *You're the Sweetest Kid I've Ever Known* (Mickey Rooney, Marilyn Maxwell) W: Ralph Blane — M: Harry Warren.

"The musical numbers, tastefully chosen and skillfully staged, are not spotted arbitrarily, but stem naturally from the situations." — *Variety*.

**1246  Summer Holiday.** GB, 1963, C, 107 m. D: Peter Yates, MS: Stanley Black, P: AIP (Kenneth Harper). Performers: Cliff Richard and The Shadows.

*All at Once* WM: Peter Myers and Ronald Cass / *Bachelor Boy* WM: Cliff Richard and Bruce Welch / *Big News* WM: Mike Conlin, Cliff Richard and Ronald Cass / *Dancing Shoes* WM: Hank Brian Marvin and Bruce Welch / *Les Girls* WM: Hank Brian Marvin, Bruce Welch and Brian Bennett / *The Next Time* WM: Phillip Springer and Buddy Kaye / *Round and Round* WM: Hank Brian Marvin, Bruce Welch and Brian Bennett / *Stranger in Town* WM: Peter Myers and Ronald Cass / *Summer Holiday* WM: Brian Bennett and Bruce Welch / *A Swingin' Affair; Yugoslav Wedding* WM: Peter Myers and Ronald Cass.

"From ... thin thread of yarn, songs, situations and dance routines arise fairly naturally. ... Richard has a warm presence and sings and dances more than adequately." — *Variety*.

**1247  Summer Magic.** US, 1963, C, 100 m. D: James Neilson, MS: Buddy Baker, P: Walt Disney (Ron Miller). Vocals: Marilyn Hooven for Dorothy McGuire.

*Beautiful Beulah* (Dorothy McGuire); *Femininity* (Hayley Mills, Deborah Walley, Wendy Turner); *Flitterin'* (Hayley Mills, Eddie Hodges, Chorus); *On the Front Porch* (Burl Ives, Chorus); *The Pink of Perfection* (Hayley Mills, Eddie Hodges); *Summer Magic* (Dorothy McGuire); *The Ugly Bug Ball*

(Burl Ives) WM: Richard M. Sherman and Robert B. Sherman.

**1248  Summer Stock.** US, 1950, C, 109 m. D: Charles Walters, MD: Johnny Green, P: MGM (Joe Pasternak). Vocals: Pete Roberts for Hans Conried. GB Title: If You Feel Like Singing.

*All for You* (Judy Garland, Gene Kelly, Chorus) W: Saul Chaplin — M: Harry Warren / *Dig, Dig, Dig for Your Supper* (Gene Kelly, Phil Silvers, Chorus); *Friendly Star* (Judy Garland) W: Mack Gordon — M: Harry Warren / *Get Happy* (Judy Garland, Chorus) W: Ted Koehler — M: Harold Arlen / *Happy Harvest* (Judy Garland, Gene Kelly, Chorus) W: Mack Gordon — M: Harry Warren / *Heavenly Music* (Gene Kelly, Phil Silvers, Chorus) WM: Saul Chaplin / *If You Feel Like Singing, Sing* (Judy Garland); *Memory Island* (Gloria De Haven, Hans Conried, Chorus) W: Mack Gordon — M: Harry Warren / *You Wonderful You* (Gene Kelly, Judy Garland) W: Jack Brooks and Saul Chaplin — M: Harry Warren.

"Whenever any of the youngsters in this venture give way to song or dance ... joy reigns and the barnyard jumps." — Bosley Crowther, *The New York Times*.

**1249  Sun Valley Serenade.** US, 1941, BW, 86 m. D: H. Bruce Humberstone, MS: Emil Newman, P: TCF (Milton Sperling). Orch: Glenn Miller. Vocals: Pat Friday for Lynn Bari.

*Chattanooga Choo Choo* (Tex Beneke, Dorothy Dandridge, Paula Kelly, The Modernaires, The Nicholas Brothers); *I Know Why* (Lynn Bari, John Payne, Sonja Henie, The Modernaires); *It Happened in Sun Valley* (Lynn Bari, John Payne, Milton Berle, Sonja Henie); *The Kiss Polka* (Female Trio) W: Mack Gordon — M: Harry Warren.

**1250  Sunday in New York.** US, 1963, C, 105 m. D: Peter Tewksbury, MS: Peter Nero, P: MGM (Everett Freeman).

*Sunday in New York* (Mel Torme) W: Carroll Coates—M: Peter Nero.

**1251 Sunny Side of the Street.** US, 1951, C, 71 m. D: Richard Quine, P: Columbia (Jonie Taps). Performer: Frankie Laine.

*I Get a Kick Out of You* (Billy Daniels) WM: Cole Porter / *I May Be Wrong But I Think You're Wonderful* W: Harry Ruskin—M: Henry Sullivan / *I'm Gonna Live Till I Die* WM: Al Hoffman, Walter Kent and Mann Curtis / *On the Sunny Side of the Street* W: Dorothy Fields—M: Jimmy McHugh / *Too Marvelous for Words* W: Johnny Mercer—M: Richard A. Whiting.

**1252 Sunny Side Up.** US, 1929, BW/C, 115 m. D: David Butler, MD: Howard Jackson, P: Fox (B.G. De Sylva).

*Anytime You're Necht on a Broad Bricht Moonlicht Nicht* (Marjorie White); *If I Had a Talking Picture of You* (Janet Gaynor, Charles Farrell, Chorus); *I'm a Dreamer, Aren't We All?* (Janet Gaynor); *Pickin' Petals Off Daisies* (Marjorie White, Frank Richardson); *Sunny Side Up* (Janet Gaynor, Marjorie White, Frank Richardson, Chorus); *Turn on the Heat* (Sharon Lynn); *You Find the Time and I'll Find the Place* (Sharon Lynn) W: B.G. De Sylva and Lew Brown—M: Ray Henderson.

"Miss Gaynor's voice may not be especially clear, but the sincerity with which she renders at least two of her songs is most appealing. . . . Mr. Farrell's singing is possibly just what one might expect from the average young man taking a chance on singing a song at a private entertainment." —Mordaunt Hall, *The New York Times.*

**1253 Superfly.** US, 1972, C, 96 m. D: Gordon Parks, Jr., MS: Curtis Mayfield, P: Warner (Sig Shore). Performer: Curtis Mayfield.

*Eddie You Should Know Better; Freddie's Dead; Give Me Your Love; Little Child Runnin' Wild; No Thing on Me; Pusherman; Superfly* WM: Curtis Mayfield.

**1254 Susan Slept Here.** US, 1954, C, 98 m. D: Frank Tashlin, MD: Leigh Harline, P: RKO (Harriet Parsons).

*Hold My Hand* (Don Cornell) WM: Jack Lawrence and Richard Myers.

**1255 Suzy.** US, 1936, BW, 99 m. D: George Fitzmaurice, MS: William Axt, P: MGM (Maurice Revnes). Vocal: Virginia Verrill for Jean Harlow.

*Did I Remember?* (Jean Harlow, Cary Grant) W: Harold Adamson—M: Walter Donaldson.

**1256 Swanee River.** US, 1939, C, 84 m. D: Sidney Lanfield, MD: Louis Silvers, P: TCF (Darryl F. Zanuck). MB: The Hall Johnson Choir.

*Beautiful Dreamer* (Al Jolson); *De Camptown Races* (Al Jolson); *Jeanie with the Light Brown Hair* (Don Ameche); *My Old Kentucky Home* (Don Ameche); *Oh, Susanna* (Al Jolson); *Old Black Joe* (The Hall Johnson Choir); *Old Folks at Home* (Al Jolson); *Ring Ring de Banjo* (Don Ameche) WM: Stephen Collins Foster.

"The latest Darryl Zanuck investigation of history . . . is a rather badly Technicolored song-slide for a half-dozen of the more famous Foster tunes. . . . Al Jolson is forever appearing at the head of a minstrel troupe to sing the Foster melodies as though they were all called *Mammy.*" —Frank S. Nugent, *The New York Times.*

**1257 Sweet Adeline.** US, 1935, BW, 87 m. D: Mervyn LeRoy, P: Warner (Edward Chodorov).

The first of 5 Jerome Kern movie musicals to star Irene Dunne. The others were: 'Roberta,' 'Show Boat,' 'High, Wide and Handsome' and 'Joy of Living.'

*Don't Ever Leave Me* (Irene Dunne); *Here Am I* (Irene Dunne); *Lonely Feet* (Irene Dunne); *'Twas Not So Long Ago* (Irene Dunne, Phil Regan, Joseph Cawthorn, Hugh Herbert, Nydia Westman); *We Were So Young*

(Winifred Shaw); *Why Was I Born?* (Irene Dunne, Winifred Shaw) W: Oscar Hammerstein II—M: Jerome Kern.

**1258   Sweet Charity.** US, 1969, C, 133 m. D: Bob Fosse, P: Universal (Robert Arthur).

*Baby Dream Your Dream* (Shirley MacLaine); *Big Spender* (Chita Rivera, Paula Kelly, Chorus); *If My Friends Could See Me Now* (Shirley MacLaine); *I Love to Cry at Weddings* (Stubby Kaye, Chorus); *I'm a Brass Band* (Shirley MacLaine); *It's a Nice Face* (Shirley MacLaine); *My Personal Property* (Shirley MacLaine); *The Rhythm of Life* (Sammy Davis, Jr., Chorus); *Sweet Charity* (John McMartin); *There's Gotta Be Something Better Than This* (Shirley MacLaine, Chita Rivera, Paula Kelly); *Where Am I Going?* (Shirley MacLaine) W: Dorothy Fields—M: Cy Coleman.

"A terrific musical film. Based on the 1966 legituner, extremely handsome and plush production accomplishes everything it sets out to do." —*Variety.*

**1259   Sweet Dreams.** US, 1985, C, 115 m. D: Karel Reisz, MS: Charles Gross, P: Tri-Star (Bernard Schwartz). Vocals: Patsy Cline for Jessica Lange. Performer: Jessica Lange.

*Blue Moon of Kentucky* WM: Bill Monroe / *Crazy* WM: Willie Nelson / *Foolin' Around* WM: Buck Owens and Harlan Howard / *Half As Much* WM: Curley Williams / *I Fall to Pieces* WM: Hank Cochran and Harlan Howard / *Lovesick Blues* WM: Cliff Friend and Irving Mills / *San Antonio Rose* WM: Bob Wills / *Seven Lonely Days* WM: Earl Shuman, Alden Shuman and Marshall Brown / *She's Got You* WM: Hank Cochran / *Sweet Dreams* WM: Don Gibson / *Walkin' After Midnight* WM: Alan Block and Don Hecht / *Young at Heart* (Frank Sinatra) W: Carolyn Leigh—M: Johnny Richards / *Your Cheatin' Heart* WM: Hank Williams / *You Send Me* (Sam Cooke) WM: Sam Cooke.

**1260   Sweethearts.** US, 1938, C,

120 m. D: W.S. Van Dyke II, MD: Herbert Stothart, P: MGM (Hunt Stromberg).

*Auld Lang Syne* (Jeanette MacDonald, Nelson Eddy, Chorus) W: Robert Burns—M: Unknown / *Every Lover Must Meet His Fate* (Jeanette MacDonald, Nelson Eddy, Chorus) W: Robert Wright and George "Chet" Forrest—M: Victor Herbert / *In the Convent They Never Taught Me That* (Jeanette MacDonald, Betty Jaynes) W: Robert B. Smith—M: Victor Herbert / *Keep It Dark* (Jeanette MacDonald, Nelson Eddy, Gene Lockhart, Kathleen Lockhart, Lucile Watson, Berton Churchill) W: Frank Pixley—M: Gustav Luders / *Little Gray Home in the West* (Jeanette MacDonald, Nelson Eddy) W: D. Eardley-Wilmot—M: Hermann Lohr / *The Message of the Violet* (Jeanette MacDonald, Nelson Eddy, Gene Lockhart) W: Frank Pixley—M: Gustav Luders / *On Parade* (Nelson Eddy, Chorus); *Pretty As a Picture* (Jeanette MacDonald, Nelson Eddy, Douglas McPhail, Chorus); *Summer Serenade* (Jeanette MacDonald); *Sweethearts* (Jeanette MacDonald, Nelson Eddy, Douglas McPhail, Betty Jaynes, Chorus); *Wooden Shoes* (Jeanette MacDonald, Ray Bolger, Betty Jaynes) W: Robert Wright and George "Chet" Forrest—M: Victor Herbert.

"Jeanette and Nelson have never sung or acted with more fire and abandon. . . . And even with 'modern lyrics' Victor Herbert's melodies are still the loveliest on Broadway, including all the legitimate stages." —B.R. Crisler, *The New York Times.*

**1261   Sweet Music.** US, 1935, BW, 100 m. D: Alfred E. Green, P: Warner (Sam Bischoff). Performer: Rudy Vallee.

*Ev'ry Day* W: Irving Kahal—M: Sammy Fain / *Fare Thee Well, Annabelle* W: Mort Dixon—M: Allie Wrubel / *The Good Green Acres of Home* W: Irving Kahal—M: Sammy Fain / *I See Two*

*Lovers* (Helen Morgan) W: Mort Dixon—M: Allie Wrubel / *Sweet Music* W: Al Dubin—M: Harry Warren / *There's a Different You in Your Heart* W: Irving Kahal—M: Sammy Fain.

**1262  Sweet Rosie O'Grady.** US, 1943, C, 74 m. D: Irving Cummings, P: TCF (William Perlberg). MB: The Leo Diamond Solidaires; St. Brendan's Choir.

*Battle Cry* (Lilyan Irene) WM: Maude Nugent / *Get Your Police Gazette* (Betty Grable, Chorus); *Going to the County Fair* (Betty Grable) W: Mack Gordon—M: Harry Warren / *Heaven Will Protect the Working Girl* (Betty Grable, Robert Young) W: Edgar Smith—M: A. Baldwin Sloane / *Little Annie Rooney* (Betty Grable, Robert Young, Frank Orth) WM: Michael Nolan / *My Heart Tells Me* (Betty Grable, Phil Regan); *My Sam* (Betty Grable) W: Mack Gordon—M: Harry Warren / *Sweet Rosie O'Grady* (Betty Grable, Robert Young, Adolphe Menjou, Chorus) WM: Maude Nugent / *Two Little Girls in Blue* (Betty Grable, Robert Young) WM: Charles Graham / *Waiting at the Church* (Betty Grable, Chorus) W: Fred W. Leigh—M: Henry E. Pether / *Where, Oh Where, Is the Groom?* (Betty Grable, Chorus); *The Wishing Waltz* (Betty Grable, Phil Regan, Chorus) W: Mack Gordon—M: Harry Warren.

**1263  Swing Time.** US, 1936, BW, 103 m. D: George Stevens, MD: Nathaniel Shilkret, P: RKO (Pandro S. Berman).

*Bojangles of Harlem* (Chorus); *A Fine Romance* (Ginger Rogers, Fred Astaire, Georges Metaxa, Helen Broderick); *Never Gonna Dance* (Fred Astaire); *Pick Yourself Up* (Ginger Rogers, Fred Astaire); *The Way You Look Tonight* (Fred Astaire, George Metaxa) W: Dorothy Fields—M: Jerome Kern.

"It's smart, modern, and impressive in every respect. ... The tunes as usual have substance and quality. ...

*The Way You Look Tonight* is the ballad outstander. ... Finale number ... is *Never Gonna Dance,* perhaps the best tune of the score, with its sweet-swing tempo." — *Variety.*

"It is a disappointment. Right now we could not even whistle a bar of *A Fine Romance,* and that's about the catchiest and brightest melody in the show. ... The others ... are merely adequate or worse." —Frank S. Nugent, *The New York Times.*

**1264  The Swinger.** US, 1966, C, 81 m. D: George Sidney, MS: Marty Paich, P: Paramount (George Sidney). Performer: Ann-Margret.

*I Wanna Be Loved* W: Billy Rose and Edward Heyman—M: Johnny Green / *Oh, So Bad* WM: Marty Paich / *Once* WM: Marty Paich and Mel Torme / *The Swinger* W: Dory Previn—M: Andre Previn / *That Old Black Magic* W: Johnny Mercer—M: Harold Arlen.

**1265  Sylvia.** US, 1965, BW, 115 m. D: Gordon Douglas, MS: David Raksin, P: Paramount (Martin H. Poll).

*Sylvia* (Paul Anka) W: Paul Francis Webster—M: David Raksin.

**1266  Take a Chance.** US, 1933, BW, 84 m. D: Laurence Schwab and Monte Brice, P: Paramount.

*It's Only a Paper Moon* was the first Harold Arlen tune to appear in a film. Earlier, with its original title, *If You Believe in Me* it had been used in a Broadway show called 'The Great Magoo.'

*Come Up and See Me Sometime* (Lillian Roth) W: Arthur Swanstrom—M: Louis Alter / *Eadie Was a Lady* (Lillian Roth) W: B.G. De Sylva—M: Richard A. Whiting and Nacio Herb Brown / *It's Only a Paper Moon* (June Knight, Charles "Buddy" Rogers, Cliff Edwards) W: Billy Rose and E.Y. Harburg—M: Harold Arlen / *Night Owl* (Cliff Edwards) WM: Herman Hupfeld / *Rise 'n' Shine* (Lillian Roth); *Should I Be Sweet?* (June Knight) W: B.G. De Sylva—M: Vincent Youmans.

**1267 Take Me Back to Oklahoma.** US, 1940, BW, 54 m. D: Al Herman, P: Monogram (Edward Finney). MB: Bob Wills and The Texas Playboys.

*You Are My Sunshine* (Tex Ritter) WM: Jimmie Davis and Charles Mitchell.

**1268 Take Me Out to the Ball Game.** US, 1949, C, 93 m. D: Busby Berkeley, MD: Adolph Deutsch, P: MGM (Arthur Freed). GB Title: Everybody's Cheering.

*The Hat My Father Wore on St. Patrick's Day* (Gene Kelly, Chorus) WM: William Jerome and Jean Schwartz / *It's Fate Baby, It's Fate* (Betty Garrett, Frank Sinatra); *O'Brien to Ryan to Goldberg* (Frank Sinatra, Gene Kelly, Jules Munshin); *The Right Girl for Me* (Frank Sinatra); *Strictly U.S.A.* (Frank Sinatra, Gene Kelly, Jules Munshin, Esther Williams, Betty Garrett, Chorus) W: Betty Comden and Adolph Green — M: Roger Edens / *Take Me Out to the Ball Game* (Frank Sinatra, Gene Kelly, Esther Williams) W: Jack Norworth — M: Albert von Tilzer / *Yes, Indeedy!* (Frank Sinatra, Gene Kelly) W: Betty Comden and Adolph Green — M: Roger Edens.

"The only hits in this 'Ball Game' are those which are danced and sung." — Bosley Crowther, *The New York Times.*

**1269 The T.A.M.I. Show.** US, 1964, BW, 123 m. D: Steve Binder, P: AIP (Lee Savin). GB Titles: Gather No Moss; Teenage Command Performance.

The first rock concert film, taped at the Civic Auditorium in Santa Monica, California. The initials comprising its name stand for Teen-Age Awards Music International.

*Around and Around* (The Rolling Stones) WM: Chuck Berry / *Baby Love* (The Supremes); *Can I Get a Witness* (Marvin Gaye) WM: Eddie Holland, Lamont Dozier and Brian Holland / *From All Over the World* (Jan and Dean) WM: P.F. Sloan and Steve Barri / *He's a Rebel* (Marvin Gaye, The Blossoms) WM: Gene Pitney / *It's My Party* (Lesley Gore) WM: Herb Weiner, Wally Gold and John Gluck, Jr. / *Johnny B. Goode* (Chuck Berry) WM: Chuck Berry / *The Little Old Lady from Pasadena* (The Beach Boys) WM: Roger Christian and Don Altfeld / *Maybe I Know* (Lesley Gore) WM: Jeff Barry and Ellie Greenwich / *Maybellene* (Chuck Berry) WM: Chuck Berry, Russ Frato and Alan Freed / *Mickey's Monkey* (Smokey Robinson and The Miracles) WM: Eddie Holland, Lamont Dozier and Brian Holland / *Off the Hook* (The Rolling Stones) / *Please, Please, Please* (James Brown) WM: James Brown and Johnny Terry / *Surfin' U.S.A.* (The Beach Boys) WM: Brian Wilson and Chuck Berry / *Sweet Little Sixteen* (Chuck Berry) WM: Chuck Berry / *Where Did Our Love Go?* (The Supremes) WM: Eddie Holland, Lamont Dozier and Brian Holland.

"The high point of artistry by the Rolling Stones (a Beatles-like quintet from England, with messy hair-dos) has their leader groaning, 'I'm all right' over and over. Son, you sure don't look it. A group called the Beach Boys (clean-cut, in striped shirts, and terrible) were another favorite. . . . But the one to see, to believe, is a shaggy-haired vocalist named James Brown, emptying his musical soul like a scalded cat." — Howard Thompson, *The New York Times.*

**1270 Tammy and the Bachelor.** US, 1957, C, 89 m. D: Joseph Pevney, MD: Frank Skinner, MS: Joseph Gershenson, P: Universal (Ross Hunter). GB Title: Tammy.

*Tammy* (Debbie Reynolds, The Ames Brothers) WM: Jay Livingston and Ray Evans.

**1271 Tammy and the Doctor.** US, 1963, C, 88 m. D: Harry Keller, MS: Frank Skinner, P: Universal (Ross Hunter).

*Tammy* (Sandra Dee) WM: Jay Livingston and Ray Evans.

**1272 Tammy Tell Me True.**
US, 1961, C, 97 m. D: Harry Keller, P:
Universal (Ross Hunter).
*Tammy Tell Me True* (Sandra Dee)
WM: Dorothy Squires.
**1273 Tea for Two.** US, 1950,
C, 98 m. D: David Butler, MD: Ray
Heindorf, P: Warner (William Jacobs).
*Crazy Rhythm* (Patrice Wymore,
Gene Nelson) W: Irving Caesar—M:
Roger Wolfe Kahn and Joseph Meyer /
*Do, Do, Do* (Doris Day, Gordon Mac-
Rae) W: Ira Gershwin—M: George
Gershwin / *I Know That You Know*
(Doris Day, Gordon MacRae, Gene
Nelson) W: Anne Caldwell—M: Vin-
cent Youmans / *I Only Have Eyes for
You* (Virginia Gibson, Gordon Mac-
Rae) W: Al Dubin—M: Harry Warren
/ *I Want to Be Happy* (Doris Day, Gor-
don MacRae) W: Irving Caesar—M:
Vincent Youmans / *No, No, Nanette*
(Doris Day, Gene Nelson) W: Otto
Harbach—M: Vincent Youmans / *Oh
Me! Oh My!* (Doris Day, Gene Nelson,
Patrice Wymore) W: Arthur Francis
[Ira Gershwin]—M: Vincent Youmans
/ *Tea for Two* (Doris Day, Gordon
MacRae, Chorus) W: Irving Caesar—
M: Vincent Youmans.
"The nostalgic numbers from the
1929 'No, No, Nanette' and other
cleffing of the period listen well." —
*Variety.*
"Good music and snappy com-
edy." —Thomas M. Pryor, *The New
York Times.*
**1274 Teacher's Pet.** US, 1958,
BW, 120 m. D: George Seaton, MS:
Roy Webb, P: Paramount (William
Perlberg). Performer: Doris Day.
*The Girl Who Invented Rock and
Roll; Teacher's Pet* WM: Joe Lubin.
**1275 The Teahouse of the
August Moon.** US, 1957, C, 123 m.
D: Daniel Mann, MS: Saul Chaplin,
P: MGM (Jack Cummings).
*Deep in the Heart of Texas* (Glenn
Ford, Eddie Albert, Marlon Brando)
W: June Hershey—M: Don Swander.
**1276 Tell It to the Judge.** US,

1949, BW, 87 m. D: Norman Foster,
MS: Werner R. Heymann, P: Colum-
bia (Buddy Adler).
*Let's Fall in Love* (Robert Cum-
mings) W: Ted Koehler—M: Harold
Arlen.
**1277 Tell Me Lies.** GB, 1968,
BW/C, 118 m. D: Peter Brook, MD:
Tony Russell, P: Mira/Walter Reade
(Peter Brook).
*Any Complaints* (Margie Lawrence,
Chorus); *Barry Bondhus* (Robert Lloyd,
Chorus); *Escalation* (Chorus); *God Is
Flame* (John Hussey, Margie Lawrence,
Chorus); *Icarus* (Chorus); *The Leeches*
(Glenda Jackson, Hugh Sullivan, Leon
Lissek, Chorus); *Make and Break*
(Glenda Jackson, Michael Williams,
Barry Stanton, Chorus); *Road Number
One* (Glenda Jackson, Margie Law-
rence, Pauline Munroe, Ursula Mohan,
Chorus); *Rose of Saigon* (Margie Law-
rence, Michael Williams, Chorus); *Tell
Me Lies* (Mark Jones, Robert Lloyd);
*When Dreams Collide* (Glenda Jackson,
Michael Williams, Robert Lloyd, Hugh
Sullivan) W: Adrian Mitchell—M:
Richard Peaslee.
"Musical numbers are shouted-
sung in a cacophonic manner that only
underscores the lyrics' vacuity." —
*Variety.*
**1278 Tell Me That You Love
Me, Junie Moon.** US, 1970, C, 112 m.
D: Otto Preminger, MS: Philip
Springer, P: Paramount (Otto Prem-
inger).
*Elvira* (Pacific Gas and Electric)
WM: Pacific Gas and Electric / *Old
Devil Time* (Pete Seeger) WM: Pete
Seeger.
**1279 10.** US, 1979, C, 122 m. D:
Blake Edwards, MS: Henry Mancini,
P: Warner (Blake Edwards, Tony
Adams).
*Don't Call It Love* (Dudley Moore,
Chorus) W: Carole Bayer Sager—M:
Henry Mancini / *Happy Birthday to You*
(Julie Andrews, Chorus) WM: Patty
Smith Hill and Mildred J. Hill / *He
Pleases Me* (Julie Andrews); *I Give My*

*Heart* (Julie Andrews); *I Have an Ear for Love* (Max Showalter); *It's Easy to Say* (Julie Andrews, Dudley Moore, Chorus) W: Robert Wells—M: Henry Mancini.

**1280  Tender Is the Night.** US, 1962, C, 146 m. D: Henry King, MS: Bernard Herrmann, P: TCF (Henry T. Weinstein).

*Tender Is the Night* (Earl Grant, Chorus) W: Paul Francis Webster—M: Sammy Fain.

**1281  Tender Mercies.** US, 1983, C, 89 m. D: Bruce Beresford, MS: George Dreyfus, P: EMI (Philip S. Hobel).

*If You'll Hold the Ladder* (Robert Duvall) WM: B. Rabin and Sara B. / *It Hurts to Face Reality* (Robert Duvall) WM: Lefty Frizzell / *I've Decided to Leave Here Forever* (Robert Duvall) WM: Robert Duvall / *Makin' Love and Makin' Out* (Charlie Craig); *Midnight Tennessee Woman* (Charlie Craig); *Off on Wednesdays* (Charlie Craig, Sherry Grooms) WM: Charlie Craig / *Overnight Sensations* (Craig Bickhardt) WM: Craig Bickhardt and E. Fries / *Over You* (Betty Buckley) WM: Austin Roberts and Bobby Hart / *Wings of a Dove* (Robert Duvall, Gail Youngs) WM: Bob Ferguson / *You Are What Love Means to Me* (Craig Bickhardt) WM: Craig Bickhardt.

**1282  The Tender Trap.** US, 1955, C, 111 m. D: Charles Walters, MS: Jeff Alexander, P: MGM (Lawrence Weingarten).

*The Tender Trap* (Frank Sinatra) W: Sammy Cahn—M: James Van Heusen.

**1283  Tequila Sunrise.** US, 1988, C, 116 m. D: Robert Towne, P: Warner (Thom Mount).

*Beyond the Sea* (Bobby Darin) Eng. W: Jack Lawrence—M: Charles Trenet / *Dead on the Money* (Andy Taylor) WM: S. Diamond and T. Cerny / *Don't Worry Baby* (The Everly Brothers, The Beach Boys) WM: Brian Wilson and Roger Christian / *Do You Believe in Shame?* (Duran Duran) WM: Taylor, Nick Rhodes and Simon Le Bon / *Give a Little Love* (Ziggy Marley and The Melody Makers) WM: D. Warren and A. Hammond / *Jo Ann's Song* (Dave Grusin featuring David Sanborn) WM: Dave Grusin / *Recurring Dream* (Crowded House) WM: Neil Finn / *Surrender to Me* (Ann Wilson, Robin Zander) WM: Ross Vannelli and Richard Marx / *Tequila Dreams* (Dave Grusin featuring Lee Ritenour) WM: Dave Grusin / *Unsubstantiated* (The Church) WM: Kilbey, Wilson-Piper, Ploog and Koppes.

**1284  Texas Carnival.** US, 1951, C, 77 m. D: Charles Walters, MD: David Rose, P: MGM (Jack Cummings). Orch: Foy Willing. MB: Red Norvo Trio.

*Carnie's Pitch* (Red Skelton) W: Dorothy Fields—M: Harry Warren / *Deep in the Heart of Texas* (Howard Keel, Chorus) W: June Hershey—M: Don Swander / *It's Dynamite* (Ann Miller); *Whoa, Emma* (Howard Keel, Chorus); *Young Folks Should Get Married* (Howard Keel) W: Dorothy Fields—M: Harry Warren.

"For tunes it has Howard Keel as a virile cowpoke baritoning his way through the footage." —*Variety*.

**1285  Thank God It's Friday.** US, 1978, C, 100 m. D: Robert Klane, P: Columbia (Rob Cohen).

*After Dark* (Patti Brooks) WM: Simon Soussan and Sabrina Soussan / *Dance All Night* (Cuba Gooding) WM: Willie Hutch / *Disco Queen* (Paul Jabara) WM: Paul Jabara / *Down to Lovetown* (The Originals) WM: Don Daniels, Michael Sutton and Kathy Wakefield / *Do You Want the Real Thing* (D.C. LaRue) WM: Bob Esty and D.C. LaRue / *Easy* (The Commodores) WM: Lionel B. Richie, Jr. / *Find My Way* (Cameo) WM: Johnny Melfi / *Floyd's Theme* (Natural Juices) WM: Dick St. Nicklaus / *I'm Here Again* (Thelma Houston) WM: B. Sutton and M. Sutton / *It's Serious* (Cameo) WM:

Gregory Johnson and Larry Blackman / *I Wanna Dance* (Marathon) WM: Pete Bellotte / *Je T'Aime* (Donna Summer) WM: Serge Gainsbourg—Arr: Thor Baldurrson / *The Last Dance* (Donna Summer) WM: Paul Jabara / *Leatherman's Theme* (The Wright Brothers Flying Machine) WM: Arthur Wright / *Let's Make a Deal* (Syreeta and G.C. Cameron) WM: Michael Smith / *Love Masterpiece* (Thelma Houston) WM: Hal Davis, Josef Powell and Art Posey / *Love to Love You, Baby* (Donna Summer) WM: Pete Bellotte, Giorgio Moroder and Donna Summer / *Lovin' Livin' and Givin'* (Diana Ross) WM: Kenneth Stover and Pam Davis / *Sevilla Nights* (Santa Esmerelda) WM: N. Skorsky, J.M. Descarano and J.C. Petit / *Thank God It's Friday* (Love and Kisses) WM: Robert Costandinos / *Too Hot ta Trot* (The Commodores) WM: William King, Jr., Ronald La Pread, Thomas McClary, Walter Orange, Lionel B. Richie, Jr., and Milan Williams / *Trapped in a Stairway* (Paul Jabara) WM: Paul Jabara and Bob Esty / *Try with Your Love* (Donna Summer) WM: Pete Bellotte, Giorgio Moroder and Donna Summer / *You Are the Most Precious Thing in My Life* (Love and Kisses) WM: Robert Costandinos / *You're the Reason I Feel Like Dancing* (The Fifth Dimension) WM: H. Johnson.

**1286  Thank Your Lucky Stars.** US, 1943, BW, 127 m. D: David Butler, MD: Ray Heindorf, P: Warner (Mark Hellinger). Orch: Spike Jones and His City Slickers; Cookie Fairchild.

*Blues in the Night* (John Garfield) W: Johnny Mercer—M: Harold Arlen / *The Dreamer* (Dinah Shore, Olivia De Havilland, Ida Lupino, George Tobias); *Goodnight, Good Neighbor* (Dennis Morgan, Chorus) W: Frank Loesser— M: Arthur Schwartz / *Hotcha Cornia* (Spike Jones) [parody of *Dark Eyes (Otchi Tchorniya)*] WM: Russian Folk Song / *How Sweet You Are* (Dinah Shore, Chorus); *Ice-Cold Katie* (Hattie McDaniel, Willie Best, Eddie Cantor, Jesse Lee Brooks, Rita Christina, Chorus); *I'm Goin' North* (Alan Hale, Jack Carson); *I'm Ridin' for a Fall* (Dennis Morgan, Joan Leslie); *Love Isn't Born, It's Made* (Ann Sheridan, Joyce Reynolds, Chorus) W: Frank Loesser—M: Arthur Schwartz / *Now's the Time to Fall in Love* (Eddie Cantor) WM: Al Sherman and Al Lewis / *No You, No Me* (Dennis Morgan, Joan Leslie); *Thank Your Lucky Stars* (Dinah Shore, Chorus); *That's What You Jolly Well Get* (Errol Flynn, Chorus); *They're Either Too Young or Too Old* (Bette Davis); *We're Staying Home Tonight* (Eddie Cantor) W: Frank Loesser —M: Arthur Schwartz.

"Too many people sing. And too few beautiful girls display their talents. It is also too much (two hours) of a show. But, in straight omnibus entertainment, that's what you have to expect." —Bosley Crowther, *The New York Times*.

**1287  Thanks a Million.** US, 1935, BW, 87 m. D: Roy Del Ruth, MD: Arthur Lange, P: TCF (Darryl F. Zanuck). Orch: Paul Whiteman. MB: The King's Men, with Ramona Rubinoff.

*Happy Days Are Here Again* (Fred Allen, Raymond Walburn, Andrew Tombes, Chorus) W: Jack Yellen—M: Milton Ager / *I'm Sitting High on a Hilltop* (Dick Powell); *I've Got a Pocketful of Sunshine* (Dick Powell); *New Orleans* (Ramona); *NRA - ABC* (The Yacht Club Boys); *Sugar Plum* (Ann Dvorak, Patsy Kelly); *Thanks a Million* (Dick Powell) W: Gus Kahn—M: Arthur Johnston.

**1288  Thanks for the Memory.** US, 1938, BW, 75 m. D: George Archainbaud, MS: Boris Morros, P: Paramount (Mel Shaver). Performers: Bob Hope and Shirley Ross.

*Thanks for the Memory* W: Leo Robin—M: Ralph Rainger / *Two Sleepy People* W: Frank Loesser—M: Hoagy Carmichael.

"In 'The Big Broadcast of 1938' ... Bob and Shirley Ross achieved a modest duet triumph with a song called *Thanks for the Memory* on which immortal circumstance the present production—probably the first full-length picture in screen history which has been given as an encore to a song—has sentimentally based its title." —B.R. Crisler, *The New York Times*.

**1289  That Certain Age.** US, 1938, BW, 95 m. D: Edward Ludwig, MD: Charles Previn, P: Universal (Joe Pasternak). Performer: Deanna Durbin.

*Be a Good Scout; Has Anyone Ever Told You Before?; My Own; That Certain Age; You're As Pretty As a Picture* W: Harold Adamson—M: Jimmy McHugh.

**1290  That Certain Feeling.** US, 1956, C, 103 m. D: Norman Panama and Melvin Frank, MS: Joseph J. Lilley, P: Paramount (Norman Panama, Melvin Frank).

*That Certain Feeling* (Pearl Bailey, Bob Hope, Eva Marie Saint) W: Ira Gershwin—M: George Gershwin.

**1291  That Darn Cat.** US, 1965, C, 116 m. D: Robert Stevenson, MS: Bob Brunner, P: Walt Disney (Bill Walsh, Ron Miller).

*That Darn Cat* (Bobby Darin) WM: Richard M. Sherman and Robert B. Sherman.

**1292  That Funny Feeling.** US, 1965, C, 93 m. D: Richard Thorpe, MS: Joseph Gershenson, P: Universal (Harry Keller).

*That Funny Feeling* (Bobby Darin) WM: Bobby Darin.

**1293  That Midnight Kiss.** US, 1949, C, 96 m. D: Norman Taurog, MS: Bronislau Kaper, P: MGM (Joe Pasternak).

*Down Among the Sheltering Palms* (Keenan Wynn, Quartet) W: James Brockman—M: Abe Olman / *I Know, I Know, I Know* (Kathryn Grayson) W: Bob Russell—M: Bronislau Kaper / *Santa Lucia* (J. Carrol Naish) Eng. W:

Thomas Oliphant—Ital. WM: Teodoro Cottrau / *They Didn't Believe Me* (Mario Lanza, Kathryn Grayson) W: Herbert Reynolds [Michael E. Rourke] —M: Jerome Kern / *Three O'Clock in the Morning* (J. Carrol Naish) W: Dorothy Terriss [Theodore Morse]—M: Julian Robledo.

**1294  That Night in Rio.** US, 1941, C, 90 m. D: Irving Cummings, MD: Alfred Newman, P: TCF (Fred Kohlmar). Orch: Bando da Lua. MB: The Flores Brothers.

*The Baron Is in Conference* (Chorus); *Boa Noite* (Don Ameche, Alice Faye, Chorus) W: Mack Gordon —M: Harry Warren / *Cae Cae* (Carmen Miranda) Eng. W: John Latouche— Span. W: Pedro Barrios—Port. WM: Roberto Martins / *Chica Chica Boom Chic* (Carmen Miranda, Don Ameche, Chorus); *I Yi Yi Yi Yi* (Carmen Miranda); *They Met in Rio* (Don Ameche, Alice Faye, Chorus) W: Mack Gordon —M: Harry Warren.

"With lavish production, brilliant Technicolor, and several tuneful songs, it's peak entertainment." —*Variety*.

**1295  That Summer.** GB, 1979, C, 93 m. D: Harley Cokliss, P: Columbia/Warner/EMI (Davina Belling, Clive Parsons).

*Another Girl, Another Planet* (The Only Ones) WM: Peter Perrett / *Because the Night* (The Patti Smith Group) WM: Patti Smith and Bruce Springsteen / *Blank Generation* (Richard Hell and The Voidoids) WM: Richard Hell / *Chelsea* (Elvis Costello) WM: Elvis Costello / *Do Anything You Wanna Do* (Eddie and The Hot Rods) WM: Ed Hollis and Graeme Douglas / *I Love the Sound of Breaking Glass* (Nick Lowe) WM: Nick Lowe, Andrew Bodnar and Stephen Golding / *Kicks* (The Boomtown Rats) WM: Bob Geldof / *New Life* (Zones) WM: Willie Gardner / *Rockaway Beach* (The Ramones) WM: Douglas Colvin, John Cummings, Thomas Erdelyi and Jeff Hyman / *Sex and Drugs and Rock and Roll*

(Ian Dury and The Blockheads) WM: Ian Dury and Chaz Jankel / *She's So Modern* (The Boomtown Rats) WM: Bob Geldof and Johnnie Fingers / *Spanish Stroll* (Mink De Ville) WM: Willy De Ville / *Teenage Kicks* (The Undertones) WM: John O'Neill / *Watching the Detectives* (Elvis Costello) WM: Elvis Costello / *What a Waste* (Ian Dury and The Blockheads) WM: Ian Dury, Rod Melvin and Chaz Jankel / *Whole Wide World* (Wreckless Eric) WM: Wreckless Eric.

**1296 That'll Be the Day.** GB, 1974, C, 91 m. D: Claude Whatham, MD: Neil Aspinall and Keith Moon, P: EMI (David Puttnam, Sanford Lieberson).

*Alley Oop* (Dante and The Evergreens) WM: Dallas Frazier / *At the Hop* (Danny and The Juniors) WM: John Madara, Arthur Singer and Dave White / *Bony Moronie* (Larry Williams) WM: Larry Williams / *Book of Love* (The Monotones) WM: Warren Davis, George Malone and Charles Patrick / *Born Too Late* (The Ponitails) W: Fred Tobias—M: Charles Strouse / *Bye Bye Love* (The Everly Brothers) WM: Felice Bryant and Boudleaux Bryant / *Chantilly Lace* (The Big Bopper) WM: J.P. Richardson / *Devoted to You* (The Everly Brothers) WM: Boudleaux Bryant / *Get Yourself Together* (Billy Fury) / *Great Balls of Fire* (Jerry Lee Lewis) WM: Jack Hammer and Otis Blackwell / *Honeycomb* (Jimmie Rodgers) WM: Bob Merrill / *I Love How You Love Me* (The Paris Sisters) WM: Barry Mann and Larry Kolber / *It'll Be Me* (Wishful Thinking) / *Linda Lou* (Ray Sharp) / *Little Darlin'* (The Diamonds) WM: Maurice Williams / *Long Live Rock* (Billy Fury) WM: Peter Townshend / *Party Doll* (Buddy Knox) WM: Jimmy Bowen and Buddy Knox / *Personality* (Lloyd Price) WM: Harold Logan and Lloyd Price / *Poetry in Motion* (Johnny Tillotson) WM: Paul Kaufman and Mike Anthony / *Red Leather Jacket* (Viv Stanshall) / *Rock On* (David Essex)

WM: David Essex / *Runaround Sue* (Dion) WM: Dion Di Mucci and Ernest Maresca / *Runaway* (Del Shannon) WM: Del Shannon [Charles Westover] and Max Crook / *Running Bear* (Johnny Preston) WM: J.P. Richardson / *Sealed with a Kiss* (Brian Hyland) W: Peter Udell—M: Gary Geld / *Slow Down* (Eugene Wallace) WM: Larry Williams / *Smoke Gets in Your Eyes* (The Platters) W: Otto Harbach—M: Jerome Kern / *That'll Be the Day* (Bobby Vee) WM: Jerry Allison, Buddy Holly and Norman Petty / *That's All Right* (Billy Fury) / *A Thousand Stars* (Billy Fury) WM: Eugene Pearson / *'Til I Kissed You* (The Everly Brothers) WM: Don Everly / *Tutti-Frutti* (Little Richard) WM: Richard Penniman, Dorothy La Bostrie and Joe Lubin / *Wake Up Little Susie* (The Everly Brothers) WM: Felice Bryant and Boudleaux Bryant / *Well All Right* (Bobby Vee) / *What'd I Say* (Billy Fury) WM: Ray Charles / *What in the World* (Stormy Tempest) / *Why Do Fools Fall in Love* (Frankie Lymon and The Teenagers) WM: Frankie Lymon and Morris Levy.

**1297 That's Life!** US, 1986, C, 102 m. D: Blake Edwards, MS: Henry Mancini, P: Columbia (Tony Adams).

*Life in a Looking Glass* (Tony Bennett) W: Leslie Bricusse—M: Henry Mancini.

**1298 That's My Boy.** US, 1951, BW, 98 m. D: Hal Walker, MS: Leigh Harline, P: Paramount (Hal B. Wallis). Performer: Dean Martin.

*Ballin' the Jack* W: Jim Burris—M: Chris Smith / *I'm in the Mood for Love* W: Dorothy Fields—M: Jimmy McHugh.

**1299 There Was a Crooked Man** ... US, 1970, C, 125 m. D: Joseph L. Mankiewicz, MS: Charles Strouse, P: Warner (Joseph L. Mankiewicz).

*There Was a Crooked Man* (Trini Lopez) WM: Lee Adams and Charles Strouse.

**1300 There's No Business Like Show Business.** US, 1954, C, 117 m. D: Walter Lang, MS: Alfred Newman and Lionel Newman, P: TCF (Sol C. Siegel).

*After You Get What You Want, You Don't Want It* (Marilyn Monroe); *Alexander's Ragtime Band* (Ethel Merman, Dan Dailey, Mitzi Gaynor, Donald O'Connor, Johnnie Ray); *Heat Wave* (Marilyn Monroe); *If You Believe* (Johnnie Ray); *Lazy* (Marilyn Monroe, Donald O'Connor, Mitzi Gaynor); *Let's Have Another Cup of Coffee* (Ethel Merman); *A Man Chases a Girl* (Donald O'Connor); *Marie* (Chorus); *Play a Simple Melody* (Ethel Merman, Dan Dailey); *A Pretty Girl Is Like a Melody* (Ethel Merman, Dan Dailey); *Remember* (Ethel Merman, Dan Dailey, Chorus); *A Sailor's Not a Sailor* (Ethel Merman, Mitzi Gaynor); *There's No Business Like Show Business* (Ethel Merman, Dan Dailey, Marilyn Monroe, Donald O'Connor, Mitzi Gaynor, Johnnie Ray); *When the Midnight Choo Choo Leaves for Alabam'* (Ethel Merman, Dan Dailey, Mitzi Gaynor, Donald O'Connor); *You'd Be Surprised* (Dan Dailey) WM: Irving Berlin.

"The orchestral-vocal treatments of the Berlin standards are so richly endowed as to give them constantly fresh values." — *Variety.*

**1301 This Gun for Hire.** US, 1942, BW, 80 m. D: Frank Tuttle, MS: David Buttolph, P: Paramount (Richard M. Blumenthal). Vocals: Martha Mears for Veronica Lake. Performer: Veronica Lake.

*I've Got You; Now You See It, Now You Don't* W: Frank Loesser—M: Jacques Press.

**1302 This Happy Breed.** GB, 1944, C, 110 m. D: David Lean, MD: Muir Mathieson, P: Universal (Noel Coward, Anthony Havelock-Allen).

*The Broadway Melody* (Charles King) W: Arthur Freed—M: Nacio Herb Brown.

**1303 This Happy Feeling.** US, 1958, C, 92 m. D: Blake Edwards, MS: Frank Skinner, P: Universal (Ross Hunter).

*This Happy Feeling* (Debbie Reynolds) WM: Jay Livingston and Ray Evans.

**1304 This Is Elvis.** US, 1981, BW/C, 101 m. D: Malcolm Leo and Andrew Solt, MS: Walter Scharf, P: Warner (David L. Wolper). Performer: Elvis Presley.

Times change, but melodies linger on. The song *Love Me Tender* was based on a ballad written in 1861 by W.W. Fosdick and George R. Poulton. Titled *Aura Lee,* it was sung by the Union Army during the Civil War. In 1865, the same tune with different words became *Army Blue*—the class song of West Point graduates.

The medley known as *An American Trilogy* included the songs *All My Trials, Battle Hymn of the Republic* and *Dixie.*

*All My Trials* WM: Unknown / *Always on My Mind* WM: Mark James, Wayne Thompson and Johnny Christopher / *An American Trilogy* Arr: Mickey Newberry / *Are You Lonesome Tonight?* WM: Roy Turk and Lou Handman / *As Long As I Have You* WM: Fred Wise and Ben Weisman / *Battle Hymn of the Republic* W: Julia Ward Howe—M: William Steff / *A Big Hunk o' Love* WM: Aaron Schroeder and Sid Wyche / *Blue Hawaii* W: Leo Robin—M: Ralph Rainger / *Blue Suede Shoes* WM: Carl Lee Perkins / *Can't Help Falling in Love* WM: Hugo Peretti, Luigi Creatore and George Weiss / *Dixie* WM: Daniel Decatur Emmett / *Don't Be Cruel* WM: Otis Blackwell and Elvis Presley / *Flip, Flop and Fly* WM: Charles Calhoun and Lou Willie Turner / *Frankfort Special* WM: Sid Wayne and Sherman Edwards / *Furry Lewis' Blues* (Furry Lewis) / *G.I. Blues* WM: Sid Tepper and Roy C. Bennett / *Guitar Man* WM: Jerry Reed / *Heartbreak Hotel* WM: Mae Boren Axton and Tommy Durden / *His Latest Flame*

WM: Doc Pomus and Mort Shuman / *Hound Dog* WM: Jerry Leiber and Mike Stoller / *If I Can Dream* WM: W. Earl Brown / *I'll Fly Away* (Albert Brumley) / *I Need Your Love Tonight* WM: Sid Wayne and Bix Reichner / *I've Got a Thing About You, Baby* WM: Tony Joe White / *I Was the One* WM: Aaron Schroeder, Claude DeMetrius, Hal Blair and Bill Pepper / *Jailhouse Rock; King Creole* WM: Jerry Leiber and Mike Stoller / *King of the Whole Wide World* WM: Ruth Batchelor and Bob Roberts / *Kung Fu Fighting* (Carl Douglas) WM: Carl Douglas / *Let Yourself Go* WM: Joy Byers / *Love Me* WM: Jerry Leiber and Mike Stoller / *Love Me Tender* W: Elvis Presley and Vera Matson—M: George R. Poulton / *Mean Woman Blues* WM: Claude DeMetrius / *Memories* WM: Billy Strange and Mac Davis / *Merry Christmas Baby* WM: Lou Baxter and Johnny Moore / *Moody Blue* WM: Mark James / *My Baby Left Me* WM: Arthur Crudup / *Mystery Train* (David Scott) WM: Herman Parker and Sam Phillips / *My Way* Eng. W: Paul Anka—Fr. WM: Gilles Thibault, Claude Francois and Jacques Revaux / *Promised Land* WM: Chuck Berry / *Ready Teddy* WM: John Marascalco and Robert Blackwell / *Rock-a-Hula Baby* WM: Fred Wise, Dolores Fuller and Ben Weisman / *Rocket 88* (Jackie Brenston) WM: Jackie Brenston / *Shake, Rattle and Roll* WM: Charles E. Calhoun [Jesse Stone] / *Stuck on You* WM: Aaron Schroeder and Leslie McFarland / *Suspicious Minds* WM: Mark James [Fred Zambon] / *Teddy Bear* WM: Kal Mann and Bernie Lowe / *That's All Right* (David Scott, Elvis Presley) WM: Arthur Crudup / *Too Much Monkey Business* WM: Chuck Berry / *Trouble* WM: Jerry Leiber and Mike Stoller / *Viva Las Vegas* WM: Doc Pomus and Mort Shuman / *Witchcraft* WM: Dave Bartholomew and Pearl King.

"Packed with enough fine music and unusual footage to satisfy anyone with an interest in the late singing idol." — *Variety.*

**1305 This Is My Affair.** US, 1937, BW, 101 m. D: William A. Seiter, MD: Arthur Lange, P: TCF (Kenneth MacGowan). GB Title: His Affair. Performer: Barbara Stanwyck.

*Fill It Up; I Hum a Waltz; Put Down Your Glasses, Pick Up Your Girl* W: Mack Gordon—M: Harry Revel.

**1306 This Is the Army.** US, 1943, C, 121 m. D: Michael Curtiz, MS: Ray Heindorf, P: Warner (Hal B. Wallis).

*American Eagles* (Robert Shanley, Chorus); *The Army's Made a Man Out of Me* (Ezra Stone, Julie Oshins, Philip Truex); *God Bless America* (Kate Smith); *How About a Cheer for the Navy?* (Chorus); *I Left My Heart at the Stage Door Canteen* (Earl Oxford); *I'm Getting Tired So I Can Sleep* (James Burell); *Ladies of the Chorus* (Alan Hale, Chorus); *Mandy* (Ralph Magelssen, Chorus); *My Sweetie* (George Murphy); *Oh, How I Hate to Get Up in the Morning* (Irving Berlin, Chorus); *Poor Little Me, I'm on K.P.* (George Tobias); *This Is the Army, Mr. Jones* (Sidney Robin, William Roerich, Henry Jones, Chorus); *This Time* (Robert Shanley, Chorus); *We're on Our Way to France* (George Murphy, George Tobias, Alan Hale, Chorus); *What Does He Look Like?* (Frances Langford); *What the Well-Dressed Man in Harlem Will Wear* (James Cross); *With My Head in the Clouds* (Robert Shanley); *Your Country and My Country* (Gertrude Niesen, Chorus) WM: Irving Berlin.

"The freshest, the most endearing, the most rousing musical tribute to the American fighting man that has come out of World War II." — Theodore Strauss, *The New York Times.*

**1307 This Property Is Condemned.** US, 1966, C, 110 m. D: Sydney Pollack, MS: Kenyon Hopkins, P: Paramount (John Houseman).

*Wish Me a Rainbow* (Mary Badham, Natalie Wood) WM: Jerry Livingston and Ray Evans.

**1308   This Week of Grace.** GB, 1933, BW, 92 m. D: Maurice Elvey, P: RKO (Julius Hagen). Performer: Gracie Fields.

*Happy Ending; Heaven Will Protect an Honest Girl; Mary Rose; My Lucky Day* WM: Harry Parr-Davies.

**1309   This'll Make You Whistle.** GB, 1936, BW, 78 m. D: Herbert Wilcox, P: C. and M. Pictures.

*I'm in a Dancing Mood* (Jack Buchanan, Elsie Randolph); *My Red-Letter Day* (Elsie Randolph); *There Isn't Any Limit to My Love* (Jack Buchanan); *This'll Make You Whistle* (Jack Buchanan, Elsie Randolph); *Without Rhythm* (Jack Buchanan); *You've Got the Wrong Rumba* (Elsie Randolph) WM: Al Hoffman, Al Goodhart and Maurice Sigler.

**1310   The Thomas Crown Affair.** US, 1968, C, 102 m. D: Norman Jewison, MS: Michel Legrand, P: UA (Norman Jewison). Alt. Titles: Thomas Crown and Company; The Crown Caper.

*The Windmills of Your Mind* (Noel Harrison) W: Alan Bergman and Marilyn Bergman—M: Michel Legrand.

**1311   Thoroughbreds Don't Cry.** US, 1937, BW, 80 m. D: Alfred E. Green, MD: William Axt, P: MGM (Harry Rapf).

*Got a Pair of New Shoes* (Judy Garland) W: Arthur Freed—M: Nacio Herb Brown.

**1312   Thoroughly Modern Millie.** US, 1967, C, 138 m. D: George Roy Hill, MD: Andre Previn and Joseph Gershenson, MS: Elmer Bernstein, P: Universal (Ross Hunter).

*Baby Face* (Julie Andrews) WM: Benny Davis and Harry Akst / *Do It Again* (Carol Channing) W: B.G. De Sylva—M: George Gershwin / *Jazz Baby* (Carol Channing) WM: Blanche Merrill and M.K. Jerome / *Jewish Wedding Song* (Julie Andrews) WM: Sylvia Neufeld / *Jimmy* (Julie Andrews) WM:

Jay Thompson / *Poor Butterfly* (Julie Andrews) W: John Golden—M: Raymond Hubbell / *Rose Of Washington Square* (Ann Dee) W: Ballard MacDonald—M: James F. Hanley / *The Tapioca* (James Fox); *Thoroughly Modern Millie* (Julie Andrews) W: Sammy Cahn—M: James Van Heusen.

**1313   A Thousand Clowns.** US, 1965, BW, 117 m. D: Fred Coe, MS: Don Walker, P: UA (Fred Coe).

*A Thousand Clowns* (Rita Gardner) WM: Judy Holliday and Gerry Mulligan / *Yes Sir! That's My Baby* (Jason Robards, Jr.) W: Gus Kahn—M: Walter Donaldson.

**1314   Thousands Cheer.** US, 1943, C, 126 m. D: George Sidney, MD: Herbert Stothart, P: MGM (Joe Pasternak). Orch: Benny Carter; Jose Iturbi; Kay Kyser; Bob Crosby.

*Daybreak* (Kathryn Grayson) W: Harold Adamson—M: Ferde Grofe / *Honeysuckle Rose* (Lena Horne) W: Andy Razaf—M: Thomas "Fats" Waller / *I Dug a Ditch* (Kathryn Grayson, Chorus) W: Lew Brown and Ralph Freed—M: Burton Lane / *In a Little Spanish Town* (Virginia O'Brien, Gloria De Haven, June Allyson) W: Sam M. Lewis and Joe Young—M: Mabel Wayne / *The Joint Is Really Jumpin' at Carnegie Hall* (Judy Garland) WM: Ralph Blane, Hugh Martin and Roger Edens / *Let Me Call You Sweetheart* (Gene Kelly) WM: Beth Slater Whitson and Leo Friedman / *Let There Be Music* (Kathryn Grayson) W: E.Y. Harburg—M: Earl K. Brent / *Should I?* (Georgia Carroll) W: Arthur Freed—M: Nacio Herb Brown / *Three Letters in the Mailbox* (Kathryn Grayson) W: Paul Francis Webster—M: Walter Jurmann / *The United Nations on the March* (Kathryn Grayson, Chorus) W: Harold Rome—M: Dmitri Shostakovich.

"Musically, there is something for all tastes." —Thomas M. Pryor, *The New York Times.*

**1315   Three Coins in the Fountain.** US, 1954, C, 102 m. D: Jean

Negulesco, MS: Victor Young, P: TCF (Sol C. Siegel).

*Three Coins in the Fountain* (Frank Sinatra) W: Sammy Cahn—M: Jule Styne.

**1316  Three for the Show.** US, 1955, C, 93 m. D: Henry C. Potter, MD: George Duning, P: Columbia (Jonie Taps).

*Down Boy* (Betty Grable, Jack Lemmon, Gower Champion) W: Harold Adamson—M: Hoagy Carmichael / *How Come You Do Me Like You Do?* (Betty Grable, Jack Lemmon) WM: Gene Austin and Roy Bergere / *I've Been Kissed Before* (Betty Grable) W: Bob Russell—M: Lester Lee / *I've Got a Crush on You* (Betty Grable, Jack Lemmon) W: Ira Gershwin—M: George Gershwin / *Which One* (Betty Grable, Marge Champion) W: Ned Washington—M: Lester Lee.

**1317  Three Little Girls in Blue.** US, 1946, C, 90 m. D: H. Bruce Humberstone, MD: Alfred Newman, P: TCF (Mack Gordon). Vocals: Carol Stewart for Vera-Ellen; Ben Gage for George Montgomery; Del Porter for Charles Smith.

*Always a Lady* (Celeste Holm); *A Farmer's Life Is a Very Merry Life* (Vera-Ellen, June Haver, Vivian Blaine) W: Mack Gordon—M: Joseph Myrow / *If You Can't Get a Girl in the Summertime* (June Haver, George Montgomery) WM: Bert Kalmar and Harry Tierney / *I Like Mike* (Vera-Ellen); *Oh My Love* (Chorus); *On the Boardwalk in Atlantic City* (Vera-Ellen, June Haver, Vivian Blaine); *Somewhere in the Night* (Vivian Blaine); *Three Little Girls in Blue* (Vera-Ellen, June Haver, Vivian Blaine); *You Make Me Feel So Young* (Vera-Ellen, Charles Smith) W: Mack Gordon—M: Joseph Myrow.

**1318  Three Little Words.** US, 1950, C, 102 m. D: Richard Thorpe, MD: Andre Previn, P: MGM (Jack Cummings). Vocals: Anita Ellis for Vera-Ellen; Helen Kane for Debbie Reynolds.

Biopic of songwriting partners Bert Kalmar and Harry Ruby who created scores for Broadway musicals and wrote Marx Brothers movies. Many of their screen songs became standards.

*All Alone Monday* (Gale Robbins) W: Bert Kalmar—M: Harry Ruby / *Come On, Papa* (Vera-Ellen, Chorus) W: Edgar Leslie—M: Harry Ruby / *Hooray for Captain Spaulding* (Fred Astaire, Red Skelton); *I Love You So Much* (Arlene Dahl, Chorus) W: Bert Kalmar—M: Harry Ruby / *I Wanna Be Loved By You* (Debbie Reynolds, Fred Astaire) W: Bert Kalmar—M: Harry Ruby and Herbert Stothart / *My Sunny Tennessee* (Fred Astaire, Red Skelton) WM: Bert Kalmar, Harry Ruby and Herman Ruby / *Nevertheless* (Fred Astaire, Red Skelton, Vera-Ellen); *She's Mine, All Mine* (Quartet); *So Long, Oo Long* (Fred Astaire, Red Skelton); *Thinking of You* (Vera-Ellen, Arlene Dahl); *Three Little Words* (Fred Astaire, Red Skelton, Vera-Ellen, Phil Regan); *Up in the Clouds* (Chorus) W: Bert Kalmar—M: Harry Ruby / *Where Did You Get That Girl?* (Vera-Ellen, Fred Astaire) W: Bert Kalmar—M: Harry Puck / *Who's Sorry Now?* (Gloria De Haven) WM: Bert Kalmar, Harry Ruby and Ted Snyder / *You Are My Lucky Star* (Phil Regan) W: Arthur Freed—M: Nacio Herb Brown / *You Smiled at Me* (Arlene Dahl) W: Bert Kalmar—M: Harry Ruby.

"The score is soothing and melodious. . . . Although the story is light as an August breeze, it serves the purpose for which it was intended, to provide some visual accompaniment for the playing of an album of songs." — Thomas M. Pryor, *The New York Times*.

**1319  Three Smart Girls.** US, 1936, BW, 84 m. D: Henry Koster, MD: Charles Previn, P: Universal (Joe Pasternak).

*My Heart Is Singing* (Deanna Durbin, Binnie Barnes); *Someone to Care for Me* (Deanna Durbin) W: Gus Kahn

—M: Bronislau Kaper and Walter Jurmann.

"Miss Durbin, 14-year-old soprano, carols most sweetly in an immature, but surprisingly well trained voice." — Frank S. Nugent, *The New York Times*.

**1320   Three Smart Girls Grow Up.** US, 1939, BW, 90 m. D: Henry Koster, P: Universal (Joe Pasternak). Performer: Deanna Durbin.

*Because* W: Edward Teschemacher—M: Guy d'Hardelot / *'Tis the Last Rose of Summer* W: Thomas Moore—M: Richard Alfred Milliken.

**1321   Thrill of a Romance.** US, 1945, C, 105 m. D: Richard Thorpe, MD: George Stoll, P: MGM (Joe Pasternak). Orch: Tommy Dorsey, Xavier Cugat.

*Because* (Male Singer) W: Edward Teschemacher—M: Guy d'Hardelot / *I Should Care* (Esther Williams, Robert Allen) WM: Sammy Cahn, Axel Stordahl and Paul Weston / *I Want What I Want When I Want It* (Lauritz Melchior) W: Henry Blossom—M: Victor Herbert / *Lonely Night* (Lauritz Melchior) W: Richard Connell—M: George Stoll / *Please Don't Say No, Say Maybe* (Lauritz Melchior, The King Sisters) W: Ralph Freed—M: Sammy Fain / *Vive L'Amour* (Esther Williams, Lauritz Melchior, Chorus) WM: Ralph Blane, Kay Thompson and George Stoll.

**1322   Thunderball.** GB, 1965, C, 129 m. D: Terence Young, MS: John Barry, P: UA (Kevin McClory).

*Thunderball* (Tom Jones) W: Don Black—M: John Barry.

**1323   Tickle Me.** US, 1965, C, 90 m. D: Norman Taurog, MS: Walter Scharf, P: AA (Ben Schwalb). MB: The Jordanaires. Performer: Elvis Presley.

*Dirty, Dirty Feeling* WM: Jerry Leiber and Mike Stoller / *Easy Question* WM: Otis Blackwell and Winfield Scott / *I Feel That I've Known You Forever* WM: Doc Pomus and Alan Jeffries / *I'm Yours* WM: Don Robertson and Hal Blair / *It Feels So Right* WM: Fred Wise and Ben Weisman / *Long Lonely Highway; Night Rider* WM: Doc Pomus and Mort Shuman / *Put the Blame on Me* WM: Kay Twomey, Fred Wise and Norman Blagman / *Slowly But Surely* WM: Sid Wayne and Ben Weisman.

**1324   Till the Clouds Roll By.** US, 1946, C, 137 m. D: Richard Whorf and Vincente Minnelli, MD: Lennie Hayton, P: MGM (Arthur Freed). Vocals: Trudi Erwin for Lucille Bremer.

*All the Things You Are* (Tony Martin); *Can't Help Lovin' Dat Man* (Lena Horne) W: Oscar Hammerstein II / *Cleopatterer* (June Allyson, Chorus) W: P.G. Wodehouse / *Cotton Blossom* (Chorus) W: Oscar Hammerstein II / *A Fine Romance* (Virginia O'Brien) W: Dorothy Fields / *How'd You Like to Spoon with Me?* (Angela Lansbury, Chorus) W: Edward Laska / *I Won't Dance* (Van Johnson, Lucille Bremer) W: Otto Harbach, Oscar Hammerstein II, Dorothy Fields and Jimmy McHugh / *The Land Where the Good Songs Go* (Lucille Bremer) W: Otto Harbach / *The Last Time I Saw Paris* (Dinah Shore) W: Oscar Hammerstein II / *Leave It to Jane* (June Allyson) W: P.G. Wodehouse / *Life Upon the Wicked Stage* (Virginia O'Brien, Chorus) W: Oscar Hammerstein II / *Long Ago and Far Away* (Kathryn Grayson) W: Ira Gershwin / *Look for the Silver Lining* (Judy Garland) W: B.G. De Sylva / *Ol' Man River* (Caleb Peterson, Frank Sinatra, Chorus); *One More Dance* (Lucille Bremer); *Only Make Believe* (Kathryn Grayson, Tony Martin) W: Oscar Hammerstein II / *She Didn't Say Yes* (The Wilde Twins); *Smoke Gets in Your Eyes* (Chorus) W: Otto Harbach / *Sunny* (Chorus) WM: Otto Harbach and Oscar Hammerstein II / *They Didn't Believe Me* (Dinah Shore, Dorothy Patrick) W: Herbert Reynolds [Michael E. Rourke] / *Till the Clouds Roll By* (June Allyson, Ray MacDonald, Chorus) W: P.G. Wodehouse / *Who?* (Judy Garland, Lucille Bremer,

Chorus) W: Otto Harbach and Oscar Hammerstein II / *Who Cares If My Boat Goes Upstream?* (Tony Martin); *Why Was I Born?* (Lena Horne) W: Oscar Hammerstein II / *Yesterdays* (Chorus) W: Otto Harbach. M: Jerome Kern.

"Picture actually opens with 'Show Boat,' a 1927 whammo. There is virtually a tabloid version of that operetta utilized for the opener . . . and the rest of the story is virtually a success-story flashback." — *Variety.*

"Why did Metro . . . have to cook up a thoroughly phoney yarn about the struggles of a chirpy young composer to carry the lovely songs of Jerry Kern?" — Bosley Crowther, *The New York Times.*

**1325  Till the End of Time.** US, 1946, BW, 105 m. D: Edward Dmytryk, MS: Leigh Harline, P: RKO (Dore Schary).

*Till the End of Time* (Perry Como) WM: Buddy Kaye and Ted Mossman — Based on Chopin's Polonaise in A-Flat.

**1326  The Time, the Place and the Girl.** US, 1946, C, 105 m. D: David Butler, P: Warner (Alex Gottlieb). Orch: Carmen Cavallero.

*A Gal in Calico* (Jack Carson, Dennis Morgan, Martha Vickers); *Oh, But I Do* (Dennis Morgan); *A Rainy Night in Rio* (Jack Carson, Dennis Morgan, Janis Paige, Martha Vickers); *Through a Thousand Dreams* (Dennis Morgan, Martha Vickers) W: Leo Robin — M: Arthur Schwartz.

**1327  A Time to Sing.** US, 1968, C, 92 m. D: Arthur Dreifuss, P: MGM (Sam Katzman). MB: Clara Ward and The X-L's. Performer: Hank Williams, Jr.

*It's All Over But the Crying* WM: Hank Williams, Jr. / *A Man Is on His Own* WM: John Scoggins and Hank Williams, Jr. / *Money Can't Buy Happiness* WM: Steve Karliski / *Next Time I Say Goodbye, I'm Leaving* (Shelley Fabares, Chorus) WM: Larry Kusik and Eddie Snyder / *Old Before My Time*

WM: Steve Karliski / *Rock in My Shoe* WM: Hank Williams, Jr. / *A Time to Sing* WM: John Scoggins.

**1328  Times Square.** US, 1980, C, 111 m. D: Alan Moyle, MS: Blue Weaver, P: EMI (Robert Stigwood).

*Babylon's Burning* (The Ruts) WM: Malcolm Owen, John Jennings, Paul Fox and Dave Ruffy / *Damn Dog* (Robin Johnson, The Cleo Club) WM: Billy Mernit and Jacob Brackman / *Down in the Park* (Gary Numan) WM: Gary Numan / *Flowers in the City* (David Johansen, Robin Johnson) WM: David Johansen and Ronnie Guy / *Grinding Halt* (The Cure) WM: Tolhurst Dempsey Smith / *Help Me!* (Marcy Levy, Robin Gibb) WM: Robin Gibb / *Innocent, Not Guilty* (Garland Jeffreys) WM: Garland Jeffreys / *I Wanna Be Sedated* (The Ramones) WM: Douglas Colvin, John Cummings and Jeff Hyman / *Life During Wartime* (Talking Heads) WM: David Byrne / *The Night Was Not* (Desmond Child and Rouge) WM: Desmond Child / *Pissing in the River* (Patti Smith Group) WM: Patti Smith and Ivan Kral / *Pretty Boys* (Joe Jackson) WM: Joe Jackson / *Rock Hard* (Suzi Quatro) WM: Mike Chapman and Nicky Chinn / *Same Old Scene* (Roxy Music) WM: Bryan Ferry / *Take This Town* (XTC) WM: Andy Partridge / *The Talk of the Town* (The Pretenders) WM: Chrissie Hynde / *Walk on the Wild Side* (Lou Reed) WM: Lou Reed / *You Can't Hurry Love* (D.L. Byron) WM: Eddie Holland, Lamont Dozier and Brian Holland / *Your Daughter Is One* (Robin Johnson, Trini Alvarado) WM: Billy Mernit, Norman Ross and Jacob Brackman.

**1329  Times Square Lady.** US, 1935, BW, 69 m. D: George B. Seitz, P: MGM (Lucien Hubbard). Performer: Pinky Tomlin.

Tomlin, a college student at the time, was discovered in Oklahoma by then popular and influential bandleader Jimmie Grier, who invited him out to the West Coast and recorded some of his compositions.

*The Object of My Affection* WM: Pinky Tomlin, Coy Poe and Jimmie Grier / *What's the Reason?* WM: Pinky Tomlin, Coy Poe, Jimmie Grier and Earl Hatch.

**1330   Tin Pan Alley.** US, 1940, BW, 94 m. D: Walter Lang, MS: Alfred Newman, P: TCF (Darryl F. Zanuck, Kenneth MacGowan).

*America, I Love You* (Alice Faye, John Payne, The Robert Brothers, The Brian Sisters, Chorus) W: Edgar Leslie—M: Archie Gottler / *Goodbye Broadway, Hello France* (Jack Oakie) W: C. Francis Reisner and Benny Davis—M: Billy Baskette / *Honeysuckle Rose* (Betty Grable, Chorus) W: Andy Razaf—M: Thomas "Fats" Waller / *K-K-K-Katy* (Jack Oakie, John Payne, Alice Faye, Betty Grable, John Loder) WM: Geoffrey O'Hara / *Moonlight and Roses* (Betty Grable) WM: Ben Black and Neil Moret [Charles N. Daniels] / *Moonlight Bay* (Alice Faye) W: Edward Madden—M: Percy Wenrich / *The Sheik of Araby* (Alice Faye, Betty Grable, Billy Gilbert, Chorus) W: Harry B. Smith and Francis Wheeler—M: Ted Snyder / *You Say the Sweetest Things, Baby* (Alice Faye, John Payne, Jack Oakie) W: Mack Gordon—M: Harry Warren.

**1331   Titanic.** US, 1953, BW, 98 m. D: Jean Negulesco, MD: Lionel Newman, MS: Sol Kaplan, P: TCF (Charles Brackett).

*Nearer, My God, to Thee* (Clifton Webb, Chorus) W: Sarah Adams—M: From the hymn *Bethany*—Arr: Lowell Mason.

**1332   To Be or Not to Be.** US, 1983, C, 108 m. D: Alan Johnson, MS: John Morris, P: TCF (Mel Brooks).

*Heart and Soul* (Anne Bancroft) W: Frank Loesser—M: Hoagy Carmichael / *Ladies* (Mel Brooks, Chorus); *A Little Peace* (Mel Brooks) WM: Mel Brooks and Ronny Graham / *Sweet Georgia Brown* (Anne Bancroft, Mel Brooks) WM: Ben Bernie, Maceo Pinkard and Kenneth Casey / *To Be or Not to Be* (Mel Brooks) WM: Mel Brooks and Pete Wingfield / *Will You Remember?* (Anne Bancroft) W: Rida Johnson Young—M: Sigmund Romberg / *You and the Night and the Music* (Anne Bancroft) W: Howard Dietz—M: Arthur Schwartz.

**1333   To Beat the Band.** US, 1935, BW, 68 m. D: Ben Stoloff, P: RKO (Zion Myers). Orch: Fred Keating. MB: The Original California Collegians.

*Eeny, Meeny, Miney, Mo* (Johnny Mercer); *If You Were Mine* (Roger Pryor); *I Saw Her at Eight O'Clock* (Johnny Mercer, Evelyn Poe); *Meet Miss America* (Joy Hodges) W: Johnny Mercer—M: Matt Malneck.

**1334   To Have and Have Not.** US, 1944, BW, 100 m. D: Howard Hawks, MD: Leo F. Forbstein, P: Warner (Howard Hawks). Performer: Hoagy Carmichael.

Did a young Andy Williams sing for Lauren Bacall in her screen debut? Or was that her own voice? According to Bacall—and Howard Hawks—it was, although Andy recorded the song before the final decision was made to go with Lauren.

*Am I Blue?* (Lauren Bacall, Hoagy Carmichael) W: Grant Clarke—M: Harry Akst / *Baltimore Oriole* W: Paul Francis Webster—M: Hoagy Carmichael / *Hong Kong Blues* WM: Hoagy Carmichael / *How Little We Know* W: Johnny Mercer—M: Hoagy Carmichael.

"[Bacall] sings a song from deep down in her throat." —Bosley Crowther, *The New York Times.*

**1335   To Live and Die in L.A..** US, 1985, C, 116 m. D: William Friedkin, P: MGM/UA (Irving H. Levin). Performers: Wang Chung.

*Lullaby; To Live and Die in L.A.; Wait; Wake Up, Stop Dreaming* WM: Wang Chung [Jack Hues and Nick Feldman].

**1336  To Sir with Love.** GB, 1967, C, 105 m. D: James Clavell, MS: Ron Grainer, P: Columbia (James Clavell).

Scottish-born Marie McDonald Lawrie began singing as Lulu in 1964. She was married for several years to Maurice Gibb of The Bee Gees.

*Stealing My Love from Me* (The Mindbenders) WM: Mark London / *To Sir with Love* (Lulu) WM: Don Black and Mark London.

**1337  The Toast of New Orleans.** US, 1950, C, 97 m. D: Norman Taurog, MD: George Stoll and Johnny Green, P: MGM (Joe Pasternak).

*The Bayou Lullaby* (Mario Lanza, Kathryn Grayson); *Be My Love* (Mario Lanza, Kathryn Grayson); *Boom Biddy Boom Boom* (Mario Lanza, Chorus); *I'll Never Love You* (Mario Lanza); *The Tina Lina* (Mario Lanza, Chorus); *The Toast of New Orleans* (Mario Lanza) W: Sammy Cahn—M: Nicholas Brodszky.

**1338  The Toast of New York.** US, 1937, BW, 109 m. D: Rowland V. Lee, MS: Nathaniel Shilkret, P: RKO (Edward Small). Performer: Frances Farmer.

*The First Time I Saw You; Ooh, La, La* WM: Allie Wrubel and Nathaniel Shilkret.

**1339  Tom Sawyer.** US, 1973, C, 104 m. D: Don Taylor, MD: John Williams, P: UA (Arthur P. Jacobs).

*Aunt Polly's Soliloquy* (Celeste Holm); *Freebootin'* (Johnny Whitaker, Jeff East); *Gratifaction* (Johnny Whitaker, Boys); *Hannibal Mo* (Chorus); *How Come?* (Johnny Whitaker); *If'n I Was God* (Johnny Whitaker); *A Man's Gotta Be* (Warren Oates, Johnny Whitaker, Jeff East); *River Song* (Charley Pride, Chorus); *Tom Sawyer* (Celeste Holm, Joshua Hill Lewis, Susan Joyce) WM: Richard M. Sherman and Robert B. Sherman.

**1340  tom thumb.** GB-US, 1958, C, 98 m. D: George Pal, P: MGM (George Pal). Vocals: Norma Zimmer for Jessie Matthews.

*After All These Years* (Jessie Matthews); *The Talented Shoes* (Ian Wallace) W: Janice Torre—M: Fred Spielman / *Tom Thumb's Tune* (Russ Tamblyn, Chorus) WM: Peggy Lee / *The Yawning Song* (Stan Freberg, Chorus) W: Kermit Goell—M: Fred Spielman.

"Film is top-drawer, a comic fairy tale with music that stacks up alongside some of the Disney classics." — *Variety*.

**1341  Tommy.** GB, 1975, C, 111 m. D: Ken Russell, MS: Pete Townshend, John Entwistle and Keith Moon. P: Columbia (Robert Stigwood, Ken Russell).

*Acid Queen* (Tina Turner); *Amazing Journey* (Pete Townshend); *Bernie's Holiday Camp* (Ann-Margret, Oliver Reed, Alison Dowling); *Captain Walker Didn't Come Home* (Pete Townshend, Margo Newman, Vicki Brown); *Champagne* (Ann-Margret, Roger Daltrey); *Christmas* (Ann-Margret, Oliver Reed, Alison Dowling) WM: Peter Townshend / *Cousin Kevin* (Paul Nicholas) WM: John Entwistle / *Do You Think It's Alright?* (Ann-Margret, Oliver Reed); *Extra Extra Extra* (Simon Townshend) WM: Peter Townshend / *Eyesight to the Blind* (Eric Clapton) WM: Sonny Boy Williamson / *Fiddle About* (Keith Moon) WM: John Entwistle / *Go to the Mirror* (Ann-Margret, Oliver Reed, Jack Nicholson, Roger Daltrey); *I'm Free* (Roger Daltrey); *It's a Boy* (Pete Townshend, Margo Newman, Vicki Brown); *Listening to You* (Roger Daltrey, Chorus); *Miracle Cure* (Simon Townshend); *Mother and Son* (Ann-Margret, Roger Daltrey); *1951 Is Going to Be a Good Year* (Ann-Margret, Oliver Reed); *Pinball Wizard* (Elton John); *Sally Simpson* (Roger Daltrey, Pete Townshend); *See Me, Feel Me* (Roger Daltrey); *Sensation* (Roger Daltrey); *Smash the Mirror* (Ann-Margret); *Sparks* (The Who); *There's a Doctor* (Ann-Margret, Oliver Reed); *Tommy, Can You Hear Me?* (Ann-Margret) WM: Peter Townshend / *Tommy's Holiday Camp* (Keith Moon) WM:

Keith Moon / *TV Studio* (Ann-Margret, Oliver Reed); *Welcome* (Ann-Margret, Roger Daltrey, Oliver Reed); *We're Not Gonna Take It* (Roger Daltrey, Chorus); *What About the Boy?* (Ann-Margret, Oliver Reed) WM: Peter Townshend.

"The enormous appeal of the original 1969 record album by The Who has been complemented in a superbly added visual dimension." — *Variety.*

**1342  Tonight and Every Night.** US, 1945, C, 92 m. D: Victor Saville, MD: Morris Stoloff and Marlin Skiles, P: Columbia (Victor Saville). Vocals: Martha Mears for Rita Hayworth.

*Anywhere* (Janet Blair); *The Boy I Left Behind* (Janet Blair, Rita Hayworth); *Cry and You Cry Alone* (Rita Hayworth, Marc Platt); *Tonight and Every Night* (Janet Blair, Rita Hayworth, Chorus); *What Does an English Girl Think of a Yank?* (Rita Hayworth); *You Excite Me* (Rita Hayworth) W: Sammy Cahn—M: Jule Styne.

**1343  Too Many Girls.** US, 1940, BW, 85 m. D: George Abbott, MD: George Bassman, P: RKO (George Abbott). Vocals: Trudi Erwin for Lucille Ball.

*'Cause We Got Cake* (Frances Langford, Chorus); *Heroes in the Fall* (Chorus); *I Didn't Know What Time It Was* (Lucille Ball, Desi Arnaz, Eddie Bracken, Hal LeRoy); *Look Out* (Frances Langford, Ann Miller, Lucille Ball, Chorus); *Love Never Went to College* (Frances Langford); *Pottawatomie* (Chorus); *Spic and Spanish* (Desi Arnaz, Ann Miller, Chorus); *You're Nearer* (Lucille Ball, Richard Carlson, Frances Langford, Ann Miller, Desi Arnaz, Libby Bennett) W: Lorenz Hart—M: Richard Rodgers.

**1344  Tootsie.** US, 1982, C, 116 m. D: Sydney Pollack, MS: Dave Grusin, P: Columbia (Sydney Pollack, Dick Richards).

*It Might Be You* (Stephen Bishop) W: Alan Bergman and Marilyn Bergman—M: Dave Grusin / *Mary's a*

*Grand Old Name* (Charles Durning) WM: George M. Cohan / *Media Zap* (Stephen Bishop); *Tootsie* (Stephen Bishop) W: Alan Bergman and Marilyn Bergman—M: Dave Grusin.

**1345  Top Gun.** US, 1986, C, 110 m. D: Tony Scott, MS: Harold Faltermeyer, P: Paramount (Don Simpson, Jerry Bruckheimer).

*Danger Zone* (Kenny Loggins) WM: Giorgio Moroder and Tom Whitlock / *Destination Unknown* (Marietta) WM: Franne Golde, Paul Fox and Jake Hooker / *Heaven in Your Eyes* (Loverboy) WM: Paul Dean, Mike Reno, Johnny Dexter and Debra Mae Moore / *Hot Summer Nights* (Miami Sound Machine) WM: Michael Jay, Alan Roy Scott and Roy Freeland / *Lead Me On* (Teena Marie) WM: Giorgio Moroder and Tom Whitlock / *Mighty Wings* (Cheap Trick) WM: Harold Faltermeyer and Mark Spiro / *Playing with the Boys* (Kenny Loggins) WM: Kenny Loggins, Peter Wolf and Ina Wolf / *Take My Breath Away* (Berlin); *Through the Fire* (Larry Greene) WM: Giorgio Moroder and Tom Whitlock / *Top Gun Anthem* (Harold Faltermeyer, Steve Stevens) WM: Harold Faltermeyer.

**1346  Top Hat.** US, 1935, BW, 99 m. D: Mark Sandrich, MD: Max Steiner, P: RKO (Pandro S. Berman). Performer: Fred Astaire.

*Cheek to Cheek; Isn't This a Lovely Day to Be Caught in the Rain?; No Strings; The Piccolino* (Ginger Rogers, Chorus); *Top Hat, White Tie and Tails* WM: Irving Berlin.

"This one can't miss and the reasons are three—Fred Astaire, Irving Berlin's ... songs and sufficient comedy between numbers to hold the film together." — *Variety.*

"Irving Berlin has written some charming melodies for the photoplay and the best of the current cinema teams does them agile justice on the dance floor." —Andre Sennwald, *The New York Times.*

**1347  Top o' the Morning.** US,

1949, BW, 100 m. D: David Miller, P: Paramount (Robert L. Welch). Performer: Bing Crosby.

*The Donovans; Oh, 'Tis Sweet to Think* (Bing Crosby, Ann Blyth); *Top o' the Morning* W: Johnny Burke—M: James Van Heusen / *When Irish Eyes Are Smiling* W: Chauncey Olcott and George Graff, Jr.—M: Ernest R. Ball / *You're in Love with Someone* W: Johnny Burke—M: James Van Heusen.

"The songs . . . are adequate to the occasion—which is adequate, in turn, to a lot of fun." —Bosley Crowther, *The New York Times*.

**1348 Top of the Town.** US, 1937, BW, 86 m. D: Ralph Murphy, P: Universal (Lou Brock). MB: The Californian Collegians; The Four Esquires.

*Blame It on the Rhumba* (Gertrude Niesen); *Fireman, Fireman, Save My Child* (Ella Logan); *Jamboree* (Gertrude Niesen); *That Foolish Feeling* (Ella Logan); *There's No Two Ways About It* (Ella Logan); *Top of the Town* (Gertrude Niesen); *Where Are You?* (Gertrude Niesen, George Murphy, Ella Logan) W: Harold Adamson—M: Jimmy McHugh.

**1349 Topper.** US, 1937, BW, 97 m. D: Norman Z. McLeod, MD: Arthur Norton, P: MGM (Hal Roach).

*Old Man Moon* (Hoagy Carmichael, Cary Grant, Constance Bennett) WM: Hoagy Carmichael.

**1350 Torch Singer.** US, 1933, BW, 72 m. D: Alexander Hall and George Somnes, P: Paramount (Albert Lewis). Performer: Claudette Colbert. GB Title: Broadway Singer.

And she sings for herself, with no dubbing.

*Don't Be a Cry Baby; Give Me Liberty or Give Me Love; It's a Long, Dark Night; The Torch Singer* W: Leo Robin—M: Ralph Rainger.

**1351 Torch Song.** US, 1953, C, 90 m. D: Charles Walters, MS: Adolph Deutsch, P: MGM (Henry Berman, Sidney Franklin, Jr.). Vocals: India Adams for Joan Crawford.

*Blue Moon* (Trio) W: Lorenz Hart—M: Richard Rodgers / *Follow Me* (Joan Crawford, Rudy Render) WM: Adolph Deutsch / *Tenderly* (Joan Crawford) W: Jack Lawrence—M: Walter Gross / *Two-Faced Woman* (Joan Crawford, Chorus) W: Howard Dietz—M: Arthur Schwartz / *You Won't Forget Me* (Joan Crawford) W: Kermit Goell—M: Fred Spielman.

**1352 A Touch of Class.** GB, 1973, C, 105 m. D: Melvin Frank, MS: John Cameron, P: Avco (Melvin Frank).

*All That Love Went to Waste* (Madeline Bell) W: Sammy Cahn—M: George Barrie / *She Loves Me, She Told Me So Last Night* (George Segal, Glenda Jackson) WM: Melvin Frank and Marvin Frank.

**1353 The Towering Inferno.** US, 1974, C, 165 m. D: John Guillermin and Irwin Allen, MS: John Williams, P: TCF / Warner (Irwin Allen).

*We May Never Love Like This Again* (Maureen McGovern) WM: Al Kasha and Joel Hirschhorn.

**1354 Town Without Pity.** US-Switzerland-Germany, 1961, BW, 105 m. D: Gottfried Reinhardt, MS: Dimitri Tiomkin, P: UA (Gottfried Reinhardt).

*Town Without Pity* (Gene Pitney) W: Ned Washington—M: Dimitri Tiomkin.

**1355 The Trail of the Lonesome Pine.** US, 1936, C, 102 m. D: Henry Hathaway, MS: Hugo Friedhofer and Gerard Carbonara, P: Paramount (Walter Wanger). Performer: Fuzzy Knight.

*A Melody from the Sky* W: Sidney D. Mitchell—M: Louis Alter / *The Trail of the Lonesome Pine* W: Ballard MacDonald—M: Harry Carroll / *Twilight on the Trail* (Fuzzy Knight, Nigel Bruce, Fred MacMurray) W: Sidney D. Mitchell—M: Louis Alter.

**1356 Trouble in Store.** GB, 1953, BW, 85 m. D: John Paddy

Carstairs, MS: Mischa Spoliansky, P: GFD/Two Cities (Maurice Cowan).

*Don't Laugh at Me* (Norman Wisdom) WM: Norman Wisdom and June Tremayne.

**1357   The Trouble with Girls.** US, 1969, C, 104 m. D: Peter Tewksbury, MS: Billy Strange, P: MGM (Lester Welch).

*Almost* (Elvis Presley) WM: Buddy Kaye and Ben Weisman / *Clean Up Your Own Back Yard* (Elvis Presley) WM: Mac Davis and Billy Strange / *The Darktown Strutters' Ball* (Anissa Jones, Pepe Brown) WM: Shelton Brooks / *On Wisconsin* (Quartet) W: Carl Beck—M: W.T. Purdy / *Sign of the Zodiac* (Elvis Presley, Marlyn Mason) WM: Unknown / *Swing Down, Sweet Chariot* (Elvis Presley, The Jordanaires) Based on *Swing Low, Sweet Chariot* WM: Unknown —Arr: Henry Thacker Burleigh / *Toot, Toot, Tootsie!* (Linda Sue Risk) WM: Gus Kahn, Ernie Erdman and Dan Russo / *Violet* (Elvis Presley, Quartet) W: Unknown —M: Tune of *Aura Lee* / *The Whiffenpoof Song* (Elvis Presley) W: Meade Minnigerode and George S. Pomeroy —M: Tod B. Galloway.

**1358   Turn Back the Clock.** US, 1933, BW, 77 m. D: Edgar Selwyn, P: MGM (Harry Rapf).

*Tony's Wife* (Lee Tracy) W: Harold Adamson—M: Burton Lane.

**1359   Twenty Million Sweethearts.** US, 1934, BW, 89 m. D: Ray Enright, MD: Leo F. Forbstein, P: First National/Warner (Sam Bischoff). Orch: Ted Fiorito.

Born in Newark, New Jersey, in 1900, bandleader Ted Fiorito was a prolific composer with at least 100 songs to his credit. Best known of the vocalists who sang with his orchestra was a young Betty Grable. June Haver also joined him for a brief time.

*Fair and Warmer* (Dick Powell, Ginger Rogers) W: Al Dubin—M: Harry Warren / *How'm I Doin'?* (The Mills Brothers) WM: Lem Fowler and

Don Redman / *I'll String Along with You* (Dick Powell, Ginger Rogers) W: Al Dubin—M: Harry Warren / *The Man on the Flying Trapeze* (Dick Powell) WM: Walter O'Keefe / *Out for No Good* (Ginger Rogers); *What Are Your Intentions?* (The Debutantes) W: Al Dubin—M: Harry Warren.

**1360   20,000 Leagues Under the Sea.** US, 1954, C, 127 m. D: Richard Fleischer, MS: Paul Smith, P: Buena Vista (Walt Disney).

*A Whale of a Tale* (Kirk Douglas) WM: Al Hoffman and Norman Gimbel.

**1361   Two for Tonight.** US, 1935, BW, 61 m. D: Frank Tuttle, P: Paramount (Douglas MacLean). Performer: Bing Crosby.

*From the Top of Your Head; I Wish I Were Aladdin; Takes Two to Make a Bargain; Two for Tonight; Without a Word of Warning; You're Beautiful* W: Mack Gordon—M: Harry Revel.

**1362   Two Girls and a Sailor.** US, 1944, BW, 124 m. D: Richard Thorpe, MD: George Stoll, P: MGM (Joe Pasternak). Orch: Harry James; Xavier Cugat.

*A-Tisket, A-Tasket* (June Allyson, Gloria De Haven) WM: Ella Fitzgerald and Van Alexander [Al Feldman] / *Babalu* (Lina Romay) WM: Bob Russell and Marguerita Lecuona / *Granada* (Carlos Ramirez) Eng. W: Dorothy Dodd—Span. WM: Augustin Lara / *In a Moment of Madness* (Helen Forrest) W: Ralph Freed—M: Jimmy McHugh / *Inka Dinka Doo* (Jimmy Durante) WM: Ben Ryan, Dave Dreyer, Harry Donnelly and Jimmy Durante / *A Love Like Ours* (June Allyson, Gloria De Haven) W: Mann Holiner—M: Alberta Nichols / *My Mother Told Me* (Gloria De Haven, Van Johnson, Tom Drake, Frank Sully, Chorus) W: Ralph Freed —M: Jimmy McHugh / *Paper Doll* (Lena Horne) WM: Johnny S. Black / *Rumba Rumba* (Lina Romay) W: Sammy Gallop—M: Jose Parfumy / *Sweet and Lovely* (June Allyson, Gloria

De Haven) WM: Gus Arnheim, Harry Tobias and Jules Lemare / *Take It Easy* (Lina Romay, Virginia O'Brien, The Wilde Twins, Chorus) WM: Albert De Bru, Irving Taylor and Vic Mizzy / *Who Will Be with You When I'm Far Away?* (Jimmy Durante) WM: Jimmy Durante / *You Dear* (Buddy Moreno) W: Ralph Freed—M: Sammy Fain / *Young Man with a Horn* (June Allyson) W: Ralph Freed—M: George Stoll.

"It just breezes along with crackling humor and the almost perpetual accompaniment of song." —Bosley Crowther, *The New York Times.*

**1363 Two Tickets to Paris.** US, 1962, BW, 78 m. D: Greg Garrison, MD: Henry Glover, P: Columbia (Harry Romm). Performers: Joey Dee and The Starliters.

*Baby, Won't You Please Come Home?* (Jeri Lynn Fraser) WM: Charles Warfield and Clarence Williams / *C'est La Vie* (Gary Crosby) W: Edward White—M: Mack Wolfson / *C'est Si Bon* Eng. W: Jerry Seelan—Fr. WM: Henri Betti and Andre Hornez / *Everytime* W: Joey Dee and Sam Taylor—M: Henry Glover / *Instant Men* (Kay Medford) W: Hal Hackady—M: Don Gohman / *Teenage Vamp* (Jeri Lynn Fraser) WM: Albert Seigal / *This Boat; Twistin' on a Liner* W: Joey Dee and Morris Levy—M: Henry Glover / *Two Tickets to Paris* (Chorus) W: Hal Hackady—M: Don Gohman / *What Kind of Love Is This?* WM: Johnny Nash / *Willy Willy* WM: Joey Dee and Morris Levy—M: Henry Glover.

**1364 Two Weeks in Another Town.** US, 1962, C, 107 m. D: Vincente Minnelli, MS: David Raksin, P: MGM (John Houseman).

*Don't Blame Me* (Leslie Uggams) W: Dorothy Fields—M: Jimmy McHugh.

**1365 Two Weeks with Love.** US, 1950, C, 92 m. D: Roy Rowland, P: MGM (Jack Cummings).

*The Aba Daba Honeymoon* (Debbie Reynolds, Carleton Carpenter) W:

Arthur Fields—M: Walter Donovan / *By the Light of the Silvery Moon* (Jane Powell, Chorus) W: Edward Madden —M: Gus Edwards / *A Heart That's Free* (Jane Powell) W: Thomas T. Railey—M: Alfred G. Robyn / *My Hero* (Jane Powell, Chorus) W: Stanislaus Stange—M: Oscar Straus / *The Oceana Roll* (Jane Powell, Chorus) W: Roger Lewis—M: Lucien Denni / *Row, Row, Row* (Debbie Reynolds, Carleton Carpenter) W: William Jerome—M: James V. Monaco.

"A frivolous excursion complete with songs and none too witty sayings." —A.H. Weiler, *The New York Times.*

**1366 Under the Cherry Moon.** US, 1986, BW, 98 m. D: Prince, P: Warner (Bob Cavallo, Joe Ruffalo, Steve Fargnoli). Performers: Prince and The Revolution.

*Anotherloverholenyohead; Christoper Tracy's Parade; Do U Lie?; Girls and Boys; I Wonder U; Kiss; Life Can Be So Nice; Mountains; New Position; Sometimes It Snows in April; Under the Cherry Moon; Venus de Milo* WM: Prince and The Revolution.

**1367 Under Your Spell.** US, 1936, BW, 62 m. D: Otto Preminger, MD: Arthur Lange, P: TCF (John Stone). Performer: Lawrence Tibbett.

*Amigo; My Little Mule Wagon; Under Your Spell* W: Howard Dietz—M: Arthur Schwartz.

**1368 The Underpup.** US, 1939, BW, 81 m. D: Richard Wallace, MD: Charles Previn, P: Universal (Joe Pasternak). Performer: Gloria Jean.

*Annie Laurie* W: William Douglas —M: Lady John Scott / *I'm Like a Bird* W: Harold Adamson—M: Unknown— Arr: Charles Previn.

**1369 Unholy Partners.** US, 1941, BW, 94 m. D: Mervyn LeRoy, MS: David Snell, P: MGM (Samuel Marx).

*After You've Gone* (Marsha Hunt) W: Henry Creamer—M: Turner Layton.

**1370  The Unsinkable Molly Brown.** US, 1964, C, 128 m. D: Charles Walters, MD: Robert Armbruster, P: MGM (Lawrence Weingarten).

*Belly Up to the Bar, Boys* (Debbie Reynolds, Chorus); *Colorado, My Home* (Harve Presnell); *He's My Friend* (Harve Presnell, Ed Begley, Jack Kruschen, Martita Hunt, Hermione Baddeley); *I Ain't Down Yet* (Debbie Reynolds, Harve Presnell, Quartet); *I'll Never Say No* (Debbie Reynolds, Harve Presnell); *Leadville Johnny Brown* (Harve Presnell) WM: Meredith Willson.

"A rowdy and sometimes rousing blend of song and sentiment, a converted stage tuner. . . . Willson's score is rather undistinguished." — *Variety*.

**1371  Untamed.** US, 1929, BW, 88 m. D: Jack Conway, P: MGM.

*Chant of the Jungle* (Joan Crawford) W: Arthur Freed — M: Nacio Herb Brown / *That Wonderful Something Is Love* (Joan Crawford, Robert Montgomery) W: Joe Goodwin — M: Louis Alter.

**1372  Untamed Youth.** US, 1957, BW, 80 m. D: Howard W. Koch, P: Warner (Aubrey Schenck). Performer: Mamie Van Doren.

*Cotton Picker* (Eddie Cochran); *Go Go Calypso* WM: Les Baxter / *Oo La La Baby* WM: Les Baxter, Eddie Cochran, Jerry Capehart and Lenny Adelson / *Rollin' Stone* WM: Les Baxter and Lenny Adelson / *Salamander* WM: Les Baxter.

**1373  Up in Arms.** US, 1944, C, 106 m. D: Elliott Nugent, MD: Louis Forbes, MS: Ray Heindorf, P: RKO (Samuel Goldwyn).

*All Out for Freedom* (Donald Dickson, The Goldwyn Girls, Chorus); *Greetings, Gates* (Dinah Shore, Danny Kaye); *Jive Number* (Dinah Shore, Danny Kaye, The Goldwyn Girls) W: Ted Koehler — M: Harold Arlen / *The Lobby Number* (Danny Kaye); *Melody in 4-F* (Danny Kaye, Chorus) W: Sylvia Fine — M: Max Liebman / *Now I Know* (Dinah Shore); *Tess's Torch Song* (Dinah Shore, Danny Kaye, Chorus) W: Ted Koehler — M: Harold Arlen.

**1374  Up in Central Park.** US, 1948, BW, 88 m. D: William A. Seiter, MD: Johnny Green, P: Universal (Karl Tunberg).

*Carousel in the Park* (Deanna Durbin, Dick Haymes); *Oh Say Do You See What I See?* (Deanna Durbin); *When She Walks in the Room* (Dick Haymes) W: Dorothy Fields — M: Sigmund Romberg.

**1375  Uptown Saturday Night.** US, 1974, C, 104 m. D: Sidney Poitier, P: Warner (Melville Tucker).

*Uptown Saturday Night* (Dobie Gray) WM: Morgan Ames and Tom Scott.

**1376  The Vagabond King.** US, 1930, C, 104 m. D: Ludwig Berger, P: Paramount (Adolph Zucker).

The Broadway stage operetta of 1925 was based on the play 'If I Were King,' about the French poet-adventurer Francois Villon.

*Huguette Waltz* (Lillian Roth) W: Brian Hooker — M: Rudolf Friml / *If I Were King* (Dennis King); *King Louis* (Dennis King) W: Leo Robin — M: Newell Chase and Sam Coslow / *Love Me Tonight* (Jeanette MacDonald, Dennis King) W: Brian Hooker — M: Rudolf Friml / *Mary, Queen of Heaven* (Chorus) W: Leo Robin — M: Newell Chase and Sam Coslow / *Only a Rose* (Jeanette MacDonald, Dennis King); *Some Day* (Jeanette MacDonald); *Song of the Vagabonds* (Dennis King, Chorus) W: Brian Hooker — M: Rudolf Friml.

"Musically, only the one number, *Song of the Vagabonds*, stands out. 'Vagabond King' as an operetta retards itself as a melodrama. Touches of grim realism are sapped of their power by girls in tights as pages in the royal court and dwarfs turning cartwheels. . . . MacDonald's performance supplies the requisite aroma of glamor." — *Variety*.

**1377 The Vagabond King.** US, 1956, C, 86 m. D: Michael Curtiz, MD: Victor Young, P: Paramount (Pat Duggan).

*Bon Jour* (Oreste) W: Johnny Burke / *Huguette Waltz* (Rita Moreno); *Only a Rose* (Oreste); *Some Day* (Kathryn Grayson); *Song of the Vagabonds* (Oreste, Chorus) W: Brian Hooker / *This Same Heart* (Oreste); *Vive Le You* (Kathryn Grayson) W: Johnny Burke. M: Rudolf Friml.

"The old songs ... are fine but 'The Vagabond King' has not aged well." —A.H. Weiler, *The New York Times.*

**1378 The Vagabond Lover.** US, 1929, BW, 69 m. D: Marshall Neilan, MD: Victor Baravalle, P: RKO (James Ashmore Creelman). Performers: Rudy Vallee and His Connecticut Yankees.

Rudy Vallee's screen debut, and quite possibly the first full-length feature with an orchestra leader as its star.

*Georgie Porgie* (Quartet) WM: Louis Herscher, Harold Raymond and Nat Simon / *Heigh-Ho, Everybody, Heigh-Ho!* WM: Harry M. Woods / *If You Were the Only Girl in the World* W: Clifford Grey—M: Nat D. Ayer / *I'll Be Reminded of You* WM: Ken Smith and Edward Heyman / *I Love You, Believe Me, I Love You* WM: Rubey Cowan, Phil Boutelje and Philip Bartholomae / *I'm Just a Vagabond Lover* WM: Rudy Vallee and Leon Zimmerman / *A Little Kiss Each Morning* WM: Harry M. Woods / *Nobody's Sweetheart* WM: Gus Kahn, Ernie Erdman, Billy Meyers and Elmer Schoebel / *Piccolo Pete* WM: Phil Baxter.

"Prefaced by a short talk from Rudy Vallee himself, who had skipped over between shows at the Paramount ... the first singing and talking film with this crooning saxophonist was offered last night at the Globe Theatre. ... It relies on fun, tuneful songs and appealing music." —Mordaunt Hall, *The New York Times.*

**1379 Valley of the Dolls.** US, 1967, C, 123 m. D: Mark Robson, MD: John Williams, MS: Andre Previn, P: TCF (David Weisbart). Vocal: Margaret Whiting for Susan Hayward.

*Come Live with Me* (Tony Scotti); *Give a Little More* (Patty Duke); *I'll Plant My Own Tree* (Susan Hayward); *It's Impossible* (Patty Duke); *Jennifer's Recollection* (Tony Scotti); *Theme from Valley of the Dolls* (Dionne Warwick) WM: Dory Previn and Andre Previn.

"Songs ... are interpolated nicely, and logically, into plot. Dionne Warwick regularly warbles title tune." — *Variety.*

**1380 Vanishing Point.** US, 1971, C, 107 m. D: Richard C. Sarafian, MS: Jimmy Bowen, P: TCF (Norman Spencer).

*Dear Jesus God* (Segarini and Bishop) WM: Segarini and Bishop / *Freedom of Ex-Pression* (The J.B. Pickers) WM: The J.B. Pickers / *Get It Together* (Jimmy Doyle) WM: Mike Settle / *I Can't Believe* (Longbranch Pennywhistle) WM: Longbranch Pennywhistle / *Mississippi Queen* (Mountain) WM: West, Lang, Pappalardi and Rea / *Nobody Knows* (Kim Carnes) WM: Mike Settle / *Over Me* (Segarini and Bishop) WM: Segarini and Bishop / *Runaway Country* (The Doug Dillard Expedition) WM: The Doug Dillard Expedition / *Sing Out for Jesus* (Big Mama Thornton) WM: Kim Carnes / *So Tired* (Eve) WM: Eve / *Super-Soul Theme* (The J.B. Pickers) WM: The J.B. Pickers / *Sweet Jesus* (Red Steagall) WM: Red Steagall / *Where Do We Go from Here* (Jimmy Walker) WM: Mike Settle / *You Got to Believe* (Delaney and Bonnie) WM: Delaney Bramlett.

**1381 Varsity Show.** US, 1937, BW, 120 m. D: William Keighley, P: Warner (Louis F. Edelman). Orch: Fred Waring and His Pennsylvanians.

And marking Fred Waring's debut, as well as those of actress-singer sisters Rosemary and Priscilla Lane.

*Have You Got Any Castles, Baby?*

(Dick Powell, Priscilla Lane); *Love Is On the Air Tonight* (Rosemary Lane, Priscilla Lane); *Moonlight on the Campus* (Dick Powell); *Old King Cole* (Johnny "Scat" Davis); *On with the Dance* (Rosemary Lane); *We're Working Our Way Through College* (Dick Powell, Chorus); *You've Got Something There* (Rosemary Lane, Dick Powell) W: Johnny Mercer—M: Richard A. Whiting.

**1382   Victor/Victoria.** GB, 1982, C, 133 m. D: Blake Edwards, P: MGM/UA (Blake Edwards, Tony Adams).

*Chicago, Illinois* (Lesley Ann Warren, Chorus); *Crazy World* (Julie Andrews); *Gay Paree* (Robert Preston); *Le Jazz Hot* (Julie Andrews, Chorus); *The Shady Dame from Seville* (Julie Andrews); *You and Me* (Julie Andrews, Robert Preston) W: Leslie Bricusse—M: Henry Mancini.

**1383   A View to a Kill.** GB, 1985, C, 131 m. D: John Glen, MS: John Barry, P: MGM/UA (Albert R. Broccoli).

*A View to a Kill* (Duran Duran) WM: Duran Duran and John Barry.

**1384   Virginia City.** US, 1940, BW, 121 m. D: Michael Curtiz, MS: Max Steiner, P: Warner (Robert Fellows).

*Rally Round the Flag Boys* (Miriam Hopkins) WM: Unknown.

**1385   Vision Quest.** US, 1985, C, 105 m. D: Harold Becker, P: Warner (Jon Peters, Peter Guber).

*Change* (John Waite) WM: Holly Knight / *Crazy for You* (Madonna) W: John Bettis—M: Jon Lind / *Gambler* (Madonna) WM: Madonna / *Hot Blooded* (Foreigner) WM: Lou Gramm and Mick Jones / *Hungry for Heaven* (Dio) WM: Ronnie James Dio and Benjamin Warner / *I'll Fall in Love Again* (Sammy Hagar) WM: Sammy Hagar / *Lunatic Fringe* (Red Rider) WM: Tom Cochrane / *Only the Young* (Journey) WM: Steve Perry, Neal Schon and Jonathan Cain / *She's on the*

*Zoom* (Don Henley) WM: Don Henley and Danny Kortchmar / *Shout to the Top* (The Style Council) WM: Paul Weller.

**1386   Viva Las Vegas.** US, 1964, C, 86 m. D: George Sidney, MD: George Stoll, P: MGM (Jack Cummings, George Sidney). GB Title: Love in Las Vegas.

*Appreciation* (Ann-Margret) / *The Climb* (The Forte Four) WM: Jerry Leiber and Mike Stoller / *C'mon Everybody* (Elvis Presley, Ann-Margret) WM: Joy Byers / *The Eyes of Texas* (Elvis Presley) W: John L. Sinclair—M: Unknown, Based on *I've Been Working on the Railroad*—Arr: Fred Wise and Ben Weisman / *If You Think I Don't Need You* (Elvis Presley) WM: Red West and Joe Cooper / *I Need Somebody to Lean On* (Elvis Presley) WM: Doc Pomus and Mort Shuman / *The Lady Loves Me* (Elvis Presley, Ann-Margret) WM: Sid Tepper and Roy C. Bennett / *My Rival* (Ann-Margret) / *Santa Lucia* (Elvis Presley) Eng. W: Thomas Oliphant—Ital. WM: Teodoro Cottrau / *Today, Tomorrow and Forever* (Elvis Presley) WM: Bill Giant, Bernie Baum and Florence Kaye / *Viva Las Vegas* (Elvis Presley, Ann-Margret) WM: Doc Pomus and Mort Shuman / *What'd I Say* (Elvis Presley) WM: Ray Charles / *The Yellow Rose of Texas* (Elvis Presley) WM: J.K., Adapted by Don George in 1955—Arr: Fred Wise and Ben Weisman.

"Hackneyed yarn provides the skeletal excuse for about 10 musical interludes." —*Variety.*

**1387   Vogues of 1938.** US, 1937, C, 108 m. D: Irving Cummings, MD: Boris Morros, MS: Victor Young, P: UA (Walter Wanger). Later Title: All This and Glamor Too.

*Aloha Oe* (Chorus) WM: Queen Liliuokalani / *Anchors Aweigh* (Chorus) W: Alfred Hart Miles and Royal Lovell—M: Charles A. Zimmerman / *Lovely One* (The Wiere Brothers, Fred Lawrence, Virginia Verrill, Chorus) W:

Frank Loesser—M: Manning Sherwin / *Siboney* (Chorus) Eng. W: Theodora Morse [Dolly Morse, Dorothy Terriss] —Span. WM: Ernesto Lecuona / *That Old Feeling* (Virginia Verrill) W: Lew Brown—M: Sammy Fain / *Turn on That Red Hot Heat* (Cotton Club Singers) WM: Paul Francis Webster and Louis Alter.

**1388 Voices.** US, 1979, C, 107 m. D: Robert Markowitz, MS: Jimmy Webb, P: MGM (Joe Wizan). Vocals: Burton Cummings for Michael Ontkean.

*Anything That's Rock 'n' Roll* (Tom Petty and The Heartbreakers) WM: Tom Petty / *Bubbles in My Beer* (Willie Nelson) WM: Tommy Duncan, Cindy Walker and Bob Wills / *Drunk As a Punk* (Michael Ontkean); *I Will Always Wait for You* (Michael Ontkean); *On a Stage* (Michael Ontkean) WM: Jimmy Webb.

**1389 Waikiki Wedding.** US, 1937, BW, 89 m. D: Frank Tuttle, MD: Boris Morros, MS: Leo Shukin, P: Paramount (Arthur Hornblow, Jr.). Performer: Bing Crosby.

*Blue Hawaii* (Bing Crosby, Shirley Ross); *In a Little Hula Heaven* (Bing Crosby, Shirley Ross); *Okolehao; Sweet Is the Word for You* W: Leo Robin—M: Ralph Rainger / *Sweet Leilani* WM: Harry Owens.

"The lei of the last minstrel." — Frank S. Nugent, *The New York Times*.

**1390 Wait Until Dark.** US, 1967, C, 107 m. D: Terence Young, P: Warner (Mel Ferrer).

*Wait Until Dark* (Bobby Darin) WM: Jay Livingston, Ray Evans and Henry Mancini.

**1391 Wake Up and Dream.** US, 1934, BW, 75 m. D: Kurt Neumann, P: Universal (B.F. Ziedman). Performer: Russ Columbo.

This was the popular singing star's last movie before his life ended suddenly at the age of 25 with a mysterious shotgun accident.

*Let's Pretend There's a Moon* WM:

Bernie Grossman, Jack Stern and Grace Hamilton / *Too Beautiful for Words* WM: Bernie Grossman, Russ Columbo and Jack Stern / *Wake Up and Dream; When You're in Love* WM: Bernie Grossman, Jack Stern and Grace Hamilton.

**1392 Wake Up and Live.** US, 1937, BW, 91 m. D: Sidney Lanfield, MD: Louis Silvers, P: TCF (Kenneth MacGowan). Orch: Ben Bernie. Vocals: Buddy Clark for Jack Haley.

*De Camptown Races* (Chorus) WM: Stephen Collins Foster / *I Love You Much Too Much, Muchacha* (Leah Ray, Chorus); *I'm Bubbling Over* (Grace Bradley, The Brewster Twins); *It's Swell of You* (Jack Haley, Ben Bernie); *Never in a Million Years* (Jack Haley, Alice Faye); *Oh, But I'm Happy* (Jack Haley); *Red Seal Malt* (Ben Bernie, Quartet); *There's a Lull in My Life* (Alice Faye); *Wake Up and Live* (Alice Faye, Jack Haley, Chorus) W: Mack Gordon—M: Harry Revel.

**1393 The Wanderers.** US, 1979, C, 113 m. D: Philip Kaufman, P: Warner (Martin Ransohoff).

*Baby It's You* (The Shirelles) WM: Mack David, Burt Bacharach and Barney Williams / *Big Girls Don't Cry* (The Four Seasons) WM: Bob Crewe and Bob Gaudio / *Do You Love Me?* (The Contours) WM: Berry Gordy, Jr. / *I Love You* (The Volumes) / *My Boyfriend's Back* (The Angels) WM: Robert Feldman, Gerald Goldstein and Richard Gottehrer / *Sherry* (The Four Seasons) WM: Bob Gaudio / *Shout* (The Isley Brothers) WM: O'Kelly Isley, Ronald Isley and Rudolph Isley / *Soldier Boy* (The Shirelles) WM: Florence Green and Luther Dixon / *Stand By Me* (Ben E. King) WM: Ben E. King, Jerry Leiber and Mike Stoller / *Stranger Girl* (Ken Wahl) / *The Times They Are A-Changin'* (Bob Dylan) WM: Bob Dylan / *Walk Like a Man* (The Four Seasons) WM: Bob Crewe and Bob Gaudio / *Wipe Out* (The Surfaris) WM: Ron Wilson, James Fuller,

Robert Berryhill and Patrick Connolly / *Ya Ya* (Lee Dorsey) WM: Lee Dorsey, Clarence Lewis and Morgan Robinson / *You Really Got a Hold on Me* (Smokey Robinson and The Miracles) WM: William "Smokey" Robinson.

**1394  The Warriors.** US, 1979, C, 90 m. D: Walter Hill, MS: Barry De Vorzon, P: Paramount (Lawrence Gordon).

*Echoes in My Mind* (Mandrill) WM: Carlos Wilson, Lou Wilson, Claude Cave II, Dr. Ric Wilson and Wilfredo Wilson / *In Havana* (Frederick La Plano) WM: Steve Nathanson and Artie Ripp / *In the City* (Joe Walsh) WM: Barry De Vorzon and Joe Walsh / *Last of an Ancient Breed* (Desmond Child and Rouge) WM: Desmond Child / *Love Is a Fire* (Genya Raven) WM: Johnny Vastano and Vinnie Poncia / *Nowhere to Run* (Arnold McCuller) WM: Eddie Holland, Lamont Dozier and Brian Holland / *You're Movin' Too Slow* (Johnny Vastano) WM: Eric Mercury and William Smith.

**1395  Way Out West.** US, 1937, BW, 65 m. D: James W. Horne, MD: Marvin Hatley, P: MGM (Hal Roach, Stan Laurel). Vocals: Chill Wills for Stan Laurel.

The best known of the four Avalon Boys, character actor Chill Wills later became successful as the voice of television's Francis the Talking Mule. The other three were Art Green, Walter Trask and Don Brookins.

*At the Ball, That's All* (The Avalon Boys); *Commence to Dancing* (The Avalon Boys) WM: J.L. Hill / *The Trail of the Lonesome Pine* (Stan Laurel) WM: Ballard MacDonald—M: Harry Carroll / *We're Going Down to Dixie* (Stan Laurel, Oliver Hardy, Rosina Lawrence) WM: William B. Bradbury / *Won't You Be My Lovey Dovey?* (Sharon Lynne, Chorus) WM: Seymour Furth and E.P. Moran.

**1396  The Way We Were.** US, 1973, C, 118 m. D: Sydney Pollack, P: Columbia (Ray Stark).

*The Way We Were* (Barbra Streisand) W: Alan Bergman and Marilyn Bergman—M: Marvin Hamlisch.

**1397  Wee Willie Winkie.** US, 1937, BW, 99 m. D: John Ford, MS: Alfred Newman, P: TCF (Gene Markey, Darryl F. Zanuck).

*Auld Lang Syne* (Shirley Temple) W: Robert Burns—M: Unknown.

**1398  Week-end in Havana.** US, 1941, C, 80 m. D: Walter Lang, MD: Alfred Newman, P: TCF (William LeBaron). Orch: Bando da Lua.

*Mama Inez* (Chorus) W: L. Wolfe Gilbert—M: Eliseo Grenet / *The Nango* (Carmen Miranda, Chorus) W: Mack Gordon—M: Harry Warren / *Rebola a Bola* (Carmen Miranda) WM: Aloysio Oliveira and Nestor Almaro / *Romance and Rumba* (Alice Faye, Cesar Romero, Chorus) W: Mack Gordon—M: James V. Monaco / *Tropical Magic* (Alice Faye, John Payne, Trio); *A Week-end in Havana* (Carmen Miranda, Alice Faye, John Payne, Cesar Romero, Chorus); *When I Love, I Love* (Carmen Miranda) W: Mack Gordon—M: Harry Warren.

**1399  Welcome Stranger.** US, 1947, BW, 107 m. D: Elliott Nugent, MS: Robert Emmett Dolan, P: Paramount (Sol C. Siegel). Performer: Bing Crosby.

*As Long As I'm Dreaming; Country Style; My Heart Is a Hobo; Smile Right Back at the Sun* W: Johnny Burke—M: James Van Heusen.

**1400  Welcome to L.A.** US, 1976, C, 106 m. D: Alan Rudolph, P: UA (Robert Altman). Performers: Richard Baskin and Keith Carradine.

*After the End; At the Door; The Best Temptation of All; City of the One-Night Stands; Night Time; Welcome to L.A.; When the Arrow Flies* WM: Richard Baskin.

**1401  We're Not Dressing.** US, 1934, BW, 77 m. D: Norman Taurog, P: Paramount (Benjamin Glazer). Performer: Bing Crosby.

*Good Night Lovely Little Lady; I'll Sing About the Birds and the Bees; It's*

*Just a New Spanish Custom* (Ethel Merman, Leon Errol); *Let's Play House* (Ethel Merman); *Love Thy Neighbor* (Bing Crosby, Ethel Merman, Leon Errol); *May I?; Once in a Blue Moon; She Reminds Me of You* W: Mack Gordon—M: Harry Revel.

**1402   West of Zanzibar.** GB, 1954, C, 84 m. D: Harry Watt, MS: Alan Rawsthorne, P: Ealing (Leslie Norman).

*West of Zanzibar* (Anthony Steele) WM: Jack Fishman.

**1403   West Side Story.** US, 1961, C, 151 m. D: Robert Wise, MD. Johnny Green and Saul Chaplin, P: UA (Robert Wise). Vocals: Marni Nixon for Natalie Wood; Betty Wand for Rita Moreno; Jim Bryant for Richard Beymer.

Based on Shakespeare's "Romeo and Juliet" and reset in New York City. The musical production opened on Broadway in September, 1957 and in London the following year.

*America* (Rita Moreno, George Chakiris, Chorus); *A Boy Like That* (Rita Moreno); *Cool* (Tucker Smith, Chorus); *Gee, Officer Krupke* (Russ Tamblyn, Chorus); *I Feel Pretty* (Natalie Wood); *I Have a Love* (Natalie Wood); *Jet Song* (Russ Tamblyn, Chorus); *Maria* (Richard Beymer); *One Hand, One Heart* (Natalie Wood, Richard Beymer); *Quintet* (Rita Moreno, Richard Beymer, Natalie Wood, Russ Tamblyn, George Chakiris, Chorus); *Something's Coming* (Richard Beymer); *Somewhere* (Natalie Wood, Richard Beymer); *Tonight* (Natalie Wood, Richard Beymer) W: Stephen Sondheim—M: Leonard Bernstein.

"The strong blend of drama, dance and music folds into a rich artistic whole." —Bosley Crowther, *The New York Times*.

"Bernstein's score, with Stephen Sondheim's expressive lyrics, accentuates the tenseness that constantly builds." —*Variety*.

**1404   What Ever Happened to Baby Jane?** US, 1962, BW, 132 m. D: Robert Aldrich, MS: Frank DeVol, P: Warner (Robert Aldrich).

*I've Written a Letter to Daddy* (Bette Davis, Julie Alldred) WM: Frank DeVol, Larry Vincent, Mo Jaffe and Harry Tobias.

**1405   What's Cookin'?** US, 1942, BW, 69 m. D: Edward F. Cline, MD: Charles Previn, P: Universal (Ken Goldsmith). Orch: Woody Herman. MB: The Jivin' Jacks and Jills. GB Title: Wake Up and Dream.

*I'll Pray for You* (The Andrews Sisters, Jane Frazee, Gloria Jean) W: Kim Gannon—M: Arthur Altman / *What to Do* (The Andrews Sisters) WM: Sid Robin / *You Can't Hold a Memory in Your Arms* (Jane Frazee) W: Hy Zaret—M: Arthur Altman.

**1406   What's New, Pussycat?** US-France, 1965, C, 108 m. D: Clive Donner, P: UA (Charles K. Feldman). French Title: Quoi de Neuf, Pussycat?

*Here I Am* (Dionne Warwick); *My Little Red Book* (Manfred Mann); *What's New, Pussycat?* (Tom Jones) W: Hal David—M: Burt Bacharach.

**1407   What's Up Doc?** US, 1972, C, 94 m. D: Peter Bogdanovich, MS: Artie Butler, P: Warner (Peter Bogdanovich).

*As Time Goes By* (Barbra Streisand) WM: Herman Hupfeld / *You're the Top* (Barbra Streisand, Ryan O'Neal) WM: Cole Porter.

**1408   What's Up, Tiger Lily?** US, 1966, C, 80 m. D: Woody Allen, P: AIP (Henry G. Saperstein). Performers: The Lovin' Spoonful.

*A Cool Million* WM: John B. Sebastian, Joe Butler, Steve Boone and Zalman Yanovsky / *Fishin' Blues* WM Arr: John B. Sebastian / *Gray Prison Blues; Lookin' to Spy; Phil's Love Theme* WM: John B. Sebastian, Joe Butler, Steve Boone and Zalman Yanovsky / *Pow* WM: John B. Sebastian, Joe Butler, Steve Boone, Zalman Yanovsky and Skip Boone / *Respoken; Speakin' of*

*Spoken* WM: John B. Sebastian / *Unconscious Minuet* WM: John B. Sebastian, Joe Butler, Steve Boone and Zalman Yanovsky.

**1409  When the Boys Meet the Girls.** US, 1965, C, 110 m. D: Alvin Ganzer, MD: Fred Karger, P: MGM (Sam Katzman). Alt. Title: Girl Crazy.

*Aruba Liberace* (Liberace) WM: Liberace / *Bidin' My Time* (Herman's Hermits); *But Not for Me* (Harve Presnell, Connie Francis); *Embraceable You* (Harve Presnell, Connie Francis); *I Got Rhythm* (Harve Presnell, Connie Francis, Louis Armstrong) W: Ira Gershwin — M: George Gershwin / *Listen, People* (Herman's Hermits) WM: Graham Gouldman / *Mail Call* (Connie Francis, Chorus) WM: Fred Karger, Ben Weisman and Sid Wayne / *Monkey See, Monkey Do* (Sam the Sham and The Pharaohs) WM: Johnny Farrow / *Throw It Out of Your Mind* (Louis Armstrong) WM: Louis Armstrong and Bill Kyle / *Treat Me Rough* (Sue Ane Langdon, Chorus) W: Ira Gershwin — M: George Gershwin / *When the Boys Meet the Girls* (Connie Francis, Chorus) WM: Jack Keller and Howard Greenfield.

**1410  When You're in Love.** US, 1937, BW, 104 m. D: Robert Riskin, MD: Alfred Newman, P: Columbia (Everett Riskin). Performer: Grace Moore. GB Title: For You Alone.

*In the Gloaming* WM: Annie Fortesque Harrison and Meta Orred / *Minnie the Moocher* WM: Cab Calloway, Irving Mills and Clarence Gaskill — Arr: Al Segal / *Our Song* W: Dorothy Fields — M: Jerome Kern / *Siboney* Eng. W: Theodora Morse [Dolly Morse, Dorothy Terriss] — Span. WM: Ernesto Lecuona / *The Whistling Boy* W: Dorothy Fields — M: Jerome Kern.

**1411  Where Do We Go from Here?** US, 1945, C, 77 m. D: Gregory Ratoff, MD: Emil Newman, P: TCF (William Perlberg).

*All at Once* (Fred MacMurray, Joan Leslie); *Christopher Columbus* (Carlos Ramirez, Fortunio Bonanova); *If Love Remains* (Fred MacMurray, Joan Leslie); *Morale* (June Haver, Chorus); *The Nina, the Pinta, the Santa Maria* (Fred MacMurray, Carlos Ramirez, Chorus); *Song of the Rhineland* (June Haver, Herman Bing, Chorus); *Where Do We Go from Here?* (Chorus) W: Ira Gershwin — M: Kurt Weill.

**1412  Where Love Has Gone.** US, 1964, C, 114 m. D: Edward Dmytryk, MS: Walter Scharf, P: Paramount (Joseph E. Levine).

*Where Love Has Gone* (Jack Jones) W: Sammy Cahn — M: James Van Heusen.

**1413  Where the Buffalo Roam.** US, 1980, C, 96 m. D: Art Linson, MD: Neil Young, P: Universal (Art Linson).

*All Along the Watchtower* (Jimi Hendrix) WM: Bob Dylan / *Buffalo Stomp* (Neil Young) Arr: Neil Young / *Highway 61 Revisited* (Bob Dylan) WM: Bob Dylan / *Home on the Range* (Neil Young) WM: Unknown — Arr: Neil Young / *I Can't Help Myself* (The Four Tops) WM: Eddie Holland, Lamont Dozier and Brian Holland / *Keep on Chooglin'* (Creedence Clearwater) WM: John Fogerty / *Lucy in the Sky with Diamonds* (Bill Murray) WM: John Lennon and Paul McCartney / *Ode to Wild Bill* (Neil Young) Arr: Neil Young / *Papa Was a Rollin' Stone* (The Temptations) WM: Norman Whitfield and Barrett Strong / *Purple Haze* (Jimi Hendrix) WM: Jimi Hendrix.

**1414  White Christmas.** US, 1954, C, 120 m. D: Michael Curtiz, MS: Joseph J. Lilley, P: Paramount (Robert Emmett Dolan).

*Abraham* (Vera-Ellen, John Brascia); *The Best Things Happen While You're Dancing* (Danny Kaye); *Blue Skies* (Bing Crosby, Danny Kaye); *Count Your Blessings* (Bing Crosby, Rosemary Clooney); *Gee, I Wish I Was Back in the Army* (Bing Crosby, Danny Kaye, Rosemary Clooney, Vera-Ellen); *Heat Wave* (Bing Crosby, Danny Kaye);

*I'd Rather See a Minstrel Show* (Bing Crosby, Danny Kaye); *Instead of Dance, It's Choreography* (Vera-Ellen, Danny Kaye); *Let Me Sing and I'm Happy* (Bing Crosby, Danny Kaye); *Love, You Didn't Do Right By Me* (Rosemary Clooney); *Mandy* (Bing Crosby, Danny Kaye, Rosemary Clooney, Vera-Ellen, John Brascia); *The Old Man* (Bing Crosby, Danny Kaye); *Sisters* (Rosemary Clooney, Vera-Ellen, Bing Crosby, Danny Kaye); *Snow* (Bing Crosby, Danny Kaye, Rosemary Clooney, Vera-Ellen); *What Can You Do with a General?* (Bing Crosby); *White Christmas* (Bing Crosby, Danny Kaye, Rosemary Clooney, Vera-Ellen) WM: Irving Berlin.

"The music of Mr. Berlin is a good bit less than inspired. Outside of the old *White Christmas* . . . there are only a couple of numbers that have a measure of charm." —Bosley Crowther, *The New York Times.*

"The directorial handling by Michael Curtiz gives a smooth blend of music . . . and drama." —*Variety.*

**1415 Whoopee!** US, 1930, C, 93 m. D: Thornton Freeland, MD: Alfred Newman, P: UA (Samuel Goldwyn, Florenz Ziegfeld).

Eddie Cantor's first full-length talking picture, Goldwyn's first musical, Busby Berkeley's first foray into film choreography and a first featured role for a fourteen-year-old Goldwyn Girl named Betty Grable.

*Cowboys* (Betty Grable, Chorus); *A Girl Friend of a Boy Friend of Mine* (Eddie Cantor) W: Gus Kahn—M: Walter Donaldson / *I'll Still Belong to You* (Paul Gregory) W: Edward Eliscu —M: Nacio Herb Brown / *Makin' Whoopee* (Eddie Cantor); *My Baby Just Cares for Me* (Eddie Cantor); *Song of the Setting Sun* (Chief Caupolican, Chorus); *Stetson* (Ethel Shutta, Chorus); *Today's the Day* (Chorus) W: Gus Kahn—M: Walter Donaldson.

"Mr. Cantor's clowning transcends even Mr. Ziegfeld's shining beauties, the

clever direction and the tuneful melodies." —Mordaunt Hall, *The New York Times.*

**1416 Wild in the Country.** US, 1961, C, 114 m. D: Philip Dunne, MS: Kenyon Hopkins, P: TCF (Jerry Wald). Performer: Elvis Presley.

*Husky Dusky Day* (Elvis Presley, Hope Lange) / *In My Way; I Slipped, I Stumbled, I Fell* WM: Fred Wise and Ben Weisman / *Wild in the Country* WM: George Weiss, Hugo Peretti and Luigi Creatore.

"Sans wiggle, Presley croons four or five songs." —*Variety.*

**1417 Wild in the Streets.** US, 1968, C, 96 m. D: Barry Shear, MS: Lex Baxter, P: AIP (James H. Nicholson, Samuel Z. Arkoff). Vocals: Unknown Voice for Christopher Jones.

*Fifty-two Percent* (13th Power); *Fourteen or Fight* (Christopher Jones, 13th Power); *Love to Be Your Man* (13th Power); *Psychedelic Senate* (The Senators); *Sally Le Roy* (Second Time); *The Shape of Things to Come* (Christopher Jones, 13th Power); *Shelley in Camp* (The Gurus); *Wild in the Streets* (Jerry Howard) WM: Barry Mann and Cynthia Weil.

**1418 Wild Is the Wind.** US, 1957, BW, 114 m. D: George Cukor, MS: Dimitri Tiomkin, P: Paramount (Hal B. Wallis).

*Scapricciatiello* (Anna Magnani) WM: Fernando Albano and Pacifico Vento / *Wild Is the Wind* (Johnny Mathis) W: Ned Washington—M: Dimitri Tiomkin.

**1419 Wild on the Beach.** US, 1965, BW, 77 m. D: Maury Dexter, P: TCF (Maury Dexter).

*Drum Dance* (Sandy Nelson) WM: Joe Saraceno and Frank P. Warren / *The Gods of Love* (Frankie Randall); *House on the Beach* (Frankie Randall) WM: By Dunham and Bobby Beverly / *It's Gonna Rain* (Sonny and Cher) WM: Sonny Bono / *Little Speedy Gonzales* (The Astronauts) WM: Stan Ross and Bobby Beverly / *Pyramid Stomp*

(The Astronauts) WM: By Dunham and Jimmie Haskell / *Rock the World* (The Astronauts) WM: By Dunham and E. Davis / *Run Away from Him* (Cindy Malone) WM: By Dunham and Bobby Beverly / *Snap It* (The Astronauts) WM: By Dunham and Jimmie Haskell / *Winter Nocturne* (Jackie and Gayle) WM: By Dunham and E. Davis.

**1420  Wild, Wild Winter.** US, 1966, C, 80 m. D: Lennie Weinrib, P: Universal (Bart Patton).

*A Change of Heart* (The Astronauts) WM: Marc Gordon and Chester Pipkin / *Heartbeats* (Dick and Dee Dee) WM: Al Capps and Mary Dean / *Just Wait and See* (The Beau Brummels) WM: Ronald C. Elliott / *Our Love's Gonna Snowball* (Jackie and Gayle) WM: Al Capps and Mary Dean / *Two of a Kind* (Jay and The Americans) WM: Tony Bruno and Victor Millrose.

**1421  Wildcats.** US, 1986, C, 107 m. D: Michael Ritchie, P: Warner (Anthea Sylbert).

*Don't Wanna Be Normal* (Randy Crawford) WM: Hawk Wolinski, James Newton Howard, David Pack and Michael McDonald / *Good Hands* (The Isley Brothers) WM: Hawk Wolinski and James Newton Howard / *Hard to Say* (James Ingram); *Love Lives Alone* (Tata Vega) WM: Hawk Wolinski, James Newton Howard and David Pack / *Molly's Theme* (James Newton Howard); *Penetration* (Brenda Russell); *Razzle Dazzle* (Michael Jeffries); *Rock It* (Sidney Justin) WM: Hawk Wolinski and James Newton Howard / *Show Me How It Works* (Mavis Staples) WM: Hawk Wolinski, James Newton Howard and David Pack / *We Stand Alone* (Joe Cocker) WM: Hawk Wolinski, James Newton Howard and Joe Cocker.

**1422  Willy Wonka and the Chocolate Factory.** US, 1971, C, 98 m. D: Mel Stuart, MD: Walter Scharf, P: Paramount (Stan Margulies, David L. Wolper).

*The Candy Man* (Aubrey Wood, Children); *Cheer Up, Charlie* (Diana Sowle); *Golden Ticket* (Jack Albertson, Peter Ostrum); *I Want It Now* (Julie Dawn Cole); *Oompa Loompa* (Chorus); *Pure Imagination* (Gene Wilder, Chorus); *The Wondrous Boat Ride* (Gene Wilder, Chorus) W: Leslie Bricusse—M: Anthony Newley.

"The film has a fair score." — *Variety.*

**1423  With a Song in My Heart.** US, 1952, C, 117 m. D: Walter Lang, MD: Alfred Newman, P: TCF (Lamar Trotti). MB: Chorus. Vocals: Jane Froman for Susan Hayward. Performer: Susan Hayward.

Biopic of singer Jane Froman, badly injured in an air crash in Lisbon in 1943 while on her way to entertain servicemen overseas.

*Alabamy Bound* W: B.G. De Sylva and Bud Green—M: Ray Henderson / *America, the Beautiful* W: Katherine Lee Bates—M: Samuel A. Ward / *Blue Moon* W: Lorenz Hart—M: Richard Rodgers / *California, Here I Come* W: Al Jolson and B.G. De Sylva—M: Joseph Meyer / *Carry Me Back to Old Virginny* WM: James A. Bland / *Chicago* WM: Fred Fisher / *Deep in the Heart of Texas* (Susan Hayward, Thelma Ritter) W: June Hershey—M: Don Swander / *Dixie* WM: Daniel Decatur Emmett / *Embraceable You* (Susan Hayward, Robert Wagner) W: Ira Gershwin—M: George Gershwin / *Get Happy* W: Ted Koehler—M: Harold Arlen / *Give My Regards to Broadway* WM: George M. Cohan / *I'll Walk Alone* W: Sammy Cahn—M: Jule Styne / *I'm Thru with Love* W: Gus Kahn—M: Matt Malneck and Fud Livingston / *Indiana* W: Ballard MacDonald—M: James F. Hanley / *It's a Good Day* WM: Peggy Lee and Dave Barbour / *I've Got a Feelin' You're Foolin'* W: Arthur Freed—M: Nacio Herb Brown / *Jim's Toasted Peanuts* WM: Ken Darby / *Montparnasse* (David Wayne) / *On the Gay White Way* W: Leo Robin—M: Ralph Rainger

/ *The Right Kind* / *Stein Song* W: Lincoln Colcord—M: E.A. Fenstad / *Tea for Two* W: Irving Caesar—M: Vincent Youmans / *That Old Feeling* W: Lew Brown—M: Sammy Fain / *They're Either Too Young or Too Old* W: Frank Loesser—M: Arthur Schwartz / *With a Song in My Heart* W: Lorenz Hart—M: Richard Rodgers / *Wonderful Home Sweet Home* WM: Ken Darby.

"Susan Hayward punches over the straight vocal-simulation and deftly handles the dramatic phases." — *Variety*.

"Miss Froman herself sings the songs ... and in her rich and generous chanting of an excellent repertory ... the most acceptable assets of the picture are contained." —Bosley Crowther, *The New York Times*.

**1424 Witness for the Prosecution.** US, 1957, BW, 114 m. D: Billy Wilder, MS: Matt Malneck, P: UA (Arthur Hornblow, Jr.).

*I May Never Go Home Anymore* (Marlene Dietrich) WM: Ralph Arthur Roberts and Jack Brooks.

**1425 The Wiz.** US, 1978, C, 133 m. D: Sidney Lumet, MD: Quincy Jones, P: Universal (Rob Cohen).

*Be a Lion* (Diana Ross, Ted Ross, Nipsey Russell, Michael Jackson); *Believe in Yourself* (Lena Horne, Diana Ross) WM: Charlie Smalls / *A Brand New Day* (Chorus) WM: Luther Vandross / *Can I Go On?* (Diana Ross) WM: Nick Ashford, Valerie Simpson and Quincy Jones / *Don't Nobody Bring Me No Bad News* (Mabel King, Chorus); *Ease on Down the Road* (Diana Ross, Michael Jackson, Ted Ross, Nipsey Russell, Chorus) WM: Charlie Smalls / *Emerald City* (Chorus) WM: Charlie Smalls and Quincy Jones / *The Feeling That We Have* (Theresa Merritt) WM: Charlie Smalls / *Glinda's Theme* (Chorus); *Good Witch Glinda* (Chorus) WM: Quincy Jones / *He's the Wizard* (Thelma Carpenter, Chorus); *Home* (Diana Ross); *I'm a Mean Ole Lion* (Ted Ross) WM: Charlie Smalls /

*Is This What Feeling Gets?* (Diana Ross) WM: Nick Ashford, Valerie Simpson and Quincy Jones / *March of the Munchkins* (Chorus) WM: Quincy Jones / *Slide Some Oil to Me* (Nipsey Russell); *Soon As I Get Home* (Diana Ross); *What Would I Do If I Could Feel?* (Nipsey Russell); *You Can't Win* (Michael Jackson, Chorus) WM: Charlie Smalls.

**1426 The Wizard of Oz.** US, 1939, BW/C, 101 m. D: Victor Fleming, MD: Herbert Stothart, P: MGM (Mervyn LeRoy). Vocals: Lorraine Bridges for Billie Burke.

*Ding-Dong! The Witch Is Dead* (Judy Garland, Billie Burke, Chorus); *Follow the Yellow Brick Road* (Judy Garland, Chorus); *If I Only Had a Brain* (Ray Bolger); *If I Only Had a Heart* (Jack Haley); *If I Only Had the Nerve* (Bert Lahr); *The Merry Old Land of Oz* (Chorus); *Munchkinland* (Chorus); *Over the Rainbow* (Judy Garland); *We're Off to See the Wizard* (Judy Garland, Ray Bolger, Bert Lahr, Jack Haley, Chorus) W: E.Y. Harburg—M: Harold Arlen.

**1427 A Woman Commands.** US, 1932, BW, 85 m. D: Paul L. Stein, P: RKO (Charles R. Rogers).

*Paradise* (Pola Negri) W: Gordon Clifford—M: Nacio Herb Brown.

**1428 The Woman in Red.** US, 1984, C, 87 m. D: Gene Wilder, MS: John Morris, P: Orion (Victor Drai). Performer: Stevie Wonder.

*Don't Drive Drunk; I Just Called to Say I Love You; It's More Than You; It's You; Love Light in Flight; Moments Aren't Moments; Weakness; Woman in Red* WM: Stevie Wonder.

**1429 A Woman's Secret.** US, 1949, BW, 85 m. D: Nicholas Ray, MD: Constantin Bakaleinikoff, MS: Frederick Hollander, P: RKO (Herman J. Mankiewicz).

*Paradise* (Gloria Grahame) W: Gordon Clifford—M: Nacio Herb Brown.

**1430 Woman's World.** US, 1954, C, 94 m. D: Jean Negulesco, MS:

Cyril J. Mockridge, P: TCF (Charles Brackett).

*It's a Woman's World* (The Four Aces) W: Sammy Cahn—M: Cyril J. Mockridge.

**1431  Wonder Bar.** US, 1934, BW, 84 m. D: Lloyd Bacon, P: Warner/First National (Robert Lord).

From a Broadway show starring Al Jolson. None of the songs were transferred to the film.

*Dark Eyes* (Al Jolson, Chorus) WM: Based on Russian Folk Song *Otchi Tchorniya*—Arr: Harry Horlick and Gregory Stone / *Don't Say Goodnight* (Dick Powell, Chorus); *Goin' to Heaven on a Mule* (Al Jolson); *Viva La France* (Al Jolson); *Why Do I Dream Those Dreams?* (Dick Powell); *Wonder Bar* (Al Jolson) W: Al Dubin—M: Harry Warren.

**1432  Wonder Man.** US, 1945, C, 98 m. D: H. Bruce Humberstone, MD: Louis Forbes, MS: Ray Heindorf, P: RKO (Samuel Goldwyn). Vocals: June Hutton for Vera-Ellen.

*Bali Boogie* (Danny Kaye, Vera-Ellen, Jack Norton, Chorus); *Opera Number* (Danny Kaye, Alice Mock) WM: Sylvia Fine / *Otchi Tchorniya* (Danny Kaye) WM: Based on Russian Folk Song—Arr: Sylvia Fine / *So-o-o-o-o in Love* (Vera-Ellen, Chorus) W: Leo Robin—M: David Rose.

**1433  Wonderful to Be Young.** GB, 1961, C, 108 m. D: Sidney J. Furie, MS: Stanley Black, P: Warner (Kenneth Harper). Performers: Cliff Richard and The Shadows. GB Title: The Young Ones.

*Algy, the Piccadilly Johnny* (Chorus) WM: Harry B. Morris / *All for One* WM: Peter Myers and Ronald Cass / *Captain Gingah* (Men) WM: George Bastow and Fred W. Leigh / *Got a Funny Feeling* WM: Hank B. Marvin and Bruce Welch / *Have a Smile* (Chorus) WM: J. Keirn Brennan, Paul Cunningham and Bert L. Rula / *Joshu-ah* (Female Singer) WM: George Arthurs and Bert Lee / *Lessons in Love* W:

Shirley Wolfe—M: Sy Soloway / *Living Doll* WM: Lionel Bart / *Nothing's Impossible* WM: Peter Myers and Ronald Cass / *Tinkle Tinkle Tinkle* (Female Singer) WM: Harry M. Woods / *What D'You Know, We've Got a Show* WM: Peter Myers and Ronald Cass / *When the Girl in Your Arms* WM: Sid Tepper and Roy C. Bennett / *Where Did You Get That Hat?* (Chorus) WM: James Rolmaz / *The Young Ones* WM: Sid Tepper and Roy C. Bennett.

**1434  Words and Music.** US, 1948, C, 119 m. D: Norman Taurog, MD: Lennie Hayton, P: MGM (Arthur Freed).

*Blue Moon* (Mel Torme); *The Blue Room* (Perry Como, Cyd Charisse); *I Wish I Were in Love Again* (Judy Garland, Mickey Rooney); *Johnny One Note* (Judy Garland); *The Lady Is a Tramp* (Lena Horne); *Manhattan* (Mickey Rooney, Tom Drake, Marshall Thompson); *Mountain Greenery* (Perry Como, Allyn McLerie); *Spring Is Here* (Mickey Rooney); *There's a Small Hotel* (Betty Garrett); *This Can't Be Love* (Cyd Charisse, Dee Turnell); *Thou Swell* (June Allyson, The Blackburn Twins); *Where or When* (Lena Horne); *Where's That Rainbow?* (Ann Sothern); *With a Song in My Heart* (Perry Como) W: Lorenz Hart—M: Richard Rodgers.

"Fortunately, the wonderful music of Richard Rodgers and the late Lorenz Hart is treated with passable justice in 'Words and Music,' a patently juvenile specimen of musical biography." — Bosley Crowther, *The New York Times*.

**1435  The World Is Full of Married Men.** GB, 1979, C, 107 m. D: Robert Young, MS: Frank Musker and Dominic Bugatti, P: New Realm (Malcolm Fancey, Adrienne Fancey, Oscar S. Lerman).

*Best of My Love* (The Emotions) WM: Maurice White and Albert McKay / *Contact* (Edwin Starr) WM: Edwin Starr and A.E. Pullan / *Get Down* (Gene Chandler) WM: James Thompson / *Heaven Must Be Missing an Angel* (Tavares) WM: Kenny St. Lewis and Freddy Perren / *Loveliness* (Paul Nicholas) / *Lovely Day* (Bill Withers) WM: Bill Withers and Skip Scarborough / *Now That We've Found Love* (Third World) WM: Kenny Gamble and Leon Huff / *Right Back Where We Started From* (Maxine Nightingale) WM: Pierre Tubbs and Vincent Edwards / *Shame* (Evelyn King) WM: John Fitch and Reuben Cross / *We Don't Make Each Other Laugh Anymore* (Gladys Knight) / *A Woman in Love* (The Three Degrees) WM: Frank Musker and Dominic Bugatti / *The World Is Full of Married Men* (Mick Jackson, Bonnie Tyler).

**1436 Written on the Wind.** US, 1956, C, 99 m. D: Douglas Sirk, MD: Joseph Gershenson, MS: Frank Skinner, P: Universal (Albert Zugsmith).

*Written on the Wind* (The Four Aces) W: Sammy Cahn—M: Victor Young.

**1437 Wuthering Heights.** GB, 1970, C, 105 m. D: Robert Fuest, P: AIP (Samuel Z. Arkoff, James H. Nicholson).

*I Was Born in Love with You* (Chorus) W: Alan Bergman and Marilyn Bergman—M: Michel Legrand.

**1438 Xanadu.** US, 1980, C, 88 m. D: Robert Greenwald, MS: Barry De Vorzon, P: Universal (Lawrence Gordon).

*All Over the World* (The Electric Light Orchestra) WM: Jeff Lynne / *Dancin'* (Olivia Newton-John, The Tubes) WM: John Farrar / *Don't Walk Away* (The Electric Light Orchestra); *The Fall* (The Electric Light Orchestra); *I'm Alive* (The Electric Light Orchestra) WM: Jeff Lynne / *Magic* (Olivia Newton-John); *Suddenly* (Olivia Newton-John, Cliff Richard); *Suspended in Time* (Olivia Newton-John); *Whenever You're Away from Me* (Olivia Newton-John, Gene Kelly) WM: John Farrar / *Xanadu* (Olivia Newton-John) WM: Jeff Lynne.

"A stupendously bad film whose only salvage is the music." —*Variety*.

**1439 Yankee Doodle Dandy.** US, 1942, BW, 126 m. D: Michael Curtiz, MD: Leo F. Forbstein, P: Warner (Hal B. Wallis, William Cagney).

*All Aboard for Old Broadway* (James Cagney, Chorus) WM: M.K. Jerome and Jack Scholl / *Belle of the Barber's Ball* (James Cagney, Jeanne Cagney, Rosemary DeCamp, Walter Huston); *Billie* (Frances Langford); *Come Along with Me Away* (James Cagney, Chorus); *The Dancing Master* (James Cagney, Jeanne Cagney, Rosemary DeCamp, Walter Huston); *Forty-Five Minutes from Broadway* (James Cagney); *Give My Regards to Broadway* (James Cagney, Chorus); *Harrigan* (James Cagney, Joan Leslie); *I'll Be True to You* (James Cagney, Jeanne Cagney, Rosemary DeCamp, Walter Huston); *I Was Born in Virginia* (James Cagney, Jeanne Cagney, Rosemary DeCamp, Walter Huston) WM: George M. Cohan / *The Love Nest* (Frances Langford) W: Otto Harbach—M: Louis A. Hirsch / *Mary's a Grand Old Name* (James Cagney, Joan Leslie, Irene Manning) WM: George M. Cohan / *Molly Malone* (Frances Langford) WM: Unknown / *Nellie Kelly, I Love You* (Frances Langford) WM: George M. Cohan / *Off the Record* (James Cagney) W: Lorenz Hart—M: Richard Rodgers / *Oh, You Wonderful Girl* (James Cagney, Jeanne Cagney, Rosemary DeCamp, Walter Huston); *Over There* (James Cagney, Frances Langford); *So Long, Mary* (Irene Manning, Chorus); *The Warmest Baby in the Bunch* (Joan Leslie); *The Yankee Doodle Boy* (James Cagney); *You're a Grand Old Flag* (James Cagney, Chorus) WM: George M. Cohan.

"It's a tribute to a grand American gentleman of the theatre whose life and songs are glorified by Warner Bros." —*Variety*.

"As warm and delightful a musical picture as has hit the screen in years."

—Bosley Crowther, *The New York Times*.

**1440   The Yellow Rolls Royce.** GB, 1965, C, 122 m. D: Anthony Asquith, MS: Riz Ortolani, P: MGM (Anatole De Grunwald).

*Forget Domani* (Katyna Ranieri) W: Norman Newell—M: Riz Ortolani.

**1441   Yentl.** US, 1983, C, 134 m. D: Barbra Streisand, P: MGM/UA (Barbra Streisand, Rusty Lemorande). Performer: Barbra Streisand.

*No Matter What Happens; No Wonder; Papa Can You Hear Me?; A Piece of Sky; This Is One of Those Moments; Tomorrow Night; The Way He Makes Me Feel; Where Is It Written?; Will Someone Ever Look at Me That Way?* W: Alan Bergman and Marilyn Bergman—M: Michel Legrand.

**1442   Yes, Giorgio.** US, 1982, C, 110 m. D: Franklin J. Schaffner, MS: John Williams, P: MGM/UA (Peter Fetterman). Performer: Luciano Pavarotti.

*Ave Maria* W: Sir Walter Scott—M: Franz Schubert / *If We Were in Love* W: Alan Bergman and Marilyn Bergman—M: John Williams / *I Left My Heart in San Francisco* W: Douglass Cross—M: George Cory / *O Sole Mio* W: Giovanni Capurro—M: Edorado di Capua.

**1443   Yolanda and the Thief.** US, 1945, C, 108 m. D: Vincente Minnelli, MS: Lennie Hayton, P: MGM (Arthur Freed). Vocals: Trudi Erwin for Lucille Bremer.

*Angel* (Lucille Bremer); *Coffee Time* (Fred Astaire, Lucille Bremer, Chorus); *This Is the Day for Love* (Lucille Bremer, Chorus); *Will You Marry Me?* (Fred Astaire, Lucille Bremer); *Yolanda* (Fred Astaire) W: Arthur Freed—M: Harry Warren.

"There's an idea in this yarn, but it only suggests itself. It becomes too immersed in its musical background." —*Variety*.

**1444   You Can't Run Away from It.** US, 1956, C, 95 m. D: Dick Powell, MD: Morris Stoloff, MS: George Duning, P: Columbia (Dick Powell).

*Howdy Friends and Neighbors* (June Allyson, Jack Lemmon, Stubby Kaye, Chorus); *Scarecrow Ballet* (Chorus); *Temporarily* (June Allyson, Jack Lemmon); *Thumbin' a Ride* (June Allyson, Jack Lemmon); *You Can't Run Away from It* (The Four Aces) W: Johnny Mercer—M: Gene de Paul.

**1445   You Only Live Twice.** GB, 1967, C, 116 m. D: Lewis Gilbert, MS: John Barry, P: UA (Harry Saltzman, Albert R. Broccoli).

*You Only Live Twice* (Nancy Sinatra) W: Leslie Bricusse—M: John Barry.

**1446   You Were Meant for Me.** US, 1948, BW, 92 m. D: Lloyd Bacon, MD: Lionel Newman, P: TCF (Fred Kohlmar). Performer: Dan Dailey.

*Ain't Misbehavin'* W: Andy Razaf—M: Thomas "Fats" Waller and Harry Brooks / *Ain't She Sweet?* (Dan Dailey, Jeanne Crain, Barbara Lawrence, Chorus) W: Jack Yellen—M: Milton Ager / *Crazy Rhythm* W: Irving Caesar—M: Roger Wolfe Kahn and Joseph Meyer / *Goodnight Sweetheart* (Chorus) WM: Ray Noble, James Campbell and Reginald Connelly / *If I Had You* WM: Ted Shapiro, James Campbell and Reginald Connelly / *I'll Get By* W: Roy Turk—M: Fred E. Ahlert / *You Were Meant for Me* W: Arthur Freed—M: Nacio Herb Brown.

**1447   You Were Never Lovelier.** US, 1942, BW, 97 m. D: William A. Seiter, MD: Leigh Harline, P: Columbia (Louis F. Edelman). Orch: Xavier Cugat. Vocals: Nan Wynn for Rita Hayworth.

*Chiu, Chiu* (Lina Romay, Chorus) W: Alan Surgal—M: Nicanor Molinare / *Dearly Beloved* (Fred Astaire, Rita Hayworth); *I'm Old Fashioned* (Fred Astaire, Rita Hayworth); *The Shorty George* (Fred Astaire, Rita Hayworth, Chorus); *These Orchids If You Please* (Quartet); *Wedding in the Spring* (Lina

Romay, Chorus); *You Were Never Lovelier* (Fred Astaire) W: Johnny Mercer—M: Jerome Kern.

**1448 You'll Find Out.** US, 1940, BW, 97 m. D: David Butler, MS: Roy Webb, P: RKO (David Butler).

*The Bad Humor Man* (Ish Kabibble); *Don't Think It Ain't Been Charming* (Kay Kyser and His College of Musical Knowledge); *I'd Know You Anywhere* (Harry Babbitt, Ginny Simms); *I've Got a One Track Mind* (Kay Kyser and His College of Musical Knowledge); *Like the Fella Once Said* (Kay Kyser and His College of Musical Knowledge); *You've Got Me This Way* (Harry Babbitt) W: Johnny Mercer—M: Jimmy McHugh.

**1449 You'll Never Get Rich.** US, 1941, BW, 88 m. D: Sidney Lanfield, MS: Morris Stoloff, P: Columbia (Sam Bischoff).

*Shooting the Works for Uncle Sam* (Fred Astaire, Chorus); *Since I Kissed My Baby Goodbye* (The Delta Rhythm Boys); *So Near and Yet So Far* (Fred Astaire); *The Wedding Cake Walk* (Martha Tilton, Chorus) WM: Cole Porter.

**1450 Young As You Feel.** US, 1931, BW, 78 m. D: Frank Borzage, P: Fox.

*The Cute Little Things You Do* (Fifi D'Orsay) WM: James F. Hanley.

**1451 Young at Heart.** US, 1955, C, 117 m. D: Gordon Douglas, MD: Ray Heindorf, P: Warner (Henry Blanke).

*Hold Me in Your Arms* (Doris Day) WM: Ray Heindorf, Charles Henderson and Don Pippin / *Just One of Those Things* (Frank Sinatra) WM: Cole Porter / *One for My Baby* (Frank Sinatra) W: Johnny Mercer—M: Harold Arlen / *Ready, Willing and Able* (Doris Day) WM: Al Rinker, Floyd Huddleston and Dick Gleason / *Someone to Watch Over Me* (Frank Sinatra) W: Ira Gershwin—M: George Gershwin / *There's a Rising Moon* (Doris Day) W: Paul Francis Webster—M: Sammy Fain / *Till My* *Love Comes to Me* (Doris Day) W: Paul Francis Webster—M: Ray Heindorf / *You My Love* (Doris Day, Frank Sinatra) W: Mack Gordon—M: James Van Heusen / *Young at Heart* (Frank Sinatra) W: Carolyn Leigh—M: Johnny Richards.

**1452 Young Frankenstein.** US, 1974, BW, 105 m. D: Mel Brooks, MS: John Morris, P: TCF (Michael Gruskoff).

*Puttin' on the Ritz* (Peter Boyle, Gene Wilder) WM: Irving Berlin.

**1453 The Young Land.** US, 1959, C, 89 m. D: Ted Tetzlaff, P: Columbia (Patrick Ford).

*Strange Are the Ways of Love* (Randy Sparks) W: Ned Washington—M: Dimitri Tiomkin.

**1454 Young Man with a Horn.** US, 1950, BW, 112 m. D: Michael Curtiz, MS: Ray Heindorf, P: Warner (Jerry Wald). Orch: Harry James. Performer: Doris Day. GB Title: Young Man of Music.

*I May Be Wrong But I Think You're Wonderful* W: Harry Ruskin—M: Henry Sullivan / *The Man I Love* W: Ira Gershwin—M: George Gershwin / *Tea for Two* W: Irving Caesar—M: Vincent Youmans / *Too Marvelous for Words* W: Johnny Mercer—M: Richard A. Whiting / *The Very Thought of You* WM: Ray Noble / *With a Song in My Heart* W: Lorenz Hart—M: Richard Rodgers.

"The unseen star of the picture is Harry James, the old maestro himself, who supplies the tingling music which flows wildly, searchingly and forlornly from Rick Martin's beloved horn. This is an instance where the soundtrack is more than a complementary force." — Thomas M. Pryor, *The New York Times.*

**1455 Young People.** US, 1940, BW, 78 m. D: Allan Dwan, MD: Alfred Newman, P: TCF (Harry Joe Brown).

*Fifth Avenue* (Shirley Temple, Jack Oakie, Charlotte Greenwood); *I*

Wouldn't Take a Million (Shirley Temple); *Tra-la-la* (Shirley Temple, Jack Oakie, Charlotte Greenwood); *Young People* (Shirley Temple, Children) W: Mack Gordon—M: Harry Warren.

**1456 Your Cheatin' Heart.** US, 1964, BW, 99 m. D: Gene Nelson, MD: Fred Karger, P: MGM (Sam Katzman). Vocals: Hank Williams, Jr. for George Hamilton. Performer: George Hamilton.

In this biopic of country singer Hank Williams, his actual band, The Driftin' Cowboys, did backup for son Hank, Jr.

*Cold, Cold Heart; Hey, Good Lookin'; I Can't Help It; I'm So Lonesome I Could Cry; I Saw the Light; Jambalaya* WM: Hank Williams / *Kaw-Liga* WM: Hank Williams and Fred Rose / *Long Gone Lonesome Blues* WM: Hank Williams / *Lovesick Blues* WM: Irving Mills and Clifford Friend / *Ramblin' Man; Your Cheatin' Heart; You Win Again* WM: Hank Williams.

**1457 You're a Lucky Fellow, Mr. Smith.** US, 1943, BW, 63 m. D: Felix Feist, MD: Charles Previn, P: Universal (Edward Lilley). Performers: The King's Men.

*On the Crest of a Rainbow* WM: Al Sherman and Harry Tobias / *What Is This Thing Called Love?* WM: Cole Porter / *When You're Smiling* WM: Mark Fisher, Joe Goodwin and Larry Shay / *You're a Lucky Fellow, Mr. Smith* W: Hughie Prince—M: Sonny Burke and Don Raye / *Your Eyes Have Told Me So* WM: Gus Kahn, Walter Blaufuss and Egbert Van Alstyne.

**1458 Ziegfeld Follies.** US, 1946, C, 110 m. D: Vincente Minnelli, MD: Lennie Hayton, P: MGM (Arthur Freed). TV Title: Ziegfeld Follies of 1946.

*The Babbitt and the Bromide* (Fred Astaire, Gene Kelly) W: Ira Gershwin—M: George Gershwin / *Bring on the Beautiful Girls* (Fred Astaire); *Bring on the Wonderful Men* (Virginia O'Brien) WM: Earl K. Brent and Roger Edens /

*The Interview* (Judy Garland, Rex Evans, Chorus) WM: Kay Thompson and Roger Edens / *Limehouse Blues* (Harriet Lee) W: Douglas Furber—M: Philip Braham / *Love* (Lena Horne) WM: Ralph Blane and Hugh Martin / *There's Beauty Everywhere* (Kathryn Grayson); *This Heart of Mine* (Fred Astaire, Lucille Bremer) W: Arthur Freed—M: Harry Warren.

**1459 Ziegfeld Girl.** US, 1941, BW, 131 m. D: Robert Z. Leonard, MD: George Stoll, P: MGM (Pandro S. Berman).

*Caribbean Love Song* (Tony Martin) W: Ralph Freed—M: Roger Edens / *I'm Always Chasing Rainbows* (Judy Garland, Charles Winninger) W: Joseph McCarthy—M: Harry Carroll / *Laugh? I Thought I'd Split My Sides* (Judy Garland, Charles Winninger); *Minnie from Trinidad* (Judy Garland, Tony Martin, Chorus) WM: Roger Edens / *Mister Gallagher and Mister Shean* (Charles Winninger, Al Shean) WM: Ed Gallagher and Al Shean / *Whispering* (Male Trio) WM: John Schonberger, Richard Coburn and Vincent Rose / *You Gotta Pull Strings* (Judy Garland, Chorus); *You Never Looked So Beautiful Before* (Judy Garland, Chorus) W: Harold Adamson—M: Walter Donaldson / *You Stepped Out of a Dream* (Tony Martin, Chorus) W: Gus Kahn—M: Nacio Herb Brown / *Ziegfeld Girls* (Judy Garland, Chorus) WM: Roger Edens.

**1460 Zoot Suit.** US, 1981, C, 103 m. D: Luis Valdez, MD: Shorty Rogers, P: Universal (Peter Burrell, Kenneth Brecher, William P. Wingate). MB: Chorus. Performer: Daniel Valdez.

*Chucos Suaves* WM: Lalo Guerrero / *Handball* WM: Daniel Valdez / *Oh Babe* WM: Daniel Valdez, Milton Kabak and Louis Prima / *Vamos A Bailar* (Chorus) WM: Lalo Guerrero / *A Zoot Suit* (Female Trio) WM: Ray Gilbert and Bob O'Brien / *Zoot Suit Boogie* WM: Daniel Valdez.

# Performer Index

# Songwriter Index

# Song Index

290